TRUMP,
TRUDEAU,
TWEETS,
TRUTH

TRUMP, TRUDEAU, TWEETS, TRUTH

A Conversation

BILL FOX

Published for the Riddell Graduate Program in Political
Management at Carleton University by
McGill-Queen's University Press
Montreal & Kingston • London • Chicago

© McGill-Queen's University Press 2022

ISBN 978-0-2280-0111-9 (CLOTH)
ISBN 978-0-2280-0247-5 (EPDF)
ISBN 978-0-2280-0248-2 (EPUB)

Legal deposit first quarter 2022
Bibliothèque nationale du Québec

Printed in Canada on acid-free paper that is 100% ancient forest free (100% post-consumer recycled), processed chlorine free

Funded by the Government of Canada   Financé par le gouvernement du Canada      Canada Council for the Arts   Conseil des arts du Canada

We acknowledge the support of the Canada Council for the Arts.
Nous remercions le Conseil des arts du Canada de son soutien.

Library and Archives Canada Cataloguing in Publication

Title: Trump, Trudeau, tweets, truth : a conversation / Bill Fox.
Names: Fox, Bill, 1947- author.
Description: Includes bibliographical references and index.
Identifiers: Canadiana (print) 20210289686 | Canadiana (ebook) 20210290110 | ISBN 9780228001119 (hardcover) | ISBN 9780228002475 (PDF) | ISBN 9780228002482 (EPUB)
Subjects: LCSH: Social media and journalism. | LCSH: Online journalism. | LCSH: Journalism—Technological innovations. | LCSH: Communication in politics—Technological innovations. | LCSH: Fake news—Political aspects. | LCSH: Social media—Political aspects. | LCSH: Press and politics. | LCSH: Mass media and public opinion. | LCSH: Trump, Donald, 1946- | LCSH: Trudeau, Justin.
Classification: LCC PN4766 .F69 2021 | DDC 302.23—dc23

This book was typeset in 10.5/13 Palatino.

Contents

Contents

A Prologue

I am a Timmins boy. And while I haven't lived in the Northern Ontario mining town for more than a half-century, I still consider it home.

My father was a hardrock miner, as were both grandfathers and most of the men I knew. Gold miners. The women were homemakers in the main, giving up the jobs they'd held during the war to be stay-at-home moms for the first wave of boomers. Some would return to the workforce during the 1960s but in the interim supported church and local charitable organizations selling the pies they'd baked and the clothing they'd bundled for rummage sales.

The families were big; the houses were small. Our family lived in a house owned by the Hollinger Mine, with a garage that backed on to a dirt lane. We didn't have a car, so the garage served as a theatre for my younger brother Robert to stage his "musicals."

The *Timmins Daily Press*, along with radio station CKGB, was housed in an art deco building on the other side of the dirt lane and had more influence on my life than I was aware of at the time.

My cousins and I sold the paper to miners coming off the day shift – bought for five cents, sold for seven cents, and if you were really lucky, the miner handed you a dime and told you to keep the three pennies change. You learned basic rules of supply, demand, inventory, and fundamental strategy lessons around risk and reward.

At night, at the ballpark, you could watch the action in the Timmins Mercantile fastball league and observe sports columnist Doug McLellan at work. And Thomson political columnist Patrick Nicholson was a must-read.

I certainly wasn't contemplating a career in journalism, or business, back then, but the seeds were sown.

R. Lindsay Crysler — editor, educator, mentor — opened the first door. And M. Brian Mulroney, Canada's eighteenth prime minister, pushed that door wide open.

I've written scores of line stories for the country's largest newspaper and am no stranger to election-night sets on network television.

As a newspaper correspondent, I was in the Paul Sauvé Arena in Montreal the night the René Lévesque-led Parti Québécois was elected in 1976. And as a political staffer, I was in Baie-Comeau the night Mulroney led the Progressive Conservative Party of Canada to the largest majority in federal electoral history.

Yet the images that linger are less the events and news that were the stuff of front pages, and more the people making that news.

Trashing the legendary Jimi Hendrix for a concert in Ottawa is an ongoing embarrassment, while any reference to Gordon Lightfoot triggers memories of a full-page feature in the *Ottawa Citizen* written with my then-roommate Richard Belec.

Grand Chief Billy Diamond introduced me to a young man named Ted Moses, who would emerge as a generational leader for the James Bay Cree.

As a White House correspondent, I did get to pull up a chair in the Oval Office to interview a president – Ronald Reagan.

And as a political staffer I got to meet a person once considered a living god – Emperor Hirohito, who only renounced his divine nature after Japan's defeat in the Second World War.

A treasured photo was taken in the ornate St. Catherine Hall of the Great Kremlin Palace. Prime Minister Mulroney is seated across from Mikhail Gorbachev, confirmed as leader of the Soviet Union scant days before. I'm seated to Mulroney's left, directly across from long-time Soviet foreign minister Andrei Gromyko, recently elevated to chairman of the Presidium of the Supreme Soviet.

Saw Terry Fox when he came through Ottawa on his Marathon of Hope to meet Prime Minister Pierre Trudeau.

Watched the incomparable David Foster work in his home studio. Came to appreciate the significance of his colleague Chris Earthy's conclusion that "the vibe is good."

Have heard the distinct sound of small arms fire that was too close for comfort in places like Teotecacinte, Nicaragua, and Sana'a, Yemen.

In a six degrees of separation moment in the late 1990s, I listened attentively as Congo strongman Laurent Kabila explained his friendship in the 1960s with revolutionary Che Guevara. In several conversations, Kabila also rationalized elaborate security procedures prior to each meeting as necessary because he could not entirely trust the people guarding him – the very people who would assassinate Kabila months later.

As a volunteer communications consultant, I learned to listen, to Kosovars whose stories of grievance are literally measured in millennia, and to a Yemeni legislator and former journalist who talked through the experience of a civil war, imprisonment, the confiscation of her home, her business.

As a corporate executive at companies such as CN Rail, Bombardier, and Bell Canada Enterprises, I sat around boardroom tables where the agendas involved bold and ambitious acquisition strategies, the reorganization of a global business, one of the largest privatizations in history, and the rebuilding of a pension fund to the benefit of literally millions of people.

And on the lighter side, I learned corporate jets are an acquired taste, and that it is alarming how quickly you acquire it.

Throughout, the opportunity to read, meet, and occasionally chat with media and communications scholars such as Christopher Dornan, Marvin Kalb, Thomas E. Patterson, Everette Dennis and James Carey has been most welcome.

Through the years, I've walked along the Great Wall of China, slept under the stars in the Saudi desert, rode a hi-rail through the Louisiana bayou, traipsed up the stairs to the Kremlin, paddled a canoe while staring at the majesty of the mountain peaks on Ellesmere Island in the High Arctic.

I would be remiss if I didn't acknowledge my professional life has been richer and more rewarding than talent warranted.

While I have had many titles in my professional career, I have only ever had one job: storyteller. This work is proposed as both exploratory and explanatory from a practitioner's perspective, intended to contribute to a conversation around the evolving place of reporting in both politics and business. The material set out in these pages will consider how public policy allowed internet giants to monetize other people's "labour," even if voluntary, take the lion's share of digital revenue, and yet avoid any of the responsibility or accountability for the "content" on its platforms. The various public policy options that might be put in place to ensure a free and rigorous news media considered essential to Western liberal democracies will be examined.

Journalistic practices themselves will have to be considered, as well as the the structure of political and corporate communications functions. New business models will require new skills that have not historically been part of the journalist's professional toolkit. Consideration will be given to emerging trends in the professional formation of journalists. Similarly, the work and business practices of the political "spinners" and corporate communications gurus will also be examined.

The work will also reflect the fact that this "practitioner" – who has spent a half-century working all three points of the media-politics-public policy triangle – lives on the wrong side of the "digital divide" and readily acknowledges that to use the term "digital" is to reinforce that fact. And in the interests of full disclosure, I should formally acknowledge that I have always been something of an outlier. Swept up in the Westerns I so enjoyed at the movies on Saturday afternoons, I always wanted to be the scout, not in the cavalry. Not a contrarian so much as someone focused on what was over the next hill.

TRUMP,
TRUDEAU,
TWEETS,
TRUTH

1

A New "Bully Pulpit"

United States President Donald Trump had the world at his finger-
tips – literally. Trump tweeted incessantly, informing the world
that he is a "very stable genius" or slagging Canadian Prime Minister Justin Trudeau.

Whether working at the White House, holed up at one of his
golf properties, or "wintering" at Mar-a-Lago in Palm Beach, Florida, the former reality television star and self-styled entrepreneur
could get his message out to his estimated eighty million-plus followers at any hour of the day or night.

The president was clear that Twitter was his mass communication channel of choice. In his bestseller *Fear*, author and Pulitzer
Prize-winning journalist Bob Woodward reports Senator Lindsey
Graham had tried to convince the president to stop tweeting.
"Tweeting," the president replied, "that's the way I operate" (Woodward 2018, 104). Woodward also attributes these statements to the
president: "This is my megaphone. This is the way that I speak directly to the people without any filter. Cut through the noise. Cut
through the fake news. That's the only way I have to communicate.
I have tens of millions of followers. This is bigger than cable news.
I go out and give a speech and it is covered by CNN and nobody's
watching, nobody cares. I tweet something and it is my megaphone
to the world" (ibid., 205). Woodward's descriptions flesh out the
extent to which Trump sees Twitter as an extension of himself. "This
is who I am. This is how I communicate. It's the reason I got elected,
it's the reason that I'm successful" (ibid., 206).

The initial 140-character limit imposed by the social media service was seemingly more than adequate for Trump to complete

his thought on any public policy issue – from firing the director of the Federal Bureau of Investigation (FBI) for having the temerity to decline to give voice to a pledge of personal loyalty to Trump, to threatening to end the daily press briefing for the White House press corps. Trump's praise of Secretary of State Mike Pompeo afforded the president the opportunity to trash Pompeo's predecessor, Rex Tillerson. "I couldn't get rid of him fast enough," Trump declared in a tweet that triggered significant follow-on commentary (Trump 2018d). On Christmas Eve 2018, Trump's tweets targeted the Federal Reserve, America's central bank, insisting, "The only problem our economy has is the Fed. They don't have a feel for the Market, they don't understand necessary Trade Wars or Strong Dollar or even Democrat Shutdowns over Borders. The Fed is like a powerful golfer who can't score because he has no touch – he can't putt" (Trump 2018e.).

In fact, Twitter's decision to expand its offering from 140 to 280 characters was a mixed blessing, as far as President Trump was concerned. "I was the Ernest Hemingway of 140 characters," Woodward quotes the president as saying (Woodward 2018, 207).

Trump's predisposition to engage in debate via Twitter provided opponent and 2016 Democratic Party presidential nominee Hillary Clinton one of her better attack lines when she told convention delegates, "A man you can bait with a Tweet is not a man we can trust with nuclear weapons," (Allen and Parnes 2017, 286).

Trump did not confine his Twitter musings to politics or affairs of state. During the 2018 World Series between the Boston Red Sox and the Los Angeles Dodgers, Trump took to Twitter to second-guess decisions by Dodgers manager Dave Roberts – in particular, Roberts's decision to pull his starting pitcher in Game 4, a decision that turned out to be pivotal to the series outcome.

To be sure, Trump wasn't the only baseball fan to question Roberts's decision. But instead of sharing his view with the person on the next bar stool, or friends gathered in a basement rec room, Trump broadened the experience. As Carleton University associate professor Christopher Dornan noted in a tweet, "A sample of how and why Trump uses Twitter. This is Trump sitting on the sofa, watching the game with his cronies, commenting on the play, complaining about strategy, bragging that he would do better. Except we're his cronies, right there on the sofa in his Fireside Chatroom" (Dornan 2018b).

The president used Twitter to make threats, strike deals, denounce critics, and declare victory, as the 31 March 2018 edition of *The Economist* noted (Economist 2018). Twitter was the president's news "network" – a network that has a reach as extensive as television without having to subject presidential declarations to the rigours of a network's editorial process. Trump's Twitter feed allowed him to outflank White House staffers whose job it is to check presidential impulses.

In a social media age, particularly with Twitter, what was once a muttered aside to a friend, family member, or confidant who could be counted on to be discreet can now be a matter of public record – parsed and passed on via the retweet.

Aggressive speech in today's society isn't restricted to politics. In the late summer, just before the launch of the 2019 season for the National Football League, star quarterback Andrew Luck decided he should heed the warnings of multiple injuries and retire. Luck, a Stanford graduate, was only twenty-nine when he made the decision, word of which leaked out via social media during a preseason game (Schefter 2019). As he trotted off the field at the game's conclusion, Luck – a bona fide star – was actually booed by the hometown fans of his team, the Indianapolis Colts (Dahlberg 2019).

Attack rhetoric with an anti-elite tinge in the legacy media as well as on social media is as prominent a feature in political discourse in Canada as it is in the United States. The SNC-Lavalin furor that flailed through the spring and summer of 2019 provides several examples. Business and academic leaders read how their networks are their Achilles heels. Former justices of the Supreme Court of Canada see the word "scandal" linked directly to their names. Their crime? Offering a legal opinion to a client on a matter of law. And the sources of this pointed criticism? Accomplished individuals such as Dr Ian Brodie, a former chief of staff to Prime Minister Stephen Harper, a tenured professor, a member of the board of directors for the Institute for Research on Public Policy. In a post 17 August 2019, Brodie tweeted, "There may be a need to regulate the post-judicial career of Supreme Court and other judges" (Brodie 2019a). "But the scandal here is that three retired Supreme Court judges, including one retired Chief Justice, thought it was okay to squeeze the federal Attorney General about a criminal prosecution!" (Brodie 2019b). "After writing all those dicta about the rule of law!" (Brodie 2019c). That individuals such as Frank Iacobucci – who has served Canada with such distinction in many iterations of his professional life – would be subject to such an attack is a sign of our times.

Veteran political columnist Martin Patriquin, *The Logic*'s Quebec correspondent, offered his own succinct zinger to describe Twitter. Appearing on a panel for CBC's public affairs program *Power & Politics*, Patriquin looked into the camera and said, "Twitter is where idiocy and entitlement meet" (CBC 2019d). Patriquin and his fellow panellists had been asked their views of a tweet posted earlier in the week by former prime minister Kim Campbell. With Hurricane Dorian headed for the Florida coast in late August 2019, Campbell tweeted, "I'm rooting for a direct hit on Mar a Lago," the reference, of course, being to President Trump's Florida home and private club (Webster and Law 2019).

The reaction to Campbell's ill-considered jibe was instantaneous and negative. Former Arkansas governor and presidential aspirant Michael Huckabee was quick to respond, as was Trump's son Eric. "Are Liberals this hateful?" Huckabee asked in his response (Huckabee 2019).

Campbell's first response to the backlash was to double down. "And no, I don't wish anyone, anywhere, the horror of being hit by a Category 4 Hurricane. But not everyone can have the protection of a fortress like Mar a Lago, built to be hurricane-proof! Trump will not bear the cost of his immoral abdication of the climate challenge!" Campbell tweeted (Campbell, K. 2019a). The exchange was of particular interest to this writer, for intensely personal reasons – a hurricane can't hit Mar-a-Lago without hitting the town of Lantana, just down the A1A and where I live some of the time. Campbell finally posted an apology. "I have deleted my tweet about the hurricane & Mar a Lago and sincerely apologize to all it offended. It was intended as sarcasm–not a serious wish of harm. Throwaway lines get a life of their own on Twitter. I shd know better. Mea culpa" (Campbell, K. 2019b).

Campbell's tweet is but one of many proof points that the sin of stating stupid stuff on Twitter is not exclusive to either conservatives or progressives.

Trump's use of Twitter to "change the channel" in terms of mainstream media coverage has convinced certain journalists and social media gurus that he is a master media manipulator.

New York Times reporter Susanne Craig, who began her illustrious career as an intern at the *Calgary Herald*, has been dealing with the Trump family for years and told a 2018 gathering sponsored by the Canadian Journalism Foundation (CJF), "They are very savvy when dealing with the media" (Canadian Journalism Foundation 2018c).

Craig cited Trump's "ability to control the media conversation" (ibid.). But while recognizing Trump's skill, Craig is clear that his skill has not been applied for the greater good. At the CJF J-Talk session, Craig told former CBC news executive Julian Sher "Trump is good for journalism in the way war is good for the economy" (ibid.).

Michael Tomasky, writing in the *New York Review of Books*, states, "Trump is in our faces, and our brains, constantly" (Tomasky 2018). Scott Adams, the creator of the *Dilbert* comic strip, is one of those who sees the strategy behind Trump's puffery, arguing that even the most erratic of Trump's moves are tactically brilliant (Winter 2017).

Twitter cofounder Ev Williams considers Trump a "master of the platform." In the course of an interview conducted for CNN Business at the Collision tech conference held in Toronto in May 2019, Williams said, "What Trump has done with Twitter is pretty genius, frankly" (O'Sullivan 2019).

New York University professor Jay Rosen begs to differ. Writing in PressThink, a project of the Arthur L. Carter Journalism Institute at New York University, Rosen (2017) acknowledges Trump's use of internet-based practices such as "sock puppetry" and "trolling." Rosen insists such behaviour "takes no genius. It takes gall. And a press willing to amplify" (ibid.).

Rosen concedes Trump's approach to media relations was shaped, in no small measure, by the fact he cannot be shamed. The president's predisposition to be "risk-friendly" in a field where most practitioners are risk-averse is a further consideration. And the overarching reason Rosen is inclined to doubt the "blinding brilliance" of Trump's earned media strategy? "Maybe it's the fact that he's gotten more negative press than any candidate or president ever" (ibid.).

A study of Trump's first one hundred days in office conducted by the Shorenstein Center on Media, Politics and Public Policy (Patterson 2017) confirmed Rosen's assessment that much of Trump's coverage in the legacy media was negative. "Studies of earlier presidents found nothing comparable to the level of unfavourable coverage afforded Trump," the study states (ibid., 14). Trump's negatives exceeded even those of former president Bill Clinton – who, astonishingly, given his electoral success, never experienced a single quarter in the eight years of his presidency where his positive coverage weighting exceeded that of the negative coverage. The Shorenstein Center study of Trump concludes, "Never in the nation's history has the country had a president with so little fidelity to the facts, so little appreciation for the dignity of the presidential office, and so little understanding of the underpinnings of democracy" (ibid., 15).

What the study also confirms is Trump's ability to exploit the legacy media's weakness for "breaking news" – especially that of television. "Through his tweets and actions, Trump exploits this habit, enabling him to change the subject when it suits his needs," the report concludes (ibid., 15–16).

There is a case to be made that Trump excelled in using a tweet as the political equivalent of a head fake in sports, a move intended to distract and displace. In July 2019, *The Economist* noted the pattern of a presidential tweet described by critics as outrageous – telling four women of colour who are members of Congress that they should go back "where they came from" – for example. His critics erupt in protest. His supporters stay silent. The provocation and response dominate the news cycle in the legacy press for days, even as the Trump administration makes a major policy change that is no less controversial but that gets lost in the shuffle (Economist 2019).

Former White House chief strategist Stephen K. Bannon argues observers are making a serious mistake if they think Trump's communications strategy was accidental. Easily overlooked by those who find Trump irksome is the fact that there is often a kernel of truth in what he says – stripped of context, to be sure, but offered up for public consumption in a manner consistent with the tradition of risk communications expert Peter Sandman's "outrage" industries (1993). "Trump understands the overwhelming power of modern mass communications. Trump gets what the media itself has forgotten about themselves," Bannon told *The New York Times* (Haberman and Rogers 2018).

While the success of these presidential "jukes" is a debatable point, the bottom line remains: Trump received three times the amount of coverage received by previous presidents, and he was the featured speaker in nearly two-thirds of that coverage, even if it was, in the main, negative coverage. Candidate Trump, by way of comparison, received far more positive coverage than his rivals for the 2016 Republican nomination when "journalists embraced him, and he returned the favor," according to the Shorenstein study (Patterson 2017, 3). The Shorenstein study, however, does underscore Trump's value as catalyst, whose successful presidential campaign exposed fault lines: in the way we do politics and business in Canada and the United States, in the way we conduct our journalism in those two related spheres, and in the communications strategies that shape public discourse.

In the same way hockey evolved from a blue-collar sport played on frozen ponds and outdoor rinks to an upper-middle-class sport played in suburban arenas, journalism in general, and political journalism in particular, evolved from trade or craft to profession. News organizations employed fewer dropouts who ran for coffee as the first rung on a career ladder and more university graduates, often with multiple degrees. Less police beat on the news pages, more urban hip. Housing prices stories crowded out housing availability stories.

The professionalization of journalism, and by extension, the communications culture that has developed to support it, led to a conversation of insiders. The mainstream media served primarily as a signalling system between interests. Data-driven politics, and the microtargeted communications activities that flowed from it, led to an increasingly diminished "circuit of communication," to cite Miller and Macintyre (1998). Whole segments of society were not "in the loop." Predictably, almost by default, the excluded engaged in their own conversations – conversations that those in the loop were unaware were even taking place. Both the Trump and Clinton campaigns in 2016 realized the list of the excluded – which had long included women and minorities – had grown. Working-class white men, for example, were now also on the list. Only Trump did something about it – at least, in communications terms.

Whatever one's assessment of Trump's effectiveness, America's forty-fifth president redefined the rules of political communication, challenged the conventions of political journalism and, in so doing, reshaped public discourse throughout Western liberal democracies.

In essence, this work is the story of a pivot: in the way we do politics, in the way we do business, and in the way we cover and talk about politics and business. And the "pivot" in this case is not the spinner's pivot of "ask me about wheat and I'll tell you about fish" but rather the pivot of an athlete – a transfer of power, of motion, of acceleration, of execution. It is also the story of a breaking point in the business model for mainstream or legacy media outlets as news organizations seek new revenue sources to offset the collapse of advertising revenue. Finally, it is the story of a distribution shift enabled by technology and a discourse shift enabled by the distribution shift.

This reordering has been and will continue to be uneven in its execution, even awkward at times. And as the media pivots, triggering a consequential public discourse pivot, the structure of political and corporate communications – and maybe the structure of politics and business itself – will have to pivot as well.

Examples of this pivot abound, from the seemingly trivial to those with profound geopolitical consequences.

Trump travelled to Washington, DC, as president-elect for his first meeting with then-president Barack Obama without letting the media pool travel with him (Hennessey 2016). Later, the president-elect headed out for a steak dinner at 21 Club after his media relations staff had assured the press he was in for the night. The "protective pool," as it is known, protested (Davies 2016). The president-elect shrugged.

In Trump's new media world, anyone with a Twitter account is potentially as current about Trump's movements or thought process as the most experienced White House correspondent, a point that seemed lost on political reporters who persisted in the practice of filing "he-said"-style stories based on Trump tweets.

His "earned media" strategy for the 2016 presidential campaign arguably objectified women, indulged in base racial stereotyping, and slandered both opponents and his own party stalwarts in equal measure. Trump's approach also generated saturation coverage for his candidacy in the mainstream press.

Trump's communications strategy was reinforced with a social media method that operationalized Bannon's belief that an electoral coalition could be built by manipulating people through the internet. Often referred to as the "weaponization of social media" (Singer and Brooking 2018), Trump and his communications strategists applied V.O. Key's "echo chamber" (1966) to the multiplatform universe of social media. Trump embraced Twitter as the new "bully pulpit," to borrow Doris Kearns Goodwin's (2013) descriptive of Teddy Roosevelt's approach to media relations.

Theodore Roosevelt found common cause with a muckraking press to push for the reforms that defined America's "Progressive

Era." Trump, in sharp contrast, used his bully pulpit to declare the media the enemy of the American people. To reinforce the idea the president saw Twitter as his bully pulpit, it is worth noting Trump tried to block critics. In July 2019, a federal appeals court upheld a 2018 district court ruling that public officials cannot turn off people "from an otherwise open online dialogue because they expressed views with which the official disagrees" (Swisher 2019).

Trump rails against a mainstream media conspiracy – with a particular focus on the *New York Times* – ignoring the fact that his public standing in America is largely a legacy media creation. If millions of Americans believe Trump is a successful businessperson, the perception was shaped in no small measure by NBC, the television network that spent tens of millions of dollars in publicity telling them so, the better to promote Trump's reality show *The Apprentice* – a Mark Burnett production. Trump, in fact, is the personification of the old joke: "I'm not a doctor, but I play one on TV." *Vanity Fair* contributing editor Fran Lebowitz once described President Trump as "a poor person's idea of a rich person" (Fox, E.J. 2016).

When *Attention Merchants*'s author Tim Wu (2016) talks about the "celebrity industrial complex," he is referring to Donald Trump-like celebrities who are known primarily for their "well-knownness," in the words of historian Daniel J. Boorstin (1962).

Globe and Mail columnist and McGill professor David Shribman observed Trump "skews every established political expectation and rule" (Shribman 2017). That Trump's son-in-law Jared Kushner and daughter Ivanka Trump occupied important advisory positions in the White House speaks to the president's lack of a sense of the appropriate. That son Eric Trump's wedding planner ran the Department of Housing and Urban Development's largest regional office in New York speaks to the absurd.

Protocol and precedent demonstrably have no place in Trump's world. The president apparently thought it appropriate to talk about TV ratings at a National Prayer Breakfast.

The president has created a cottage industry of fact checkers – most notably the *Toronto Star*'s former Washington bureau chief

Daniel Dale. Dale, who has since joined the cable news network CNN, did an exemplary job holding President Trump to account for his public utterances. As the 2020 US presidential campaign unfolded, a case could be made that Dale's coverage was having an impact on the broader electorate. That said, these media efforts to address the record of the Trump administration would seem to have had little or no effect on Trump's hard core of base supporters – estimated at fully 35 per cent of the US electorate. Or on the Republican Party, for that matter.

Michael Wolff suggests part of the explanation is that Trump's supporters were never under any illusions about the president. "That was almost his appeal: he was what he was," Wolff writes. "Twinkle in his eye, larceny in his heart" (Wolff 2018, 20). Trump understands intuitively how irrelevant journalists' investigative findings can be in a post-truth world, a world that plays out on mobile devices and screens with doctored Facebook videos of House Speaker Nancy Pelosi.

American voters endorsed Trump's call for change on 8 November 2016; albeit tepidly. Trump won the Electoral College vote decisively, lost the popular vote by more than 2.8 million votes (Kentish 2016), but for all intents and purposes swept the "fly-over" states of Middle America.

His bid to become the de facto political leader of the Western world – as unsettling to some as it was improbable to most – has media sociologists reconsidering the role of media in general, and social media in particular, in civic discourse.

A Knight Foundation report released in October 2018 analyzed the extent of Twitter as a platform for the dissemination of disinformation. The study, led by George Washington University researcher Matthew Hindman, analyzed ten million tweets from 700,000 Twitter accounts with help from the social media intelligence firm Graphika (Hindman and Barash 2018).

The report states 6.6 million tweets linking to fake and conspiracy news published in the month before the 2016 election had been posted. "A supercluster of densely interlinked, heavily followed accounts plays a large role in the spread of fake news and disinformation on Twitter," the study concludes (ibid., 43). "Social bots likely make up the majority of the accounts in the supercluster" (ibid.). The study revealed "a large majority of fake news came from supposedly pro-Republican and pro-Donald Trump accounts in the month before the election, smaller but still substantial amounts of fake news were passed on by liberal or Democratic-identified accounts" (ibid., 4).

Trump's tweets can affect business conversations as well. A morning tweet denouncing Boeing (Trump 2016) for cost overruns in a proposal to replace Air Force One caused a sag in Boeing's share price. Similar tweets citing cost overruns for the F-35 fighter jet program created similar investment "opportunities" for high-frequency traders. Selective disclosure sections in securities law tend not to take the impact of presidential pronouncements on Twitter into account. More substantively, Trump's tweets in the spring of 2018 threatening a trade war with China caused the long-running bull market to lose steam. When the president stepped up his Twitter attacks on China in December 2018, the perceived threat of a trade war between the two superpowers triggered the worst December declines for market indices since the Great Depression (Bayly 2019). A story in *Bloomberg Businessweek* entitled "The Chaos Cycle: Powell Speaks, Trump Tweets, China Reacts, Markets Freak. Repeat" published in August 2019, and edited by Pat Regnier, states, "The ups and downs of asset prices on any given day are being determined, more and more, by the words and actions of three men" (Regan 2019). The three identified in the piece? Trump, Federal Reserve Chair Jerome Powell, and Xi Jinping, president of China (ibid.).

But the article cedes Trump's pride of place.

"First, of course, is Donald Trump who has rediscovered his power to send markets soaring – or into a tailspin – with less than 280 characters on Twitter" (ibid.).

Canadians in general, and Prime Minister Justin Trudeau in particular, now have a heightened appreciation of President Trump's skill of turning "words into weapons," as an article in the *Guardian* so artfully described Trump's use of Twitter (Lakoff and Duran 2018).

Having taken his leave of the G7 summit of the world's most industrialized nations, which Canada was hosting in the town of La Malbaie, Quebec, in June 2018, Trump switched on one of the "20 television sets" he said they have on the presidential aircraft, Air Force One, to catch Trudeau's concluding news conference. Trump, on his way to his self-declared "historic" summit with North Korean leader Kim Jong Un, was enraged by Trudeau's answer to a media query about a Canadian response to US plans to impose tariffs on Canadian steel and aluminum entering the United States (Laughland 2018).

Trump's decision to invoke "national security" as the rationale for the tariffs was particularly irritating to Canada. Trudeau, as he had on several occasions in the days leading up to the summit, made it clear if the US persisted in applying these tariffs – which Trudeau described as "kind of insulting" – Canadians would respond in kind. Speaking on behalf of all Canadians, Trudeau said, "We're polite, we're reasonable, but we also will not be pushed around" (Papenfuss 2018).

Trump, basically, blew a gasket. He ordered US administrators to not sign the joint declaration worked out by G7 leaders that Trump had agreed to scant hours before. The president first accused the Canadian prime minister of making false statements (Trump 2018a) and then fired off a tweet describing Trudeau as "very dishonest" (Trump 2018b). For one G7 leader to call another a liar is unusual to say the least. But Trump wasn't finished. Subsequent tweets mocked Trudeau as having "acted so meek and mild" when the two met face to face. The implication was clear: Trudeau was a milquetoast when Trump was in the room and only found his tough-talk voice once he thought the president was safely in the air and on his way to Singapore.

Lest anyone miss the true intent of Trump's tweets, the president unleashed two of his most senior advisers to appear on US public affairs television the following Sunday morning. Larry Kudlow, director of Trump's National Economic Council, said of the Canadian prime minister, "Here's the thing … He really kind of stabbed us in the back" (Chiacu and Lynch 2018). Trade adviser Peter Navarro went even further, declaring "there is a special place in hell for any foreign leader that engages in bad faith diplomacy with President Donald J. Trump" (Watkins 2018).

The Twitter-triggered attack from the president and his advisers against the Canadian prime minister unleashed a media feeding frenzy in Canada. As former CTV commentator Don Martin put it, in Trump's new world, North Korea is lionized even as Canada is demonized (Martin, D. 2018). The spat led to significant coverage in the US media as well.

The harsh language introduced an even harsher reality: the dispute raised the risk of a broader trade war between Canada and the United States, a trade war that would cost Canada more dearly than it would the US. Trump's threat to retaliate by imposing tariffs on the automotive sector was particularly problematic, given the importance of the auto industry to Ontario's manufacturing sector. Trump's tweets literally threatened the livelihoods of tens of thousands of Canadians and, in a worst-case scenario, threatened to tip the Canadian economy into recession.

To add insult to the injury, public opinion research suggested Americans do not hold Canadians in quite as high a regard as they did before Trump fired up his thumbs.

Trudeau was later asked if he shared Senator Lindsey Graham's view that the president should give it a rest from time to time. Trudeau was at his diplomatic best when he answered, "I think it's important for people to be authentic and he's certainly authentic" (Press 2018).

My former boss Brian Mulroney often said a Canadian prime minister has two overarching concerns: national unity and the relationship with the United States. Mulroney would likely add the relationship with China to the list if the question was put today.

Trump and Trudeau are fundamentally different people. Yet Trudeau offered a candid and insightful explanation of the relationship between the two in an interview with *New York Times* reporter Ian Austen: "We're very different in our approaches and in our ideologies. But we also know the relationship between the two countries is bigger than any one person, and because of that, we get along as fine as we need to" (Austen 2019).

As *The Economist* observed in its 12 November 2016 edition, if Trump did not rewrite the rules of campaigning, he certainly got away with flouting most of them (Economist 2016b).

Jay Rosen's assessment notwithstanding, Trump sees himself as skilled in the exercise of traditional media relations. By way of illustration, in the early days of transition, Trump summoned network news anchors and executives to Trump Tower. Trump insisted the session be off the record. Once the network types agreed, the president-elect lectured and berated them all, dismissed them as "liars," then arranged for a one-sided account of the dressing-down to appear the next morning in the *New York Post*, to ensure that the collective humiliation of the broadcaster grandees was part of the breakfast conversation as people gathered in Manhattan over coffee and bagels.

While Trudeau's primary social media tool is Facebook, his communications team is careful not to ignore Twitter and other digital platforms. Indeed, Trudeau's former principal secretary Gerald Butts was an early, and frequent, interlocutor on Twitter. Butts understands today's "spin cycle" begins before news accounts are posted, that political advisers who wanted to steer a narrative in a particular direction needed to nudge the story along through early and repeated social media engagement. Butts's frequent tweets led more traditional political operatives to wonder how anyone that active on Twitter could find time to do their job. Butts understood earlier and better than many that these tweets were a big part of his job. As the prime minister's closest adviser Butts also knew that if Twitter was the hook to get the attention of activists and the engaged, Facebook and Instagram were the platforms of choice for the "persuasion" stage of political communications for the broader public.

Facebook continued to be central to both Trump and Trudeau's communications strategies while in office. In sharp contrast to Mr Trump, the Liberal leader's messaging reflected his "sunny ways" narrative, a narrative that fits with Facebook and the social network's roots. Trudeau's shift was no less a tectonic event than Trump's, even if the Liberal leader's appeal was to our "better angels." Mainstream media certainly had a role in both the Trudeau and Trump election campaigns. Where once mainstream media provided *the* forum, now the legacy press provided *a* forum. With the shift to social media platforms, politics changed fundamentally. Trudeau's early rock-star-like standing internationally speaks to the top line success of his social media strategy, even as the first cracks of disapproval started to appear on home ice on issues as varied as pipeline expansion, crippling tariffs on Canadian steel and aluminum, or the SNC-Lavalin affair where the prime minister's advisers were accused of applying "undue pressure" on former minister of justice and attorney general Jody Wilson-Raybould; a saga that will be explored in some further detail in a later chapter.

Conservative critics love to criticize Prime Minister Justin Trudeau for his love of selfies – the implication being the Liberal leader is all about photo ops and not substance. Yet the two are not necessarily mutually exclusive. Massachusetts Senator Elizabeth Warren's unsuccessful bid for the Democratic nomination for president in 2020 was lauded as policy-rich. "Warren has a plan for that" was so common a refrain that she sold T-shirts and other merchandise emblazoned with it. And according to the media intelligence firm Zignal Labs, Warren was also the candidate "most associated with the term 'selfies'" (Kolhatkar 2019). Indeed, she often spent hours at the end of events in selfie marathons.

This shift from mainstream or legacy media to social media reflects the evolution of political communications with implications for public discourse. And it is decidedly a mixed blessing for all. *Toronto Star* columnist Susan Delacourt captured the emerging reality when she stated, "2018 may well come to be known as the year of buyers' remorse when it comes to politicians and social media" (Delacourt 2018).

Trump and Trudeau, as political leaders of neighbouring countries seeking common cause despite sharply different political philosophies and approaches to public life, will be considered as catalysts of this new era. Their respective earned media strategies exposed both the fault lines and the opportunities inherent in the way we discuss politics and business. While supporters of both men would recoil in horror at the mere suggestion they have anything in common, the fact is both Trump and Trudeau have a touch of the narcissist about them. Even though Trump and Trudeau express radically different worldviews, they share the ability to obtain and maintain attention.

For purposes of this book, their respective success or failure matters less than the fact that as candidates, they are changing the conventions and practices of media relations and, in doing so, are affecting political discourse.

The professionalization of political and business communications over the last four decades led to the cultural splintering that *Data Smog* author David Shenk warned about two decades ago (1997). As British academic Aeron Davis (2000) observed in the latter decades of the twentieth century, journalists and institutional communicators created a hybrid media world that moved away from the traditional media effects, a one-to-many model, yet stopped short of social media's many-to-many potential.

Davis described this hybrid as an "elite discourse network" (ibid.). More familiar descriptives from the US cited "inside the Beltway" political conversations – a reference to the ring road freeway system that surrounds Washington, DC. NYU professor Jay Rosen identified the "church of the savvy" (2009) in this regard. Media relations in this new world became an exercise in elite discourse management. Institutional communications resources were allocated to feed an ever decreasing pool of working reporters. The consequence was a conversation between an established order – largely older, male, and white – of people who had attended the

same schools, read the same books, lived in the same neighbour-
hoods, shared the same globalist free-market worldview. This
"discourse" excluded the general population because "people"
weren't the object of the exercise. The "politics" of the policy or
program initiative came to dominate political discourse, the effect
of the program in specific communities discussed only in that limited context. Not surprisingly, the ever growing numbers excluded
from these "inside the Beltway" conversations found voice in other
outlets – talk radio initially; then specialty TV channels, blogs, and
internet-based news sites. Political parties – such as the Reform
Party of Canada – that could not find a pew in the "church of the
savvy" instead seized the opportunity to fashion a decidedly different discourse for their own platforms.

Any study of media – legacy or social – is a study of power; political and economic power, primarily.

Media scholars have long identified the concept of "media effects"
as a core tenet of communications research. Yet the extent of the
media's influence or effect has been the subject of spirited, even divisive, debate among communications scholars for more than a century.

Much of the media effects research to date, as reflected in Thomas
C. Leonard's work, for example, has focused on the media's role
as a primary site of political discourse in Western liberal democracies, assigning the mainstream media pride of place as the
post-Enlightenment's agora or public commons.

As American political scientist Harold D. Lasswell stated, "rational
choices depend on enlightenment, which in turn depends upon
communication and especially upon the equivalence of attention
among the leaders, experts and rank-and-file" (1948, 51). For that
reason, the mass media's role in shaping public opinion has been
a particular focus of media effects research. The legendary Walter
Lippmann argued, "We shall assume that what each man does is
based not on direct and certain knowledge, but by pictures made
by himself or given to him" (1922). Individuals, according to Lippmann, form opinions based "on the pictures in our heads" (ibid.).
The mass media – for the better part of two centuries – played a

central role in the creation of those pictures. Symbols, therefore, are an important part of the machinery of human communication. The media's role in symbol creation, in turn, has implications for the way society organizes itself, including, but not limited to, the way society organizes both politically and in terms of financial markets.

Not surprisingly, the main body of scholarly evidence in the media effects field examines the legacy or traditional media model of top down, one-to-many mass communication. Society's institutions – governments, courts, financial markets – organized their communications functions accordingly.

The mainstream media fulfilled a central role as the gatekeepers of public discourse. And because of that gatekeeper function, the mainstream media played a central role in defining political agendas. Problems featured in evening newscasts or on the front pages of daily newspapers were problems political and business leaders were expected to take up (Iyengar and Kinder 1987). Issues outside the glare of the media searchlight were problems political leaders could safely ignore. Institutional communications brought a laser-like focus on the media's gatekeeper function. Institutional communications were designed to advance a "command and control" agenda by influencing the news gathering process.

To paraphrase the late communications scholar James Carey, media managers and institutional communicators alike understood that society constructs a reality through communications and then takes up residence in the reality we've collectively constructed. And therein lies the cornerstone of the media's power: its ability to construct and then distribute "reality."

To distill the better part of a century of media effects theory scholarship to a series of bumper stickers, a few people made the news – sources. And fewer still decided what the news would be – gatekeepers. The business model that supported the mainstream media was equally straightforward. The media's product was eyeballs, sold to interests with paid messages to convey.

In the later part of the twentieth century, television established itself as the information media of choice. A whole industry built up around the art of stagecraft – political communications directors as executive producers. Stagecraft is the reason former Richard Nixon chief of staff H.R. Haldeman described the job of "advance man" as one of the most demanding jobs in politics (Whipple 2017).

The "reach" got bigger, and the number of people able to make news got even smaller, leaders mostly. And the gatekeepers were even fewer. In Ronald Reagan's White House in the 1980s, the media strategy each week was able to focus on as few as a dozen journalists.

This focus on a remarkably few people meant "inside the Beltway" became more than a Washington insider disclaimer. Talking-head television meant the tall foreheads of the pundit class – of which I was a member for many years – talked to and about themselves. The general public was, in the main, excluded from the conversation and, if referenced at all, were discussed in largely anthropological terms.

And then along came the World Wide Web, which blew both the operational model and the business model to smithereens, albeit not overnight.

Harold Innis (1950) observed that with each new communication technology, a new empire emerges that harnesses the innovations and power that new media affords. And Marshall McLuhan (1964) argued, "the medium is the message": the overall impact of a medium is far greater than the content that medium carries. We certainly see this with social media, even if we are only now starting to understand it; collectively slow to appreciate how revolutionary the new pipeline would prove to be.

As new social media platforms began to emerge, we persisted in the one-to-many model of communication. Our political leaders set up Twitter accounts to show they were hip, and then, unaware of the premium social media ascribes to "authenticity," let their staff craft the tweets. Conservative leadership hopeful Peter MacKay's tweets during the early days of the 2019–20 campaign to succeed Andrew Scheer are a textbook example of how not to.

Meanwhile, the true revolutionaries built new sites for groups that had been excluded or marginalized from the legacy media discourse. Women, racialized people, and young people were able to organize and amplify their voices. They discovered they could bypass the gatekeepers, have political conversations that political leaders were barely aware of and, in the case of Arab Spring, literally overthrow governments in politically oppressed countries such as Yemen, Egypt, and Tunisia despite a "lapdog" legacy media that was anything but a free press. These activists also discovered the harsh truth that the power of social media to disrupt could give rise to the power of armed conflict.

Voices in North America who believed they, too, were excluded from that mainstream media conversation saw the same opportunity in emerging technologies – with one major difference. Unlike the civil society groups in Yemen, for example, some of the people in America who did not see their worldview reflected in the legacy media were not disadvantaged, either socially or economically. In fact, they had more money than everyone else combined. So they spent their money on new media and created outlets such as Breitbart News.

In many ways, certain of these online gatekeepers resemble a racetrack tout – someone who offers advice about betting on horses – either to influence the odds or to share in some of the winnings. These digital touts – including algorithms – offer eyeballs a content tailored to their particular worldview, and that tailoring is fashioned by detailed information provided by the "consumer" themselves. The messaging is at once an exercise in opinion reinforcement and the creation of a distinct community that, in turn, impacts public discourse and, by extension, public opinion. And in a perversion of James Carey's democratic ideal, they created an alternative reality and took up residence in it; a world shaped by fake news where belief mattered more than reason.

With the emergence of social media platforms and applications that make it possible for people to create, share, and exchange information, constructing reality has been altered fundamentally. Journalism is being disaggregated. The one-to-many model of mainstream media has given way in theory, if not in practice, to the many-to-many constellation of social media. The gatekeeper function is no longer the domain of a select few editors – overwhelmingly of a dominant white male demographic. But ironically, the selection and distribution of texts now rests in the hands of even fewer social media platforms. The "editor" has given way to the "algorithm." The "boys on the bus," so endearingly chronicled in Timothy Crouse's book on the same name on the 1972 US presidential campaign, have given way to "trending" topics. And while the algorithms that decide which topics are trending may lay claim to being fair and impartial, it's not difficult for them to be "gamed" or manipulated, and often for profit. A great example of this are the "boys" in the Macedonian city of Veles with its population of 45,000 – home to some 140 American political websites – effectively trolls for Trump (Silverman 2016a).

Algorithms have power, the platforms they enable have near monopolies, which in turn gives rise to what British scholar Helen Kennedy describes as "data-driven" discrimination (Kennedy, H. 2017).

A world where news conformed to a concise and relatively precise definition largely made by "knowns" has given way to what Clay Shirky (2008) describes as an "ecosystem" of information generators.

News, despite journalistic claims to the contrary, wasn't always about truth. News is, and always was, more about accuracy than veracity. Ironically, in the context of the 2016 US presidential campaign or Britain's Brexit referendum on leaving the European Union, this fixation on accuracy proved to be the mainstream media's Achilles heel.

The Trumps and the Nigel Farages – former head of the UK Independence Party – of the world fully understood that their promises and warnings of apocalyptical outcomes in the heat of presidential or referendum campaigns didn't have to be true or ever happen. The "news" test was met if they simply said so. The journalist's job too often was stenographic: accurately recording the assertion, infrequently testing the veracity of the assertion in follow-up stories.

When the original declaration occurs on a social media platform, even the minimal accuracy tests of traditional journalism are not a precondition to distribution. Instead, emotion and an expression of existing belief tend to motivate distribution via social media. Legacy journalism, built as it was for the better part of a hundred years on an advertising-based business model, has long wrestled with the challenge of finding a balance between the interesting and the important. Social media sites came down decidedly on the "interesting" side of the equation.

Facebook is a particular focus of attention in election campaigns and the follow-on postmortems in the United States. According to a *New York Times* piece by Mike Isaac (2016), a private chat sprang up among Facebook executives on election night in 2016 when it became obvious that Trump would win; they were asking each other what role the company had played in shaping the election outcome. Subsequently, company chair and chief executive officer Mark Zuckerberg said it was "a pretty crazy idea" to think Facebook affected the outcome. Others scoffed at Zuckerberg's assertion. University of North Carolina associate professor Zeynep Tufekci flat out declared, "Of course Facebook had a significant influence in this last election outcome" (ibid.).

The "influence" argument proceeds on twin tracks; the first, an argument of scale: more than one-quarter of the world's population has a Facebook page. Further, a majority of Americans state they get their news from social media. Which is interesting because Facebook executives, including Monika Bickert, head of global policy management (Bell 2019), and Kevin Chan, Facebook's head of public policy for Canada, speaking as a panellist at a Massey College event, insist they are not in the news business (pers. notes). Facebook says it is a technology company, and as such it doesn't have to engage in the fact checking that news organizations build their brands on.

The second track is linked to the business model of social media platforms and the impact that business model has on traditional legacy media outlets. If advertising was indeed the midwife of a free press (Curran and Seaton 2003), the advertisers have found a new and vastly more efficient vehicle for their commercial messages.

Facebook's business model is its prisoner's dilemma. As John Naughton (2016) observed, "Facebook has a conflict of interest in these matters. It makes its vast living, remember, from monitoring and making money from the data trails of its users." The more an item is "shared" on Facebook, the higher the financial reward for the self-described "social network." Fake news may be bad for democracy but, as Naughton and others have pointed out, for social media platforms, it's good for business. In an analysis of Facebook activity by *BuzzFeed* (Silverman 2016b) for the three months before the 2016 US election, bogus election news stories appearing online and in social media appeared to have greater reach than the most popular articles generated by major news websites. Fake stories declaring both Pope Francis and the actor Denzel Washington had backed Donald Trump's presidential bid are two such examples. "Among the 20 most popular fake election stories identified by *BuzzFeed*, all but three favored Mr. Trump or denigrated Hillary Clinton" (Harris and Eddy 2016).

The *New York Times* or the Canadian Broadcasting Corporation are accountable for the news they produce. Google and Facebook are not accountable for the news they distribute, incredibly, as a direct result of federal law.

Outgoing president Barack Obama expressed his concerns about the impact of fake news on democracy. "If we are not serious about facts, and what's true and what's not, and particularly in an age of social media where so many people are getting their information in soundbites and off their phones, if we can't discriminate between serious arguments and propaganda, then we have problems" (ibid.).

Western liberal democracies need to have a meaningful public policy discussion around the role of journalism in general and social media in particular when it comes to enabling or hindering civic discourse. While Europe has developed the General Data Protection Regulation (GDPR), acknowledging that innovations in governance need to keep pace with innovations in technology, the Canadian and US governments have fallen behind, creating a policy deficit with regard to social media accountability on issues as varied as interference in the election process and the integrity of content to data mining and artificial intelligence (Hirsh 2018).

The Europeans seem more prepared to engage in a substantive policy debate on the issues. The Germans, for example, want to know more about the "secret sauce" of social media – the algorithms that determine what we'll see when we log on. Outgoing German Chancellor Angela Merkel stated, "I believe we should not underestimate what is happening in the context of the internet and with digitalization; this is part of our reality. We have regulations that allow for our press freedom, including the requirement for due diligence from journalists. Today, we have many that experience a media that is based on very different foundations and is much less regulated" (Tharoor 2016).

The fake-news debate around social media and the online news organizations distributed by the platforms are but one component part of these campaign postmortems. The abject failure of the mainstream media is being chronicled in equal detail. *New York Times* columnist Nicholas Kristof believes he and his colleagues are too out of touch with working-class America. The voting public, in the words of *The Economist*, "repudiate the media – including this newspaper – for being patronizing, partisan, out of touch and as elitist as the politicians" (Economist 2016c). *Columbia Journalism Review* editor Kyle Pope says of Trump's triumph, "Simply put, it is rooted in a failure of reporting" (Pope 2016).

Pope's assertion is worth exploring in a broader conversation focused on the impact of an increasingly threatened mainstream media and an ever expanding and evolving social media on public discourse and public institutions through the public policy panel of the prism.

Trump's electoral success in 2016 triggered an insightful and compelling body of "post-game analysis." *The Economist* noted, "an apparently amateurish and chaotic campaign has humiliated an industry of consultants, pundits and pollsters" (Economist 2016c).

Trump's electoral success also triggered an existential crisis in the legacy media. Having blown the story, the mainstream media "is reviled, financially desperate, and undergoing a crisis of faith about the very efficacy of gathering facts," according to journalist, novelist, and playwright George Packer, writing in the *New Yorker* (2016).

Former Trump strategist Bannon says political journalists "still do not understand why Donald Trump is the president of the United States" and refers to the 2016 presidential campaign as a "humiliating defeat" for the mainstream press (Grynbaum 2017).

To some extent, Trump's subsequent travails were entirely predictable. Republican rival Jeb Bush had warned Trump would be a "chaos president." As Tom Axworthy, principal secretary to former prime minister Pierre Trudeau, wryly observed at a Massey College gathering at the University of Toronto, "When you elect a clown, expect a circus" (Axworthy 2017).

And the melodrama continues. The release of Michael Wolff's *Fire and Fury* in January 2018 is one example. Much of Wolff's work has been challenged on a fact-by-fact basis. Yet its defenders argue that it feels true or speaks to a larger truth. The fact remains, the American electorate has turned the executive branch of their government over to people who literally cannot spell Denmark in an official communiqué. And yet the error-filled executive orders emanating from the White House signal major domestic and foreign policy shifts from positions held by every president of the United States since Harry Truman.

Trump basically threatened a trade war with Canada in a tweet. And Canada's political and economic landscape shifted dramatically as a result.

Any meaningful postmortem, therefore, must include all participants in the civic discourse process – from the individuals who have voice, to the individuals who provide the song sheet.

The emergence of broadcast technology triggered an extended consideration of public policy options here in Canada in the early part of the twentieth century; a similar engagement of thought leaders is warranted in the social media era. The implications of the new shape of public discourse – exemplified by the Trudeau and Trump electoral successes – has implications beyond political journalism. If there is a post-truth world in politics, why would we assume financial markets will be spared a similar fate?

New York Times columnist Thomas Friedman says this policy conversation around social media should have occurred in 2007; it didn't, Friedman states, because of our collective preoccupation with the global economic crisis then beginning to emerge. Arguably, the failure to conduct that policy conversation altered the ground rules for the current conversation that goes to the heart of the existing political, economic, and social global order, a conversation shaped significantly by social media. There are legitimate questions to be considered: Is the policy playing field for social and legacy media fair or is it tilted in favour of the newer platforms? How does Facebook chair and CEO Mark Zuckerberg's worldview defence stand up against Fred Siebert's "social responsibility" theory of the press (Siebert, Peterson, and Schramm 1956)? In Richard Lanham's "economics of attention," is clickbait any different than page 3 pin-ups (2007a)?

How many of the legacy media's wounds are self-inflicted? Scholars such as Kathleen Hall Jamieson, as far back as the 1980s, were warning editors that they were crafting the kind of political coverage that would destroy them. And if today's newsrooms came equipped with electronic scoreboards to tell the journalists there assembled which stories are "trending," how does that square with Wilbur Schramm's (1947) definition of what constitutes news?

As mainstream journalism struggles to identify a new business model, where is the debate on the existing policies that are impacting the marketplace? Here in Canada, what are the implications for liberal democracy if the strongest news gathering body is state-owned and state-funded? How are private news organizations to generate revenue from content if federal government subsidies allow the public broadcaster to offer digital content for free? Is a free press one of the "institutions" liberal democracies need to prosper?

And what of journalists themselves? Do today's journalists have the skills required to be the entrepreneurs they will have to be?

And are our schools of journalism shaping curricula to build those professional skills? Technologies have displaced people in every segment of our society. Artificial intelligence research points to a marked acceleration of that trend over the next decade. If driverless cars are a near future reality, what journalistic tasks will be taken over by machines? Are journalism's "stenographic" functions – reports on monthly jobless figures – best covered by algorithm?

Legislators have barely begun that policy exploration. The House of Commons Standing Committee on Canadian Heritage, for example, spent sixteen months in 2016–17 studying the future of local news (Parliament of Canada, House of Commons 2016–17). In the spirit of Graham Spry, a broader debate from a Canadian perspective is warranted.

The discussion in this book will be guided by James Carey's "ritual" view of communications, that of "a conversation" where there are no final thoughts, and there is no last word.

2

Reflections: The "Grist" for the Mill

On a spring day in 1987, I found myself on a sidewalk in Ottawa – unemployed. For the first time since I ran away to the newspaper twenty years earlier, I didn't have a job.

Meandering along, I heard a car horn sound and someone called out my name – Ontario premier David Peterson, in Ottawa for the first ministers meeting that would produce the Meech Lake constitutional accord. Peterson asked if news reports I was no longer a PMO staffer were true, made a few personal comments intended to salve a bruised ego, explained he was on his way to meet Prime Minister Brian Mulroney and other premiers at Willson House, and as he headed back to the car said, "Don't go anywhere. You'll hear from us." And I did, mere hours later. David MacNaughton, who most recently served as Canada's ambassador to the United States but was then a senior adviser to Peterson, was on the phone with a range of options for discussion, including the possibility of joining Public Affairs International, the company he, Allan Gregg, and Michael Robinson built before it was sold to Hill+Knowlton. If memory serves, there was a reference to a Jaguar as a signing bonus. Still think about that Jag. But the exchange with Peterson and MacNaughton restored some confidence and helped focus the mind on next steps.

The evening before, I had met with Derek Burney, a career diplomat who had recently agreed to come into the Prime Minister's Office as chief of staff. Burney had sagely insisted on the right to make any and all changes in PMO personnel he deemed necessary – and I was one of those changes. As is often the case with governments at midterm, the cabinet and caucus had been pressing Mulroney to shake up the

PMO. Mulroney had asked that I travel to Washington, DC, personally to recruit former CTV bureau chief Bruce Phillips, then serving
with distinction as the head of public affairs at our embassy there,
to return to Canada and take over my duties as the prime minister's
director of communications. I was to begin a new job. Assigned the
office next to Mulroney's Centre Block office, I was to function as
a "gatekeeper" and the prime minister's contact person. However,
the warning signs began flashing even as the announcement of these
changes went out. First, it was decided I would be a "special adviser"
and not "senior adviser" as might have been expected if the media
line that the move constituted a promotion was to have any credibility or traction. And second, within days, colleague Geoff Norquay
dropped by to tell me he had met with Burney, had been asked to
stay, but that others in the PMO would not be.

Shortly after, Burney asked that I come to his office in the Lan-
gevin Block, which houses the office of the prime minister. The
meeting was short and to the point. "I invite you to leave," Burney said, an invitation accepted on the spot. Burney's remit was
to bring order to what was perceived by outsiders as disorder in
the Prime Minister's Office. That task would be complicated if
the office structure included multiple "gatekeepers" to the prime
minister. In only a few days in the post, I had quickly concluded
I was ill-suited both in temperament and in terms of professional
formation for the gatekeeper job. And as an enthusiastic supporter
of Burney's appointment in the first instance, I was equally supportive of the idea he should have the right to pick his own team.
So I was fully prepared to take my leave of the PMO – effective
immediately. And in Ottawa, that means you are a person without
standing or status – effective immediately.

The job market for political people publicly identified as the
problem, rather than the solution, can be challenging – which is
why Peterson's shout out on the proverbial morning after triggers
a smile to this day.

With Prime Minister Mulroney's active encouragement and support, the preferred path forward suggested a professional focus on

product, personal control of that product, and a period of intro-spection. My friend and much-admired colleague Harry Near literally took me off the street. And the third amigo – Hugh Segal – and his colleagues at Camp Advertising provided the proverbial roof over my head.

As a reporter, I had spent much of my work life covering politics, followed by three intense years of doing politics, only to emerge wondering if there were aspects about the interaction between the two that I had not fully understood. And that thought process led to Ottawa's Carleton University and its School of Journalism and Communication. Like other dilettantes who came of age in the late 1960s, a desultory undergraduate experience led me to leak away to an entry-level copy boy job at the *Ottawa Citizen* before graduation. Now, the lack of a university degree loomed large as a hole in the CV worth plugging. Legendary journalist Anthony Westell, then head of Carleton's journalism program, cited an "old wheeze" track that allowed experienced journalists to be admitted directly into the master's program on a probationary basis.

The first class I attended focused on television and was led by the late Paul Attallah, an exceptionally talented professor. Subsequent courses with people such as Eileen Saunders and Christopher Dornan reinforced the view that I had identified the right path, a path that included a stop in the office of a long-time friend and mentor, the late Stuart Adam.

Adam was a fellow *Toronto Star* alum. And, of equal interest to me, he held a doctorate in politics from Queen's University in Kingston, Ontario. Adam understood the world of media and the world of politics in a way few do and therefore was a logical per-son to put questions intended to deepen my understanding of a whirlwind world so recently left.

My questions flowed at the pace of a game of pepper on a baseball diamond. Adam didn't attempt to respond within that constraint. He simply got up from his desk, reached into the bookshelf behind him, and pulled out a book by Thomas C. Leonard entitled *The Power of the Press: The Birth of American Political Reporting* (1986).

And so it began: a quest that started in the lecture halls of Carleton went on to the Shorenstein Center on Media, Politics and Public Policy at Harvard's John F. Kennedy School of Government and the Freedom Forum Media Studies Center, housed in Pulitzer Hall at New York's Columbia University, and then back to the lecture halls at Carleton.

The physical journey was twinned with readings and personal conversations with media and communications scholars such as Herbert Gans and Michael Schudson, James Carey and Neil Postman. There was plenty of time for discussion and debate with fellow travellers – people like Warren Mitofsky, who invented exit polls for the US television networks, and *New Yorker* and CNN staffer Jeffrey Toobin, who went from famous to infamous in a single Zoom call. Marion Just's work on television challenged long-held assumptions about the inherent superiority of print. Maimouna Mills sharpened sensitivities around considerations of race and diversity. A reading list led me to the work of activist Jesse Hirsh, who I would later meet courtesy of my friend Allan Gregg. A lasting bond and friendship with Hirsh ensued, nurtured by long discussions about media, politics, and public policy as we walked the fairways of Toronto's Weston Golf and Country Club.

Through the readings, the articles in academic journals, the quick conversations in social settings with the scholars whose works were included in the syllabus for the coursework, a pattern emerged, like the number hidden in those circle tests for colour blindness.

Certain of the insights of these scholars confirmed long-held personal views. Others led to new ways of considering past experiences. Some were genuinely revelatory. All contributed to a broadening of perspective and a deepening suspicion that certain of the communications theories developed in an old media world weathered the journey to the other side of the digital divide just fine.

What follows in this chapter does not meet the academic test of a literature review. Rather, this chapter puts in place certain building blocks of information, understanding, and insight about the mill that is journalism and political communications strategies that produce much of the grist for that mill that struck me as relevant enough to be jotted down over the years in margin notes and Moleskin notebooks for further reflection. The observations are personal, even idiosyncratic. Certain scholars reappear throughout the text like points of punctuation. The explanation is simple enough; their work helped me connect some of the dots.

Media as Primary Site

Leonard (1995) identified the media as a primary site of political discourse in any liberal democracy, whether that site is the front page of the *Globe and Mail*, the couch on the set of *Jimmy Kimmel Live!*, or a celebrity's Twitter feed. In fact, journalism provides much of the vernacular for that discussion – a kind of conversational shorthand. Headline writers for newspapers do much of the crafting of the code. To hear "Brexit" is to know that what follows is related to the decision of the British electorate to pull the UK out of the European Union. And thanks to the tabloid press, we know we should be keeping up with the Kardashians even if the reasons why continue to elude some of us.

News is a direct output of the Enlightenment, as much a product of the Industrial Age as a tin can. Liberal theorists asserted an informed and engaged public is a key to self-government. Communication, then, is central to the exercise of power in any liberal democracy. Communication is the bridge, with information flowing from the governors to the governed and from the governed to the governors.

What's News

News is a particular form of communication that can have a direct influence on public opinion. News is intended to tell you what you want to know, what you need to know, what you should know. But the work of generating that news is split between journalists and the institutional communications professionals who provide much of the grist for the journalistic mill.

The aforementioned Stuart Adam and his colleague Roy Peter Clark (Adam and Clark 2006) identified two types of news: civic news – the events, issues, and institutions that define public life – and literary news – news of the individual. News at its most powerful, they state, combines elements of both.

Political leaders typically try to generate both; in fact, the ability to generate literary news is an important rung on the ladder to elected office. Donald Trump knew how to make news long before he was the subject of civic news as a candidate for the Republican Party nomination.

Walter Lippmann warned "news" and "truth" are not the same thing, and Thomas Patterson extended the thought with his description of news as a "highly refracted version of reality" (Patterson 1994, 29). News is not what happened, as the media sociologists observed, but what someone says has happened or will happen. Reporters on Parliament Hill do not attend cabinet meetings or the weekly party caucus sessions. So, by definition, any account of what happened at the Wednesday morning gathering of the Conservative caucus reflects what someone inside the room described. And that version may or may not align perfectly, if at all, with someone else's description of what went on behind closed doors. The secondhand nature of much of what we consider political news in particular is decidedly a factor in the current "fake news" debate, which will be addressed in more detail later in this work.

News is mostly about people and certain kinds of people at that. It is largely made by "knowns" – individuals who are in a position to feed the media beast by virtue of the position or standing they enjoy in a community. As a consequence, news historically has reflected an older, white, male order.

Women, racialized people, and youth were all but excluded from mainstream media coverage. These key elements of society did not see themselves on evening newscasts, hear their voices on radio, or read accounts of their views on the op-ed pages of newspapers. By virtue of this exclusion, mainstream media forced these marginalized members of society to carry on their conversations elsewhere. Social media created the opportunities for these individuals to do exactly that.

Media Effects

News, in the end, is about power: the power of the text and the power inherent in controlling the distribution of texts. News, as a consequence, is a contested space, and the contest historically had certain rules of engagement – rules rooted both in communications theory and in the conventions of news gathering.

News matters, not so much because news tells us what to think but more precisely because news tells us what to think about (Cohen, B.C. 1963). Or, what not to think about (Gitlin 1980). And over the past five decades, television news in particular emerged as news that mattered.

News helped shape the political agenda, primed the public to measure political leaders against the agenda the news helped set, and then created a bandwagon effect by reporting on how fellow citizens were reacting to the first two factors.

The legacy media acted as gatekeepers for that public discussion, and these gatekeepers – the people who were deciding what we would see, hear, or read – were precious few in number. Larry Speakes, deputy press secretary in the Reagan White House, could execute media relations strategies intended to dominate weekend news cycles by reaching out to as few as a dozen key White House correspondents on a Thursday with the background information that would shape their weekend analysis pieces and inform their commentary on the Sunday network public affairs programs.

Agenda setting is about issue salience and politically speaking is a precondition to agenda building. If electors are not seized of a societal problem, they are not particularly inclined to engage in a discussion around proposed solutions.

Framing is at the heart of agenda setting. Framing refers to the construction of a communication – its language, its visuals, its messages. Framing is an exercise in semiotics, at a most basic level.

The "Cold War" – a phrase first articulated by author and journalist George Orwell in his essay "You and the Atom Bomb," published in *Tribune Magazine* on 19 October 1945 (Orwell) – was the dominant news frame for all foreign and defence policy news in Western liberal democracies for more than fifty years and enjoyed something of a renaissance as a result of the debate around President Trump's relationship with Russian President Vladimir Putin. But in the main, the "Cold War" frame gave way to the "war on terror" following the 9/11 terrorist attacks on the United States.

Frames, as Robert Entman's (1993) work helps us understand, define problems, diagnose causes, make moral judgments, and suggest remedies. Frames are also contested spaces where various interests seek to clamp a particular frame around a newsworthy event. In the 2018 Ontario election, for example, "change" emerged as the dominant news frame of the campaign. And while frames are neither permanent nor temporary and are always works in progress, political leaders or others in the news can be at a decided disadvantage if the dominant news frame runs counter to their core message. Former Ontario premier Kathleen Wynne, as the incumbent leading a government that had been in power for fifteen years, faced a near impossible task in the 2018 campaign in trying to be heard in a political conversation focused on a "change" narrative.

Author David Moscrop, building on the work of Shanto Iyengar and Donald Kinder, observes, "Media effects are mostly about commanding attention and changing the criteria for judgment, not changing minds" (Moscrop 2019, 122). The political scientist goes on to make the case that "we know from behavioural science research that people will make different decisions based on wording alone" (ibid., 98). By way of illustration, it is worth noting that in his book, Moscrop describes Colten Boushie, an Indigenous man who was shot to death as he sat in a car on a rural family farm in Saskatchewan, and the people who were with him as "visitors." Others might describe them as "trespassers" or worse.

Framing also has a direct impact on how governments go about their business, including how governments allocate resources –

both human and material. Prime Minister Justin Trudeau's personal commitment to a political agenda to advance the causes of women and diversity is self-evident. But when President Trump imposed punitive tariffs as a means of forcing changes to the North American Free Trade Agreement (NAFTA) in the summer of 2018, voters expected the prime minister's time and attention to shift to the looming threat to the Canadian economy.

Any shift in the political or policy agenda triggers a similar shift in the public's assessment of a political leader. Trudeau has made a meaningful, potentially historic commitment to redefine Canada's relationship with Indigenous peoples. By the summer of 2020, in the context of Black Lives Matter and a national debate around systemic racism in Canada, Trudeau's rhetoric was being assessed in practical, program, and policy terms.

The actual impact of the media on public opinion has been a matter of extensive debate among communications scholars for the better part of a century. An initial belief, based on a "magic bullet" or "hypodermic needle" model, took hold as part of the "total war" concept that emerged in the First World War, focused in the main on propaganda. That theory gave way to a "minimal effects" school of thought first articulated by Paul Lazarsfeld and his colleagues in the 1950s. Eventually, like a skier working down a slalom course, a "third wave" of theorizing emerged that asserted that, in certain circumstances, the media can have significant effects. This nuanced view, articulated by Mount Royal University's David Taras among others, suggested the media may not have the power to trigger conversions to rival the biblical account of Saul on the road to Damascus but can generate a series of minor effects that in aggregate can have a significant influence.

The 2016 US presidential election provides a clear example of the argument advanced by media effects theorists that, in election terms, small shifts can be meaningful. Even decisive. NBCNews.com reported the Russians launched a pro-Jill Stein social media blitz to help Donald Trump by boosting Stein, the Green Party presidential candidate, as a means of siphoning away votes from Democratic

Party nominee Hillary Clinton (Windrem 2018). In three states that proved pivotal in US Electoral College terms – Pennsylvania, Wisconsin, and Michigan – Stein's vote totals may have been a factor in determining the national outcome. In Pennsylvania, Stein received 49,678 votes, and Trump won the state by 46,765 votes; in Wisconsin, Stein received 31,006 votes, and Trump won the state by 22,177 votes; in Michigan, Stein received 51,463 votes, and Trump carried the state by 10,704 (Soufan 2018). One cannot assume all Stein votes would have gone to the Democrats had the Green Party leader not been on the ballot. Nor is it possible to measure the true impact of the Russian bot campaign. But the broader point about the potential significance of small shifts stands.

These theories were all predicated on old media models – one to many, media as megaphone. Not surprisingly, debate around media effects triggered thinking as to how best to ensure there was some effect on public opinion, and these theories, in turn, provided the foundation for the professionalization of political communication.

Harold Lasswell (1935) declared that effective communications of any kind comes down to five basic questions: Who? Says what? To whom? Through which channel? To what effect?

The clarity of Lasswell's thinking and the facility of his language can obscure the detailed work required to exercise a communications strategy against the tests he sets out. Who? involves control analysis. Says what? is an exercise in content analysis. To whom? involves audience analysis. Through which channel? requires media analysis. To what effect? leads to response analysis.

Carl Hovland (Hovland, Janis, and Kelley 1953) and his colleagues at Yale University further identified four factors that can impact the effectiveness of any communication. The communication is first influenced by the credibility or expertise of the message source. Ontario Premier Doug Ford is deemed a credible source if the message is focused on concern for tax dollars, not so much if the issue is climate change. Stimuli matter – how motivated is the audience to receive the message. A news story about WestJet launching a new discount airline is of interest to discount travellers, less so for the folks who fly up front as a matter of routine. Audience makeup is a third factor – a consideration Donald Trump excelled at identifying and exploiting. The president invariably appeared before audiences that reflected his voter base. If official Washington was critical of Trump's ongoing humiliation of former attorney general Jeff Sessions, a rally in West Virginia provided a more receptive audience. The response to a communication is the last factor. And, as Lippmann advised, the same word or phrase will not trigger the same response in everyone who hears it. Trump crowds may have roared their approval when the president made a reference to "Crooked Hillary" even as others reacted with anger or dismay. During the Brexit referendum in the UK, former chancellor George Osborne warned a vote for Britain to leave the EU could cause housing prices to drop. Osborne's "fear" message might have been bad news for certain of his Conservative constituents, but it was good news for anyone – especially younger voters – who wanted to get into the housing market (Shipman 2016).

In the rush to embrace the creative and connective possibilities afforded by social media, political communications strategists overlook long-standing communications principles at their peril.

The 2017 travails of then-federal finance minister Bill Morneau and his boss Prime Minister Justin Trudeau provide illustrations of why the credibility of the messenger is such a key element in the findings of Hovland and his fellow Yale researchers mentioned previously.

The Trudeau government decided Canada's tax law needed an overhaul to catch unscrupulous tax filers looking to reduce their tax bill by sneaking income through certain loopholes. "Income sprinkling" – where small business owners spread income among family members to reduce tax bills for the principals – was one targeted area among others. There was an obvious political angle to the story. Income sprinkling is appealing to small business owners and farmers, for example – folks who tilt small "c" conservative.

In a battle cry intended to signal the Trudeau government's determination to crack down on tax cheats on behalf of the middle class, Morneau tabled new rules to deal with income splitting, as the practice is also known. As finance minister, Morneau was decidedly the logical candidate to make the case for the changes. As an individual of significant personal wealth, Morneau was decidedly a less than ideal candidate to champion the cause.

Morneau's world is a world of tax lawyers and learned accountants, whose advice is focused on a single objective – keeping his tax bill to the strict minimum. There isn't anything illegal about any of this. There isn't anything immoral about any of this. But the *optics* of an individual whose fortune is held in numbered companies, offshore property, and trust funds leading a political conversation on flushing out tax evaders would strike Hovland et al. as being as ill-considered as it is ill-advised.

The prime minister decided he would come to his beleaguered finance minister's defence, which served only to compound the problem. Trudeau, like Morneau, is a person of wealth. He, too, has a net worth tied to numbered companies (McGregor, G. 2015). Tory finance critic Pierre Poilievre dubbed Trudeau and Morneau the "trust-fund twins" (Dickson 2018).

The Liberals, who, like progressives the world over, tend to see themselves as better people dedicated to a higher purpose, were outraged at opposition attacks on Morneau's personal integrity. But the Liberal defence was complicated by a series of facts that came to light: the fact Morneau had not placed his holdings in the family company Morneau Shepell in a blind trust as he might have, the fact the company benefited directly from contracts with the federal government, the fact Morneau used an Alberta-based numbered company as the vehicle to hold on to his shares.

CBC political correspondent Aaron Wherry, in his work *Promise and Peril, Justin Trudeau in Power*, notes Morneau had disclosed the fact that he owned a villa in France to the ethics commissioner "but he had failed, it turned out, to disclose the numbered company he'd set up to hold the ownership of that villa" (Wherry 2019, 104). Adds Wherry, "Then it emerged that he [Morneau] had not put his personal investments including shares he owned in

Morneau Shepell into a blind trust. The assets were held in a numbered company registered in Alberta" (ibid.). Morneau's memory, it turns out, did not improve with time and led directly to the end of his career in elected politics as a consequence of the WE Charity scandal, which will be dealt with in more detail later in this work.

Morneau's family, including his wife, who is a member of the McCain family of frozen French fry fame, has every right to keep its tax burden to the minimum required by law. To do otherwise would be irresponsible and prejudicial to the interests of other family members who did not choose a career path that involved elected office or public service. Morneau's political narrative created a situation where political attacks along the "do as I say not as I do" line of thought were inevitable.

Perhaps observers should set aside the tone-deaf assumption. The Liberal strategists are smart people. It is more likely they are as aware of the dissonance as the rest of us and proceeded anyway.

The larger and more problematic problem in political communications terms with Morneau's strategy around tax reform was that it constitutes a threat to the Liberal master narrative – as champions of the middle class.

The Liberal electoral successes in 2015 and 2019, and to some extent 2021, were to some extent 2021, were due in no small measure to the campaigns' success in establishing a dominant news frame around campaign coverage that advanced the Liberals' middle class agenda. Morneau may be a lot of things, but what the debate around his personal situation during the fall of 2017 established beyond all else is that he is not middle class, which in turn compromised his ability to be a champion for that same middle class. In late 2017 Morneau did finally create a blind trust for his personal holdings (Akin 2017).

Trudeau's holiday controversy in 2016 posed a similar threat.

Like Morneau, the prime minister is a person of means. Theirs is a world of privilege and that world of privilege is far removed from the world of the middle class that Trudeau and Morneau purport to champion. They are largely immune from the vagaries of daily life. Layoffs, corporate downsizing, overheated housing markets, the "gig" economy are familiar to them only in a one-step-removed way. Their spouses aren't seated at the kitchen table at night doing the "company" books. But they share with all Canadians the desire to escape the harshness of winter. And it is a measure of the country's relative economic success in recent years that many ordinary families were able to enjoy that respite, whether by driving to Florida or Arizona or packing onto Air Canada Rouge flights for an "all-in" week at a resort in Cuba, the Dominican Republic, or the Mexican Riviera. Prime ministers are no less entitled to such a break. And political reporters are entitled to always ask if and where the prime minister of the day might be vacationing. The questioning invariably is in three steps: Where is the prime minister going; where is he or she staying; and who is picking up the tab?

Unlike their White House counterparts, Canadian reporters rarely follow the prime minister south if they are given answers to those questions in advance of the trip. Every once in a while, a major news organization such as the *Toronto Star* or the CBC will spring for the cost of a reporter and/or photographer to travel south, get a picture of the house where a PM is staying, and interview local waiters, bartenders, and resident busybodies about any sightings. But in the main, party leaders are left alone. Unless the answers to their questions aren't forthcoming.

Over the Christmas holidays in 2016–17, Trudeau decided he and his family needed just such a break. The PMO was a bit evasive in responding to media queries. Veteran parliamentary correspondent David Akin's curiosity was piqued. In time, Akin was able to break the story that the prime minister had vacationed on a private island in the Bahamas owned by the billionaire philanthropist Aga Khan. And Trudeau invited a few friends to tag along – Liberal Party of Canada president Anna Gainey, her husband Tom Pitfield, and Newfoundland MP Seamus O'Regan who now serves as minister of natural resources.

The subsequent furor has been well chronicled in the mainstream media. In the end, Ethics Commissioner Mary Dawson, after a yearlong investigation, ruled Trudeau was in violation of his own ethical guidelines.

Trudeau, who positioned the Aga Khan as a family friend of long standing, was visibly shocked by Dawson's decision. His defenders were quick to cite the fact the Aga Khan had been a pallbearer at Trudeau's father's funeral and that there was no link between the visit and a decision by the government of Canada to award a $15 million grant to the billionaire philanthropist's pet project, the Global Centre for Pluralism – ironically, a grant originally approved by the Harper government (Dawson, M. 2017).

As was with the case with Morneau, much of the defence put up by Trudeau's supporters fit under the thematic umbrella of F. Scott Fitzgerald's admonition that "the very rich ... they are different from you and me," which is precisely the point.

Forget the legality, forget any discussion of benefit. The real failure in Trudeau's defence of his "excellent adventure" was in making it clear for all the world to see that he is not – and has never been – middle class. And that reality, like Morneau's before, threatens the dominant news frame the Liberals had so carefully and successfully established. In terms of the long-term political implications, that fact may prove the most telling.

Dawson's statement became a refrain in news stories about Trudeau's ill-advised Christmas vacation; specifically, the statement that "there was ongoing official business between the Government of Canada and the Aga Khan at the time each invitation was accepted ... the vacations accepted by Mr. Trudeau or his family might reasonably be seen to have been given to influence Mr. Trudeau" (Quinn 2017).

The prime minister clearly didn't see it that way. As *Globe and Mail* reporter Campbell Clark noted, "Mr. Trudeau has a tendency to think he's a good guy and that everyone should see him that way" (Clark, C. 2017). Good guys, typically, see themselves as being above base motive.

In a subsequent press availability session, the prime minister looked like the proverbial deer in the headlights when responding to questions from Rosemary Barton, the CBC's chief political correspondent. In a clip posted on Twitter for all to see, the prime minister looked a touch Stepford-y when he paused at one point and said, "Let me try to just reorder the thoughts" (CBC 2017b).

Political communicators tend to be disciples of Sun Tzu's philosophy, set out in his treatise *The Art of War*, that every battle is won before it is ever fought (1964).

Former US Air Force colonel John Boyd, a fighter pilot in the Korean War, is credited as the brainchild behind the "OODA" strategy, which applies equally well to political communication: observe, orient, decide, act (Shipman 2016, 93).

When it comes to the strategy element of politics, the tyranny of the pen rules. As UK pollster Andrew Cooper stated, "If you've not written it down, it's not a strategy" (ibid., 64).

Cooper, the strategist for former prime minister David Cameron and the pollster for the Remain campaign in the Brexit referendum, says: "The War book is everything we know, the segmentation, our strongest messages ... this is our message in a sentence, this is our message in a paragraph, this is our message in a page, the media strategy, the campaign grid, that's the bible" (ibid.).

A political communication initiative rolls out in distinct phases; the first involves getting the electorate's attention through media coverage. The second focuses on comprehension – does the target audience understand the message you are trying to convey. The final phase is acceptance – does the audience buy the point you are trying to make. Too many political communicators make the mistake of stopping after the first phase. Once they've had a "media avail" session, appeared on CBC's *Power & Politics* with Vassy Kapelos, talked to Evan Solomon on CTV, pretaped an appearance on Global's *The West Block* with Mercedes Stephenson, and sat down for a backgrounder with an influential columnist or two, they think the job is done, assuming of course that a colleague has covered off the French-language media side of things if the minister is a unilingual English-language speaker.

This approach – the Moses school of communication – is fatally flawed. As the Bible reminds us, Moses came down from the mountain, carrying the two stone tablets inscribed with the Ten Commandments, and was basically ignored and left to wander the desert for the next forty years. If the "big reveal" approach didn't work for Moses, it isn't any more likely to work for a federal cabinet minister trying to convince Canadians to instantly embrace a policy or program related to an issue as complex as, for example, Canada's relationship with Indigenous peoples.

Political conversation occurs within a "circuit of communication" (Miller and Macintyre 1998). That includes social and political institutions, media organizations, the public, and decision makers. It is within this circuit of communication that the joust to control the dominant news frame occurs – which is why corporate or government communications must be treated as a strategic function and not simply an exercise in tactical execution if it is to be effective. As Robert J. McCloskey states in a piece carried in the *Washington Post*, "It ought to be an iron law that government spokesmen be there, as it was once said, at the takeoff as well as the landing. Regrettably, it isn't" (as cited in Hess 1984, 60).

Institutional communications as an organizing function – whether in politics or business – involves two primary assignments: content creation and content promulgation. Any product crafted for communications purposes should have three component parts: a statement of core values, the specific policy objective being addressed, and specifics as to what you intend to do to achieve the policy objective. There is both art and science to the task. Content creators can come up short on both fronts. Communication as a function suffers from the curse of the gifted amateur. Everyone thinks he or she is expert, elected officials even more so because in their minds the "people" endorsed their sense of self when they voted the MP, MPP, or city councillor into office. The science, much of it rooted in social psychology or behavioural science, is ignored at the communicator's peril. As Ronald Coase observed, there is "no fundamental distinction" between "the market for goods and the market for ideas" (as cited in Hesmondhalgh 2007, 31).

On the promulgation side, political communications efforts can be undermined by public power struggles and/or confusion at the top, mixed messages from multiple experts, from the late release of information, from paternalistic attitudes on the part of those speaking for the institution, as well as from the failure to counter urban myths in real time – a particular challenge in a social media world.

Certain theories are particularly relevant to political communications: message repetition enhances message processing. Consonance and cumulation matter (Noelle-Neumann 1973). Motivation is significant, as personal relevance is the most important variable in any communication.

Social cognitive theory asserts that limits on human capacity require people to rely on "mental shortcuts" to make sense of an increasingly interconnected and complex world (Gilliam and Bales 2001). Myths, metaphors, and parables are the instruments of choice to help people process information (ibid.) and achieve what Lasswell described as an "equivalent enlightenment." Lasswell acknowledged the public would never have enough detailed knowledge to be president or prime minister, but they could know enough to have a view as to whether the solution being advanced by the political leadership was in their collective interest.

Robert Reich (1987), who served as labour secretary in the Clinton administration, suggested four parables dominate political discourse: rot at the top, the triumphant Individual, the benign community, and the mob at the gates. These competing narratives help explain how people's perceptions of the same political person can be radically different. For readers of the *New York Times*, and columnist Paul Krugman in particular, news accounts of the Trump administration as a kleptocracy fit the rot at the top construct. Trump supporters in the "red states" were more likely to see the president as the personification of the triumphant individual.

Successful political communicators create a "master narrative" for their communications strategy, and that narrative can be as simple, and as simplistic, as "Make America Great Again." There are parallels between political communication and music. As legendary blues guitarist B.B. King observed, "If you are going to play more than two or three notes, you have to have a story to tell" (Fini Zanuck 2017). The master narrative is supported by a story arc that provides episodic expressions of "news" in support of the master narrative. Any announcement by Donald Trump, whether the specifics dealt with trade tariffs or the nuclear threat posed by North Korea, was addressed in a manner that spoke to and supported Trump's campaign pledge to "Make America Great Again."

The language Trump used is worth parsing. For the professional class, globalists in the main who have seen their personal circumstances improve as a result of multilateral trade agreements and technological innovations, Trump's promise rang hollow. It is no accident that in the 2016 presidential election, Trump lost those parts of America that produce about 65 per cent of the nation's wealth. But for those individuals who feel threatened by climate change initiatives that directly target the coal they mine, Trump's promise to restore the world they once knew resonated in a powerful and intensely personal way.

We all process storytelling on twin tracks – known as the "elaboration likelihood model" (Petty and Cacioppo 1986). There is a central route of engagement, where we process information through a thoughtful consideration of an argument. The ongoing debate in Western liberal democracies on immigration policy in general, and the treatment of refugees in particular, provides a useful example. We accept the rule of law, and we think people who would like to call Canada home should respect the law and apply to emigrate according to those rules. And in that context, we decry queue jumpers on reading news stories about individuals looking to circumvent the system. But we also take in information through what Petty and Cacioppo describe as an "affective association" route – basically the communication of peripheral cues, often emotional. In this context, assertions their parents are queue jumpers do not matter when viewers are confronted with images of children in cages, forcibly removed from their parents by border authorities.

As the "caged children" controversy illustrates, a single word in a headline has the potential to impact public perception. On 20 June 2018 the *Globe and Mail* carried a headline that read, "Trump signs executive order ending family separation policy at Mexican border" (Morrow 2018). The story outlined the executive order

Trump had signed the day before advising border guards to stop taking children away from their migrant parents and putting the children in cages. Now, an economy of language is always a factor in newspaper headlines. But the *Globe* headline had the effect of creating an opening for Trump supporters to push their claim the president was solving a problem of someone else's creation. The headline might have had a different impact on the reader if a single word had been added so that the headline read, "Trump signs executive order ending *his* family separation policy."

Images can matter more than words when it comes to political communication. Eye trumps ear. The White House sent first lady Melania Trump to Texas to do some damage control on the caged children controversy that flared across front pages in America in June 2018. Incredibly, Mrs Trump boarded the plane for her return trip to the White House wearing a fashionista green jacket with a message written across the back in bold white print that read, "I really don't care, do U?"

Given the predisposition of social media mavens to parse every tweet for meaning, a debate broke out immediately as to whether Melania's wardrobe choice was a tone-deaf goof or a statement.

Initially, the commentariat was gobsmacked. As CBC anchor Rosemary Barton tweeted: "Um. I don't understand how this happened" (Barton 2018). But the second wave wondered if the whole thing was either a hoax or a set-up. Liz Plank posted the assertion the jacket "was 100% bait. This is an effective strategy to get the media to criticize her wardrobe so that they can criticize the media for criticizing her wardrobe and delegitimize us as fake news," she warned (Plank 2018). "Nope," Christopher Dornan weighed in. "This gives them too much credit" (Dornan 2018a).

The first lady's official spokesperson insisted the media not read anything into the message on the back of the jacket. Only to have the president himself, moments later, insist that we should. The message, said Trump, "refers to the Fake News media. Melania has learned how dishonest they are and she truly no longer cares" (Trump 2018c).

Former staffers, with experience in advancing trips for the political leaders they served, were inclined to think that if Mrs Trump's advisers had done their jobs to even a minimal professional standard, there would not have been a green jacket with a charged message on the back for the media to focus on. But it is possible the decision to wear the coat was deliberate, to invite criticism, to allow *Fox & Friends* types to launch the type of attack that worried Liz Plank. All a bit Kafkaesque.

What is a fact is that no news consumer will ever remember anything else about Melania Trump's trip to Texas. And the ensuing controversy over the first lady's coat did overshadow the circumstances of the children being held in custody.

Political communication requires a disciplined approach to determining what is immediate and what is important, in terms of a political agenda. While that assertion might strike some as a statement of the blindingly obvious, political communications staff routinely get the balance wrong; although as an old wall poster once declared, "When you are up to your ass in alligators, it is hard to remember you were sent in to drain the swamp."

Any media conversation occurs in a context, and a political communications plan must reflect that fact. Strategists need to think about where the story they want to tell fits in terms of what else is going on locally, regionally, nationally, internationally. As stated in the previous chapter, the official communiqué from the G7 Summit in June 2018 hosted by Prime Minister Justin Trudeau at La Malbaie, Quebec, was lost when Trump took exception to something Trudeau said at a news conference on a separate issue. The reason Trump was so incensed is that the president was on his way to Singapore to meet North Korean ruler Kim Jong Un. Trudeau's insistence that Canada wasn't going to be pushed around by the US on tariffs took on a broader meaning in the context of the Singapore summit. And the story developed "legs" as journalists contrasted the way Trump treats once traditional enemies of the United States compared to the way he deals with allies and friends.

The impact of the mass media is more pronounced on new and emerging story lines when news consumers are accumulating knowledge. And it is a fact that the more direct experience we have with an issue, the less potential there is for media coverage to impact our opinion.

Interpersonal relations are more powerful than media at the persuasion stage. Campaign strategists, for example, dream of news stories based on public opinion polls showing their party with momentum late in a campaign and just before the family gathers for Sunday dinner or a barbecue over a long weekend.

Political communication today ascribes value to "issues management." Many political crises are the results of failed issues management.

In the spring of 2019, for example, politicos and pundits alike were sharply critical of the way Trudeau's PMO responded to a story that appeared in the 7 February 2019 edition of the *Globe and Mail* alleging recently demoted cabinet minister Jody Wilson-Raybould was subjected to undue pressure over her handling of the SNC-Lavalin case while she was attorney general and justice minister. As one Ottawa wag put it, "there was no crisis until the PMO responded" (pers. com.).

Risk and crisis communication warrant a specific reference. There is a tendency to conflate the two when in fact they are very different communications exercises. Risk communication involves the broader public, usually concerning a health risk such as the COVID-19 pandemic that literally shook the world's public health and economic order to its very foundation in the spring of 2020. A crisis is something else entirely. Carleton professor Josh Greenberg identifies crises as "attacks on an organization that compromises its ability to execute against its mandate" (pers. com.).

Iterative news stories invariably include references to previous stories. Internationalists may be disappointed in the decision by the United States to withdraw from the United Nations Human Rights Council but accounts of the Trump administration's decision include references to the council's many conflicts and general ineffectiveness.

Conceding the obvious point that lies are not rare in the president's world, the fact is there is often a kernel of truth in what Trump says. Canadians may scoff at the suggestion steel and aluminum exports to the United States constitute a "national security" threat but when

Trump links the tariffs in question to Canada's supply management system in general, and the protectionist practices around dairy in particular, commentators in Canada are quick to concede the president has a point, not on steel but on milk. The fact the presidential comments constitute a misdirection gets lost in the shuffle.

Media capital can be accumulated by political leaders either on an institutional basis, based on the job they hold, or on an individual basis, based on their personal appeal as a news maker. Trump and Trudeau excel on both fronts.

These "truths" about media, media effect, and communication strategies for the public discourse they seek to shape grew under an old media order – what James Carey described as the "transmission model" of mass communication, involving the transmission of ideas, over distance, for the purposes of control.

And then along came the web.

Social Media: A New Media Model

Carleton professor Christopher Dornan made a telling point in a paper prepared for UNESCO that living with media is one of the main things we do. Whether sitting in an airport terminal, or on a train, or a bus, in a restaurant, in our room or our car – the law against texting while driving notwithstanding – we're constantly on our mobile devices. "Every tweet, every Yelp review, every snapshot posted on Instagram [which now has more than a billion active users each month] is both a trace and an expression of one's self," as Dornan so accurately observed (Dornan 2017a, 3). To be alive in the twenty-first century, he says, is to leave a data trail whether we wish to or not.

The social media world we operate in today has, or at least had, the potential to embrace a new approach to communications built on what Tim O'Reilly describes as "an architecture of participation" from a top down one-to-many model to a more inclusive many-to-many, iterative model.

Believers in the new media order argue it is a revolution and not an evolution, and its impact is so significant that society's institutions will be altered by it. The new media landscape is defined by interconnectedness, media portability, integrated experiences. The traditional reporter's role of occupying a front row seat as witness has given way to a world of front row participation that by definition includes more players.

Clay Shirky (2008) describes this new media order as an ecosystem, with new roles for intervenors to fill, more messages to share, more paths to connectedness, and for those long marginalized by the mainstream media, more opportunities to speak. Instead of "audience," communicators now need to think "community." Instead of message delivery, the task involves building a connection.

At the invitation of my friend Jesse Hirsh, I found myself attending "salons" hosted by producer, professor, and digital journalist Ramona Pringle at Ryerson's Transmedia Zone. An incubator for innovation and experimentation in multiplatform storytelling, the zone encourages students and other participants to be at their entrepreneurial and creative best, and they were. The struggle by this old dog to even follow the conversations led me to conclude there wasn't enough professional runway left in my life to master these new storytelling arts.

A social media conversation, supporters insist, is more about authenticity than authority, which is why campaign strategists and party talking heads use the word like a point of punctuation whenever they speak of their digital offerings.

"Facts" are no longer accepted as such. Triangulation – the analysis of information from multiple media sources – is the order of the day. A generational divide emerges in the conversation about "fake news." Trump's admission he routinely makes stuff up preoccupies a generation that accepts hyperbole in public speech but is troubled by invention. An editorial in *The Economist*, for example, declared, "Trump lies so frequently that it seems like a tic" (Economist 2019f, 4). Younger intervenors are less fussed, influenced perhaps by the postmodern argument that all truths are partial and a function of one's perspective. They wonder why anyone would accept any statement from any political figure at face value. The new rules would have you post the point on a platform of choice, and if it survives the scrutiny that follows, it is more likely to be closer to the truth.

Scholars such as Emily Bell have described Twitter as the greatest journalistic tool since the invention of the printing press. Twitter has turned the world of rapid response into a world of real-time response. Journalism has been transformationally altered by platforms such as Twitter, not replaced but certainly displaced. Journalists, to quote Jesse Hirsh, are no longer the source of the initial capture of an image or observation. Journalists must now move up the information value chain, making relevant requests for more information and then filtering and contextualizing the results of their inquiries. Twenty years ago, journalist, author, and angel investor Esther Dyson anticipated a media landscape with journalists as facilitators of a community conversation (Dyson 1997).

Journalism's gatekeeper function is now widely shared with others in the profession to be sure but also with "citizen journalists," with the blogosphere, social media activists, and, significantly, algorithms. The media has long wrestled with the dilemma of how much coverage weight to give the interesting, relative to the important – a challenge linked directly to advertising as the subsidizer of news. Eventually, the law of large numbers gave way to the law of right numbers, which in turn, triggered a shift in what news organizations covered. Page 3 pin-ups in tabloid newspapers were an earlier, cruder version of clickbait. But "clicks" are now a management tool for editors trying to decide what stories should be played prominently in their daily news lineup.

News gathering today, according to the emerging model, involves more collaboration, more integration, more transparency, more interactivity, all in aid of trying to get into the everyday conversations of people.

Social media has also altered the hierarchy of dissemination of news. A media availability session will generate live tweets. The first, more complete account of the event will then appear on a website of a national news organization such as Postmedia or the

CBC, then on the website of the local outlet of the news organization, and finally, in the actual physical newspaper delivered to
increasingly fewer doors.

This social media revolution, like all revolutions, carries a cost,
and, as Dornan reminds us, the technologies that have made mass
participation possible have also compromised traditional anchors of
authenticity, which is tied directly to the debate around fake news.

In a social media age, communications hiccups can trigger a
global conversation in an instant. Queen Elizabeth II triggered a
bit of a tempest with her 2018 Christmas message. The issue didn't
have anything to do with the message itself but rather the gold leaf
piano in the background. Presumably when you walk by a gold
leaf piano every day, the fact it is gold leaf doesn't register. It is
your normal if you are the Queen. Except it isn't normal for most,
and it was the producers' collective jobs to realize that fact and
have the piano removed before the taping began.

The character limit on Twitter affords limited opportunity for
nuance or context. Declarative statements are the order of the day.
Provocative statements help those posting to be heard. Excess is
rewarded. Before he was elected to Parliament in the 2011 federal
election, Chris Alexander was considered a rising Canadian star in the
world of diplomacy. In late 2018, the former MP offered this thought:
"When Trudeau kills pipeline projects & drives business away from
Canada's oil patch, he costs us jobs, lowers our standard of living &
empowers dictators like Putin" (Alexander, C. 2018). The first several
assertions constitute fair comment politically. The reference to the
Russian president in that context is curious to say the least.

Fake news is an issue significant enough today that it is now
a "beat" for journalists such as *BuzzFeed*'s Craig Silverman who
covers the phenomenon in the same way reporters used to cover
city hall.

For some, including the president of the United States, any piece of
reporting that doesn't support a particular worldview is "fake news."

News consumers are well aware of the ongoing controversy in
the US as to the role Russian bots played in the 2016 presidential

election. Lest anyone in Canada succumb to the notion that we are somehow immune to the same disruption, Darrell Bricker of Ipsos Public Affairs cited the example of the 2018 Ontario election. "Our social media analysis shows that nearly 20% of all social media activity in this campaign [was] generated by bots," Bricker stated in a tweet (Bricker 2018). Bots, which can have a human component, typically follow the "outrage" industry approach of marshalling half-truths to camouflage the whoppers, "falsehoods in a forest of facts" to borrow the phrase of John Scott-Railton (Deibert 2017), director of the Citizen Lab at the University of Toronto's Munk School of Global Affairs and Public Policy.

Mainstream media has also been swept up in this rush to post. "In a world where everyone is a publisher, no one is an editor," bemoaned former CBS anchor Scott Pelley. "We have entered a time when a writer's first idea is his best idea. When the first thing a reporter hears is the first thing he or she reports" (Beaujon 2013).

And while fake news may find initial purchase in social media, it is laundered through the conventions of responsible reporting embraced by the legacy media. In fact, much of what the general population knows about political social media sites is gleaned from news accounts carried in the legacy press. We may not subscribe to Breitbart News, but we can follow Breitbart's more topical offerings from stories carried in the *New York Times*. Again, this wash, rinse, repeat cycle isn't new. Mainstream media has been recycling stories that first appeared in supermarket tabloids for years.

If the phenomenon of fake news isn't news, the speed and extent of the ability to spread the false news is unprecedented. A century ago, Mark Twain observed "a lie can travel halfway around the world while the truth is putting on its shoes." Social media can spread a lie around the world in less time than it takes a person to blink.

A 2018 study by professors at Massachusetts Institute of Technology (MIT) concluded fake news stories "diffused significantly farther, faster, deeper and more broadly than the truth" (Vosoughi, Roy, and Aral 2018, 1). The researchers discovered that a lie is 70 per cent more likely to be shared on social media (ibid.) and that the truth takes six times longer than fake news to reach 1,500 people on Twitter (ibid., 2).

Lawmakers in Western liberal democracies are seized of the issue. But politicians also make extensive use of social media platforms such as Facebook for their own purposes. Kory Teneycke, campaign manager for the Ontario Progressive Conservatives in 2018, says the digital focus of the campaign was decisive. The Conservatives were able to take leader Doug Ford's message directly to voters – through their own TV "news" feed and cheap and cheerful online ads – without having to push their narrative through the filter of the mainstream media. In today's world, political communicators use Twitter to draw attention to an issue and tailored messages on Facebook to "close the deal."

While campaign operatives have embraced social media enthusiastically, strategically they seem wedded to the traditional one-to-many model, which raises a question as to whether the "revolution" might be closer to "evolution" as Mark Bauerlein (2008) suggests.

The success of political parties in getting their "message" directly to the voters shouldn't distract from a focus on the message itself. Thomas Patterson (2013) astutely observed reporters don't always understand the broader thematic messages inherent in their news stories.

In Canada, for example, the modern Conservative political mantra of less government may produce transactional, rather than transformational, governments. But for conservatives that is not a negative.

So why does any of this matter?

Start with Peter Drucker's observation that society's basic economic resource today is knowledge and that reality demands that for the first time in history people with knowledge take responsibility for making themselves understood by people who do not have the same knowledge base.

V.O. Key Jr. (1966) observed, "the output of an echo chamber bears an inevitable and invariable relation to the input," and Walter Lippmann warned, "there can be no liberty for the community that lacks the information by which to detect lies"

(Lippmann 1920). From the early days of the American republic, James Madison wrote, "A popular government without popular information, or the means of acquiring it, is but a prologue to a farce or a tragedy; or, perhaps both" (Barry and Madison 1822). Critics of Donald Trump argue we are all now living Madison's farce or tragedy or both. Legendary CBS anchor Walter Cronkite once observed, "We [as a nation] are not educated well enough to perform the necessary act of intelligently selecting our leaders" (Martelle 2005). Reality is socially constructed. And media – whether legacy or social – is where our reality is constructed, increasingly via social media platforms.

The FAANGs – Facebook, Apple, Amazon, Netflix, and Google – see news as important to their business. Google executive Richard Gingras put it succinctly when he told the 2 May 2018 gathering hosted by the Canadian Journalism Foundation, "The future of Google and the future of news are inextricably linked. Building trust in news matters to Google" (Canadian Journalism Foundation 2018b).

Which brings us back to classic liberalism, journalism, and its place in public discourse. Pulitzer Prize-winning journalist Alex S. Jones says journalism's first obligation is to the truth, its first loyalty is to citizens, and its essence is the discipline of verification.

Neil Postman, in *Amusing Ourselves to Death* (1985), identified the societal risk with this question: "Ignorance is always correctable, but what do we do if we take ignorance to be knowledge?"

3

Boorstin's World: A Shift in the Balance of News Gathering and News Making

Increasingly, if we aren't sleeping or actually working our day jobs, we are in the media torrent. And that reality has implications for the way we organize ourselves politically. As Nick Couldry of the London School of Economics and Andreas Hepp observed, "If we do politics, for instance, it is politics by and through media" (Couldry and Hepp 2011). Because the journalistic product we consume is a decisive factor in how we do politics, it matters how we gather news and how society's leaders make news.

Journalism must provide the nation's early warning system, according to Robert McChesney (2013), so that problems can be anticipated, studied, debated, and addressed before they grow to crisis proportions.

The University of Illinois professor concedes it is impractical to expect every media outlet to provide all of these services to their communities, but McChesney insists "it is necessary, however, that the media system as a whole makes such journalism a realistic expectation for the citizenry. There should be a basic understanding of the commons – the social world – that all people share, so that all people can effectively participate in the political and electoral processes of self-governance" (ibid.). McChesney believes the true test of a free press is measured by how well that press provides citizens with the information they need to preserve their freedoms and rights.

Harvard scholar Thomas Patterson extends Walter Lippmann's thought and argues journalists "are in the daily business of making the unseen visible, of connecting us to the world beyond our direct experience" (Patterson 2013, 6).

Communications scholar Ben Bagdikian – who, as an editor at the *Washington Post*, received parts of the Pentagon Papers from Daniel Ellsberg and, more importantly, convinced editor Ben Bradlee and publisher Katharine Graham to ignore threats from the Nixon administration and publish the information – states that great journalism requires great institutions. By the same token, liberal democracies must see "civic journalism" as a great institution in and of itself: an institution as foundational to civil society as an independent judiciary or a robust electoral system. And civic journalism requires material resources. Great journalism requires the organizational muscle to stand up to governments and corporations. And finally, great journalism requires competition.

News Gathering

Journalists, in the words of former CBC anchor Knowlton Nash, like to see news as a first rough draft of history. Matthew Arnold preferred the descriptive of journalism as "literature in a hurry." More formal definitions of news were crafted by scholars such as Wilbur Schramm, who described news as "an attempt to reconstruct the essential framework of an event" (Schramm 1949).

Patterson says news is more accurately the story of how today is different from yesterday – however you define "different." Even a cursory analysis of US presidential campaigns lends credence to Patterson's observation. Daily news accounts from the campaign trail frequently highlight some difference in a candidate's statement today from a statement on the same subject or issue in the days prior. Legendary CBC correspondent Joe Schlesinger summarized the different approaches to news coverage succinctly over lunch one day. As a foreign correspondent, Schlesinger says he looked at the world through a telescope; as a national political correspondent, he looked at the world through a microscope.

News highlights the exception, the aberration, not the rule. My hunch is the last time a newspaper headline declared "Plane Lands" was when Charles Lindbergh touched down at Le Bourget in Paris the better part of a century ago. Planes are supposed to land safely; it is only news when they don't.

There is a "Top 10" list of criteria used by journalists to determine "what's news," none of them particularly surprising. Timeliness, proximity, consequence, and human interest all count. Conflict helps, as does the prominence of the news maker. The weird can be wonderful, from a news perspective. Funny works. Topicality matters, and visuals are always welcome.

Alex S. Jones, the former executive director of the Shorenstein Center on Media, Politics and Public Policy at Harvard's John F. Kennedy School of Government (and not to be confused with InfoWars' Alex Jones), has identified a hierarchy of news.

The first tier involves "bearing witness" – the meat and potatoes of accountability news: reporters going places, seeing things first-hand, looking things up, digging into public records, developing sources, checking, double-checking. Deteriorating balance sheets at legacy news outlets constitute a "clear and present danger" to journalists' ability to bear witness.

The second tier is the follow-up. Given the five Ws of journalism – who, what, when, where, why – the second tier focuses on the why.

The third tier is explanatory news, the news that goes deeply into a subject, the news that focuses on the transcendent issues of our time; climate change, for example.

Investigative reporting is a tier unto itself, at the top of the reporting chain. This reporting is time-consuming, it is risky, it is expensive, it is irritating to those under investigation. Bill Clinton's press secretary Mike McCurry was of the view that "investigative reporters are by definition conspiracy theorists" (quoted in Kurtz 1998, 37). McCurry's comment is certain to bring a smile to the face of anyone who had the good fortune to meet the legendary investigative reporter I.F. Stone. It is also essential and threatened for one simple reason; the business model that has sustained this kind of journalism for more than 200 years is broken.

News – the communication instrument of choice for political discourse – is a by-product of classical liberalism.

Harvard's Alex S. Jones (2009) states newspapers have borne a disproportionate share of the burden of "accountability" reporting – the on-the-ground reportage that shapes the public record, which Jones has dubbed the "iron core" of news. Jones estimates 85 per cent of this work – the assembly of the basic facts that provide the fodder for public discussion and debate – is done by newspapers. And newspapers, basically, are shrinking and withering on the vine, with obvious implications for other democratic institutions.

In January 2017, the prestigious *Boston Globe* announced it would no longer be a "newspaper of record" but would evolve, instead, to "an organization of interest" (Kennedy, D. 2017). The *Boston Globe*'s evolution is most certainly of interest. And suggests it may be time to revisit some of James Carey's ideas as to how mainstream journalism as it has evolved may have missed its true calling.

Historically, mainstream journalism held to certain standards: accuracy, balance, and holding government accountable with a clear separation between news, editorial opinion, and advertising context. The degree to which the news organization sought to maximize profit was a factor in each news organization's weighting of each of these factors.

Communications scholar Robert Entman offered a further list, a compartmentalized categorization of journalism: traditional journalism, tabloid journalism, advocacy journalism, and entertainment (Jones, A. 2009, 43). But as the stress fractures began to appear in the business model for mainstream journalism, distinctions between Entman's categories became more difficult to identify. And that, in turn, began to influence the news gathering process itself, and the editorial content that process produced.

News gathering is, by its very nature, inefficient, says James Fallows, who denounces what he described as the "counting-house mentality" (1996a, 70) of media chain ownership "determined to 'downsize' newsrooms and cut expenses to satisfy quarterly earnings demands" (ibid., 70–1).

As Edward Jay Epstein states, "Despite the more heroic public claims of the news media, daily journalism is largely concerned with finding and retaining profitable sources of pre-packaged stories" (1975, 9). Media sociologists note journalism, in practice, is a matter of the representatives of one bureaucracy – a mainstream media outlet – picking up prefabricated items from representatives of another bureaucracy – governments, school boards, stock exchanges, the courts.

Reporters cannot know in advance what the news of the day will be, as communications scholars James S. Ettema and Theodore L. Glasser (1984) concluded, but they can know where to find it. The "beat" system evolved as a result. Beats can be organized around physical spaces such as the cop shop, the White House, or a parliamentary press gallery, or areas of expertise such as the environment or health or, in the world of financial reporting, mergers and acquisitions.

USA Today founder Al Neuharth identified a complacency that bordered on the smug in terms of how journalists saw themselves and the content they were producing. "The message I kept hearing over and over was that newspaper people thought they were putting out better newspapers than newspaper readers thought they were reading," Neuharth said (1989). Years later, Richard Stursberg, the former executive vice-president of English services, would make substantially the same comment about the CBC (2012).

This tension between the cost of news gathering and quarterly returns for investors changed fundamentally when newspapers, basically, went to the financial markets. A broad and diverse shareholder base is unlikely to even be familiar with, never mind espouse, Siebert's "social responsibility" foundational mandate of the press. Further, this base's assessment of what constitutes a reasonable return on investment may be set slightly higher than one might expect in a "journalism as public trust" construct. The pressure to produce quarterly returns leads inevitably to a focus on cost, which in turn leads to a focus on the lowest cost for news gathering. This focus tilted the field in favour of news makers, given their ability to generate "news" at a relatively low, (and equally important) predictable, or even fixed cost.

Historically, news is about people, as distinct from groups or social processes. And it's mostly about certain people, people who are "knowns" by virtue of their own celebrity status – think Angelina Jolie – or by virtue of their job – a senior government official, for example.

News isn't what happened but, more precisely, is what someone says happened or will happen, according to Leon Sigal. The folks telling reporters what happened are afforded the elevated descriptive of "source."

"Knowledge deficiencies" on the part of journalists leave them "vulnerable to manipulation by their sources," says Patterson (2013), and those sources will play the "subject-matter expert" trump card to their advantage.

The fact is, the source need only tell a reporter what the source deems to be in his or her self-interest (Epstein 1975). Because of the voluntary nature of the relationship, the supply of information continues only if the source is satisfied with the way the journalist used the information. James Fallows likens this "access" bargain to a plea bargain in court. This creates a core conundrum for the reporter.

A journalist's dependency on sources is a bargain with a price. NBC political correspondent Katy Tur, who covered Trump's presidential campaign, offered this analysis in her bestseller *Unbelievable*. "Access is seductive. Access means good nuggets from a campaign. Access means your calls answered. Access is safe and secure because you're the one at your organization who can always get a comment, a confirmation, or an exclusive interview. But access is barely journalism" (Tur 2017, 171).

Tur's observation buttresses Anya Schiffrin's conclusion: "The pressure to deliver news and inside information is at odds with the imperative to cover powerful institutions and their leaders without fear or favour" (Schiffrin 2011, 73). Sources typically see the relationship as a two-way street, with the elite source on "receive" as much as he or she is on send. Journalists can be less aware of this reality and routinely give away valuable information about what the other side is up to in exchange for minimal considerations. The "source" conundrum will be addressed in more detail in the next chapter.

Journalists see their mission in life as "bringers of light." Lippmann encourages us to see journalism more like a flashlight in a dark room (Graber 2001, 22).

Journalists and government officials have more interests in common than professionals in either discipline are inclined to admit.

As media sociologists have observed repeatedly, journalists and politicians are, figuratively speaking, joined at the hip. This reality of political journalism stands in sharp contrast to the situation in financial reporting, where business leaders and the business reporters who cover them have significantly less in common.

As a by-product, perhaps, of the emergence of schools of journalism and the consequential professionalization of what was once a craft, journalists tend now to be lumped in with politicians as members of the technological, globalist elites that Trump ran against in 2016. They are the "professional class" Thomas Frank writes about in *Listen, Liberal* (Frank 2016). And if 2016 Democratic presidential nominee Hillary Clinton was slow to realize that a distemper had seized Middle America, the national press corps wasn't any quicker on the uptake – for many of the same reasons.

Yet in the adversarial culture nurtured in newsrooms, reporters and politicians tend to trumpet their differences. The late and legendary Liberal senator and strategist Keith Davey once said, "I honestly believe that a healthy, wholesome tension between politicians and the fourth estate is the essence of democracy" (Davey 1986, 184). That tension flows – to the extent it exists – in part from the fact reporters and politicians have fundamentally different jobs.

Politics and public policy are a collaborative affair; in essence, an exercise in aggregation and accommodation, a role that traditionally was filled in democracies by the political party. For reporters, the basic job is to discover and highlight disunity. Douglass Cater described the reporter as Hegelian; that is, he or she thinks in terms of thesis and antithesis (Cater 1959).

These differences notwithstanding, journalism is an integral part of the government process. Journalistic institutions and mainstream political parties are largely dedicated to the preservation of the socioeconomic status quo. Journalists and politicians both tend to speak in the voice of free-market capitalism. Political revolutionaries see the two groups as symbiotic and dismiss the clashes between the two as little more than an affectation to allow participants on each side to sleep a little better at night. Indeed, in today's social media world, it is increasingly difficult to see where the line is drawn between what Daniel Boorstin (1962) describes as news gathering and news making, particularly when it comes to political reporting.

A short history underscores the nature of the mutually dependent relationship.

In Canada, reporters and politicians began to "bunk in" together in the late nineteenth century when the Speaker of the House of Commons set aside space for the distinguished members of the Parliamentary Press Gallery.

In the United States, William Price of the *Washington Star* began stationing himself outside the White House so he could interview then-president Grover Cleveland's visitors. Woodrow Wilson was the first US president to hold regular news conferences (Hess 1996, 114).

Further, there has always been a direct link between political communication and advances in communications technology.

Franklin Delano Roosevelt was the first American president to appear on television but was better known for maximizing the opportunities to communicate directly with voters through radio. FDR, who had poets and playwrights on the payroll to help him with his messaging, also used the "backgrounder" interview to great effect.

Dwight Eisenhower was the first president to formalize the position of press secretary, naming James Hagerty to the position. John Fitzgerald Kennedy held the first televised news conference, and Mike McCurry, in turn, was the first White House spokesperson to allow his daily briefing to be televised.

There has always been a political price exacted from party leaders who did not adjust to changes in communications technology. Liberal Prime Minister Louis St-Laurent was effective on radio and used it extensively, earning the nickname "Uncle Louis." But as media historian Allan Levine (1993) noted, St-Laurent's charm did not make a successful transition to television.

The 1960 presidential debates in the United States are now the stuff of journalistic legend. Radio listeners thought Richard Nixon had prevailed. Television viewers thought John Kennedy had won decisively. Suddenly, political commentary included references to Nixon's "five o'clock shadow."

Pierre Trudeau, inspired by classical liberal theorists such as John Locke and John Stuart Mill, looked to parliamentary correspondents for a genuine exchange of ideas. "Gotcha" journalism failed to meet Trudeau's expectations. To put it mildly, Trudeau did not always think the Canadian press corps held up their end of the bargain, with the notable exception of the "poetry war" that broke out between the Liberal leader and Jim Travers, Jim McLean, and Derek Hodgson – aka Team Grunt – on the campaign plane in 1980 (pers. notes). The former Liberal leader either did not understand or was dismissive of journalistic processes. Further, it was never clear to this writer that he fully appreciated the differences in journalistic culture between Canada's French-language and English-language presses.

What Pierre Trudeau did understand was the power of television as the information medium of choice during his time in office. Levine (1993) references Trudeau's decade-long correspondence with University of Toronto scholar Marshall McLuhan. The former Liberal leader fully appreciated television's ability to literally put him directly in people's living rooms.

The impact of television will be dealt with in more detail later, in the chapter on news and power.

Personal relationships have always been a subject of debate in media relations in politics, particularly the "revolving door" between journalism, politics, and government.

In his introduction to a paper written by James McEnteer and published by Harvard's Shorenstein Center, Fred Schauer asked, "Can insider information and the insider perspective be obtained in such a way that the journalist does not become part of the very enterprise whose evaluation and criticism is almost definitional of the job?" (McEnteer 1991, i).

As former *Maclean's* editor-in-chief Robert Lewis (2018a) captures so vividly in his work, successive Liberal leaders sought the advice and counsel of distinguished political journalists such as the *Vancouver Sun*'s Bruce Hutchison or *Maclean's* correspondent Blair Fraser.

Conservative Prime Minister Brian Mulroney's long-standing friendship with Peter C. Newman predated Mulroney's selection as Progressive Conservative Party leader and election to Parliament. Mulroney believed Newman was a journalist he could trust, until the former *Maclean's* editor-in-chief wrote *The Secret Mulroney Tapes*, released in 2005 (CBC 2006).

Mulroney and US president George H.W. Bush shared a belief these personal relationships would be a significant factor in shaping media coverage – and both, in the end, were disappointed. Both leaders were reluctant to accept an operating principle among media relations advisers: that a journalist is neither friend nor foe but rather a professional intermediary between politicians and the people they are trying to reach. Senator Davey put it well: "No matter how close your relationship with any member of the working press, that person will put his craft ahead of your friendship" (Levine 1993).

Media bias has also been a matter of intense debate for politicians. Liberal governments of the 1950s, for example, thought the CBC constituted a dark, chronic conspiracy to malign the government. Stephen Harper's Conservative government of 2006–15 held substantially the same view. Yet academic studies have established that any "slant" in the news pages is more likely to reflect the political makeup of potential readers. Ownership plays little or no role in determining any slant in news stories.

On occasion, despite the fact it has no constitutional or legislative basis to do so, the media may claim the mantle of an "unofficial opposition" for its own, usually in situations where election results produced overwhelming majorities for one party or another: Quebec after the 1973 provincial election and Ottawa after the 1984 federal election are two such examples.

Media bias is rarely ideological in North America; rather, as Nate Silver (2012) observed, the bias is in favour of the story. However, the media, writes Daniel Kahneman (2011), does not simply shape public opinion but is also shaped by it. Canadian recording artist Shania Twain's statement to the *Guardian* that she would have voted for Donald Trump in 2016 triggered a public reaction significant enough to generate a second wave of news coverage in the Canadian media the next day. Twain took advantage of the political communication technique known as the "walk back" to dampen the furor.

In terms of the day-to-day routine of the news gathering process, government press operations grew as the press corps grew. Press officers were usually described as "flacks" and treated by working reporters as something of a lower species, especially if the press officer had once been a journalist. Yet a comprehensive study by Brookings Institution fellow Stephen Hess (1984) confirmed the extent of the dependence of the news gatherers on the news makers – Washington-based reporters covering the US federal government contacted press officers on more than half their stories.

In a political leader's office, such as the Prime Minister's Office in Ottawa, the division of labour around the political communication that is the purpose of news making is relatively straightforward.

The director of communications serves as the strategist, develops the strategic communications plan, and generally restricts personal contact with, or availability to, the "A" list of political correspondents. However, in recent years, as the influence of "the centre" has grown in Ottawa and leaders' offices increasingly include both a chief of staff and a principal secretary, the principal secretary often plays a lead role in terms of the communications strategy.

The director of communications must be, and be seen to be, part of the senior management group. Media disasters ensue when senior staff members – without media expertise – decide what the press should or should not be told. In the early 1980s, the tall foreheads in Reagan's White House instructed deputy press secretary Larry Speakes to deny a US invasion of Grenada was imminent. Bill Plante's report on the CBS *Evening News* included Speakes's denial – along with news US troops had landed in Grenada (Stahl 1999).

Press secretaries, in the main, assume responsibility for tactical execution of communications plans. The litmus test for press secretaries is access; they have to be seen as being "in the loop."

Marlin Fitzwater (1995), who served both presidents Reagan and Bush, said, "The Press Secretary to the President stands between the opposing forces, explaining, cajoling, begging, sometimes pushing both sides to a better understanding of each other." Press officers have to be responsive, and the execution function rolls out on two tracks. The first involves content, the preparation and distribution of background and supportive material on government announcements. The second is more logistical – "wagon masters" charged with the transportation, logistical support, and care and feeding of the media entourage.

Political communications staff in Washington and Ottawa use different phrases to describe the same activity. In Washington, you "feed the lions"; in Ottawa, you "feed the goat." An official spokesperson in Washington trying to extricate themselves from a challenging exchange with a reporter is "dancing," while in Ottawa – true to our Canadian heritage – they are "skating."

What is common to both capitals is that there is never any shortage of senior staff people who know they would be better at media relations than either the director of communications or the press secretary, and they are uniformly willing to take on the assignment – unofficially, of course, on a background, not-for-attribution basis only, with the freedom to duck, dive, and deny any involvement at the first sign of trouble.

Media critic Howard Kurtz (1998) says the modern presidency is above all a media presidency, which is as convenient an explanation for Donald Trump as anything else.

If journalism and government are mutually dependent on each other, communications and policy are similarly dependent within government, the faint condescension of the policy types toward their communications colleagues notwithstanding.

Management guru Peter Drucker suggests we'd all be well-advised to find a mirror when giving thought to societal problems. "I don't know why people are so fixated on the subject of leadership," Drucker observed. "What we really need to think about is followership" (Economist 2019a, 49). Drucker's point is well-taken. Donald Trump, so far as we know, only got to cast one ballot in the 2016 and 2020 presidential votes. As offensive as his character may be to some, Trump did not launch a military coup. Trump was sworn in as the forty-fifth president of the United States in 2016 because tens of millions of his fellow citizens cast ballots in support of his candidacy.

The fact is, a government's failure to explain itself clearly and candidly to its citizens is a failure for democracy. Pro-European Union supporters within the former David Cameron government in the UK may wonder how Brexit supporters prevailed. They need only look in a mirror to explain the failure. If residents of the northeastern city of Sunderland who voted overwhelmingly for Brexit were unaware of the risk a Leave vote posed to the Nissan car manufacturing plant in their town that has produced thousands of jobs since 1986, the fault lies not just with them.

The philosopher and educator John Dewey believed "no policy, however sound, could survive a flawed 'process,' and the communication of the policy is central to that process" (Fox B. 1999, 31). Policy experts invariably seek refuge in the argument of complexity and are quick to denounce the "bumper sticker mentality" of their communications colleagues. The fact is, workers on a steel factory floor are perfectly capable of assessing the implications of trade tariffs slapped on their industry (as president Trump did on Canadian steel and aluminum in 2018) and may even have a better grasp of the complexities of the business than the policy wonks in the capital. It is no accident that when Canada succeeded in having the tariffs lifted, Prime Minister Trudeau headed to a steel plant in Hamilton, Ontario, to share the news with unionized workers.

The "permanent campaign" has become a feature of modern government (Caddell 1976). As stated earlier in this work, communications are now seen as almost as much a role of government as fiscal policy (Lilleker 2006). In fact, Trudeau's critics argue the prime minister doesn't actually do much else. As Lilleker states, "Modern democracies need to be increasingly responsible to their publics and at the heart of responsiveness is dialogue" (ibid.).

The media plays a decided role in that process. As James Carey put it so eloquently, job one is "simply to make sure that in the short run we don't get screwed" (as cited in Adam 2009).

From the government side of the equation, the strategic objective of any communications plan is to influence the news agenda.

A more substantive challenge flows from the fact policy often lacks the novelty that news requires.

Government communications has long been plagued by the particular and peculiar vernacular of the English language known as "bureaucratese."

Queen's University politics associate professor Jonathan Rose argues people might have a better understanding of what government is trying to tell them if governments used language that citizens use (Rose 2017). Rose posted a photo of a sign put up by the City of Kingston to illustrate the point. The sign urged people to "Offer input now! On the revised draft of the public engagement framework" (ibid.).

You couldn't make this stuff up. As Rose noted in his tweet, "Few will want to offer input on a revised draft of a framework" (ibid.). What is even more unsettling is the fact someone was paid professional fees to craft this example of bafflegab. And someone else was paid to approve it.

John Lanchester, writing in a 2016 edition of the *New York Times Magazine*, offered this assessment of how public communication ought to be crafted: "As a rule of thumb, texts aimed at a general audience must be written at a 10th-grade level or below" (Lanchester 2016).

As we all know, journalism is not the only provider of political information or stimulant for informed debate and participation. Political information also comes from the creative and performing arts, the visual arts, academic research, entertainment media, conversations with family and friends. Yet, as McChesney states, "All of those other avenues are much more effective and valuable if they rest atop a strong journalism and support that journalism" (McChesney 2013). Late-night talk shows have emerged as a place for political debate, but it is the news in the mainstream media that has provided the raw material for the opening monologues as far back as when the late Steve Allen was inventing the genre.

The exercise of media relations is, therefore, essential to the governance process, and it is why the tilt in the balance between the world of news gathering to Boorstin's world of news making is so important.

Social Media and the Scribes

The social media model is the story we are in the process of writing today, on platforms such as Facebook, Twitter, Reddit, Instagram, TikTok and with tools such as WhatsApp. The emergence of new technologies and new media platforms has led to an evolution, even a revolution, in the way information flows in society.

Proponents of the "revolution" school of media theory believe the democratization of the production process of "content" will be the salvation of us all.

The web-based, network-enabled revolution in text production and distribution we are in the process of fashioning constitutes a fundamental shift in the power paradigm.

In this new model, control over production is no longer completely in the hands of professional journalists, according to Clay Shirky (2008). To speak online is to publish, and to publish online is to connect with others.

This process of "creative collaboration" has led to a fundamental shift in the very definition of news, in theory at least, from news as an institutional prerogative of those in control of systems of production, to news as part of an interactive process conducted on a global scale.

Traditional media, with its megaphone model of top-down, one-way communication to a largely passive audience, is spectacularly ill-suited to this new definition of news. Some years ago, University of Missouri fellow Michael Skoler (2009) stated, "The old journalism, with its overreliance on the same experts and analysts, is out of touch with a culture of information sharing, connection and the collective wisdom of diverse voices passing along direct experience." Would that the executive producers of the network election specials for the 2016 US presidential campaign had read Skoler.

This reality, predictably, is a cause of concern for professional journalists.

Changes triggered by social media platforms at least have the potential to create new channels and new types of public discourse, where everyone is a creator of content and everyone has a hand in shaping the discussion. Reporters now routinely take to Twitter to ask for help from followers for stories the journalist is working on. David A. Fahrenthold did just that when he began his investigation of Trump's charitable work (Bilton 2016). In 2017 Fahrenthold won a Pulitzer Prize for his work with the help of "ordinary citizens."

Anyone with a mobile device witnesses daily the mass amateurization of news gathering activities previously reserved for media professionals, whether the news event involves a natural catastrophe, a conflict with police, a political rally, or a demonstration. Widely circulated cellphone videos taken by witnesses are central elements of news accounts of the killing of George Floyd and were introduced as critical evidence in the trial of Derek Chauvin, the former Minneapolis police officer convicted of Floyd's murder.

Floyd's death, which occurred after he was pinned to the ground with the police officer's knee on his neck for more than nine minutes as witnesses pleaded for his life, triggered legacy and social media demands for racial justice across America and beyond. And the images captured by traumatized citizens on their phones enabled millions to witness a confrontation that began over a counterfeit twenty-dollar bill. The cellphone footage put people everywhere on the sidewalk outside the Cup Foods store with direct implications for the broader societal debate around the use of force by police officers.

Obviously, this isn't the first time a breakthrough in communications technology has prompted observers to proclaim a new platform as the salvation of democracy. My friend and Carleton colleague Susan Delacourt, in her book *Shopping for Votes* (2013), quotes former prime minister William Lyon Mackenzie King's assessment of radio's potential: "May we not predict that as a result of this carrying of the living voice throughout the length and breadth of the Dominion, there will be aroused a more general interest in public affairs, and an increasing devotion of the individual citizen to the commonweal." Added the legendary Graham Spry, radio "should make the home not merely a billboard, but a theatre, a concert hall, a club, a public meeting, a school, a university" (ibid.). Radio did, in fact, become an important medium of public discourse, although Donald Trump's appearances on Howard Stern may not have been precisely what Willie King had in mind.

Twitter, in no small measure because of Trump, has been a focus for discussion about the impact of social media on news gathering. Former *Toronto Star* public editor Kathy English, for example, asks if Twitter's real-time dimension compromises standards of accuracy (English 2010). Journalists wonder if they should tweet rumours and by extension ask if all tweets must be verified or does the "wisdom of the crowds" – to quote James Surowiecki – take care of that? Print journalists in particular wonder if you can say anything meaningful in 140 characters, while social media gurus ask what happens to the authenticity of Twitter if it moves from 280 to 10,000 characters?

So what does this shift mean for political communicators? It means a fundamental shift in the relationship between politicians and the journalists who cover them, and a shift that once again favours the news maker at the expense of the news gatherer.

Digital communications are challenging, even destroying,

long-standing journalistic conventions. Mainstream media "news values" and production processes are evolving as well, the emergence of citizen journalists being but one example. Content distribution today is dominated by gorillas, like Facebook, and guerrillas who are sophisticated in their use of these platforms, such as Breitbart News.

As Esther Dyson (1997) predicted twenty years ago, power has been swept away from mass media and big government alike, and big business may not be far behind. Trump had no particular credential to lead a government, and a plurality of the American electorate didn't particularly care because in 2016 many saw big government as part of their problem and not part of the solution – Obamacare being a flashpoint for the discussion. The internet is redefining who is and is not informed, even as it redefines information, and what it means to be "informed."

On the good-news side of the ledger, social media is empowering those who have been marginalized by mainstream media: women, racialized people, Indigenous people. On the less constructive side, voices that were marginalized by media gatekeepers for good and valid reasons can also find voice for hate speech, personal attacks, rumour.

In political terms, this multiplicity of platforms and voices has also created pools of people with different political agendas, different sets of expectations, different standards of government performance, and different levels of attachment to common institutions and values. The key to political communication now, as then, is understanding which media are right for which message at which time.

There are a host of issues associated with the democratization of news for political or public discourse. The agenda-setting process is more complex, the digital divide means uneven access to information, there is a more fundamental questioning of the idea of an informed citizen, and whether that classic liberal ideal is achievable. There is also the issue of a generation gap, people whose media consumption habits are mostly passive versus the millennial, activist content creator.

Carey's Conversation: Today's Strategic Communications Plan

Gerald Butts, Prime Minister Justin Trudeau's former principal secretary, was the de facto master of the Liberal government's message track. A big part of his job, done with then-PMO communications executive director Kate Purchase, was to shape and influence Canada's political conversation. Twitter is an instrument of choice. As it is for Donald Trump.

The media, as stated repeatedly in this work, is a primary site of political discourse in Western liberal democracies. But with today's social media, not only has the number of sites increased dramatically, the exercise of strategic communications has changed fundamentally. And the reason for that is the fact social media has altered the relationship of the engaged, just as television did before it.

James Carey's transmission model was at the heart of old media: a top-down model, built on a premise of a megaphone, that involved getting the right audience the right message through the right channel. This model involved passive consumption, never more so than when television emerged as our information medium of choice. In this transmission model, senior media editors served as the gatekeepers of public discourse. And in exercising that function, they set political agendas, structured the way electors assessed the elected, then reported on those assessments as "public opinion." Political communications plans through this era, predictably, reflected this transmission media model.

Carey, however, privileged the "ritual model" of communication: a process through which a shared culture is created, modified, and transformed. Social media provides for Carey's ritual model and affords a new twist to the theorists' view that the central function of news is the creation of community.

Social media, at least in theory, constitutes a shift from passive consumption to active participation. When building a communications plan in this environment, strategists should be thinking about building connections, rather than delivering messages.

A social media conversation is more about authenticity than authority, and that simple fact poses challenges for news gatherers wedded to the traditional "first witness" approach. Too often, the lead item on a national newscast is a story unfolding in Istanbul or Damascus being told by a correspondent in London or Washington. How "authentic" can such a report be?

A political junkie today can follow a campaign or a candidate minute by minute. And digital media platforms such as Twitter and Facebook are at the heart of this change.

Twitter in Three Takes

The 2012 US presidential election campaign was considered by communications experts as a continental divide of sorts. Twitter effectively took over the campaign. Today, in a Donald Trump world, we have a better appreciation of how truly transformational the 2012 Twitter takeover of presidential politics was.

The perspectives of a news maker and a news gatherer on this phenomenon warrant further reflection. Michael Slaby (2013), a driving force behind the successful integration of digital platforms for the 2008 and 2012 Obama presidential campaigns, and later a Shorenstein fellow, focuses on the democratic idea of engagement. Peter Hamby (2013), who covered these races for CNN, examines in some detail how that ideal translated into actual media coverage. Their findings help inform any consideration of media effects of subsequent US presidential campaigns.

Slaby acknowledges that everyone from technologists to sociologists has attempted to articulate the shift that is occurring and how that shift is impacting the "voices" of public discourse – organizations, media companies, political parties, movements, governments.

Retweeting occurs all day long. You may still read a column from the *New York Times*, but you are likely to have accessed the column through a link from your Twitter feed, and the link is more likely to have been sent to you from a friend or someone you follow.

Operationally, Twitter turned rapid response into real-time response. One example in a campaign context is that conventional wisdom concerning who won and who lost coalesces on social media before televised leaders' debates even end.

The shift in media behaviour from passive consumption to active participation forces all publishers into a new posture of participant. This transition is proving more difficult for legacy media, who privilege a journalistic model more closely aligned with Robert Heinlein's "Fair Witness" character in his 1961 science fiction novel *Stranger in a Strange Land* – an individual trained to observe events and report exactly what he or she sees or hears.

Even people who do not share, or tweet, consume more content from indirect and/or unpredictable sources. The significance of this shift is not to be underestimated as it represents a massive content creation challenge. The fact political conversation is now about authenticity rather than authority means political leaders must be personal, embracing, and articulating coherent values, conveying a meaningful sense of purpose. Presidential candidate Hillary Clinton failed consistently in this regard.

Michael Slaby's advice to communications planners is basically to burn the boats and strike out for new ground as there is no going back.

Peter Hamby's perspective provides an important counterweight. A political reporter for CNN and also a Shorenstein fellow, Hamby decided a belief among veterans of the Mitt Romney 2012 presidential campaign warranted further consideration. In a campaign postmortem, a top Romney strategist decried what Hamby called "the media's declining interest in weighty matters and its growing obsession with process and trivia in the internet age" (Hamby 2013).

In the aftermath of the 2012 presidential campaign, Hamby states, many reporters and political professionals alike were sharply critical of Twitter's impact on the Washington conversation; specifically, with the cynical tone of the online conversation.

Social media has accelerated the "run and gun" pace of reporting. The most important thing about political journalism today is to be first. "Scoop" is the coin of the social media realm, and the need for speed means more tweets go out based on a single source.

Margaret Sullivan, media columnist for the *Washington Post*, says this approach to news coverage is a mistake. "Speed kills," Sullivan said in a conversation with *Globe and Mail* editor-in-chief David Walmsley at a Canadian Journalism Foundation event in Toronto on 28 May 2019. News consumers, Sullivan says, don't care who had the story first. They just want the story to be right. Hamby's study concluded the numbers of stories from unnamed sources are rising. And invariably retweeted.

One clear sign of Twitter's ascendancy is that campaign operatives seem to care more about tweets than the final story journalists were writing or linking to. The mainstream media's traditional offerings are being marginalized in the electoral process. People are more likely to be familiar with the views of leading columnists from their Twitter feeds than from anything that appears in the publication that actually employs them or the network newscast they anchor. CBC anchor Rosemary Barton has more than 249,000 followers.

Social media creates a snowball effect. A well-placed leak starts to roll on Twitter, forcing rival news organizations to chase the story, turning it into a much bigger story than the substance warrants. The "boys on the bus" has given way to the "noise on the bus." Pack journalism predates social media, but like everything else impacted by new technologies, pack journalism can now take shape quicker and more broadly.

Campaign operatives – as news makers – now enjoy more success at setting the agenda than the media, according to the Pew Research Center (Hamby 2013). As Margaret Sullivan said, "We do rise to President Trump's bait far too often." The media, she says, let Trump "become our de facto assignment editor" (Canadian Journalism Foundation 2019a).

Twitter, of course, is not representative of the general public; it skews younger, activist, and liberal, Trump notwithstanding. In a tweet posted in the early days of the 2019 federal election, Ipsos Public Affairs CEO Darrell Bricker noted, "I'm looking at the numbers and see what I see. There's no votes to gain going right. As for Twitter, about 1% of Canadians Tweet on a regular basis. Tells you how representative it is" (Bricker 2019b). Twitter may indeed be a platform for insiders to talk to insiders, but if that conversation is where the news stories get "baked" and distributed later in the cycle through legacy media outlets, Twitter's impact on public discourse is both significant and meaningful.

Most reporters interviewed by Hamby for his paper expressed some form of regret about how they used Twitter during the 2012 campaign, as a Twitter conversation thrives on incrementalism, self-involvement, snark. A Pew Research study cited by Hamby concluded Twitter was far and away the most negative of platforms.

Joe Klein, *Time* correspondent and author of *Primary Colors*, worries journalism has slid from skepticism to cynicism. And the late David Carr, in an open letter to the journalistic tribe, advised, "Tweet less, dear colleagues" (Hamby 2013). The *New York Times* columnist stated he "unfollowed a lot of political colleagues, because you are tweeting for your colleagues, you are not tweeting for me" (ibid.). Carr's bottom line? "Be willing to play off the ball" – in other words, old-style contrarianism (ibid.).

Modern political managers have all worked to manage the media component of their mandate to govern. Each government has had its successes, each has had moments when they were convinced the media was conspiring against them.

There has always been a battle between political communications advisers and the media over the dominant news frame but, historically, it was a battle of engagement.

IRPP President Jennifer Ditchburn, a long-time parliamentary correspondent for the Canadian Press, conducted academic research for her master's degree in journalism and concluded that during the Harper years, the joust was fundamentally a battle of nonengagement. Campaign operatives saw social media platforms as enhancing their abilities as "news makers" while reducing the need to engage with or rely on the "news gatherers."

In the United States, Donald Trump made it quite clear he is substantively rewriting the rules of engagement for his administration with the Washington press corps.

Convinced as they are that emerging technologies make them less dependent on legacy news organizations, the news makers believe they need the news gatherers less and less. And as a consequence, legacy or traditional media continues to be *a* site of political discourse but not necessarily *the* primary site of political discourse in Western liberal democracies.

Social media is redefining who is, and who is not, informed.

Which brings us back to Gerald Butts.

Canada's federal Liberals literally went to school on the 2012 Obama campaign in the US and then pioneered some of their own techniques. Campaign operatives on both sides of the border today seem to care more about the tweets than the stories that finally appear in the *New York Times* or the *Toronto Star*. They now understand that journalists think the important thing about today's journalism is to be first and that, because of our ever diminishing newsroom resources, more and more one-sided information is being repackaged as news.

Butts, however, was equally aware of William Gibson's admonition that "The future is already here – it's just unevenly distributed" (Economist 2001). For that reason, Liberal strategists pay as much attention to the photo op as they did to the Google Hangout when it was the new next thing.

Prime ministers have long engaged the services of an official photographer. Adam Scotti – Justin Trudeau's official photographer – has elevated the function to the next level and operates as a "photojournalist." Every photograph reflects a communication strategy behind the picture released. As an aside, Scotti's father, my friend Bill McCarthy, served as Prime Minister Mulroney's official photographer.

Journalists aren't going to disappear. As Anderson et al. put it, "The availability of resources like citizen photos doesn't obviate the need for journalism or journalists, but it does change the job from being the source of the initial capture of an image or observation to being the persons who can make relevant requests, and then filter and contextualize the results" (Anderson, Bell, and Shirky 2012, 24).

The mobile device has emerged as the connector to the world. The amount of time we spend online has exploded. Hachten and Scotton observed, "Long-distance mass communication has become a rudimentary central nervous system for our fragile, shrinking, and increasingly interdependent, yet fractious, world" (2011, 2).

Going forward, communications planners may have to think more "ritual" and less "transmission" even as they are mindful of Carey's rules, that no one has the last word, no one has final thoughts.

While it may be tempting to throw out everything we know or have known about media effects, my personal inclination is not to do so. The old top-down, one-to-many megaphone model of communication focused on the right audience, the right message, the right channel. And there is evidence this traditional "transmission model" of top-notifications is still being used in the social media age. Kory Teneycke, campaign manager for Doug Ford's Conservatives in Ontario, talked about messages so tailored a wife would get a campaign message that would be different from her husband's.

Clearly, however, the mainstream media has a lot of adjusting to do if journalism is to prosper in a social media age. And that means a fundamental rethink of how the media goes about its business, which will be considered in more detail later in this work.

Strategic Communications Planning

The academic term for what is at the heart of strategic communications is "elite discourse network" management, a phrase coined by Aeron Davis (Davis 2000) to describe the interactions of Miller and Macintyre's "circuit of communication" (1998). Harold Lasswell (1948) states one function of communication is to provide intelligence about what other elites are doing and about the strength of each.

A story, the details notwithstanding, is not the same to all who hear it; each of us will enter the story at a slightly different point; each of us will consider the information against the backdrop of our personal experiences, circumstances, beliefs. Walter Lippmann set out the overarching challenge inherent in any political communication when he wrote, "For the most part we do not see first, and then define, we define first, and then see" (1922). He explained that political discourse as conducted through the media involves "the triangular relationship between the scene of the action, the human picture of that scene, the human response to that picture working itself out upon the scene of the action" (ibid.).

In other words, whatever we believe to be the true picture, we treat as if it were the actual picture. This predisposition predates social media platforms such as Facebook and the use of algorithms.

Today's media is less about authority and more about authenticity. Control of the gatekeeper function no longer rests exclusively with legacy media journalists. Niche news sites are increasingly important, from the *Drudge Report* to *Canadaland*. The proliferation of voices makes it more difficult to agree on a common set of facts. The proliferation of echo chambers has led to a fundamental challenge to the very idea of "facts." Political communicators today need to be guided by Nate Silver's observation that there is no big secret, there are 1,000 little secrets (Silver 2012, 239).

More generally, there are certain home truths that guide media relations work in the political sphere, identified by media critic Howard Kurtz (1998).

First, journalists love politicians who reinvent themselves. Pierre Trudeau was a master at creating different media personas. Politicians on the rise are invariably portrayed in glowing terms. The reverse is also true. As Kathleen Hall Jamieson notes, "A long and honourable tradition of academic research says that as someone drops in the polls, the press coverage becomes more hostile. The danger always with reporters covering a candidate based on polls is that they create a self-fulfilling prophecy" (Hall Jamieson 2000). Conservative Party Leader Erin O'Toole's challenges in the spring of 2021 are one illustration of Hall Jamieson's point.

Reporters are suckers for a politician who knows how to work the press. And journalists respond to someone who gets in their face, a fact that Donald Trump figured out early on. Attacking the press is a surefire way to get press, as Trump reaffirmed.

Bare-knuckle press manipulation can work, even when you get caught at it. Mudslinging works best when there are two or more participants.

No personal dirt remains unearthed when someone becomes newsworthy. David Axelrod describes an election campaign as an MRI for the soul. Whoever or whatever you are will, in the end, be revealed. By way of illustration, Conservative Party leadership candidate Kellie Leitch surprised many of her earlier supporters – this writer included – with her proposal to screen immigrants for "anti-Canadian values" during the 2017 Conservative Party leadership campaign (Tunney 2016).

In recent years, sex is no longer off limits for the mainstream press as the coverage afforded porn star Stormy Daniels and her affair with Donald Trump underscores. And in 2017 and early 2018 sexual harassment emerged as a dominant media story line in coverage of sports, politics, media, and business. By 2021, the Canadian Armed Forces faced a leadership and culture crisis as a direct result of media reports of the way complaints from women serving in the armed forces were either ignored or covered up by the military's chain of command and their political masters.

The press has a limited appetite for ideas. The media likes scandal stories, especially if big names are involved. But they prefer sound bite flaps to a complex scandal that involves a lot of long, hard work. Trump's sexcapades are easier to follow than his financial situation.

A significant subset of any communications strategy is crisis communications. And once again, Donald Trump rewrote the rules.

In any crisis, you need to establish exactly what it is you are dealing with, which will prove to be more of a challenge than it should be. The information available to you will be incomplete and often contradictory, so you really need to drill down to the root of the problem. That process will be complicated by human, even personal considerations and may involve someone you have known or worked with for some time: an ally, a business associate.

You need to define a story arc, create a master narrative, understand the multiple constituencies you are dealing with, figure out the players in your "circuit of communication." You need to remind yourself that all facts will not be received the same way in all quarters. You need to remember people turn to the media in a time of crisis. You need to fight the tendency for a siege mentality to set in: withdrawing to the modern equivalent of the medieval keep and raising the drawbridge is a mistake.

And you need to appreciate the value of the symbolic arena. Axelrod acknowledges President Obama sometimes came up short on the symbolic arena front; Obama's response to the "underwear bomber" who unsuccessfully tried to blow up a flight bound for Detroit – when the president heeded advisers and let Janet Napolitano, then director of homeland security, provide the official government response – being an example cited by the strategist (Axelrod 2015, 398).

Axelrod further advises crisis communicators be sensitive to the liberal technocrats' excess of faith in government's ability to solve a problem.

Test your strategy with contrary opinions, what former United States Army general David Petraeus described as a "red team" challenge to your plan. Make certain your messages address all three stages of a communication process: attention, comprehension, acceptance. Remember, media dependency is higher when there is a high degree of conflict or change. The potential for mass media messages to achieve broad effect increases when the media functions as a central information system in a time of conflict.

Think about Nate Silver's divide between foxes and hedgehogs (Silver 2012). Foxes are better forecasters; hedgehogs are better TV guests. Tailor your messages and designate your spokesperson accordingly. Factor in advocacy media outlets that profile advocacy advertising; in Ottawa, this could be the *Hill Times* or *iPolitics*.

If you are dealing with a political story, remember Axelrod's observation that "Washington is a terrible place to be when the story line has turned against you. The town is one big echo chamber"

(Axelrod 2015). Substitute Ottawa for Washington, add the name "Harper" and a reference to Syrian refugees, and you get the point.

Follow another Axelrod suggestion: candour, not pander.

A major long-term risk in any crisis communication situation is the "tick-tock" – the media's demand for a minute-by-minute accounting of events. In the early days of the Trump administration, White House spokespeople proved particularly inept in this regard. The 2020 COVID-19 pandemic is but one example. For that reason, remember the worst time to deny anything is when you don't know everything.

Strategic communications staffers can conflate crisis and risk communications. In fact, they are very different worlds. The late Joe Scanlon, a long-time Carleton professor, was recognized as an international expert on the distinction.

As Ulrich Beck (1986) observed, we have transitioned from an industrial society to a risk society. Political conflict and cleavages as defined by the logic of the distribution of good have given way to a society where cleavages are increasingly defined by the distribution of bad. Trump's 2020 campaign message suggested a Biden victory would result in certain classes of Americans having to accept a disproportionately larger share of the risk.

Comprehensive multilateral trade agreements will create winners and losers in any political geography. Debates around trade pacts, such as the debate during and after the 2016 presidential campaign on NAFTA, for example, focus less on the advantaged and more on the constituencies who would be stuck with the tab.

As a consequence, in today's Western liberal democracies, we get a lot of government by risk avoidance or, as a fallback position, government leaders hiding behind the shield of plausible deniability.

Governments increasingly try to conduct public business in private. And that is easier to do than newspaper subscribers may suspect. Media focus on the interesting can result in limited coverage of the important.

For example, the media fixated on guilty pleas from Michael Cohen, President Donald Trump's former lawyer, for breaking campaign finance and financial laws, including helping make hush money payments to a porn star and a former Playboy bunny to keep their alleged extramarital affairs with Donald Trump out of the 2016 election campaign coverage (Feuer 2018). That fixation, inevitably, meant less coverage of the broader issues of what Trump was doing to government writ large. Robert Reich, labour secretary in the Bill Clinton administration, posted a tweet that stated, "We have become so overwhelmed by the corruption and attacks on democracy emanating from the White House that the EPA can roll back clean air laws, potentially killing thousands of Americans, and it goes barely noticed. The damage being done to the country is truly unfathomable" (Reich 2018).

A *Forbes* magazine investigation of former commerce secretary Wilbur Ross's business dealings is a further example. *Forbes* described Ross as a "grifter" and suggested Ross had improperly helped himself to an estimated $120 million from his various business holdings, and the story was barely covered in the mainstream media (Alexander, D. 2018).

Every prime minister's office has had its share of critics when it comes to assessing crisis management skills. Justin Trudeau's PMO gets poor grades for its handling of the prime minister's vacation on the Aga Khan's private island in the Bahamas. Stephen Harper's PMO came in for similar criticism from seasoned observers such as *National Post* writer John Ivison, who, in a piece carried 22 October 2013, quipped, "Not the first time, the generals in the Prime Minister's Office have made a Little Bighorn of it," referring, of course, to General George Armstrong Custer's ill-fated engagement with Lakota and Cheyenne warriors in the foothills of Montana (Ivison 2013). And as for my stewardship of the communications team in Brian Mulroney's PMO, "Tunagate" was oft-cited as an example of our collective incompetence.

Rahm Emanuel, Obama's first chief of staff and subsequently the mayor of Chicago, provided some important context for these considerations, however, when he said, "If it's between good and bad, somebody else will deal with it. Everything that gets into the Oval Office is between bad and worse" (Whipple 2017).

Typically, crisis managers forget a critical component part of any communications strategy – evaluation. The evaluation has to be goals-based; it must meet predetermined objectives. The process must also be evaluated; specifically, the rollout plan and how it will work. And finally, outcomes must be measured. Did the plan produce the desired result?

Feeding frenzies are an element of political crises, the phrase having been coined by Larry Sabato (1991), who compared the way the media go after a wounded politician with sharks in a feeding frenzy. These feeding frenzies are usually triggered by a self-inflicted wound, tend to occur when things are relatively quiet on the news front, and are fed by "wiggle" disclosures: small bits of news that facilitate the retelling of the central point of the original story in follow-up pieces.

Bill Clinton's communications team had a tight checklist to handle crisis situations: be first, be right, be credible, express empathy, promote action, show respect. The former president would have been well-advised to share the checklist with Hillary Clinton's 2016 campaign team. The Democratic nominee's team turned a spell of physical weakness triggered by a flu bug into a three-day crisis of alarmist speculation as to the former first lady's health. The campaign's response touched on most of the most common mistakes strategists make when faced with a crisis: mixed messages from multiple sources, information that was released late, paternalistic attitudes, failing to counter urban myths in real time on social media, public power struggles and confusion.

Why bother with communications planning in the first place? Because there are important and traceable interactions between media, public opinion, and policy-makers. Changes in reigning ideas help to constitute changes in policy content.

The formation of belief systems of political elites plays a significant role in shaping public policy (Davis 2003). And the politics of an issue are determined in large part by how the benefits conferred are distributed and the costs incurred imposed (Oliver, T.R. 2006).

This shift has had a direct impact on news and public discourse.

Institutional coverage can easily slip into a limited discourse involving like-minded souls. Political communicators invariably have journalists they favour over others, the basis for that favouritism often philosophical if not ideological. Predictably, journalists who are deemed to share a worldview with those in power are more likely to be on the receiving end of insider information. Astonishingly, political communicators can be quite vocal about the fact they don't even read news from organizations deemed to be either too progressive or too conservative, and, when confronted on this point, look startled when asked how they can be any good at their jobs if they are blissfully unaware of what is being written or said about their issue in certain media quarters.

Public perceptions of journalism and journalists have shifted over time, from the lapdog era of an early compliant press, to the watchdog era of Watergate and the Pentagon Papers, to the more recent junkyard dog construct. The *Washington Post*'s Margaret Sullivan says today's media needs to emphasize the "watchdog" role (Canadian Journalism Foundation 2019a).

ABC news anchor and former White House communications director George Stephanopoulos wonders why "every political reporter has become an amateur psychologist" (Stephanopoulos 1996). James Fallows (1996b) described the "reporter as wise guy" persona.

But many of these preoccupations flowed from the old media model, the linear, top-down process from leaders to the led.

Everyone in politics assumes there is such a thing as media effects, that most of the beliefs that come to affect political behaviour are likely developed by way of communication, that there is an audience that is listening. Sir Craig Oliver, communications adviser to former British prime minister David Cameron, believes that decades of anti-European Union coverage in the British press was certainly a factor in shaping public opinion about the UK's membership in the union, which in turn shaped the debate in the Brexit referendum campaign (Oliver, C. 2016, 83). But they are equally aware of Lippmann's (1922) caution that the people who are the target of a media relations strategy are like an audience of any other kind – they attend differently. Lippmann's conclusion that messages are received differently by different people applies equally to visual communications, as anyone who has worked advance for a political leader or candidate can attest. Photo ops are carefully considered, yet images that trigger a smile for one viewer run the risk of a guffaw in another.

The media balance today is shifting, and as a result, there are new variables to consider in the media effects construct.

Republican strategist Frank Luntz, for example, believes people don't vote for specific policies, but for intangible personal traits they ascribe to candidates – trust, consistency, stability. Ironically, small "c" conservative voices are also among the loudest in denouncing "values" signalling.

Media outlets themselves are redefining the relationship with their audience. *Politico*, when it was launched, saw itself as the voice of, and the mirror to, a certain type of reader – in the main, self-styled influencers and decision makers.

Social media was, and may still be, in a position to change all that.

Social media users actually know you cannot believe everything you read on the internet. They know you have to stitch together knowledge, as the late David Carr told a Canadian Journalism Foundation dinner. They know the story is never finished, that the story is always evolving, that retweeting goes on all day, and that your view of any story is shaped in no small measure by whether the story came from someone you know. Paul Lazarsfeld's (Katz and Lazarsfeld 1955) two-step flow theory of communication is enjoying a renaissance in the social media age. Lazarsfeld and his colleagues concluded media messages are received first by opinion leaders from every walk of life. These opinion leaders have higher levels of media consumption, and they pass on media messages to less active members of society. But only after the "message" has gone through the opinion leader's personal filter. The opinion leader watches the newscast or reads the newspaper, and then the opinion leader shares the "news" with a coworker who didn't. The coworker's "knowledge" of the event is therefore shaped by their colleague's account of the news more than the news story itself. Anyone who has played the parlour game of broken telephone understands the theory.

But there are risks. As Katherine Fulton states, "We live in a world in which original journalism is a smaller and smaller component of a larger and larger media and communications system" (Fulton 2000). Fallows (1996a) some time ago identified the risk inherent in the temptation for journalists to write stories about events they didn't report on. That temptation has grown in the social media age.

This phenomenon plays into the world of American historian Daniel Boorstin's pseudo-event. In his seminal work *The Image*, (1962) Boorstin, a former librarian of the United States Congress, explained we, as a society, increasingly embrace news gathering over news making. The power to make a reportable event is, therefore, the power to make an experience. As Lippmann observed, the art is in the intruding. Social media has given a whole new meaning to that phenomenon.

Boorstin argues that the making of illusions that "trump" the experience of life – my pun intended – has become the business of America; a business that finds expression in advertising, public relations, public opinion research, journalism, reality television, and the creative arts.

Technologies and platforms such as Facebook and Twitter have multiplied and magnified the world of pseudo-events, which leads some – on all sides of the political divide – to conclude that what we are being fed through the mainstream media is a politics of illusion. Which raises a core question: What are the implications for democracy if our shared concept of reality is an artifice?

Boorstin states a pseudo-event is not spontaneous but comes about because someone has planned it, planted it, or incited it primarily for the purpose of being reported. A pseudo-event's relation to the underlying reality of the situation is ambiguous at best.

An interview is a classic example of a pseudo-event; Horace Greeley's interview with religious leader Brigham Young in Salt Lake City, Utah, in July 1859 is oft-cited by media historians as the first full-fledged modern news interview. A planned news leak is a pseudo-event par excellence, with distribution made all the more easy in the Twitter-verse.

The political "leader's tour" is another example of Boorstin's pseudo-event. The leader's tour also serves as a visual cue for voters, what Graham Fraser (1989) described as the "campaign correlative." The basic proposition holds that if you can't get the tour bus to the campaign rally on time, you probably can't govern either.

Audiences do crave spontaneity, authenticity. They love "scrums." So, there is a fine line between media management and media manipulation. A political agenda and a media agenda are not one and the same. A political leader cannot allow "the bus" to control the communications agenda. The message is lost if the leader is constantly reacting to developments elsewhere. As Larry Speakes once said, "Don't tell us how to stage the news, and we won't tell you how to cover it."

An election campaign plane – a by-product of the television era – was a unique phenomenon, basically *Animal House* with wings. The late Jim Travers once likened a visit from a campaign press corps "to a semi-civilized visit from the Hells Angels" (as cited in Fox, B. 1999, 53). The concept of a campaign plane may now be as dated as a Walkman.

Seeds of difficulty, if not destruction, for newly elected governments are invariably sown in the hothouse atmosphere of the campaign. Rhetorical excesses on the hustings tend to be rewarded with heavier coverage weights. There is a need to move the story forward for subsequent news cycles. And invariably, these same candidates once in office become hostage to their campaign trail declarations.

Pseudo-events produce more pseudo-events: interviews with anchors from major network television, for example, invariably result in follow-on news stories in other media outlets.

Boorstin drew a sharp distinction between a pseudo-event and propaganda: the former is an ambiguous truth, the latter an appealing falsehood.

When it comes to the public, a pseudo-event tends to be more compelling than a spontaneous event in the same field. Boorstin's pseudo-events became the rule of news generation, rather than the exception.

Pseudo-events are typically more dramatic in a political context; televised leaders' debates are of more interest to viewers than mainstreeting, for example. Boorstin warned of the menace of "unreality," and he foreshadowed a world of pseudo-events packaged as news that would give rise to a world of candidates for elected office with pseudo-qualifications. Critics of both Trump and Trudeau constantly question their qualifications for the offices they hold.

Ironically, news making has, in its own right, become news. As Boorstin observed, "The story of the making of our illusions – 'the news behind the news' – has become the most appealing news of the world" (1962, 5). The late Neil Postman noted that media debunk the image and the image-maker yet, in the end, accept them as the only reality we have left. The strategists, the pollsters, the spin doctors, the data miners are now deemed newsworthy. The political equivalent of "magicians," these operatives dominate public affairs panels and op-ed pages. We know there is an element of misdirection to their craft and, far from being offended by that fact, we really want to know more about just how they do it. The CBC – Canada's public broadcaster – positions The Insiders, its political pundit panel, as subject matter experts in the art of news making.

President Trump, in choosing candidates for positions in his White House, considered whether or not they were photogenic, whether they looked the part. Somehow former press secretary Sean Spicer passed the test.

A celebrity – such as Donald Trump – is the human pseudoevent, a person who is well-known for their well-knownness. There is a democratic element to pseudo-events; anyone can become a celebrity if only he or she can get on the news and stay there. Here in

Canada, television personality Kevin O'Leary became the immediate front-runner when he declared his candidacy for the leadership of the Conservative Party in 2017 despite a lifetime of avoiding partisan politics or public policy debates.

Yochai Benkler (2006) believes the way a society produces its information environment goes to the very core of freedom.

Carey (2000) argued there is no shortage of good journalism today, but this journalism is hard to find because it is so surrounded and submerged in the trivial and the inconsequential. Carey didn't live long enough to experience the Kardashians, but they would certainly qualify as an illustration of his point.

Distinguished journalists have been ringing alarm bells about this slide toward infotainment for some time. "Journalists are now creating the coverage that is going to lead to their own destruction," Kathleen Hall Jamieson warned more than thirty years ago (as cited in Glaberson 1994). "If you cover the world cynically and assume that everyone is Machiavellian and motivated by their own self-interest, you invite your readers and viewers to reject journalism as a mode of communication because it must be cynical, too" (ibid.). The title of former political columnist George Bain's book said it all: *Gotcha! How the Media Distort the News* (Bain 1994). Bain, it is worth noting, is a member of the News Hall of Fame. Public journalism advocate "Buzz" Merritt wrote about journalism's headhunting tendencies: "Scalps on the belt, particularly government scalps, were the sign of rank and the measure of testosterone at gatherings of the tribe" (as quoted in Fox, B. 1999, 75). This "cult of savviness," as NYU's Jay Rosen (Rosen 2011) describes it, gives the reader journalism with attitude, an attitude "with malice toward all" (as cited in Patterson 2013, 17).

News makers seized of the market-driven approach to news can, in fact, create some fundamental and troubling distortions that impact civil discourse and ultimately public policy.

Crime and accidents, for example, get a disproportionate share of local TV news coverage, with "hook and hold" being the operative strategy. As a consequence, Americans believed that crime was rising sharply, triggering a call from some members of the public for more prisons and longer sentences. Thomas Patterson (2013) says the prob-lem was not their deductive logic. These news consumers believed crime in American was something it was not. A parallel story line emerged in Canada during the Harper years. Statistics showed that crime was falling. Yet yearly statistics have no shot in public opinion terms against nightly newscasts that feature local crime.

"Spin" was once an element of political discourse. As "spin" gave way to "talking points," which in turn gave way to "alterna-tive facts," political debate suffered accordingly.

For anyone growing up in the early 1960s, Soviet Premier Nikita Khrushchev was a fixture in the news – whether the specific was the threatening nuclear holocaust during the Cuban Missile Crisis or the spectacle of Khrushchev banging his shoe on a desk before the General Assembly of the United Nations. But Khrushchev did offer an insight of value when it comes to that slice of society that gener-ates news on a daily basis – the elected. "Politicians are the same all over," the Soviet leader reportedly said in 1963. "They promise to build a bridge even where there is no river" (from Wikiquote.org).

The bottom line remains: the media and the political communica-tor have two distinct jobs. The media see the assignment as airing the government's dirty linen. The political communicator is hoping to run it through the wash before the linen goes up on the clothesline. Ten-sion between the two is constructive, but a relative equilibrium in the power relationship between news gatherer and news maker is vital.

What looms as an overarching concern in this social media age is that emerging media technologies have tipped the scale in favour of news makers at the expense of news gatherers. News makers have their own "distribution" system on platforms such as Twit-ter. Donald Trump could get his message out directly to people without that message being subjected to the journalistic tests of the news gatherers. The "fact checkers" catch up to the tweet even-tually, but not before the unfiltered version has reached literally millions of followers.

4

News and Its Relationship to Truth

From the days of the Enlightenment, there has been a consensus in Western liberal democracies as to the centrality of journalism to public discourse, and public life.

As Mitchell Stephens observed in his work *Beyond News: The Future of Journalism*: "Argumentative, opinionated journalism helped create the United States of America" (Stephens 2014, 28). For German philosopher Jürgen Habermas, this "circulation of opinion … was nothing less than the creation of his treasured 'public sphere,'" Stephens states (2014).

A uniform definition of what constitutes news has proven more elusive.

Patterson argues journalism is an intentionally short-sighted discipline.

The legendary Walter Lippmann called the press a "beam of a searchlight that moves restlessly about" and said the news is simply where the searchlight settles. The news agenda shifts abruptly when the restless beacon moves on. Novelty is an integral component part of the news gathering process, the journalist ever on the lookout for the unusual, the sensational.

Lippmann was always careful to distinguish between news and truth, and quipped that "the two could coincide only in a few limited areas, such as box scores" (as cited in Fox B., 1999, 59).

Back in the days when there were enough journalists to hang off the edge of the press club bar, the wags had their own self-deprecating definition: news is largely about proclaiming Lord Acton's death for the benefit of readers who were blissfully unaware that Lord Acton was ever alive. Long-time Southam News columnist Don

McGillivray in conversation often offered this practical definition: "News is what you didn't already know" (pers. notes).

Another Canadian icon was more caustic. An obituary for Robertson Davies, the legendary writer and first master of Massey College, that appeared in the 4 December 1995 edition of the *New York Times* quoted the novelist and essayist as saying, "The news is what you can squeeze in before you have to go to press; it's not what is happening in the world" (Flint 1995).

Earlier definitions were more hopeful.

In 1947, the Hutchins Commission on Freedom of the Press defined news as "a truthful, comprehensive, and intelligent account of the day's events in a context which gives them meaning" (Commission on Freedom of the Press 1947). Charles Prestwich Scott, editor of the *Manchester Guardian* from 1872 to 1929, offered this British perspective: "The function of a good newspaper, and therefore of a good journalist, is to see life steady and to see it whole" (as cited in Fallows 1996a, 47).

Media sociologist Michael Schudson (1995) sees news as a form of culture, that the central function of news is the creation of community. In today's social media-filter bubble world, that creation of community has taken on a new meaning.

Thomas Patterson suggests that "journalistic truth is a 'sorting out' process that occurs over time through interaction 'among the public, newsmakers and journalists'" (Patterson 2013, 61), a point underscored by legendary *Toronto Star* editor Borden Spears who said, "The marvel really is not that newspapers get some things wrong, but that in the face of confused events, conflicting information, self-interested motives, reluctance to disclose, and pressure to publish before today fades into history, they get so many things right ... The mistake is to expect that any one news report, or any one newspaper, contains the final truth. Every journalist knows that truth is cumulative" (Debates of the Senate 1995).

As McDaniel (1987) observed, there is a structure to the reporting and writing of news, and this structure historically determined the kind of news we read, heard, or watched. McDaniel notes that for the better part of a century journalism operated "out of its own conventions and understandings, and within its own set of sociological, ideological, and literary constraints," a construct often described as the "para-ideology" of journalism.

In other words, legacy media in North America philosophically spoke to a certain or particular "truth."

Herbert Gans, author of *Deciding What's News*, posits American journalism is far from ideologically neutral, that journalism reflects a set of values shaped in no small measure by the progressive movement of the early twentieth century. Readers of Doris Kearns Goodwin's masterpiece *The Bully Pulpit* (2013) will be familiar with the code. Journalism in this construct is ethnocentric, it values its own nation above all else. In Canada, that view of "nation" was defined in the English- and French-language press long before politicians settled on what constituted a "nation" or a "distinct society."

Further, this journalism believes in altruistic democracy, that politics should follow a course based on public interest and public service. This credo allowed journalists – when it comes to the office of the president of the United States, for example – to support the office but attack the office holder.

Journalism treats politics as a contest but insists all participants be scrupulously honest, which explains why the media is fixated on campaign skulduggery, whether the specific is the Conservative Party's "in and out" approach to transferring funds within the party to circumvent election spending limits during the 2006 Canadian federal election or voter suppression campaigns in the 2016 US election.

Journalism in Western liberal democracies embraces the notion of responsible capitalism but has precise notions of what constitutes acceptable ways of earning a living or amassing a fortune. Microsoft founder Bill Gates is heralded as a leader of the information economy and the Bill & Melinda Gates Foundation is celebrated for its good works. Berkshire Hathaway CEO Warren Buffett is afforded the same treatment. Hedge fund managers, not so much. And the $150 million-plus in speaking fees earned by Bill and Hillary Clinton since he left office in 2001 is often positioned by the mainstream media in a most unfavourable light.

Small-town pastoralism is trumped as a magic kingdom, although the sharp reduction in the ranks of employed journalists in smaller communities means the mainstream media largely missed the transition from Norman Rockwell's idealized America to the Rust Belt.

Rugged individualism is celebrated; extremes either of the left or the right, less so.

Order-restored narratives dominate broadcast newscasts, particularly local news at the supper hour.

Beginning with former US president Ronald Reagan, political discourse in North America has been dominated by individuals who champion the cause of the "middle class" even though the personal circumstances of these individuals would suggest they themselves are far removed from that very political constituency. President Donald Trump and Prime Minister Justin Trudeau provide two recent examples.

News also incorporates certain modes of explanation, with motive serving as a primary construct for political coverage. The media deems stories to be of greater or lesser importance and offer them to audiences in an order of priority. Voters tend to endorse that priority (Iyengar and Kinder 1987).

Journalists are rarely in a position to establish the truth of something themselves, one of the reasons Walter Lippmann was always so careful to distinguish between news and truth.

The reliance on sources is determinant when it comes to news. Peter Donolo, Jean Chrétien's highly regarded communications director, operated on the basis of this simple truth: if you aren't part of the story before it is written, you aren't part of the story. Donolo's premise is even more relevant in a social media-dominated public square. Carleton University professor Eileen Saunders describes this phenomenon as "sources as primary definers" (pers. notes), and that, too, has had a determinant effect on "news" and "truth." Given these circumstances, news has historically been the domain of elite institutions and elite individuals.

Legacy news organizations typically have in-house rules to guide reporters and editors in the handling of sources. The *Toronto Star* policy, as articulated by former public editor Kathy English, states, "The public interest is best served when news sources are identified by their full names" (English 2017, IN10). However, the *Star* policy also acknowledges the public interest can, on occasion, be best served if information provided by unidentified sources is published. In those instances, *Star* reporters are expected to take specific steps to determine the reliability of those sources.

The *Star*'s then-Ottawa bureau chief and now public editor Bruce Campion-Smith gave readers a look behind the veil of anonymity. "First off, a confidential source is generally someone we know very well and have a track record with and built on a relationship usually over years," he told English. "The source has to absolutely be in a position to know what they are talking about" (ibid.).

Journalists protect sources at all costs. Journalists who in the fall of 2019 were demanding Prime Minister Justin Trudeau waive cabinet confidentiality in the SNC-Lavalin affair refused to identify the sources for the news stories that triggered the controversy in the first instance. Campion-Smith insists reporters do not "allow someone to anonymously trash another individual" (English 2017). The political classes would argue Campion-Smith's assertion is more aspirational than factual.

The Associated Press (n.d.) provides a handy guideline of terms for news sources that anyone planning to interact with the legacy media should be familiar with. "On the record" means the information can be used with no caveats and the source can be quoted by name. "Off the record" means the information cannot be used for publication. "Off the record" is an oft-used phrase, but most people who use it mean something else entirely. These sources typically want the information used; they just want to ensure that their fingerprints won't be on the story.

"Not for attribution" means comments can be quoted directly, the source is not identified by name but can be referred to by position. News consumers will be familiar with descriptives such as a "White House source" or "a source in the PMO."

"Background" is a more precise term. This "information can be published but only under conditions negotiated with the source. Generally, sources do not want their names" to appear in the reportage but will usually "agree to a description of their position."

"Deep background" means the information can be used but without descriptive attribution. In this case, the source does not want to be identified in any way, even with a general description of their role or function. Reporters given information on a "deep background" basis often use it to shake the proverbial tree in an effort to find other sources who may be more willing to go on the record or speak on background.

Where the ground gets trickier is when reporters have to give the reader some sense of the motivation behind sources providing information. The *Star*'s Queens Park bureau chief Robert Benzie notes, "As we have seen from the *New York Times*' superb reporting on the current president, off-the-record sources are essential to understanding what is going on in the White House" (English 2017, IN10). But Benzie adds, "I do think we need to explain in stories why we are giving sources the right to withhold their names" (ibid.). It is the correspondent's reliance on those sources, including White House sources who insisted on anonymity, that triggered certain of Trump's tweets about "fake news."

The SNC-Lavalin affair that dominated Canada's political conversation through the early months of 2019 is a textbook example of this "motivation" conundrum.

The word in the headline seemed innocuous enough: "pressed" (Fife, Chase, and Fine 2019). The front-page account in the 7 February edition of the *Globe and Mail* provided more detail on how Prime Minister Justin Trudeau's office attempted to press former justice minister and attorney general Jody Wilson-Raybould "to intervene in the corruption and fraud prosecution of Montreal engineering and construction giant SNC-Lavalin Group Inc." (ibid.).

The story cited "sources" who told the reporters who broke the story that Wilson-Raybould "refused to ask federal prosecutors to make a deal with the company that could prevent a costly trial" (ibid.). Curiously, the story did not include the fact that the minister and the director of public prosecutions had already rejected the federal prosecutor's recommendation that they do just that. The story stated that these same sources said that the former attorney general "came under heavy pressure to persuade the Public Prosecution Service of Canada to change its mind" and enter into negotiations with the company for a "deferred prosecution agreement" that allows prosecutors to suspend criminal cases (ibid.).

The prime minister was quick to declare the allegations in the story false, stating, "At no time did I or my office direct the current or previous attorney-general to make any particular decision in this matter" (ibid.). In the time-honoured tradition of politics, Trudeau was answering an assertion that had actually never been made. As the *Globe* noted, "The *Globe and Mail* never reported that officials in Trudeau's office had directed Ms. Wilson-Raybould to take action – only that she was pressured to do so and declined" (ibid.). Which begs the question – who exactly decided the former minister was under "heavy pressure"?

The *Globe* story triggered the first real political crisis for the Trudeau government. The SNC-Lavalin affair, as it became known, literally dominated federal political discourse for months. Readers of the 17 January 2019 edition of *Bloomberg Businessweek* would be familiar with the descriptive "Overton window," attributed to Joseph Overton. "The term refers to the range of ideas that are at any given time considered worthy of discussion" (Coy and Dmitrieva 2019). In Canada, at the federal level, the range of ideas considered worthy of discussion through February and March of 2019 was pretty much restricted to the SNC-Lavalin affair. The federal budget, in sharp contrast, did not make it near the top of the list.

As the story unfolded, Wilson-Raybould resigned from the Trudeau cabinet. Her colleague Jane Philpott, considered by observers to be one of the more effective ministers in Trudeau's cabinet, also resigned, convinced that her former colleague had been subjected to undue pressure from Trudeau and his advisers. Michael Wernick, clerk of the Privy Council and a central player in the saga, resigned his position as the head of Canada's public service. Gerald Butts, Trudeau's principal secretary and most senior adviser, also decided to resign his post.

The Liberal caucus was at first unsettled by the furor, then turned on Wilson-Raybould and Philpott and demanded they be kicked out of caucus – a decision the prime minister took in early April 2019.

Commons justice committee hearings into the affair were dismissed by opposition MPs as a farce and a cover-up. The official Opposition Conservative Party used a series of tactics to delay the debate on the federal budget to keep the focus on the SNC-Lavalin affair.

Maclean's columnist Paul Wells dismissed the prime minister as an "imposter" (Wells 2019). Emboldened by the Wilson-Raybould and Philpott resignations, pundits argued Trudeau's 2015 pledge to do politics differently and his declared commitment to women and diversity were undermined by his actions.

Regional tensions were enflamed, as individuals in Western Canada denounced the special treatment being afforded a Quebec-based company, arguing the treatment SNC-Lavalin received would not have been extended to companies in the beleaguered oil and gas sector if the companies were to find themselves in similar circumstances.

The governing Grits saw their standing in public opinion polls drop like a stone. As the "he said, she said" stories appeared, pollster Darrell Bricker of Ipsos Public Affairs said Canadians were on the "she said" side – Wilson-Raybould's version – by a margin of two to one over Trudeau's version (Bricker 2019a). And all as a result of a scoop uncovered by *Globe* reporters from sources that have not been identified to this day. Wilson-Raybould has stated unequivocally and on the record that she was not the source, although she also stated under oath in her testimony before the

Commons justice committee that she did in fact believe she was subjected to undue pressure on the SNC-Lavalin file.

The *Globe* stated in the very first story that the sources for the piece were "granted anonymity to speak directly about what went on behind-the-scenes in the matter" (Fife, Chase, and Fine 2019). Predictably, the story led to a sidebar debate about who the sources for the story were and why they were granted anonymity.

To its credit, the *Globe and Mail* dealt with the anonymous source issue head on. Public Editor Sylvia Stead, in an article entitled "In Defence of Confidential Sources," acknowledged some readers were pushing the paper to reveal its sources (Stead 2019). Stead argued subsequent confirmation of the details negated the need. Stead made an important distinction for readers, describing the sources as "confidential" not "anonymous." The sources for the story are "known to the reporters, two of whom are very experienced Ottawa hands with dozens of years of experience covering federal politics" (ibid.). The two reporters – Robert Fife and Steven Chase – most certainly warrant Stead's description. And the third byline on the original story is that of Sean Fine, a reporter with extensive experience covering justice issues. Added *Globe* Editor-in-Chief David Walmsley, "We have no agenda other than a belief in our institutions and because of that belief we are motivated to demand better of them. Focusing on firm independent journalistic inquiry is our duty" (ibid.).

The fact the *Globe* did not identify the sources for the story continued to be an issue for certain readers, in no small measure because the accusation itself – that the former minister was subjected to undue pressure – was highly subjective. Readers were expected to accept the judgment of someone that was not identified for them. The sources were, however, known to the *Globe* reporters and editors. The paper's editorial leadership clearly concluded they were authoritative. A tweet posted by David Hamer summarized the concerns of many readers with the *Globe*'s use of anonymous sources: "My point is that Mr. Fife [coauthor Bob Fife] might want to ask why they're leaking and what axes his sources are grinding before he publishes" (Hamer 2019).

What has tended to be overlooked in the post-publication analysis is a paragraph attributed to a second group of sources – sources identified by the *Globe* as being from SNC-Lavalin. The 7 February bombshell story states these company sources "told the *Globe* the PMO was furious with the justice minister's intransigence on the remediation agreement and that the company was pleased to see her moved out of the portfolio" (Fife, Chase, and Fine 2019).

The significance of these statements cannot be underestimated. First, the SNC-Lavalin sources confirmed the PMO was unhappy with the minister. Second, the SNC-Lavalin sources confirmed they were happy to see Wilson-Raybould shifted from the twin justice and attorney general portfolios to Veterans Affairs and associate minister of national defence. The SNC-Lavalin sources did their company serious harm; first, by presuming to speak for the PMO and second, by confirming the company was happy to see Wilson-Raybould shuffled. The SNC-Lavalin "sources" were critical for the *Globe* story for a number of reasons, including the fact their comments, for all intents and purposes, provided the second source for the story's core assertion regarding "undue pressure" on the former minister.

The minister herself had provided the first clue that there was more to her new assignment than a simple cabinet shuffle. In a statement issued at the time, she noted, "It is a pillar of our democracy that our system of justice be free from even the perception of political interference and uphold the highest levels of public confidence. As such, it has always been my view that the Attorney General of Canada must be non-partisan, more transparent in the principles, that are the basis for decisions, and, in this respect, always be willing to speak truth to power. This is how I served throughout my tenure in that role" (Proudfoot 2019).

Globe reporter Steven Chase subsequently confirmed, during a panel appearance on the CBC public affairs program *Power & Politics*, that the minister's statement caused the *Globe*'s Ottawa bureau to pursue the issue further (CBC 2019b).

The identity of the sources for the original *Globe* story notwithstanding, there is no question coverage in the mainstream media has reflected Wilson-Raybould's dominant news frame of "whistleblower."

And that is no accident, according to Josh Greenberg, director of Carleton University's School of Journalism and Communication. "Finally, there's no doubt in my mind that JWR [Jody Wilson-Raybould] and JP [Jane Philpott] received effective tactical advice about how to hit back at PMO with maximum impact: Fife leak [Robert Fife, one of the coauthors of the original *Globe* story], drip release strategy, Wells interview [interview by Philpott with *Maclean's* Paul Wells], published caucus letter &c. All calculated and carefully executed with sharp precision" (Greenberg 2019b). He elaborated in an earlier tweet, "I would also note the important broker role played by a key intermediary – the PR strategist – both within and outside parties, advising on media relations, timing of announcements, key messaging, etc." (Greenberg 2019a). Added *Toronto Star* columnist Susan Delacourt, "Though Wilson-Raybould asserts she had no hand in the original leak of her story to the *Globe and Mail* back in February, her version of events around SNC-Lavalin has asserted itself since the beginning as the prevailing narrative" (Delacourt 2019a).

Certain media voices have questioned just how this reality came to pass. "The story they hammer home repeatedly has been swallowed uncritically across the country," wrote Janice Kennedy in the *Ottawa Citizen*. "The real truth here is that there is no single truth and no sainted truth-teller. With a narrative involving shades, nuances, interpretations, and bigger-picture considerations, the assumption that Wilson-Raybould and Philpott are the only ones with a lock on the truth and principle is irrational … the kneejerk and wholesale dismissal of testimony by anyone else involved in this sorry drama is the real ethical breach" (Kennedy, J. 2019).

A number of communications theories explain how the "whistleblower" narrative took hold, Kennedy's concerns notwithstanding, as it most emphatically did.

Media scholar Andie Tucher identified the phenomenon known as the "congenial truth." According to Tucher, we take in information that conforms with a truth we are collectively comfortable with, and then ignore facts or information that are inconsistent with that "truth" (1994).

Once that truth takes hold, Elisabeth Noelle-Neumann's "spiral of silence" begins. Attempts to challenge the congenial truth are met with such hostility that the challengers of the conventional wisdom simply stop intervening (Noelle-Neumann 1974). In recent years the spiral of silence has been fuelled by characterizing certain voices as "elites."

In a poll taken in early March, a month after the scandal broke, 75 per cent of respondents agreed there was inappropriate political interference on the SNC-Lavalin file, and 62 per cent believed the prime minister had lost the moral authority to govern. Finally, 85 per cent would support a public inquiry into the affair, and 84 per cent wanted an RCMP investigation into the matter (Bricker 2019a).

But an important fact remains: the success of Wilson-Raybould in establishing "her truth" is a direct consequence of a failure on the part of the prime minister's advisers.

As an aside, and ironically, Wilson-Raybould's statement that she was subjected to undue pressure from the Prime Minister's Office on the SNC-Lavalin file was, with few exceptions, accepted by the media at face value. Her further assertion that there was no political interference in the Vice-Admiral Mark Norman case, less so.

Even his defenders were troubled as to why Trudeau's version of what occurred seemed to change daily. The prime minister and his advisers were never able to establish a narrative of their own. Framing, as Robert Entman reminds us, is the central power in the democratic process, which is precisely why political elites – in this case, warring factions within the Liberal family – struggle to control the framing of issues (Entman 1993).

Wilson-Raybould, supported by her former cabinet colleague Jane Philpott, succeeded brilliantly in establishing her "whistle-blower" status as the dominant news fame. Further, both proved skilled at rolling out the "wiggle disclosures" that University of Virginia scholar Larry Sabato says are essential to give a scandal "legs" (Sabato 1991). Each development of the story, however minor, allowed journalists to repeat the core allegation of undue pressure at each retelling.

The decision by the Commons justice committee to summon Wilson-Raybould as a witness, and then limit her testimony to one four-hour session, lent credence to the cries from media pundits that the government was engaging in a cover-up (Harris, K. 2019).

Media texts are polysemic, that is they are open to multiple and different meanings to different people. But as Clay Shirky reminds us, "communication of any kind fails if it does not align with the audience's interpretation of reality" (pers. notes).

How might the debate have rolled out if the prime minister's communications team had established "animus" rather than "whistleblower" as the dominant news frame? What if the team had argued that this story wasn't about speaking truth to power or the rule of law? What if it was instead framed as a story about a disgruntled former cabinet minister who decided to take down the prime minister politically for demoting her?

The prime minister's inability to settle on a single story line emboldened media pundits to pursue a second congenial truth they'd long believed but lacked supporting arguments to advance – that Justin Trudeau is an "imposter," the political equivalent of a ventriloquist's dummy. And the government's disarray generated a subtext: that principal secretary Gerald Butts was the ventriloquist controlling the dummy PM and Butts simply wasn't up to the job.

Epstein makes the telling observation that what passes for investigative reporting "is really just the development of sources 'within the counter-elite'" (as cited in Fox, B. 1999, 69). The Wilson-Raybould saga is a prime illustration of Epstein's observation.

James Fallows, for many years the national correspondent for *The Atlantic*, provided interesting insights into journalistic practice when a scandal surfaces in *Breaking the News*. "When the first hint of a scandal breaks, reporters and editors know there is far less risk in over-covering it than in playing it down" (1996a, 132). Fallows says if journalists hype a story that turns out to be "no big deal" they lose very little. "But if they overlook the early indications of what later turns into a bona fide scandal, they run the risk of going down in history as 'the reporter who missed the next Watergate'" (ibid.). Fallows concludes "during times of scandal, our media abandon the pretense of maintaining perspective, and in times without scandal it hopes for a scandal to come" (ibid.).

Journalists seeking to keep governments and the people who run them accountable are deeply dependent on whistleblowers – sources who draw a reporter's attention to untoward activity. The proverbial brown envelope – or its electronic equivalent in this mobile device age – is one instrument of choice. Donald Trump's White House leaked like a sieve. Author Michael Wolff states former adviser Steve Bannon, former chief of staff Reince Priebus, and son-in-law/adviser Jared Kushner each "became an inveterate and polished leaker" (Wolff 2018, 121).

Canada's political class underscored the importance of sources to freedom of expression by passing legislation in the fall of 2017 further protecting anonymous sources from police investigations. The Journalistic Sources Protection Act, conceived by a Conservative senator but supported by all sides in the House of Commons, "raises the bar for the issuance of search warrants" (Galloway 2017). The legislation, which amended both the Criminal Code and the Canada Evidence Act, forces police to persuade a Superior Court judge "that the information cannot be obtained through any other means" (ibid.). The legislation protects both journalists and their sources when pursuing issues of public interest.

As mentioned in a previous chapter, historically, news gathering, in essence, involved the representatives of one bureaucracy – a newspaper or a television network – picking up prefabricated news items from the representatives of another bureaucracy – business or government. Yet that structure is less benign than it looks. The beat system, in practice, circumscribes how reporters will know what they know. What you know depends on who you know, and that in turn, depends on where you are.

Time constraints inherent in the news gathering process leave little time for verification. Slashed newsroom budgets are a factor. And social media, Twitter in particular, has sharply reduced the time between gathering and distribution. So reporters strive for accuracy. The craft is in reproducing a politician's statement accurately. When, during the Brexit referendum campaign, then-Conservative cabinet minister and now Prime Minister Boris Johnson declared the UK's exit from the European Union would save British taxpayers hundreds of millions of pounds every month, news accounts reproduced the statement. To be fair, some reporters, columnists, and other opinion writers dismissed the assertion as folly. But Leave strategists are disciples of the "eye beats ear" axiom of political communications. A bus painted with bright slogans claiming the EU cost British taxpayers £350 million a week provided an effective backdrop for Johnson and company.

In the world of "sources," bureaucrats are known as "self-evidently competent knowers" (Ettema and Glasser 1984). By convention, journalists choose authoritative sources over other potential sources: the more senior, the better. A prime minister's policy adviser is a good source, a prime minister's chief of staff even better.

Because sources shape news stories, they influence events as a consequence, according to former Ontario Securities Commission chair Ed Waitzer. "You can't help but be influenced in how you see things by who gives you access," Waitzer said. "And one of the costs of no access is that [the lack of access] maybe influences how the reporter sees something" (pers. notes 2012).

The theory of primary definition holds that "certain elites, based on social hierarchies, enjoy a privileged access to the media and hence hold the ability to define topics in a preferred way" (Driedger 2008). *Washington Post* editor Marty Baron, in the course of an interview with Code Media that was subsequently posted on YouTube, says, "a source should be somebody who has actual direct knowledge of something" (Recode 2017).

Sources are the key to news, and, because of that, news is weighted toward sources willing to provide information. The relationship between the reporter and the source, the academics say, is like a dance – with the source doing most of the leading.

Coverage of Senator Mike Duffy's expense claims is a textbook case in point. Judge Charles Vaillancourt's decision basically states the reporters missed the real story because they were so dependent on a few sources operating with a clear political agenda, all of which came out at trial and will be explored in more detail in the next chapter.

Reporters obviously have a series of "tests" they use in assessing information provided by a source: Has the source provided information that proved to be of value in the past? Can they speak to the issue at hand with authority? Is the source productive? Reliable? But as Google vice-president Richard Gingras observed at a CJF event in Toronto on 2 May 2018, "the known sources are not necessarily the right sources" (Canadian Journalism Foundation 2018b).

Leakers are good examples. Journalism celebrates the whistleblower, the individual in a government or any large institution with the courage to call out unacceptable behaviour – a person like Edward Snowden, who in 2013 leaked highly classified information from the National Security Agency regarding global surveillance programs. Yet leakers can have their own agenda – animus leaks being but one example. The challenge for the reporter is to provide enough information about the source to satisfy the news consumer that the information meets the twin tests of authority of providence and legitimacy of motive without going so far as to "out" the source.

The case of Vice-Admiral Mark Norman referenced earlier in this chapter is informative in the context of the media's treatment of whistleblowers.

The saga generated front-page headlines for years. The RCMP alleged that the senior Royal Canadian Navy officer tipped off Chantier Davie Canada in the fall of 2015 that the new Liberal cabinet had questions about a sole-source contract awarded by the previous Conservative government with Davie for the Quebec shipbuilding firm to convert a commercial ship into a desperately needed temporary naval supply vessel. Norman was leading the project on behalf of the navy. The story of the cabinet delay in finalizing the Davie contract was also leaked to the media, specifically to CBC reporter James Cudmore (Cudmore 2015), who soon after would take a job with the Liberal government at National Defence.

Certain ministers were ticked, to say the least. The public service was made aware of the government's displeasure. The obvious security questions were raised about the leaking of cabinet secrets. The RCMP was called in, and over time their investigation focused on Norman. Once the RCMP informed General Jonathan Vance, chief of the defence staff, in January 2017 that Norman was under investigation, he was immediately placed on leave with pay (Canadian Press 2019). That decision – in and of itself – stands up to scrutiny. Any organization, on being informed a senior executive is under police investigation, has little choice but to ask the executive to take a leave or to suspend the person. But the presumption of innocence is also fundamental, and for that reason, even if the individual is suspended, he or she is granted leave with pay.

Subsequently, the vice-admiral was charged with a single count of breach of trust in March 2018.

A series of accusations from Norman's defence team, led by the renowned lawyer Marie Henein, kept the story in the news. Defence lawyers argued Norman's ability to defend himself was being hampered by the Crown's refusal to turn over certain documents. Allegations of political interference were used as points of punctuation by Norman's lawyers and reported extensively by a press gallery.

The Norman story took an even more dramatic turn in the spring of 2019 when the Department of Justice's director of public prosecutions decided to drop the charge against the vice-admiral. Some Ottawa observers quickly drew a straight line from the trial date, which had been set for August, and the fixed date for the 2019 federal election. The prosecutor said that while certain of Norman's actions were secretive and inappropriate, as lead prosecutor Barbara Mercier stated, "Inappropriate does not mean criminal" (Brewster and Harris 2019).

The Public Prosecution Service press release stated that, to convict, the Crown must prove the accused person's conduct represented "a serious and marked departure from the standards expected of a person in his position of trust" and that the person acted outside the public interest for a dishonest, corrupt, or oppressive purpose.

Norman's defence, stripped to its essentials, is that Ottawa leaks like a sieve, and therefore Norman's conduct – without ever being specific as to exactly what the conduct involved – didn't mark a "serious and marked" departure from the standards expected. Follow-up news stories included statements from experienced former journalist Greg Weston who told one and all that he essentially lived off the proverbial plain brown envelopes for the better part of a successful and rewarding thirty-plus year career.

Norman was afforded full martyr status. Alberta Premier Jason Kenney, who, as defence minister in the Harper government, worked directly with Norman on the Davie contract, tweeted, "Congrats to Vice-Admiral Mark Norman on his exoneration. The charges brought against him were an outrage. I was proud to work with him on a successful supply ship procurement. Government effort to block and politicize the project should be investigated" (Kenney 2019).

Kenney's former colleague Peter MacKay, himself another Conservative defence minister, was equally outraged and suggested Norman should be returned to duty, preferably as the next chief of the defence staff (CBC 2019c).

Conservative commentators contrasted the treatment of Norman to Omar Khadr's circumstance and argued if the Trudeau government decided it had to pay Khadr $10.5 million to right wrongs, Norman was entitled to at least as much to assuage the personal torment and the damage to his reputation (Madison 2019).

Norman's legion of defenders pointed out he had brought that supply ship contract in on time and on budget, and asked aloud whether anyone could remember the last time that occurred on a Canadian defence procurement contract (Pugliese 2018). Rival shipbuilding companies, specifically Irving Shipbuilding, were portrayed as "friends" of the Trudeau government.

Norman himself said he wanted his old job as No. 2 (immediately under General Vance) at the Department of National Defence back and said, "I am confident that at all times, I acted with great integrity, I acted ethically and I acted in the best interests of the Royal Canadian Navy, the Canadian Forces and, ultimately, the people of Canada" (Brewster and Harris 2019). What Norman didn't say is whether or not he was one of the leakers.

Canadian public opinion was on Norman's side on the issue, with many believing the vice-admiral was owed an apology at a minimum.

The prosecutor's statement that the vice-admiral's actions crossed the line were covered by the media, but because the prosecutor's comments did not align with the "congenial truth" about the vice-admiral, the comments were not part of the Norman narrative going forward.

Norman defence attorney Marie Henein tore a strip off Prime Minister Justin Trudeau over Norman's travails without ever mentioning Trudeau's name. At the news conference called to confirm the Crown had decided to drop the charges, Henein said, "Before we get started, I'd just like to introduce the ... *all female* team that represented Vice-Admiral Norman ... Fortunately Vice-Admiral Norman didn't fire the females he hired" (Warnica 2019).

The Conservative opposition moved quickly to maximize the damage in terms of the link to the Wilson-Raybould/Jane Philpott saga.

The Trudeau government added to the public perception that the Liberals had done something untoward by rushing out an announcement that the federal government would foot all Norman's legal bills. General Vance's response welcoming his former colleague back with open arms added to the impression Norman had been badly treated (Pugliese 2019).

Lost in the story was a first principle – the principle of responsible government.

Norman undoubtedly did a first-class job shepherding the supply vessel procurement process involving a single supply ship as a temporary fix to a successful completion. And he did, according to published news reports, have clear instructions from the previous Conservative government to deal directly with Davie Shipbuilding (Brewster 2019). And while the Conservatives were in power, published reports state Norman was authorized to deal directly with former prime minister Stephen Harper's office. But there was a federal election in the fall of 2015. The Harper Conservatives were defeated. Trudeau's Liberals were elected. Ministers were duly sworn in. Certain other shipbuilders complained.

That the new government might have a question or two about a sole-source contract in a riding held by a cabinet minister in the previous government on the eve of a general election is hardly surprising. That new ministers get to discuss the issue at cabinet is their right. That others might seek to limit cabinet's options with strategic leaks may well be a regular or even everyday occurrence in Ottawa. In early 2019, Matthew Matchett, a federal procurement official, was charged with breach of trust in regard to leaking cabinet secrets about the Davie ship contract (Berthiaume, 2019). It is not a right for any civil servant to leak the specifics of cabinet discussions.

In the end, Norman and the Department of National Defence issued a joint statement saying the vice-admiral would retire from the Canadian Armed Forces after reaching a "mutually acceptable" agreement, the details of which will remain confidential. Warren Winkler, the former chief justice of the Ontario Court of Appeal, assisted the two sides in coming to terms.

The Conservative opposition denounced the settlement, arguing the Trudeau government had bought Norman's silence while sticking Canadian taxpayers with the tab. Interestingly enough, no Ottawa reporters appear to have followed up on the prosecutor's assertion that certain of Norman's actions were "inappropriate" (Brewster and Harris 2019). Why – if the officer had more to say – did Norman agree to a settlement that stipulated details would remain confidential? And no one asked Norman at his news conference whether he had, in fact, leaked information about the Liberal cabinet's discussions (CPAC 2019). Norman, under terms of the agreement negotiated by Winkler, probably couldn't have answered the question anyway. But the question could and should have been put for the record.

The Ottawa press corps appears to have settled on a narrative for the Norman story. And as Sir Craig Oliver, communications adviser to former British prime minister David Cameron, observed in the context of the Brexit campaign, "I've been around long enough to know that if something takes root in journalism, no matter if it is wrong, it is almost impossible to dislodge" (Oliver, C. 2016, 79).

There is a cautionary tale regarding whistleblowers. As an inquiry into the treatment of Maher Arar, a telecommunications engineer with dual Syrian and Canadian citizenship, established, "whistleblowers" can also have an agenda. Arar was detained while in transit at John F. Kennedy International Airport in New York, held without charges, sent to Syria where he was jailed and tortured. The inquiry report states, "This case is an example of how some government officials, over an extended period of time, used the media to put a spin on an affair and unfairly damage a person's reputation" (Government of Canada 2006, 257).

The report states, by definition, only those officials with access to classified information could have been responsible for the leaks. And despite the fact these organizations "boast highly skilled investigators" they were never able to establish who was responsible for the leaks (ibid., 261). "Everyone asked about the leaks decried the fact that government officials would leak classified or confidential information to the media, but no one seems able to do anything about it" (ibid.). The report goes on to state, "The obvious implication of the failure to identify the source of leaks is that there is no deterrent to others who may be inclined to leak classified or confidential information in the future. If no one ever gets caught, those who are prepared to leak this type of protected information for purposes that suit their own interests will probably continue to do so" (ibid.).

Being a good and steady source matters in terms of media relations. Individuals are advised to be a source before they are a story; building a bank account of good will is a factor in media relations.

Sources define reality; that is the reason why media effects are more pronounced on new or emerging issues.

The media will highlight voices of dissent – Donald Trump or Senator Bernie Sanders, for example – but the dissent is usually shades or variations on capitalist/liberal democratic societies. Only in America, among Western liberal democracies, would Bernie Sanders be considered a radical.

Trump, as president, was predisposed to see the exercise of media relations as akin to war. But *Washington Post*'s editor Marty Baron was quick to counter with the assertion, "We're not at war with the [Trump] administration, we're at work. We're doing our jobs" (Recode 2017).

The interaction between most political leaders and journalists evolves around what Daniel Boorstin (1962) described as "pseudo-events" – interviews, media availability sessions, press releases, and leaks. On the latter point, legendary *New York Times* columnist James "Scotty" Reston observed, "a ship of state is the only vessel that leaks from the top."

The purpose of a media relations strategy is to create a reportable event, and the power to make a reportable event is therefore the power to make an experience (Edward L. Bernays as cited in Boorstin 1962). These two factors – source dependency and staged events – are root causes of the news content that has triggered the current debate concerning "fake news." The balance in political coverage has shifted to the staged.

Hossein Derakhshan, a Canadian journalist, has an interesting approach to the "fake news" debate. In a paper he coauthored with Dr Claire Wardle, a leading expert on social media, entitled "Information Disorder," Derakhshan distinguished between different kinds of bad information, suggesting the differences could be summarized in three categories (Wardle and Derakhshan 2017). The first – misinformation – is false or incorrect information, with no intent to harm. A mistake in a news story would be an example. Malinformation, the second, is information that is true but is intended to harm. Revenge porn is one example.

But the current public debate has tended to evolve around the third category: disinformation, which Derakhshan described as false information intended to cause harm – disinformation foreign intelligence agencies, among others, have raised to an art form. This type of manipulated or fabricated information has been around forever, Derakhshan says, but what has changed is that fake news "can easily and cheaply be amplified" through social media, he explained, appearing at a Canadian Journalism Foundation discussion on the topic of "Building Trust in Media" held in Toronto 2 May 2018 (Canadian Journalism Foundation 2018b). Further, "the consumption of news has become a public act," Derakhshan says, and that, too, is new.

Picking up on the theme, *Buzzfeed*'s Craig Silverman says, "we share things because we are trying to convey something about ourselves" (ibid.). Derakhshan says, "we have entered the post-Enlightenment era," where people "are not talking about facts anymore, people are talking about faith" (ibid.).

In his bestseller *Munich*, novelist Robert Harris shares an observation that speaks to today's political conversation: "Truth was like any other material necessary for the making of war: it had to be beaten and bent and cut into the required shape" (Harris, R. 2017, 90). There is a lot of beating and bending of the truth on Twitter.

President Donald Trump showed an uncanny ability to make news. And often, the news he made was about the news. The Canadian Journalism Foundation hosted an interesting panel discussion in Toronto 24 April 2018 under the heading "When the Media Becomes the News: Covering Media Power and Politics" (2018a), most ably moderated by the CBC's Ioanna Roumeliotis. Emily Steel, a key member of the *New York Times* Pulitzer Prize-winning team that helped put sexual harassment on the public agenda, and Michael Calderone, senior media reporter for *Politico*, explored a world where journalists have now become truth defenders as well as truth tellers.

Steel walked the audience through the rigorous reporting and editing practices that were brought to bear on her stories that exposed the series of settlements related to sexual harassment allegations against former Fox News host Bill O'Reilly. And Calderone spoke of the effort and energy that went into the coverage of Alabama Republican Senate hopeful Roy Moore, who was accused of sexual misconduct with teens. Both spoke to the risk of how honest mistakes by journalists can become news in itself and feed into the public debate around "fake news."

A 2018 media controversy in Saskatchewan is one such example. The backstory involves the shooting death of Colten Boushie, a Cree man from the Red Pheasant First Nation, two years before by farmer Gerald Stanley, who was acquitted of the charge of second-degree murder. The family of Colten Boushie subsequently filed lawsuits against Stanley, the RCMP, and the attorney general of Canada.

The CBC ran a story 6 March 2018 alleging the RCMP did a sloppy job of investigating Boushie's death (Common and Gomez 2018). The story was featured prominently on all CBC platforms. Critics, including Saskatchewan radio personality John Gormley, argued the story was also substantively wrong. Gormley called out the public broadcaster in a withering commentary carried on private radio stations across the province. Gormley, a former Progressive Conservative member of Parliament, is an influential voice in the world of Saskatchewan public affairs. He writes a weekly column for the *Saskatoon StarPhoenix* and the *Regina Leader-Post*, and, in addition, his radio show is carried weekdays on talk radio stations in Saskatoon and Regina. "Canada's state broadcaster has an agenda," Gormley thundered during one of his broadcasts. "They're not entitled to make stuff up" (Gormley 2018).

For Gormley, and presumably certain of his listeners, the CBC report was a textbook example of "fake news." For the public broadcaster, the report's shortcomings were mistakes, made with no malice aforethought. The CBC's assertion to the effect "we stand by the remainder of our reporting" was dismissed by Gormley as a "shameful misrepresentation."

Even when news accounts contain factual errors, they can communicate a broader truth. Michael Wolff, author of *Fire and Fury*,
the bestselling look into the Trump White House, has been challenged on certain specifics. Having read the tome, one is left with
the impression that while the work may contain certain factual
errors, it does speak to a broader truth. One particular insight that
commended itself was Wolff's observations about Trump and fake
news. "There is no happenstance news, in Trump's view," Wolff
states (2018). "All news was manipulated and designed, planned
and planted" (ibid.). For that reason, Trump believes all news is
fake to some extent and helps explain why he cottoned on to the
"fake news" label with such ease. Trump liked to brag that he had
spent much of his adult life making stuff up for the press "and they
always print it" (ibid., 215).

President Trump was an early leader of the "fake news" attack
on the legacy media, a deliberate strategy on his part, according to
author David Frum. Trump has told political journalists that if he
undermines the credibility of the mainstream media, Americans
will be less inclined to credit what the mainstream media writes and
says about him. The president has declared the press the enemy of
the people. "The FAKE NEWS media (failing @nytimes, @NBCNews, @
ABC, @CBS, @CNN) is not my enemy," Trump tweeted, "it is the enemy
of the American people" (quoted in Frum 2018, 106).

In late August 2019, Americans had a sense of how a group of
Trump supporters planned to take up arms against the media as
enemies of the people. The plan, according to the *New York Times*,
involved leaking details about the private and professional lives
of the journalists themselves (Vogel and Peters 2019). The *Times*
responded responsibly, stating, "No organization is above scrutiny,
including *The Times*. We have high standards, own our mistakes,
and always strive to do better. If anyone – even those acting in bad
faith – brings legitimate problems to our attention, we'll look into
them and respond appropriately" (Sulzberger 2019).

Conservative commentator and columnist S.E. Cupp issued
an effective challenge to Trump's denunciation of the press as

an enemy of the American people. In a tweet, Cupp wrote, "The press is not the enemy of the people. The press is the enemy of the powerful, unaccountable and corrupt. The unjust, unethical, and dishonest. The bully, the blowhard. The cover up, run around and false pretense. Let's be clear: that's made the press the enemy of one person" (Cupp 2018).

Frum argues what Trump really wants "is more bias, not less; more fake news, not less. What he demands from the media is not objectivity, but complicity" (Frum 2018, 122).

The real news about fake news is that it isn't – news, that is. Gordon Allport and Leo Postman first reported in 1947 that a "rumour public" exists wherever there is a community of interest and that much of urban society constitutes a weave of cliques and circles where opinion formation occurs (Allport and Postman 1947).

Publisher William Randolph Hearst is generally – if erroneously – "credited" with starting the Spanish-American War in 1898. According to journalistic folklore, when the famous illustrator Frederic Remington cabled Hearst to say there was no sign of unrest in Spanish-controlled Cuba, Hearst allegedly cabled back, "You furnish the pictures and I'll furnish the war" (McCullough 1991). Hearst's biographer Kenneth Whyte questions the veracity of the story (Rosenthal 2009). Whyte notes neither telegram was ever found and concludes the only account of this exchange is wrong.

Carleton professor Christopher Dornan reminds us that legacy newspapers weren't above making things up in a bid to win the attention of readers. "Famously, in 1844, the *New York Sun* broke the news that the Atlantic Ocean had been crossed in three days by a manned balloon," Dornan wrote in a March 2017 reflection paper for the Canadian Commission for UNESCO. "The story was a fabrication, written by Edgar Allan Poe. At the time, the name for this was 'sensationalism.' Today, we call it clickbait" (Dornan 2017a, 5). Attendees at a conference co-sponsored by Harvard's Shorenstein Center on Media, Politics and Public Policy in February 2017 were told an article on "fake news" appeared in *Harper's* in 1925 (Lazer, et al. 2017, 4).

Legacy media has a distinct role to play in addressing the growing concern over "fake news." In an opinion piece entitled "How
to Protect Against Fake 'Facts,'" posted 23 November 2017 on
the *Washington Post* site, David Ignatius states, "We need to work
harder to make sure that we're unbiased truth-tellers, not a series
of echo chambers" (Ignatius 2017).

There is no question, as the conference's final report states, "the
spread of false information became a topic of wide public concern during the 2016 U.S. election season" (Lazer et al. 2017, 4).
The report states social media platforms "provide a megaphone
to anyone who can attract followers," even as long-standing
media institutions are weakened (ibid., 5). Conference presenters,
including such distinguished scholars as Yochai Benkler, Michael
Schudson, and Emily Thorson, concluded this development was
problematic, even dangerous, for two reasons: the abundance of
sources and the creation of echo chambers and filter bubbles.

We humans are "biased information seekers" (Sunstein et al.
2016, as cited in ibid., 6). Further, source credibility "profoundly
affects the social interpretation of information" (Swire et al. 2017,
as cited in ibid.). As a result, challenging or "correcting misinformation does not necessarily change peoples' beliefs" or opinions
(Nyhan and Reifler 2010; Flynn et al. 2016, as cited in ibid.).

Media researchers have identified the phenomenon of people
reversing long-held beliefs if the political leader or party they
support pivots on a policy or program. Fox News provides examples literally on a nightly basis, with popular host Sean Hannity
being Exhibit A. Even Donald Trump's lawyer Rudy Giuliani, in
1998, was on record as stating, "Too many immigrants work and
pay taxes but are still being deprived of the basic benefits they
deserve ... It's simply unfair to target hard-working people simply because they have yet to become citizens" (Siegel 2018). That
statement, of course, predates his defence of President Trump and
the president's promise to build a wall along America's southern border and the practice of separating children from parents
attempting to enter the country without proper documentation

and then placing those children in cages. Giuliani now appears on *Meet the Press* insisting "truth isn't truth."

Bots constitute a further complication, designed as they are to amplify the reach of news even if it is fake (Shao et al., as cited in Lazer et al. 2017, 7). At its most basic, a bot is a software application that performs simple and repetitive tasks at a higher rate of speed than a human is capable of, even as the app creators hope you will assume the product is coming from a human. The appeal of bots in a political communications context is self-evident. Oracle will help you build your own. Author David Moscrop, outlining the threat posed by bots, states bots can "mislead or manipulate internet users by flooding online spaces with questionable if not outright false information, by simplifying the message of one side or another to make its position seem more popular than it is, or by forcing that position to the front of people's minds – hijacking their overloaded brains" (Moscrop 2019, 52).

Governments are no strangers to the world of fake news. Philippine President Rodrigo Duterte has turned Facebook into a weapon through a process identified by *Bloomberg Businessweek* writer Lauren Etter as "patriotic trolling," where governments use social media to attack dissenting voices and, in the process, take full advantage of corporate policy at Facebook. After he was elected, Etter states, Facebook "began deepening its partnership with the new administration, offering white-glove services to help maximize the platform's potential" (Etter 2017). So Duterte and other authoritarian strongmen use Facebook as "a tool to wage war against a wide range of opponents – opposition parties, human-rights activists, minority populations, journalists" through "targeted harassment and propaganda," often by true believers (ibid.).

An article entitled "Spreading Fake News Becomes Standard Practice for Governments Across the World," written by Craig Timberg for the *Washington Post* (2017), is worth noting. Timberg states, "Campaigns to manipulate public opinion through false or misleading social media postings have become standard political practice across much of the world with information ministries, specialized military units, and political operatives shaping the flow of information in dozens of countries" (ibid.).

To put the current circumstance in context, Dornan makes the point the invention of Gutenberg's printing press led to the notion of public opinion, and once the connection between the opinion of the masses and the exercise of power was established, public opinion became "an arena of contestation and manipulation" (Dornan 2017a, 5).

Journalism, once the product of a partisan press, became instead a product of mass markets, Dornan observes. And as a result, "capturing widespread attention became the imperative" (ibid.). In a social media age, the attention-getting process has morphed, even mutated, to the point where "the information environment surges with content whose sole purpose is to engineer attention" (ibid. 3). This rich vein of information and expression is not only mined for profit but is "pressed into the service of persuasion," Dornan observes (ibid.). In this new media order, mainstream media "no longer command anything approaching the resources, revenues or respect they once did," the Carleton professor writes (ibid., 7).

Adam Gopnik's 1995 assertion in the *New York Times* that facts and analysis are the bricks and mortar of responsible reporting (Frankel 1995) is at the heart of the present debate over "fake news." Former US senator Daniel Patrick Moynihan once famously said, "Everyone is entitled to his own opinion, but not his own facts" (Clinton 2017, 8). In 2011, David Frum observed, "Now we are all entitled to our facts and conservative media use this right to immerse their audience in a total environment of pseudo-facts and pretend information" (Frum 2011). Former president Barack Obama suggested the new media ecosystem means "everything is true and nothing is true" (Remnick 2016).

In Donald Trump's world, if he says there were more people who attended his inauguration than mainstream media reported or that can be seen in photographs, that's the truth, the visual evidence to the contrary notwithstanding.

Former White House aide Karl Rove during George W. Bush's presidency dismissed critics who insisted they lived in a "reality-based community" as naive, insisting, "We're an empire now, and when we act, we create our own reality" (Clinton 2017, 9). Rove's worldview may have contributed to the fiction around "weapons of mass destruction" that emerged as a key justification for the US and British governments to invade Iraq in 2003. The more compelling case is advanced by Yale history professor Timothy Snyder in a book entitled *On Tyranny: Twenty Lessons from the Twentieth Century*. "To abandon facts is to abandon freedom," Snyder states (Snyder 2019, 65). "If nothing is true, then no one can criticize power because there is no basis upon which to do so. If nothing is true, then all is spectacle" (ibid.).

A defining moment in the Trump administration's media relations strategy was accidental, according to author Michael Wolff. Presidential senior counsellor Kellyanne Conway asserted the new president's right to claim "alternative facts." According to Wolff, Conway was supposed to say "alternative information" (Wolff 2018).

As the late Neil Postman stated so eloquently in his work *Amusing Ourselves to Death* (1985), the media conundrum around whether to give news consumers the "interesting" at the expense of the "important" predates the internet and the emergence of social media platforms such as Facebook and Twitter.

Long before there was a World Wide Web, social media, or alt news sites, legendary CBS anchor Walter Cronkite was worried by what he described as the "gullibility of the American electorate" (Brinkley 2012, 536). "We need courses, beginning in junior high, on journalism for consumers," Cronkite opined. "How to read a newspaper. How to watch television. People have got to be taught to be skeptical so that they don't become cynical about all news sources" (ibid.). Cronkite's concern is echoed by others, including Wayne C. Booth who argued, "Any nation is in trouble if its citizens are not trained for critical response to the flood of misinformation poured over them daily" (Booth 2009).

Here in Canada, the House of Commons Canadian Heritage standing committee held hearings over the winter of 2016–17 on the issue of fake news. Committee chair Seamus O'Regan, subsequently promoted to the Trudeau cabinet, said people are worried about fake news. "By the time a fabricated story about the pope endorsing president-elect Trump was proven bogus, it had been shared one million times," he said (Leblanc 2016). "With great powers come great responsibilities," he added, referring to Facebook's reach (ibid.). Facebook Canada's spokesperson Kevin Chan, echoing his company CEO Mark Zuckerberg, told committee members, "I want you to know, and I want the parliamentary committee to know, that obviously Facebook takes very seriously our responsibilities" (ibid.).

Chan's assurances notwithstanding, the refrain from Facebook executives that the social media site is not a media organization is getting a bit tired, even irritating. The Pew Research Center asserts 44 per cent of Americans get their news from Facebook (Solon 2016). Speaking at Web Summit in Lisbon, tech investor Dave McClure said, "It's clearly a source of news and information for billions of people. If that's not a media organization, then I don't know what is" (ibid.).

The problem, according to Claire Wardle, then with the Tow Center for Digital Journalism, is that "Facebook stumbled into the news business without systems, editorial frameworks, and editorial guidelines and now it is trying to course-correct" (ibid.).

Facebook's motto once urged employees to "Move fast and break things." Mission accomplished, at least as far as the legacy media is concerned. Small wonder there is a growing consensus that Facebook's power needs curbing. And the social media platforms, to date, have proven incapable of regulating themselves.

While Walter Lippmann's descriptive of the media as the beam of a searchlight that settles on a single subject, leaving all else in shadow, is almost one hundred years old, it stands up even in today's social media world, as Zuckerberg and his colleagues at Facebook have discovered.

The "searchlight" has settled on Facebook in a way that it hasn't on other social media companies. Facebook's business and corporate practices have been subjected to more intense media scrutiny and, as a consequence, more extensive public scrutiny. In its hurried attempt to be seen publicly to be addressing the problems critics link to Facebook's distribution algorithms, inconsistencies have surfaced in the company's positioning – its own "truth."

Facebook's business model is a root cause. The social media platform's algorithms reward "likes" more than "truth," it trades in "likes" and "shares," and if the numbers benefit from clickbait – the social media platform equivalent of steroids – then so be it. Ads, in turn, are placed next to stories that attract the most attention. Advertisers are routinely embarrassed by news reports drawing their attention to the fact their ad appeared next to stories they'd rather not be associated with. That said, advertisers can fend for themselves. Any advertiser displeased with placement can take up the issue with Facebook directly. And Facebook – like any other commercial enterprise – is responsive to customer complaints.

Al Franken's resignation under pressure from the US Senate, triggered by allegations of sexual misconduct, overshadows his prescient interrogation in 2017 of Facebook's chief legal officer on the issue of Russian meddling in the 2016 presidential election.

The Democrat posed the question that should continue to bedevil Facebook's leadership, specifically: "How did Facebook, which prides itself on being able to process billions of data points and instantly transform them into personal connections for its users, somehow not make the connection that electoral ads paid for in rubles were coming from Russia?" (Pullen 2017). (A November 2017 article in the *New York Times* cited a number of Russian-financed ads linking Clinton with the devil, for example (Kang, Fandos, and Isaac 2017). Added Franken, "Those are two data points: American political ads and Russian money, rubles. How could you not connect those two dots?" (Pullen 2017). A sheepish Colin Stretch admitted, "Senator, it's a signal we should have been alerted to" (ibid.). Stretch then promised the firm would not allow political advertising by foreign actors (ibid.).

The exchange triggered significant media commentary, much of it reflecting the proposition that social network platforms such as

Facebook can't have it both ways. Their business model is predicated on an assertion they can connect interests. In fact, as any road warrior can attest, stop once at a motel off an interchange on I-95 and be prepared for a barrage of ads from other hotels located around the same interchange. The assertion, therefore, that the platforms couldn't connect Franken's two dots are either an outright bit of dissembling or Facebook's business model is a fraud.

At congressional hearings being held simultaneously in the Senate and the House of Representatives, legislators on both sides of the aisle expressed their frustration at the answers being provided by witnesses from the social media companies. Facebook executives mutter a *mea culpa*, coupled with a promise the company is working hard to address the fake news issues that bedevil its platform. Perhaps most telling of all is the fact that even as elected representatives were trying to get to the bottom of the Russian intervention, Facebook CEO Mark Zuckerberg and Chief Operating Officer Sheryl Sandberg had decided to give the hearings a miss so they could report "blockbuster" quarterly earnings to Wall Street analysts (Kang, Fandos, and Isaac 2017). Months after standing up British and European politicians who wanted to question Zuckerberg (Chan 2018), both he and Sandberg declined an invitation to appear before a Commons committee in Ottawa in May 2019, sending Kevin Chan to appear in their stead. Chan's answers to their questions failed to impress the parliamentarians in general and NDP MP Charlie Angus in particular. Zuckerberg and Sandberg will be served with a formal summons should they "decide to come to Canada to go fishing," said Angus, a parliamentarian for the left-leaning New Democratic Party. "It's not good enough for them to blow us off" (Scherer 2019).

British parliamentarians have proven elected officials can be effective in addressing the big policy issues presented by digital platform giants. The subheading of an article written by the *Guardian*'s Carole Cadwalladr stated, "The doggedness of a Commons select committee has played a major role in one of the great political scandals of our time" (Cadwalladr 2018).

Other obvious developments around the issue of "truth" in a political context did not generate the media coverage one might have expected. Canadian mainstream media outlets, for example, pursued a story first published in *BuzzFeed News* (Le Conte and Waterson 2016) (Waterson 2016) and the *Guardian* (Cadwalladr, Graham-Harrison, and Townsend 2018) that linked a small Canadian company located on Vancouver Island to Britain's Leave campaign of the Brexit referendum as aggressively as this writer might have expected. AggregateIQ, cofounded by Jeff Silvester and Zack Massingham and reportedly funded in part by Robert Mercer, a billionaire backer of Donald Trump, had been hired to help influence voters with targeted messages. The Canadian media initially filed follow-up stories but showed limited interest in how it came to be that a small analytics firm with twenty employees was paid 2.7 million British pounds ($4.6 million Canadian) for political work out of the Leave campaign's total budget of 6.8 million pounds. Some months later, privacy officials in Britain and British Columbia announced they were on the case (Freeze 2017). Led by UK Information Commissioner Elizabeth Denham, the two privacy commissions have launched an investigation into the company's activities. Denham is Canadian and headed the BC commission for six years before being named Britain's privacy commissioner (ibid.).

Social media algorithms also reinforce political polarization.

McGill University professor Taylor Owen, then working with Emily Bell at Columbia's Tow Center, has written extensively and insightfully that you cannot understand the success of social platforms such as Facebook unless you understand behavioural economics, more precisely a behavioural approach to persuasive communications. In 2016, Owen tweeted that if people think fake news "is a problem now, wait until @facebook builds a metaverse" (Owen 2016).

Fake news is largely manufactured and, on occasion, sponsored. But even more troubling, author and *New Yorker* correspondent Jane Mayer provides a whole new definition of "pay news" in a chillingly important work published in 2016 entitled *Dark Money*.

A phrase that originated as an advertising jingle to tell view-ers/listeners/readers the sponsoring news organization would pay for news tips now refers to the practice of paying organiz-ations to cover designated public policy issues. According to Mayer, "The company that syndicated [Rush] Limbaugh's show, Premiere Networks, meanwhile, was getting paid a handsome $2 million or so a year by the Heritage Foundation to push the think tank's line on issues" (Mayer 2016, 211). The "radical rich" Republicans funded "investigative news services" such as the Franklin Center for Government and Public Integrity, Mayer writes. Franklin Center reports frequently "attacked government programs, particularly those initiated by Obama" (ibid., 427). If the media's power flows in part from its ability to set a political agenda, the Heritage Foundation is paying talking heads to set a particular agenda.

The 20 October 2020 edition of the *New York Times* carried a story under the headline "As Local News Dies, a Pay-for-Play Network Rises in Its Place," which outlined in some detail how a national operation of 1,300 local sites "publishes coverage that is ordered up by Republicans and Corporate P.R. firms" in news deserts (Alba and Nicas 2020).

Former *Globe and Mail* columnist Tabatha Southey informed read-ers that no less an authority than Oxford Dictionaries had selected "post-truth" as its international word of the year in 2016. States Southey, "It defines the word as an adjective 'relating to or denot-ing circumstances in which the objective facts are less influential in shaping public opinion than appeals to emotion and personal belief'" (2016). Southey asserts, "bullshit is a demand problem, not a supply problem" (ibid.).

Social media sites steer material our way based on algorithms that are, in turn, shaped by our own user profiles. Content teases are the direct consequence of our browser habits. As one wag put it, "you are what you click."

And then there is the whole issue of the different definitions of what constitutes "truth."

In the early 1990s, I spent some of the most enjoyable days of my life in the company of legends in Mexico City.

The occasion was a week-long series of panels and discussion groups organized by the Mexico City daily *El Universal* focused on the role of the official spokesperson. Pierre Salinger, long-time ABC correspondent and press secretary to US President John F. Kennedy, had called personally to extend the invitation to attend and participate. The lineup included Marlin Fitzwater, who served presidents Reagan and Bush, Gennady Gerasimov, spokesperson for Mikhail Gorbachev, the last president of the USSR, and Husain Haqqani, who would go on to a distinguished career as a diplomat for Pakistan.

As anyone who has ever spent time on a team bus can attest, some of the more interesting conversations occurred on the bus as we rolled from event to event. Listening to Fitzwater and Gerasimov compare notes on the 1986 Reykjavik Summit, for example, was literally the stuff of history.

Fitzwater is a compelling figure: quick, smart, strong values, and a down-home perspective on life that served him extraordinarily well in the White House.

In his memoirs, Fitzwater cites a journalism professor who famously told him, "There are two kinds of truth: the kind you can prove in court and the kind any fool can plainly see" (Fox, B. 1999, 111).

Fitzwater observed, "It has always astonished me how many times the government tries to establish courtly truth without establishing the kind that any fool can plainly see" (ibid.). Prime Minister Justin Trudeau and his cabinet colleagues would have been well-advised to heed Fitzwater's advice in their handling of the long-running case of Omar Khadr.

Canadians will remember that in the first week of July 2017, an unidentified source in the federal government leaked news to the *Globe and Mail* that Canada was to pay Khadr $10.5 million in compensation for actions by government officials that the Supreme Court of Canada ruled had violated Khadr's constitutional rights (Fife 2017).

Khadr's story was well-known to many Canadians. Born in 1986 in Toronto, he was a child when he and his siblings were taken to Pakistan by their parents. In 1995, Khadr's father, ostensibly a charity organizer in Pakistan and Afghanistan, was charged in Pakistan with aiding terrorism. He was freed, reportedly after then-prime minister Jean Chrétien inquired on his behalf. Soon, he was living closely with Osama bin Laden and accused of being a senior member of al Qaeda by Canada and the US. (Ahmed Khadr was killed in a shootout in 2003 on the Afghan border. His son Omar was either a child soldier or unprivileged enemy belligerent, depending on your perspective.)

27 July 2017 marked the fifteenth anniversary of a firefight in Afghanistan that claimed the life of US Delta Force member Sergeant First Class Christopher Speer. Omar Khadr, then fifteen, was seriously wounded and captured in the same fatal skirmish. Considered an enemy combatant by the US government, Khadr was subsequently taken to its detention facility at Guantánamo Bay in Cuba where he insists he was subjected to repeated torture and mistreatment. During his time at Guantánamo, Khadr was questioned by Canadian intelligence service agents who shared their findings with US authorities.

In 2005, the US charged Khadr with the murder of Christopher Speer as well as other crimes, though that authority was invalidated the next year by the US Supreme Court. In 2007, he was charged again under a new military act. Meanwhile, his lawyers launched an overlapping series of court cases in Guantánamo, the United States, and Canada, including against the government of Canada over recordings of those interviews. In 2008, the Supreme Court of Canada ruled the Conservative Harper government had illegally withheld them from Khadr's defence lawyers and ordered them released.

In addition, Khadr's legal team insisted Canadian officials violated his rights when they interrogated him at Guantánamo in 2003 and 2004. Specifically, they asserted the Canadian officials conducted the interrogations knowing Khadr was a minor, was without his legal representation, and had been subject to torture.

The Supreme Court, in a January 2010 unanimous ruling, agreed that Khadr's rights had been denied during those interviews. Later that year, US military prosecutors offered him a plea deal on the condition that he confess to killing Speer. In October 2010, on the advice of counsel, Khadr pleaded guilty to five war crimes including murder.

In 2012, Khadr was repatriated to Canada to serve out the remainder of his term in a Canadian prison. In 2013, he launched an appeal in the US of his convictions and in 2015 was freed on bail in Edmonton (Friscolanti 2015). (As he was released, a $134 million default judgment against Khadr was awarded to Tabitha Speers, the widow of Christopher Speers, as well as another US soldier wounded in the battle.)

There is much confusion as to what exactly happened on that fateful day in Afghanistan. Khadr himself now says he doesn't know and hopes he didn't throw the grenade that led to Speer's fatal wounds. But in the context of the court cases against Canada, Khadr's lawyers argue these specifics are of no consequence, that the case is centred on Khadr's constitutional rights and whether the government of Canada violated those rights.

In their legal brief and supporting media strategy, Khadr's lawyers successfully established the issue of his constitutional rights as the dominant news frame. The issue, they asserted, was clear and relatively straightforward. In the context of his constitutional rights, Khadr is the victim, the Supreme Court agreed, twice, and as a consequence he is entitled to compensation.

The lawyers cited the precedent of Maher Arar, another Canadian whose rights were violated when, in 2002, the RCMP gave misleading information to American authorities, which handed him over to Syria, where he was tortured. Arar, who spent a year in Syria, was awarded $10.5 million in compensation plus legal fees, as well as a formal apology from then-prime minister Stephen Harper, in 2007.

For the Trudeau government, the "truth" as established in a court of law was self-evident. The government could either seek a settlement with Khadr or keep fighting in the courts with the inherent risk of a subsequent award that might be significantly higher in dollar terms.

So confident was the Trudeau government of the merits of the court-established truth that when word of the settlement was leaked, the government didn't bother to make a minister available to speak to the issue for days. A press release was prepared to be issued in the name of Public Safety Minister Ralph Goodale and Foreign Affairs Minister Chrystia Freeland (Tasker 2017).

Unfortunately for the Trudeau government, Fitzwater's journalism professor proved to be a wise owl.

Many Canadians were outraged. News that Khadr was to receive $10.5 million in compensation and an apology from the Canadian government sparked a heated public debate. And it is worth noting that Ralph Goodale – who acknowledged Canadians were "deeply divided" in their views of Khadr – and former justice minister Jody Wilson-Raybould, who was pressed into service for the news conference itself, couldn't bring themselves to actually articulate the apology included in the government's press release before the cameras.

In the ensuing debate, certain of Khadr's defenders implied anyone who opposed or questioned the settlement was an Islamophobe or worse.

Most certainly, there were legal and media voices who shed much light on the Khadr story, notably law professor Craig Forcese (2008) and former *Toronto Star* reporter Michelle Shephard, who may know more about the Khadr story than anyone on the planet, including Khadr.

But the fact is media coverage was indeed a factor in shaping public responses to news of the $10.5 million settlement. While Khadr's lawyers brilliantly framed their case, and their media strategy, as an issue of constitutional rights, news coverage painted a broader picture. What happened in the firefight of July 2002 was irrelevant to the court case but not irrelevant to the public. There may indeed always be confusion about what exactly happened during the firefight and there may be legitimate doubt as to whether Khadr ever threw the grenade that killed Sergeant Speer. But there was no doubt about the footage, aired on YouTube (2013), of a smiling Omar Khadr helping build roadside bombs similar to those improvised explosive devices that claimed Canadian troops and maimed Canadian Armed Forces personnel during a ten-year combat mission in Afghanistan. In news terms, the Khadrs are the gift that keeps on giving. In the fall of 2020, news stories appeared reporting Khadr's sister Zaynab – a Canadian citizen – was suing the government of Canada in an effort to have her name taken off the "no-fly list" so she can return to Canada and be reunited with her children who were allowed entry (CTV 2020).

Since the settlement announcement, views on Khadr have hardened. He remains a divisive figure for many Canadians. In an Abacus poll conducted a few weeks after the announcement, only 33 per cent of respondents gave the federal government a good or acceptable rating for its handling of the Khadr matter (Anderson and Coletto 2017b).

Given the Supreme Court rulings, the federal government may well have made the correct legal decision. But the government's initial response would suggest that its ministers failed to understand the public debate was never going to be as narrowly or as neatly defined as the court case.

A Liberal government was in power when Khadr's rights were violated during those interrogations in Guantánamo. A Liberal government had a responsibility to explain to the public why Canadian officials did what they did in 2003 and 2004. Ironically, Goodale, who announced the Khadr settlement, was in Jean Chrétien's cabinet when the offending interrogations occurred, yet if any of the reporters who attended his settlement announcement asked him for an explanation as to why Canadian officials followed a course of action that violated Khadr's constitutional rights, the answer didn't generate any coverage.

The federal government clearly assumed their court-established truth would carry the day and in so doing missed the opportunity, and indeed the obligation, to speak to the truth that "any fool can plainly see." The fact the federal government did not have a designated cabinet spokesperson in place the day there was news of the settlement speaks volumes.

Finally, there is the issue of "false equivalency."

Presidential aspirant Hillary Clinton's relationship with the legacy media in many ways reflects the complexity of her relationship with the American electorate. Clinton, whether in the context of her work as first lady, as a US senator from New York, or as secretary of state, was often afforded editorial endorsements from august media organizations such as the *New York Times*. But the subtext of the headlines over many news stories was "Hillary pilloried."

Clinton believes part of the explanation lies in a media structural bias she dubs a "tidy false equivalency" (Clinton 2017, 342) – a phenomenon created by network television's "point/counterpoint" structure. "Balanced doesn't mean strictly equal," Clinton states. "It means reasonable. It means asking smart questions backed by solid reporting and making decisions about coverage that will help people get the information they need to make sound decisions … Picking the mid-point between two sides, no matter how extreme one of them is, isn't balance – it's false equivalency" (ibid., 229). Clinton cites a study by the Shorenstein Center's Thomas Patterson to buttress her argument. "If everything and everyone are portrayed negatively, there's a levelling effect that opens the door to charlatans," Patterson states. "The press historically has helped citizens recognize the difference between the earnest politician and the pretender. Today's news coverage blurs the distinction" (ibid., 230). A proof point for Clinton is the fact the media treated the issue of email security on her part in much the same way the media covered the Trump campaign's contact with the Russians.

Legendary CBS broadcast journalist Edward R. Murrow, who Tim Wu describes as "the first bona fide star of broadcast news," offered a perspective on objectivity that modern-day political reporters might reflect upon in the context of today's issues around false equivalences.

Murrow's broadcasts from Europe during the Second World War provide the context. "The journalistic approach, while objective, was not neutral," Wu states. "The war was not a subject that he thought deserved a balanced presentation of both sides" (Wu, T. 2016, 107). The CBS icon was a model of consistency on this specific issue. In the 1950s, he would bring the same approach to his coverage of "communist-hunting" Senator Joseph McCarthy.

Journalism's embrace of "fair and balanced" as an objective test of the quality of its editorial content can be a slippery slope. In the words of author Joan Didion, journalistic balance is a "scrupulous passivity, an agreement to cover the story not as it occurred, but as it is presented" (Patterson 2013, 52). Such balanced reporting devolves into James Fallows's definition of "false equivalencies – the side-by-side placement of statements of differing factual integrity" (as cited in ibid., 52). Television's point/counterpoint structure for virtually every panel favours the news maker over the news gatherer. Television studio debates in the 1960s over the medical consequences of smoking or, more recently, climate change are examples. A decided majority of scientists has reached consensus on climate change. There are dissenting scientific voices to be sure, but the dissenters are a minority. Yet with the "false equivalency" format, the two sides are afforded equal treatment and standing.

"Be truthful, not neutral," advises Christiane Amanpour, CNN's distinguished correspondent (Amanpour 2017).

In *Amusing Ourselves to Death*, Postman (1985) compared George Orwell's view of culture as a prison to Aldous Huxley's perspective on culture as a burlesque and concluded devastation was more likely to come from an enemy with a smiling face. Postman's worldview enjoyed a renaissance with the election of Donald J. Trump as the forty-fifth president of the United States.

Hannah Arendt, in the seminal work *The Origins of Totalitarianism*, could have been writing about the world today when she states, "The ideal subject of totalitarian rule is not the convinced Nazi or the convinced Communist but the people for whom the distinction between fact and fiction (i.e. the reality of experience) and the distinction between true and false (i.e. the standards of thought) no longer exist" (Arendt 1968).

The satirist Jonathan Swift summarized the societal cost of falsehood when he states, "Falsehood flies, and truth comes limping after it, so that when men come to be undeceived, it is too late, the jest is over and the tale hath had its effect … like a physician who hath found out an infallible medicine, after the patient is dead."

5

News and Power

News and the media organizations that produce and distribute journalistic content have been the subject of intense analysis over the years through a particular panel of the prism – power. The economist Joseph Stiglitz advances a fundamental proposition in the context of news and the exercise of power: the function of the media is to convey information to readers that enables them to make better decisions – as consumers, as managers, as workers, as owners, as investors, as voters. And better individual decisions are likely to produce better societal outcomes.

For some, power flows through the control of production and distribution of texts; for others, power is exercised through the texts themselves. The debate revolves around a core question: the media as social institution, as Miliband would have it, or the media as business, as Robertson Davies believed (Flint 1995). As Barton Swaim, the opinion editor of the *Weekly Standard,* noted, "It was Foucault who held that political power structures were really just a matter of 'competing discourses'" (Swaim 2015, 30).

Media ownership is somewhere between "a" factor and "the" factor in the consideration of media effects for communications theorists. British scholar Ralph Miliband (1973), for example, argued that pure economic determinism suggests that control of the means of production determines the content. Miliband saw mass media as an ideological tool of the ruling class: the key consideration being the media's practice of marginalizing dissent.

Miliband saw the media as a watchdog, but what the media was protecting most ferociously was the status quo. The media, according to Miliband, fulfilled a conformist rather than a critical role.

And the "gatekeeper" was motivated by essentially inescapable commercial imperatives.

New Zealand academic Peter A. Thompson cites the "propaganda model" developed by Edward Herman and Noam Chomsky (Herman and Chomsky 1988), which holds that news media coverage is tilted in favour of media and corporate elites through five filters:

- ownership arrangements
- reliance on advertising revenue
- dependency on elite sources
- concern to avoid flak
- ideological conformity

"There is plenty of empirical evidence from sociological studies of media organizations available to support the proposition that the various filters can and do shape news content," Thompson states (Thompson, P.A. 2009, 76).

Recently, the emergence of social media platforms prompted a personal return to the writing of James Carey and, in particular, Carey's transmission versus ritual view of mass communications.

Heavily influenced by Canadian scholars Harold Innis and Marshall McLuhan, Carey believed communication was really about a philosophy of inquiry. This "ritual" view of communications – the idea of sharing, of participation, of association – seems well-suited to the more ideal view of the potential of social media platforms. Social media, at least initially, afforded people a platform for "ritual" conversations, but, in time, that potential mutated to a communication structure that fostered communities that constituted alternate universes.

Harvard scholar Yochai Benkler opens his work *The Wealth of Networks* with the assertion, "Information, knowledge, and culture are central to human freedom and human development" (Benkler 2006, 1). The key consideration in a networked sphere involves the cost of becoming a "speaker" (ibid., 210) and when everyone can speak, "The central point of failure becomes the capacity to be heard" (ibid., 238). Benkler acknowledges that "there is no guarantee that networked information technology will lead to the improvements in innovation, freedom, and justice that I suggest are possible" (ibid., 18). It is now clear that commercial considerations continue to largely determine who and what gets heard on social media platforms. Miliband's preoccupation with control of the means of production has been expanded in a social media age to include concern over the control of the means of distribution.

Critical theorists tended to focus on the power inherent in controlling the means of production. Press barons past – such as Lord Beaverbrook and, more recently, Conrad Black – emerged as the metaphorical villains of the piece. Former British prime minister Stanley Baldwin, in a sentence reportedly suggested to him by his cousin Rudyard Kipling, once declared, "What proprietorship of these papers is aiming at is power, and power without responsibility – the prerogative of the harlot throughout the ages" (Curran and Seaton 2003, 38). Baldwin's description is equally relevant today in the context of social media "barons" such as Facebook's Mark Zuckerberg and Twitter's Jack Dorsey.

Carey saw communication as a symbolic process whereby "reality is produced, maintained, repaired and transformed" (Carey 1989, 23). Yet to Carey's dismay, American social sciences has represented communication within an overarching transmission view, looking at each new advance in communications technology, from radio to television to the internet, as an opportunity to conduct politics and economics within a command-and-control structure. Much of the media scholarship of the "administrative" school has emerged from American academia, with a focus described by Carey on the "transmission of signals or messages over distance for purposes of control."

To the dismay and even disdain of cultural theorists, the "administrative school," building on the work of Walter Lippmann, focused on a different expression of power – media effects. Adherents of this approach cite American political scientist Bernard C. Cohen (Cohen, B.C. 1963) to the effect that media is powerful, not because media tells us what to think but, more precisely, because media tells us what to think about. Columbia's Todd Gitlin (1980) offers the critical theorists' counterpoint: that the media's real power lies in what we do *not* think about, that the legacy media wields what influence and power it has in a staunch defence of the economic and political status quo.

Media influence on public opinion and voter intentions is of particular interest to the political community and the political press.

The conventional wisdom in academic circles in the late 1970s held that media coverage had little to no impact on voter intentions during election campaigns. As a member of the national campaign team for two federal elections in the 1980s, I can attest the earned media strategy was afforded less significance and less attention than other elements of the campaign. The sense at the time was "play for a tie" in terms of campaign news coverage, and let your ground game, advertising, and the televised leaders' debates decide the issue. This "media as necessary evil" view was reflected in the campaigns in operational terms as well. In the 1984 election campaign, access to candidate Brian Mulroney for the travelling press corps was strictly limited, to the point that reporters were on the verge of open rebellion as the campaign entered the late stages. In 1988, the concept was taken a step further. White ropes were put up at events in the expectation reporters would know enough to stay behind them.

Ever mindful of the old admonition that to a person with a hammer everything looks like a nail, my sense was that media coverage mattered more than other campaign strategists appreciated; hardly surprising, given my background in political journalism.

The 1993 federal election campaign turned that "sense" into a belief, and this has become the dominant "frame" for my ongoing interest (with occasional lapses into obsession) in politics and political communication.

Though the Conservatives had been in power since 1984, the new prime minister Kim Campbell went into the 1993 campaign basically tied in terms of public support with the Jean Chrétien-led Liberals. But an ill-considered comment Campbell made on the lawn of Rideau Hall with the campaign scant minutes old – that unemployment would remain high until the "end of the century" – began an unravelling that would culminate in the electoral collapse of the once powerful Progressive Conservative Party (Farnsworth 1993). And the events that triggered Campbell's collapse all occurred before the other variables – specifically advertising and the televised leaders' debates – had rolled out.

Canadian communications scholar Marshall McLuhan made the point that any new means of moving information will alter the power structure. McLuhan came up with the idea that "we shape our tools and thereafter they shape us," although the actual quote was written by John Culkin, a professor of communications at Fordham University and a friend of McLuhan (Culkin 1967). And social media advocates certainly believe the political and economic institutions that constitute today's power structure are most emphatically being altered.

Journalist A.J. Liebling's oft-quoted assertion that "freedom of the press is guaranteed only to those who own one" has – in theory at least – been overtaken with the emergence of social media platforms (Dornan 2017a, 6).

Appearing as a panellist at an event organized by the Canadian Journalism Foundation, Richard Gingras, Google's vice-president of news, stated, "The internet put a printing press in everyone's hands" (Canadian Journalism Foundation 2018b). Today's world includes literally a billion-plus websites – a total that is growing daily. And as an extension of that reality, panel participants agreed that popularity is at the core of much of what social media participants are exposed to. In his work *The Economics of Attention*, Richard Lanham argues the internet "constitutes a pure economics of attention" (2007a, 202). As a result, style and substance have basically traded places in the economic pecking order. "Push style to its extreme and it becomes substance," Lanham observes (ibid., 255).

That emerging communications technologies continue to threaten what Benkler describes as "the incumbents of the industrial information economy" is self-evident (2006, 2). And the radical increase in the ranks of storytellers has increased both the number and the diversity of stories told, as Benkler notes. But his description of this new media universe as "not as easily corruptible by money as were the mass media" is now revealed to have been overly optimistic (ibid., 56).

Emerging technologies have led to a shift in the gatekeeper function in the media ecosystem. A shift in public discourse did follow. But the speed at which the shift occurs is, and will continue to be, uneven. "Progress" will not be linear nor consistent. Cellphone technology, by way of example, was first developed the year I was born – 1947 – but didn't become a device you could carry in a pocket for another four decades (Dyroff 2018).

Postman long held that "every technology is both a burden and a blessing; not either-or but this-and-that" (Postman 1992, 4–5).

The explosion of web platforms has dramatically increased the number of sites for public discourse and in so doing has fundamentally altered the relationship of the engaged, with obvious implications for politics and public policy.

Communications scholar James Carey's admonition that "no one has the last word; there are no final thoughts" is a helpful guide as we contemplate this tectonic shift (as quoted in Clark, R.P. 2006).

In critical theory terms, the power of the FAANGS – Facebook, Apple, Amazon, Netflix, and Alphabet's Google – in terms of the production and distribution of texts is self-evident. As part of that broader process, journalism is being disaggregated today and is in the process of being brought back together differently. By way of illustration, Facebook is the de facto distributor for the new media ecosystem. One example of how legacy news organizations have ceded control of distribution to Facebook was highlighted in a tweet slugged "Outrageous" posted by Rob Walsh, a former parliamentary counsel to the House of Commons. Walsh expressed his irritation over the fact "I can't access a @CBC podcast without joining Facebook ... And @CBC is a taxpayer's media outlet!" Walsh fumed (2018).

Further, Facebook has somehow convinced us all that it is in our collective interest to produce for free the content they slice, dice, and sell to advertisers. Wired "serfs" we are. Facebook's 2.4 billion active monthly users include more than half of all humans with internet connection.

News and Reality

Harvard's Thomas Patterson (2013) describes journalists as our "chief sense-makers," helping us understand the world of public affairs beyond our experience.

Media scholar Gaye Tuchman states, "The news frame organizes everyday reality and the news frame is part and parcel of everyday reality ... it is an essential feature of news" (Tuchman 1978, 193).

Political conversations are rarely based on direct knowledge. Most of us have limited involvement in political activities or public policy. Most Canadians are not members of a political party, do not attend council meetings at city hall, and aren't active in volunteer organizations. As a result, political conversation is usually shaped by a secondhand experience, something created for us by mass media.

Having been forced to leave Yemen where I was doing some volunteer work for the National Democratic Institute after the outbreak of the civil war there in 2015, I found myself in the following days watching a panel of experts assembled for a conversation with Peter Mansbridge, then anchor of the CBC's *The National*. Each of the panellists was considered a subject matter expert and each displayed an impressive command of the broader geopolitical issues at play in the region. But none of the panellists had been in Yemen during that country's post-Arab Spring renewal and extensive public consultation process that saw ordinary citizens and activists alike produce a new draft constitution, the specifics of which were factors in triggering Yemen's civil war. The panellists understanding of the situation was shaped to some degree by news reports and the observations of others – and not from firsthand, on-the-ground knowledge.

Jörgen Westerståhl states, "News reporting must be factual and impartial in order to provide a foundation for independent and rational decision-making" (1983, 407). Adds Tuchman, "The news media set the frame in which citizens discuss public events ... the quality of the debate necessarily depends on the information available" (Tuchman 1978). Walter Lippmann says news is a "powerful instrument of social control" precisely because it defines the reality we all operate in (Fox, B. 1999, 251).

So the question arises, is the news we consume today rich enough for the robust debate needed for a vibrant democracy?

Virtually every student of political communications can quote Bagdikian's axiom that "the democratic consent of the governed is meaningless unless the consent is informed consent" (Bagdikian 1992, xxvii).

Former *Columbia Journalism Review* editor Joan Konner put the challenge well: "The legitimacy of our democracy depends on having everyone participate in our deliberations. The challenge to journalism is how they can help us to construct a democratic conversation" (pers. notes).

Ironically, Lippmann articulated the cost of less news almost one hundred years before the wheels started to wobble on the traditional media's business model. "All that the sharpest critics of democracy have alleged is true if there is no steady supply of trustworthy and relevant news," Lippmann stated. "Incompetence and aimlessness, corruption and disloyalty, panic and ultimate disaster, must come to any people which is denied an assured access to the facts ... No one can manage anything on pap. Neither can a people" (Lippmann 1920, 11).

Media sociologist Herbert Gans (1980) reminds us that democracy functions whether the electorate is informed or not. US President Barack Obama during his time in office literally saved the auto industry, a critical component part of the Michigan economy. The auto bailout was a news story of significance. Yet by the time of the 2016 election, that economic rebound wasn't enough to sway a majority of voters in that state who chose the Republican nominee, Donald Trump. In the 2020 campaign, Trump was insisting he was the leader who saved the auto industry (Dale 2020).

For the better part of fifty years, television dominated the news and as a consequence, was a central element in the exercise of political power. Television news, as Shanto Iyengar and Donald Kinder (1987) observed, is *News That Matters*. Writing in the early 1980s, George Gerbner observed, "Television is the central and most pervasive mass medium in American culture and it plays a distinct and historically unprecedented role." Here in Canada, Peter Desbarats, a long-time journalist and former dean of the school of journalism at Western University, said, "Television has become the most important and influential medium of news and information for most Canadians" (Desbarats 1996). US media commentator Ken Auletta (1992), author of *Three Blind Mice*, says television has become a basic American utility. In fact, in all but the most underdeveloped economically deprived communities, television is as accessible as water, gas, or electricity (Hood and Tabary-Peterssen 1997).

Television, as we know it, is an expression of public policy. A bargain was struck. Networks were given access to the publicly owned airwaves and in return agreed to meet an ill-defined and constantly evolving test of "public service." Not everyone was convinced of television's potential. The philosopher Bertrand Russell once declared, "Television will be of no importance in your lifetime or mine" (as cited in Blackwell and Ruja 1994, 569). Yet television most emphatically contributes to the viewer's concept of reality in specific and measurable ways, as Gerbner et al. (1980) concluded.

Given the centrality of communication to the political process, television, as the information medium of choice for the last forty years of the twentieth century and well into the current one, plays a pivotal role in our politics.

Senator Keith Davey was constantly reminding his Liberal colleagues that in politics, perception is reality. Davey's oft-repeated observation underscores the importance of the symbolic arena in politics, and television dominates the symbolic environment of life (ibid.).

Television revolutionized the world of political communication. Television brought candidates for office directly into people's homes and, in particular, allowed politicians to be in direct contact with low-involvement voters. Candidates with access to network television news could speak "personally" to couch potatoes and the political literati alike. Political communications staff wave off journalistic protests about the use of stagecraft to manage messages.

In the wake of the 2016 US presidential campaign, much analytical attention was focused on President Trump's use of social media, especially Facebook and Twitter, and justifiably so. In today's social media world, a case can be made that television matters less.

Yet it is worth reminding ourselves that Donald Trump is a creation of network television, especially his role as a ruthless business leader on NBC's *The Apprentice. The Economist* and the *New York Times* may question whether Trump is, in fact, as successful an entrepreneur as he claims to be, but all acknowledge Trump played a successful business mogul on network television for twenty years.

The amount of exposure each of us has to television is an important indication of the strength of television's influence on the ways we think and act.

Ironically, television as a medium is an educator without peer (Neuman, Just, and Crigler 1992). Some may question this assertion, especially if suppertime news shows inform your view of TV news. The problem with television news isn't inherent to the medium; the problem is a direct consequence of the way content creators use the medium.

Brevity is the major cause for concern. TV's ninety-second rule, now even shorter, "reduces TV news to a kaleidoscope of shocks and sensations, portends and propaganda, gossip and titillation" (Gilder 1994). The vast majority of political news stories on television are not framed in a manner consistent with the way ordinary viewers tend to take in information. Further, many of the visuals shown in television news are totally uninformative.

The seminal Crigler study (Neuman, Just, and Crigler 1992) established that television succeeds better than newspapers in communicating substantive information. The visuals help. Graber (1988) concludes the public's fondness for the medium is fully justified.

A founding editor of the journal *Political Communication*, Doris Graber also challenges another of the orthodoxies around the TV generation; specifically, she challenges the assertion that most average citizens are political dunces. Issue salience is the key. When it comes to functionally useful knowledge, Graber finds average citizens are moderately well-informed in policy and program areas such as affirmative action, government support for troubled industries, and foreign policy regarding the Middle East.

Despite television's potential as an educator without peer, television executives decided the medium was better suited to other purposes. The late NBC executive Reuven Frank, for example, believed, "The highest power of television journalism is not in the transmission of information but in the transmission of experience" (Epstein 1974, 39).

Television's potential to provide a public sphere has long been acknowledged, as has the role humans play in creating its limits. Edward R. Murrow, who was less successful on television than he was on radio, said, "This instrument can teach, it can illuminate; yes, and it can even inspire. But it can do so only to the extent that humans are determined to use it to those ends" (Wu, T. 2016, 160–1).

Legendary CBS executive producer Fred Friendly echoed Murrow's observations, with a particularly pointed observation of what happens when journalistic values clash with commercial considerations. "That's the tragedy of television," Friendly said. "At its best, it is so very good. But television can make so much money doing its worst that it can't afford to be at its best" (Brinkley 2012, 5).

Power and Framing

The legendary military strategist Sun Tzu presaged media framing theory when he made the point in *The Art of War* (1964) that every battle is won before it is fought, and it is won by choosing the terrain on which it is fought.

Robert Entman (1993) believes the ability to frame an issue is the central power in the democratic process, which is why political elites struggle to control that frame. Frames basically involve choosing the terrain on which the political battle is fought.

TV news is largely about frames: episodic frames that focus on a specific event or a thematic frame of a more general construct. Most television news stories include both types, but one is always dominant. Frames, frankly, are everything when it comes to media coverage and the political conversation that flows from that coverage.

Thomas Pynchon famously said if you can get people asking the wrong question, the answer actually doesn't matter. This truism surfaced in the spring of 2018 in the course of a radio interview on the CBC Radio public affairs program *The Current*. Host Anna Maria Tremonti was asking guest and former prime minister Jean Chrétien about the so-called sponsorship scandal that swirled around the awarding of advertising and public relations contracts in Quebec following the near miss of the 1995 referendum campaign on Quebec independence (Tremonti 2018).

Chrétien challenged the very description of the sponsorship flap as a "scandal," insisted there was never any proof that any parliamentarian was lining his or her pockets, and concluded with a spirited defence that if anyone thought he was going to accept criticism for spending money to tell Quebecers they have the best of all worlds in a united Canada, they should think some more (ibid.).

A Chrétien tour de force, mixing patriotism, passion, and non sequiter in equal measure. And if you accept Chretien's "framing," his defence makes all the sense in the world. So you spent some money to buy TV time to keep the country together. And maybe the bookkeeping around the campaign wasn't as tight as it should have been. And yes, maybe the odd rogue's hourly billings were higher than they should have been. As the cost of keeping the country together, this hardly constitutes a "scandal."

But what if the story isn't a story about sponsorship or advertising or parliamentarians lining their pockets? What if the story is a story about election fraud? What if the ad firms in question were being paid for "volunteer" work during the 1997 federal election campaign? What if the real story is that these agencies were told to send people into campaign offices in Quebec where party leader Jean Charest was bringing the Progressive Conservative Party back from the dead? And what if the understanding was that the agencies' costs were to be covered after the votes were counted and the account books on election spending were closed? (CBC 2005).

Was the Canadian political media – and the commission of inquiry headed by Justice John Gomery – chasing the wrong angle? And was it chasing the wrong angle because someone put a "sponsorship scandal" frame on the story instead of an "electoral fraud" frame? And was that someone a Liberal strategist who thought Thomas Pynchon (Pynchon 1973) was on to something because padded billings are one thing, flouting election spending laws is something else again.

Media strategy is intended to frame the earned media coverage in line with a particular party's ballot question. This process rolls out in three distinct phases.

The first – agenda setting – has an almost immediate impact on those directly affected by the problem and is a precondition to agenda building. Stories about inner-city crime in Toronto are more immediately relevant to those who live in the downtown club district than to those who live in the leafy tranquility of Forest Hill or Lawrence Park.

Agenda setting has more influence on those with a more independent view than on those with strong partisan leanings. The key function here is the role of the gatekeeper, once the domain of a relatively small group of senior editors but now, in a social media context, a more broadly held responsibility.

The second phase – priming – involves our assessment of political leaders based on what we have now agreed is the agenda. Priming effects are stronger on issues that are relatively new to the media agenda but impact the deeply partisan and the more independent minded similarly. The COVID-19 pandemic in 2020 is a textbook example. In a campaign setting, winnability is often the "agenda." Trump, for example, made winnability his master narrative for both the Republican primaries and the 2016 presidential campaign.

The third phase – the bandwagon effect – involves the expression of our opinion. There are clear limits to television's power; television could not sustain a story that was radically at odds with stories on radio or in the newspapers, although the emergence of the "fake news" phenomenon constitutes a new test for the assertion. Social media was subjected to the same test in the 2020 US presidential campaign.

A further key to understanding this process is to appreciate that news frames are neither temporary nor permanent but are always works in progress.

And as discussed in an earlier chapter, congenial truths (Tucher 1994) are a factor in framing theory as well. Congenial truths, in essence, involve a pact between the reporter and the reader, an understanding that is mutually acceptable. These "truths" can be different in French Canada than in English Canada or Nova Scotia versus Alberta. They can also lead reporters to attach less importance to established fact if that fact is in contrast with conventional wisdom. This collusion is quiet rather than conspiratorial. It can be highly localized and is part of the reason reporters can be slow to jump on a big story, such as Donald Trump's appeal in the "fly-over states" in 2016.

Television news also focuses on accountability, either a causal construct focusing on the origins of the problem or a treatment construct that focuses on the person or institution with the power to solve the problem or not.

Television news prefers an episodic/treatment construct frame, largely for commercial reasons. The episode provides the novelty a news story requires, and the treatment construct puts a face to the problem. President Trump made extensive use of this construct. He used the "episode" of a threatened plant closure in the US automotive sector to position himself as the person who could come to the rescue of the plant workers. He summoned the executives of the Big Three automakers to Washington. He threatened border duties on cars assembled elsewhere that are earmarked for sale in the United States (Boudette 2017). The CEOs, in the Trump version of events, capitulate. Problem solved – by President Trump, just like he promised he would in the 2016 election campaign. In 2020, the construct worked against Trump in terms of the president's handling of the pandemic.

Television news is leader-centric, and it creates a "hegemonic model" of public communication, one that disseminates information in a manner that ensures existing societal power structures are maintained through an elaborate code control process.

Cognitive scientists tell us that information that individuals can more easily retrieve from their memory bank tends to dominate judgment. Because people rely heavily on the media for political information, patterns of news coverage are critical determinants of accessibility (Tversky and Kahneman 1974). The significance of accessibility bias, Amos Tversky and Daniel Kahneman explain, flowed from the fact a person's judgment is shaped, in part, by what comes to mind (ibid.).

"People tend to assess the relative importance of issues by the ease with which they are retrieved from memory," Daniel Kahneman states in *Thinking, Fast and Slow*, "and this is largely determined by the extent of coverage in the media. Frequently mentioned topics populate the mind even as others slip away from awareness" (Kahneman 2011).

Adds Kahneman, "In turn, what the media choose to report corresponds to their view of what is currently on the public's mind" (ibid., 9). "The media do not just shape what the public is interested in, but also are shaped by it," Kahneman observes. "Editors cannot ignore the public's demands that certain topics and viewpoints receive extensive coverage" (ibid., 138). "It is no accident that authoritarian regimes exert substantial pressure on independent media" (ibid., 9). Donald Trump would undoubtedly chafe at any suggestion his administration was an authoritarian regime, but there is no denying the president and his supporters were trying to exert pressure on the independent press such as the *New York Times* or CNN.

McGinniss (1969) once stated television "seems particularly useful to the politician who can be charming but lacks ideas." And given the way the candidate's voice has largely disappeared from newscasts, audiences have little more to go on than charm.

Political conversations on television are not restricted to news and current affairs programming. In the United States, satirical news show hosts such as Bill Maher and John Oliver are significant influencers of public opinion, as is Fox News pundit Sean Hannity.

In 1963, NBC and CBS expanded their nightly news shows to thirty minutes. ABC followed suit. Not coincidentally, 1963 was also the first year that a majority of Americans said they relied on TV over newspapers as their primary news source.

TV news has its critics. Frank Lloyd Wright described TV news as "chewing gum for the eyes." Neil Postman (1985) reminded us TV's voice was the voice of entertainment.

Elly Alboim, a professor at Carleton University who enjoyed a long and distinguished career at CBC News, acknowledged that "our narrative form requires drama, conflict, the denouement" (pers. notes). As a consequence, politics on TV must consider entertainment codes. Michael Deaver, Ronald Reagan's deputy chief of staff, was a master of the art. Deaver was known in political circles as "the vicar of visuals."

In a TV-dominant era, a political communications strategist becomes a de facto "executive producer." Inspired by semioticians such as Christian Metz, these communications strategists must replicate Hollywood's multilayered sign system, integrating five channels of communication: image, written language, voice, music, sound effects.

Television and cinema are neighbouring sign systems. Any "message" is lost if contradicted by the visuals, which is why stagecraft is an important component part of news making. As a newly minted political staffer, I was on the receiving end of a tutorial on the importance of stagecraft by Brian Mulroney, then an opposition leader on his way to becoming prime minister.

In the spring of 1984, the Liberal Party was busy picking a successor to Pierre Trudeau. Not surprisingly, the national media was completely preoccupied with the Liberal leadership race. On any given night, stories featuring leadership contenders dominated the lineups of network newscasts. Given the relative lack of interest in the opposition parties and their leaders, Mulroney and his advisers decided the best use of his time was to hit the road – literally.

The "boonies tour," as it became affectionately known, saw Mulroney, his wife Mila, and a small support staff campaign extensively in smaller towns and cities from Castlegar, British Columbia, to Timmins, Ontario; from les Cantons-de-l'Est in Quebec to Shippagan in New Brunswick. The size of the halls, the height of the stage, the lighting, the discipline of those asked to introduce Mulroney were uneven to say the least. It was my job to see to it that each event met certain standards. And if it meant pissing off a local grandee or two, that was better than assuming the sound system provided by the bigwig's brother-in-law was adequate.

So, at each stop, as Mulroney put the finishing touches to his speech, I would meet with the then-volunteer advance team to ensure all was good to go. Over time a verbal shorthand evolved. As he'd get ready to leave his hotel room to stand stage left, waiting for the introduction to conclude, Mulroney would look at me and say, "Have you checked the podium?" I would answer, "Yes sir, the podium is fine." With that reassurance, Mulroney would head to the elevators on his way to centre stage.

One night in Winnipeg in the spring of 1984, emotions were running high. Mulroney was set to deliver one of the defining speeches of his leadership – a ringing defence of minority language rights. It was a message many Manitoba Conservatives who had packed the hall didn't want to hear, including at least one member of Mulroney's caucus. And so a larger than usual number of key fundraisers and local organizers were milling around the corridor outside Mulroney's hotel room determined to make certain the staff – and ultimately the leader – knew what a political mistake Mulroney was about to make.

As I listened to the emotional, even angry representations, and came to understand someone was going to have to hear these folks out however long that took, I asked my friend and colleague Bill Pristanski – then Mulroney's "body man" – if he would go down and check the hall.

Finally, the corridor was cleared of hangers-on. It was showtime. As we started to head toward the elevator, Mulroney looked over and asked, "Have you checked the podium?" "Pristanski says it is fine," I replied. Mulroney stopped dead in his tracks, looked me right in the eye, and said, "That wasn't my question."

Chagrined, I asked the Mulroneys to hold and give me a few minutes, and I bolted down the corridor, took the elevator being held for the leader, and went down to do my job. Back minutes later, I reported everything was fine; we headed to the hall, and Mulroney went on to deliver one of the most powerful and defining speeches of his political career.

Mulroney had every confidence in Pristanski – a friend of long standing – whom the former prime minister continues to work with to this day. In fact, Bill would subsequently be named director of tour and scheduling in the PMO with a job jar that included "checking the podium." But Mulroney was making a broader point about stagecraft. If the venue, crowd, and visuals on a political tour are ever changing, the person charged with ensuring they meet the "stagecraft" test cannot.

One set of eyes. One definition of minimal standards. One "executive producer."

There is a price paid when a political leader and his or her advisers get the stagecraft wrong. The Conservative campaign's decision in 1988 to construct a "boy in the bubble" tour for Mulroney was counterproductive, for example. By severely restricting access to the Conservative leader, the Tory campaign strategists were inadvertently signalling that their leader needed to be protected against vocal critics of the Canada-US free trade proposal at the heart of Mulroney's campaigning. The campaign strategists were following the tried and true tour axiom neatly summarized by the old Holiday Inn slogan: no surprises. Yet what voters were seeing was a visual that suggested the people who knew Mulroney best – his political advisers – didn't trust him to defend the key plank of his electoral platform against all comers. Both Mulroney and his media adviser Marc Lortie – a career diplomat – knew this "bubble" was a mistake. Tour director John Tory, who would go on to be elected and re-elected as Toronto's mayor, heeded Mulroney's advice, ignored instructions from headquarters, and invited network cameras to film an impromptu debate in Victoria between Mulroney and anti-free trade activists that was, with hindsight, a defining moment of the campaign.

Another reason political operatives ascribe value to stagecraft is that when a political leader makes a public appearance, the eyes of the world are literally upon them, a lesson brought home to me most effectively by Larry Speakes, deputy press secretary to US president Ronald Reagan.

In the spring of 1986, an advance team preparing for a prime ministerial visit to Washington, DC, weeks later was gathered in Speakes's office to review details on the White House welcome, to be held on the South Lawn. Speakes, aware I had spent time as a White House correspondent for the *Toronto Star*, knew I was familiar with the pomp and circumstance that would be part of Reagan's welcome for Mulroney. Ever the gracious host, Speakes took a few minutes to remind us of the highlights: a marine colour guard, a military marching band, national anthems as the respective delegations stood at attention, assembled on the lawn – television visuals to die for.

As Speakes spoke, one image summoned from a memory of White House welcomes past surfaced.

When it was the turn of others to carry the briefing forward, I asked Speakes in a whispered exchange if we could have a private discussion once the meeting broke up. He quickly agreed. Once the other attendees had left his office, I asked my counterpart if the Rose Garden welcome still involved the two leaders standing on a small riser overlooking the assembly. Speakes quickly confirmed this was indeed the protocol. I quietly explained that was a problem for me. Prime Minister Mulroney suffered from a chronic inner ear issue that triggered bouts of vertigo if he found himself on a riser or platform above a certain height. PMO stagecraft, as a matter of operating procedure, ensured the riser or platform was never more than six to eight inches high. As staffers, we also usually insisted that Mila Mulroney stand next to her husband. The protocol types bristled at this, their irritation exacerbated because an explanation for why we were so insistent was never forthcoming. We had our own view of what constituted "need to know." But Speakes clearly needed to know. So I told him that if we went with the six-foot riser, my guy was likely to end up head-first in the tuba as the military band marched past.

As we considered options, I asked if we could simply place a chair or two on the riser. That way, if the prime minister needed to, he could steady himself on the chair back. Speakes said we could do that. But he'd have to leak the fact the chair was for Mulroney. Startled, I asked why. Speakes explained that foreign powers, particularly the then-Soviet Union, had intelligence units dedicated to a frame-by-frame analysis of the US president, literally searching for any signs of weakness or a change in health. Particularly after John Hinckley's assassination attempt in 1981, Reagan's handlers were determined there would be no images of the president that would suggest he was in anything but robust good health. And while I understood completely, I wasn't looking forward to going back to Ottawa and telling the prime minister our stagecraft secret would soon be public.

In the briefing that followed on my return to Ottawa, Mulroney responded with his usual good humour and this instruction: If you have to leak it, make sure you leak it to someone interesting. ABC White House correspondent Sam Donaldson fit the bill perfectly.

More recently, Prime Minister Justin Trudeau's decision to visit Carleton University's student newspaper office in May 2019 was sound. The advance person's decision to sit him down under a bright yellow wall painted with the paper's title – the *Charlatan* – less so.

If getting the stagecraft wrong extracted a political price in the television age, it continues to do so in the 24-7 media age – Justin Trudeau's ill-fated trip to India in February 2018 being a prime example. Visuals from the trip continue to circulate on social media to this day. Trudeau and his entire family wore traditional Indian clothes. The Indian officials didn't. The visuals had a Griswolds'*National Lampoon's Vacation* feel to them.

Media coverage in general, and television coverage in particular, helps set the political agenda, determining what problems a political leader must take up and what problems he or she can safely ignore. And the lineup for a television newscast is influenced in no small measure by the stories featured prominently in daily newspapers. If television news shapes a political agenda, historically, newspapers shape television's agenda.

The Syrian refugee crisis of 2015 is but one example. The iconic photograph of the lifeless body of three-year-old Alan Kurdi lying on a beach in Bodrum, Turkey, after his family's failed attempt to flee the ravages of war in an overcrowded lifeboat trying to cross the Mediterranean put the plight of the displaced and dispossessed on the political agenda. The fact the boy had family in Canada placed it higher on the Canadian political agenda.

The public picks up on the problems the media identify as important; issue salience for the media does lead to issue salience for the public.

Politics of the air more readily becomes an active experience for the viewer/listener than politics in the newspaper does for the reader. Yet ironically, television is a primary information source that does not generate as much original information in the form of civic journalism as newspapers.

TV news privileges holders of power and therefore becomes a powerful force for conservative hegemony (Kellner 2018). However, TV's power is arguably on the wane. The nightly newscast is largely obsolete, as is appointment television. After CBC anchorman Peter Mansbridge retired in 2017, audiences for the network's relaunched *The National* nightly news broadcast are noticeably smaller than they were in Mansbridge's era.

Ken Auletta (2014) points out that the audience for broadcast networks is only one-third of what it was in the late 1970s, lost to a proliferating array of viewing options. PVRs allow people to skip the ads, leading advertisers to conclude television airtime for all but "live" events isn't worth what it once was.

Information channels have at once proliferated and become more individualized. News and current affairs programming can be accessed or ignored on multiple platforms. As audiences become subsets, opinion reinforcement is a more likely outcome.

But TV still holds significant power; all-candidates debates for the 2015 federal elections in Canada and the 2016 primary and presidential campaigns in the United States still attracted large and meaningful audiences.

Television gave us the phenomenon of the "double dose," which occurs when what we see on the TV screen aligns with the social reality we have constructed.

Media scholars have identified how television contributes to the cultivation of common perspectives. Television viewing leads to a more homogeneous view of the world, regardless of individual starting points. That truth may, in fact, be the most critical consequence of living with television.

Television's dominance as a news venue of choice for the better part of four decades is a factor in the exercise of political power. In a TV-centric universe, the leader of the government is the dominant news makers in any democracy. This fact represents a particular challenge in Canada, a constitutional monarchy with a system of "responsible government."

Where both the critical and the administrative schools of communication theory come together however is on the core question for political managers: Does media coverage matter? The answer – from both camps – is an emphatic yes.

For the administrative school, as stated earlier in this work, media coverage matters not so much because the media tells you what to think but more precisely because the media tells you what to think about (Cohen, b.c. 1963, 13). And in telling you what to think about, the media is nudging you along the road toward what to think (Entman 1989).

The critical school argues media matters because of what it ensures you *don't* think about (Gitlin 1980). The gatekeeper function is key for both schools of thought. For the administrative school, the gatekeeper function rests with the journalist; for the critical school, the gatekeeper function rests with those who control the process of production, that is, the owner.

But in today's social media world, that control of the gatekeeper function has evolved further still and now rests largely in the hands of those who control distribution, and it is less completely in the hands of "news professionals." Algorithms are now an integral part of the gatekeeper mix. And as a consequence, there are real questions about the implications of the new axis of media, politics, and public policy about our ability to govern ourselves. The 2016 presidential campaign demonstrates the consequences of population pools with markedly different information bases, sets of expectations, standards of government performance, and markedly different political agendas.

The "Power" of News

One of the more compelling subtexts of the 2016 presidential campaign in the context of the power of media coverage was the dramatic – if questionable – intervention of former FBI director James Comey as the campaign entered its final days.

For poll aggregator Nate Silver, an analysis of the data leads to one inescapable conclusion: Comey cost Democratic Party nominee Hillary Clinton the presidency. The creator of FiveThirtyEight. com says a letter from Comey to Republican congressional leaders "announcing that the FBI had 'learned of the existence of emails that appear to be pertinent to the investigation' into the private email server that Clinton used as secretary of state" sent eleven days before voting day shifted public opinion. Silver's analysis suggests late-deciding voters broke strongly against Clinton in swing states, enough to cost the former secretary of state narrow victories in Michigan, Wisconsin, and Pennsylvania. "I'll put it like this," Silver tweeted: "Clinton would almost certainly be President-elect if the election had been held Oct. 27" (Silver 2016a).

Clinton, for her part, shares Silver's view and explains why in some detail in her bestseller *What Happened*.

The backstory behind Silver's assertion will be the subject of post-election analysis and will feed conspiracy theorists for years. Clinton's email practices as secretary of state had been the subject of an extensive investigation by the FBI, focused on potential breaches of national security. In July 2016, after Clinton had secured her party's nomination, Comey announced he would not recommend any prosecution of the one-time senator from New York and former first lady. The FBI director concluded Clinton's handling of classified information did not constitute a crime. In an unusual and arguably unacceptable "editorial" comment by a law enforcement officer, Comey stated Clinton had been "extremely careless" in the way she blended email accounts on personal and government electronic devices and servers but said "no reasonable prosecutor" could bring a case against her.

Comey's conclusion did not sit well with Republicans who summoned him to several Capitol Hill hearings where he was subjected to intense interrogation.

On the hustings, Clinton's cavalier attitude toward which email accounts were used in communicating to her the business of the American state became a key component of Republican nominee Donald Trump's stump speech, along with that infamous "Lock her up" chant.

The attack against Clinton played out against a broader narrative about the Clintons' collective casual approach to the truth – a concern rooted in former president Bill Clinton's public assertions about the nature of his relationship with then-White House intern Monica Lewinsky and Hillary Clinton's personal attacks against the women who had identified her husband as a serial philanderer.

News analysts concluded the email controversy was largely "baked in" to the electoral equation. Those already convinced Hillary Clinton was being evasive at best needed no further proof. Those who considered the issue a tempest in a teacup seized on the "no criminal charges warranted" conclusion for comfort.

Then, with eleven days to go before the 8 November 2016 election day, Comey upset the electoral apple cart. That letter to congressional Republicans was in regard to an unrelated case (Toobin 2016). A series of leaks from within the FBI confirmed that the investigation Comey referenced was a probe into the "sexting" practices of former congressman Anthony Weiner, the estranged husband of key Clinton adviser Huma Abedin and one of the most loathsome figures in contemporary American politics (his political career imploded because of earlier sexting).

Comey admitted in an email he sent to FBI agents that the bureau does not ordinarily tell Congress about ongoing investigations. Indeed, in sending the letter, Comey violated a long-standing Justice Department rule. There are those who argue Comey's hand was forced, that he did it to avoid a bigger scandal by the story being leaked to the Trump campaign by the Republican-dominated US attorney's office in New York that was leading the Weiner investigation.

Subsequent news accounts established the FBI had nothing to back up its decision as there was no new evidence against Clinton. In fact, at the time Comey sent the letter to the congressional Republicans, the bureau didn't even have the necessary warrant to open the emails in question.

In a textbook illustration of the "cover your ass" instincts so prevalent in government towns, Comey sent out another letter – thirty-six hours before voting day – reconfirming what he had said in July: that no criminal charges against Clinton were warranted. But by then the electoral price had been exacted. Silver states categorically that Comey "had a large, measurable impact on the case" (Silver 2016b). Silver also argues the legacy media must accept some responsibility for the outcome as well. "The story dominated news coverage for the better part of a week, drowning out other headlines, whether they were negative for Clinton (such as the news about impending Obamacare premium hikes) or problematic for Trump (such as his alleged ties to Russia). And yet the story didn't have a punchline: Two days before the election, Comey disclosed that the emails hadn't turned up anything new" (Silver 2017).

In analyzing media effects, it is helpful to remind oneself that the test is not a conversion as dramatic as the biblical account of Saul on the road to Damascus. Trump was elected the forty-fifth president of the United States despite losing the popular vote by almost three million ballots. He did so by winning three key states and their electoral college electors – the aforementioned Michigan, Wisconsin, and Pennsylvania – by a combined total of 77,000 votes.

In the ongoing debate among media theorists about the impact media coverage can have on public opinion, Neuman and Guggenheim (2011) assert small shifts can have a meaningful impact. And according to Silver's analysis, Comey's letter triggered just such a shift.

For Canadians, there is an element of déjà vu to the Clinton-Comey saga, although in the Canadian case, the police were following the money, not the emails.

In the 2005–06 federal campaign, the RCMP intruded into Canada's electoral process, with a not dissimilar result.

On 23 November 2005, after financial markets closed, then-Liberal finance minister Ralph Goodale made an announcement about income trusts – an announcement viewed on Bay Street as good news for the sector. The news was less good for Paul Martin's government. The fact that the value of units in income trusts surged following Goodale's announcement was hardly news. The fact that trading in income trusts had surged in the hours before the announcement was.

Former Conservative cabinet minister Monte Solberg, then an opposition MP, said rumours of a leak were circulating in the corridors of power in Ottawa. "The markets had started to go a little bizarre and there was quite a bit of commentary in the media about it," Solberg said in an interview (pers. notes 2012). "The business guys picked up on it right away … people suspected that there was a leak somewhere in the Department of Finance because they were the only ones who would know" (ibid.).

The NDP was equally suspicious. "A series of unusual trades" convinced Brian Topp, then the party's national campaign director, "that players on Bay Street had foreknowledge of the finance minister's announcement" (Topp 2010, 87).

The RCMP commissioner, however, was to fundamentally alter the equation by changing the dominant news frame around the income trust saga from "leak" to "scandal."

On 23 December 2005, RCMP Commissioner Giuliano Zaccardelli wrote New Democrat Judy Wasylycia-Leis a three-sentence letter responding to a question from the NDP finance critic. In his letter, the commissioner confirmed the RCMP's "review of the matter has been completed" and stated that the RCMP "will be commencing a criminal investigation" (Sallot 2006, A8).

Zaccardelli had faxed his letter. And when the Mounties didn't hear back from the NDP for a few days, concerns arose that NDP staff might not be in the office over the holiday season. The RCMP then reached out to ensure NDP staffers were aware the fax had been sent (pers. notes 2012).

Zaccardelli's letter, arising as it did in the middle of the election campaign, was a gift for the media and opposition parties alike. Solberg agrees the RCMP confirmation that a criminal investigation had been launched "was really unusual ... the Liberals were furious" (ibid.). The RCMP announcement constituted "a major new development ... a scandal," said Ian Brodie, a former chief of staff to Conservative Prime Minister Stephen Harper. "And in the middle of the campaign, which I don't think anybody in a million years would have predicted" (ibid.).

The RCMP, in turn, issued a press release confirming the letter's contents, making it clear the federal force would investigate whether there was a leak that allowed insiders to make unfair profits in market trading because of insider information. Incredibly, the RCMP press release also stated explicitly that there was "no evidence of wrongdoing or illegal activity" by Goodale and further stated the finance minister was not the target of the probe (Globe and Mail 2005, A14). While I have the highest personal regard for Goodale – who would later go on to serve as Canada's High Commissioner to the United Kingdom – how the national police force could arrive at such a conclusion before the criminal investigation was completed was an unavoidable question.

The RCMP decision, not surprisingly, was the subject of editorial comment and scrutiny. Former *Globe and Mail* columnist Jeffrey Simpson, for example, wrote, "You don't have to be a shill for the Liberals to ask what the heck the Mounties thought they were doing in announcing a criminal investigation during an election campaign" (Simpson 2006, A15). The Mounties did offer a "damned if you do, damned if you don't" defence. The propriety of the RCMP's decision to go public about the criminal investigation they had launched was debatable. The media assessments of the impact of the intrusion into the federal campaign were decidedly one-sided.

The context, of course, was the continuing fallout from the Quebec-focused sponsorship scandal that had plagued the last years of the Chrétien government. Martin's advisers had worked to build a firewall between the former prime minister and the daily revelations from the sponsorship scandal commission of inquiry headed by Justice John Gomery, who issued his last report months before the election began.

The RCMP announcement jumped the firewall. As then-CBC commentator Rex Murphy noted, "Post-Gomery, any RCMP investigation that involved the Liberals as a party of government was going to be big news. But such an announcement in the absolute still centre of a tight election was bound to be a political trumpet blast … It had seismic resonance," Murphy concluded (2006, A23).

When word got around that the RCMP had decided to pursue a criminal investigation, it came as a surprise even to the people who had asked for it. "We weren't expecting a response from the RCMP at any point because normally, they don't disclose whether or not they are pursuing a criminal investigation," said Brad Lavigne, a veteran NDP staffer who served as director of communications for the campaign team (pers. notes 2012).

Liberal campaign strategist David Herle summarizes his reaction to the announcement in a single word: "horror" (ibid.). Because the Liberal campaign had decided to slow down nightly tracking over Christmas, Herle had no objective measure to help him assess how damaging the news might be to Martin's campaign. When the Liberal leader called Herle at his cottage as the news broke, Herle tried to buck up Martin's spirits, but Martin wasn't buying. "He said to me, 'Oh fuck, David, this is really bad! We're in trouble,'" Herle recalled (ibid.).

Herle says as far as he is concerned, there is no question the news of the criminal investigation was the turning point of the campaign. "Is there any question that that was the turning point?

None whatsoever. And was I absolutely convinced we were going to win the election until that day? Yes, I was ... But it wouldn't have had that impact had sponsorship never happened" (ibid.).

Elly Alboim, a long-time political journalist and professor at Carleton University and a principal at Earnscliffe, says categorically that "it [the election] turned on that single event [the RCMP investigation]." "The game had been lost with that single announcement," Alboim, a key adviser to Martin, said in an interview (ibid.). "It didn't take ten minutes for all of us to be in touch with each other ... for the consensus to emerge" (ibid.). A former CBC Ottawa bureau chief, Alboim says he was "horrified and angered" at the RCMP decision. "My absolute and immediate thought was that it was deliberate and conscious" (ibid.).

Solberg and other Conservatives are more inclined to see the RCMP investigation as the proverbial last straw, a factor in the election outcome but not necessarily the factor in the result. Ian Brodie agrees the income trust issue's salience in the campaign shifted when the dominant news frame became one of "criminal investigation" or "scandal" instead of "leak." "I think that's fair," he said. "Something broke" (ibid.). Says Brodie, "It's nice because everyone here can have an opinion and we don't have enough data to tell but yeah, I think it was ... it was a heavy piece. I don't think it was the only piece, but I think it was a heavy piece" (ibid.).

My friend and former colleague Darrell Bricker takes strong exception to any analysis that suggests the income trust investigation impacted the election outcome.

The president and CEO of Ipsos Public Affairs worldwide, Bricker responded on Twitter in support of a post from former Harper adviser Ken Boessenkool who argued the rise in Conservative fortunes in the 2005–06 federal elected predated the RCMP election (Boessenkool 2019). "It's tedious how these lazy stories become accepted history," Bricker observed. "The Goodale issue did not decide the election. Gun crime moved the 905 [905 is the area code for the ridings that ring Toronto]. Law and Order carried the day" (Bricker 2019c).

This writer is one of the people who developed the "story" Bricker is dismissing as "tedious." And having spent hours analyzing literally hundreds of news stories from a cross-section of Canadian media outlets that dealt with the income trust affair and analyzing overnight polling data from reputable public opinion research firms, as well as conducting multiple interviews with campaign strategists from three federal parties who were central to the story, I bristle at Bricker's use of the word "lazy" to describe the work.

Bricker's sweeping assertion ignores Elisabeth Noelle-Neumann's (1974) research on the impact of consonance and cumulation on public opinion.

There is a legitimate debate as to whether the income trust scandal was "a" or "the" factor in the 2005–06 federal campaign. But to suggest it was of no account or consequence is a stretch.

The bottom line is that party strategists for the Conservatives, the Liberals, and the New Democrats all agree the income trust issue was a factor in moving public opinion in the course of the federal campaign, but all equally agree the impact only occurred after the dominant news frame on the story changed from "leak" to "scandal."

The power of the penny or tabloid press warrants particular consideration in any discussion of media effects. In a discussion with CBC's *The Fifth Estate* cohost Gillian Findlay, investigative reporter Nick Davies of the *Guardian* likened the power of tabloids "to the power of the playground bully" (Canadian Journalism Foundation 2015). "The power of the tabloids derives from fear," Davies explained (ibid.). People perceive tabloids as a threat to "their private lives, particularly their sex lives" (ibid.). This "fear" took an interesting twist in the case of candidate Trump, who asked his friend, the *National Enquirer*'s David Pecker, to pay hush money to a former Playboy bunny to keep Trump's sex life out of the tabloids.

Celebrity Politics and Media Capital

The "symbolic" arena is important in politics.

In early 2016, Mr Trudeau went to Washington – Prime Minister Justin Trudeau, that is. Everyone, including Trudeau's political opponents, conceded the photo ops were fabulous. The South

Lawn of the White House. Then-president Barack Obama and his secretary of state John Kerry heralding the prime minister's leadership on issues as varied as climate change and international security. There was a celebrity-studded White House dinner, selfies all round.

Expectations around more contentious issues such as the ongoing softwood lumber dispute were carefully managed, handled with exceptional skill by Canada's then-ambassador to Washington, David MacNaughton.

The Canadian press corps was hanging off every word, the headlines qualified as a hallelujah chorus. Experienced Washington hands suggested Canada's interests might have been better served had the prime minister spent a little less time with Hollywood A-listers and a little more time with congressional leaders. And when the government Challenger jet took off from Andrews Air Force Base for the return flight to Ottawa, interim Conservative Leader Rona Ambrose suggested there wasn't much substantive work being done behind the photo ops. Published work by media scholars such as Aeron Davis would give Ambrose only part marks for her analysis because of the inherent value in leaders' summits as a means of engaging bureaucracies.

Trudeau's visit to Washington showcased the phenomenon of celebrity politics and media capital.

Author Tim Wu makes a compelling argument that the military-industrial complex of president Dwight D. Eisenhower's America has given way to the "celebrity industrial complex" of today. Actor George Clooney's causes are deemed of interest because of his attractiveness on small and big screens. Presidential nominee Donald Trump trotted out Todd Rundgren to (try to) counter Bruce Springsteen's support for Hillary Clinton. As measured by album sales, the comparison is decidedly one-sided in favour of the Boss. In a red state/blue state breakdown, less so. There is an irony in that Springsteen's music over forty-plus years has given voice to the very people Hillary Clinton stood accused of losing touch with in 2016.

Davis, a professor of political communication at Goldsmiths, University of London, examines the symbolic and cultural forms of communication between politicians and their publics.

The celebrity politician is hardly a new phenomenon – the late Sonny Bono, the homely half of the 1960s pop duo Sonny & Cher, being but one example. Bono capitalized on his fame to launch a political career and was elected to Congress in California. And their celebrity isn't necessarily linked to their likeability. Vladimir Putin, Silvio Berlusconi, Nicolas Sarkozy, and, of course, Donald Trump would qualify as celebrity politicians, yet each alienates large numbers of electors in their respective countries. The fact that Trump lost the popular vote in the 2016 election to Hillary Clinton by almost three million votes irks him no end and will always be an "inconvenient truth" for the Republican. But Trump and the others use their celebrity to acquire political capital, drawn from "several audiences," a fact that seems to escape pundits looking for a single, simple explanation for Trump's electoral triumph.

A key to understanding this phenomenon is to appreciate the fact the news media and reporters are primary conduits for this accrual.

Media scholars identify two types of media capital: institutional media capital, which is usually associated with the position held, and individual media capital, which is self-evidently personal in nature and linked to the political figure's charisma.

Institutional media capital is the most straightforward in terms of accumulation. Her Majesty Queen Elizabeth II has serious institutional media capital (Bourdieu 1991 as cited in Davis and Seymour 2010). As does whoever is the president of the United States.

When a Washington-based reporter for the *Toronto Star*, I found myself sitting on a small charter jet with Democratic nominee Walter Mondale, who was heading to St. Louis, Missouri, for a private fundraiser in 1984. During the flight, I asked what it was like to campaign against an incumbent president, namely Ronald Reagan.

A Mondale strategist smiled and said the following: Imagine a bright sunny day. A huge crowd has assembled out on the tarmac at a local airport. There is a small speck in the sky, a long distance away. As it gets closer to the airport, the speck gets bigger, and in time, the crowd realizes it is Air Force One – the president's plane. The plane lands, taxis toward the crowd, then comes to a halt. The door is opened, revealing the presidential seal. A marine honour guard snaps to attention, a military band strikes up "Hail to the Chief." The president steps out, smiles, and waves to the crowd. "How do you think he's doing so far?" The strategist quipped.

Individual media capital is harder to accrue. And it is the holy grail for political strategists; it is what political organizations or parties are looking for when they select leaders and spokespeople. Washington reporters may have sniggered when the Trump transition team let it be known photogeneity would be a factor in considering candidates for White House spokesperson positions, but in fact it was a consideration for all positions in the Trump administration, including cabinet posts.

The 2016 funeral for former first lady Nancy Reagan triggered this personal observation. Before he was elected president in 1980, the chattering classes had long tended to dismiss Ronald Reagan as a B-list actor, thereby missing the point entirely. While Reagan's abilities as a film actor probably didn't add to Sir Laurence Olivier's anxieties, Reagan's regular appearances on television put him directly into the living rooms of millions of Americans as television was establishing itself as our information and entertainment medium of choice.

That was the basis of Reagan's connection with his core constituency, a phenomenon Donald Horton and Richard Wohl (Horton and Wohl 1956) described as a "parasocial" relationship. The viewer assumes a personal relationship with the television personality, even though they have never met. Stand next to former CBC anchor Peter Mansbridge at a luggage carousel and watch the number of people who feel perfectly free to engage him in a personal conversation. And people who have never met the network's Rosemary Barton greet her with the familiar "Hi Rosie!"

And that's the point too many pundits miss, in the same way the Republican establishment missed Trump. The forty-fifth president

of the United States was created by network television. His show –
The Apprentice – appeared on NBC for years. Trump was positioned
as the celebrity you love to hate. *The Apprentice* filled a hole in NBC's
Thursday night lineup at a time when the iconic comedies *Friends*
and *Frasier* were ending their runs.

So who watches appointment TV on legacy networks anymore,
you ask? The people who grew up on TV, who are now disproportionately aging, low-income, disenchanted, disillusioned. People
who live in "fly-over" states. People who voted Trump.

There are two ways to accumulate this media capital. The first,
journalist-based social capital, is relationship based. Read any
story that states "sources say," for example; the "sources" are
building up their accounts. The second type of media cultural
capital flows from an understanding of how news production
works and journalists operate. Trump as candidate displayed a
mastery of the latter.

Individual media capital can reflect a mismatch between perceived and actual power.

Prime Minister Justin Trudeau generated significant political
capital during his 2016 visit to Washington; his host, president
Obama, whose term of office was running down, not so much.

Rona Ambrose's characterization of the Washington visit as
being all about pomp and circumstance is certainly an accurate
analysis of the news coverage. But that is the nature of news, something Trump understood much better than Hillary Clinton did, her
long stint in politics notwithstanding.

To be fair, it is hard for reporters to cover a policy or program
initiative that is still in the conceptual stage.

The Shamrock Summit held in Quebec City in March 1985,
when Prime Minister Brian Mulroney hosted US president
Ronald Reagan, is a case in point. The summit's most significant outcome was a decision to embark on negotiations for a
comprehensive trade agreement between Canada and the US.
Proponents and opponents alike agree the subsequent agreement fundamentally shaped the Canadian economy for a

generation. Yet the shiny object many reporters present were chasing that day was a sidebar issue about US fighter jets operating in the Arctic. And the visual coverage was determined when Mulroney and Reagan (both of Irish background) went onstage for the finale of a nationally televised gala on St. Patrick's Day to sing the last lines of "When Irish Eyes Are Smiling."

Figuring out what is going to attract a presidential or prime ministerial eye is as much art as science.

Former US president Lyndon Johnson had a straightforward approach to accruing political capital in his home state – he had heads of government and heads of state come to Texas to visit him at his ranch. Canada's Lester B. Pearson was one such visitor. And Pearson caught Johnson's eye when he arrived in a Department of Transportation JetStar – one of the world's first corporate jets. This showpiece of technology fascinated Johnson, who ordered one for himself. Whatever was discussed during the visit, Pearson's foray clearly got the president's attention.

Once politicians have accrued the individual political capital, their success or failure is largely determined by what they do with it. Johnson, for example, inherited political capital as a direct result of the tragedy of the assassination of John F. Kennedy in Johnson's home state of Texas. And Johnson decided to use that political capital for transformative initiatives – the Civil Rights Act and the Voting Rights Act.

Media strategists over the last fifty years have talked about the centrality of television in political communication. Johnson understood the role of media in terms of what he was looking to accomplish as president. Communications adviser Bill Moyers's desk occupied a corner of Johnson's private office at the LBJ ranch.

Wu's work *The Attention Merchants* provides an excellent synopsis of what he calls "the epic scramble to get inside our heads."

Building on the theories of crowd psychology first articulated by Gustave Le Bon, British propagandists are credited with pioneering work during the First World War: developing propaganda as an element of the concept of total war. In the US, individuals such as George Creel soon followed suit.

Walter Lippmann's experience working with Creel was formative in his seminal work *Public Opinion*, published in 1922, in which Lippmann first gave voice to the notion of "manufactured consent" (Lippmann 1922). Lippmann challenged the central dogma of democracy, that the "knowledge needed for the management of human affairs comes up spontaneously from the human heart" (Wu, T. 2016, 47). A cynic for some, a realist to others, Lippmann nonetheless helps us understand a core practice of political communication in the context of the exercise of power – the use of metaphor by political leaders to make the complexities of modern society more accessible to citizens who have less time to parse the particulars of policy proposals.

What is different about Trump – who is decidedly of the metaphor world – is that there is ample evidence he does not get the complexity of the issues he seeks to speak to.

But that's getting ahead of the story.

The world of Creel and Lippmann, Edward Bernays and Claude Hopkins, pioneers in the field of public relations and advertising, was a world of relatively few media sources and, therefore, relatively few gatekeepers.

The internet changed all that.

Bill Gates's assertion that "content is king" emerged as a core truth; what changed is the number of actors who could create that content and the relatively small number of actors distributing that content. As Clay Shirky, who specializes in the social and economic effects of internet technologies and journalism, notes, "Social tools remove older obstacles to public expression, and thus remove the bottlenecks that characterized mass media. The result is the mass amateurization of efforts previously reserved for media professionals" (ibid., 269).

Social media platforms such as Facebook became information sources of choice. In the 2019 Canadian federal election, candidates from all parties were being held to account for social media postings dating back years.

Google's influence became so pervasive, the verb form has replaced "research" in everyday discourse. And Twitter provided everyone with a personal podium – albeit, one limited to 280 characters, not including image. A Facebook page and Twitter account were enough to establish a personal brand, even if that brand's appeal was relatively limited.

Clicks became the new measure of success; clickbait, an inevitable consequence.

The social media platforms also changed the relationship between the information consumer and the advertisers hoping to reach them. Advertising was essentially a one-way experience in legacy media, though tailored, to be sure. At one point, before General Motors decided to make over the car entirely for a new demographic, Cadillac spent its advertising budget on what was then known as the "seniors' tour" rather than the main tour, round bellies being more inclined to purchase traditional Cadillac products.

What the Googles of the world started to do was to mine the data of your searches, then sell your declared interest to potential advertisers. Where the traditional media once sold eyeballs, with no guarantees to the advertiser that those eyeballs would linger on the paid message, social media platforms parlayed a self-declared interest into more targeted messages. Political communicators were quick to seize on the potential of that shift in the attention market.

Former Canadian television personality Mike Duffy likely owes his appointment to the Senate to his celebrity status. Yet the controversy over his expense claims became a national news story for the same reason.

As Daniel Boorstin observed in *The Image* (1962), celebrities invariably present an "image" to us: it is synthetic, planned, and created to serve a purpose, to make a certain kind of impression. The image must be believable, or it serves no purpose; it must not violate rules of ordinary common sense; it must be current and not aspirational; it must be vivid, concrete, and simplified. Boorstin says it must not offend but can be ambiguous, in his words, floating somewhere between the imagination and the senses.

Donald Trump parlayed an image as a successful businessperson into the presidency, the evidence of the true extent of his business acumen notwithstanding.

But in fairness to the general public, a major US television network – NBC – spent tens of millions of dollars in publicity over more than a decade to convince Americans that Trump *was* a successful business tycoon, the better to sell his reality television show.

If Trump's presidential perch is built on celebrity, then for some, the best way to knock him off that perch is to counter with a bigger celebrity: I'll see your Trump and raise you an Oprah Winfrey.

Internet strategist Jesse Hirsh said in a discussion of the impact of social media on political discourse that narcissism is now the skill set required for leadership, "all self, all the time." And lest Canadians see themselves as immune, consider the fact newly minted New Democratic Party Leader Jagmeet Singh invited the Canadian Press and *Toronto Life* to cover his marriage proposal to his girlfriend (Wherry 2018).

The premium, in this worldview, lies in the ability to get attention. The problems arise once you get the job: just ask former Canadian heritage minister Mélanie Joly, who was deemed not ready for prime time and shuffled to a less demanding cabinet job.

Boorstin suggests there is a cautionary tale from celebrities of all types. Their fate, Boorstin says, is preordained; he or she will be destroyed as he or she was made – by publicity. British journalist Tim Shipman, author of *All Out War*, a riveting account of Britain's Brexit referendum campaign, states, "Behavioural psychologists teach us to infer motive from behaviour, not the other way around" (Shipman 2016, 217). As the author James Lee Burke once opined in his bestselling thriller *Robicheaux*, "People are what they do, not what they think, not what they say" (Burke 2018).

Hand-wringing around the impact of social media underestimates the extent of the social change required for any meaningful reform. An article entitled "Social Media and Politics" carried in *The Economist* begins with the assertion "Facebook, Google and Twitter were supposed to improve politics" but concludes, "Something has gone very wrong ... Far from bringing enlightenment, social media have been spreading poison" (Economist 2017d, 11). The article concedes that German philosopher Jürgen Habermas warned social media would erode the public sphere in democracies, and further acknowledges social media "does not cause division so much as amplify it." The article also quotes James Williams, a doctoral student at Oxford and former Google employee, to the effect "digital technologies increasingly inhibit our ability to pursue any politics worth having" (ibid.). But the observation that leaps off the page is Williams's assertion that to save democracy, "we need to reform our attention economy." Tim Wu, come on down.

Having spent my entire professional life in the triangle of press-politics-public-policy, media effects is a natural interest, as is the strategic communications function that is an integral component of public discourse and the exercise of political power.

The issue that bedevilled academic research into media effects, identified by British professor Kenneth Newton (Newton 1999) among others, is the difficulty in isolating the variables, which, in a campaign context involved advertising, party leaders' tours, televised debates, local candidates, and geopolitical factors, as varied as the state of the world economy and, the COVID-19 pandemic.

Eventually, the limited-effects view gave way to a more nuanced perspective that argued the media could, in fact, have quite strong effects but only on certain people and in certain circumstances (McCombs and Shaw 1972). This work underscored a critically important point: there is science as well as art to strategic communications and you ignore the science at your peril. It is hardly a surprise that my worldview includes a belief in media effects. As social psychologist Angus Campbell et al. (1960) observed, important shifts in public attitudes occur between election campaigns, and most beliefs that come to affect political behaviour are probably developed by way of a communication process that is dominated by social and mass media. They also made an observation that underscores the notion of effect. Mismanagement or corruption are not political issues that are easily kept alive after a change in government, a point that is lost on many new governments. The electorate, bluntly put, believes it did its job when they threw the bums out. Now they'd like the new government to get on with its job. As a result, defences of current practices that include references to sins of the past do not resonate with voters.

As societies grow more complex and as the quality of media technology improves, the media continuously takes on more and more unique information functions (Ball-Rokeach and DeFleur 1976). Our dependency is heightened when a relatively high degree of change and conflict is present in a society; even more so when the media serves a central information function.

Earlier conventional wisdom about limited media effects was effectively challenged by Elisabeth Noelle-Neumann (1973), who asserted consonance and cumulation impacted media effects. Where consonance is highly developed in media coverage patterns, there will be a stronger influence on opinion formation because, among other things, the protective mechanism of selective perception is eliminated. Cumulative effects of media coverage is a further factor. It is no accident candidate Trump made repeated references to "Crooked Hillary," altered for the 2020 presidential campaign to asserting Democratic nominee Joe Biden was part of a "corrupt family."

The combination of consonance and cumulation can create a "spiral of silence" whereby individuals find it increasingly difficult to articulate another opinion without becoming isolated in their social circle. Canada's Senate expenses scandal is one example. With a few notable exceptions, support for senators such as Mike Duffy or Pamela Wallin, under media attack from their own caucus colleagues, tended to be expressed privately, if at all.

Because our reality is socially constructed, television makes specific and measurable contributions to viewers' conception of reality, and, therefore, television is a factor in the exercise of political power (Berger and Luckmann 1966).

Two-Step Flow and Power

The "two-step flow" theory of communications is considered by scholars as the dominant paradigm of mass communication (Gitlin 1980). First developed by Lazarsfeld et al. (1944) and developed further by Elihu Katz and Lazarsfeld (1955), the theory posits that mass media messages reach audiences in two phases, a fact with obvious implications in the world of the retweet. Lazarsfeld believed information from the media first reached opinion leaders with higher levels of engagement, who in turn passed on those messages to others with less developed media consumption habits – after the information had gone through the personal filters of those opinion leaders. In the era of the retweet, we may not have seen the interview with a political figure featured on a network newscast until the next day when a friend sent along the link, set up with a personal observation or two.

Opinion leaders identified by Lazarsfeld and his colleagues have certain characteristics (Rogers, E. 1962). They have greater exposure to mass media than their followers, are more cosmopolitan, have greater contact with change agents, have greater levels of social participation, have higher socioeconomic status, and are more innovative.

Lazarsfeld further believed social characteristics were more determinant when it comes to political preferences. In fairness to Lazarsfeld, he did post the idea in a footnote that television could result in a fundamental change to his equation. But in a social media world, where we are as likely to read news that is referred to us by a friend or peer, his two-step flow theory is worth revisiting. Lazarsfeld's two-step flow is operationalized by today's campaign strategists through Twitter and Facebook. A remarkable number of people today say they get their news "from Facebook." It might be more accurate to say "off Facebook" because, as Facebook is quick to assert, it is not a content creation company.

For critical theorists, there has been a significant concentration of power in this evolving social media age.

Speaking at a conference at Cambridge University, Emily Bell, founding director of the Tow Center for Digital Journalism, said news publishers have lost control over the distribution of their own product, their editorial content now filtered through algorithms and platforms that are at once opaque and unpredictable and, more significantly, beyond their control.

Bell (2016) offers a new definition of the Four Horsemen of the Apocalypse: Google, Facebook, Apple, and Amazon. "Our news ecosystem has changed more dramatically in the past five years than perhaps at any time in the past five hundred" (ibid.). Artificial intelligence bots are but one illustration. More than 40 per cent of adults in America consider Facebook a source of news. Said Bell, "social media hasn't just swallowed journalism, it has swallowed everything" (ibid.) – from political campaigns to banking systems.

Ed Herman and Noam Chomsky (1988) admonished that corporate media is not controlled by big business; it is big business. Mainstream media does not watch over the concentration of power; it is power.

Former Harvard University president Richard Neustadt (1960) argued, "The power of the presidency is the power of persuasion." Abraham Lincoln came to a similar conclusion a century earlier. "Public sentiment is everything," Lincoln said. "With public sentiment, nothing can fail. Without it, nothing can succeed" (Lincoln 1894).

Long-time presidential adviser David Gergen says the most memorable American presidents of the twentieth century "have been excellent communicators" (2000, 210). And with some advice president Trump might have been well-advised to heed, Gergen states, "A president's capacity to lead rests squarely upon a reputation for openness and candor" (ibid., 93). Truth, says Gergen, is the glue that holds governments, indeed civilization itself, together (ibid., 139). And he quotes Thomas Jefferson to the effect that "great initiatives cannot be built upon slender majorities" (ibid., 304). Not surprisingly, Gergen emerged as a forceful and articulate critic of President Trump.

6

News as a Signalling System for Elites: A Case Study

The Scoop

Media effects theory typically considers the power of the news in the context of its influence or impact on the multitudes: a traditional top-down, one-to-many model. Aeron Davis, a professor at Goldsmiths, University of London, suggests we also need to consider news as a signalling system for elites, a channel of negotiation as much as a channel for promulgation. And a takeover bid of an iconic Canadian corporation proves Davis's point that in some situations, news isn't about the masses at all.

The saga began with a leak and a mistake. The leak was fed to Canada's leading business news organization, the *Globe and Mail*'s Report on Business. The significance of the story resulted in editions that flared a headline across the front page of the paper on 29 March 2007 declaring, "U.S. Equity Firm Stalks BCE, Plots Takeover; Kohlberg Kravis Roberts Deal Worth at Least $24.3 Billion Would be Largest in Canadian Corporate History" (Reguly and Willis 2007, A1). Written by ROB reporter Eric Reguly and columnist Andrew Willis, it described New York-based KKR as "the world's most powerful private equity firm" and stated the company – which had gained a certain notoriety as the "barbarians at the gate" in the RJR Nabisco leveraged buyout in the late 1980s – was hoping to launch a "friendly takeover bid" (ibid.). The story stated KKR had met with BCE Inc. CEO Michael Sabia on two separate occasions; the most recent within two weeks of the Reguly-Willis story appearing.

"I got a tipoff that day from an investment banker," Reguly said to this writer in an interview (pers. notes 2012). "I remember phoning you on deadline ... you pissed me off royally. I think

I said, 'Bill, I really like my source on this one.' And you know my source. I'm not going to tell you who it is, but I think you know him very, very well." This writer, at the time, was executive vice-president corporate development and communications at Bell Canada Enterprises.

Reflecting back on the conversation, Reguly – now the *Globe*'s European correspondent – said, "I don't think you ever said it was untrue. But you left me with a lot of doubt."

Reguly said, after ending the conversation, "I thought, 'Just fuck it! I'm going with it.'" The telephone exchange "didn't put me off enough that I wasn't going to phone another source." He placed a call to a source within the Ontario Teachers' Pension Plan. "It was someone very senior at Teachers that confirmed it for me. That's why the story appeared the next day."

Reguly asked his colleague Andy Willis to work his contacts to seek further confirmation. "We needed a triple-check on a story this big," Reguly explained. "He [Willis] got a sort of comfort phone call from … someone who wasn't directly involved," Reguly added.

Reguly said he decided at one point to tell *Globe* publisher Phillip Crawley about the story he was working on, "more as a courtesy because you don't want to surprise your publisher. Because you know, at the time, we [the *Globe* newspaper] were partly owned by BCE." Reguly said, "I went down to Phillip and said, 'Look, I have the story and I'm going with it.' And he said – because Phillip is a journalist at heart and spent most of his career as a journalist – he said, 'If you're happy with your sources go with it' … He did not, in any way, try and talk me out of it," Reguly added.

Reguly quickly volunteered the fact that breaking the BCE story – as big a story as it was – did not involve a lot of legwork on his part. "It wasn't that hard to break," Reguly said. "I mean, I didn't phone anyone. You know, someone phoned me and delivered the story on a platter" (ibid.).

That Reguly and Willis were the reporters who broke the BCE story was no accident. While Reguly may have been on the receiving end of the leak, he and his colleague, who wrote the Streetwise column, had spent years developing the relationships with their sources; in Reguly's case, with the primary source.

"Reguly and I began to pick up that there were overtures being made to BCE – seen as undervalued – from groups such as KKR," Willis explained in an interview (ibid.). "So Reguly and I wrote some of those stories, based largely on conversations with investors and bankers surrounding BCE, and it kind of went from there." Willis acknowledged, "We made a small factual error that KKR had teamed up with Teachers to come forward with a friendly bid. What we didn't realize, but subsequently found out, was in fact that there were at least two groups circling BCE with serious intent to try and take the whole thing private." The fact the *Globe* afforded the story front-page treatment "started a fuse burning at Teachers," Willis said (ibid.).

The assertion KKR "has been in talks with leading pension funds, including the Ontario Teachers' Pension Plan" was mistaken (Reguly and Willis 2007, A1). Teachers, owners of 5.3 per cent of BCE's outstanding shares, was the company's largest single shareholder. The *Globe* story further included a quote attributed to "an executive close to the pension plan": "Certainly, no one thinks anyone could buy BCE without Teachers getting involved" (ibid.). That factual error was significant in terms of how subsequent events would unfold.

The wall poster message conveyed through the leak was clear: the biggest acquisition in Canadian corporate history and arguably the world's biggest leveraged buyout to date was in the offing, and Teachers was part of the play. The leak was strategic, intended to signal to an increasingly disgruntled shareholder base that a takeover premium for their shares was available. The *Globe* report of takeover talks created a buzz in the market the day it appeared, to the point where BCE was asked by TSX Market Regulation Services to respond. That day, shares jumped as much as $3.47, or 11.2 per cent, to $33.60 (Yahoo Finance 2007). The company issued a statement "to confirm the fact that there are no ongoing discussions being held with any private equity investor with respect to any privatization of the Company or any similar transaction"

Chart 1
Bell Canada Enterprises (BCE) March 2007 daily high

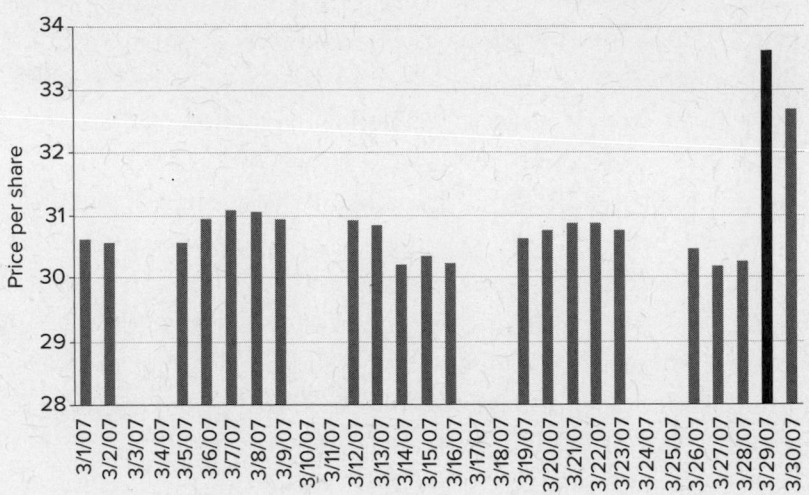

Source: Historical chart data provided by Thomson Financial Network.

Chart 2
Bell Canada Enterprises (BCE) March 2007 daily volume

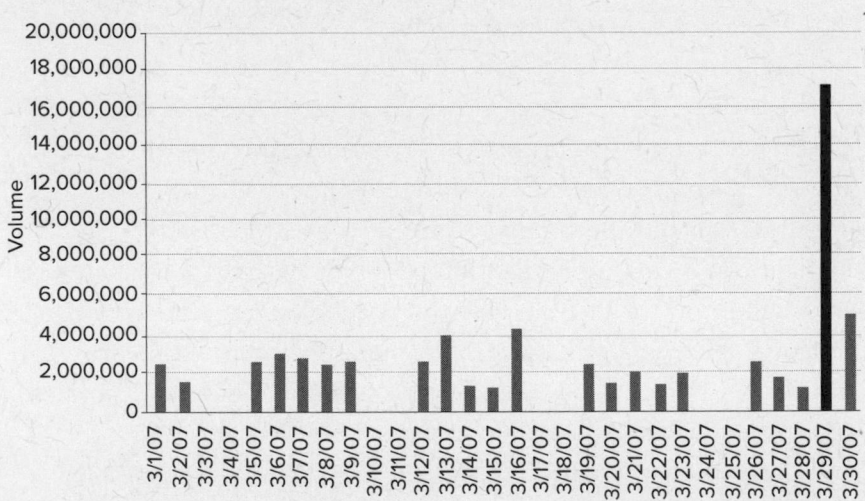

Source: Historical chart data provided by Thomson Financial Network.

(Bell Canada Enterprises 2007a). Further, the statement declared the company "has no current intention to pursue such discussions" (ibid.). The key words in the two sentences: "ongoing" and "current." That companies are approached about transactions is a matter of routine; if talks are "ongoing," it is a matter of some significance. Similarly, the word "current" is used to reinforce the notion that there isn't any "ongoing" negotiation.

In his bestseller *The Big Short*, Michael Lewis states, "Financial markets are a collection of arguments" (Lewis, M. 2010, 79). The BCE saga is a story of arguments and signals.

As stated earlier in this work, the significance of media effects on various "publics" has long been debated in scholarship circles. Many argue that media effects are minimal to inconsequential, that controlling the means of production and distribution matters more than the messaging itself – a hypothesis being debated once again in the context of today's social media world.

Even for those inclined to see media content as a factor that matters in public opinion, research has been bedevilled "by the difficulties of unraveling cause-and-effect relations" (Newton 1999, 582). However, the BCE case, selected originally for the author's doctoral dissertation, focuses on the world of financial reporting and financial markets – a public opinion expression of a different sort – in a considered attempt to reduce the variables. First, there are more "rules" set out in disclosure laws and advisories from securities exchanges that circumscribe public pronouncements around publicly traded companies. Second, "opinionation" in equity markets is expressed in relatively straightforward fashion – the buying and selling of equity instruments such as common shares. Further, these expressions of opinionation are measured, in terms of both price and trading volumes. That trade activity is a matter of public record and can be compared on a minute-by-minute basis with financial news reports.

The detailed analysis of the BCE case in this chapter seeks to apply Aeron Davis's (2007b) "inverted" paradigm research model to explore the role of "elite discourse networks" within traditional or legacy media, testing his proposition that the real "effect" of mainstream media lies in its value as a "signalling" system between elites. Elite discourse networks, basically, involve the exchange of information or messages between "insiders" with minimal consideration of the impact those conversations may have on a broader population.

Richard Lanham (2007a) coined the phrase "the economics of attention" to describe a world where we used to make stuff and sell it with fluff, and now the fluff is the stuff. The facility of Lanham's language should in no way diminish the significance of his insight: the "value" proposition in today's economy lies less in the production than in the ability of the producer to command the attention of the consuming public – whether the factor commanding attention is the brand value of a legacy media organization such as the *New York Times* or the secret sauce of Facebook's algorithms.

A media relations strategy, whether crafted in support of a political candidate or a merger and acquisition play, is one instrument used to gain attention.

The Backstory

In fact, the story's first chapter was written a few months prior, when the leadership team of Bell Canada Enterprises (BCE) took to the stage at Toronto's Carlu event space in February 2007 for the annual "Investors' Day" presentation. BCE executives believed better days were ahead. In the five years since Michael Sabia had been appointed president and chief executive officer, the company had weathered one of the most challenging periods in its history.

BCE, in the period immediately prior to Sabia's appointment, had lost its strategic focus, in the opinion of market analysts. Foreign interests owned 20 per cent of the company's core asset – Bell Canada. The company had invested heavily in non-core businesses, spending $8 billion in share currency to purchase Teleglobe, for example, which soon after found itself in dire straits, filed for bankruptcy protection, and was sold for $250 million – a fraction of BCE's purchase price.

While Bell remained heavily regulated by the Canadian Radio-television and Telecommunications Commission (CRTC), Bell's marketplace had become more competitive with new service providers for traditional telephony, mobile devices, and internet services. The disruptive innovations Harvard's Clayton Christensen had written about were decimating legacy services, such as long-distance telephony, while forcing Bell Canada to invest heavily in new growth services, such as wireless and video services. The challenge was more simply stated than met – BCE needed to develop a plan to "balance" the decline in revenues from its highly profitable legacy services with the increase in revenues from its growth services, all the while maintaining margins and managing capital intensity.

Sabia's executive team – which latterly included this writer[1] – had been told by the company's board of directors to knock down the "wall of worries" confronting BCE. In incremental steps, the executive team returned BCE to its core competency, telecommunications; first, by buying back the 20 per cent of Bell Canada held by US interests. The directories business – Yellow Pages – was sold at a premium. BCE exited its ownership stakes in Emergis, CGI, Bell Globemedia and Telesat – all under premium prices and conditions. The list is illustrative, not exhaustive. These actions surfaced more than $9 billion in capital. A restructured cost base identified $1.6 billion in savings in operating expenses. Dividends were first reinstated, then increased twice in twelve months. BCE paid down $1.4 billion in debt, introduced two successful normal course issuer bid initiatives – or share buybacks – and introduced a new business strategy that resulted in more than half of Bell Canada's annual revenue being generated from the new growth services. As a result of those changes, executives insisted the company had a substantial, improving revenue growth trajectory and a balance sheet strong enough to fund that growth.

Yet for all the changes, Bay Street wasn't impressed. BCE's appeal in the equities market continued to be limited, and the stock price

---

[1] William John Fox served as executive vice-president, office of the CEO; executive vice-president, Communications and Corporate Development for BCE; and an officer of BCE Inc. from May 2005 to 11 July 2008.

languished behind its peers. Former Ontario Securities Commission chair Ed Waitzer says "the bankers" had been sending signals to the company, its board, and CEO Michael Sabia for several years that something had to change. "There was a lot of that signalling going on, right?" Waitzer said (pers. notes 2012). "It was only when Teachers sort of started doing it in a public way that ... the choices became quite constrained." The company's share-price performance remained a preoccupation for market analysts, a fact that was reflected in the analysts' ongoing coverage of the company, which in turn helped shape the coverage in the business press. A publicly traded company's share price is like a box score in baseball and is often the hook for a news story. Despite the fact BCE's actions had freed up billions of dollars with a view to increase earnings, dividends, and share price, a public perception persisted of an enterprise facing more challenges than opportunities. Richard Currie, BCE board chair from 2002 to 2009, summarized the situation succinctly in his acceptance speech at the Ivey Business Leader Award ceremony, months after he'd stepped down from the firm: "At BCE, a near hysterical level of criticism was directed at the company, especially the CEO, during my time as chairman" (Currie 2009).

Ironically, Sabia's success in selling off non-core assets – such as Bell Globemedia and Telesat – had the net effect of putting the company in play as the transactions had swelled BCE's coffers. The company was holding billions of dollars of cash, cash that could be used by potential buyers of BCE to reduce the amount of debt required to finance a takeover. As James Surowiecki explained in a column published in the 30 January 2012 edition of the *New Yorker*, financial engineering has always been a component part of leveraged buyouts. "In a typical deal, the private-equity firm buys a company using some of its own money and some borrowed money," Surowiecki states (2012, 21). The late Stanley Hartt followed a variation on this model in the BCE transaction. "Here was a company that could be bought with its own money, or largely with its own money," said Hartt in an interview with the writer. Hartt, then the chair of Citigroup Global Markets Canada, had advised BCE on the sale of Telesat in 2006 and as a consequence had an informed view of the company's financial circumstance as well as its strategic plan.

In a conversation later that year with BCE's CEO, Hartt suggested Michael Sabia consider a management-led bid to take the company private. Hartt and his colleagues at Citigroup worked up a model to show how the transaction could be done. Sabia decided to give Hartt's suggestion a pass, believing it was time for BCE's shareholders to reap the rewards of an improving "story." Hartt said he, in turn, asked Sabia if Hartt could show the model to other people. "That was how the Teachers thing got started," Hartt said (pers. notes 2012). Further, Hartt and his team knew they weren't likely to be the only investment bankers to develop a takeover model for control of BCE.

The Ontario Teachers' Pension Plan and Citigroup subsequently approached BCE's board to explore the board's interest in a takeover of the company. Other private equity players – notably New York-based Kohlberg Kravis Roberts (KKR) – expressed a similar interest. The approaches were rebuffed by the BCE board. Having, in their view, done the proverbial heavy lifting, BCE's board of directors was not inclined to let private equity interests reap the financial rewards of that hard work.

Sabia met with both consortia – the KKR/Canada Pension Plan Investment Board (CPPIB) and Teachers/Providence Equity Partners – to inform them that BCE's board of directors was not interested in pursuing such a transaction. "I remember I asked at the end of each meeting, 'I am assuming that you are not going to launch this on a hostile basis,'" Sabia said in an interview (ibid.). The KKR/CPPIB consortium told the BCE CEO that hostile bids were "not really our style," he recalls. The Teachers-led consortium did not reply, "which was obviously an answer," Sabia said on reflection.

When the blockbuster Reguly-Willis story about a possible buyout appeared in the *Globe* on 29 March 2007, Sabia concluded that for at least one of the interested parties, "being hostile was fine. And, therefore … essentially, we were at the beginning of a war."

After the *Globe* story appeared, Hartt said, "My first reaction was validation of the fact that … this company with too much cash and no strategic use for it was a target."

An Elite Discourse Network Takes Shape

The leak and subsequent confirmation to Reguly and Willis were intended to force BCE's hand by informing the markets that there was a private equity option to create shareholder value. As media critic Howard Kurtz observed, "In business, unlike politics, the reporting of rumours is deemed fair game, since rumours, even bogus ones, move markets" (2001, xii).

The *Globe* story dutifully noted the fact that BCE, as a matter of policy, does not comment on market rumours and therefore would neither confirm nor deny whether the company had been approached by potential buyers. However, in this case, BCE had a message of its own for the market. The *Globe* story quoted "an official close to Mr. Sabia" to the effect that "private equity firms are told categorically no to offers." The "official" in this case was the author. In baseball parlance, the statement was a "purpose" pitch, the strength of the denial of interest intended to stem media speculation about the bid in an effort to ensure the story didn't "have legs." BCE executives' use of the term "categorical no" was intended to dissuade private equity interests from coming forward with new offers. Company officials were more hopeful than confident the intervention would have the desired effect.

Davis (2003) states elites – including business elites – are often in conflict with each other. Public negotiations are a component of the conflict resolution process. And that negotiation, on occasion, takes place in and through the mainstream press. "Together, these points suggest a scenario in which elites are simultaneously the main sources, main targets, and some of the most influenced recipients of news," Davis states (ibid., 673). "If this is so, it could be concluded that a major function of the news media is to act as a communications channel for the regular negotiations and decision-making that take place between different elite groups –

to the exclusion of the mass of consumer-citizens" (ibid.). As a consequence, Davis states in an earlier study "that a significant proportion of corporate PR in Britain is not particularly focused on the 'masses' or the mainstream news at all" (Davis 2002, 57).

Davis's conclusions reflect Driedger's (2008) work on the disproportionate influence of elites in shaping the news – both political news and financial news. Driedger's (2008) theory of priming definition would seem to have a direct application for the elite discourse network that took shape during the BCE transaction. Driedger states that elites with privileged access to the media have the ability to define topics in the news in a way that reflects the elite participants' preference or bias.

Elite discourse network considerations on occasion are reflected in the very structure of the deal itself and were certainly an element of the takeover strategy developed by the Teachers-led consortium in the spring of 2007, according to Stanley Hartt. Hartt advised Teachers' executives, "You are going after a Canadian icon here." Federal regulators stipulate Canadian interests must hold a majority position in any domestic telecommunications company. Hartt said, "The Canadian ownership could've been anyone; it happened to be Teachers." Control was an issue, as Hartt explained, because, for the federal government, actual control in fact is as important as control as defined in law. An investor with extensive experience running telecommunications companies was a further requirement; in this case that role was filled by Providence Equity Partners. "They had run telephone companies and Teachers had never run a telephone company," Hartt explained (pers. notes 2012).

Hartt, a key adviser on the transaction, suggested the Teachers-led consortium would be well-advised to retain expert public affairs advisers. Hartt recommended Edelman Canada; its then-president and CEO, Charles Fremes, was an experienced crisis communications adviser, while its senior vice-president, John Capobianco, would lead the government relations campaign. As Fremes – a personal friend of this writer – was dealing with serious health issues at the time, Freda Colbourne, his long-time associate who would replace him as CEO, was brought into the file. Colbourne worked most closely with Teachers' communications director Deborah Allan, Capobianco with Jim Leech, then the head of Teachers' private equity unit and subsequently CEO. Message alignment was key. "When you have consistent messaging with government officials, it flows up," Capobianco said (pers. notes).

Capobianco quickly concluded officials in Ottawa had concerns that the proposed transaction raised foreign control issues. Hartt says he knew Colbourne and Capobianco had been successful in addressing those concerns when Hartt showed up at the US ambassador's residence in Ottawa in 2007 for a July Fourth party. Then-Liberal leader Stéphane Dion approached Hartt at the party and basically reiterated Capobianco's public line that Teachers would emerge as the controlling shareholder, "which I thought was brilliant. I hadn't said a word and I agreed fiercely, of course … because I had every interest to," Hartt says. Dion was, in fact, "playing me back my own music. We hadn't gone to see him. He got it from the media" (pers. notes 2012).

Optics matters in transactions such as the BCE bid because of the heightened public interest.

Edelman advisers were careful to position the Teachers' offer as coming from its 280,000-plus schoolteachers, both active and retired, and not from some faceless private equity firm. "We wanted it to be a 'teacher in the classroom' versus KKR," Colbourne explained. "We were worried about a possible backlash from long-term BCE shareholders. We didn't want to be perceived as hotshot private equity at all." Edelman also encouraged Teachers to be more aggressive in terms of media relations than the pension fund had been in the past, "much more than they were comfortable doing," Colbourne said. The media advisers further recommended Teachers make more use of formal written statements to articulate the pension fund's positions, rather than simply responding verbally to media queries (ibid.).

The Teachers-led consortium's media relations strategy was predicated on the assumption KKR was the true competition. Partners such as US-based Providence Equity Partners were kept in the background until BCE's review of strategic alternatives was truly launched and the requirement to establish Providence's expertise in telecommunications presented itself. Even then, Providence's media exposure was primarily focused on US media outlets such as the *Wall Street Journal* and the *New York Times*.

Edelman executives were active in providing reporters assigned to the BCE story with background briefings. Elite discourse network management was integral to the exercise.

In the days following the initial leak to Reguly and Willis, Teachers had to send a signal of its own to the elite discourse network being created around BCE in response to BCE's rejection. As BCE's largest single shareholder, with more than 5 per cent of its shares, Teachers was required by US securities law to inform the markets as to the fund's intent because BCE is listed on both the Toronto and New York stock exchanges. Specifically, Teachers had to formally declare any intention to move from a "passive" to an "activist" shareholder. The form is known as a "Schedule 13D." Teachers had informed BCE of its intention to file a 13D with the US Securities and Exchange Commission (SEC) just before the Easter weekend in 2007. Sabia asked Jim Leech to hold off on the filing until he and BCE board chair Richard Currie could meet with the pension fund executives. Leech and then-Teachers' CEO Claude Lamoureux agreed to meet Sabia and Currie on Easter Monday, "which in retrospect was absolutely hopeless," Sabia said. "By then, the die were cast" (ibid.).

Currie and Sabia had hoped to convince the pension fund not to proceed with the SEC filing and expressed a willingness to work with Teachers to address the pension fund's concerns about BCE's performance and intentions. Teachers, however, made it clear to Currie and Sabia that the filing would proceed. "Teachers figured Mr. Sabia was stonewalling and would have none of it," according to a source the *National Post* described as "familiar with the discussions who asked not to be identified" (Tedesco 2007a, A1).

Further, Teachers ensured that reporters covering the story were aware of its intention to do so. Reporters' calls to BCE asking for comment on the discussion with Teachers were placed before Sabia and

Currie were back at BCE's offices – mere blocks away. The filing 9 April 2007, for all intents and purposes, put the company on the block.

Headlines and Share Prices

What followed was a saga former *Globe* editor-in-chief John Stackhouse – then the editor of the ROB – declared was "the most important story we will cover over the next year" (pers. notes 2012). Information flows at the *Globe* were organized at three points during the working day: the morning and afternoon meetings of the *Globe*'s editors and "a little bit of a caucus around the front page at 5:30 or 6 p.m." Former *Globe* editor Edward Greenspon said he would meet with ROB editors in the third instance "only if they had something that was front-pageable." But in an interview, Greenspon quickly added, "BCE was always potentially front-pageable ... BCE is huge, big. Bell is iconic. Everybody owned Bell stock at some point ... whether through a pension plan or individually" (pers. notes 2012).

As economist R.J. Shiller observed in his (2005) work *Irrational Exuberance*, the news media are "naturally attracted to financial markets because, at the very least, the markets provide constant news in the form of daily price changes ... The stock market has star quality. The public considers it the Big Casino ... The only other regular generator of news on a comparable scale is sporting events" (ibid., 86).

As was a Report on Business trademark for such a huge story, the *Globe* assigned a large team of reporters to the BCE saga. Says Reguly, "We just threw people at it." Former *Globe* reporter Boyd Erman describes the writing process as "organic." The issue of who was holding the pen on a particular story was largely decided by the reporters themselves. The reporters covering the BCE story worked in the same section of the newsroom, which meant communication between them was both face to face and instant. "When it worked, it was beautiful," Erman said (pers. notes 2012).

Reporter Sean Silcoff, who is now with the *Globe*, worked the BCE takeover story for the *Financial Post*, the business section of the *National Post* and the ROB's direct competitor. While business columnist Theresa Tedesco contributed significantly to certain major stories, in particular sharing certain contacts with her colleague, the day-to-day coverage was left primarily to Silcoff, then the only business reporter in the *Financial Post* Montreal bureau. Rather than being overwhelmed by the sheer force of numbers on the other side, the then-*Post* reporter tried to make the most of the "flexibility and freedom of being basically the only guy on the story for the *Financial Post*."

Silcoff says he began his pursuit of the BCE story from the perspective of the proverbial "widows and orphans" who historically held the stock for its dividend but who hadn't "seen a rise in their dividend cheque in ten years ... That was the story that mattered to people. That is the story that I pursued," Silcoff said. As the saga unfolded, Silcoff came to appreciate that the story had, in fact, evolved into a story of competing institutions and an exercise in elite discourse. "We were talking as much to those people ... as the great unwashed ... the 2,000 people that matter," said Silcoff. Access to these elites, to paraphrase the tagline from an iconic Smith Barney television ad, was gained the old-fashioned way, said Silcoff: you earned it. "I called every [BCE] director a hundred times," Silcoff said. "Most won't return your calls. But you might get one breakthrough" (ibid.).

Motives on a story as big as the BCE transaction, Silcoff conceded, can vary. Reguly says he does not know what motivated his source to leak the BCE takeover bid story in the first instance. "Honest to God, Bill, you know this guy. He's an investment banker, but I still don't know what his motive was, I really don't. I know he worked for a big bank at the time." Sometimes sources were driven by "self-interest"; on other occasions an individual was anxious to set the record straight on a particular issue or development. Principals did have to consider selective disclosure laws, Silcoff observed, "but there seemed to be some wiggle room. Some disclosures they feel they can make as long as it [attribution] doesn't come back to them." (ibid.).

Breaking a major story is a key to getting access to elites, said Silcoff, who broke a major development in the BCE saga when he reported the fact Telus Corp. was going to join the auction for control of BCE. "Everyone remembers we had that story first," Sil-coff said. "When you get a story right and you really nail it, that becomes a huge calling card." Sources, Silcoff said, then start to reach out to journalists, including elite sources who are privy to sensitive information. "You build relationships ... they start point-ing you in certain directions," Silcoff said. These contacts lead a reporter to new story lines or different angles on a current story line: the "wiggle" disclosures that feed reporters' search for novelty.

The use of elite discourse networks is commonplace in other sectors of society. The political community, for example, has long communicated through the mainstream media. Former president George H.W. Bush press secretary Marlin Fitzwater states, "In Washington, unlike anywhere else in America, people talk to each other through the press" (Fitzwater 1995, 338).

In the BCE transaction, the "circuit of communication" included interests as varied as Prime Minister Stephen Harper's min-ority Conservative government, various federal departments, opposition parties, institutional investors, bidding consortia mem-bers, BCE retail shareholders, employees, customers, competitors, and bondholders (Miller and Macintyre 1998).

Ed Waitzer, who advised the strategic oversight committee of BCE's board of directors on the transaction, said in an interview the media plays multiple roles in elite discourse networks. "The media have, in effect, become a new class of deal intermediaries, the same way investment bankers are," Waitzer explained (pers. notes 2012), echoing Davis (2007b). In fact, Waitzer says the "media have, to some extent, supplanted the role of the bankers who used to sort of carry the messages back and forth and get paid." The bankers are still getting paid, Waitzer says, while journalists are not – at least, not for their work as the messengers in the elite dis-course networks. Waitzer believes journalists may not "even know the role they are playing" much of the time. But he believes con-tent analysis of news stories in any transaction would reveal the pattern. "Put them [the messages] at points in time in the deal and you can see how influential they were," Waitzer said.

The BCE case study supports Aeron Davis's proposition that the traditional forms of media effects research on mass audiences can be overly restrictive. As stated earlier, Davis (ibid.) was among the first to suggest the traditional model of assessing media effects – by focusing on a mass or general audience – be turned upside down. Presaging Waitzer's point, Davis argues a major function of the mainstream media is to act as a conduit for insiders: a communications channel where elite interests negotiate and take decisions "to the exclusion of mass consumer-citizens" (Davis 2003, 673). While elites – market analysts, shareholders, directors, investors – all have access to rival and / or exclusive sources of news, all "did have access to, and regularly consulted, certain mainstream news sources" (Davis 2006a, 608).

The BCE case aligns well with Davis's hypothesis. Further, Davidson's (1983) "third person hypothesis" predicts people will overestimate the influence mass communications – such as news reports – will have on others. They expect the "news" to have a greater impact on others than on themselves; news reports may prompt others to sell a stock, for example, and that in turn will cause others to buy or sell *in anticipation* of the reaction of others. Similarly, Driedger's (2008) theory of priming definition has a particular application to Davis's model. Based on the premise that certain elites enjoy privileged access to the media, Driedger contends these elites have the ability to define topics in a "frame" of their choosing. Journalists in a competitive, deadline-driven environment assigned to a major business story with a relatively short list of primary or informed sources are particularly beholden to these elites. Thus, news management is "vital" during takeover activity, according to Davis (2006b, 10).

Finally, "framing" theory (Entman 1993) also has a direct application to the BCE case study. While a company's share price is an expression of the market's assessment of its future profitability, there are two distinct paths to valuation. The first is based on an assessment of the company's future operations; the second "looks at the company purely as a commodity to be speculatively bought and sold" (Davis, 2007a 171). The BCE case falls in the second category. Like gamblers at a roulette wheel, shareholders in companies that are takeover targets essentially decide whether or not to "play the red." The deal closes, or it doesn't, a fact that will be determined by a relatively small number of individuals who communicate with each other through the mainstream media in a manner reminiscent of the "wall posters" of China's Cultural Revolution.

Signals Sent

Content analysis of coverage of the BCE saga in the *Globe and Mail* and the *National Post* reveals the extent to which elites used the mainstream media to send signals to each other even as their financial and legal advisers interacted on a minute-by-minute basis in the course of the major transaction. Of the 430 stories analyzed, 121, or better than 30 per cent, included a specific message from one elite group – the company, potential bidders, elected officials, regulators – to another. Further, each "Morse code" message – to cite the phrase used by investment bankers – shaped the news coverage in terms of the dominant news frame for certain periods of time. And each had a direct impact on the company's share price during the news cycle in which the signal or coded message was sent.

First, there was the mistaken signal included in the first news story – the leak to Reguly and Willis, which Willis described as including a "small factual error." The *Globe* had reported KKR had in fact teamed up with Teachers and had made a friendly overture to BCE. In the post-mortem "how the deal was done" stories, Teachers' Leech confirmed that, in the wake of the Reguly-Willis story, the first message the pension fund had to send through the elite discourse network was that Teachers was not in partnership with KKR, even though the two parties had partnered on BCE-related transactions in the past: notably, the Yellow Pages transaction. Teachers had been hearing rumours dating back to November 2006 that KKR had been "sniffing" around BCE, according to a post-mortem report carried in the *Globe* (DeCloet and Stewart 2007). The news account goes on to state, "When those rumours were confirmed in a *Globe and Mail* story in late March, Mr. Leech says he believed he had to start talking to partners like U.S. media buyout specialist Providence Equity Partners Inc. so the fund wouldn't be caught sleeping by a surprise takeover bid for one of its largest investments" (ibid.). Leech made a similar statement to the *Post*'s Sean Silcoff. "We said to ourselves, we can't be caught sleeping at the switch here" (Silcoff 2007h).

The next major development in the saga built on Teachers' declaration of interest in becoming a "player" in any transaction and that a Teachers-led initiative to take the company private was the best option for BCE shareholders.

In the news cycles immediately following the 9 April 2007 filing of the 13D, stories began to appear in both the *Globe* and *Post* signalling the fact Teachers had become "frustrated" with BCE's relatively stagnant stock price (Tedesco 2007a). The statements were attributed to a source "who spoke on condition of anonymity" (ibid.). The source was further quoted as saying, "Looking at all of its options, and the most promising is a Canadian-led privatization" (ibid.). The same day, 10 April, Teachers also signalled to *Globe* reporters Boyd Erman, Sinclair Stewart, and Jacquie McNish that the pension fund was willing to pay an "eye-popping" price close to $40 a share – a significant premium for a stock that had been trading around $30 in mid-March (Erman, Stewart, and McNish 2007). Once Teachers filed the 13D, the makeup of the shareholder base was transformed, according to former Edelman Canada CEO Colbourne. Retail shareholders – the proverbial widows and orphans – were displaced by hedge funds and risk arbitrageurs. Teachers, said Colbourne, had already gone and made the case for change to large institutional shareholders. "The analysts and media thought it was good news that something would happen at Bell," Colbourne said in an interview. The next day, the *Post* reported that Teachers had full financing for its bid from Citigroup, the US bank conglomerate (Tedesco and McLeod 2007). Further, the *Globe* reported in a separate story that BCE's largest institutional shareholders were lining up behind Teachers. Market reaction was immediate and positive for shareholders.

Other interested parties were reacting to the news stories about BCE as well. Bondholders, for example, signalled their discontent with the potential BCE leveraged buyout (Koza 2007) based on the fact that more leverage means more credit risk.

The federal government had its own signals to send about the proposed transaction. Then-finance minister Jim Flaherty told reporters: "As you know, there are rules that apply with respect to potential acquisitions ... There's no intention to change that law ... This is a situation that the Government of Canada will monitor, and is monitoring closely" (Chase 2007). Earlier news accounts had raised the public policy issue of foreign ownership restrictions on telecommunications companies. Former industry minister Maxime Bernier had recently proposed that members of Parliament review foreign ownership rules. The BCE deal was described as having the potential to accelerate the Harper government's reform agenda around telecommunications companies (Tuck and McCarthy 2007). The *Financial Post*'s Sean Silcoff asked in print, "Could the buyers count on Ottawa changing the foreign ownership rules so a Verizon or an AT&T could buy BCE?" (Silcoff 2007a).

Strategic buyers also began to signal their interest in being part of any play for BCE. Telus, the Western Canada-based telecommunications company, was touted as a potential suitor in *Financial Post* stories following the Reguly-Willis scoop (Tait and Deveau 2007). On 30 March, the *Globe and Mail* cited sources claiming BCE executives and directors were revisiting options in the wake of the KKR approach "that include a transformational deal to join the country's two telecommunications giants [BCE and Telus]" (Willis, McNish, and McLean 2007). The story also flagged the fact the two companies' overlapping wireless businesses "would trigger competition issues" (ibid.).

Teachers made extensive use of the elite discourse network and dominated headlines for several days after the initial *Globe* story appeared, with a series of tactical leaks intended to convey and then confirm the pension fund's front-runner status in the BCE sweepstakes. First, Teachers confirmed it had put together a consortium to potentially launch a bid (Silcoff 2007b). Then, the media reported the pension fund had effectively blocked KKR's ability to launch a bid by tying up many key Canadian sources of funding (ibid.). The reports were followed up with a 16 April story that Teachers had the support of institutional shareholders "that together control more than one-third of BCE Inc.'s stock" (Willis and Stewart 2007a). The story included details that could only have come from a highly placed source, such as the fact Teachers was considering the option "to pressure BCE's board with a 'bear hug letter,' in which large shareholders publicly express their support for a buyout offer at a heady premium" (ibid.).

Teachers' effective control of the communications exercise at this point was leading to a perception in the market that the pension fund was positioned to run the table – to borrow a phrase from snooker. "What I've learned subsequently, in fact even very recently, is that there were attempts by Teachers to minimize competition … to try and get anyone with the firepower to go after this asset all working together so they could keep the price down and maximize the upside," Willis said. "The last thing any bidder wanted, particularly Teachers, was a contested auction."

BCE, in turn, had to reassert control of the media agenda as a first step in reasserting the board's control of the transaction agenda. In a 2012 interview, Sabia said that his judgment – then and now – was that BCE's board "lacked the gumption to really fight them through a proxy battle (pers. notes 2012). Because of foreign ownership restrictions and a limited Canadian equity pool, Sabia was convinced BCE's board had to move aggressively to "put something together and have a contest here." Otherwise, "we'll just be a battleship, with no engine, no rudder, waiting for the torpedoes to hit."

Surprisingly to Sabia, there was little debate at the board as to a course of action. The option of a proxy fight, for example, was not discussed. "Now, when I look back on it, I keep asking myself: So how come that dog didn't bark?" Sabia says.

The newspapers of 18 April 2007 reported the details of BCE's response to the takeover proposals. The company announced a review of strategic alternatives – effectively confirming the fact a "for sale" sign was hanging outside the corporate headquarters on rue de la Gauchetière in Montreal. Further, the company announced it had entered into non-exclusive negotiations with a consortium that included KKR, the Canada Pension Plan Investment Board, and La Caisse de dépôt et placement du Québec. The *Globe* reported "the stage is set for the biggest takeover battle in Canadian history" (Erman 2007a). The *Post* added "colour" that Teachers had hoped to persuade BCE that the pension fund was the "white knight," but "Mr. Sabia and BCE's board of directors, led by highly respected chairman Richard Currie, were not about to sit back and hand the company to Teachers" (Tedesco 2007b).

Messaging between elites is, of course, subject to interpretation. The 17 April 2007 BCE press release (Bell Canada Enterprises 2007b) that informed the 18 April coverage (which Sabia coauthored with this writer) is an example of a communication crafted for an elite discourse network, as much as it was for public consumption. The drafting of that news release triggered a spirited discussion at the BCE board. "In a way, the debate was about what elite network matters," said Sabia (pers. notes 2012). Certain board members pushed for a plain-vanilla press release – with a single review of strategic alternatives message – targeting a single constituency, BCE shareholders, specifically institutional shareholders. To the visible consternation of certain of the board's legal advisers, Sabia and other BCE executives, including this writer, were pushing drafts intended to address a broader elite discourse network with multiple constituencies, including federal policy-makers and regulators.

A series of stories fed to reporters by other interests included repeated references to the risk of a "busted auction." Teachers, in particular, was incensed. Leaks led to new stories citing "sources," including one in a 23 April *Globe* story who said, "Teachers is now reconsidering its options, including whether it will join the process" (Stewart 2007). For the next several days, the *National Post* and the *Globe* reported that the odds were growing that the Ontario Teachers' Pension Plan would not make a takeover bid for BCE Inc.

Teachers, Waitzer said, was active with the media, "trying to make sure the auction went their way ... we called their [Teachers'] bluff," Waitzer said, but concedes, "It hurt. I think at least Michael's [Sabia] credibility and it hurt the board's credibility unnecessarily. We kind of looked like we didn't know what we were doing" (pers. notes 2012).

Subsequent stories in both the *Globe* and the *Post* raised the prospect of a "one-horse race" (Tedesco 2007b; Yakabuski 2007b). BCE was encouraged by sources cited in other stories "to do everything in its power to shut down any co-operation among bidders," as Andrew Willis described it (2007b). BCE management, and Sabia in particular, were sharply criticized for their interventionist ways, which allowed some sources to feed an impression the management team favoured the KKR/CPPIB consortium.

The *Globe* reported pressure was mounting on BCE "amid concerns that the race to control the country's largest telecommunications company would become one-sided" (Willis, Stewart, and Erman 2007): The *Globe* quoted "one investment banker working with a potential buyer" as saying, "BCE board members are aware that the process seemed to create a favoured bidder, and they want to get rid of that perception" (ibid.). Sabia stated that individual board members were clearly talking directly to reporters. News accounts that focused on the role Sabia played in the strategic review process were, in his view, a case in point. "How is it that almost instantaneously, people in the media seemed to know the specifics of the role that I played?" Sabia asked rhetorically. "There was no press release to that effect, but all of a sudden, everybody seemed to know. My hypothesis is that people who did know what was going on were talking; or their emissaries were talking" (pers. notes 2012).

Sabia, according to Willis, became a target of pointed criticism. "There became a fairly significant number of voices saying that Michael wasn't the right CEO anymore and that the board should look at new CEO candidates" (ibid.).

BCE's board, having created a strategic oversight committee chaired by board member and corporate governance expert Donna Soble Kaufman, signalled that the board and its advisers were considering "an innovative move that could potentially widen the field of bidders for the company" (Silcoff 2007c). This innovation, known as "equity shared financing," created a capital pool of the smaller Canadian pension funds by telling them they would not be allowed to pick a side in the takeover battle, and would have to make capital available to any winning bidder instead. Said Kaufman, "Our goal from the beginning has been to foster a competitive process by seeking to ensure that no one party is able to assemble a disproportionate share of available Canadian equity" (Willis, McLeod, and Erman 2007).

Anxious to ensure that a single bidder did not take full advantage of foreign ownership restrictions by locking up available pension funds and thereby limiting the number of potential bidders, BCE's board and management in the end effectively put a pool of Canadian pension funds on a "bench" to be available for any successful bidder.

The significance of this strategic initiative was largely lost on reporters covering the BCE story – in no small measure because of the constraints placed on BCE executives by the board regarding contact with the media, which limited the ability to conduct background or follow-up briefings to explain the move in some more detail. The media's preoccupation with, and uncritical acceptance of, the "broken process" narrative perplexes Sabia to this day. "They [reporters] never understood that to create competitive pressure – which I think is the obligation one has in those circumstances – given how big the company was relative to how small the equity pool is in Canada and the foreign ownership limits, you've got to intervene," Sabia said. "If you just let the natural process play out, you probably won't get an auction. You're going to have to allocate people to various groups in a pretty hands-on way." Journalists, Sabia believes, got so convinced of the broken process narrative "that they could never see the other side of this: that a quote-unquote 'traditional process' wouldn't work here or at least there was a very high risk that it wouldn't work."

To be fair, there was a *Globe* story crediting Sabia with "doing the right thing," citing "one person close to the talks." "He's negotiating with the group with the higher number knowing that Teachers might increase their price" (Erman 2007a). A price per share range was established for news consumers in the *Globe* story, stating the KKR/ CPPIB bid was expected to be in the $40 to $42 range, while the Teachers-led consortium was talking $38 to $40 per share (ibid.).

Sabia concedes the board decision to restrict BCE management's communication and interaction with reporters assigned to the story was, at a minimum, a contributing factor. "We were just like a punching bag," Sabia said. He describes the board decision as "weird." "To this day, I really don't understand why," he said. The coverage was intensely personal and focused on Sabia. "Maybe their view was, let him take it, it's not us," Sabia said. "But at the end of the day, okay, I was being beaten up, sure, but they didn't look good either in this" (pers. notes 2012).

Sabia said the tactic constituted a gang-up on BCE's board, with the hope that eventually they'd crack under pressure. "In retrospect, not a bad strategy," he added. "At the end of the day, it kind of worked." Teachers *formally* came into the process several weeks later, "and pretty much on their terms," Sabia observed (ibid.).

Waitzer concedes the BCE board and management likely paid a personal price in regulation terms for the considered decision to limit approved contact with reporters concerning the story – at least officially.

The BCE board decision to restrict contact between journalists working the story and BCE's management team didn't mean there weren't leaks from the BCE side, Waitzer concedes: "We [BCE] leaked like a sieve"; and while his personal bias was to be more accessible, he thinks the strategy – at least officially – to stay out of the media is defensible. Former BCE executive Scott Thomson agrees BCE's side of the takeover saga had its share of leaks. "It was weird how we would talk about things and variations on that would appear in the paper," Thomson said in an interview (pers. notes 2012). "You could tell me right now that the leaks were coming from one of five directors," said BCE adviser Waitzer, who has his own theories. "On some I wouldn't be surprised that they were that Machiavellian, and others, I wouldn't be surprised if they were that naive" (pers. notes 2012).

"We got to a good outcome," Waitzer said. "Actually, I think an exceptional outcome. At times, I think we ended up doing it the hard way and sometimes in spite of ourselves. But you know, at the end of the day, the outcome speaks louder than the process" (pers. notes 2012).

"The media likes to have heroes and villains and victims," said Waitzer. Referring to the BCE team leading the transaction, Waitzer said with a laugh, "We alternated between being the villain or the victim, but we were never the hero." Teachers, said Waitzer, tried "to position themselves ultimately as heroes or victims." Telus CEO Darren Entwistle "tried to position himself as hero, or mostly as victim, I guess" (pers. notes 2012).

Other constituencies surfaced other concerns. The *Globe*'s Quebec correspondent Konrad Yakabuski, for example, reported the Quebec government's concern the sale of BCE might result in the head office being moved out of Montreal (Yakabuski 2007a). Edelman's Colbourne advised Teachers to respond with a leak to the effect the pension fund had no plans to move the head office to Toronto.

Analysts were speculating BCE's potential buyers were banking on changes to foreign ownership rules. "The market is bidding this stock up to a level that doesn't make sense on a leveraged buyout basis," National Bank financial analyst Greg MacDonald told the *Globe* (McLean 2007a).

The *Post* reported a potential privatization of BCE would create a tax conundrum for federal Finance Minister Jim Flaherty, as the privatization could cost the federal treasury an estimated $800 million in lost tax revenue (Vieira 2007). And finally, Scotia Capital's analyst John Henderson created a new story line when he published a report suggesting a BCE-Telus merger – which he dubbed Belus – was the best possible outcome: "a true made-in-Canada solution" (Greenwood 2007). Former *Globe* reporter Andy Willis said John Henderson was an important card in the elite discourse network. "He came out with that Belus concept," said Willis. "To John's credit, he did the homework. He figured out where the savings would come from" (pers. notes 2012). Henderson's reportage predated any formal signal from Telus as to the company's intensions.

However, a relatively small item in Willis's Streetwise column of 19 April 2007 provided an important indication of one of the stories behind the story. Willis declared the fees paid to investment bankers and legal advisers on a transaction the size of BCE were estimated at $400 million. "A half dozen banks and law firms have picked sides, signing up months ago to advise the principal players in what promises to be the biggest deal in Canadian history," Willis reported (2007a). Further, Willis stated the transaction was, in effect, a play in two acts. "And at the end of the rainbow, five or six years from now, comes the final pot of gold when Bell Canada goes public again" (ibid.). Journalists chasing stories are trained to follow self-interest and the money. In the case of the BCE transaction, both were factors for transaction advisers. What they needed was a game, and when the prospects for a spirited contest seemed threatened, these denizens of the second concentric circle responded by creating media noise.

The intensity of the competition between the *Globe* and the *Post* contributed to the coverage weights. Stories, on occasion, were played more prominently than the substance of the news account might otherwise warrant.

One particular element of the BCE saga is that two parties to the transaction – BCE Inc. and Teachers – were part owners of the *Globe*: in BCE's case directly a majority owner of Bell Globemedia; in Teachers' case indirectly. Yet Greenspon says the ownership positions weren't "really a terribly complicating factor" (pers. notes 2012). Teachers, said Greenspon, "was a pretty passive investor," as was BCE. In fact, BCE CEO Michael Sabia had reached out to Greenspon the day of his appointment as the *Globe*'s editor-in-chief to congratulate him – but also to state, "I just want you to know this is the first time and the last time I'm going to phone you," Greenspon recalled. Sabia told Greenspon he was cognizant of the *Globe*'s status as a national institution and declared there would be no corporate influence in the way the *Globe* conducted its news operation.

Teachers continued to express its annoyance with BCE's management to reporters (Reguly 2007, B8). But reporters were waiting for the second shoe to drop: a decision by Telus whether or not to enter the bidding war (Silcoff 2007d). And, predictably, as news accounts began to speculate as to the likelihood of a busted auction, the short-sellers entered into the market, in effect betting that the takeover bid would fail and the rising share price, reflecting an unexpected takeover premium, would slump (Silcoff 2007e).

The Auction

By 19 May 2007, media reports of fears of a one-horse race were set aside. News accounts reported Teachers was, in fact, ready to make a bid (Silcoff 2007f). By 6 June, Teachers' bid was confirmed (McLean, Willis, Erman, and McLeod 2007), squaring off against the bid from the KKR / CPPIB consortium as well as one from a group led by Cerberus Capital Management LP, that included CanWest Global. All three groups officially signed non-disclosure agreements to gain access to data rooms. This writer, as BCE's spokesperson, issued a statement to the effect that "the strategic oversight committee of the board is pleased that three groups have signed non-disclosure agreements and entered into discussions on taking the company private ... Our goal from the beginning has been to foster a competitive process," the statement concluded (ibid.). The story quoted "one source close to BCE" to the effect that "there is significant Canadian equity to support three bids" (ibid.). The company message was designed to reassure shareholders that despite news accounts of the "noise" about the process, there would in fact be a competitive bidding process for BCE. Sabia, the next day, reminded reporters a private equity takeover was not the only option to create shareholder value on the table (McLean 2007b). Reporters then turned their attention to the only potential strategic buyer – Telus. Strategic buyers can be willing to pay more than a financial buyer if the acquisition has the potential to enhance existing operations.

Telus's decision to enter the fray was leaked to the *Post*'s Silcoff and Theresa Tedesco (Tedesco and Silcoff 2007a) and quickly matched by the *Globe*. The following story the next day suggested that private equity suitors might "soon be headed for the exits ... There may be a party, and only Darren Entwistle [Telus CEO] shows up ... Absent a regulatory intervention, this thing is worth more to Telus," one source explained (Willis and Reguly 2007). Private equity sources, in turn, reached out to reporters to probe if a Bell-Telus merger was "a done deal. And if so, have we just been set up as a stalking horse?" (McLean, Stewart, McNish, and Chase 2007).

Because any bid by definition would involve a merger of two major Canadian telecommunications companies, Telus turned its attention to Ottawa, asking the Competition Bureau to ensure its bid would not be placed at a competitive disadvantage to private equity bids as a result of the bureau's approval process (Nowak 2007). The *Post* follow-up piece portrayed Telus's bid as "corporate nationalism" but included a warning to the federal government that Telus would not proceed with a bid if the Competition Bureau ordered a divestiture of wireless assets (Silcoff 2007g). Once again, senior Telus sources told reporters that Telus would pull the plug on its bid if it was forced to sell wireless assets "belonging to either company" (Tait 2007a). Then, within hours, Telus announced it would not proceed with a bid, citing dissatisfaction with the way BCE had run the process.

Even as they were reporting Telus's decision to withdraw, journalists assigned to the story were being told the phone firm might consider returning to the table if BCE's independent directors were to exercise more authority. Citing "one person involved in the takeover discussion," the *Globe* story stated, "Telus is in a no-lose situation ... It can sit back and watch the action and make a move when it wants, while the board is in a no-win situation of trying to make a messed-up auction look like it's working" (McNish, McLean, and Stewart 2007).

Third parties questioned Telus's insistence that "the inadequacies of BCE's bid process did not make it possible for Telus to submit an offer" (ibid.). Bay Street observers told reporters the Telus move

didn't make sense. "You either want to do this massive transformation deal or you don't" (Tait 2007b). The street's instant analysis:
the move was a stalling tactic by Telus in the hope of forcing BCE's
board to extend the deadline for the submission of bids.

Sabia cites the Telus intervention as an example of how a member
of the elite – in this case Telus CEO Darren Entwistle – can misuse a
discourse network. "He just completely misplayed his cards," Sabia
said. "He completely misunderstood his position" (pers. notes 2012).

Not only was Telus and Entwistle late to declaring an interest, the
signal to Ottawa that he was only interested in a Bell-Telus merger if
the Competition Bureau agreed no remedies would be exacted from
the new entity, particularly in the context of the wireless business, was
poorly received. "The competition lawyers threw up all over it," Sabia
said. Then, Entwistle used the mainstream media to signal BCE's board
he wanted the deadline for the strategic review process extended.
"Those were, I think, his two fundamental miscalculations," Sabia
said, "all of which were based, I believe, on the perception on his part
that he was the preferred path, and therefore he could write the script.
It turned out to be anything but," the former BCE CEO concluded (ibid.).

When the *Globe*'s Sinclair Stewart reported that certain members
of the KKR / CPPIB bid had pulled out, questions were once again
raised as to the consortium's ability to mount a bid (Stewart, Willis,
and McNish 2007).

BCE's board, seized of their responsibility to shareholders, could not
let the perception of a flawed process go unanswered, and instructed
this writer to state, "In a deal of unprecedented complexity and size
in Canada, we have succeeded in creating a truly competitive process … It is not surprising that some party seeking its own advantage
wants to complain, because we have not tipped the process in any
one direction. We have run the process in a manner that seeks to
encourage maximum participation with a view to achieving the best
results for BCE shareholders" (McNish, McLean, and Stewart 2007).

By 23 June 2007, BCE's advisers were sending signals that the
board would move quickly to a decision. Quoting an "executive
who works with one of the parties that has been pursuing BCE," the

Globe reported the board of directors would have a recommendation for shareholders within seventy-two hours. "This thing is over at the end of the next week," the source is quoted as saying (Stewart and Willis 2007). Subsequent news stories confirmed three bidding consortia – Teachers/Providence, KKR/CPPIB, and Cerberus/Can-West – had tabled formal offers to take BCE private (DeCloet 2007).

Determined to placate shareholders that a value-creation transaction was still achievable, sources were quoted as saying the BCE board was favouring all-cash bids and discounting the more complex Cerberus proposal (Willis and Stewart 2007b). The *Post* was also reporting the all-cash bids from Teachers/Providence and KKR/CPPIB were both in the $41 a share range (Tedesco and Silcoff 2007b).

On Friday, 29 June 2007, BCE's directors gathered in the boardroom at the telco's Montreal headquarters to consider its options. Earlier in the day, BCE's advisers had approached Teachers one more time and asked them to "'sharpen their pencil' – Bay Street speak for putting more cash on the table," as the *Globe* reported in its postgame analysis (Stewart and DeCloet 2007, B1). Both the *Globe and Mail* and the *Post* had put their Saturday, 30 June print editions to bed as the BCE board's deliberations continued into the late evening. For that reason, while the *Globe* was the first to electronically report the news on Saturday that Teachers had won the battle for BCE, both it and the *Post* had to wait until 2 July to run extensive "how the deal was done" stories in their print editions (ibid.).

Those front-page stories featured more elite messaging: specifically quoting Telus sources to the effect the battle for BCE might not, in fact, be over (McLean, Stewart, Reguly, and McNish 2007). Teachers CEO Claude Lamoureux used an interview with the Montreal daily *La Presse* to signal his dissatisfaction with the role BCE executives played in the auction process, and was particularly critical of Sabia, suggesting the company's management should have been reined in by directors (Yakabuski 2007b). BCE board chair Richard Currie responded in kind, denouncing Lamoureux's attack as "graceless, unfortunate and beneath the dignity of the person running Ontario Teachers" (Tedesco 2007c). Further, Currie responded to Telus's assertion that the inadequacies of BCE's bid process precluded Telus from presenting an offer. Targeting Telus's executive leadership, Currie told *Post* columnist Theresa Tedesco "they were complete amateurs" (ibid.).

More ominously, as shareholders contemplated a $42.75 offer per share (Bell Canada Enterprises 2007f), BCE's angry bondholders had one last message: announcing their intention to sue BCE (Erman 2007b). The bondholders cited the company's statement of 29 March following publication of the Reguly/Willis story to the effect "the company has no current intention to pursue such discussions" (ibid.). The bondholders argued "what makes this situation a little bit unusual are the company's comments in March. It may have been factually correct on that day, at that time. But it sent a certain signal to the market," the bondholders told the *Globe* (ibid.). It fell to this writer to respond with the statement that "the press release of March 29 was an accurate representation of the company's position at that time" (ibid.).

The exchange illustrates the extent of elite discourse network activity throughout the BCE saga. Interested parties, including sophisticated investors with access to the most able legal and financial advisers and numerous back channel communications options, nonetheless routinely used the mainstream media in general, and the *Globe and Mail*'s Report on Business and the *National Post*'s financial section, in particular, to send messages to each other.

Reflections

Reguly said that working on the BCE saga was "a thrill. In that era … I felt that my job was chronicling the eradication of corporate Canada." Icons such as Alcan and Falconbridge were being acquired at significant premiums by large multinational corporations, Reguly said. BCE, one of the biggest companies in Canada and its largest telecommunications company, was about to be taken private. "I really did feel this was an end-of-an-era story" (pers. notes 2012).

Willis says the BCE story "was the single wildest story I've ever worked on. I couldn't believe the number of interested parties who were feeding me information." Sources in the hedge fund community were also major suppliers of information on the BCE transaction. And with three competing private equity consortia in the play, "within each of them there were one or two individuals who felt it would be useful for their cause to have a good relationship with the press. So, they talked a little bit too" (ibid.).

The extensive experience of the *Globe* team assigned to the BCE transaction was a factor in the paper's coverage. "We had very, very experienced business journalists, so they weren't easily going to be fooled," Greenspon said. "We had a lot of confidence that they were well-sourced. We knew that these were people who were in the play."

Willis said outside public relations firms were not significant sources in the BCE story; reporters could rely on principals – actual members of the elite discourse network – to be primary sources. Referring to Teachers' Jim Leech, Willis said simply, "You always knew where to find Jim." Hartt, in essence, confirms Willis's assessment. "A lot of people at Teachers didn't think that this was something that they needed to phone the bankers about," Hartt said. "So I didn't get a lot of phone calls at the time of this media ping-pong game that you're referring to. I remember it absolutely, but I wasn't involved in it," he said (ibid.).

Communications theorist James Carey argued journalists "write not for the public, but for one another, for their editors, for their sources, and for other insiders who are part of the specialized world they are reporting" (1997, 153). Carey, in essence, was describing elite discourse networks. Carey, focusing on political reporting, states, "Washington news is valued precisely because it is an insider's conversation, one interest group speaking to another, with reporters acting as symbol brokers coding stories into a conversation only the sophisticated few can follow" (ibid., 153–4).

Failure to manage elite discourse networks can prove costly to a potential takeover.

Former *Globe* reporter Jacquie McNish describes the "seismic events" that were elements of the BCE story: the federal government taking a policy decision regarding income trusts, an activist shareholder in Teachers, "what appeared on the outside to be fault lines in the boardroom" (pers. notes 2012). The timing was a factor, as the transaction occurred "at the top of this unsustainable bull market," McNish said, followed by the greatest financial collapse in the last seventy years. The legal issues in the BCE transaction proved to be extraordinary, the multiple National Newspaper Award-winning reporter added. "It was this wild roller-coaster ride that had more twists and turns," McNish said, and as a result, "no one really controlled the process." McNish likened the BCE transaction to a ship out on the ocean being buffeted in different directions by giant waves. The result, for McNish, "made for great journalism, great stories, but the whole thing became unpredictable. When you get in a situation like that, my experience as a journalist is that you tend to get a lot more different voices, a lot more frustration, and the media becomes a tool if you will, of all the different interests to either express their frustration, to have their point of view expressed ... People had a lot of axes to grind."

McNish agrees the BCE case created an active elite discourse network unique to the transaction, but instead of seeing the creation of that network as a result of the work of one mastermind, McNish suggests it was a discourse born of frustration. "At various points, you could see, you know, like the BCE side ... think they need to send a signal that there is going to be an actual auction here," McNish said. "The Teachers side sends a signal back saying, if I think you're interfering too much, I may not be in it and you may have a busted auction here." McNish said the signalling between the various interests through an elite discourse network may seem neat and organized, but from her perspective the discourse was messy and unpredictable. While McNish's assessment as to the reasons why an elite discourse network was required in the BCE saga may be irritating to BCE's former management, including the author, her statements do, in fact, confirm such a network was created around the transaction.

While one side of the BCE transaction was talking and the other side wasn't, *Globe* reporters had to write the story anyway. "We always attempted to explain the motivation of the groups that we were talking about, but the stories got written nonetheless," Willis explained.

Willis further concedes, "There were a number of occasions where one party's vested interest would have dominated a headline. But I would also point out in hindsight the BCE side at the board level and at the senior level, they don't stoop to much off-the-record stuff."

Carleton University professor and communications consultant Elly Alboim has a decidedly different perspective on the role journalists played in the elite discourse network around the BCE transaction and argues, "the ability to bear fair witness is their primary responsibility." In the BCE case, "there should have been a narrative on both sides," Alboim said. But because "the only people reading or caring were people in the market who had a stake in what was going on," the coverage, in his opinion, was decidedly one-sided. "We couldn't get a break on the business pages," Alboim added. As an adviser to BCE CEO Michael Sabia during the saga, Alboim concluded the anti-Sabia narrative that dominated the business press was shaped by "an implacable attack from someone very sophisticated about how markets operated and more particularly, how market journalism operated." This media-savvy individual was ably assisted by a "number of malevolent self-interested actors," according to Alboim, including investment bankers looking for bragging rights on the street and lawyers determined to add to the complexity of the issue in the interest of billable hours. The reporters, argues Alboim, "were carrying water for each of these guys."

Market Reaction

News that a change-of-control premium might be available to BCE shareholders had an immediate impact on the company's share price. On the trading day prior to the initial Reguly-Willis story, the company's share price traded in a relatively narrow band just over $30 a share. The day after the *Globe* story appeared, the opening price was above $33.

Further, an analysis of TSX share-price changes for BCE on days the elite discourse network created around the transaction was active establishes a direct link between the headline and share price movement, and trading volumes.

The 29 March 2007 news accounts of a potential transaction, for example, triggered an increase in the share price. Subsequent announcements from the company – such as the 17 April 2007 announcement that BCE was "reviewing strategic alternatives" – pushed the share price over $35. The announcement three days later – 20 April 2007 – that the board had established "a committee of independent directors to oversee the company's evaluation of a range of strategic alternatives" pushed the share price over $38; as news surfaced that the Teachers-led consortium was developing a fully financed offer, BCE's share price topped $40.

News accounts critical of BCE's handling of the strategic review process also had an impact on the share price. After news stories in the *Globe and Mail* and the *Financial Post* appeared the week of 23 April 2007 raising the spectre of a broken auction, BCE's share price began to drift downward, with the company's shares trading just above $37 in early May.

Once again, announcements from the company relating to the strategic review process caused the share price to move. The 23 May 2007 (Bell Canada Enterprises 2007c) press release announcing a consortium led by Cerberus Capital Management LP and a group of Canadian investors had signed agreements to explore the possibility of taking the company private pushed the share price back to almost $40. A subsequent announcement on 5 June 2007 that the Teachers-led consortium had signed a similar agreement (Bell Canada Enterprises 2007d) kept the share price in the $39.50 range.

The announcement on 20 June 2007 that Telus Corporation had entered into an agreement to explore the possibility of a merger with BCE (Bell Canada Enterprises 2007e) pushed BCE's share price over $40.50 the next day. In the days following Telus's withdrawal, BCE's share price drifted back below $39.50, only to move back to the $41.50 range on the first trading day following the Saturday, 30 June 2007 announcement that BCE had signed an agreement with Teachers to sell the company for $42.75 a share (Bell Canada Enterprises 2007f). Further news stories of significance in the BCE saga also generated a spike in the volume of shares sold.

As stated earlier in this chapter, a publicly traded company's share price reflects one of two things: a projection of the company's future earnings potential or the potential for a change-of-control premium. In the BCE case, the projection of the company's future earnings potential was largely moot once Telus withdrew from the strategic review process, as the opportunities left for consideration involved taking the company private. Further, BCE's operational performance, with results reported on 2 May 2007 for the first quarter, were simply not a factor. BCE's board could, in theory, have decided to decline the privatization options. To do so would have denied shareholders the second opportunity for a return – the change-of-control premium. As Sabia stated in an interview, the board did not give a lengthy consideration to a "just say no" option, and as a consequence, from the time of the first story of a potential transaction appeared in the *Globe* on 29 March – a full three months before the sale to Teachers was finally announced – fluctuations in BCE's share price reflected the market's assessment of whether or not the transaction was likely to occur. When the market determined a successful conclusion to the strategic review process was more likely, BCE's share price increased; when doubts surfaced, the share price dropped. And the charts cataloguing share price moves during the BCE saga establish a direct link to the headlines of the day – headlines generated by the elite discourse network that had grown up around the BCE transaction.

7

New Media Order and Public Discourse

When Donald J. Trump was officially sworn in as the forty-fifth president of the United States on 20 January 2017, much of America was still in a state of shock.

As David Shribman (2017) noted in a column carried in the *Globe and Mail*, Trump was an outsider with no political, government, or military leadership experience, with no meaningful party affiliation, no long-term political allegiances or alliances, no sense of historical custom, and no particular sense of ceremony.

Trump did succeed in positioning himself as an agent of change during the presidential campaign, having promised to "make America great again." The specifics as to just how he intended to do that included tearing up trade agreements, repealing Obamacare, building a tall wall along America's southern border, and "draining the swamp" in Washington.

Despite a lot of early talk about impeachment, the lengthy overhang of the Mueller inquiry into Russian interference in the 2016 election, links between Trump associates and Russians, and an admission by his personal lawyer that he broke electoral laws at Trump's express behest, the American electorate and the broader international community had a full term of office to assess whether Trump could deliver on his campaign promises.

The challenges Trump faced are both self-evident and self-inflicted. Candidate Trump told the electorate his government would cut taxes dramatically, pay down the national debt, protect Social Security and Medicare, and rebuild the military. As *Bloomberg Businessweek* noted in late 2016, "fulfilling any one of those four promises is possible, but doing all four at once defies logic" (Coy 2016). By November of 2017, as the first anniversary of his electoral triumph approached, Trump was pushing a tax reform plan through a Republican-controlled Congress that would dramatically reduce income taxes for corporations and the hyper-rich, while driving America's budgetary deficit into a stratosphere measured in the trillions of dollars.

How candidate and then President Trump turned conventional political wisdom on its head, and in so doing flouted and forced a reconsideration of many of the rules of political communications, is worthy of detailed consideration.

A few disclaimers.

First, consider the source of what follows. The 2016 class from the Riddell Graduate Program in Political Management at Carleton University can attest that I spent much of the 2016 fall semester telling students that in my considered opinion, Donald Trump would not, and could not, be elected president. Several students pushed back, from both the conservative and the progressive sides of the political spectrum. There was a lot of "Mama said" in their arguments (to quote the lyric from the Shirelles' 1960s hit single), underscoring candidate Trump's connection to those parts of America that felt ignored. Further, this author is one of the "elites" Trump railed against; a long-time political reporter, a one-time White House correspondent, a political staffer and campaign insider, a pundit, a lobbyist, a corporate executive in heavily regulated industries.

Philosophically, I am predisposed to eighteenth-century liberalism and not the mercantilist view of an earlier era now espoused by Trump. Everything this author heard from candidate Trump, or President Trump, is considered from that particular perspective. By way of example, I have supported and defended the trade liberalization agreements such as NAFTA that Trump wanted to tear up, or improve, depending on the moment.

Trump may have spent more time on Twitter than he did talking to the White House correspondent for the *Washington Post* but from a communications theory perspective, his messaging included elements of each of the four steps and each of the three phases in the Yale school communication process described in detail in an earlier chapter.

The president understood the importance of the symbolic arena. When speaking to immigration issues, for example, he was hyperaware of the power of the image of a porous border, understood the stimulative properties of a reference to a giant wall, knew how his target audience would respond to the image, and knew the power that audience response could have on a broader community. Writers such as Annette Gordon-Reed argue Trump had a better grasp of how to develop themes on social media than his competitors (2018). Trump's communications strategists may have used the most sophisticated of data mining techniques to identify niche audiences but they never lost sight of Lasswell's (1948) classic communications construct. The difference in today's world of social networking platforms is that the range of answers to the "through which channel" question has dramatically more options.

Consider these specifics.

President Trump, like candidate Trump before him, saw the mainstream news outlets as his adversaries and that the way to win against them was to direct the presidential "bully pulpit" against them. Trump clearly was seized of the *Washington Post* columnist E.J. Dionne Jr.'s observation that having an elite as an enemy is an enormous political asset. And an East Coast-based, small "l" liberal media establishment is easily portrayed as "elite" in fly-over states. Media critic Howard Kurtz (1998) has been arguing for years that one of the best ways to get press is to attack the press.

Trump's instrument of choice was his Twitter account. Twitter, by way of definition, is a "form of mass instant messaging, that specializes in recording the details of life in the moment" (Brown, I. 2009, F1). Twitter founder Jack Dorsey has described the social network as the "people's news network." Twitter may well be the niche platform Wall Street analysts insist it is. But the platform's impact on public discourse is disproportionate to its user numbers because it is a platform of choice for celebrities, politicians, and journalists alike; the perfect platform for the "celebrity" culture Boorstin predicted.

Political people looking for a way to connect more directly with their fellow citizens were seized of Twitter's potential long before The Donald came to the White House. Former Toronto mayor David Miller was an early user. Current Ottawa Mayor Jim Watson – whose daily schedule makes the Energizer bunny look like a half-miler – uses Twitter to great effect. Follow his feed for an hour or so and you're exhausted for him.

Trump tweeted unsolicited advice to former British prime minister Theresa May on diplomatic appointments or on how to negotiate Brexit. He tweeted to complain when North Korean dictator Kim Jong Un referred to him as "old" and also to praise the brutal leader's "great and beautiful vision for his county" (Trump 2019b). The parsing of Trump's presidential tweets is a reminder of the days of China's Cultural Revolution, when news correspondents and Western diplomats were forced to read wall posters to interpret government edicts during the Mao Zedong era. *Dazibao*, big-character, handwritten posters, were prominently displayed on the walls that ran along city streets. Initiated as a mass propaganda campaign by the Communist Party, dissidents came to use them to undermine authority.

A few stats to back up the sweeping assertion. According to Bloomberg, Trump posted fifty-one tweets in a single day during an official visit to South Korea in November 2017 (Kochkodin 2017). While he was relatively restrained at the start of his time in the White House, tweeting just 134 times in January 2017, that didn't last. By October 2017, he was up to 300 per month, and, except for a few dips, that upward trend continued. By June 2019, he was blasting out more than 650 tweets (including retweets) in the month (Social Blade 2019).

Trump's tweets reflected a pattern of behaviour, succinctly summarized in a column carried by *The Economist* in its 1 April 2017 edition: "You have only to follow his incontinent stream of tweets to grasp Mr. Trump's paranoia and vanity," the story states (Economist 2017a). "The press lies about him; the election result fraudulently omitted millions of votes for him; the intelligence

services are disloyal; his predecessors tapped his phones. It's neither pretty, nor presidential" (ibid.).

Trump's 2016 campaign manager and communications strategist
Kellyanne Conway might have been talking about her candidate
when she said, "I've noticed a lot of people are very bold and blus-
tery on Twitter, because it is very easy to do that with a poison
keyboard and a hundred and forty characters" (Lizza 2016).

Trump's tweets could reveal a lack of understanding of geopolitical situations. Bestselling author Harlan Coben posted this tweet
about Trump: "On Aleppo, he sounds like a fifth grader giving a
book report on a book he has never read" (Coben 2016). And on
occasion, the president could come across as positively obtuse.
While Notre-Dame cathedral in Paris was ablaze in April 2019,
Trump tweeted advice that the French should send in the water
tankers (which experts noted would likely have collapsed the fragile structure) (Trump 2019a).

Many of Trump's tweets didn't stand up to scrutiny, as journalists including former *Toronto Star* Washington bureau chief
and current CNN correspondent Daniel Dale has established. The
14 March 2017 edition of *Bloomberg Businessweek* cited the example
of a tweet the president sent out about a contract with Boeing for
two new aircraft to serve as Air Force One. "Costs are out of control, more than $4 billion. Cancel order!" the president decreed
(Graff 2017). Except no one involved with the program knew what
the president was referring to. Trump's subsequent claim at a cam-
paign-style rally in Melbourne, Florida, that his intervention saved
$1 billion forced a spokesperson for the US Air Force to concede he
had no idea what Trump was talking about. (By August 2019, the
cost of replacing the two aging planes that serve as Air Force One
had reached $5.3 billion) (Milbank 2019).

Trump's tweets caused the president to step on his own "message" repeatedly and created an aura of chaos and confusion around
his decision making. Former defense secretary James Mattis said,
"All the victories were becoming just submerged by this mercurial,
capricious, tweeting form of decision making" (Woodward 2020,

81). Attorney General William Barr complained Trump's tweeted instructions to the Justice Department made it "impossible for me to do my job" (ibid., 244).

What Trump figured out is that Twitter allows candidates and office-holders to assert their voice back into political conversation.

An insightful study by Kiku Adatto (1990), published by the Shorenstein Center at Harvard's Kennedy School, charted how the candidate's voice had basically disappeared from network television political coverage. Whereas in the 1968 presidential campaign, viewers of network newscasts would hear voice clips from candidates that ran just under a minute, by the 1988 campaign, the candidate's voice had been reduced to less than ten seconds. Instead of hearing from George H.W. Bush or Michael Dukakis directly, viewers were presented with a visual with the candidate in the background, but the camera focused on the correspondent who was telling viewers what the candidate was saying (ibid.).

Voters did not have to wonder what was on Donald Trump's mind. He told them. On Twitter. And if they didn't have a Twitter feed, Facebook posts or mainstream reporters kept voters appraised of the latest presidential tweet – a social media wrinkle on Lazarsfeld's two-step flow theory of mass communication.

Just after the 2016 election, *Washington Post* media columnist Margaret Sullivan used Trump's use of Twitter as a "bully" pulpit to issue a call to arms to her colleagues in the mainstream media. "In many ways, Trump can bypass the traditional press – using YouTube or Twitter to take his messages to the world without pesky journalistic fact-checking or filtering," Sullivan wrote. "He has masterfully manipulated the media for the past 18 months – bullying reporters, garnering billions in free publicity and portraying journalists as part of the corporate structure that must be brought down so that the people can triumph" (Sullivan, M. 2016). Sullivan's conclusion is "that U.S. citizens need an independent press more than ever ... Journalists, and their corporate bosses, shouldn't allow themselves to be used as props in Trump's never-ending theatre" (ibid.).

Harvard professor Thomas Patterson agrees citizens need an independent press more than ever because of the mass of conflicting information that is out there. "There is something worse than an inadequately informed public and that's an ill-informed public," Patterson states (2013).

A free press and free speech were afforded constitutional protection in the United States with the First Amendment to the Declaration of Independence. In Canada, the Charter of Rights and Freedoms in the 1982 Constitution included similar protections for a free press.

Political journalists are accustomed to and even comfortable with the fact their work can be challenged, even sharply criticized, by the very people they write about. The folks in the parliamentary press gallery, almost without exception, have been on the receiving end of a call from an editor or executive producer who has, in turn, been on the receiving end of a blistering call from a story subject or one of their minders.

Politicians of every stripe have been known to use the media, or an individual reporter, as a reference to make a point in a speech to an audience. The practice takes on a particular meaning when that speech is before a partisan crowd and the reporters covering the event are being denounced as enemies of the people. Donald Trump took the practice a step further still, his rants about "fake news" often articulated with specific attacks aimed at individual reporters on-site covering the event. It is chilling that in her work *Unbelievable*, NBC correspondent Katy Tur reported, "Everyone covering Trump [during the 2016 campaign] at NBC is under armed protection outside the venues" (Tur 2017, 190). Think about that. How free is a press where reporters covering presidential campaigns have to travel with personal security?

In August 2019, Cesar Sayoc, who frequently attended Trump's rallies and was called a "Donald Trump superfan" by his lawyers, was sentenced to twenty years in prison for mailing sixteen bombs to people and organizations he considered the president's enemies. Many of those named, including CNN and prominent Democrats, had been attacked by the president on Twitter (Weiser and Watkins 2019).

The *Boston Globe* launched an initiative supported by more than 350 dailies in the United States that set out a defence of a free press on the newspapers' editorial pages. The *Globe* editorial noted president Trump's sustained assault on a free press was "a central pillar of President Trump's politics" (Boston Globe 2018). In Trump's view, journalists are not classified as "fellow Americans" but rather as "the enemy of the people," the editorial noted. Further, 51 per cent of Republican respondents to a poll shared Trump's opinion. The 2018 editorial quoted former Republican president Ronald Reagan, who said, "Our tradition of a free press as a vital part of our democracy is as important as ever" (ibid.). The editorial concludes, "The greatness of America is dependent on the role of a free press to speak truth to the powerful" (ibid.).

Trump wasn't the first tenant of 1600 Pennsylvania Avenue to declare war on the mainstream media. Cronkite biographer Douglas Brinkley cites a 1969 speech written by Pat Buchanan, edited personally by President Richard M. Nixon, and delivered by former vice-president Spiro Agnew that decried "a small group of men, numbering perhaps no more than a dozen anchormen, commentators and executive producers [who] settle upon the 20 minutes or so of film and commentary that's to reach the public." The text goes on to read, "it is time that the networks were made more responsive to the views of the nation and more responsible to the people they serve" (Brinkley 2012, 441). That both Nixon and Agnew had to resign their offices in disgrace as a result of the work of these same journalists is a matter of historic record. But the "elitist" attack on the mainstream media penned by Buchanan and delivered by Agnew is a pejorative descriptive used by certain candidates for political office to this day.

The legacy media may have sniped at Trump's practice of articulating policy in a series of inarticulate tweets, but the fact is, they then fired up their own mobile devices and wrote news stories based on the tweet for their audiences.

His presidential predecessor, Barack Obama, cautioned against underestimating Trump, and the evidence would suggest Trump –

or someone around him – is a more sophisticated thinker about media and political communication than the commentariat is inclined to give him credit for. For starters, the public persona that is Donald Trump is a creation of the traditional or legacy media. From his earliest years, Trump demonstrated a heightened ability to get his name in the news. His critics may claim Trump has never read a book in his adult life, but by turning the task over to ghost-writers, Trump figured out how to claim authorship of a bestseller.

Corporate titans and the business press question his business acumen. *The Economist*, for example, describes Trump's business empire as small, middle-aged, and largely a domestic property business: half the Trump Group's entire worth is in five buildings, 66 per cent of the company's value is in New York, and 93 per cent of its value is in America (Economist 2016d). We're not talking Samsung, Apple, or General Motors here.

Trump – for all the right and all the wrong reasons – rarely has any trouble getting our collective attention. Trump and his media advisers also understood and played off certain of the scholarly principles of communication set out in earlier chapters:

- that news is about accuracy, not veracity
- that news is not what happened but what someone says has happened or will happen
- that legacy media, particularly network television, is hostage to the notions of "balance" and "fairness"
- that the broadcast media is hostage to "false equivalencies" – the structure of news and current affairs programming dictates the networks need to have as many of your "whisperers" as they allo-cate for the other side (Kellyanne Conway, come on down)
- that, as Edward Bernays observed almost a century ago, the power to make a reportable event is the power to make the experience

Trump also understood certain of us get as much of our political information from Howard Stern's radio show or Jimmy Fallon's late-night TV couch than we do from news and opinion pages.

Trump may have little in common with Harvard's Robert Reich, labour secretary in the Clinton administration, either in terms of political philosophy or personal character, but the president reflected a core understanding of Reich's (1987) observation that political communication makes extensive use of parables.

Salena Zito (2016), writing in *The Atlantic* near the end of the 2016 election campaign, perhaps summarized the situation best when she wrote, "The press takes him literally, but not seriously; his supporters take him seriously, but not literally." The wisdom of Zito's observation was underscored in a piece carried in *Politico Magazine* in November 2017. Trump's core supporters readily admitted he had not as yet delivered on many of his campaign promises. And they didn't care (Kruse 2017).

Trump and his advisers demonstrated an understanding of Elisabeth Noelle-Neumann's (1973) theories that cumulation and consonance in media coverage is a factor in opinionation – the "crooked Hillary" refrain cited earlier being but one example. They also understood Amos Tversky and Daniel Kahneman's (1974) theories of accessibility bias and ensured their messaging aligned with the images triggered by daily headlines.

Trump and his advisers knew "reality" is socially constructed, that almost none of us have direct experience with the events that dominate the news. As Trump told an audience in Kansas City in July 2018: "Don't believe the crap you see from these people, the fake news ... What you're seeing and what you're reading is not what's happening" (Cillizza 2018). They understood the gatekeeper function – once held by a relatively small band of senior journalists – is less clearly in the hands of media professionals in a social media world and now includes people such as former Trump strategist Steve Bannon, who continued to make headlines long after his departure from the White House.

They understood news has expanded from an institutional prerogative of those in control of production of legacy media outlets to a new prerogative of those in control of distribution through social networking platforms. They further understood news today is a collaborative, interactive process that might involve traditional "known" news makers such as a secretary of state or minister of finance but might just as easily involve a Russian hacker or WikiLeaks founder Julian Assange.

Team Trump understood this new media order rewards those who can turn noise into signal, to quote aggregator Nate Silver, and further understood that for a significant percentage of the population, legacy media and political elites are one and the same. Not surprisingly then, Trump's 2016 campaign made certain the establishment media were on the presidential ballot as much as Hillary Clinton as the personification of everything that is wrong with Washington insiders. For the 2020 presidential campaign, Trump substituted the name Joe Biden and repeated the refrain. And finally, Trump and his advisers knew that one means of undermining legacy media claims to fairness and objectivity was to make the media a story.

Here in Canada, anti-Trudeau voices worked to make reporters an element of the 2019 federal election, a development that will be explored in more detail in a later chapter.

As a further assertion of his unconventionality, Trump said repeatedly in the course of the 2016 campaign that he did not have any pollsters on his payroll – which begs the question, what did he think his campaign manager Kellyanne Conway did for a living? Trump insisted he didn't need to pay people to tell him what to say. Like much of what Trump has to say, the truth lies elsewhere. In addition to having polling experts on his payroll in 2016, Trump also had data miners, and if they weren't telling the Republican nominee what to say, they were most certainly telling Trump what swing voters in swing states wanted to hear, while forwarding literally tens of thousands of targeted messages to them. Dubbed "Project Alamo," the team headquartered in San Antonio, Texas, operated on two fronts. Consistent with strategist Steve Bannon's assertion that the path to victory rested with the campaign's ability to manipulate people through the internet the data miners identified 13.5 million voters in sixteen battleground states deemed "persuadable" (Morris 2016) – presumably some of the same people Hillary Clinton dismissed as "a basket of deplorables."

Simultaneously, the data miners conducted three major voter suppression operations targeting idealistic white liberals, young women, and African Americans. Brad Parscale, the digital consultant who played such a key role in Project Alamo, was Trump's first campaign manager for the president's 2020 re-election bid.

Americans increasingly get their news from social media sites such as Facebook and Google. Polls show that many of us have burrowed into our own echo chambers of information, a process made easier by filter bubbles, which in turn lend themselves to "dog whistle" politics. The true value of this kind of information lies in its ability to fit within a narrative.

There is no denying that when it comes to getting news about politics and government, liberals and conservatives inhabit different worlds. The "cultural splintering" author David Shenk predicted more than twenty years ago in his work *Data Smog* (1997) has certainly occurred in the world of political discourse.

Trump figured out that in today's evolving media ecosystem, spending hundreds of millions of dollars on television ads was a less effective way of connecting. Candidate Trump wasn't the first to question the impact of political advertising in the legacy press on public opinion.

In *The Gamble: Choice and Chance in the 2012 Presidential Election*, authors John Sides and Lynn Vavreck concluded: "When either [Democratic nominee Barack] Obama or [Republican nominee Mitt] Romney was able to out-advertise the other, the polls could move – but the effects of the ads typically wore off quickly" (2013, XV). In fact, later in the piece, Sides and Vavreck state the effects of the ads wore off "within a day" (ibid., 9).

By 2020, Trump's presidential campaign was using artificial intelligence to "text up to 100,000 message variables a day" (Woodward 2020, 268). *Washington Post* associate editor and author Bob Woodward cites Brad Parscale as stating the Trump campaign could contact a voter on their phone "100 times for about 11 cents" (ibid., 210).

As a consequence, as society moves increasingly online, look to the "spend" on legacy broadcast media to drop dramatically in subsequent campaigns everywhere in Western liberal democracies. In an important "canary in the coal mine" statement, Kory Teneycke, manager of the successful Conservative campaign in Ontario in 2018, said in an interview with Liberal campaign strategist David Herle that network television advertising is "now more dead than not, with some niche, but diminishing value" (Herle 2018).

The provincial Conservative campaign response, in part, included the party's own "news" crew, which allowed the campaign to file its own "reports" from the field directly to interested voters from a "correspondent" who concluded each report with a "stand up." And if the offering looked as if it was "journalism" from a news organization, so be it. The footage was also used to create "a constant pipeline of advertising content" (ibid.) – ad content that was brief, authoritative, built around "streeters" with actual voters on camera expressing their desire for change from the Liberal incumbent.

Radio, by contrast, is still seen as an interesting property from a campaign perspective. Radio is an "intimate" medium in many ways. Listeners can feel they are part of the conversation. And in major metropolitan areas, long commutes in a car can be more bearable if the radio is on.

President Trump's team also understood concepts of "framing" and succeeded in establishing "change" as the dominant news frame. In many ways, Trump is the personification of what Daniel Boorstin predicted in *The Image*, published in 1962 – a world of pseudo-events, where celebrities have replaced heroes, where people are well-known for being well-known, and where the world of pseudo-events gives rise to candidates with pseudo-qualifications.

The premium on the ability to get attention in a social media world would, inevitably, introduce the notion of narcissism into the equation of leadership, particularly at the political level. To quote Jesse Hirsh, "all self, all the time."

The problems surface once the aspirant for office is elected and his or her limitations are the subject of daily coverage in the legacy media. Trump actually had the job of president for four years. And he had to wrestle with the realities his predecessors discovered before him: that leadership is about the individual, at particular moments of time, dealing with events, many of which may have been out of his or her control – events as varied as the terrorist attacks on 9/11 to the Syrian refugee crisis of 2015. In Trump's case, the "event" was the COVID-19 pandemic. The people's "ask" can shift in a second. Winston Churchill was needed as the leader of all of Britain and arguably, the rest of the free world during the dark days following Dunkirk in 1940. He was shown the door electorally as soon as the Second World War was successfully concluded.

Fair is rarely part of the equation, as Barack Obama discovered during the financial crisis of 2008–09. But purpose, principle, and policy are. None of these three "Ps" seem to be Trump strengths.

Perhaps William "Bull" Halsey, a fleet admiral of the US Navy during the Second World War, put it best when he said, "There are no great men. Just great challenges which ordinary men, out of necessity, are forced by circumstances to meet" (United States Government 1971).

Financial markets, fundamentally an expression of expectations of future profits, loved Trump in the early going, anticipating reduced corporate taxes, which would lead to massive share buybacks and increased corporate profitability. But as far as certain of America's allies and trading partners were concerned, a casual reader of publications such as *The Economist*, the *Guardian*, or the *Financial Times* might wonder if America's role as the guarantor of the liberal postwar order still holds.

Much of America does not see itself in Trump's cabinet – made up in the main of older, white males: billionaires used to giving orders and generals used to following them.

Old-style free market liberals struggle to understand how voters could endorse promises to cut taxes for the richest, while imposing tariffs and trade protection measures that would raise prices for the poorest on everything from cars to cans of beer. One headline, riffing off Don McLean's classic "American Pie," summarized

Trump's tariff on steel and aluminum succinctly: "Hit the Chevy with a levy, tax your whiskey & rye" (Eltzroth 2018).

Campaign rhetoric notwithstanding, political life isn't as simple as promising to build a wall and getting someone else to pay for it, as Trump himself discovered over the 2018–19 holiday season when the US government basically shut down. And it is at least in the realm of the possible that climate change isn't just a Chinese conspiracy. But one of the other things the president figured out about political communication is that his foibles, flaws, and inconsistencies could be trumped by a larger truth certain voters wanted to believe – that the America they knew somehow had slipped but could be made great again.

Trump understood that while we receive political information through a central route that is largely fact-based and leads to a thoughtful consideration of the arguments, we also receive political information through a second, more emotional route that involves peripheral cues and affective associations.

If attention is the currency of the Information Age and television entrances the masses, social media engages individually.

Media effects theory holds the media is more effective in influencing public opinion on new or emerging issues; Team Trump understood the importance of creating new issues.

As stated earlier in this work, communication, as an organizational function, involves two primary tasks: content creation and content promulgation. Team Trump approached both through a social media lens but executed in a manner consistent with traditional media effects theories.

University of Toronto professor Clifford Orwin's cautionary observation that Trump didn't win the election only because Hillary Clinton lost it is a pointed reminder Trump's approach to media relations warrants more careful consideration (Orwin 2016).

Communications / Public Discourse

Charles Horton Cooley made the point, "communication is the mechanism by which society organizes itself" (Mattelart 1994, 31). Yet Boorstin quotes Max Frisch, who believed technology involved "the knack of so arranging the world that we don't have to experience it" (1962, i). As Boorstin states, "In this book I describe the world of our making; how we have used our wealth, our literacy, our technology, and our progress, to create a thicket of unreality which stands between us and the facts of life" (ibid., 3). Boorstin said the making of the illusions "which flood our experience has become the business of America" (ibid., 5).

In recent years, even prestige publications have had to answer criticism they'd used technology to alter reality for storytelling purposes. *Time* magazine was called out for a cover portrait of a blurry and unshaven O.J. Simpson at the time of his 1994 arrest in connection with the murders of his ex-wife Nicole Brown Simpson and her friend, Ron Goldman. The mug shot was taken by the Los Angeles Police Department. The credit read, "Photo-Illustration for Time by Matt Mahurin." *Time* later conceded the "illustration" involved darkening Simpson's skin in the image, which had the effect of creating a more sinister appearance, according to critics. The critics said *Time* had made a marketing decision designed to sell more newsstand copies (Carmody 1994). The fact *Newsweek* used the same mug shot without any alterations reinforced the case being made by critics.

In the run-up to the 2019 Canadian federal election, the Conservative Party of Canada ran a social media ad stating, "Justin Trudeau has made it clear that he wants to 'phase-out' Canada's oil & gas sector" (Conservative Party of Canada 2019). But as Edwin Mundt tweeted, "So @CPC_HQ memed a doctored photo by combining a picture of Justin Trudeau with a Getty Images stock photo and ran a Photoshop Plug-in to darken his skin tone. I suspect we'll see more of this" (Mundt 2019; Howse 2019). The denunciations of the Conservative ad peppered Twitter feeds all day. What was not addressed is whether the Conservatives considered the decision to make Trudeau look more sinister was a net benefit to their re-election prospects.

National Geographic's February 1982 cover featured a camel train in front of the pyramids at Giza. The original photograph was horizontal. The photo was altered to better fit the vertical cover, and in doing so, the final image effectively showed the Pyramids closer together than they are in fact (Nickle 2017).

Former Liberal Party leader Michael Ignatieff, before his stint in electoral politics, penned his lament for this transition to the world of pseudo-events as follows: "In place of thought, we have opinion; in place of argument, we have journalism; in place of polemic, we have personality profiles ... in place of ... public dialogue, we have celebrity chat shows" (cited in Jennings 2002, 111).

The heroes of antiquity have given way to the celebrity, which Boorstin describes as a "person well-known for their well-known-ness" (1962, 221). "In the democracy of pseudo-events, anyone can become a celebrity, if only he can get into the news and stay there" (ibid., 60).

Trump's positioning as a businessman is a prime example of the phenomenon. The world is largely uninformed as to the legitimacy of Trump's business credentials for a number of reasons, not the least of which is his ability to dismiss any public reporting of the specifics of his world. Trump's businesses are private and therefore most are not subject to public disclosure laws. He refuses to make his income tax returns public. And the defence from his supporters as to why the president hasn't paid any personal income tax in years invariably involves deductions of business losses in the hundreds of millions if not billions of dollars – which might fall short of a traditional benchmark of business acumen or success.

New York Times reporter Susanne Craig, who with two colleagues painstakingly followed a financial trail that began with three pages of Donald Trump's 1995 income tax returns and included a veritable mountain of documents from the New York property tax system, uncovered what Craig describes as the "foundational lie" of the Donald Trump saga (Canadian Journalism Foundation 2018c).

Trump claimed he borrowed $1 million from his father Fred Trump, whom Craig describes as "one of the great post-war builders in the United States" (ibid.). Trump insists he parlayed the loan, which he says he repaid, into a multi-billion-dollar empire. The

truth, says Craig, is Fred Trump had his son's back at every step of
the way and came to his rescue repeatedly, most notably in 1990
when Donald Trump was basically bankrupt.

In their 2018 follow-up blockbuster investigation of Trump's
finances, Craig and her colleagues discovered that Trump
received in excess of $60 million in loans from his father, received
in excess of $400 million in today's dollars in total benefits, and
was an active participant in schemes to avoid estate taxes that ran
the gamut from tax avoidance, to tax evasion, to outright fraud
(Barstow, Craig, and Buettner 2018).

The 1995 tax return claims Trump lost $916 million that year (Bar-
stow, Craig, Buettner, and Twohey 2016) and, as a consequence,
Craig says, "it is our belief he never paid a penny of (income) tax
since then" (Barstow, Craig, and Buettner 2018). In 2019 Craig and
her colleagues were subsequently awarded a Pulitzer Prize for
their later work.

As president, Trump certainly sought out Frisch's state of
arranging the world so that he didn't have to experience it. The
technology of Twitter allowed the president to communicate with
the American people in bumper sticker terms. By refusing to meet
the mainstream press in structured news conferences prior to the
coronavirus pandemic, Trump was able to avoid exchanges that
might reveal the limits of his understanding of the requirements of
his job or his grasp of detail on specific issues. By choosing news
organizations such as Fox News for the vast majority of interviews, Trump forced the broader public to listen to a conversation
constrained by the political and ideological limits of his "base."

It was the political scientist V.O. Key Jr., riffing off Plato perhaps, who advanced the notion of the "voice of the people" as an
"echo." In his 1966 work *The Responsible Electorate*, Key states, "The
output of an echo chamber bears an inevitable and invariable relation to the input" (1966, 2). Key went on to observe, "The people's
verdict can be no more than a selective reflection from the alternatives and outlooks presented to them" (ibid.). Key's observations
reflected a period when legacy media provided the political water

cooler around which political conversation occurred. His analysis asserted the public can only form opinions based on the information presented to them.

Social media, particularly social network platforms, has reshaped the contours of the echo chamber. Our friends tend to be like-minded souls, families perhaps less so. The links embedded in our tweets tend to support our worldview. Friends are more likely to click on a link we send them for precisely that reason. We read a piece because someone we respect and/or hold dear has posted it for our consideration, and having read it, we like or retweet or share the post with our network.

Social media platforms were certainly a factor in the 2018 Ontario provincial election.

In fact, Jeff Ballingall, founder of Ontario Proud, told *iPolitics*, "We were pivotal ... There's no longer a monopoly on political discourse," Ballingall told reporter Marieke Walsh. "We're able to reach people and mobilize them ... Social media is allowing people to fight back, we're able to tap into growing resentment about affordability issues, about government waste, about corruption and scandal" (Walsh, M. 2018).

According to Ontario Proud, the group has a bigger following on Facebook than all of the provincial parties and leaders combined. During the campaign period – from 9 May to 7 June – the group, which advocates a centre-right perspective on political issues, claims to have generated 63.6 million Facebook impressions while 3.7 million minutes of Ontario Proud videos were viewed (ibid.). Ontario Proud is, in some ways, a direct response to third-party organizations of a "progressive" political philosophy formed during the past provincial campaigns such as the Working Families coalition.

Public affairs firm Hill+Knowlton's analysis suggests Ballingall's boasts were well-founded. "Ontario Proud dominated every single social and digital channel and conversation during the election," Lindsay Finneran-Gingras told *iPolitics* (ibid.).

The third-party group sent more than one million text messages and generated 2.5 million phone calls during the campaign.

With the defeat of the Kathleen Wynne-led provincial Liberals in Ontario, Ballingall and company turned their firepower on federal Liberal Leader Justin Trudeau in time for the 2019 federal vote, with less success.

Ballingall can certainly draw a straight line between his site's messaging and the themes deemed determinant in the election of the Doug Ford-led Progressive Conservatives. However, the group's "master narrative" aligned with the dominant news frame for the campaign in the legacy media as well – change. It remains to be seen if third parties such as Ontario Proud are as successful if their messaging is not aligned with legacy media story lines. By May 2019, public support for the Ford government had melted like a snowbank in spring, as measured by published public opinion research (D'Mello 2019). Ontario Proud, in the immediate term at least, doesn't seem to be able to do anything to improve Ford's "negatives." Further, subsequent filings after the provincial election suggest Ontario Proud may be more Astroturf than grassroots – an organization relying on professional fundraisers and largely funded by large Toronto-area property developers (Crawley 2018).

Contrarian views are less likely to penetrate the bubble and therefore are less likely to find "echo" in our political conversations. Communications scholar Todd Gitlin asks, "Does democracy require a public or publics? A public sphere or separate public sphericules?" (1998).

By attacking the editorial product of all news organizations that fall outside the president's imposed parameters as promulgators of "fake news," Donald Trump got to refute the charges without engaging in the specifics.

Obviously, Trump's attempts to dismiss any and all journalistic criticism of him, his family, or his administration as "fake news" weren't always successful. As he headed to the UK for a visit in 2018, to be followed by a round or two of golf at the Turnberry course he owns in Scotland, Trump was greeted by an editorial in *The Scotsman* under the headline, "A Denunciation of Donald Trump." The piece went on to describe Trump as "an appalling human being" as well as "a racist, a serial liar and either a sexual abuser or someone who falsely brags about being one" (Scotsman Leader Comment 2018).

Daniel Dale, formerly the *Toronto Star* bureau chief in Washington, established himself in the political conversation in the United States by carefully tracking Trump's pattern of falsehoods. Dale is hardly alone. But Dale is arguably the best Washington-based reporter at it by the way he includes a presidential falsehood as well as the truth in the same tweet. His Twitter threads of Trump rallies and remarks regularly go viral (Dale 2019). When President Trump asked the television networks for prime time on 8 January 2019 to discuss the impasse with Congress that forced a partial shutdown of the US government, CNN invited Dale to appear live to comment on the veracity of the president's address to the nation. The news network hired Dale soon after to continue his political fact checking (CNN 2019).

Washington Post media columnist Margaret Sullivan says of the president, "The problem is, he lies all the time" (Canadian Journalism Foundation 2019a). Former defense secretary Jim Mattis says President Trump "doesn't know the difference between the truth and a lie" (Woodward 2020, 69). NBC correspondent Katy Tur, one of the first journalists assigned full-time to the Trump 2016 campaign, offered this observation about the most unlikely of presidential candidates: "To me, he has a compulsive desire to be the best, smartest, and in this case toughest" (Tur 2017, 71).

Trump's media relations raise a core question. Boorstin reminds us of the famous axiom widely attributed to Abraham Lincoln that "You may fool all of the people some of the time, you can even fool some of the people all of the time; but you can't fool all of the people all the time," Boorstin states (1962, 36). "This has been the foundation-belief of American democracy" (ibid.).

Trump clearly believes he can fool enough of the people enough of the time to succeed. Yet Boorstin points to a reality that, in the end, may lead to Trump's ultimate undoing. "The very agency that first makes the celebrity in the long run invariably destroys him. He will be destroyed, as he was made, by publicity," Boorstin asserts (ibid., 63). Once Trump tells people he has spent a lifetime feeding reporters stuff he has made up, reporters will have to consider everything the president says from that perspective.

Trump's success at dominated earned media coverage begs the question: Is his success an accident or by design?

In a thought-provoking piece carried in the 9 December 2017 edition of the *New York Times* entitled "Trump's way: Inside Trump's Hour-by-Hour Battle for Self-Preservation," correspondents Maggie Haberman, Glenn Thrush and Peter Baker state, "For most of the year, people inside and outside Washington have been convinced that there is a strategy behind Mr. Trump's actions" (Haberman, Thrush, and Baker 2017). Yet the writers conclude "there is seldom a plan apart from pre-emption, self-defence, obsession and impulse" (ibid.). The report states, "Occasionally, the President solicits affirmation before hitting the 'tweet' button." And in an important insight, the journalists also state, "The ammunition for his Twitter war is television" (ibid.).

President Trump, despite his age, is a child of television. Author Michael Wolff asserts, "Trump didn't read. He didn't really even skim ... He was post literate – total television" (Wolff 2018, 113–14). Trump, reportedly, spends many hours of every day glued to a television screen, swilling Diet Coke. He watches CNN and MSNBC to inform himself as to what the enemy is up to and Fox News for commentators he sees as the forces of truth and light.

Presidential viewing habits notwithstanding, it is a challenge to accept the *Times* correspondents' assertion that there is no plan. Trump's public declarations reflect a real understanding of the way legacy media outlets cover and report the news. For critics disinclined to give Trump credit for anything, it is a reach to argue his presidential campaign reflected a core understanding of how mainstream media – particularly network and cable television news – conducts its business. But the evidence suggests otherwise.

When the *Access Hollywood* tape of Trump having a lewd conversation with TV host Billy Bush surfaced in the 2016 presidential campaign, Trump's crude comments toward women were considered by the chattering classes to be the proverbial last straw.

As Trump and Clinton prepared for a televised debate, much of the coverage leading up to the event focused on how Republican nominee Trump planned to explain the unexplainable.

When reporters arrived in St. Louis, Missouri – the site of the event – they were invited to a nearby hotel where the Trump campaign had gathered three women who accused former president Bill Clinton of forcing himself on them, plus one whose rapist was defended by lawyer Hillary Clinton.

Trump planned to put the women in the Trump family box for the debate – right up front. Bill Clinton – and his wife, the Democratic nominee – would have to come face to face with his accusers. "It would also mean that when Trump is questioned about the 'pussy' tape, which he very obviously will be, he'll have a visual response: four allegedly abused women, something for people to see not just hear," NBC's Katy Tur reports. "The man knows television. No disputing that" (Tur 2017, 236).

Trump's triumph in the 2016 presidential campaign should have triggered an industry-wide "examination of conscience" (to use the Catholic Church's term) on the part of the political press and the sources that feed it. The mainstream media did an effective job of chronicling Trump's many shortcomings, both in personal and policy terms. But in tracking the trees, the mainstream press missed the proverbial forest – the forest that is the American electorate. "In terms of our bellwether moments, this is our anti-Watergate," stated Kyle Pope, editor of the *Columbia Journalism Review* (English 2016). Added *Washington Post* media critic Margaret Sullivan, "To put it bluntly, the media missed the story. Make no mistake. This is an epic fail" (ibid.).

The political press's predisposition to see the fourth estate's role as truth tellers put them at a bit of a disadvantage in media relations terms when reporters found themselves dealing with Trump campaign operatives such as Steve Bannon, who believed the media's claim to be the protector of probity and all that is factual and accurate was, in itself, a sham (Wolff 2018, 47).

Bannon, whose strategic approach to public discourse is predicated in no small measure on an assertion of media incompetence, says news organizations were "humiliated" by the outcome of the 2016 presidential campaign. "The paper of record for our beloved republic, *New York Times*, should be absolutely ashamed," Bannon states. "They got it 100 per cent wrong" (Grynbaum 2017). Referring to publications such as the *New York Times* and the *Washington Post*, Bannon said, "The media has zero integrity, zero intelligence and no hard work" (ibid.). Bannon says the mainstream media simply doesn't understand the country and wonders why none of the journalists assigned to cover the Trump campaign weren't terminated for cause.

There may, however, be another explanation for the disconnect between the media and the electorate. The election of a Doug Ford-led Progressive Conservative government in Ontario on 7 June 2018 underscores the complexity in the differences between what reporters think they are telling the public and what their new stories are actually communicating.

On the surface, Ford's media coverage during the provincial campaign was negative. The media mocked Ford in the weeks leading up to the campaign when he launched his bid for the hastily vacated party leadership from the basement of his mother's house. How hopelessly suburban.

Then, Ford defied campaign convention by informing the press there would be no media bus made available for the leader's tour. Reporters would simply have to find their own way to campaign events. And to make that task even more difficult, the campaign was less than forthcoming with a schedule of events. Certain days, the itinerary listed a single event, forcing reporters to determine how many other "unscheduled" events Ford had appeared at that day.

Reviews of Ford's performances during televised leaders' debates were uniformly critical. His stump speech was dismissed as a litany of bromides, simplistic in the extreme.

And the soap opera that is the Ford family added to the tone and tenor of the coverage, culminating in the final days of the campaign with news the widow of Ford's brother – the late Toronto mayor Rob Ford – was suing the PC leader for his failures as executor of Rob Ford's will. Renata Ford's claim, in essence, was that she and her two children were destitute, and Doug and brother Randy Ford's mismanagement of the family business was the root cause. In a later episode of the Ford family soap opera, Renata announced her intention to be a candidate for Maxime Bernier's libertarian People's Party of Canada in the 2019 federal election.

The coverage weights did have an impact on public perceptions of the PC leader. Public opinion research during the campaign suggested the more news consumers knew about Doug Ford, the less they liked about what they saw. Conservative strategists reacted to this emerging reality effectively. In the waning days of the campaign, the strategists surrounded Ford with star Conservative candidates – Christine Elliott, Caroline Mulroney, Rod Phillips, Peter Bethlenfalvy.

The tactic succeeded. The steady slide in Conservative support in tracking polls was first arrested and then reversed (CBC 2018). While every Conservative candidate elected was perfectly entitled to say they won *despite* Doug Ford, not because of him, the fact is, Doug Ford is premier.

But the impact on the broader public of this negative media campaign coverage of Ford was undermined in part by a broader, more fundamental fact of mass communication. News highlights the exception. And the exception when it comes to political government news often involves a failure of some type. The anti-government construct of much media coverage during fifteen years of Liberal governments in Ontario not only created problems for former premier Kathleen Wynne but generally aligns completely with Ford's core small "c" conservative message that the best thing government can do for people is get out of their way. William D. Eggers and Paul Macmillan talk about the "solution revolution," but a subtext of that story line is a growing belief on the part of the public that people and not governments will have to solve society's problems (Eggers and Macmillan 2013).

When governments embrace an overarching strategy of risk avoidance, with a subtext of plausible deniability, the potential for government to be seen by the electorate as a force for good is minimized. Green energy initiatives get buried in an avalanche of headlines about the business boondoggles around the letting of contracts for alternate energy sources. So why not campaign on simplistic promises of cheap gas and buck-a-bottle beer? Those kinds of campaign commitments align with the everyday lives of people. This "bread and circuses" approach dates back to the Roman Empire. Doug Ford's election suggests the strategy can still succeed.

Many of Ford's strategists had previously earned campaign medals in Stephen Harper's Ottawa and they know from firsthand experience that a cut in taxes – Harper trimmed the federal goods and services tax in 2005 – might be bad economics but good politics.

The dominant news frame for the Ontario election was "change" – making it virtually impossible for incumbent Liberal Premier Kathleen Wynne to even be part of that conversation. And that desire for change was stronger than the reservations voters had about Ford personally.

Campaign canvassers uniformly reported that when they would knock on a door, the message coming back to them was basically, "we don't like Ford, but we want change," and the strength of the Conservative team had more appeal than the Andrea Horwath-led New Democrats.

In Canada, the modern Conservative Party's mantra of less government may produce transactional, rather than transformational governments. But what some of the *commentariat* fail to appreciate is the fact that for conservatives, that is not a negative. On the contrary, minimal government is precisely their objective – the very "transformation" they seek. This brand of conservatism sees people, and not governments, as the true agents of change. Individuals are the innovators, and government's role is to create the winning program and policy conditions that will allow people to do what they do best.

Ford campaign manager Kory Teneycke, for example, would scoff at mainstream media analysis that dismissed the party leader's promise to get government out of people's lives as simplistic. Teneycke understood Ontarians had grown tired of the nanny state, were increasingly irritated with Kathleen Wynne as scold, and believed flashpoints such as high hydro bills were the direct result of government doing a bad job of something the private sector can do more efficiently and effectively.

Teneycke understood Ford's message was exactly what Ontarians anxious for change wanted to hear and that they didn't need to hear much else. That said, the Ontario Conservatives, like Donald Trump, have discovered the vague generalities of campaign promises around "cutting waste" can prove problematic in government. Buyers' remorse has set in with certain Ontarians who voted on change but struggle with Ford's specifics of change. In fact, Ford's record in office was a factor in the 2019 federal election.

Conservatives also understand there is a pace to change and that pace for the broader community is slower than social activists would like. The introduction of the Charter of Rights and Freedoms as part of the 1982 constitutional patriation process did create circumstances where court decisions could accelerate that change – judges as social architects. But certain politicians, whether large "C" Conservatives such as Stephen Harper or Liberals such as Jean Chrétien, understand that the public needs to take a deep breath and rest every once in a while.

In these circumstances, political parties campaigning on ambitious, interventionist agendas may find the broader public doesn't share their sense of immediacy around issues such as gender or diversity.

The mainstream or legacy media must address the issue of its fading credibility if it is to continue to have a viable role to play in shaping public discourse. As Katy Tur states, "We can tell the truth all day, but it's pointless if no one believes us" (Tur 2017, 199). In a blog posted in the wake of Trump's successful presidential bid, Charlie Beckett, a professor at the London School of Economics, argued American journalism "has to face up to the fact that half of the voters appear to hate them, the other half despair of them. Few trust them" (Beckett 2016). Beckett's post-game analysis concludes political journalists need to listen more and talk less.

The mainstream media's preoccupation with horse-race coverage is also a factor in this disconnect, according to John Sides and Lynn

Vavreck (2013). In their study of the 2012 presidential campaign, the authors state, "Polls do not move for no reason ... Polls move in response to new information about the candidates" (ibid., 41). News stories are a key source of that new information, and much of that new information relates to the horse race. Public opinion polls, according to author Nick Moon (Moon 1999), are the most reported form of public political communication. "During the 2012 primary campaign, the Pew Center's Project for Excellence in Journalism (PEJ) estimated that nearly two-thirds of news coverage (64 per cent) was framed around horse-race topics" (Sides and Vavreck 2013, 41). The *Washington Post*'s Margaret Sullivan says horse-race coverage "is not very helpful and not very good journalism" (Canadian Journalism Foundation 2019a). The typical pattern for coverage of individual candidates in primaries followed an arc: discovery, scrutiny, decline – especially if the candidate begins to look like an "also ran" in the horse race. "As horse-race political coverage and polling has become dominant, the news media have ignored the people and focused on the political celebrities and the stats" (Beckett 2016). And he quotes *Columbia Journalism Review* editor Kyle Pope who states, "Reporters' eagerness first to ridicule Trump and his supporters, then dismiss them and finally to actively lobby and argue for their defeat have led us to a moment when the entire journalistic enterprise needs to be rethought and rebuilt" (ibid.).

Pope considers the 2016 presidential campaign the "anti-Watergate" moment for political journalism, and he believes the "original sin" is rooted in a fundamental failure of reporting (ibid.). Hillary Clinton wasn't the only one flying over red states instead of touching down for a firsthand look.

One of the more troubling elements of the "echo chamber" phenomenon is the "pack journalism" practices so prevalent in the legacy media. What Matthew Yglesias describes as "the pundit's fallacy" is one of the consequences of what Thomas Patterson describes as the game versus governance schema dilemma. Yglesias defines the fallacy as the belief on the part of many political commentators that their pet issues are, miraculously, the very same issues that matter most to the electorate (Yglesias 2018). During the early days of the 2019 Canadian federal election, political reporters were left wondering if the voters shared their preoccupation with the SNC-Lavalin affair.

The "inside the Beltway" phenomenon in American politics is an expression of Lippmann's observation that the amount of public attention paid an issue by political insiders is an unreliable index of either public awareness or familiarity.

This tendency for media insiders to fashion a discourse based almost exclusively on conversations with political insiders can have disastrous consequences for both sides. David Cameron's communications guru Craig Oliver put it this way: "One of the things I have learned in this job is that there are about 3,500 people who live in the political/media village. Their values, what they think and believe, are often dramatically different to the 35 million voters we have to win over. What I have learned is that people who focus on the 3,500 and not the 35 million are almost always the ones that fail" (Oliver, C. 2016, 217).

Political leaders, regardless of their partisan stripe, routinely bristle at the kind of coverage they receive. Author Michael Wolff states the media long ago wrote Donald Trump off as a lightweight and a wannabe, but Trump's real mistake, according to Wolff, was that in his earlier years he tried to curry favour with the media too much (Wolff 2018). If Wolff is correct, Pierre Trudeau's barely disguised disdain for the political press may have been the more effective strategy.

As stated earlier, former Canadian prime minister Brian Mulroney and former US president George Herbert Walker Bush both believed personal relations should count for something in the exercise of media relations. But what Bush found more deeply disturbing were the press practices of the pack: "Then too, you [are] always reminded of the 'pack' and how the 'pack' works. They write the same things, say the same things, rub their hands in the same concerned way, yell the same way now on these talks shows" (Meachem 2015, 436).

Mulroney was equally befuddled by the pack mentality, mused about the questions on politics or public policy the media didn't ask, and deplored the pack's predisposition to accept a narrative or Andie Tucher's "congenial truth" about certain of his political opponents or opposing political parties. Why, for example, are small "l" and large "L" liberals just assumed to be better people than those who espouse a more conservative or leftist worldview?

Economist Robert Shiller was struck by Robert K. Merton's observation that there are two kinds of people in the world: cosmopolitans and locals. The cosmopolitans, according to Merton, orient themselves to the whole world; the locals, to their village or town. Merton's observation succinctly describes much of the division in political discourse today, whether the subject is trade agreements, international alliances, or climate change (Shiller 2005, 104).

Management guru Peter Drucker was the first to articulate a core requirement for leaders of any description in an information age, which "demands for the first time in history that people with knowledge take responsibility for making themselves understood by people who do not have the same knowledge base" (Lanham 2007b, 134).

International trade agreements, tackling climate change, and membership in the European Union may well be worthy public policy initiatives. But the failure of progressive leadership to not just explain but also successfully sell the opportunities in these initiatives by political and business leaders from Hillary Clinton to David Cameron to Angela Merkel lead to Trump, Brexit, a US withdrawal from the Paris Accord, and threats of trade wars with China.

If free traders recoil in horror at the rhetoric of Donald Trump or Britain's Brexiters, they need only consider their own failures to communicate. In his seminal work *Listen, Liberal*, Thomas Frank (2016) offers a sharp rebuke of the worldview as espoused by the tight little group of credentialed professionals, their world of technocratic unity, their world of post-partisan thinking, focused on the benefit of the new order to them, with scant heed paid to those disproportionately burdened with the cost of this new global order.

Public discourse also needs to develop an ability to discuss the personal traits of political leaders in a manner that rises above the schoolyard taunt.

Peter Wehner, a senior fellow at the Ethics and Public Policy Center in Washington, DC, served in three previous Republican administrations. And in an opinion piece in the 25 August 2018 *New York Times* that carried a headline and deck of "The Full Spectrum Corruption of Donald Trump: Everyone and Everything He Touches Rots," Wehner wrote, "We have to distinguish between imperfect leaders and corrupt ones, and we need the vocabulary to do so" (Wehner 2018).

Harvard scholar Yochai Benkler saw the evolution of the internet as an opportunity for individuals to change the way "we create and exchange information, knowledge and culture." In his work *The Wealth of Networks*, Benkler foreshadowed a shift "from the mass-mediated public sphere to a networked public sphere" (Benkler 2006, 18). Where individuals "are less susceptible to manipulation by a legally defined class of others – the owners of communications infrastructure and media" (ibid., 9). Done right, the twenty-first century can offer "individuals greater autonomy, political communities greater democracy, and societies greater opportunities for cultural self-reflection and human connection" (ibid., 473). However, Benkler realistically asserts, "I offer no reassurances, however, that any of this will in fact come to pass" (ibid., 18). The current debate around Facebook's algorithmic control of what content we see, even from content posted by friends, underscores the wisdom of Benkler's caution. Is manipulation by algorithm any less threatening than the manipulation of old-style press barons?

The shift to an Internet-driven public discourse may presage a parallel shift in attitudes toward authority, and by extension, political institutions, according to internet strategist Jesse Hirsh. Describing a shift from institutional authority to cognitive authority, Hirsh says data is the most authoritative element of the internet. "We are addicted to, and obsessed with, screens," Hirsh says. "An individual can gain global attention with a tweet, and we seek out the individual in our society who delivers a signal amidst the noise" (pers. notes).

Predictably, as a former newspaper correspondent, print publications constituted a cornerstone of my consideration of these issues. James Carey argued the substance of democratic conversations must come from public sources, and the newspaper "is the historically central source" (cited in Schudson 1995, 305). The daily publication of a record of news and commentary constituted, for Carey, "a first step toward the reflection necessary for wisdom in democratic life" (cited in Adam 2009, 855). The press, said Carey, best carried out that assignment by encouraging the condition of public discourse and public life.

And in the spirit of Carey's philosophy of communications, Indigenous leader Gwen Phillips, responsible for guiding the Ktunaxa Nation's transition to self-government, made an observation in the course of her keynote address at a Data Power conference at Carleton University in June 2017 worthy of reflection by political journalists and communicators alike. "Be careful with our words," Phillips advised the scholars and researchers in attendance, "because words create worlds" (Phillips, G. 2017).

In Canada, political discourse has historically been shaped by linguistic and regional considerations. The French phrase *"il parle à sa paroisse,"* which translates as "he speaks to his own parish," was oft-cited when a political leader's message in Quebec seemed somewhat different than the message used to address the same issue in English Canada. Hardly surprising, given that Canada, as presently organized politically, celebrated its sesquicentennial in 2017. A federal system, to be sure, chosen instead of Britain's unitary state model to accommodate regional differences, real and perceived.

Yet a study published by the Institute for Research on Public Policy (Montpetit, Lachapelle, and Kiss 2017) suggests those regional differences are less determinant in policy terms. Based on 1,000 interviews with respondents in five regions – Quebec, Ontario, British Columbia, the Prairie provinces, and Atlantic Canada – authors Éric Montpetit, Erick Lachapelle, and Simon Kiss report "Canadians are first and foremost divided over values not regions," according to the report's summary (ibid., 1). "Disagreements on policy issues exist because of Canadians' different values, not because of territorial fracture lines" (ibid.). Conversely, the authors assert, "Individuals who share the same values, regardless of where they live, have similar policy preferences" (ibid.). The study's conclusion speaks to Merton's cosmopolitans/locals division.

In a country long accustomed to the puzzled "What does Quebec want?" or the assertive "The West wants in!" form of political discourse, the authors conclude that to be successful, "public policy has to be framed on values not regions" (ibid.) – although they do concede policy-makers "sometimes need to adopt regionally sensitive communications strategies" (ibid.). Alberta Premier Jason Kenney has enthusiastically embraced the notion of "regionally sensitive communications strategies."

Liberal strategist Tiffany Gooch called for the creation of "a culture of mutual respect" in the Twittersphere in a 25 June 2017 column in the *Toronto Star*. "At its best, I consider political Twitter to be the modern version of the public square," Gooch stated. "When Twitter works, it is now a powerful engagement tool influencing public policy and political strategies." Though, as Gooch conceded, "It doesn't always work" (Gooch 2017).

Twitter's properties as a public space trigger concerns beyond the baseline of respect for opinion. Twitter can also provide a pulpit for those self-appointed guardians of a truth – whether that truth is cultural, political, or scientific in nature. Twitter callouts – by everyone from Donald Trump to professional athletes – now trigger news stories in mainstream media outlets.

In the old media order, when news was made by "knowns," those "knowns" had a certain standing or status that was a factor in assessing the value in the information they were providing. In time, the symbiotic relationship between political leaders and political journalists created its own echo chamber. The megaphone, one-to-many communication model of the "transmission" tradition gave way to a signalling system between leadership factions. Political communication and political journalism evolved to Aeron Davis's system of elite discourse networks (2002), which in turn gave rise to Jay Rosen's "church of the savvy" (2009). The public wasn't "savvy" enough for the inside-baseball conversation and therefore found itself increasingly excluded from it. And to pick up on Thomas Patterson's (1994) astute observation, political journalism's increasing dependency on a "game" schema for the media narrative became less relevant for a public more interested in a "governance" narrative.

Predictably, citizens initiated political conversations of their own that attracted minimal interest from the mainstream media because these did not conform to the political press's "game" schema. The Academy of the Impossible, founded by activist Jesse Hirsh and writer Emily Pohl-Weary, provided one Toronto venue for these public conversations. The academy's salons attracted individuals interested in public policy as it impacted the community – however that community was defined. The sessions attracted political personages familiar to consumers of mainstream media. Yet the conversations were rarely, if ever, the subject of mainstream media coverage.

In the new universe of tailored messaging, authority or authenticity doesn't necessarily reflect professional standing or political power but rather a perspective or point of view that is claimed or asserted for reasons that range from ideology to cultural identity.

Not surprisingly, a subtext of the debate around the value of social media interventions is a debate around who the voice claims to speak for. In fact, the polarization of political discourse has left increasing numbers of citizens in Western liberal democracies with a sense that the parties have stopped speaking to them. A Twitter post 17 November 2018 from Astrid K read, "I'm not married, have no kids, have a job that pays well, and have investments. There isn't a major party who offers me anything, I'm basically nothing more than an ATM for them" (K 2018).

The hyper-partisan nature of political discourse in Western liberal democracies today is problematic on a more fundamental level. "Democracy depends on the ability to manage conflict constructively," argues Jeffrey Mirel. "Learning how to deal with conflict in a civil manner is one of the great lessons that schools in a democracy must teach" (Wu, T. 2016, 99).

The debate over the proposed expansion of the Trans Mountain pipeline that moves oil from Alberta to its Vancouver-area terminal is but one example. Trans Mountain wasn't simply about adding more pipeline; it was a metaphor for the more fundamental question of whether Canada's various levels of government could in fact come to agreement on a major initiative of any kind.

There is no shortage of sarcasm and snark in tweets posted by Canada's elected officials. In the wake of General Motors' announcement that the automaker would be closing its plant in Oshawa, Ontario, and laying off nearly 3,000 workers, Alberta MP Michelle Rempel Garner saw it all as some kind of left-wing plot. "This is a sentiment that is pervasive among a set of the leftist elite political class in Canada," Rempel Garner tweeted. "'Cars are soooo outdated, why should we make them?' 'Oh Alberta, you and your dirty little jobs, it's about time this industry collapsed.' The 'let them eat cake' ideology of the left" (Rempel Garner 2018). A few months later, Liberal MP Adam Vaughan suggested it was time to "whack" Ontario Premier Doug Ford for his government's cuts to education, a descriptive that evoked images of Martin Scorsese's *The Departed*.

Literary critic Wayne Booth (2009, 89) argues any nation is in trouble if its citizens are not trained in critical response. But NYU professor Clay Shirky makes an equally key point in a piece carried in the January/February 2011 edition of *Foreign Affairs* when he states, "Political freedom has to be accompanied by a civil society literate enough and densely connected enough to discuss the issues presented to the public" (Shirky 2011).

Political communication is an integral component in the rise of populism politics in Western liberal democracies. In a paper entitled "Political Journalism in a Populist Age," published by Harvard's Shorenstein Center, fellow Claes H. de Vreese notes the political debate that gives rise to populist parties is often focused on the twin threats of economic uncertainty and cultural disruption (de Vreese 2017). De Vreese, a professor and chair of political communication at the University of Amsterdam, states populism does not have a "mother ideology" and tends to surface on political fringes on both the left and the right. However, there are three distinct elements to populist rhetoric, de Vreese states: there is always a reference to the "people," there is invariably a reference to a "corrupt elite," and there is an element of "out-group" exclusion.

Reason in political discourse doesn't always prevail.

Media sociologists long ago established as fact the predisposition of groups in society to change their position on a public policy or program if the political party they support does an about-face. Television viewers in the United States can amuse themselves by watching Fox News host Sean Hannity – a close friend and confidant of Donald Trump – turn himself into a pretzel to support Trump on a decision Hannity loudly denounced when former president Barack Obama suggested the idea was worthy of consideration. And here in Canada, old-timers were undoubtedly bemused to watch Trudeau Liberals mount a spirited defence of the North American Free Trade Agreement – given the fact that thirty-one years earlier, Liberals fought the 1988 federal election in opposition to NAFTA's predecessor agreement, the Canada-US Free Trade Agreement. An article carried in *The Economist* (2016a) provided a timely reminder that political parties are never monoliths; they are always fractious and often fractured.

The concept of the "tyranny of the majority" is well-established and to some extent was a factor in the move to include a Charter of Rights and Freedoms in the Canadian Constitution of 1982. But in electoral terms, in liberal democracies with a "first-past-the-post" system, the tyranny of the majority is in fact a tyranny of the plurality. And when it comes to which candidates carry a party's banner in an election, the tyranny of the plurality gives way to the tyranny of a micro plurality.

Ontario Progressive Conservative Premier Doug Ford likes to talk about "Ford Nation" – an electoral coalition begun by his father Doug Ford Sr. and his brother and former Toronto mayor, the late Rob Ford. Yet Ford Nation, for all its strength, wasn't large enough to put Ford over the top in the March 2018 leadership contest of the provincial Progressive Conservative Party. It was a boost from Tanya Granic Allen's social conservative supporters that provided Ford with his margin of victory. A similar boost from social conservative supporters of candidates Leslyn Lewis and Derek Sloan allowed Erin O'Toole to emerge victorious in the 2020 federal Conservative Party leadership contest. And the list of public policy issues that preoccupy these citizens is relatively short.

President Trump's response to the violent confrontation between white supremacists and protesters in Charlottesville, Virginia, when he said there were "very fine people" on "many sides," is a textbook example of "dog whistle politics," a political strategy that begins with former Alabama governor and presidential aspirant George Wallace, a Dixie Democrat, according to Ian Haney López. In his book *Dog Whistle Politics: How Coded Racial Appeals Have Reinvented Racism and Wrecked the Middle Class*, Haney López asserts the connection between race, Southern white politicians, and the Republican Party "is not accidental" (2014, 2). Adds Haney López, "Dog whistle politics trades … in studied ambiguity, where the lack of a smoking-gun racial epithet allows for proclamations of innocence" (ibid., 130). Trump's speech to supporters in Phoenix, Arizona, on 22 August 2017, in the aftermath of the deadly violence in Charlottesville, would be one such example, when he repeated his remarks but omitted his incendiary "on many sides" phrase (Naylor and Keith 2017). The game, says Haney López, is simple: "a willingness to manipulate racial animus in pursuit of power" (2014, 113).

Writing in the 6 April 2017 edition of the *New York Review of Books*, Michael Tomasky asserts this new and evolving media ecosystem favours the right. "Democrats and the 'liberal' media simply do not have the power to shape the terms of discourse in the same way that the congeries of talk-radio hosts, web sites, blogs, and social media outlets of the right do," he states (Tomasky 2017, 12–13).

In the 21 June 2017 *New York Times*, columnist Thomas L. Friedman quoted Dov Seidman, author of *How*: "What we're experiencing is an assault on the very foundations of our society and democracy – the twin pillars of truth and trust" (Friedman 2017).

British scholar Helen Kennedy, a professor of digital society at the University of Sheffield, offered attendees at a Data Power conference at Carleton University in June 2017 a humorous yet insightful point of comparison for the new media society. The world of truth, according to Kennedy, is the world of Descartes: "I think, therefore I am" (Kennedy, H. 2017). In the post-truth world, Descartes's reason-based approach gives way to the talk TV perspective: "I believe, therefore I am right."

A tweet from friend Nancy Jamieson (Jamieson 2016) included a link to an article by Farhad Manjoo entitled "How the Internet is Loosening Our Grip on the Truth" that appeared in the *New York Times*. Manjoo states, "the Internet is distorting our collective grasp on the truth" (Manjoo 2016). He cites a Pew Research Center survey as proof "that many of us have burrowed into our own echo chambers of information." In 2008, Manjoo argued the internet would "usher in a 'post-fact age.'" Today's political discourse doesn't just involve different policy positions but more fundamentally, different "basic facts." The true value of information doesn't matter in this new order, according to Manjoo, who quotes Walter Quattrociocchi: "All that matters is whether the information fits in your narrative" (ibid.).

In a compelling work that challenges certain elements of conventional wisdom around campaigns and political communication, John Sides and Lynn Vavreck (2013) note campaigns are increasingly scientific in and of themselves. And, as a result, long-held beliefs about the effectiveness of traditional campaign tools are being challenged. The kind of campaign effects that preoccupy political journalists – such as performances in televised leaders' debates – are relatively small in determining the outcome than larger, fundamental factors such as the economy that affect an election. "It is hard to beat an incumbent in a growing economy," the authors state (ibid., 12). In the 2012 presidential campaign, the study concluded, "Partisans were very loyal and the vast majority stuck with their party's candidate throughout the campaign" (ibid., 8).

There can be some shift in the polls, invariably in response to new information about the candidate. And those shifts, and the horse-race coverage they tend to generate, can have an impact, particularly in presidential primaries. As Trump established in 2016, the dominant news frame for the Republican primaries was that he was the front-runner, coverage that in the end proved to be a self-fulfilling prophecy. By focusing on the "horse race," the mainstream media's coverage of candidate Trump was strategically positive for his campaign.

The wise owls in the field insist behavioural economics will increasingly drive digital communications strategies; that successful political messaging will require as many "nudges" as Amazon uses to advance its various business lines.

Concern over the impact social network sites are having on public discourse is growing. In his 2016 autobiography *Born to Run*, Bruce Springsteen makes a reference to "the new digital world of three-second attention spans" (2016, 424).

The 2017 Dalton Camp lecture on journalism was delivered at St. Thomas University by then-UBC assistant professor Taylor Owen, now an associate professor at the Max Bell School of Public Policy at McGill University. An edited version of the speech was carried later on CBC Radio's *Ideas* program. Owen stated, "I think there is something wrong with what I will call the character of our civic discourse" (Owen 2017b). As Neil Postman did twenty years earlier, Owen urged his audience to "think Huxley, not Orwell" (ibid.).

Journalism long enjoyed a position "at the centre of democratic discourse," Owen said (ibid.). The gatekeeper function rested with a relatively small group of professionals. This largely "exclusionary" model fostered the media's agenda-setting capabilities.

However, "journalism was ground zero for the disruptive potential of the internet," Owen stated (ibid.). The democratizing potential of the internet has given way to a reality that is largely one of control, Owen argues. The ecosystem is now dominated by a small number of companies, giving rise to a new layer of power in our global system.

Former *Guardian* editor and academic Emily Bell is one of those who believes Facebook's news feed operations are bad news for democracy. "No other organization in the history of the world has had the impact Facebook has on the news ecosystem," Bell states. "The bland social networking site most of us use to post pictures of dogs and children and to complain at length about other people, has become a critical traffic source for many digital news organizations and the default news source for most of its users" (Bell 2018).

Author Michael Wolff believes the mainstream media's preoccupation with "iron core" news may have led inexorably to the demise of the legacy press. "It might be a central tragedy of the news media that its old-fashioned and even benighted civic-minded belief that politics is the highest form of news has helped transform it from a mass business to a narrow-cast one" Wolff states. "Politics has gone one way, culture another" (Wolff 2018, 250).

The very notion that the media has a fundamental role to play in any democracy is being questioned by Trump's Republican base. A March 2017 study conducted by the Pew Research Center asked a specific set of probes with this preface: "… is very important in maintaining a strong democracy in the United States" followed by a list of rights (Pew Research Center 2017). Only 49 per cent of Republicans believed it was very important that news organizations are free to criticize political leaders as opposed to 76 per cent of respondents who identified as Democrat (ibid.). In a PBS/NPR/Marist poll from July 2017, 42 per cent of Republican respondents said freedom of the press has expanded too far, whereas 32 per cent of Democrats thought "freedom of the press has been restricted too much" (Taylor 2017).

This shift in attitudes among Republicans explains how people like Newt Gingrich or the assembly of hosts on *Fox & Friends* feel comfortable in urging the White House to deny access to news organizations that criticize the president or attack the "snowflake" reporters who they say can't take their criticism.

In an important story carried in the 9 June edition of the *National Post*, a strategist, who was not identified by name, insisted that Doug Ford's victory in the 2018 Ontario provincial election was a sure thing, thanks to literally thousands of targeted online ads produced in-house and inexpensively. The strategist told reporter

Tom Blackwell, "Doug Ford won the Ontario election on Google and Facebook, and was never in any danger of losing – despite what some public polls indicated" (Blackwell 2018). Public opinion research, relatively early in the campaign, had detected a bit of a surge in support for the Andrea Horwath-led New Democratic Party (ibid.).

Given the ability to slice and dice the electorate by demographic and geographic groups through Facebook and Google, the online spots were more important than any traditional media coverage, earned or paid, the campaign official insisted. Meanwhile, the political journalists documenting the election are "increasingly irrelevant," according to the Conservative insider (ibid.). The campaign operatives believe the mock TV news items produced by the Ford team and posted on Facebook were more influential for their target audiences than the actual news coverage by the television networks.

The Ford campaign also refused to answer mainstream media demands for a fully costed electoral platform. "The party felt the result would have been too messy," Blackwell quotes the source as saying. "We didn't take the bait to get into a conversation about hypothetical budgets" (ibid.).

A degree of caution would seem warranted, however, in considering the sweeping assertions of the Conservative campaign strategist.

First, Harvard professor Stephen Ansolabehere's observations about the need for ad content to align with news coverage may apply as much in a social media era as it did in the old mainstream media model. The dominant news frame for much of the media coverage in the 2018 Ontario election was "change" – a message that reinforced the dominant media frame in the Conservative spots. It is an open question if the targeted Tory online ads would have been as effective if the mainstream media story line had been something other than "change."

In Canada's 2015 federal election, Liberal Leader Justin Trudeau catapulted his third-place party to power with a campaign conversation that was largely about tone, a tone that spoke to values.

Trudeau articulated a new political agenda that put a premium on what he understood to be core Canadian values – the pledge to dramatically increase the number of Syrian refugees who would be welcomed to Canada being but one example. A poll late in the campaign by Abacus Data for *Maclean's* found that those voters most concerned about their government's values were more than twice as likely to support the Liberals as the Tories (Geddes 2015).

Ironically, in her failed Conservative leadership bid in 2017, Kellie Leitch also used the language of "Canadian values" for her own purposes. But where Trudeau's appeal was to our better angels, Leitch's appeal was positioned as a test: fail, and you don't get to come to Canada.

Too many campaign narratives flow from an attempt to "reverse engineer" a platform to reflect what opinion research suggests the public wants to hear. But as Steve Jobs once famously said, "People don't know what they want until you show it to them."

A Social Media-fed Uprising

Political discourse typically extends beyond official channels, particularly in parts of the world where the exercise of democratic practices is limited and where the state exercises an inordinate control over the traditional/legacy press and therefore disproportionate control over the information available to citizens.

Social media proved a godsend for reformers operating within totalitarian regimes where the mainstream media was controlled by power elites.

The Arab Spring uprisings in 2011 constitute one such example, where civil society groups led populist uprisings against entrenched regimes in places such as Libya, Tunisia, Egypt, and Yemen.

As a volunteer with the Washington-based National Democratic Institute (NDI), my personal experience is with the situation in Yemen, having made repeated trips into the country to work with civil society groups there looking to put the building blocks of democracy – a new national constitution, free elections, voter registration, extensive public consultation – in place as an alternative to the corruption of the Ali Abdullah Saleh regime. One assignment specifically involved work to support the rollout of a new draft constitution for the United Nations Development Programme (UNDP) – an event that literally triggered the Houthi rebellion that degenerated into a full-scale civil war aided and abetted by outside interests.

Yemen, home of an ancient civilization, is one of the world's poorest countries.

For the better part of forty years, President Ali Abdullah Saleh wielded power, including a forced unification of North and South Yemen in 1990. Saleh positioned his regime as a strategic ally of the United States of America, parlaying America's preoccupation with the threat posed by al Qaeda in the Arabian Peninsula into massive injections of foreign aid, little of which reached the Yemeni people. Estimates of his personal wealth top $50 billion.

The 2011 uprising in Yemen was initiated by student leaders but soon included significant elements of civil society. Social media was a key component part of the public discourse that supported the uprising as Saleh controlled the national broadcaster and much of the traditional or legacy press.

The uprising forced Saleh to resign, replaced by his deputy, President Abdu Rabbu Mansour Hadi. But, as a condition of his resignation, the agreement stipulated Saleh, his family, and his supporters would face no prosecution.

Yemenis, supported by international organizations such as NDI, began the ambitious program of democratization. Laura Nichols, as NDI's country director for Yemen, played a lead role in this process, as did her husband Jeff Fox – my brother – who served as NDI's political program director in Yemen. The civil society groups, supported by the internationals, led a two-year national dialogue that produced a draft of a new constitution, a framework for free elections, and the establishment of a national voters' list.

All of this work, which would have represented a formidable job jar even in an established liberal democracy, was largely completed within three years in a society with no real notion of media relations, no tradition of a watchdog role for the press, with a culture of violence where political assassinations, kidnapping, and armed conflict were daily occurrences, and with a strong exile community whose leaders issued directives to supporters from afar.

These governance challenges were exacerbated by practical infrastructure challenges: electricity, water, food, medical supplies. I saw firsthand how central social media platforms were to the reform process. While relatively few people in Yemen had internet access, almost everyone has a cellphone, making SMS and instant messaging critically important.

And then there were cultural challenges with which people in Western liberal democracies have less familiarity. Tribal leaders in Yemen, for example, enjoy significant power and expect to be dealt with separately, apart from government institutions. Further, the notion of women in leadership roles constituted an emotional and difficult choice for certain culturally conservative segments of Yemeni society.

Despite myriad challenges, the Yemeni people were making real progress. A draft constitution, which flowed from the national dialogue process, was to be delivered to president Hadi on Saturday, 17 January 2015 (Ghobari 2015) and rolled out to the general population the following Thursday (pers. notes).

The rebel insurgency, aided and abetted by Saleh, was launched to thwart the process. President Hadi's chief of staff, who was en route to the presidential palace on a Saturday afternoon to deliver the draft constitution, was kidnapped. Media outlets were occupied by Houthi rebels. Ministers in Hadi's government were denied access to the national broadcaster. Sana'a, the Yemeni capital, was the scene of intense street fighting over the weekend.

Social media was a primary source for news of developments. In fact, it was social media that first reported on Monday, 19 January 2015 that a coup was underway with Houthi rebels laying siege to the presidential palace in Sana'a.

The small arms fire that could be heard so distinctly shortly after 7 a.m. soon gave way to artillery fire. As the situation became increasingly unstable through the day, the conversation for "internationals" shifted to how and when to make a break for the airport – provided commercial flights were available. The weapons fire was like hearing the soundtrack to an action film, without seeing the images because of the need to stay away from windows.

Consistent with Clay Shirky's description of today's media ecosystem, these social media accounts from Yemenis and internationals alike provided the raw material to structure reports on CNN from Nick Paton Walsh, a senior international correspondent for the network who happened to be on assignment in Sana'a. He was the only Western television correspondent in the city as the firefights flared into civil war.

Unable to identify a secure route to the airport, we monitored CNN reports that the president was safe and that the prime minister had been attacked but had escaped unharmed. Later in the day, reports on Twitter indicated that a ceasefire between government troops and the Houthi rebels had been worked out, followed quickly by word that the ceasefire wouldn't hold.

Options were limited. Sit and wait and hope for the best or make a run for it. We gathered at the compound where we were housed before midnight, then climbed into a convoy of SUVs for the trip to the airport, leaving the compound at 2 a.m. The trip to the airport in the pitch black of early morning was like a scene out of the movies, as flames flickered from fires lit at the checkpoints along the route. We were stopped on seven separate occasions by AK-47-toting Houthi rebels who would open the doors of the SUVs, flash lights in everyone's eyes, repeat the mantra of "God is great," then "Death to Americans," then "Death to Jews." As the rebels checked everyone in the vehicles out, their "chase vehicles" armed with machine guns idled nearby, ready to give pursuit to anyone foolish enough to try and drive through the checkpoint without stopping. Our Yemeni security personnel gave the rebels an agreed upon story intended to create the impression that we were medical personnel. There were repeated references to "Dr Fox" – which is technically accurate and totally misleading.

On arrival at the airport, we were advised the scheduled Turkish Airlines flight out of Yemen was delayed. But incredibly, the flight began boarding shortly before 7 a.m. The crew were in a hurry. Not because of the small arms fire or because of the artillery fire or because of the escalation toward a full-blown civil war but because a major dust storm was threatening.

As Paul Simon sang in "The Boy in the Bubble," "these are the days of miracle and wonder." Scant hours after sitting in the back seat of an SUV in the early hours of what would become a horrific civil war, with an AK-47 pointed at my nose, and someone praising God and threatening reprisals in the same sentence, I walked into the business class lounge at the airport in Istanbul for a hot shower, hot food, and a direct flight to Toronto. My brother Jeff and sister-in-law Laura were able to secure seats on a later flight.

The fighting in Yemen continues to this day, although famine now poses a more significant risk than gunfire. Geopolitics is a determinant, competing tensions rendering a difficult situation even more complex: the US versus al Qaeda, Saudi Arabia versus Iran, North Yemen versus South Yemen.

Political communication in Western liberal democracies typically is not carried out against a soundtrack of heavy artillery. But in Yemen as in North America, social media has carved out a central role in the political discourse and by extension, the exercise of power.

8

Old News, New News, Old Scribes, New Scribes

A wise owl once observed that every trade is also a tribe, and journalism is no exception.

Journalists want to be, and often are, seen as the high priests of society, the watchdogs. Reporters, particularly those who came of age professionally when Watergate dominated political news in America, have tended to see the practice of journalism as something akin to a religious vocation. As James Squires, former editor of the *Chicago Tribune*, stated, "You hadn't taken a job, you had answered a calling" (Squires 1993, 8).

This romantic, somewhat nostalgic view of journalism was always a bit of an affectation.

The clash of commercial considerations with journalism's higher calling did not originate with Donald Trump. And indeed, at least one major US network made no bones about the fact that candidate Trump was good for ratings. In February 2016, at the start of the election season, CBS board chair Les Moonves, later forced to resign when allegations of sexual harassment surfaced, said simply, "The money's rolling in and this is fun … It's a terrible thing to say. But bring it on, Donald. Keep going" (Collins 2016).

But in the not so distant past, media proprietors historically subscribed to professor Fred Siebert's "social responsibility" theory of the press. Proprietors were allowed to accumulate wealth – as long as it met the test of the Progressive Movement's philosophy of "responsible capitalism." Media owners typically lived in the community, held prominent positions in local charity organizations, and were connected to the business and cultural leadership of that community. The publisher personified the higher calling journalism aspired to represent. As a copy boy at the *Ottawa Citizen* in the late 1960s, I stood straighter and tried to appear smarter at the mere sight of publisher R.W. Southam walking through the newsroom to visit editor-in-chief Christopher Young. We copy boys probably should have tried to look busier as well, but the fact is, Mr Southam was such an impressive and imposing figure, we mostly just stood and stared.

However, the ongoing battle between the public service/business halves of journalism has been decidedly one-sided of late (Carper 1995). In the past thirty years, the business side of journalism has assumed an unyielding dominance. Alison Carper argues reader surveys and focus-group testing have led to a journalistic product that subverts the very notion of a democratic press. Newspapers used these market research techniques to find out what readers wanted, and then proceeded to give it to them. Steve Crosby, at the time editor of the *Wausau Daily Herald* in Wisconsin, summarized the shift succinctly: "News is what our readers say it is" (ibid., 3).

Corporate concentration is cited by media scholars as a root cause of the decline of the "social responsibility" role of the press. The "dirty little secret" about corporate ownership, says Squires, is that it is incompatible with good journalism (Squires 1993, 8). Hedge fund ownership created a new order of magnitude.

Major areas of concern emerge. First, there is an issue when editorial budgets are reduced to enhance profitability. Paul Godfrey's stewardship of Postmedia and what appears to the outside world as a "harvest strategy" necessitated by debt servicing charges is an obvious example. Newsroom budgets are being slashed even as the public's appetite for minimalist, fact-based accounts is waning. We know a woman stepped off a streetcar in Toronto and was hit by a dump truck. We've seen the footage posted on YouTube minutes later. By the time we get to our *Toronto Star* or the *Toronto Sun*, we are looking for more. And more costs more, not less, to produce.

The same pattern is impacting foreign news. Canadians look at the world through a particular panel of the prism – and that panel is not American or British or French. When events in the world unfold, we look for a Canadian perspective. But instead of reportage from resident Canadian correspondents, we are now fed a steady diet of "parachute journalism."

Then, there is the potential for corporate conflicts of interest. Former Bell Media president Kevin Crull's interference in the newsroom at CTV News over a story about a decision by the Canadian Radio-television and Telecommunications Commission (CRTC) that had a direct impact on Bell Media's parent company, BCE Inc., is one notorious example. Crull was fired after news of his attempt became public (Bradshaw and Dobby 2015). Only the most naive believe the 2015 incident was the first time Crull – a friend and former colleague at BCE – had instructions for CTV News president Wendy Freeman as to how a story with a "Bell" angle should be covered.

Even before we'd heard about Facebook or Snapchat or Twitter, the press had shifted from matters of importance to matters of interest. John McManus, then a professor at Santa Clara University, said, "The economics of the business favour breadth of appeal over depth" (McManus 1994). In a culture of what McManus has dubbed "market-driven journalism," the line between entertainment and news has steadily blurred. McManus's overarching concern is that "the public can't get out of the news what is not put in" (ibid.). Media proprietors offer the classic defence "there is no use preaching to an empty church" to justify their approach. But former Shorenstein Center fellow Judith Lichtenberg states, "It is disingenuous for the press to claim it simply gives people the information they want, when their desire for it is partly a function of press coverage" (Fox, W. 1997, 11).

This current trend to narrowcasting, whether it is embraced by Trump or progressives or the far left, does constitute a threat to democracy, according to Doris Graber. "If citizens do not drink from the same well of information, will they splinter into communications ghettos?" (Graber 2001, 166).

If news is largely about how today is different from yesterday, what happened today is a much more complex question than it used to be. The news agenda has become increasingly idiosyncratic, to the point where it is now largely possible to conduct public business in private. Kathleen Hall Jamieson's warning back in 1989 that the media was in the process of fashioning the kind of coverage that would destroy us (Hall Jamieson 1989), ignored in the main by legacy media, is linked to Hesmondhalgh's observation that "recent trends in journalism represent a collapse of the standards of professional reporting founded on the goals of objectivity and public service" (Hesmondhalgh 2007, 284). Sophisticated information consumers are increasingly turning away from legacy news media such as the local newspapers, which leads to a diminished shared information experience and governments that basically want to stay out of the news on the really important, substantive, societal issues. President Trump clearly did not want a national conversation about gun control in the wake of the mass shootings in El Paso, Texas, and Dayton, Ohio, in the summer of 2019. So, Trump blurted out an offer to buy Greenland from the Danes. And as Tim Wu later tweeted, "Purposefully or not, Trump has successfully changed the national political conversation from gun control to Greenland" (Wu, T. 2019).

Journalism is predicated, to some extent, on an assumption that the reporters know of what they speak or write about. Yet subject matter experts sometimes question whether that is, in fact, the case.

The Senate spending scandal that beset Stephen Harper's Conservative government offers one illustration. Media mining of access to information requests had uncovered what can most charitably be described as profligate spending on the part of certain senators, including high-profile Conservative appointees Mike Duffy, Pamela Wallin – a close personal friend – and Patrick Brazeau. To say the spending totals were a problem for the Harper government would be to understate the case. Harper wore his frugality like a badge of honour. Respect for taxpayers' money was integral to his brand.

The Senate's board of internal economy was expected to hold the senators to account. The way the board went about the task bordered on farce.

Duffy's case became the media focal point, for a number of reasons, starting with the fact Duffy was told by the Prime Minister's

Office he would have to repay $90,000 in expenses he had claimed. When Duffy said he didn't have the ability to repay, and the party's fundraisers refused to pay, Harper's chief of staff Nigel Wright wrote the senator a cheque to cover the amount. When the Crown attorney laid criminal charges against Duffy following an RCMP investigation, the long-time political reporter found the media searchlight had settled on him.

The media covered the scandal extensively, fed by sources that included individuals from the senior Senate leadership. In fact, Senator Wallin's counsel, Terrence O'Sullivan, built a timeline grid recording the number of times he and/or Senator Wallin were contacted by reporters asking for comment on a particular decision taken by the Senate's board of internal economy before Senator Wallin had in fact been informed of the board's decision.

The reports reflected what sources were telling reporters, and a master narrative emerged. These senators were seen as swanning around the country at the taxpayers' expense. Duffy's "travel" status was a particular focus of the media coverage. How could the former television journalist, familiar to millions of Canadians, claim daily travel expenses when he was living in the house he owned with his wife Heather in the Ottawa suburb of Kanata, a house he had been living in for decades.

Public opinion turned against the senators. Individual Canadians offered the view the senators would be fired if they worked anywhere else. Which is precisely the point. The senators didn't work anywhere else; they were members of the Senate, where the rules are different and, as was subsequently established, applied unevenly.

The narrative, at this point, began to shift. Core principles from the rule of law to the presumption of innocence were set aside. A single senator, the Honourable Hugh Segal, rose to speak against a government motion to suspend the three senators without pay. Speaking without notes of any kind, Segal made the point the motion "moves to a consideration of punishment before the nuances about what might have constituted the violation ... have been addressed." In Senator Wallin's case, he said, the auditors had applied new rules regarding travel retroactively to come up with the total she allegedly overspent. Senator Segal noted, "That is, in fact, imposing a retroactive, arbitrary, unfair judgment in a fashion that has the equivalent of professional capital punishment ... We're in the process of, in my judgment, imposing a very arch, difficult, unfair judgment in a fashion that constitutes pretrial sentencing," Segal concluded (Senate of Canada 2013).

Segal's speech did receive some media coverage. But the "congenial truth" around the Senate spending scandal had taken hold. The story was the journalistic equivalent of low hanging fruit: rot at the top, aligned with the "elite" narrative, and well-sourced.

However, as the venue shifted from the Centre Block of Parliament Hill to a courtroom on Elgin Street a few blocks away, journalists covering the story lost sight of the truism that a court of public opinion is not a court of law. The rules of what constitutes "evidence" are different in a trial than they are for a news story. Journalists were stunned at trial when Senator Duffy was acquitted on all thirty-one charges. They shouldn't have been, according to Duffy's lawyer.

Donald Bayne, who successfully defended Senator Duffy against the thirty-one criminal charges relating to Senate expenses, consulting contracts, and a payment by Stephen Harper's chief of staff, had this to say about the journalists covering Duffy's trial: "It was troubling to discern that these prominent, experienced and respected journalists ... were reporting the criminal trial of a 'generation' to the Canadian public without understanding criminal trial fundamentals," Bayne stated (Bayne 2017). Bayne's observations had a particular relevance and resonance for this writer. Duffy and I used to cover city hall together in Ottawa in the early 1970s and prior to that had both spent time on the "police beat" there.

Even worse, said Bayne, is that the parliamentary press missed the story in the Duffy case. The prominent defence counsel conceded two years of vilification of Duffy in the daily press "had done their work" (ibid.). "Most in the public believed what the media told them, the judge did not" (ibid.). "Judge [Charles]

Vaillancourt, who presided over a lengthy and difficult trial in a dignified and error-free fashion did his job impeccably well. The media did not" (ibid.).

Bayne, of course, was referring to the judge's findings that the real story in the Duffy affair was the conduct and attempted cover-up by individuals in the Prime Minister's Office of Stephen Harper, which Vaillancourt described as "mind-boggling and shocking ... I find based on all of the evidence that Senator Duffy was forced into accepting Nigel Wright's funds so that the government could rid itself of an embarrassing political fiasco that just was not going away" (Russell, A. 2016). Duffy's expenses may not have passed the "smell test" of another employer – God knows, I had my own issues with media scrutiny of expense accounts when I worked in the Prime Minister's Office – but Vaillancourt's point is the media had to consider Duffy's claims in the context of Senate expense rules, not those of the *Globe* and *Post*. And his further point is that the Senate "sources" fed the media beast in a way intended to deflect attention away from the Harper PMO.

The "reporter-as-stenographer" approach to much of day-to-day journalism is predicated on an assumption that journalists themselves cannot establish the "truth" of anything; therefore, their professionalism lies in the accuracy of their account. Unable to ascertain the "truth" of a political claim, they seek to satisfy their professional obligation by accurately capturing and reproducing the statement.

In this, the era of Donald Trump, who repeatedly utters falsehoods, observers are challenging that perspective as a cop-out. "Dear journalists, you don't have to let liars use you as loudspeakers," Dan Gillmor urged in a tweet posted 15 June 2018 (Gillmor 2018).

Thomas Patterson (2013) argues the knowledge deficiency of journalists means they are vulnerable to manipulation by sources. And that knowledge deficiency is due, in no small measure, to shrinking editorial budgets. Reporters have less time to develop a deeper understanding of the policy and program issues they cover, which forces them to either concentrate on the politics of the matter or rely on their "sources" to provide the expertise.

At the risk of sounding like an old-timer whining about expansion of the original six-team National Hockey League, the fact is when news bureaus were larger, reporters assigned to them were operating from a deep knowledge base. In the early 1980s, for example, reporters in Ottawa covering then-prime minister Pierre Trudeau's constitutional reform initiative – people like the *Globe*'s Jeffrey Simpson or the CBC's Stuart Langford – knew the subject matter. They could discuss the specifics of various proposals with experts such as C.E.S. (Ned) Franks or Ronald Watts at Queen's University in some detail.

In Britain, Remain activist David Chaplin put questions to the BBC in the wake of the Brexit referendum that could be applied to all journalists in Western liberal democracies when he asked, "I think the BBC has some real questions to answer about whether they see themselves as an information-aggregation service, or providing editorial analysis of news and content for their viewers?" (Shipman 2016, 309).

Going forward, a consensus is emerging among media scholars that journalism will have to reassert itself as a knowledge profession. The journalistic culture that has emerged in North America will need to be fundamentally transformed if journalism is to hold its place in civil discourse. The old days of the 5Ws – who, what, when, where, why – have been rendered obsolete by technology. These historically bare-bones accounts will not provide enough value to meet the test of the paywall.

While there are differences in journalistic practices in both Canada and the United States – and indeed, between journalism in English Canada and French Canada – the similarities between the two prevail, particularly with the emergence of journalism as a profession, rather than a trade or craft as it was thought of in the 1960s.

As an aside, the whole concept of journalism as profession was a struggle for some industry old-timers. Columnists Pete Hamill and Jimmy Breslin were New York's primary storytellers through the 1970s and 1980s. In an HBO film documenting his illustrious career,

Hamill sais he saw writing for a newspaper as "a craft. It is teachable." Added Hamill's contemporary and fellow journalistic colossus Jimmy Breslin: "Journalism ... that's a college word" (Block, Alter, and McCarthy 2018).

Journalism will have to evolve from Robert Heinlein's "fair witness" model of initial observation to a more exacting role of verification and interpretation, according to Thomas Patterson.

The life-threatening risk to journalism is a public that concludes the offering is no more valuable than information coming from other sources. As media critic Tom Rosenstiel and former *New York Times* editor Bill Kovach observed, "Journalists need to focus on people and their problems, not on politicians and theirs" (Kovach and Rosenstiel 2007, 221–2).

Susan Delacourt's compelling *Shopping for Votes* (2013) examines how political parties position citizens as consumers. Political messaging addresses voters as private citizens and not as members of the public. Targeted tax cuts, such as deductions for minor sport, are one expression. Yet the need for someone to speak to the "public" interest hasn't gone away.

Political parties having established themselves as news makers gave further impetus to this shift away from "journalism" by creating their own media outlets. Former Mississippi governor Haley Barbour, when he was running the Republican National Committee, believed "your message is only as good as your ability to get the message heard" (pers. notes 1995). In the mid-1990s, Barbour and his colleagues were convinced that mainstream television networks, with an East Coast liberal bias, were a major reason Republicans weren't getting their message out. So they created their own channels, starting with Barbour's brainchild "GOP TV" and eventually, under Republican strategist Roger Ailes's leadership, Fox News.

Marshall McLuhan (1964), as every Canadian communications student knows, coined the phrase "the medium is the message" – advancing the notion of technological determinism.

Canadian communications scholar Harold Innis, often described as a technological determinist, might be more accurately considered a "communications determinist," according to scholars such as Menahem Blondheim of the Hebrew University of Jerusalem. Advances in communication technology were the main determinants of change for Innis, and as Philip Massolin observes, "since communication media shaped social and political organizations, a change in the means of communication entailed a change in the very make-up of the civilization" (Massolin 1996, 95).

Harold Innis first published *The Bias of Communication* in 1951, the year before he died. His was a contrarian view to the conventional wisdom of the time regarding media effects. "I have attempted to suggest that Western civilization has been profoundly influenced by communication," Innis states modestly, "and that marked changes in communication have had important implications" (Innis 1991). The latter observation presaged the influence television would have on North American society in general, and political discourse in particular. The University of Toronto scholar concluded the demands of new media are imposed on older media; at the time, radio on newspapers and books (ibid., 82–3). Yet his observation applies equally to the impact of digital platforms and apps such as Twitter or Snapchat. Innis further suggested changes to the medium would trigger changes in any assessment, again presaging the impact of social media on civil discourse. "[A] change in the type of medium implies a change in the type of appraisal and hence makes it difficult for one civilization to understand another" (ibid.).

McLuhan and Innis's theoretical constructs pose two interesting propositions for a social media age. The first is that social media means that in theory, at least, we all own the press. And to follow up on Innis, if TV produces a person with different characteristics, then what kind of a "person" does social media produce? And what kind of person do we need to produce journalistic content in this emerging, evolving, social media world?

If politics is a contest to define the characteristics of public discourse, how does that contest play out in a social media world?

Picking up on James Carey's "ritual transmission" model, the question comes down to this: Whose version of reality will be displayed and honoured?

Media technology analyst Jesse Hirsh sees a shared gatekeeper function in the new media world, involving professional journalists, citizen journalists, the blogosphere, social media, and independent news venues. The gatekeeper process will involve more collaboration, more integration, more transparency, and more interactivity. *ProPublica*, for example, teams up with major news organizations, finances local journalists, and focuses on problems that affect people in specific areas. It's service journalism. Its Intuit online tax series (how it tricked US residents into paying to file taxes that they should have been able to do for free) forced Congress to back down on a law (Elliott, J. 2019). *ProPublica* awards include the 2019 Pulitzer for writing on international gang MS-13.

David Frum, a senior editor at *The Atlantic* and former speechwriter to George W. Bush, articulates the point slightly differently. A tweet by CNN's *Reliable Sources* program, hosted by Brian Stelter, in December 2017, shows Frum on the show making the case that mistakes in the mainstream media, far from being a reason to distrust the outlet, should be seen instead as a concerted, professional effort to get at the truth (Reliable Sources 2017). "I'm saying look, journalism is a process," Frum states. "The way you discover the truth as a consumer of news is not by reading any one story and thinking, 'aha, here's the truth.' You have to be engaged in it, you have to be an active consumer" (ibid.).

Emerging newsroom leaders readily embrace the potential of social network sites. Michael Gruzuk, senior director of CBC News content experience, programming and innovation, told an audience at Massey College in 2017 there is "so much work that needs to be done in Canadian newsrooms on diversity of voices." Social media can be valuable in identifying those voices. *Policy Options* editor Jennifer Ditchburn has introduced new voices from Canada's Indigenous communities to the debate on Canada's relationship with its Aboriginal peoples.

Pessimists about this new world order worry that social media users seek out only like-minded views, a subtext of much of the analysis after the US presidential election. But the more pointed conceptual question is how to understand the role in politics of the everyday talk of citizens among themselves? Data mining, in other words.

Political journalists and communications strategists alike will need to focus on how the political system is embedded within a larger world, especially in an era of networked spaces. Danielle Allen and Jennifer Light (2015) understand all public forms of expression on matters of common concern can be influential.

The art of politics is the process of people needing to decide what to do about matters of common concern in the face of uncertainty. Politics is the practice of deciding what to do when a society or a community has no basis for agreement. The problem becomes a political one precisely because there is no a priori truth to which we, collectively, can agree to, which addresses the question that confronts us.

The facts alone rarely settle a political argument. Cathy J. Cohen and Joseph Kahne (Cohen and Kahne 2012) remind us participation politics is being able to exert "both voice and influence on issues of public concern." And that, in turn, flows from social media's potential for a richer conception of democratic politics.

The modern public sphere includes conversations that occur in print, broadcast, and now digital media; a reimagining of Jürgen Habermas's (1989) public sphere, which he originally defined as constituted of conversations.

Those who are immersed in new media – regardless of age – have two powerful tools at their disposal. The first is the new mental architecture that new media are helping to create: increasing creativity and the ability to attend to many different things at once as well as imagining and participating in communities that transcend old political boundaries. The second is the networked public sphere itself, with its burgeoning connectivity and variety of digital tools and platforms for creating, organizing, and collaborating. The end of exclusivity for Big Media's model of one-to-many and the shift to the new media model of many-to-many allows for robust, uncentred engagement in social and political life.

To paraphrase Prince, the "people formerly known as the audience" can choose from a variety of sources, create their own content, disseminate news and ideas, aggregate, share, rank, tag, and critique content across all platforms.

Rethinking journalism in this transformed news landscape is an imperative.

Media scholars have examined ways in which today's digital technologies are often credited with – as well as criticized for – influencing the scope of journalistic innovation. Precisely what counts as journalism in a given context is a matter of perspective. James Carey suggested decades ago that society may need a new form of journalism to solve new problems. If we follow Carey's train of thought, journalism needs to be reinvented in the public interest. If journalists are to remain competitive in the media market of the future, they will have to move up the value chain, from reporter as witness with initial observations to journalist with sufficient expertise to be competent at verification and interpretation.

Elmira, Ontario's Malcolm Gladwell may personify what journalism will look like in future. While Gladwell, author of such bestsellers as the *Tipping Point*, believes all his work is still journalism, he is quoted in a piece written by Amy Chozick to the effect, "You can't be a reporter forever" (Chozick 2019). Gladwell, who began his writing career with the *Washington Post* and the *New Yorker*, says he has grown up and gotten "a little more entrepreneurial" (ibid.). With Jacob Weisberg, the former chairman and editor-in-chief of the Slate Group, Gladwell has developed a podcast for Pushkin Industries entitled *Revisionist History* that has drawn as many as three million listeners an episode. But it is Gladwell's approach to his journalism that points a path forward. "He was never interested in the traditional profile of a C.E.O. or an investigative piece on the malfeasance of some bank or company," observes his former editor David Remnick (ibid.). "He got intrigued by the combination of reporting, thinking, reading, storytelling, telling two stories at once that lead you to a revelatory conclusion" (ibid.).

Collectively, we need to be thinking about news reporting that it is much more improvisational than has historically been acknowledged in academic scholarship.

There is a risk tomorrow's journalism may look a lot like independent television production today – far removed from Henry Ford's centralized assembly line and more aligned with the complex professional era identified by French media theorist Bernard Miège (1987). The independent artist – or journalist – is afforded a degree of independence in terms of the product, but the work is carried out under the control – even suppression – of creative managers. Miège argued that creative workers bear the cost of conception on behalf of cultural industry companies by being willing to forgo the benefits of secure working conditions and in nearly all cases, earning relatively little when they do.

A personal experience working with CTV morning show host Ben Mulroney is illustrative of how this world works. Mulroney, the son of former prime minister Brian Mulroney, built his broadcast career in the entertainment field. As host of CTV's *eTalk*, Mulroney was a familiar figure interviewing celebrities on the red carpet at the Academy Awards extravaganza each year. But at one point, Mulroney, a long-time family friend and at the time a neighbour in the same condo complex in downtown Toronto, began to think of next steps in his career. Working together, we developed a concept for a television special with the working title "Sons" and partnered with producer Craig Thompson of Ballinran Productions and the talented photojournalist Mike Nolan.

The idea was to explore the lives of individuals who are making their way in a world where their fathers have already enjoyed some measure of success – the Villeneuves in Formula One racing, the Bush family from US politics, Leonard and Adam Cohen from the worlds of verse and music. "Daughters" presented itself as the obvious sequel.

CTV was interested enough to sign a development deal – for $25,000. Research was conducted, potential participants were confirmed, a treatment was commissioned and completed. But the network executives clearly had another project in mind. They liked the idea of a special with Mulroney, but they were more interested in a special built around the concept of Ben as modern dad. And they thought the script might be better left in the hands of a comedy writing team.

In this post-Fordist world, the network executives exercise the real power. And independent producers learn to acquiesce to their suggestions in the "notes." The Lennon-McCartney lyric from "Paperback Writer" is instructive: the creative type offers to make the text longer if you like the style, or change it round, because "I want to be a paperback writer." And so it goes in independent television. You change it round or the network finds someone who will.

While I had no issue with CTV's right to make the special that its creative managers wanted, I had no interest in the new proposal and therefore, bowed out once the contractual obligations set out in the development deal were met. As it turned out, the network wasn't that interested in the treatment from the comedian writers either. And Ben Mulroney's career continues to flourish as host of the CTV network morning show.

In terms of the world of content creation, independent producers proliferated even as large corporations became dominant. By way of illustration, David Hesmondhalgh noted 80 per cent of the Hollywood film industry is made up of companies with four employees or fewer. And while these independent producers have a degree of creative freedom, the power rests in the main with the folks who control distribution, budgets, marketing, and financing (Hesmondhalgh 2007). Most creative workers in this post-Fordist world are either underemployed or underpaid, or both.

There are winners in this model, to be sure. And the winners are compensated most generously. But there is every chance this approach, if adopted by journalists, will tilt the journalistic playing field even more decisively in favour of the "interesting" at the expense of the "important" civic journalism that a healthy democracy requires.

An advertisement that appeared on page 41 of the January/February 2017 edition of *The Walrus* speaks to the direction journalism educators think the business is heading. The messaging had a decided entrepreneurial cast to it. "Own your journalism career – build your own journalism business," the ad stated. "Develop the digital skills and business acumen required to spot the opportunity in creative turmoil with the Master of Journalism (New Ventures)," the ad continued. "Learn how the journalism business works and how you can make it work for you ..." at the University of King's College in Halifax.

Rob Steiner is the director of the Fellowships in Global Journalism program at the Munk School of Global Affairs at the University of Toronto and his objective is to help shape journalists who are subject matter experts and therefore of immediate value to news organizations. Steiner starts the fellows with a "boot camp" where instructors with distinguished careers in journalism – people like Colin MacKenzie, a former managing editor of the *Globe and Mail*, and Bernard Simon, a long-time correspondent for the *Financial Times* – hone reporting, writing, editing, and presentation skills. Fellows are also taught data journalism, investigative journalism, and smartphone photography. The program operates like a news bureau, pitching stories to news organizations as varied as the BBC World Service and *Policy Options* magazine. But what Steiner's program really sets out to do is to help reporters move to a new, more flexible cost structure for their journalism. Like technology start-ups, Steiner sees a new model of news organizations built around a small corps of full-time staff, supported by a large number of contributors.

Steiner encourages his students to start with a question or untested idea but to hold the "pitch" until the writer has done some initial research. A competitive idea, according to Steiner, is subjected to a series of tests. Is the issue important and not just interesting for your target audience and/or is it counterintuitive or surprising or weird? The idea has to relate to a current discussion of debate and should be timely and/or urgent for the intended audience. The piece should advance a view that is not well-known by the specific audience, should include some tension, a conflict or a debate that signals something is changing. And the story has to have meat – information – and not just opinion.

Steiner's group of fellows includes lawyers, historians, and other subject matter experts. And while the students have enjoyed some measure of success in getting their stories picked up in an impressive range of journalistic platforms, it is still not clear this new generation of entrepreneurial reporters can generate the kind of revenue they would require to sustain their professional activity on a full-time basis.

Catherine Wallace, a former Atkinson Foundation fellow, says more collaboration between universities and media outlets could also help counter the depopulation of the nation's newsrooms. Noting Canada has lost a third of its journalists in the last six years, Wallace believes the reporting void could be filled, in part, with academics. "While methods differ, researchers and journalists can be seen as two sides of the same coin – each working to establish truths and publish facts," Wallace writes in the *Toronto Star* (Wallace 2017, IN1).

Clay Shirky's (2008) concept, likening today's media environment to an ecosystem, by definition implies new and creative forms and forums for news gathering.

And finally, the storytelling or narrative will include voices from outside mainstream journalism.

Too many reporters remain locked in a mindset where a relatively limited list of sources is still relied upon to gather the evidence or "facts" for most important stories. Journalism needs to develop an appreciation for the role of the crowd, to collect data, to provide the first photographs from live events, for on-the-ground information.

Jesse Hirsh has been a leading voice in the discussion around the role of algorithms in news. Stories that come from structured data may well be written mostly by machines – an estimate that 90 per cent of these types of stories in future being automated is not far-fetched. This shift would allow news organizations to swing more resources to the kind of investigative and interpretive work that only people can do: humanizing the data, not mechanizing the process.

Knowledge-based journalism is very much part of the future. The extent to which a journalist now needs to have an in-depth knowledge about something other than journalism is increasing. The complexity of information and the need for speed leaves little room for the generalist.

Newsrooms still reflect a military-style "command-and-control" hierarchy. The news business in the twentieth century was a fairly linear process. Reporters gathered facts and observations, turned them into stories, which were edited and then distributed through paper or the airwaves to an audience. The process was like a pipeline; reporters and editors worked upstream; the audience was downstream. The newsroom structure reflected Carey's "transmission model" of communication, with editors fulfilling the gatekeeper function and news was "authoritative." Experts argue their failure to rethink workflow means news organizations live with all the drawbacks of digital processes while achieving none of the benefits. The command-and-control approach is no longer viable or valid. Journalism in the future will have to adopt Carey's "ritual model."

New journalism may have to look a bit like guerrilla warfare. Resource allocation will be an ongoing challenge. But in the spirit of Lippmann's searchlight, a news organization can keep multiple constituencies honest if these constituencies never know where the spotlight will settle next.

Media studies often describe journalists as subscribing to, and upholding, certain shared norms, values, and beliefs. Social media raises questions about this set of assumptions. WikiLeaks, for example, sparked a controversy over who may claim the right to be a journalist in the digital age. Overshadowed to a significant extent by founder Julian Assange's controversial role in the Russian hacking of Democratic Party servers that emerged from the 2016 US presidential campaign, WikiLeaks initially came to the broader public's attention as a bold, new, collective experiment in whistleblowing. WikiLeaks surfaced stories in situations where it was difficult to get the attention of the Western press on subjects as varied as judicial killings and disappearances in Kenya and an

Apache helicopter attack on a neighbourhood in Baghdad. The international consortium of news organizations that collaborated on the story that became known as the "Panama Papers" is another example. Each news organization pursued elements of the story connected to their primary sphere of activity but collectively told the broader story of international offshore tax havens. WikiLeaks, for some, represents the thin edge of the information wedge: if WikiLeaks can't run a story, then who can or will?

WikiLeaks is also, as NYU scholar Jay Rosen (2010) notes, the first stateless news organization. WikiLeaks has effectively positioned itself between source and publisher. Assange insists he did not receive the bounty of emails – which hackers intercepted from the Democratic National Committee or Clinton campaign chair John Podesta's email account – from a Russian state source but will provide no further detail.

These "practices" cause people like George Packer, a former staff writer at the *New Yorker* who now writes for *The Atlantic*, to argue WikiLeaks and others like it are not news organizations but cells of activists intent on releasing information "designed to embarrass people in power" (Carr 2010). This debate was re-engaged in April 2019 when Ecuador withdrew the asylum it had granted Assange in 2012, allowing him to be led out of its London Embassy in handcuffs by police, facing extradition to the United States, and charges including violating the Espionage Act (Breuninger and Mangan 2019).

Even legacy news organizations, such as the *Guardian* and the *New York Times*, are moving beyond national boundaries to circumvent gag orders on the basis that "only a free and unrestrained press can effectively expose deception in government."

Penelope Muse Abernathy (2014) has examined this evolving media landscape from a particular perspective – community journalism. Abernathy is seized of the irony that the dramatic decline in print advertising revenue has limited funds to invest in digital efforts. Her preoccupation is with Harvard's Alex Jones's (2009) "iron core," the economic, health, education, and quality of life issues in any community that define our collective future. These stories are the "vitamin" supplements for their communities. If local media don't cover these issues, who will?

There is a significant shortcoming in citizen journalism models, however. Journalism requires news organizations with the financial wherewithal to stand up to the most powerful interests in society. Alex Jones makes the point "a marginally profitable news organization is too weak to withstand the kind of punishment that comes from publishing news that makes powerful people mad" (2009, 199).

Citizen journalists, states Abernathy, rarely have the know-how, the tenacity, and the resources to pursue and write about the public policy issues simmering below the surface. As a result, in many communities we now face a shortage of professional accountability reporting, particularly beat reporting. "News deserts" is the term used to describe what follows, now numbering 1,300 communities in the US without local news coverage, and counting (Waldman and Sennott 2019).

Buzzfeed's Craig Silverman, speaking at a Canadian Journalism Foundation event (2018b), said local media are struggling more than other elements of the media ecosystem in today's wired world. And a study released 25 September 2018 by the Public Policy Forum underscores the consequence of that struggle for democratic institutions.

Building on its earlier study the "Shattered Mirror," the report entitled "Mind the Gaps: Quantifying the Decline of News Coverage in Canada" (2018) studied twenty small and midsized Canadian cities. The communities selected reflected regional and linguistic balances aligned with Canada's demographics. The conclusion was straightforward: the number and depth of newspaper articles about civic affairs declined sharply between 2008 and 2017, leaving citizens less well-informed about their democratic institutions.

The study found the number of English-language newspaper articles in all five regions of Canada fell by almost half. News organizations are retreating from city hall, from the courts, from the legislature. Coverage of civic affairs declined by almost a third. Most significantly, the study discovered there were fewer articles about the community per year in every community examined. "While some digital-only publications have enriched the news ecosystem, so far they have tended to lack the journalistic intensity of the news media system of the previous century," the study states, acknowledging that one possible explanation is that the scale necessary to prosper in the digital world is difficult to achieve in Canada (Public Policy Forum 2018, 2).

Effective communities require more than just facts; they need to know what those facts mean to the lives of the diverse people who make up the communities. As Ron Heifetz of Harvard's Kennedy School of Government states, "A newspaper reminds a community every day of its collective identity, the stake we have in one another, and the lessons of its history" (cited in Muse Abernathy 2014).

During the years Kathleen Wynne was premier of Ontario, Torstar board chair John Honderich would say, with sadness, the *Star* had the largest bureau covering the Ontario legislature at Queen's Park – two people. More journalistic resources allocated to provincial politics in Ontario might have better served democracy if more reporters had been available to probe party platforms in the 2018 provincial election. And after a year in office, Premier Doug Ford's Conservative government – in news terms at least – is the proverbial gift that keeps on giving when it comes to generating news opportunities of interest to the public.

A Pew Research Center study reports newsroom staffing levels decreased by around 25 per cent in the US between 2008 and 2018 (Grieco 2019). Canada's Postmedia is a textbook example of what happens when a "harvest" strategy plays out – retention bonuses for corporate executives, massive layoffs for editorial staff.

Idealists believe in a rough rule of thumb: the more government waste, the more local corruption there is, the more serious the community problems that are likely to emerge.

The digital revolution, in the words of Charles Dickens, represents the best of times and the worst of times: a time of tremendous innovation, even as the business models for sustaining full-time professional accountability reporting have collapsed.

Post-industrial Journalism

On one level, there is no such thing as a news industry anymore. As stated earlier, advertisers today have other – arguably, better – options to sell us goods, ideas, and opinions.

That core assertion guided a project at Columbia's Tow Center that looked at post-industrial journalism. Led by Chris Anderson, Emily Bell, and Clay Shirky, the project further asserted we can no longer assume that making information public can be done only by professionals and institutions, given the explosion of tools and techniques over the past fifteen years (Anderson, Bell, and Shirky 2012). Michael Maier (2007) encourages us to think about journalism without journalists.

Current changes in the news ecosystem have led to a reduction in the quality of news. Anderson, Bell and Shirky conclude "on present evidence, we are convinced that journalism in this country will get worse before it gets better" (Anderson, Bell, and Shirky 2012, 1). Further, the new possibilities afforded by emerging technologies will require new forms of organization.

As a subtext, the authors hold that journalism plays an irreplaceable role in both democratic politics and market economics, but there is no way to preserve journalism in its current construct. To date, direct fee models, whether paywalls, service payments, or other forms, have either failed or underperformed, with a few notable exceptions such as the *New York Times*. Understanding the extent of the disruption to news production and journalism and deciding where effort can be most effectively applied will be vital for all journalists.

Michael Lewis's 2014 bestseller *Flash Boys* presaged things to come in the world of political communication and, by extension, political journalism (2014). Lewis was most insightful in his consideration of how technology in general, and algorithms in particular, had changed financial markets – particularly equity markets – forever. "The financial markets were changing in ways even professionals did not fully understand," Lewis states. "Their ability to move at computer, rather than human, speed had given rise to a new class of Wall Street traders, engaged in new kinds of trading." High-frequency trading basically created a private space within public markets, the *Moneyball* author observes. "Every day, the markets were driven less directly by human beings and more directly by machines" (Lewis, M. 2014).

Algorithms identified areas of interest and distributed the commodity at speeds news desks could not and cannot match. Bot-fed sites created access to limited yet specific "audiences" within the public sphere. Where required, political conversations were taking place below legacy media radar screens. Political journalism, as a consequence, was changing in ways political reporters didn't completely understand, just like the Wall Street floor traders before them didn't see what was coming.

Going forward, journalists will have to come up with the answers to two questions: What can new entrants in the news ecosystem do better now – compared with what journalists were producing under the old model – and what roles can journalists themselves now play?

For many news events, even major news events, it is increasingly more likely the first description will be provided by a connected citizen and not a professional journalist. As the Tow Center report observed (Anderson, Bell, and Shirky 2012), it was Sohaib Athar, an IT consultant in Abbottabad, Pakistan, who provided the first public "report" when US Navy Seals stormed Osama bin Laden's compound, fatally killing the al Qaeda leader in 2011. Athar first tweeted about hearing a helicopter and then a blast. But Athar didn't realize what he had. He tweeted later, "Uh oh, now I'm the guy who live-blogged the Osama raid without knowing it" (Mullen and Saifi 2016).

Athar's experience points to a new reality: the journalist has not been replaced but displaced. Journalism will have to move up the content chain, from the production of initial observations to a role that emphasizes verification and interpretation. And as a consequence, the professional formation of journalists will evolve as well.

Old News versus New News

In terms of network television, the evening newscast is obsolete, as is any "appointment" television. There are a few exceptions around live events – such as the Remembrance Day ceremonies from Ottawa each 11 November or anniversaries such as the seventy-fifth anniversary of the D-Day landing in 2019 – and a clinging adherence to sporting events. But in the main, technology allows individuals to consume editorial and entertainment products at a time of their choosing, on a device of their choosing, and without commercial interruptions.

The physical, printed version newspaper will soon be an archival curiosity. The Montreal daily, *La Presse*, is now entirely digital, owned by a social trust. Subscribers to other public affairs publications such as the *New Yorker* or *The Economist* are constantly bombarded with email messages to move to online editions.

A parallel, and equally transformative, shift has occurred on the editorial side.

The gatekeeper function – in many ways the raison d'être of traditional journalism – shifted first from the editor to the reporter and now, because of social media, to the broader community. British journalist and author George Pitcher describes a parallel universe of alternative authorities (from Fitzpatrick and Bronstein 2006, 73).

New Yorker writer Ken Auletta (2013) speaks to a concept of "open journalism" whereby the news organization invites readers to participate in the journalistic venture itself. Even on day-to-day stories, reporters are asking news consumers for help. In the summer of 2019, when the Liberal majority on the House of Commons ethics committee voted down an Opposition motion to call Ethics Commissioner Mario Dion as a witness to speak to his conclusion Prime Minister Justin Trudeau had broken Canada's ethics laws in the SNC-Lavalin affair, Global Television's Mercedes Stephenson asked the #cdnpoli Twitterverse if anyone could think of a precedent. Crowd-sourced research (Stephenson 2019). *Globe and Mail* reporters put out similar appeals on breaking stories as a matter of routine.

Postmedia's former editor-in-chief Lou Clancy called on my brother Jeff Fox to give readers an on-the-ground account of Yemen amid the civil war there. Jeff, a long-time political activist, is not trained as a journalist but he is trained in the art of narrative.

His eyewitness accounts of the price paid by Yemeni civilians in the ongoing conflict helped broaden readers' understanding of the reality on the ground.

The social grid – how people share stories – has shifted.

Journalism was too long wedded to its top-down, one-to-many model. Going forward, journalism will privilege new professional roles: aggregators, curators, experts. The news experience will have more in common with scientific discovery. The winners will be those who can take an immense amount of data, slice it, dice it, and, to cite Nate Silver (2012), turn noise into signal. Algorithms are a key factor in both the creation of content and its distribution.

The late *New York Times* columnist David Carr (2011) talked of a journalism that was less about authority and more about authenticity. That journalism can't actually know everything, so knowledge in any given subject area will have to be stitched together (Harvard Kennedy School 2011).

Politico reflects the different media and journalism Auletta referenced. Founded by individuals with deep traditional political reporting experience, *Politico*'s content reflects a key discovery – stories generating an echo online were not the stories that appeared on page one of the august *Washington Post*. *Politico* has positioned itself as the voice of, and mirror to, a certain style of reader: the self-styled influencers, decision makers, fixers. *Politico*'s audience serves a dual purpose: they are at once readers and feeders, an expansion of the traditional pool of "sources." *Axios* is the latest expression of how the thinking of *Politico*'s founders has evolved.

BuzzFeed is another example of Auletta's difference. The news organization unabashedly uses all the promotional tools available online, from "top 25 lists" to other clickbait material. *BuzzFeed* staffers are young, tend to the cool. They take the work seriously, themselves less so. These emerging news organizations all reflect Shirky's (2008) media "ecosystem."

Basic data literacy will have to improve. The iconic status that journalists accord the Watergate story doesn't change the fact it was based on the acquisition of secrets from a primary source. But that source dependency can cause mainstream journalism to miss big stories. Outsiders, and not journalists, detected some of the most significant big business stories in recent years; from the Bernie Madoff financial pyramid scheme (Clark, A. 2010), to the fixing of the LIBOR rate by big banks (Keenan, D. 2012).

In his bestselling novel *The Scarecrow*, author and former reporter Michael Connelly refers to a "mojo" – which he describes as "a mobile journalist nimbly able to file from the field via any electronic means" (Connelly 2009). But new-generation reporters will also have to have project management skills.

News organizations need to start thinking of themselves as organizations that do things and not simply "cover" things. They will be smaller than they are today, operating on new forms of funding from a number of sources.

News in the twenty-first century will reflect a different reality because news organizations no longer control the news as it has been traditionally understood. Content will be endlessly reusable, designed for perpetual levels of iteration. "Fair use" means every outlet, in practice, is a wire service. The days when every news organization has to cover the same things – such as question period in the House of Commons – are over. Of course, people have been making this claim as far back as my own days as the Ottawa bureau chief of the *Toronto Star* in the early 1980s.

News organizations can't beat Facebook or Twitter for speed or spread, so political journalists in particular will have to shift from covering secrets to uncovering mysteries.

Controlled distribution will give way to superdistribution, and that process will be more squarely in the hands of individual journalists. You can subscribe to *Axios*, for example, or you can watch the *Axios* documentaries on HBO. Journalism will always include a core of full-time practitioners, but there will be an increasing participation by people working at it part-time or as volunteer subject matter experts.

These stories will be distributed by people who will be concerned less with the question of what is news and more with questions like, "Will my friends or followers like this?" (Anderson, Bell, and

Shirky 2012). The authors conclude what is going on in journalism today is a revolution not an evolution – a revolution "so large that the existing structure of society can't contain it without being altered by it" (ibid.).

The Case for "Value" Journalism

The 2016 US presidential campaign, with its subtext debates about fake news and media bias, reignited the debate as to whether mainstream journalism's editorial content was substantive enough to achieve the democratic ideal of informed consent.

Former Harvard professor Robert Picard (2006) argued well before that election that the answer to the question is an unequivocal and resounding *no*! The reality, according to Picard, "is that the average person is not now – and never has been – deeply interested in news" (ibid., 5). For most readers, viewers, and listeners, news consumption is brief and consists primarily of scanning major developments.

Media scholars have identified three types of knowledge that find expression in the news: knowledge about things, knowledge about how to do things, and knowledge about why things happened and their implications.

The primary focus of contemporary journalism is conveying knowledge of the first type, even though most of us have some of that knowledge about events before newscasts air or newspapers go to press. As Mitchell Stephens wrote in "Beyond News: The Case for Wisdom Journalism," information about virtually every major event now appears fast and free on Google, Yahoo, or a hundred other websites (2009, 3). Television newscasts are a prime example of the limitations inherent in this approach. The lead item might be a story about something that occurred in Atlanta. The reporter covering the story is in Washington. The reporter's knowledge "about things" is restricted to what he or she was able to pick up off the internet – which the viewer in Toronto can do for themselves. This type of reportage fails both the "authority" test of traditional journalism and the "authenticity" test of today's journalism.

News organizations need to shift to the third type of knowledge if they are to be relevant in future. Stephens's colleague Sarah J. Hart described the kind of shift civic journalism must make when she observed, "News is what happened; journalism is what it means" (as cited in Stephens 2014, 153). And they need to do so by answering the traditional question that has shaped coverage in the *Toronto Star* for generations: What does this mean to our audience?

News and information that help people understand the effects of policies, global trends, economic developments, and security threats are clearly relevant regardless of location. But much of the daily reporting on distant events fails to make clear connections between those events and people's lives. Too much of the content of news organizations is basic, raw information and not the kind of information that promotes understanding.

In the new environment, news organizations must become more customer friendly, have a greater degree of intimacy with viewers, listeners, and readers. Instead of telling news consumers everything there is to know, news organizations will increasingly need to tell their customers where they can get what they need and want to know, whether the source for that information is the news organization itself or other sources that the news organization certifies as credible.

Future news organizations will have to live with dramatically less revenue from advertisers and provide content that is more closely focused on the communities the news organization purports to serve.

Journalists, says Stephens (2009, 13), must offer something less common, less cheap. His answer? "Wisdom journalism"; that is, content that is informed, intelligent, interesting, insightful, and interpretive and original. The last point cannot be emphasized enough. The legendary *Baltimore Sun* political reporter Jack Germond (Patterson 2013) characterized Washington coverage as falling under the 90/10 rule: 90 per cent of the coverage was a rehash of the 10 per cent of stories that involved some original reporting.

Alex Panetta, former Washington bureau chief for the Canadian Press, *Politico Canada*, and now a correspondent for the CBC, is one of the generators of original reporting Germond talks about. The North American Free Trade Agreement, under attack from the Trump administration, was as important an economic story for Canada in 2018 as the future of resource extraction. Network public affairs shows routinely featured panels of experts to dissect what the latest pronouncement from the president really meant and the implications for the Canadian economy. Yet much of this expert opinion and learned analysis was built on a basic understanding of the situation of the moment shaped by Panetta's exceptional coverage. Few of the panellists or pundits had spoken directly with any politician or official directly involved in the talks. All were examining tea leaves placed in their cups by Panetta's reporting (and that of other specialist reporters). No Panetta, no iron core.

Wisdom reporting, says Stephens, not only produces knowledge, it requires knowledge. "Our best journalism needs to aim higher, needs to be more ambitious for itself and its audience," he said (2014, 11). Sir Martyn Lewis, a former BBC news anchor, sees a future in "solutions-driven journalism" (Cahalane 2012).

This new journalism model will impact political discourse. Harvard's Cass Sunstein, a charter member of the elites that the American electorate allegedly turned on in the 2016 campaign, offered one view in his work *Simpler: The Future of Government* (Sunstein 2013). Sunstein saw a government rooted in policies that preserve freedom of choice. Governments of the future, said Sunstein, will provide "nudges," thereby encouraging people to make choices that will help them rather than harm them. "Nudges" are seen as libertarian because they preserve freedom of choice. The field of behavioural economics is one expression: you don't ban junk food; instead, you have the school cafeteria put fruit at eye level.

Donald Trump used Twitter to nudge. When a Republican majority in the House of Representatives, emboldened by Trump's election, decided their first act of 2017 should be a vote to eviscerate the Office of Congressional Ethics, a tweet from the then-president-elect was enough to "nudge" a reversal (Walsh, Raju, and Collinson 2017). Political conversation will be engaged in similar fashion.

Exit polls in the 2016 presidential campaign suggested people don't vote for specific politics as much as they are swayed by intangible personal traits; people they feel they can trust, people who promise to bring a measure of stability to their lives.

While mainstream journalists were somewhere between bemused and befuddled as to why voters would believe anything candidate Trump said, they overlooked the fact a significant proportion of the electorate had already decided they didn't believe a single thing candidate Clinton said. And when Trump promised to "Make America Great Again," the assertion resonated with those electors who believed their recent experience was one of economic and personal instability.

Patterson is critical of the approach educators in North America have taken to journalism education. Joseph Pulitzer, who founded the Columbia School of Journalism, envisioned journalism as an intellectual profession, producing graduates with the same status as those educated in medicine or the law. Instead, says Patterson, university administrators set up schools of journalism as trade schools. As someone who holds a graduate degree from Carleton's School of Journalism and Communication, it is hard for me to not see Patterson's assessment as a little harsh. But his point, that the curriculum offered is not intensely practical enough to qualify as an apprenticeship and not deep enough to be considered scholarly, is insightful.

Anderson et al. concluded journalism schools today are more like film schools than law schools, "which is to say that the relative success or failure of a J-School grad is going to be far more variable than it used to be" (Anderson, Bell, and Shirky 2012, 111). For that reason, the authors go on to predict "the fate of journalism in the United States is now far more squarely in the hands of individual journalists than it is of the institutions that support them" (ibid., 112).

The new media template will require new skills. Columbia University, for example, now offers a dual degree in computer science and journalism. Today's reporters need to understand programming and data. Mathematics is a core competency.

Journalists now have to be entrepreneurs; they will have to develop a public persona. The late Southam News chief Charles Lynch figured this out sixty years ago. But where TV, radio, and speaking appearances were once the domain of high-profile columnists like Lynch, it will be part of the job jar for every journalist in future.

Carleton's School of Journalism and Communication has taken the idea of providing a professional formation that includes skills better suited to a digital age a step further – with a new program geared to a world of storytelling beyond the professional codes and conventions of journalism. The bachelor of media production and design degree program welcomed its first students in the fall of 2018. "It's not journalism, it is storytelling online," the program's first director, Christopher Waddell, explained in an interview (pers. notes).

Journalism schools, not surprisingly, include a concentration of courses intended to hone reporting and editing skills within the structures of legacy journalism – how to cover the police or the courts, for example. "We're not doing that in this course,' Waddell, a distinguished former journalist and director of Carleton's journalism program, explains. Graduates of this new program will bring a different perspective entirely; storytelling decisions rather than journalistic decisions. Graduates are expected to go on to work as media producers for mainstream and new digital media as well as in governments, corporations, or not-for-profits.

What the program does recognize, however, is the broader reality that in today's digital world, storytelling is not confined to mainstream media and that journalists are no longer the sole or even primary gatekeepers of public discourse.

In ancient Celtic culture, the history and laws of the people were not committed to paper, according to research websites, but instead were captured in long, lyrical poems, and were memorized and recited by bards known as Scealai or Seanchai. Storytelling, in other words, has always had its place in public discourse. Some question whether it should have a place for journalism. NYU professor Jay Rosen wonders how journalists came to see their role as "society's storytellers." In a Twitter post thread, Rosen goes on to ask, "What are the costs of this misfit self-conception?" (Rosen 2018).

Rosen points to an article penned by Jeff Jarvis on Medium.com. Jarvis writes, "In journalism, the story too often becomes a self-fulfilling creation" (Jarvis 2018). Jarvis quotes Bernhard Pörksen, who wrote, "You have the story in your head, you know what sound readers or colleagues want to hear. And you deliver what works" (ibid.). Instead of asserting themselves as society's storytellers, Jarvis argues the job of the journalist is "to inform the public conversation … to convene communities into civil, informed, and productive conversation … This means our first job is not to write but to listen to that conversation so we can find out what it needs to function. Then we report" (ibid.).

Jarvis's reference to news stories as "self-fulfilling creations" triggers reflections on Andie Tucher's (1994) concept of a "congenial truth" – decidedly a fact in the Canadian mainstream media's coverage of the SNC-Lavalin affair.

The new media model also suggests a theoretical shift.

Communications scholar James Carey's transmission model involved transmitting ideas over distance for the purpose of control. "Because we have looked at each new advance in communications technology as an opportunity for politics and economics, we have devoted it, almost exclusively, to matters of government and trade," Carey wrote (Carey 2008, 27). However, the emergence of social media – at least in theory – opens the possibility of a ritual model of communication, a process through which a shared culture is created, modified, and transformed. Instead of imparting information, the ritual model evolves around the idea of sharing, of participation, of association: a representation of shared beliefs.

In portraying Lippmann as the villain of the piece, Carey argues the construct of news and political communication articulated in *Public Opinion* frames the issue as one of human psychology, which kick-started the field of inquiry that became known as "effects" theory. This style of journalism reduced citizens to the object, rather than the subject of politics and public discourse, according

to Carey (1989). And in so doing, it reduced journalism to a signalling system (ibid.).

Carey was a sharp critic of old media, arguing, "The press, by
seeing its role as that of informing the public, abandons its role as an
agency for carrying on the conversation of our culture" (ibid., 82).

Carey's ritual model of communications would see journalism
move away from the practice of imparting information and adopt
instead a philosophy of inquiry, a representation of shared beliefs.
Social media, potentially, affords the opportunity of facilitating the
cultural conversation Carey pined for. And that conversation can
only be led by a new style of journalism crafted by professionals
with new skills.

Black Lives Matter

The debate focused on the new form of journalism James Carey said
we needed to have swept through the newsrooms of North America in the summer of 2020. The visceral reaction to the police killing
of George Floyd in Minneapolis triggered a societal examination of
conscience focused on systemic racism – structural bias identified as
a root cause, arguably more problematic than individual acts; white
supremacy a bigger problem than white supremacists.

The institutions being challenged in this debate about the future
form of journalism included the most cherished titles in publishing
and the most revered newsroom leaders. As *The Economist* observed in
a piece carried in the Books and Arts section of its 16 July 2020 edition,
"Have you heard the news? It's about the news" (Economist 2020b).

The *New York Times*, in the words of one staffer who resigned,
found itself in the grip of a "civil war" between the "wokes," mostly
younger staffers, and the liberals, mostly those over forty (Weiss
2020). *Washington Post* editor Marty Baron, whose leadership in
newsrooms from Miami to Los Angeles to Boston to the *Post* is
literally the stuff of legend, found himself accused of driving Black
journalists out of these same newsrooms (Smith, B. 2020a).

The demands for change focused on a foundational tenet of
Western journalism – the notion of objectivity. The *Oxford English*

Dictionary describes objectivity as "to not be influenced by personal feelings or opinions in considering and representing facts" (CBC 2020a). Objectivity is a cornerstone of the CBC's Journalistic Standards and Practices bible (ibid.). It is also, for journalists from the Black, Indigenous, and People of Colour communities, as well as the LBGTQ+ communities, an affectation, largely unattainable.

Describing objectivity as "the view from nowhere," UBC journalism professor and scholar Candis Callison, coauthor with Mary Lynn Young of *Reckoning: Journalism's Limits and Possibilities*, says objectivity is "really impossible, as everybody comes from somewhere" (ibid.). Bestselling author and former *Toronto Star* journalist Desmond Cole argues objectivity props up white supremacy (ibid.).

Radiyah Chowdhury, an assistant editor at *Chatelaine*, made a compelling and considered case for questioning objectivity in an essay entitled "The Forever Battle of a Journalist of Colour," deemed the best essay on the subject of media and democracy by the Friends of Canadian Broadcasting (Chowdhury 2020). "I've been grappling with the decision to leave journalism for a while now," wrote Chowdhury. "These days, it feels like Canadian journalisms asks something almost impossible of people of colour" (ibid.). As a journalism student, Chowdhury says objectivity "as it was presented to us seemed to be tailored for a specific type of person, one whose capacity to be dispassionate about certain issues came from a place of privilege that was unfamiliar to me" (ibid.). Journalists from the Black, Indigenous and People of Colour communities, Chowdhury states, are asked "to set aside the traumas they face on a daily basis for the sake of an industry largely created by white people. To legitimize viewpoints that denounce their very existence in the name of balance. To be less human in the most important ways they know how." Chowdhury asserts: "to be racialized is to be politicized" (ibid.).

Former *Washington Post* reporter Wesley Lowery, now with CBS News, says journalism needs to be built around "moral clarity," which the Pulitzer Prize-winning journalist says "means ending its attempt to see all sides of a story, when there is only one" (Sullivan,

A. 2020a). Lowery believes "no journalistic process is objective. And no individual journalist is objective, because no human being is … a better pledge would be an assurance that we will devote ourselves to accuracy" (Lowery 2020).

Social media in general, and Twitter in particular, is a factor of significance in the current debate on the future of journalism. "What's different now, in this moment, is that editors no longer hold a monopoly on publishing power," Lowery states (ibid.). "Individual reporters now have followings of our own on social media platforms, granting us the ability to speak directly to the public … black journalists are now making demands on Twitter" (ibid.).

Lowery's op-ed, carried in the *New York Times*, was described by executive editor Dean Baquet as "terrific" (Lammer, Linsky, and Ratliff 2020). "I'm closer to agreeing with him than some people would think," Baquet continued (ibid.).

As the holder of one of the most powerful jobs in American journalism, Baquet believes the notion of objectivity has "gotten turned into a cartoon" and that, in his mind, journalism's future rests with "the independent and fair reporter" who gets on a plane "with an empty notebook" (ibid.). Baquet, a Black journalist originally from New Orleans, differentiates between what is "core" and what is "habit." What is core, he says, defines who and what you are. What is habit can change (ibid.). Journalism, says Baquet, "is supposed to reflect its time" (ibid.). And in these times, younger journalists feel more comfortable speaking out than journalists of previous generations. "Twitter has given people voice and power and that is a good thing," Baquet says (ibid.). Baquet considers his new mission as the leader of a 1,600-staffer newsroom is to let the new-generation journalists "teach the Times" (ibid.).

The *Wall Street Journal* argues something else entirely is going on in the nation's newsrooms. In a lead editorial published 22 June 2020, which carried the imprimatur of the editorial board, the paper spoke to what the editorial described as "America's Jacobin Moment" (Wall Street Journal 2020). This cultural "putsch" in American institutions, the paper argued, strikes at liberal values and constitutes "a ferocious campaign of political conformity sweeping across American artistic, educational, business and entertainment institutions" (ibid.). The editorial settled on the Jacobin descriptive "because it has the fervour and indiscriminate judgment of the revolutionary mind" (ibid.). "The guillotine isn't in use, but the impulse is the same to destroy careers, livelihoods and reputations." The editorial went on to assert "apologists for cancel culture can find reason to stigmatize or banish anyone" (ibid.).

Where both sides of the debate agree is that the clash "is essentially about power and control" as the editorial states (ibid.).

For the institutional voice that is the *Wall Street Journal*, "as they march through liberal institutions, they are also laying waste to liberal values of free speech, democratic debate and cultural tolerance." The editorial concludes with a dire prediction: "If liberals don't stop the Jacobin left, expect a political backlash and social fracture that will make Donald Trump's presidency look like a tea party" (ibid.). Critics including Wesley Lowery argue in effect that liberalism itself is a form of systemic racism and therefore a form of white supremacy (Sullivan, A. 2020a).

Even industry icons like Baron at the *Washington Post* are being challenged, judged against a new set of criteria. In a column carried in the *New York Times* 28 June 2020, media columnist Ben Smith described the *Post* as "a top-down institution whose constrained view of what journalism is today has frustrated some of the industry's creative young stars" (Smith, B. 2020a). Smith described the *Post* as "a faceless institution in an era of influencers and personal brands."

Baron not surprisingly, believes "The Post is more than a collection of individuals who wish to express themselves. The reputation of The Post must prevail over any one individual's desire for expression." As Smith concluded, so "stubbornly retro" (ibid.). The *Post* reporters who spoke to Smith insisted on anonymity "because The Post prefers that its employees not talk to the media" (ibid.). The irony of news reporters speaking to other journalists on condition of anonymity is striking. Further, it is worth noting reporters at organizations such as the *Post* or the *New York Times* want the benefit of the institutional prestige of these publications, even as they insist the publications change both their cultures and their content to espouse this emerging worldview.

The decision by the *New York Times* to run an op-ed from Senator Tom Cotton that advocated the use of federal troops to restore order in cities besieged by protest triggered an internal revolt at the *Times* and a debate of international proportions elsewhere.

The NewsGuild of New York, which represents employees at the *New York Times,* issued a formal statement that declared, "We find the publication of this essay to be an irresponsible choice" (Murphy and Haylock 2020). More than 1,000 *Times* staff members signed a letter protesting the essay's publication (Lee, E. 2020), insisting the op-ed page piece "puts black @nytimes staff in danger" (Economist 2020b). Editorial page editor James Bennet resigned days later (Lee, E. 2020). Op-ed columnist Bari Weiss – considered a "conservative" voice – tendered her resignation as well and posted a 1,500-word letter she had written publisher A.G. Sulzberger on her Facebook page denouncing what she described as a "hostile work environment" (ibid.). Weiss claimed she was subjected to "bullying" by colleagues who had created an "illiberal environment" (ibid.). Coworkers, Weiss said, had insulted her and called for her removal on Twitter. "I do not understand how you have allowed this kind of behavior to go on inside your company in full view of the paper's entire staff and the public" (ibid.). A former staffer at the *Wall Street Journal*, Weiss claimed "intellectual curiosity" was "now a liability at The Times" (ibid.). And in a pointed acknowledgement of the power of social media in general, and Twitter in particular, Weiss declared, "Twitter is not on the masthead of The New York Times. But Twitter has become its ultimate editor" (ibid.).

One of the more intriguing story lines in the debate involved an open letter to appear in the Letters section of the October 2020 issue of *Harper's Magazine*. Entitled "A Letter on Justice and Open Debate," the letter states, "Our cultural institutions are facing a moment of trial ... The forces of illiberalism are gaining strength throughout the world" (Harper's Magazine, 2020). The letter goes on to state, "The democratic inclusion we want can be achieved only if we speak out against the intolerant climate that has set in on all sides ... It is now all too common to hear calls for swift and severe retribution in response to perceived transgressions of speech and thought" (ibid.). The letter was signed by more than 150 writers, journalists, academics, individuals from the performing arts; names as well-known as Martin Amis and Margaret Atwood, Todd Gitlin and Noam Chomsky, Dexter Filkins and Malcolm Gladwell, Gloria Steinem and J.K. Rowling.

The signatories were immediately denounced as rich, privileged, and out of touch.

HuffPost enterprise director Richard Kim, who was asked to sign the letter, refused to do so and took to Twitter to dismiss the letter as "fatuous, self-important drivel" (Kim 2020).

Conservative columnist Andrew Sullivan posted a farewell letter in *New York* magazine July 17, 2020 entitled "See You Next Friday: A Farewell Letter" (Sullivan, A. 2020b). Sullivan said he had in effect been shown the door by a magazine that had every right to do so. "What has happened, I think, is relatively simple: A critical mass of the staff and management at *New York* Magazine and Vox Media no longer want to associate with me" (ibid.). A once and future blogger, Sullivan stated, "They seem to believe, and this is increasingly the orthodoxy in mainstream media, that any writer not actively committed to critical theory in questions of race, gender, sexual orientation, and gender identity is actively, physically harming co-workers merely by existing in the same virtual space" (ibid.). Sullivan balks at what he describes as the "mainstream media's increasingly narrow range of acceptable thought" (ibid.) and cites George Orwell to the effect that "if liberty means anything at all it means the right to tell people what they do not want to hear" (ibid.).

The debate triggered by the *Times* and *Post* sagas has extended to other Western liberal democracies.

A comment piece carried by the *Sunday Times* and written by Joanna Williams, author of *Academic Freedom in an Age of Conformity*, carried the subtitle, "The sad capitulation of The New York Times is part of a stifling culture of woke conformity" (Williams 2020). The Gray Lady, as the *New York Times* is known, had shifted "from publishing 'all the news that's fit to print' to only views with which she wholeheartedly concurs," Williams stated. "It seems that America's national newspaper of record, winner of more Pulitzer prizes than any other, no longer has room for disagreement on its comment pages" (ibid.). The new journalism, from Williams's perspective, insists commentators "fall into line or shut up."

A letter from a reader to the editor of the *Times* summarized the liberal view of public discourse succinctly and effectively. Under the headline "Agree to Disagree," Alan Hawkes from Saffron Walden, Essex, wrote, "Sir, There were several articles in Saturday's comment section (Jun 20) with which I profoundly disagree. Keep up the good work."

This debate on the future of journalism is unlikely to come to a quick conclusion. Achieving consensus may prove elusive. The debate may have a particular relevance in countries with public broadcasters supported directly by taxpayers, such as Canada or the United Kingdom.

The Canadian Broadcasting Corporation / Société Radio-Canada is Canada's largest media organization. The CBC receives an annual subsidy of more than $1 billion from the federal government. But in a journalistic world of "moral certainty," who gets to decide the definition of moral certainty: the journalists in CBC newsrooms or the taxpayers who fund them? In a world of "activist" journalism, who decides what issues to be "active" about? In a world where language is a weapon, who decides what vocabulary or descriptive is acceptable? And if Canadians vote to change the federal government, does that democratically expressed desire for change get reflected in the way the public broadcaster defines activism?

Ironically, a tenet of classic liberalism – free markets – may be a factor, if not a determinant factor, in resolving the issue. Baquet's observation that journalism should reflect its time is fundamental (Lammer, Linsky, and Ratliff 2020). Communities long ignored or marginalized in the mainstream press have other channels to find voice and other gatekeepers to curate that conversation.

BIPOC journalists – like their peers in the legal community – want access to jobs and want corporate cultures to change to incorporate and accommodate their worldview. The latter demand may constitute more of a challenge for incumbents than the inclusion argument. As the *Times* executive editor Dean Baquet observed, "We thought these diversely talented people wanted to be just like us – and they do not!" (Rosen 2020a).

Lowery says the media industry has turned a deaf ear when BIPOC journalists raise their concerns. "Collectively, the industry has responded to generations of black journalists with indifference at best and open hostility at its frequent worst" (Lowery 2020). "Frequently, when we speak out about coverage that is inaccurate or otherwise lacking, we are driven from newsrooms" (ibid.). In Canada, *Chatelaine* executive editor Denise Balkissoon says that there haven't been enough BIPOC journalists in leadership positions. Black Lives Matter, the former *Globe* columnist says, just not in the newsrooms of the nation (Balkissoon 2020). To underscore Balkissoon's point, Unifor, the bargaining unit at the *Globe and Mail*, says the entire top of the house at the *Globe* is white, and as a consequence, the union served notice future collective agreements will demand formal quotas on diversity (Unifor 2020). The negotiations, presumably, will have to include consideration of factors such as seniority and "bumping rights" for current union members.

James Carey had a vivid descriptive of the role of journalism in a democracy. "News can only give, like the blip on a sonar scope, a signal that something is happening" (Carey 1989). Former Carleton University professor Christopher Dornan extends the thought in a paper entitled "Science Disinformation in a Time of Pandemic" written for the Public Policy Forum in June 2020. "Journalism in a free society such as Canada is reflexively sceptical of political authority," Dornan states (Dornan 2020, 23). "Its mandate is to subject government and business to informed scrutiny on behalf of the public, and the news media employ as columnists and commentators a class of opinionaters characterized by a quick intelligence, an oppositional disposition and a talent for commanding attention" (ibid.). In a liberal democracy, opinions are freely held. As Dornan states, "In a free society people are entitled to believe all manner of nonsense" (ibid., 28).

Tom Rosenstiel issued this warning to those who would set aside objectivity as a foundational tenet: "If journalists replace a flawed understanding of objectivity by taking refuge in subjectivity and think their opinions have more moral integrity than genuine inquiry, journalism will be lost" (Economist 2020b).

9

A New Public Policy Framework for a New Business Model

Paul M. Tellier, my friend, mentor, and former boss, believed government was the single biggest variable in anyone's business. Once the country's top public servant and a member of the Canadian Business Hall of Fame, Tellier is uniquely positioned to comment on the impact program or policy decisions by governments at any level can have on the business plan of any enterprise. Media companies – whether legacy or social – are no exception.

Governments, as David Hesmondhalgh reminds us, can intervene in communications, media, and cultural markets in any one of three main ways: legislate, regulate, or subsidize. My classroom notes from a graduate course in communications, culture, and regulation, taught at the time by Sheryl Hamilton at Carleton University, records the point that policies are not neutral, they are political, and they have an effect.

In fact, governments in Canada began subsidizing public affairs journalism before there was a Canada. Books, newspapers, and magazines were eligible for postal subsidies – the de facto distribution system of the era – as far back as 1849. Policy-makers have long considered broadcasting a matter of public interest and because of its power, in need of some measure of political control. The policy debate in Western liberal democracies is now focused on digital platform companies. For reasons that are self-evident, that someone living in a developed country might not have a Facebook page borders on the inconceivable, particularly any individual who aspires to elected office.

"You'd be hard pressed to find a politician who's been elected in the past 10 years who didn't use Facebook," according to David

Kirkpatrick, author of *The Facebook Effect*, a history of the social media site. Two presidents, Barack Obama and Donald Trump, won elections in no small part thanks to Facebook, states *The Economist* (Economist 2019e).

In recent years, developments in telecommunications policy "have had a profound impact on cultural production," writes David Hesmondhalgh (2007, 107).

With the rise of the internet, news, education, and entertainment began to blur together (Castells 2009, 364). While the right of free expression of views is a "fundamental aspect of democratic liberal thought," according to Hesmondhalgh (2007, 109), the proliferation of texts over the last thirty years did not necessarily translate into a diversity of views.

Canada's media landscape is at once highly concentrated and vertically integrated.

Bell Canada Enterprises, for example, simultaneously produces content through Bell Media's CTV subsidiary and distributes that content through other subsidiaries such as Bell Canada through broadband, fibre, and wireless. Further, companies such as BCE contribute to and, in doing so, effectively control content creation funding through the Canadian Media Fund. This structure affords the broadcasters a de facto veto over the content creation process as applicants are expected to have a broadcast partner, which means firms like BCE have disproportionate market power.

Creators have to show a significant degree of flexibility when dealing with a broadcaster such as CTV or Global. Independent producers learn to twist their original idea into a pretzel if network programmers are so inclined because there is limited funding available to any creator who doesn't have a broadcaster onside.

From a creative perspective, federal government policy, arguably, is a "jobs" policy as much as it is a "content" policy. Franchise shows, such as *The Amazing Race Canada*, qualified as Canadian content (Vlessing 2013). To be sure, these programs generated a lot of work for skilled production personnel, and did attract large audiences (ibid.). Whether they gave "voice" to Canada or Canadians is a separate issue, host and Olympic gold medallist Jon Montgomery notwithstanding.

Television's role through the late twentieth century as an electronic public sphere fell victim to audience segmentation. Political economy's preoccupation with power identifies the key consideration in this equation with the observation "symbol creators continue to exercise relatively high levels of operational autonomy but very low levels of power when it comes to the circulation of texts" (Hesmondhalgh 2007, 302). In an internet age, relatively few cultural companies "have very quickly found ways of re-establishing control over circulation" (ibid., 303). In terms of political news, control over circulation rests disproportionately with digital platform companies.

Facebook, according to scholar Taylor Owen, has largely won the platform war. "They have become the infrastructure for the free press," he declared, in an edited version of the Dalton Camp Lecture in Journalism delivered at St. Thomas University and carried on the CBC Radio program *Ideas* (Owen 2017b). Legacy media, says Owen, "gave up many of the things unique to them" in a Faustian bargain with social media to extend distribution of their editorial content, "and I don't know how they get those back" (ibid.).

What is arguably a little different about today's debate around the threat posed by social media monopolies to business monopolies past is the positioning of the power of Facebook et al. as a direct threat to democracy.

Unsuccessful presidential candidate Elizabeth Warren is one elected official focused on the size and scale of digital platform companies and the implications of that corporate strength on public policy. The Democratic senator from Massachusetts stated in the summer of 2019, "When corporations get so big that they can start to squeeze the government, then democracy no longer works" (Green 2019, 38).

The risk inherent in the broader policy process is that lawmakers, whether in Canada or the US, will be preoccupied with issues that arose during the last election cycle rather than anticipating the issues that might arise in the next. The result could be the policy equivalent of France's infamous Maginot Line – defensive battlements inspired by the trench warfare of the First World War that proved spectacularly ineffective against the German blitzkrieg of the Second World War.

Many of the policy solutions advanced would treat digital platform companies like media companies. Communications scholars such as Carleton University's Dwayne Winseck argue to do so is old thinking and misses the point entirely. The policy challenges posed by digital platform companies are large – data protection, privacy, and market dominance to cite three identified by Winseck.

In a February 2019 article, Jesse Hirsh quotes Winseck to the effect that "if any existing regulatory framework should regulate technology companies, it should be those that regulate banking and financial services – not media companies" (Hirsh 2019). "For Winseck, the relationship is quite simple: data has become a kind of currency, a commodity of considerable value, and much like a relationship with a bank, our relationship with a technology company is based on trust" (ibid.). Adds Hirsh, "A technology company manages data on our behalf in the same way that a bank manager manages money on our behalf" (ibid.). Winseck, says Hirsh, sees a parallel to the rules governing financial institutions around deposits, governance, even social and economic stability (ibid.).

The prescience of Winseck's thinking was underscored in July 2019 when Facebook announced it was to launch a new cryptocurrency – Libra – in 2020. The value of the Libra will be pegged to a basket of major currencies (Economist 2019b, 9). If even a fraction of Facebook's users take up the company's offering, Facebook would quickly become one of the world's largest financial institutions, with real implications for the economic sovereignty of governments.

Winseck and fellow scholars will press their case for new thinking. But for purposes of this work, issues related to civil discourse, the electoral process, the ability of national governments to hold digital platform companies to account will provide the framework.

A key question to be confronted is whether the public policy process can keep pace with the rate of technological change. The University of Ottawa's Elizabeth Dubois says the policy challenge in Canada is basically that we have rules, regulations, and norms designed for a media system that simply doesn't exist anymore. Appearing as a panellist at an event hosted by the IRPP on 7 May 2019, Dubois added that the challenge is compounded by the fact there is a disconnect between young people and people in policy-making roles in government.

Fellow panellist Taylor Owen credited the federal government with at least making a serious effort to engage in the last year or two, but as Dubois noted, the most recent amendments to the Canada Elections Act that took effect 30 June 2019 are insufficient (Dubois, McGuire, and Owen 2019). Dubois says, "As bot detection improves, bot creators get better at masking their identify." As a consequence of these various challenges, "we no longer know what reliable information is in society," according to McGill's Owen (ibid.).

A secondary consideration involves an acknowledgment that public policy and the business models for both legacy and social media going forward are inextricably linked.

In its infancy, the press was "partisan," funded by political parties or movements espousing a particular philosophy. As referenced earlier in this work, James Curran and Jean Seaton credit advertising as the midwife of press freedom, creating the opportunity for financially independent newspapers to become, according to the *New Cambridge Modern History*, "great organs of the public mind" (Curran and Seaton 2003, 44). The value proposition was driven by maximizing the size of the audience – readers, in the case of newspapers – and the consequence of that, according to Curran and Seaton, was a cumulative downgrading of political coverage. "For the press barons, profits mattered more than politics," they concluded (ibid., 44).

With the exception of state-financed broadcasters, the press is a private enterprise empowered as a public trust. Advertising allowed the daily press to move past its partisan beginnings, a mixed blessing for certain scholars. The size of the audience determined the depth of the revenue stream. In time, the law of large numbers gave way to the law of right numbers. Advertisers became more interested in the socioeconomic profile of the news consumer: performance-car companies sought out broadsheets with meaningful business sections; the sound-system manufacturers loved the tabloids.

Today, the midwife is moving on. Joseph Schumpeter's "creative destruction" – described as a process of industrial innovation that incessantly revolutionizes the economic structure from within, incessantly destroying the old one, increasingly creating a new one (Environmental Protection Agency 1973, 186) – appeared for legacy print organizations in the form of free online advertising.

The "virtuous" circle of profitability and public service that sustained traditional media for the better part of 200 years has been broken, with direct implications for public discourse.

Canadian communications scholar Marshall McLuhan predicted the demise of the business model for print journalism back in 1964. Recognizing – accurately – that classified ads were the lifeblood of newspapers, McLuhan presciently observed, "Should an alternative source of easy access to such diverse daily information be found, the press will fold" (Public Policy Forum 2017, 16). Kijiji and Craigslist proved to be just such "an alternative source of easy access."

Ad-supported business models appear doomed, given the way the big five tech companies such as Facebook are soaking up digital ad dollars.

In an interview with *Toronto Life*, Postmedia chair and CEO Paul Godfrey said print advertising "has fallen off the cliff," and, given the fact advertising represents 80 per cent of Postmedia's revenue stream, the trend line is clear. As Godfrey said, "we can only hike the price of the paper so much" (Johnston 2017).

Research conducted by the leading Canadian polling firm Abacus (Horgan 2017) underscores the conundrum facing news producers and news consumers alike. The research suggests millions of Canadians say they talk about politics daily, yet newspapers are struggling to identify the business model that will allow these outlets to produce the quality, original content that is as essential to that conversation as water is to life.

Advertising's subsidization of news, current affairs, and cultural content has always been a source of unease in the creative classes. Erik Barnouw, an acclaimed observer of broadcasting, is quoted by Tim Wu as saying, "The real question is whether we can afford to have our cultural and artistic life become a byproduct of advertising. My answer is that we can't" (Wu, T. 2016, 150).

Godfrey was one of the media proprietors to ask the Commons Standing Committee on Canadian Heritage (Parliament of Canada 2016a) to recommend federal help for the beleaguered news business. In a subsequent interview with *Toronto Life*, Godfrey said, "I'm asking for the same breaks they give the film industry" (Johnston 2017). From a public perspective, it is hard to imagine a less appealing spokesperson for print publications than Godfrey. Despite the fact he has been employed by different media companies since the mid-1980s, Godfrey describes himself as a "businessman" and former politician and not as a media executive. He believes he is fully deserving of compensation that touches $5 million a year (CBC 2019a), insisting "there are not many people in Canada who can run a newspaper chain … The job is hard and full of heartache" (Johnston 2017). Godfrey clearly is untroubled by optics, accepting a $900,000 "retention bonus" (Ibid.) in 2016 alone even as scores of journalists at Postmedia properties were being shown the door – or "downsized" to use the jargon of the HR weenies. The juxtaposition did not go over well in political Ottawa.

Similarly, Godfrey affects a "that was then, this is now" posture when asked about a promise he made to the Competition Bureau (2015) when Postmedia acquired the Sun chain that he would not combine the newsrooms of the two organizations. And the Postmedia CEO is chillingly candid when asked about the impact all this corporate downsizing has had on the group's member papers. "Are our papers as good as they used to be? No, but they haven't become unacceptable" (Johnston 2017). In August 2019, Postmedia

CEO Andrew MacLeod was accused of hatching a plan to "muffle moderate voices at Canada's largest newspaper company" in a story by Sean Craig in *Canadaland* (Craig 2019). MacLeod, according to Craig's reportage, doesn't believe the flagship *National Post* is conservative enough. Postmedia declined Craig's request to comment on his story.

Weeks later, further controversy erupted when the *Vancouver Sun* ran an opinion piece entitled "Can Social Trust and Diversity Co-exist?" that questioned immigration policies based on inclusion, diversity, and tolerance. The paper's own journalists denounced the piece, as did reporters at the sister publication *The Province*. Editor-in-chief Harold Munro's apology to readers made the feeble argument he hadn't read the piece prior to publication. Presumably, somebody else in the *Sun*'s editorial chain of command had (Gul 2019).

Godfrey's appointment to the Canadian News Hall of Fame may have triggered a lot of arching of eyebrows in Canada's journalistic community, but his matter-of-fact assessment of the state of Canadian news organizations can't be as easily dismissed. His statement to *Toronto Life* to the effect that "if we hire more staff, we'll be out of business in three months" may exasperate but has the aura of authenticity (Johnston 2017).

Former Torstar board chair John Honderich had a similar message for the Commons Standing Committee on Canadian Heritage when he appeared before them in September 2016. "My message to you is a simple one," Honderich said in an opening statement. "There is a crisis of declining good journalism across Canada. At this point, we only see the situation getting worse" (Parliament of Canada 2016b).

A former Ottawa and Washington bureau chief for the *Star*, Honderich told committee members fewer municipal council meetings are being covered in Canada. "The implications of this trend for an informed citizenry and for local communities gaining access to the information they need are profound," Honderich said. "If you believe, as we do, that the quality of a democracy is a direct function of the quality of information citizens have to make informed decisions, then this trend is indeed worrisome" (ibid.). The former publisher of the *Toronto Star* said desire for the content newspapers produce is far from dead; close to 90 per cent of Canadians read newspaper content on some platform every week. "Readership is not the issue. It is the business model," Honderich said (ibid.).

In the spring of 2017, Honderich carried his case for government action to a public meeting sponsored by the Macdonald-Laurier Institute to debate the issue. "You could not have a more fundamental public good than making sure the Canadian population is well-informed," Honderich argued. "That is an absolutely fundamental tenet of how a democracy works" (Ballingall, A. 2017). The former Torstar chair's comments echoed remarks made by then-US president Barack Obama at a memorial service for CBS legend Walter Cronkite when Obama said, "Journalism is more than just a profession. It is a public good vital to our democracy." Honderich stated the functioning of any healthy democracy is predicated on the participation of a well-informed population. Newspapers "provide, when well run, the means for a populace to examine itself, a channel to ferret out lies and abuse and corruption, and a vehicle to give voice to those whose voices are not often heard," he concluded (ibid.).

Former *National Post* columnist Andrew Coyne, now at the *Globe*, who espoused a contrarian view at the event, made the uncomfortable if important point than many of the problems of legacy media are self-inflicted. "People do not value the thing we are selling at a price sufficient to cover its cost," Coyne said (ibid.). Rejecting the notion of any government subsidy of the news, Coyne said simply, "If the government can't subsidize everyone, it shouldn't subsidize anyone" (ibid.).

Columbia University professor Tim Wu, author of *The Attention Merchants* (2016), argues the business model for modern media has always been based on the reselling of human attention. More recently, Google has become the most profitable "attention merchant" in history.

Elected in 2015, the Liberal government was sufficiently seized of the threat to local news posed by the decline of print publications that it charged the non-partisan Public Policy Forum with investigating the situation. The Public Policy Forum (PPF) report, "The Shattered Mirror: News, Democracy and Trust in the Digital Age" (Public Policy Forum 2017), echoes Honderich's assertion that real news is in crisis.

On its splash page, PPF states "foreign giants" are getting more than the lion's share of the advertising money "that news outlets rely on to pay for quality journalism." In a report issued in February 2017, PPF quotes from the 2009 Knight Commission on the Information Needs of Communities in a Democracy that concluded news is as vital to democracy as "clean air, safe streets, good schools and public health" (Public Policy Forum 2017, 4). But the new media landscape, according to the PPF, is littered with "clickbait, fake news and recycled stories ... The Internet, whose fresh and diverse tributaries of information made it a historic force for openness, now has been polluted by the run-off of lies, hate and the manipulations of foreign powers," the PPF report asserts (ibid., 3). The "truth neutrality" of digital platforms such as Facebook and Google is "incompatible with democracy," the report continues (ibid.). The PPF report includes a series of program and policy options whereby government could help Canada's media companies. The report includes a specific admonition: "Those who fear the state will take up residence in the newsrooms of the nation should realize it has been well ensconced there for a long time – although generally at a safe distance from the journalists" (ibid., 8).

In Quebec, a coalition of newspapers called for government intervention in a meaningful way. Owners of other newspaper groups joined the chorus. Yet the policy conversation took a decidedly different turn in Quebec than the debate in English Canada. The issue was framed as a "cultural" issue. Newspapers were seen as essential to the preservation of French language and culture. Government support did not trigger the same kind of denunciations that appeared in the English-language media in the rest of Canada where working journalists were less sure the idea of government support had merit. In December 2017, former premier Philippe Couillard's government set aside $24.4 million over five years to help community papers survive and build digital platforms, and created a second $12 million program to improve the papers' capacity to recycle newsprint (CBC 2017a).

Quebecor CEO and president Pierre Karl Péladeau, a former leader of the Parti Québécois, was quick to denounce the programs as "flagrant favouritism" for media companies with "Liberal [read federalist] connections" (Everett-Green 2017). The pushback argument from the government took the form of an assurance Péladeau's print media properties were equally eligible to participate.

Canadians still trust journalists, and journalism. An overwhelming majority of respondents to a survey and focus groups conducted for the PPF by the Earnscliffe Strategy Group consider current affairs, community and political news as important (pers. notes 2016). But respondents think they get more of that news than ever. Thanks to the internet, they believe they are awash in news, even if they are less certain as to its source or its reliability.

The Earnscliffe research included an online survey of 1,500 adults conducted 22 September to 2 October 2016 and six focus group discussions conducted in Montreal, Toronto, and Regina.

Earnscliffe principal Allan Gregg says the challenge facing the Trudeau government as it considers options to support Canadian journalism is that people don't believe there is a problem, and therefore have little appetite for any program or policy solution. "Canadians feel they are inundated with news," yet fewer than half "have heard, read or seen anything about the news organizations facing business and financial difficulties," Gregg stated (ibid.). "The notion that the news is in peril therefore is counterintuitive and runs contrary to their actual experience and is not part of public consciousness" (pers. notes 2016). Respondents to the Earnscliffe research initiative consumed news with a "fair degree of scepticism" according to Gregg, with fully 83 per cent of them believing "a lot of bogus and untrue news and information appears online" (pers. notes 2016).

Gregg's findings are seconded by a survey conducted by Abacus Data (Anderson and Coletto 2017a). Some 56 per cent of respondents said there is no need for the federal government to get involved to ensure there are strong local media serving communities across Canada. "The biggest takeaway thought is that many people seem to shrug at what could be seismic events in the history of Canadian newspapers," stated Abacus principal Bruce Anderson (ibid.). Fully 86 per cent of respondents to the Abacus poll thought they would still be able to get the news they need if their daily newspaper went out of business, the Abacus report states (ibid.). In a piece published in *Maclean*'s 21 July 2017 entitled "Why Canadians Are Closer to Losing Their News Than They Think," author Colin Horgan says the obvious follow-up question to the Abacus poll is "From Where?" (Horgan 2017).

Facebook is a site of choice for many looking for news. But Facebook executives are the first to tell you they are not in the news business, that they are not publishers, that they are not a media company, that they are simply a distribution network. So where is the original news supposed to come from?

According to *Toronto Star* reporter Joanna Chiu, "At least 250 Canadian newspapers have shut down since 2013, turning swaths of Canada into 'news deserts,' where there are few or no journalists covering those communities at all" (Chiu 2020b).

The good people of Guelph, Ontario, have been finding out for themselves since the *Guelph Mercury*, the local daily, closed its doors in January 2016. In a compelling piece published in the 21 July 2017 edition of the *Globe and Mail*, media reporter Simon Houpt states his investigation into the *Guelph Mercury* closing "found high anxiety at the overall drop in news, despair over a growing sense that city politics are becoming nastier and more polarized without the moderating influence of a daily, and a creeping dread that fact-free US-style politics – enhanced by the canny use of social media by those in power – could be spreading north" (Houpt 2017).

A proof point for any argument over the importance of local news to civil society is the 2019 National Newspaper Award to Grant LaFleche of the *St. Catharines Standard* in recognition of a year-long investigation that uncovered evidence of political interference in the hiring process for the Niagara region's top bureaucrat as well as the uncovering of a contract awarded in secret at more than $1 million (St. Catharines Standard 2019).

Google News head Richard Gingras believes these are the early days of a renaissance in journalistic creativity. "New news experiences must be created," Gingras said in November 2016. "I am passionately optimistic about the future of news" (Gingras 2016). Gingras concedes the web "challenges our understanding of the economics of information" (ibid.). Yet he insists with the right content and tools, journalism will find a new business model.

Equity market analysis – like the public policy debate – has tended to focus on the decline of print legacy media. Analysts believe that decline will continue and that efforts by print publications to enhance revenues through the use of paywalls will enjoy limited success because of the proliferation of free content on the internet.

Television networks, long the beneficiaries of a bottleneck in distribution, are now in a prolonged period of structural decline. People do not watch TV in the "appointment" way they used to, and this change in viewing habits is having a direct impact on networks such as Global and CBC. At the same time, on-demand services such as Crave or Netflix are seeing meaningful growth.

Interestingly enough, radio continues to be a viable platform.

But in all cases, legacy media outlets have been followers rather than leaders in shaping their businesses going forward. The focus on content creation, like Bernard Miège's artisans, affords an aura of independence of thought while ceding the actual economic power and control to social media platforms – a classic illustration of the post-Fordist world.

Certain media outlets are succeeding as a "brand" – the *New York Times*, most notably. But each of these companies finds itself in business lines not traditionally associated with print publications.

The events business, for example, is now big business for publications as varied as the *Times*, *Politico*, and *The Walrus*.

Digital technology is no longer the disrupter; it is the driver. The mobile device is the platform of choice.

Owen argues we, as a society, "need to know what is true" (Owen 2017b). Yet as a direct result of the "pernicious effect" of Facebook's platform on our civil discourse, the social network site has "created a toxic public sphere" (ibid.). Referring to former president Barack Obama's warnings about the need for truth in civil discourse – linking it to Dwight D. Eisenhower's warning in the 1950s of the dangers of the military-industrial complex – Owen believes we stand on the cusp of a new age of government intervention, but readily admits "I don't really have adequate solutions" to the societal challenges created by digital platforms (ibid.).

Facebook executives insist the social network site is just one of many places people get their news. But like prime ministers at a cabinet table in a system of responsible government, Facebook is decidedly first among "equals." Research from the Pew Research Center suggests almost half of American adults rely on Facebook for their news (Lichterman 2016), underscoring the potential for influence. Further, the company trips on its own rhetorical shoelaces when it touts its ability to sway users to potential advertisers.

Zuckerberg's questioning of Facebook's impact on the US presidential campaign is dismissed out of hand by academics. University of North Carolina associate professor Zeynep Tufekci states flatly, "Of course, Facebook had a significant influence on this last election's outcome" (Isaac 2016). Max Read took it a step further in a *New York* magazine article published the day after the election, which stated, "It's not just that Facebook makes politics worse, it's that it changes politics entirely" (Read 2016).

Former US president Barack Obama issued this warning about the effects of fake news on democracy during an appearance in Ottawa, hosted by Canada 2020 in June 2019: "The marketplace of ideas that is the basis of our democratic practice has difficulty working if we don't have some common baseline of what's true and what's not." Obama went on to say he personally knows the people who created and run the major social media platforms and added, "I think that the amount of power they now have, as essentially a common carrier of ideas, it means that there has to be some sort of collective conversation about how that works" (Zilio 2019).

Guardian columnist John Naughton makes the point that fake news may be problematic for many, but it is big business for Facebook (2016). Picking up on founder Mark Zuckerberg's observation that "identifying the 'truth' is complicated," Naughton states, "Zuckerberg's problem is that he doesn't want to engage in that kind of fact-checking, because it would be a tacit acknowledgment that Facebook is a publisher rather than just a technology company and therefore has some editorial responsibilities" (ibid.). Facebook's conundrum is its inherent conflict of interest, Naughton argues. The social media site makes money from the digital fingerprints of its users. "The more something is 'shared' on the internet, the more lucrative it is for Facebook," he states (ibid.). "If you run a social networking site, fake news is good for business even if it is bad for democracy," Naughton concludes.

In a column posted Sunday, 28 May 2017, Naughton revisited the threat Facebook's quest for speed poses for democracy. "'Fake news' was the tool of choice for micro-targeting voters with personalized political messages," Naughton writes (2017). In the ensuing debate, Facebook's various lines of defence – starting with its assertion that it is a technology company, "merely a conduit" – proved inadequate. Facebook insists it is working on a technical fix to its problems, which also include content that is racist, hateful, misogynistic, and worse. Naughton warned the social networking site hasn't much time. "If we discovered that the output of an ice-cream factory included a small but measurable quantity of raw sewage, we'd close it down in an instant," Naughton states (ibid.). "Message to Zuckerberg: move quickly and fix things. Or else" (ibid.).

Technosociologist Zeynep Tufekci, in a TEDGlobal session in New York City, summarized Facebook's prisoner's dilemma: either the story to advertisers about the site's ability to identify interested parties is a giant con, or the power of the influence of its algorithms should be a matter of great concern (Tufekci 2017).

Facebook's corporate reputation took a serious hit as a result of the election advertising controversy, in which the company admitted in 2017 that Russian operatives published around 8,000 posts on Facebook aimed at influencing the election and that they were seen by 126 million Americans – roughly half the voting public. The company proved it was spectacularly inept at issues management, despite its hip, tech-savvy positioning. As Dylan Byers, then with CNN, noted, Facebook's timeline around the Russian ad issue was a textbook case in how not to handle a crisis:

> FACEBOOK timeline
> – didn't happen
> – happened, but was small
> – ok, semi-big
> – ok, it reached 126 million, but no evidence it influenced them
> (Byers 2017)

Digital companies have certainly been more active in launching government relations initiatives. Twitter Canada named Michele Austin, one of the country's most able government relations practitioners, as its head of government, public policy, and philanthropy. In 2020, Facebook hired the highly regarded Rachel Curran as the public policy manager for Canada (Curran 2020). But a controversy flared in October 2020 when news accounts appeared claiming Facebook Canada's Kevin Chan had emailed a senior official at Canadian Heritage earlier in the year asking if there were "promising senior analysts" in the public service who might be interested in jobs at the social media company even as Ottawa was considering how best to regulate the internet companies (Boutilier 2020b).

McGill's Taylor Owen says governments, and not just Facebook, have to face the broader policy issues – a challenge the Trudeau government has only recently seemed inclined to meet (Owen 2017a).

In a speech delivered in Paris intended to presage his government's "digital charter," Prime Minister Trudeau said social media platforms and tech giants have failed Canadian consumers and it is time the government stepped in. "Now, citizens are living more and more in a digital space that's unregulated," the prime minister stated. "This leaves people incredibly vulnerable" (Boutilier 2019).

Trudeau's declaration was, in part, an indirect response to a question put to Taylor Owen at an IRPP function scant days before. "We know publicly traded monopolies do not self-regulate," Owen said (Dubois, McGuire, and Owen 2019), which raises the question whether we, as citizens, should be outsourcing public policy decisions to large, non-Canadian corporations.

Social media companies can't and won't fix the problem of fake news. For example, Monika Bickert, Facebook's head of global policy management, told a British parliamentary committee, "Our community would not want us, a private company, to be the arbiter of the truth" (Digital, Culture, Media and Sport Committee 2018, 16). Chan, director of policy for Facebook Canada, insists "we very much don't want to have an editorial voice." A participant on a panel organized by the journalism fellows at Massey College on 28 March 2017, Chan insisted, "We are not in the business of telling friends what to tell each other." Yet with the use of algorithms, Facebook is in fact doing just that. Another participant, Jesse Hirsh, encouraged the audience to "see algorithms as a gateway" (pers. notes 2017).

The folks at Facebook did not invent the law of unintended consequences. But it is a bit much for Facebook's leadership to assume that the law doesn't apply to them or that in instances where it is a factor in their business, they are entitled to an exemption of some sort.

Columbia University professor Emily Bell says the lines between technology companies and publishers can no longer be blurred. Writing in the *Guardian*'s 2 April 2017 edition, Bell states Facebook is "being unmasked as the world's largest repository for made-up stories and 'fake news'" (Bell 2017). Bell says these new digital platforms with their algorithmic gatekeepers need to face reality. In a separate paper published by the Tow Center, Bell and her colleagues argue the platforms are "explicitly editorial" (Bell, Taylor, Brown, Hauka, and Rashidian 2017, 10). These companies, have in fact, taken over the publishers' role. As the subhead over Bell's *Guardian* piece states, "Google, Facebook, *et al* are in reality media companies and must accept the responsibilities that go with it" (Bell 2017).

Indeed, the masquerade that social networking companies are merely technology companies has been debunked so successfully in so many forums some observers think it is inevitable both Facebook and Google will soon pivot and proclaim themselves not just media companies but *the* media companies.

Academics were sounding alarms about the impact that digital platforms were having on civil discourse well in advance of the 2016 US presidential campaign. Harvard Law scholar Jonathan Zittrain, for example, writing in the June 2014 edition of the *New Republic,* advanced the proposition that Facebook could decide the 2016 election without anyone finding out (Zittrain 2014). Others argue, "Facebook's draw is its ability to give you what you want," which is a concern given the fact they have taken over the news ecosystem (Madrigal 2017).

Facebook has, in fact, taken over media distribution from the content creators.

A quote attributed to Jason Kint, CEO of the industry trade group Digital Content Next, undoubtedly sent chills down spines in newsrooms across North America: "Media companies are like serfs working Facebook's land" (Frier and Smith 2017, 21).

Facebook has caught the attention of German authorities, according to the *New York Times*, "for allowing the spread of hate speech in postings that would be illegal in traditional media" (Harris and Eddy 2016). Further, Chancellor Angela Merkel has said algorithms used by social networking sites must be transparent in informing the public how they rank news "so that interested citizens are also aware of what actually happens with their own media behaviour and that of others" (Mozur and Scott 2016).

Critics insist social media companies have done little themselves to address emerging concerns about the ease with which interests can abuse their systems.

The 23 October 2017 edition of *Bloomberg Businessweek*, for example, carried a story that proclaimed, "Twitter is crawling with bots and lacks incentive to expel them" (Wang 2017, 22). Twitter, the story stated, was designed to be friendly to bots; indeed an estimated 9 to 15 per cent of Twitter's 300 million-plus active accounts are bots, according to the business newsmagazine. "Now Twitter is scrambling to explain how bots controlled by Russian meddlers may have been used to impact the 2016 president election" (ibid.). By way of example, the story states tweets that mentioned a candidate's name received coordinated replies with disparaging comments.

A 2017 edition of *The Economist* entitled "The World in 2018" predicted a shift in the balance between governments and markets will occur. And the first indication of that shift is the phenomenon the author described as "techlash" (CISION 2017). Across the rich world, "politicians will turn on the technology giants – Facebook, Google and Amazon in particular – saddling them with fines, regulation and a tougher interpretation of competition rules," the article states (ibid.). It will be the "21st-century equivalent of the antitrust era," the piece continues.

Internet platform company executives are reacting to the flashing yellow light from government. Former Google CEO Eric Schmidt predicted "excesses" are "likely to result in greater regulation of internet platforms in the coming years" (De Vynck 2020). In a *mea culpa* of sorts, Schmidt said, "The context of social networks serving as amplifiers for idiots and crazy people is not what we intended" (ibid.). Schmidt went on to say, "Unless the industry gets its act together in a really clever way, there will be regulation."

Jesse Hirsh has argued Canada needs a government entity responsible for digital policy as well. Hirsh, for example, says policy-makers need to focus on the role of algorithms in social media. A former CBC technology commentator, Hirsh has been arguing for some time that "algorithms are a kind of media and should be regulated much like other forms of media." In a paper entitled "Algorithmic Media and Transparency," Hirsh states: "We are witnessing the rise of algorithmic authority and if we are to remain democratic, this authority must be transparent and accountable." Hirsh notes algorithmic media is now the primary source of news for a majority of people and as a consequence, algorithms are now playing a growing role in the construction of our reality. "On Facebook, we don't see everything our friends post, but rather that which the Facebook news feed algorithms selected for us" (ibid.). If, as communications scholars argue, media has a central role in shaping reality, the algorithm dictates of digital platforms are shaping a particular, and arguably peculiar, reality. Search engine manipulation effect is now a fact in public discourse, says Hirsh.

Hirsh reports some policy-makers are now arguing democracies require an entirely new and dedicated agency to deal with these issues, an agency along the lines of the Food and Drug Administration in the United States. Hirsh argues regulation of algorithms is inevitable; the question is whether this regulation takes the form of self-regulation or state-based regulation.

In a column carried in the 20 March 2018 edition of *Bloomberg Businessweek*, Paul Ford asks "Where's Our Digital EPA?" – referring to the Environmental Protection Agency (Ford 2018). Noting the European Union's commission on fake news is having some impact, Ford states, "Let's stop pretending big internet companies can police themselves" (ibid.). Later, in the same column, Ford underlines the fact the news feed is now a core service of Facebook – an issue of some significance for policy-makers everywhere given the fact Facebook now reaches virtually half the world's internet-connected population.

A second policy area of broadening concern is the immunity that social network platforms enjoy in terms of liability. In the earliest days of the web, a tweak to existing communication law exempted online conversation from the libel and slander laws applied to mainstream media. And at the time, according to Nancy Watzman, editor at Trust, Media and Democracy, the "carveout" made a certain amount of sense (Watzman 2017). The exemption had little to do with free speech; rather the intent was to help tech start-ups deal with the "safe harbor" provisions of the Telecommunications Act regarding forward-looking statements.

Section 230 of the Communications Decency Act allows internet companies to police their own sites on the one hand but allows these same companies to avoid liability on the content they host on the other (New York Times 2020c). In May 2020, President Trump signed an executive order calling for a federal review of the statute (ibid.).

Digital company executives, such as Google's Richard Gingras, express concern the debate around fake news is being used to "impose regulations that will constrain free speech. Free expression is under attack," Gingras says. "Democracy is under attack" (Canadian Journalism Foundation 2018b).

While the public policy issues before governments in Western liberal democracies regarding social media apply to each of the "big five," the spotlight, to use Walter Lippmann's descriptive, has settled on Facebook in a way that it hasn't with the others.

Facebook executives are at least partly responsible. Kevin Chan's insistence that he did not need to register as a lobbyist in Ottawa because he spends less than 20 per cent of his time on government relations (Hemmadi 2018) may have met the test of the federal Lobbying Act but failed the legacy media smell test.

Guardian journalist Carole Cadwalladr, whose investigative work uncovered the role Cambridge Analytica played in aiding the Leave campaign in the Brexit referendum in the UK, courageously called out the tech titans in their own lair – the annual TED Talks gathering in Vancouver (Cadwalladr 2019a). "I did tell them that they had facilitated multiple crimes in the EU referendum. That as things stood, I didn't think it was possible to have free and fair elections ever again," Cadwalladr wrote in a follow-up piece that appeared in the 21 April 2019 edition of the *Guardian* (Cadwalladr 2019b). The *Guardian* journalist insisted liberal democracy is broken, and "the Gods of Silicon Valley" – Facebook, Google, and Twitter executives – are the ones who broke it. "We in Britain are the canary," Cadwalladr said in that TED Talk. "Our democracy is broken. It is subversion, and you are accessories to it … the hand-maidens to authoritarianism" (Cadwalladr 2019a).

While media coverage weights reflect a preoccupation with the story of Russian interference in the 2016 presidential campaign in the US, a House of Commons committee in the UK reported, "We heard evidence of Russian state-sponsored attempts to influence elections in the U.S. and the U.K. through social media" and "of efforts of private companies to do the same, and of law-breaking by certain Leave campaign groups in the U.K.'s EU referendum in their use of social media" (Digital, Culture, Media and Sport Committee 2018, 3).

The Select Committee on Digital, Culture, Media and Sport, in an interim report issued 29 July 2018, flatly asserted Britain's electoral laws are not fit for a digital age. The report notes the backers of data-mining companies such as Cambridge Analytica or the Canadian-based AggregateIQ circumvented election spending laws by putting millions into the company or project, and then charging the campaign a fraction of the true cost of the work.

Committee members made every attempt to examine the role of platforms such as Facebook and messaging software such as WhatsApp in these campaigns of disinformation and intrusion. The report notes, "Time and again, Facebook chose to avoid answering our written and oral questions to the point of obfuscation" (ibid., 45).

For those in other Western liberal democracies, the most chilling aspect of the inquiry was the evidence uncovered of Russian meddling in the electoral process in Britain as well as in the United States. Predictably, the mainstream media in America has focused on the Mueller report in domestic political terms – did the Trump campaign collude with the Russians, did the Russian interference decide the 2016 US presidential campaign, and is there sufficient evidence to impeach Donald Trump?

As David Cole stated in his review of the report carried in the *New York Review of Books*, "Mueller found 'sweeping and systemic' intrusions by Russia in the presidential campaign, all aimed at supporting Trump's election ... The report establishes beyond doubt that a foreign rival engaged in a systemic effort to subvert our democracy. Tellingly, the Russians referred to their actions as 'information warfare'" (Cole 2019, 4).

The *Globe and Mail* offered a particularly succinct and effective summary of Mueller's report in the headline of its editorial, "Donald Trump Isn't a Secret Russian Agent. He's Just a (Very) Bad President." It went on: "Did agents of the Russian government, largely operating online, try to influence the 2016 election? Yes. Did they try to undermine Hillary Clinton's campaign? Of course. Did they try to sow discord in American society? Repeatedly" (Globe and Mail 2019). The Russian campaign, opines the *Globe*, was all about sapping confidence in democracy by sowing chaos and "Mr. Trump was the official candidate of chaos" (ibid.).

The situation in Canada is no better. Canada's commissioner of elections, Yves Côté, certainly believes the country must do more to prevent foreign interference in elections in this country. "The abuse of social media and its proven potential to create serious problems with democratic processes raise questions of fundamental importance," Côté said in August 2018 (Thompson, E. 2018). "Political parties, candidates, Elections Canada, third parties, NGOs, mainstream media and the social media platforms themselves, all have a role to play in preventing the spread of misinformation" (ibid.). *National Post* columnist Terry Glavin used his Twitter account to predict, "And by the way, there will be foreign interference in the October federal election. The Liberal government is quite right about that. But it won't be Russia making the most mischief. It will be China. It will be in spades, and the target will be Andrew Scheer's Conservatives" (Glavin 2019). Glavin's warning takes on added weight in the context of Chinese propaganda activities during the COVID-19 pandemic.

A year before, Cameron Ahmad, a spokesperson in the Prime Minister's Office, told the *Globe and Mail*, "The amount of

deception, fake and misleading information and accounts targeting elected officials and diminishing the debate on social media
platforms, particularly on Twitter, is increasingly concerning and
frankly unacceptable" (Leblanc 2018).

Parody and deceptive accounts on Twitter, as well as the circulation of false information, are a particular irritant for the Trudeau
government. Ahmad's comment included a warning: "Social
media companies should immediately take action to fight back
against those who deceive and manipulate for political gain ...
Right now it remains clear that more action must be taken" (ibid.).

Data breaches are another focus for federal officials. The evolution of Google's "privacy policy" points to the kind of work
legislators in Western liberal democracies should be undertaking.
According to an opinion piece by Charles Warzel and Ash Ngu
carried in the *New York Times*, Google's privacy policy in 1999
stated, "Google may share information about users with advertisers, business partners, sponsors and other third parties. However,
we only talk about our users in aggregate. Not as individuals"
(Warzel and Ngu 2019). Months later, that particular paragraph
was gone, and by June 2004, Google's privacy policy read, "If you
have an account, we may share the information submitted under
your account among all of our services in order to provide you
with a seamless experience and to improve the quality of our services" (ibid.). State Warzel and Ngu, "This is how we all 'consented'
without having a clue that we had done so" (ibid.).

In April 2018, Canada's privacy commissioner was forced to
take Facebook to court over data breaches. Daniel Therrien and
his team launched an investigation in March 2018, which concluded Facebook's privacy framework was so "elastic" that they
afforded no meaningful protection of personal data. Incredibly,
Facebook dismissed Therrien's findings as "opinion" and basically
shrugged off the privacy commissioner's concerns. "It is untenable
that organizations are allowed to reject my office's legal findings as
mere opinion," Therrien said (Curry and McMahon 2019). "Facebook should not get to decide what Canadian privacy law does

or does not require" (ibid.). Therrien's point is well-taken. But the fact remains multinational corporations are hyper-sensitive to the precedent-setting potential for policy decisions at the national or subnational level. And for tech giants such as Facebook, the Canadian market isn't significant enough to allow Canadian lawmakers to set rules the company might not want to follow worldwide

On one level, social media platforms such as Facebook have become prisoners of their own rhetoric. Having insisted they are not media companies, that theirs is a neutral platform, and that, as a consequence, they have no role nor right in determining the accuracy of statements transmitted through their network, they are hard pressed to explain how they might correct misinformation.

Frank Pasquale, a professor of law at the University of Maryland and author of *The Black Box Society*, argues the courts actually limit the government's ability to stop lies (Pasquale 2015).

Government support for homegrown journalism is one obvious response to the challenges of global conglomerates as having any responsibility for the "fake news" being distributed on their digital platforms.

In 2018, then-finance minister Bill Morneau unveiled a series of measures to support the Canadian media sector. It started in February, with the budget, which stated, "To ensure trusted, local perspectives as well as accountability in local communities, the Government proposes to provide $50 million over five years, starting in 2018–19, to one or more independent non-governmental organizations that will support local journalism in underserved communities. The organizations will have full responsibility to administer the funds, respecting the independence of the press" (Government of Canada 2018a). Alas, the budget document provided no insight as to who these "non-governmental organizations" might be or how the $50 million pie would be sliced up. The budget also stated, "Further, consistent with the advice laid out in the Public Policy Forum's report on news in the digital age, over the next year the government will be exploring new models that enable private giving and philanthropic support for trusted, professional, non-profit journalism and local news. This could include new ways for Canadian newspapers to innovate and be recognized to receive charitable status for not-for-profit provision of journalism reflecting the public interest that they serve" (ibid.).

In his follow-up November 2018 economic statement (Department of Finance Canada 2018), Morneau had unveiled a proposal allowing non-profit news organizations "to receive charitable donations and issue official donation receipts."

Former Torstar chair John Honderich had a suggestion as to how to make that happen. In remarks delivered at a Canadian Journalism Foundation gala on 13 June 2019, when he received the CJF's Lifetime Achievement Award, Honderich addressed what he described as "a growing crisis" in journalism today. "Everyone in this room appreciates the link between quality journalism and a healthy democracy," Honderich said (Canadian Journalism Foundation 2019b). Quoting former *Toronto Star* reporter Ernest Hemingway, who said "the best ammunition against lies is the truth" (ibid.), Honderich asked the audience in attendance to consider the role philanthropy could play in journalism.

"For several decades, the US has considered philanthropic funding of quality journalism as both worthy and legitimate," Honderich said (ibid.). Honderich, who also filled a number of managerial and executive positions at the paper including editor-in-chief, said there are now more than 150 independent, non-profit centres doing investigative journalism in the United States, including *ProPublica*. Honderich said this approach is different from crowdfunding, which tends to be project-specific. "These charitable gifts can and are used to fund the necessary infrastructure – salaries, rent, equipment – to make a news centre sustainable," Honderich added (ibid.). "In Canada, we have no such tradition," he said, for a number of reasons, including the fact Canada didn't have the necessary laws, a situation Honderich said would be rectified in 2020 (ibid.). Riffing on the late US president John F. Kennedy's inaugural address, Honderich concluded by saying, "Think not on what journalism has done for you, but rather ask what you might do to make sure quality journalism thrives in Canada" (ibid.).

A few months after February's federal budget rolled out the first supports, the Desmarais family announced that *La Presse* – North America's largest and oldest French-language daily – would be converted into a not-for-profit entity, seizing the newly available opportunities. The Desmarais family also pledged to give the new entity $50 million from its holding company, Power Corporation, to ease the transition. But then, the Desmarais family – which has owned *La Presse* since 1967 – will back away.

Public Policy Forum CEO Ed Greenspon, a driving force behind the federally commissioned report into the future of news, "Shattered Mirror," which Morneau cited in his financial documents, said, "I think we're in a period where even exceptionally smart business people, like the Desmarais family, are finding that they can't figure their way around the obstacles in the face of the industry, at least on a short-term basis" (Serebrin 2018, F1).

The decision by the Desmarais family isn't without its political consequences. *La Presse*'s leadership had positioned the paper as the main media voice for federalism in Quebec – in sharp contrast with the editorial voice of Quebecor's dailies that reflect owner Pierre Karl Péladeau's support for an independent Quebec.

Carleton University associate professor Christopher Dornan, in a Creative Commons podcast posted by the School of Journalism and Communication, stated the journalistic community is not united on the issue of government subsidies to mainstream media organizations. Said Dornan, "Journalism itself is essential to the well-being of the country, from the national level all the way down to the community level." That said, Dornan also acknowledges, "It would actually be political poison to give private sector companies public funds just because they are losing money" (Dornan 2017b).

The Morneau funding announcements triggered the expected response from critics. Former Harper chief of staff Ian Brodie, for example, tweeted, "I hope the new federal subsidy program will let Canadian reporters get right on top of this story" (Brodie

2018a), attaching a *Wall Street Journal* article on how a warming climate was allowing farms to plant new crops further north, then following up with "High quality journalism will want to show how climate change is expanding ag [agricultural] production in Alberta" (Brodie 2018b).

In 2017, as funding models were first being debated, *Post* columnist Andrew Coyne made the case against his own bosses. "We should be clear where this is leading: not to the temporary, transitional aid claimed, but to the permanent clientization of the news media," Coyne wrote in a column entitled "Why the Media Should Say No to a Government Bailout." "This is a watershed moment for the industry," Coyne continued. "Once we take the cash, we will – inevitably – get hooked on it" (2017). Coyne states the Trudeau government commissioned "Shattered Mirror" from the Public Policy Forum to and for a purpose: "The industry wants to be helped, and the government wants to be seen to be helping it" (Coyne 2017).

The harrumphing of Postmedia columnists over the Trudeau government's eventual $595 million fund to support Canadian media is particularly bemusing. Set aside for a minute the fact Paul Godfrey, CEO of Postmedia, was among the company leaders pushing the government to provide aid. What these columnists are really saying is that we, their readers, should assume their coverage will be influenced by government dollars. If these columnists have so little confidence in the integrity of their editorial leadership, the honourable thing to do is resign.

And if they don't resign, be still.

In journalism, at least, hypocrisy should know bounds.

News accounts suggested the Liberals themselves were concerned the federal funding initiative would be seen as an attempt to influence journalists and their coverage, and that a program to bail out a failing newspaper industry in particular was more political trouble than the program was worth.

However, as *Globe and Mail* writer Barrie McKenna pointed out in an opinion piece published before the debate even began, the federal government isn't quite the disinterested party it claims to be (2017, B1–2). Ottawa's financial support for the CBC's "digital shift" put the public broadcaster in direct competition for online readers and advertising, McKenna argues. The key point here is the first use of this subsidized product is digital – not television or radio. And unlike newspapers such as the *Globe*, the CBC does not charge for its digital services. Given the fact the CBC receives subsidies from taxpayers of over $1 billion a year – well in excess of the long-standing, if modest postal subsidies for magazines in Canada – the public broadcaster's digital initiative constitutes "predatory behaviour" underwritten by the federal government, according to McKenna.

The Broadcasting Act calls on the Canadian Broadcasting Corporation, as the national public broadcaster, to provide "radio and television services." That's all.

In June 2018, the Trudeau government commissioned a joint review of the Telecommunications Act and the Broadcasting Act by a seven-person panel led by former telecommunications executive Janet Yale. Citing the degree of vertical integration across the two sectors – some of Canada's largest broadcasters and also the country's largest telecommunications carriers – the government rightly decided it was important to have a coherent review of both pieces of legislation so that each set of issues was not examined in isolation. The terms of reference for the panel notes the Broadcasting Act in particular was enacted "before the rise of the internet" (Innovation, Science and Economic Development Canada 2018, 8).

The mandate document states, "The new open, global communications environment creates opportunities for Canadian content on the world stage but also poses challenges at home with respect to the creation of and access to Canadian cultural content, as well as, reliable news and information content" (ibid.). The specific reference to news and information content is referenced later, in a section entitled "Democracy, News, and Citizenship" (ibid., 11).

The government acknowledges "Canadian news media are in the process of a disruptive and dramatic change" (ibid.). The mandate letter posts the concern that "the phenomenon of online disinformation has the potential to undermine our democratic institutions, compromise the integrity of our elections and erode public trust" (ibid.).

The letter puts two specific questions for that section to the panel:

- Are current legislative provisions sufficient to ensure the provision of trusted, accurate, and quality news and information?
- Are there specific changes that should be made to legislation to ensure the continuing viability of local news? (ibid.).

Yet the mandate letter does not address the specifics of Alex Jones's finding about the "iron core" of civic journalism: that the overwhelming majority of this news originates from newspapers.

The mandate letter makes specific reference to the CBC / Radio-Canada as Canada's national broadcaster and states: "Canadians expect our national public broadcaster to show strong leadership and fully renew its rich tradition of excellence in the digital world" (ibid., 12). But the fact remains, the national public broadcaster largely bailed on local television news a long time ago. And while the current leadership is taking steps to put more professional journalists into the local news field, they are few, and new.

My friend and colleague Lawson Hunter, who for a decade led Canada's Competition Bureau, put the challenge facing legislators considering public policy solutions to the societal problems emerging from social media habits elegantly when he asked, "How do we break the mould of incrementalism and end the act of muddling through?" (pers. notes). The answer to his question must address a core reality that "technology is more powerful than the regulator will ever be" (ibid.)

Hunter, who has spent meaningful time considering policy options in the cultural space, has written insightfully about how the emergence of media provided over the internet poses a considerable challenge for a defining feature of Canadian regulation – the promotion of Canadian content. He argues the transition from a "push" network, where choices are limited, to a "pull" network, where content is available on demand, renders many of the traditional policy tools obsolete, ownership regulations and exhibition and expenditure quotas being prime examples.

In years past, broadcasters either directly or indirectly subsidized Canadian content production and were in a position to do so because of the market power they exercised over distribution channels. Disrupters such as Netflix challenged and, in so doing, forced a change to business models. As a result, content policies will have to be supported through direct subsidies to content creators.

Former CBC executive Richard Stursberg called for the creation of a "Canadian Content Investment Agency" in early 2017 (Stursberg 2017, FP7). The agency would replace Telefilm Canada and the Canadian Media Fund and "would be platform-, content- and producer-agnostic." Netflix and other similar companies operating in Canada should be required to charge HST, pay taxes, and make a financial contribution to the production of Canadian content, Stursberg argues (ibid.). Similarly, digital advertising should also involve an HST payment (Stursberg 2016). Production subsidies for foreign competitors should be abandoned (ibid.). Combined, these measures would yield significant new revenues, Stursberg states (Stursberg 2017, FP7). Stursberg would go on to make the case for taxing Google and Facebook to help Canadian media in his book *The Tangled Garden: A Canadian Cultural Manifesto for the Digital Age*, written with Stephen Armstrong. In a review published in *The Tyee* 5 September 2019, which first appeared in the CCPA's *Monitor*, communications scholar Marc Edge challenges Stursberg's core premise that big media companies have incurred "losses as far as the eye can see" (Edge 2019). Edge and others argue the conglomerates that own Canadian content producers and distributers – such as BCE – have robust balance sheets.

The fact remains, Ottawa's policy and program decisions have had, and continue to have, a direct impact on the media market place.

Ottawa has increased the budget for Canada's public broadcaster significantly. Much of that new – or restored – funding has been earmarked by the CBC for digital offerings. Canadians may pay less for their public broadcaster than citizens in most industrialized countries. A position paper prepared by the CBC and released in November 2016 by then-president Hubert Lacroix supported his campaign to make the CBC ad-free in exchange for more government funding. He stated the CBC/SRC is the "third worst-funded public broadcaster in the world among comparable countries, with only New Zealand and the US receiving lower per capita funding" (Ireland 2016). According to the CBC report, the UK spends $114 per person annually to support its public broadcaster, the British Broadcasting Corporation (BBC), compared to only $34 per person here in Canada (ibid.). Yet, by financing the public broadcaster's move into digital news, Ottawa is directly subsidizing a competitor to news organizations as varied as the *Globe and Mail* and *Canadaland* (Craig 2016).

Federal voices, whether from the Commons Heritage committee or the Finance Department's budget papers, all publicly recognize the importance of a free and independent media and local news reporting.

Accepting Clay Shirky's descriptive of today's media environment as an "ecosystem," the fact remains, not all elements of that system are of equal value. And for that reason, the threat to civil society posed by the decline in traditional print media outlets may be underappreciated by the general public.

As Alex Jones pointed out in *Losing the News: The Future of the News That Feeds Democracy* (2009), the overwhelming majority of the "iron core" of news that feeds democracy – fully 85 per cent – comes from newspapers. This is the news of verification, the news from the planning committee meeting at city hall, the news about a local school board's decision on reading lists for students, the news of conferences and learned societies, the news from smaller and more isolated communities.

Both Walter Lippmann's administrative school of media effects theory and American philosopher John Dewey's cultural studies perspective would have seen the iron core as essential to a vital democratic life. The legendary journalist Bill Moyers, who took a sabbatical from the industry to serve as President Lyndon B. Johnson's press secretary, spoke to the core belief of a generation when he stated that "the quality of democracy and the quality of journalism are deeply entwined" (Democracy Now 2005). And while CBC has declared a commitment to local news, the fact remains that most local TV stations have all but abandoned providing in-depth coverage of politics and public policy, as Jones observes.

Citizen journalists, to be sure, can fill some of this void, but their coverage will be largely episodic and less well positioned to iden- tify themes and patterns.

Talk radio hosts have real influence on political conversation. And we are all exposed to pundits' panels of various sizes and descript- ives. Here in Canada, for example, members of CBC's At Issue panel or The Insiders are recognizable from coast to coast to coast. Yet the very existence of these media voices is predicated on an assumption their audience has a basic knowledge of the matter or issue at hand. And that basic knowledge flows from Jack Germond's 10 per cent of original reporting, not the 90 per cent that spend much of the rest of the news cycle talking about what the 10 per cent unearthed.

Ottawa's bottom line consistently in any conversation around protection of journalistic independence or local news is that the Trudeau government has no interest in any option that involves more direct cost to consumers. As the 2019 election loomed, Ottawa still hadn't even put Facebook and Google on the same footing in terms of tax obligations. For example, a business placing an ad with a Canadian newspaper or television station cannot deduct the expense if the media outlet is foreign-owned. Somehow, the same rules do not apply to Facebook.

An interesting illustration of how far Facebook has fallen in terms of its perception among opinion leaders is an ad placed by Friends of Canadian Broadcasting that appeared on page A6 of the 2 May 2019 edition of the *Globe and Mail*. Under the heading "Unfriend Facebook," the ad declared, "The Privacy Commissioner says Facebook broke the law. As if breaking democracy wasn't enough" (Friends of Public Broadcasting 2019, A6).

A champion of the CBC, Friends of Canadian Broadcasting for years fought the good fight against budget cuts for the public broadcaster proposed by various federal governments, particularly Conservative ones. Today, it has a new foe: Facebook. The ad copy reads, "Did you know that a tax loophole subsidizes foreign internet media companies like Facebook with $1.6 billion of our tax dollars every year. This disgraced company pollutes our democracy and siphons billions of dollars away from professional Canadian journalism," the ad declares. "It's time to close the internet advertising loophole" (ibid.).

The new media ecosystem has its strengths: more roles, more messages, more paths, more opportunities, more gatekeepers all functioning within an architecture of participation. But this does not obviate the need for news professionals who can give voice to Jones's philosophy that journalism's first obligation is to the truth, its first loyalty is to citizens, its essence is the discipline of verification.

As the script for Steven Spielberg's movie *The Post* reminds us, when, in 1971, the US Supreme Court ruled in favour of the right of news organizations to publish the Pentagon Papers, the court reaffirmed the premise that the media's obligation is to the governed and not the governors.

As stated earlier in this chapter, media companies more open to innovative revenue models have enjoyed some measure of success. The reordering of the media universe triggered by the internet in general and social networking platforms in particular resulted in role changes even for the "knowns" that had historically been part of the legacy media ecosystem, but as sources and not as primary content producers.

The Institute for Research on Public Policy (IRPP) is one such example. The IRPP is home to *Policy Options*, the institute's monthly magazine. *Policy Options* was long a source of content for leading Canadian newspapers such as the *Globe and Mail* or the *Toronto Star*. Distinguished former editors such as William Watson and L. Ian Macdonald appeared frequently on the op-ed pages of leading

Canadian dailies. Furthermore, IRPP studies and reports provided the foundation for news stories.

"*Policy Options* was always a unique offering," says former IRPP president Graham Fox, who, in the interests of full disclosure, is my son. "But three or four years ago, we came to the realization that we are our own media" (pers. notes 2017). Fox says, "going digital was superbly liberating for us." The challenge, says Fox, lies in the answer to a fairly straightforward question: "How do you take the basic piece of research and break it down into consumable bits?"

Policy Options once had a circulation of around 2,000 subscribers for its ten issues a year and got attention by placing op-ed pieces in mainstream dailies, as well as being used as the basis for the odd news story. *Policy Options* is now available daily, with monthly page views that routinely exceed 100,000 page views. "The audience has completely exploded," says former *Policy Options* editor-in-chief Jennifer Ditchburn (ibid.). And that wider and more diverse audience "now sees itself and reads itself in the diverse group of authors who publish with us."

Ditchburn saw it as a central component of her job as editor to find voices overlooked by the traditional press, especially on emerging issues such as the relationship with Indigenous peoples. "We're smaller, so we can give more love to the writers," she says with a laugh.

The increase in traffic to the IRPP media centre as well as *Policy Options* sites and podcasts is attributable in no small measure to those new "authors, who have their own social media profiles and bring new networks with them," according to Ditchburn. The institute posts a podcast every two weeks, usually involving a discussion with an author who has written on a particular topic for *Policy Options*, in part to draw more attention to an article or a study.

Ditchburn, who has tens of thousands of followers on Twitter, makes good use of the platform to draw wider attention to *Policy Options* pieces; Ditchburn herself personifies the changing media landscape. With undergraduate and graduate degrees in journalism from Concordia and Carleton, Ditchburn distinguished herself as a parliamentary correspondent for the Canadian Press and the CBC and appeared frequently as a panellist on public affairs programs such as CBC's *Power & Politics* and its At Issue panel on *The National*. In her *Policy Options* role, Ditchburn looked to cut out the political journalist as "middleman," get past the small "p" politics of who is winning and who is losing and how much time is left in the game, and instead, hear from the subject matter expert more directly. "Obviously, our readership is a different breed," Ditchburn says (ibid.). *Policy Options'* audience is less interested in the politics of a policy or program and more interested in the core question of whether what is being advanced is good or bad public policy. And as for an underlying philosophy, Fox and Ditchburn are guided by a belief that values coalitions are more interesting than political coalitions.

Podcasts, like those of that Canadian site, are increasingly a venue of choice for civil discourse.

Liberal campaign strategist David Herle's podcast, *The Herle Burly*, attracts some 10,000 listeners – successful, but not enough to eliminate the need for a day job. Yet Herle's influence in the village of political candidates, consultants, and journalists is more significant than the weekly numbers would suggest. By way of illustration, pre-recorded hour-long interviews with former Ontario premier and interim federal Liberal leader Bob Rae and Conservative icon and public intellectual Hugh Segal over the 2018–19 holiday season were shared and spread by the pundit class on various social media platforms for the better part of the following month.

On a grander, international scale, Michael Bloomberg invented a media empire even as the business model for legacy media companies was cracking along the advertising fault line. Yet Bloomberg perhaps succeeded in part because he was not a media person. The former mayor of New York holds an electrical engineering degree: "He was a scientist by avocation," according to his friend and colleague Matt Winkler. Bloomberg had developed a machine, the Bloomberg Terminal, to sell financial information. He quickly realized he needed to add news for his system to truly succeed. But he also realized his news would have to meet the market's "value test." As the legacy media wonders if its future is measured in months, Bloomberg – with 2,700-plus journalists and analysts in 120 countries around the world, and 100 billion pieces of data processed by Bloomberg Terminal every day – has built one of the world's most successful media empires because he realized very early on that the business he wanted to be in needed one ingredient above all else – a different type of news.

Appearing at a Canadian Journalism Foundation J-Talks session in Toronto, editor-in-chief emeritus Matt Winkler (Canadian Journalism Foundation 2016) explained how Bloomberg did it. There is a "Bloomberg Way" to cover stories. Bloomberg understood the power of data. Bloomberg may or may not have been familiar with Elisabeth Noelle-Neumann's theories of consonance and cumulation but he and Winkler – who Bloomberg lured away from the *Wall Street Journal* – did know "the more rigorous the elements of style, the greater the authority of the reporting" (ibid.).

Bloomberg News stories reflected "five Fs":
first word
fastest word
most factual word
final word
future word

This approach to its journalism became an organizing base of knowledge. Winkler says Bloomberg News reporters "write for their 'Aunt Agatha' but in such a way that the dope can understand it and the professional can appreciate it."

As an organization, Bloomberg News focuses on data – how good the data is and what you do with the data you have. Data can test conventional wisdom, or consensus. "We can do things with that data to tell a story," Winkler said. An analysis of the data led Bloomberg News to challenge the "congenial truth" on Greece's debt crisis for example. "Greek bonds were the best investment of any asset class," Winkler said.

News organizations, said Winkler, should concentrate on delivering more truth every day, although he conceded the truth is hard to come by. "J.P. Morgan [a major US bank] knows more about what is going on in your town than you do, and you live there," he added.

Bloomberg News' offering focused on delivering more truth every day.

The implications of a business model that tries to compensate for the loss of advertising dollars with digital dimes continue to reverberate through legacy media organizations. The shrinking of newsrooms is a North America-wide phenomenon. A study released in July 2019 concluded newsroom employment in the United States dropped by a quarter between 2008 and 2018, with the sharpest decline at newspapers (Grieco 2019). In 2008, there were 71,000 newsroom employees at US newspapers; by 2018, that number had plummeted to 38,000. While there was some growth in digital-only newsrooms, the growth was more than offset by job losses in the print sector.

In April 2019, the Cleveland *Plain Dealer* announced the paper's intention to lay off one-third of its unionized newsroom staff (Feran 2019). One of those laid off was Tom Feran, who not only volunteered to leave after a thirty-seven-year career in order to save a younger journalist's position but also wrote the paper's article about the cuts. Two decades ago, the newspaper employed 340 unionized journalists (ibid.). When I was assigned to cover the White House for the *Toronto Star* in the early 1980s, the *Plain Dealer* had a full-time staff in Washington, as well. Today, its non-management editorial staff is down to thirty-three journalists (ibid.).

As advertisers flee, newsrooms start to look like mining towns when the ore runs out.

Where newspapers once accounted for six in ten newsroom jobs in America, today that figure stands at a third. In 2016, Rogers

Media began selling or closing the vast majority of its media titles, leaving just a handful of consumer magazines in its portfolio (Masthead 2016). Then, in June 2018, Rogers Media announced the company was terminating literally one-third of its digital content and publishing team – seventy-five jobs (Jackson, E. 2018). The widely respected Steve Maich, Rogers Media's senior vice-president of digital publishing and content, left the firm, as did Lianne George, editor-in-chief of *Chatelaine*, who, weeks earlier, had been selected Canada's magazine editor of the year.

The company press release cites the pressures on the print industry generally and the loss of advertising revenues as the root cause of the layoffs. "We have reorganized our digital content and publishing structure to reflect the headwinds the industry is facing and make the business sustainable," said Andrea Goldstein, senior director of communications, in a statement (Shufelt 2018). Then, incredibly, the statement from Rogers also said, "Today's changes do not impact the quality of the content or the frequency of our print issues" (ibid.). In other words, the seventy-five skilled employees being let go had made absolutely no contribution to the quality of Rogers Media publications. Not even Postmedia chair Paul Godfrey would try and get away with such a claim.

Two months later, the second shoe dropped when news broke Rogers Communication Inc. – the parent company of Rogers Media – wanted out of the magazine business altogether. The company retained investment bankers from CIBC to solicit bids for venerable properties such as *Maclean's*, *Chatelaine*, and *Canadian Business*. The background paper distributed to potential buyers indicated the titles collectively had generated $12 million in print advertising revenue and $9.5 million in digital ad revenue, with print and online circulation adding another $17.1 million (Krashinsky Robertson 2018), triggering a tweet from *Maclean's* former editor-in-chief Robert Lewis that the "total magazine revenue, for @rogers publishing less than half of what Maclean's alone generated in 1980s" (Lewis, R. 2018b). St. Joseph Communications, the company that owns *Toronto Life*, ultimately emerged as the buyer for the last Rogers' publishing properties.

The financial challenges facing Canadian-owned news organizations are compounded by the fact digital advertising flows disproportionately to Facebook and Google.

In a social media age, a content conversation invariably includes references to clickbait. Yet the media's decision to speak with a voice of entertainment has been a content consideration since the emergence of the penny press.

As Earnscliffe research conducted for the Public Policy Forum (PPF)'s "Shattered Mirror" initiative confirms, people are reading more news than ever; just are not paying for it in traditional ways. The Reuters Institute for the Study of Journalism's 2019 "Digital News Report" confirmed a number of consumer trends identified in various news stories: the fact people are spending less time on Facebook and more time on WhatsApp or Instagram, that smartphones are increasingly the dominant delivery device of choice, that devices are driving the popularity of podcasts, and that public trust in the news is falling (Newman, Fletcher, Kalogeropoulos, and Nielsen 2019).

However two findings in particular leapt off the screen in the key findings section, findings based on 75,000-plus online news consumers in thirty-eight markets.

The first is that the "pivot to paid" is a modest success for news organizations at best. In Canada, for example, only 9 per cent of respondents pay for online news. And among those who do pay, the vast majority only have one subscription – which underscores the likelihood of a "winner take all" end result (ibid.). Equally chilling is the fact 32 per cent of respondents are for all intents and purposes news dropouts, saying they actively avoid the news (ibid.).

While conventional wisdom suggests our search for truth can easily be distracted by light, frivolous clickbait stories advising on surefire ways to lose thirty pounds in three days, some observers ask if the real issue is that people don't care for serious stories or if the real issue is that people don't care for the way digital journalism presents serious stories? (pers. notes).

As exciting as the content creation opportunities presented by emerging technologies are, studies conducted in the United States point to two trends carried over from legacy media that are particularly troublesome. First, the vast majority of digital sources available to people contains no original reporting. As a result, "we face a situation in which sources of opinion are proliferating, but sources of facts on which those opinions are based are shrinking" (Public Policy Forum 2017, 48). In other words, the journalists that are responsible for the content that fuels the discussion are disappearing, even as those who seek to opine are proliferating. The second trend, or subset concern, is driven by an analysis by Earnscliffe Strategy Group principal Allan Gregg, who concludes it is the source of the news, and not the platform or channel on which it is seen or read, that confers trust and authority (Gregg 2017).

The business model for Google is relatively straightforward: anytime anyone clicks on an ad, Google gets paid (Smith, Levin, and Bergen 2017). And in a "noblesse oblige" kind of way, Google, like Facebook before it, has made an effort to help print media monetize content (Bergen 2017b). A headline on a story carried in the *Globe and Mail* in 2017 declared that both companies were looking to introduce subscription tools catering to print media companies (Bergen 2017a). All agree newspaper publishers can't live on advertising alone, and while the digital behemoths are happy to discuss subscription tools, the parties haven't sat down for the trickier discussion around revenue tools.

A panel discussion focused on news and truth organized by the Canadian Journalism Foundation on May 2, 2018, opened with a declaration by a spokesperson for Google Canada that "the future of Google and the future of the news business are inextricably linked" (Canadian Journalism Foundation 2018b).

Having ceded control of distribution to the digital powers, news organizations are now hostage to algorithms that profess "neutrality" when it comes to truth.

News, particularly local news, to state the obvious, is tough to scale. Yet civic news is overwhelmingly produced by the daily newspapers that are shrivelling away to nothingness. As the PPF report concludes, the result is more clickbait, fake news, and recycled stories.

The "billionaire bailout model" of newspaper ownership is a mixed blessing. The good burghers of Buffalo, New York, were undoubtedly happy Warren Buffett's Berkshire Hathaway conglomerate bought up the *Buffalo News*, only to see the paper sold a few years later. Canadian news consumers are the better for the Thomson family's private ownership of the *Globe and Mail*. But in Las Vegas, casino billionaire Sheldon Adelson bought the *Las Vegas Review-Journal* to hound his enemies. And Jeff Bezos's personal ownership of the *Washington Post* put Bezos and the *Post* in direct conflict with President Trump and makes it possible the *Post* will be caught up in broader political and policy considerations around Amazon's growth in the context of corporate concentration.

In today's social media world, we don't yet know whether there is a future for journalism as a profitable business in the tradition way of measuring profitability. And for that reason, media companies and public policy advocates alike may need to identify, and then embrace, new approaches. "Ultimately, it won't be the angry bloggers or the clueless citizen journalists, not the crazy kids from YouTube or the dark forces behind MySpace who will decide the fate of journalism," Michael Maier, CEO of Blogform Publishing, wrote in 2007. "Ultimately, readers and advertisers will show what they are willing to pay for" (Maier 2007, 13).

The PPF report asks the core question at the heart of the debate: Is a crisis for the traditional news industry necessarily a crisis for democracy? "I am optimistic about journalism. I am not optimistic about newspapers," says media scholar Kara Swisher (Shorenstein Center on Media, Politics and Public Policy 2015). Kelly Toughill, a former *Toronto Star* editor who is now an associate professor in the journalism program at the University of King's College in Halifax, offers this provocative assessment. Toughill says she no longer believes newspapers are essential to civil society (Toughill 2016).

Toughill argues the future of newspaper companies should not be confused with the future of journalism. "The demise of newspapers breaks my heart – but it won't break democracy," she says (ibid.).

Google's Gingras cautions, "there are no silver bullets here" in terms of setting a new business model for civic journalism. "There is not going to be a solution that will happen overnight" (Canadian Journalism Foundation 2018b). Subscription and/or membership models are likely to be foundational. But if "civic journalism" is to continue to be integral to an informed public, then governments in Western liberal democracies will have to recognize the importance with appropriately supportive legislative, regulatory and tax policies and programs.

One area of public policy regarding social network companies that begs to be addressed relates to election campaigns.

Canada's Commissioner of Elections Yves Côté acknowledges more has to be done to present social media disruptions of elections and in fact has already started to work with Facebook, Twitter, and other interested third parties. His 2018 annual report quotes Côté to the effect that "the abuse of social media and its proven potential to create serious problems with democratic processes raise serious questions of fundamental importance … Political parties, candidates, Elections Canada, third parties, NGOs, mainstream media and the social media platforms themselves, all have a role to play in preventing the spread of misinformation" (Thompson, E. 2018).

As *Attention Merchant* author Tim Wu notes, "Social media has as much impact as broadcasting on elections, yet unlike broadcasting it is unregulated and has proved easy to manipulate" (Wu, T. 2017). Wu says, at a minimum, new rules should be introduced barring social media companies from accepting money from foreign governments or their agents for political advertising. Further, Wu says the US needs more aggressive anti-bot laws. "A robust and unfiltered debate is one thing; corruption of the debate itself is another," he states. "A country where speaking one's mind always results in death threats is not a country that can be said to be truly free" (ibid.).

Canada's Election Act sets out a series of rules governing election advertising on radio and television. These rules have been altered over the years, and have been subject to extended debate and discussion as a component part of the public hearings held by the Royal Commission on Electoral Reform and Party Financing chaired by Pierre Lortie in the early 1990s. These hearings considered many of the issues that have surfaced in the context of the current debate around social media platforms – offshore ad buys, spending limits, the need to identify the name of a campaign ad sponsor and also clearly state the ad was authorized by sponsors. The specifics matter less than this overarching point: there are rules governing political advertising on radio and television; there are no such rules governing political advertising on social media platforms.

Election reform would seem to be a worthy cause for the minority House of Commons that was elected in 2019, as it would be in the interest of all political parties to have a rigorous legislative regime in place to protect the integrity of our electoral processes.

A second report published in August 2018 by the Public Policy Forum entitled "Democracy Divided: Countering Disinformation and Hate in the Digital Public Sphere" sets out the extent to which the "disruption" has come to democracy (Greenspon and Owen 2018). Written by PPF president Ed Greenspon and McGill's Taylor Owen, the report notes the open internet has, in fact, been consolidated by a handful of global companies. The business model for these companies "aligns well with the dissemination of false and inflammatory information," the report states (ibid.). "The economic incentives of this new system have led to a prioritization of emotion over reason, opinion over facts, snap judgment over deliberation, anonymity over identity and the globally scalable over the locally relevant" (ibid.).

In a direct warning to the Trudeau government, the coauthors assert that "digital attacks on democracy can no more be tolerated than physical ones" (ibid.). The report states self-regulation on the part of the platform giants will be insufficient, and that there is a necessary role for government and government regulation.

The easiest fix for the Canadian government is to address inequities in current tax law. "The current situation is neither fair nor sensible," the report states, recommending taxes imposed should be based on the location of the customer, and not the location of the business (ibid.).

The coauthors also call for publishers of online content to identify themselves in clearer terms, and that platforms be held liable to ensure the content they carry confirms with legal and regulatory requirements.

A strategy to sustain journalism as a public good is recommended, as is a long-term, large-scale civic literacy and critical thinking campaign, echoing similar calls from Walter Cronkite in an earlier era.

On the broader issue of public policy, federal lawmakers need to identify "civic journalism" as a policy priority.

As I argued in an op-ed page piece published in the *Toronto Star* on 22 July 2018 (Fox, B. 2018), social media companies either can't or won't address the myriad of policy problems that have surfaced. And in recent years, governments in Western liberal democracies have been more focused on how to exploit social media than on how to regulate it. If news organizations are just another business, then their survival is of little importance or significance. But if civic journalism is as central to democracy as classic liberal theory asserts, then the situation warrants a fresh think on the part of federal policy-makers, both political and bureaucratic.

The Canadian government can easily introduce a series of tax measures that would make civic journalism a more viable business proposition. The tax system is but one instrument of choice.

In May 2019, then-Heritage minister Pablo Rodriguez announced the government had named a committee, to advise the government who to name to a committee, that would ultimately decide which media entities would share in the hundreds of millions of dollars of support. Specifically, that committee would suggest eligibility criteria for the disbursement of the government largesse. In particular, Rodriguez asked "eight associations that represent Canadian journalism to submit the name of a candidate to take part in the work of the independent panel of experts" (Canadian Heritage 2019).

One of those organizations was Unifor. As the union that represents thousands of Canadian journalists, the appointment made sense on one level. As a union openly, vehemently, and consistently opposed to the Conservative Party and its leader Andrew Scheer, the appointment made no sense at all. The ensuing furor created yet another circumstance where working reporters were denouncing both their employers and the union that represents them for even approaching Ottawa looking for financial assistance.

As of January 2020, "qualified Canadian journalism organizations" (QCJOs) would be able to register with the Canada Revenue Agency for "qualified donee status," meaning the entities could accept donations and issue tax receipts like registered charities (Lundy and Cardoso 2019). QCJOs would also qualify for a 25 per cent labour tax credit on salaries paid to newsroom employees – capped at $13,750 per employee each year (ibid.). News accounts stated certain broadcast outlets, as well as organizations already receiving funding from the Canada Periodical Fund will not qualify for the labour tax credit (ibid.). And as a final element, digital news subscribers to QCJOs will be eligible for a temporary personal tax credit (ibid.).

The package was derided by the Conservatives and denounced by journalists themselves.

"If you were searching for a way to kill the news business, you couldn't do a better job," wrote then-*National Post* columnist Andrew Coyne, who has been consistently vocal in his criticism of the initiative. "It's when you see the details of how they propose to go about it [the media bailout] that the chill really sets in … if this goes through, everything will be subsidized: print, broadcast, the works – a whole industry of CBCs" (Coyne 2019a). Added Coyne, "taking money from the people we cover will place us in a permanent and inescapable conflict of interest" (ibid.). Coyne is a regular on CBC's At Issue panel, and the CBC does, to use his term, "take money from the people we cover." The CBC News and Current Affairs division is, and has been, home to some of Canada's finest journalists for decades. That said, CBC journalists are also accustomed to having their personal and professional integrity questioned by critics based on an assumption – offensively mistaken in my view – that public funding leads invariably to bias.

The complexity of the federal government's approach to funding news organizations made it a virtual certainty any and all applications for support would get bogged down in bureaucracy. By the time the *Toronto Star* was sold to new owners in August 2020, not a single cent from Ottawa had found its way into Torstar's balance sheet – two-plus years after the promised relief in the February 2018 federal budget (Gallant 2020).

Given the number of questions the federal initiative to support journalism raised, both in the news and political communities, Carleton professor Christopher Waddell asked the best question: Why do it? (Waddell 2019).

The problem with the Trudeau government's approach, from this author's perspective, is that the "qualification" determination will be managed by an independent panel and a new administrative body that will be created to handle status designation. In other words, a body appointed by government will, in effect, pick winners and losers – a recipe for a highly politicized debate if ever there was one.

Any government subsidy for journalism is bound to be the subject of heated debate.

Universality is the only approach in policy terms that can silence critics who will argue any program supporting journalism is simply a way for incumbent governments to reward their media friends. Any program put in place should be as available to small online start-ups or relative newcomers such as *Canadaland* as it is to Postmedia or Torstar.

Ottawa could also improve the ability of Canadian news organizations to negotiate with mega-multinationals like Google and Facebook by amending Canada's competition laws. Canadian law, at present, prohibits media companies from organizing a negotiating bloc. The News Media Canada lobby group wants Ottawa to allow media outlets "to band together to bargain collectively with the tech giants" (Chiu 2020a). The industry is challenging the Trudeau government to follow Australia's lead with an initiative that can be implemented "at no cost to taxpayers" and involve no "new user fees or subsidies" (ibid.).

The Canadian government should also be thinking of something bolder in terms of facilitating Canadian civic discourse.

Author Chris Hedges provides a philosophical justification for the need for a more robust public policy framework to regulate social media. Positioning the internet as "the latest technological instrument of control," Hedges argues "technology is morally neutral. It serves the interests of those who control it. And those who control it today are destroying journalism, culture, and art, while they herd the population into clans that fuel isolation, self-delusion, intolerance, and hatred" (Hedges 2010, 214).

Political theorist David Moscrop summarized today's conundrum that is the relationship between media and democracy succinctly when he wrote: "Without a free and independent media, liberal democracy would not be possible" (Moscrop 2019, 154). That said, Moscrop adds, "new communications technologies, including social media, mean that living within one's own little world is easier than ever" (ibid., 155).

In the last century, Canadians engaged in a public policy debate triggered by the perceived threat to our culture posed by merging broadcast technologies. Graham Spry summarized the issue succinctly: "It is a choice between commercial interests and the people's interests and it is a choice between the state and the United States" (Fox, W. 1997, 3).

In the UK, opinion pieces have appeared in leading publications such as the *Financial Times*, penned by writers such as Diane Cole, advocating for a publicly funded rival to Facebook and Google.

Why couldn't Canada contemplate as ambitious an initiative?

Canada subsidized the distribution of civic journalism when the post office constituted the delivery system. In an internet age, why wouldn't the federal government build a public platform for Canada?

The federal government already has a prototype in place. CANARIE, a world-class 100-gigabyte-per-second network, provides the national backbone of Canada's ultra-high-speed National Research and Education Network. Created in 1993, CANARIE receives most of its funding from the federal government. More than one million Canadians already have access to the network at some 2,000 connected institutions such as research centres or universities (pers. notes).

CANARIE may afford Canada a unique opportunity to create a digital platform for civil discourse. While a made-in-Canada alternative to Facebook has certain appeal, there is no particular public policy purpose in matching the relatively benign and highly personal uses most users make of Facebook – posts that are of primary interest to family and friends. And Facebook's appeal may well be fading with younger people. By way of illustration, a Twitter post in August 2019 asked if anyone knew any high school students that were on Facebook (Safia Khan 2019).

Michael Binder, a former senior civil servant at the federal departments of communication and industry, said CANARIE flowed directly from the recommendations set out in a report from the Information Highway Advisory Council chaired by then-university president and former governor general David Johnston. The advisory council identified a clear need for a communications network that would connect Canada's university and research communities. "It was not meant to be commercial," Binder said in a personal conversation. Policy-makers in Ottawa understood that if a pan-Canadian network wasn't created, Canada's scholars and researchers would simply join networks in the US.

Today, there is a policy opportunity to build on CANARIE's success, with a network dedicated to civic discourse that is accessible and available to individual Canadians, a primary site for political and civic discourse in Canada, in both official languages as well as

Indigenous languages. A country that had the foresight to launch CANARIE in 1993 before most of us were active on the internet surely has the expertise to create a Canadian platform that can serve as a genuine "common carrier" for the country. There will undoubtedly be voices to explain how this can't or shouldn't be a priority for government.

What Canada needs is one voice to say how it can.

The Canada Infrastructure Bank – with its specific mandate to kick-start recovery after the COVID-19 pandemic – could be that voice.

10

Brownface, Blackface: Two-Faced?

The irony is striking. In a social media age, an old high school year-book and a US legacy-based media outlet arguably provided the defining media moment of the 2019 Canadian federal election.

In the early evening of Wednesday, 18 September 2019, news broke *Time* was going to run a photo of Prime Minister Justin Trudeau in brownface (Kambhampaty, Carlisle, and Chan 2019). The photo dated from 2001, taken at a fundraiser for West Point Grey Academy where Trudeau was a teacher at the time. The gala had a theme – 1001 Arabian Nights. Trudeau, ever the amateur thespian, attended the black tie event in costume, as Aladdin. Trudeau posed for the picture with four other attendees. The Liberal leader is nothing if not thorough. The brownface makeup looked as if it had been laid on with a trowel. Even his hands were darkened for effect; one was clearly visible in the photo, laid on the chest of a colleague, which as a standalone proposition caused considerable social media commentary.

Time had received the photo some weeks before. Word the newsmagazine was about to go to press with the photo rocked the Liberal campaign.

Reporters travelling with Trudeau, already sensitive to attacks they were being too easy on the incumbent, demanded "a media avail," as scrums are now known. Trudeau agreed to meet the press on board his campaign plane before it took off for Winnipeg. The prime minister apologized unconditionally, and told the country he was "pissed off at myself" (Dawson and Subramaniam 2019).

While getting Trudeau in front of the media immediately was the correct call from a crisis communications perspective, the campaign-plane media availability session was a limited success for one overarching reason. In response to a question from CBC reporter David Cochrane that startled the assembled scribes and voters watching the exchange on television, Trudeau admitted there were other photos of him in blackface, specifically a photo that appeared in the yearbook of Collège Jean-de-Brébeuf. Trudeau, then a high school student, had appeared in a school production wearing "makeup," to use the prime minister's term, and singing "Day O," also known as the Banana Boat song (CBC 2019e).

In the same news cycle, reporters were told the Conservative Party had shared a video of the prime minister in blackface with Global News (ibid.). Conservative Party Leader Andrew Scheer said they had given the news organization the video for "verification" (Stephenson and Armstrong 2019). This video was reportedly taken while Trudeau was working at a whitewater rafting business nearly thirty years before (D'Amore 2019a).

Problematically, the prime minister said that he was reluctant to declare definitively there were no more such images in circulation (CBC 2019e). The whole purpose of a *mea culpa* media session is to confirm the facts, take ownership of the problems, apologize abjectly, and move on. Trudeau's inability to say whether or not there were more blackface photos out there precluded any possibility of the media moving on.

For some in the media, Trudeau's political opponents, and his social media critics, the images made a mockery of the Liberal government's commitment to diversity.

As news stories featuring the blackface photos dominated front pages and nightly newscasts, New Democratic Party Leader Jagmeet Singh was visibly shocked and spoke movingly to and for every individual who has had to endure the slights or acts of institutionalized racism that constitute life for racialized Canadians (Global News 2019).

The implosion of Trudeau's "woke" persona made news around the world. When President Donald Trump was asked about it, he replied, "I'm surprised. I was more surprised when I saw the number of times" (Jackson, H. 2019b). But if the blackface scandal was a defining election moment for Canadian political journalists in terms of airtime, tweets, or column inches devoted to the subject, it is less clear the news was a defining moment for voters.

As the story unfolded, Canada's political class was eager for a more scientific assessment of the impact of Trudeau's "bozo eruption" on voter intentions. Darrell Bricker, for example, was convinced there wasn't much the Liberal campaign could do to counter the impact of the blackface narrative. Bricker's analysis of his own research suggested enthusiasm among Liberal voters was already muted before the campaign was launched and he speculated on Twitter whether the blackface storyline would diminish their enthusiasm even further. "No ad, no war room trick, nothing campaign controls will change this," he tweeted (Bricker 2019d). Bricker's basic contention was that the Liberals needed other parties to screw up to emerge victorious. His analysis proved to be prescient, and a flawed earned media strategy on the part of the Conservative Party may have been the screw-up.

The pollsters took to the field in an attempt to determine what, if any, effect the blackface revelation would have. In the immediate aftermath, the short answer appeared to be not much. Abacus research published an online poll on 23 September 2019 that put decided and leading support for the parties at 34 per cent for the Conservatives, 32 per cent for the Liberals, 15 per cent for the NDP, and 11 per cent for the Greens – roughly in line with a previous poll conducted by Abacus before the photos surfaced (Anderson and Coletto 2019).

The poll made it clear the news stories about blackface had the attention of the electorate: 53 per cent of respondents said they had "heard a lot" about the story, with a further 34 per cent of respondents saying they had paid "some" attention to the story. Only 13 per cent of those polled said they had paid no attention at all (ibid.). So the story, in effect, was afforded saturation coverage here. Consistent with Shanto Iyengar and Donald R. Kinder's (1987) theories of agenda setting, the media coverage of the blackface photos ensured Canadians were consuming news stories that focused on diversity and race in an election context. And while 24 per cent of respondents aware of the scandal said they were truly offended and the photos had changed their view of Trudeau for the worse, another 34 per cent of respondents said they thought Trudeau's apology was enough to allow them to move on even if they didn't like the images of their prime minister captured in the photos and video. Most tellingly, 42 per cent said the photos didn't really bother them, which suggests the need for a broader conversation another day (Anderson and Coletto 2019).

Almost half – 48 per cent of respondents – said the published pictures wouldn't affect their vote, although 40 per cent of the respondents said they weren't planning to vote Liberal anyway. Only 12 per cent said the publication of the photos was making them reconsider voting Liberal, a relatively low number in absolute terms but potentially significant in a tight election.

Progressives were both aggrieved and troubled by the photos. Members of Trudeau's Liberal caucus – particularly those seeking re-election – were visibly anguished as they asked Canadians to repudiate the act but not the Liberal "values" agenda.

As *Toronto Star* columnist Vinay Menon observed, "You get the feeling he's talked his way out of many jams in the past" (Menon 2019). But Menon went on to state, "That doesn't necessarily mean he [Trudeau] is a racist – but it does suggest he is a narcissist. When I look at the photos, I honestly don't see malice or evil intent. I see ignorance. I see a jackass. I see a blowhard who craves attention" (ibid.). Once the initial shock subsided, Menon's observations would echo in terms of the response of the electorate. Trudeau, politically speaking, lived to fight another day.

Basically, the prime minister pleaded for the forgiveness he and the Liberal campaign were not prepared to extend to other candidates for other parties embarrassed by social media postings from their past.

Trudeau's apology was couched in language that spoke to an isolation of sorts born of privilege. Given the fact many Canadians see the prime minister as a child of privilege, the framing of his abject apology aligned with the public's perception of his "real-ity," a precondition for any successful political communications strategy. In fact, Trudeau continues to make public amends. In February 2020, during an interview with broadcast journalist Marci Ien at an event to mark Black History Month, Trudeau raised the issue himself, encouraging Canadians to take a hard look at their own actions in the context of racism. "For me, taking that hard look certainly came to a head last fall during the election campaign and reflection on my own choices of many years ago that have actually hurt people today" (Bryden 2020). The prime minister went on to say "I made really dumb choices that I didn't under-stand the consequences for" (ibid.). Trudeau's explanation was clearly good enough for Ien. Later in the year, the CTV journalist would be elected as a Liberal MP in Toronto Centre.

What is most significant about Trudeau's statement was his acknowledgement the blackface controversy is now part of his story (ibid.).

The blackface controversy affords an interesting case study of political journalism, political communication, and the impact of each discipline on public opinion in a campaign context.

The approach of reporters covering the story, the Liberal defence, and the opposition parties' strategic decisions as to how best to respond to the blackface controversy were all factors in the public response.

Conservative Party Leader Andrew Scheer, for example, took a hard line, accusing Prime Minister Trudeau of racism (CBC 2019e). Conservative commentators on public affairs television panels worked to link the controversy to the message in the party's cam-paign commercials and the tag line that argued Trudeau was "not as advertised" (ibid.). On one level, both responses seemed reason-able, even appropriate.

On the podcast *The Herle Burly*, Jenni Byrne, a former adviser for Conservative Prime Minister Stephen Harper, made the valid point that if similar pictures of any other candidate for any other federal party had emerged, that candidate would be gone (Herle 2019b). In a similar vein, campaign veteran Jason Lietaer tweeted,

"If the CEO of Tim Hortons were found to have been in blackface, the same people defending Mr Trudeau would mount a ferocious online campaign and boycott its coffee and donuts. The CEO would be gone in less than 24 hours. Any CEO would be fired by the Board. That is a fact" (Lietaer 2019).

That said, prime ministers and presidents aren't like any other candidates, or any other CEOs. After all, former US president Bill Clinton not only survived reporting of the Monica Lewinsky affair and subsequent impeachment vote but saw his popularity increase to more than 70 per cent (Desilver 2019).

And Trudeau – described by *Globe and Mail* journalist Simon Houpt as "the first Instagram Prime Minister of Canada" (Houpt 2019) – stands out as different even in a leadership crowd. Conservative Party campaign manager Hamish Marshall told *The Herle Burly* host David Herle that Trudeau is "an extremely polarizing figure" and therefore "not a normal politician" (Herle 2019a).

As communications guru Scott Reid noted, the double standard by which others judge Trudeau infuriates his critics. For years, they've raged that he is a phony, the political equivalent of a community theatre actor. Yet that's not how he is perceived by Canadians. "It's about the inescapable fact that, for whatever reason – his surname, his celebrity, his good looks, his values or whatever in hell it is – the public is simply willing to grade him differently," wrote Reid. "Why? Because that's the way it rolls for some people" (Reid, S. 2019).

The prime minister's political opponents could barely contain their exasperation with the way the blackface story was playing out. Former Harper chief of staff Ian Brodie, for example, tweeted, "At the rate this story is disappearing, I doubt we'll see a question about it at the debate. Back to climate change, abortion, and white supremacy, all with a straight face" (Brodie 2019d).

What drives Trudeau's critics to distraction is a belief that the prime minister is judged by a different standard than the rest of us. And they may have a point. Reid, a former director of communications for Prime Minister Paul Martin, certainly thinks so.

"By any established standard, he [Trudeau] should be done" (Reid, S. 2019). But Reid quickly added, "For some people, the rules are different. They just are."

Conservative advertising strategist Dennis Matthews extends the thought, saying of Trudeau, "He's not a normal political candidate, he's a brand. A celebrity who has built, and continues to build, something that can withstand even the most damaging circumstances" (Matthews 2019a).

Trudeau's "brand" building began the day he was born – to a sitting prime minister and his wife, Margaret, on Christmas Day, 1971. He, his brother Sasha, and his late brother Michel were featured in photo ops for years. Justin Trudeau's political career for all intents and purposes was launched with the eulogy he delivered at his father's funeral. Images helped shape public impressions of who and what Justin Trudeau is. And those public impressions were integral to the public response to the blackface scandal: the frat boy behaviour being but a few frames in a kaleidoscope that includes many other, more favourable images.

In the same campaign Canadians were confronted with the blackface photos, Trudeau literally paddled a canoe to a campaign event in northern Ontario. The Liberal leader used the occasion to announce an incentive program to make it easier for families with reduced means to go camping – an electoral promise that inspired the *National Post's* John Ivison to tweet, "I think that might be the stupidest thing I've heard so far in this election" (Ivison 2019b). But if the policy proposal bordered on the goofy, Trudeau's "brand" was advanced with the photo. What was clear to anyone who saw the visuals is that Justin Trudeau, like his father, is skilled and comfortable in a canoe. You do not master that skill an hour before the photo op. And Canadians have always had a historical, even emotional, bordering on the spiritual, connection to canoes. As irritating as it might have been for Trudeau's political opponents, the images spoke to today's preoccupation with "authenticity."

Critics will cringe at the mere suggestion photos of Trudeau in blackface and images of the prime minister paddling a canoe should ever be considered in a single train of thought. Yet in the communications world of "peripheral cues" – emotional rather than rational cues – both are elements of any voter assessment as to the kind of person the Liberal leader is.

In their comments about Trudeau, both Reid and Matthews are speaking to the phenomenon that Andie Tucher identified as a "congenial truth" (1994). We, collectively, come to a view about something or someone based on a body of evidence over a period of time. As news consumers, we consider any new fact against that body of evidence, and decide whether that new fact is in and of itself enough to change that perception. News frames have a central role in creating "congenial truths." Journalists, in deciding whether a particular fact is included in any news story, are influenced by "congenial truths."

Congenial truths can also be reinforced by "slanting," a concept introduced by Samuel Hayakawa in 1940. Slanting is defined as "the process of selecting details that are favourable or unfavourable to the subject being described" (Mullainathan and Shleifer 2005, 1031). Slanting is an element of media competition. "Competition forces newspapers to cater to the prejudices of their readers, and greater competition typically results in more aggressive catering to such prejudices as competitors strive to divide the market" (ibid., 1042). Residents of the Greater Toronto Area can compare accounts of the same news event in the *Toronto Star* and the *Toronto Sun*.

As described earlier in this work, Iyengar and Kinder (1987) identified a three-step process to analyze media effects on the public. As a first step, the news story puts the issue featured on our collective agenda. The second phase "primes" us to assess political leaders against the "agenda" the news has set. The "priming" process is influenced directly by the dominant news frame clamped over the event. The third and final phase is the "bandwagon" – our collective response to the first two steps. All three steps apply in the blackface case.

The Abacus election poll mentioned previously reaffirms the media success in setting an agenda with the blackface story. But Carleton University associate professor Elly Alboim argues the political press and the Conservatives tripped themselves up when they tried to take agenda setting a step further. And the tripwire was the attempt to establish "racist" as the dominant news frame around Justin Trudeau. "In this case journalism moved beyond its normal agenda setting role of telling people what they might think about to telling them what to think," Alboim states (Alboim 2019a). "Media became an articulate actor in the drama ... an unspoken assertion of media entitlement" (ibid.). In a newsletter penned for clients of the Earnscliffe Strategy Group, Alboim concluded, "Trudeau seemed to receive the benefit of the doubt on intent and whether he harbours racist feelings. His various apologies combined with his previous focus on diversity and inclusion likely pre-empted wider and deeper anger" (ibid.).

Which is not to say the story did not have a measurable impact on the 2019 federal election. Alboim argues that as a direct result of the blackface story, the contextual frame of the 2019 federal election changed. The campaign, for Alboim, became a virtual referendum on Trudeau. The election became a leadership-driven campaign. And for that reason, the televised leaders' debates had the potential to take on more significance than might otherwise have been the case (ibid.), a consideration that will be addressed in more detail later in this chapter.

Abacus Data CEO David Coletto shared Alboim's view: "I'm increasingly convinced that the blackface controversy may end up helping the Liberals and Trudeau," Coletto posted in a tweet on 26 September 2019, a week after the scandal broke (Coletto 2019b). The election, Coletto argued, had become about values and character (Coletto 2019a), which Coletto concluded created an advantage for the Liberals. Coletto stated the Liberals are more comfortable fighting a "values" election. In contrast, the Conservative platform, built in the main on Harper-era boutique tax cuts, was largely transactional.

Post-election news accounts stated research conducted by Liberal campaign strategists led to an important and early discovery about the blackface controversy. "To some people's surprise, and the Liberals' relief, the focus group participants – even those from visible minorities – weren't all that fussed," *Toronto Star* political columnist Susan Delacourt reported (Delacourt 2019c). "They had seen the apology, believed Trudeau was sincere, not a racist, and many said it was time to move on."

"This is why it is good to have focus groups," Dan Arnold, the Liberal campaign's director of research, later explained. "Because it shows you how people actually feel, when you see their tone and facial expressions as they talk about an issue" (ibid.). Without giving away too many trade secrets, strategist Tom Pitfield also confirmed the Liberals had engaged in extensive "resonance testing" during the campaign (ibid.). Resonance testing is intended to take the guesswork out of campaign communications by determining whether messages targeted at voters are having the intended effect. Trudeau's second-day response to the blackface controversy was clearer, crisper, and more effective than his first.

Significantly, the Conservative campaign did not make extensive use of focus group research. Campaign chair Hamish Marshall told podcast host David Herle that he doesn't believe in focus groups much, convinced the research technique produces too much "group think" on the part of participants who all turn into film critics (Herle 2019a). The Liberals – and Herle, for that matter – disagree.

At least a few Liberals knew well ahead of the election beginning that the blackface photos were in the possession of a major international media outlet, as did a number of Conservatives. Marshall says he was made aware that photos of Trudeau in blackface existed a full year before the 2019 federal election was called (ibid.). The substantive point here being both major parties had ample time to develop comprehensive "issue management" strategies to deal with the blackface revelations. The responses of both parties, therefore, must be seen as considered.

Ironically, Conservative Leader Andrew Scheer created an opportunity for the Liberals to limit the damage even before news of the blackface photos surfaced. Responding to questions about certain public utterances from his own candidates, including one who shared homophobic and anti-Muslim posts online, Scheer made it clear he was prepared to forgive past sins, provided the candidate apologized (Jackson, H. 2019a).

Trudeau could have seized the moment to agree with Scheer, and make a generic reference to the fact many people have done or said things in their past that they now regret and are not reflective of their attitudes. Green Party candidate Greg Malone, for example, told reporters that in his days with the satirical troupe CODCO, he would wear brownface when portraying Indian activist Mahatma Gandhi. Further, Malone make the point the skits were carried on Canada's public broadcaster – the CBC (Shah 2019a). Malone expressed his regret and apologized unreservedly. Malone's apology was accepted. The matter – in his case – was closed.

Leaders, however, are held to a higher standard than local candidates. And it would have been immeasurably more difficult for Trudeau to issue any kind of disclaimer regarding past behaviour without inviting a media feeding frenzy fuelled by legitimate media demands for specifics.

What the Liberal campaign had to do – and after an initial stumble in the end did effectively – was to come up with a strategy to help progressive voters see past the blackface revelations. And in keeping with the potential of social media to allow parties to control a channel of distribution, their instrument of choice was a tweet.

In an age of Trump as a dominant presence in the Twitterverse, a tweet by his predecessor Barack Obama may have helped Trudeau get through the blackface controversy and in doing so, contributed to the Liberal victory. *National Post* columnist John Ivison, for example, says Liberal strategists are convinced Obama's endorsement was vital to Trudeau's electoral success (Ivison 2019d). According to Ivison's well-sourced account, the mood in the Liberal war room was decidedly despondent going into the Thanksgiving weekend. The nightly tracking suggested the Liberals were stalled. However, according to Ivison, a reported Tory promise to cut government services had caused some swing voters to take another look at Trudeau. Then, on Wednesday, 16 October, Obama weighed in with a laudatory tweet: "I was proud to work with Justin Trudeau as President. He's a hard-working, effective leader who takes on big issues like climate change. The world needs his progressive leadership now, and I hope our neighbors to the north support him for another term" (Obama 2019).

Ivison argues the Obama intervention paved the road to redemption on the blackface issue for the prime minister. Obama's tweet received 325,000 likes and 45,000 retweets, huge for a Canadian political tweet, though relatively standard for a former president with 113 million followers. Traffic to the Liberal Facebook page "soared 1,300 per cent," Ivison adds (Ivison 2019d). The party spent thousands of dollars to ensure supporters saw the endorsement. Obama's intervention recharged the Liberal base, particularly those Liberal supporters who were angered and embarrassed by the blackface issue.

Ipsos Public Affairs CEO Darrell Bricker challenged the analysis that suggests the Obama intervention was electorally significant. "Ah, no. A smart move with marginal impact," Bricker tweeted (Bricker 2019e). "CPC vote actually grew a little through the weekend, not the other way around." Bricker's reportage on the rolling overnight polls is undoubtedly accurate. But there may be a broader point to consider.

Long-standing communications theories were most certainly at play in the blackface controversy. An opinion poll published by Abacus Data measured the impact of the Obama endorsement on voting intentions. The top line concluded 63 per cent of Canadians have a positive impression of Barack Obama (Coletto 2019c), significant in the context of the Yale school's conclusion the messenger matters when it comes to political messaging.

More importantly, 62 per cent of Liberal supporters said they were more likely to vote Liberal as a result of Obama's tweet (ibid.). Liberal strategists were quite open about the fact they had reached out to Obama hoping he could help. The former president's tweet more than met their expectations, extending the helping hand the prime minister needed to address the blackface backlash. In effect, Obama was saying, I can get past this, and I hope you can as well.

The Liberal campaign had an informed view of how the prime minister's apology was being received by voters, the Conservatives less so. Because of their research, the Liberals knew how the blackface controversy was playing out.

The Conservative Party's political messaging was curious, even questionable, and may have had the effect of reducing the electoral impact of the blackface scandal. The party, through Andrew Scheer, took a hard line, branding Trudeau a racist. But that hard line was at variance with public opinion and therefore public reaction. Canadians, in the main, do not see Justin Trudeau as a racist. Pampered, yes. Privileged, for sure. A jerk, perhaps. Lacking in self-awareness, definitely. But a racist, no. The question is why the Conservative campaign didn't know the "racist" framing used by Scheer wasn't connecting with voters generally in quite the same fashion as it was with the chattering classes, and the party's base.

Veteran campaign strategist David Herle argues, "Don't base your campaign on a proposition your opponent can disprove" (Herle 2020e). Similarly, don't base your earned media strategy on a dominant news frame you cannot establish. An attack that positioned Trudeau as a pampered child of privilege might have proved more resonant with voters than the "racist" construct.

Two-Faced

The emergence of a "values" campaign in 2019 also had implications for Andrew Scheer. Scheer's curriculum vitae and the questions raised as to its completeness and authenticity became a campaign story of significance in terms of voter reaction.

The Conservative Party decided "trust" was one of the party's key messages, only to have Scheer himself undermine the "trust" message. Scheer – or someone acting on his behalf – fudged his CV. There were at least two answers to the question as to which university Scheer graduated from. And the Conservative Party leader was less than forthcoming about his dual Canadian-American citizenship. Noteworthy for a number of reasons, including the fact

Scheer had criticized former governor general Michaëlle Jean for holding dual citizenship (Fife and Dickson 2019).

As the campaign unfolded, Campbell Clark and Adam Radwanski filed a story to the *Globe*, published online on 28 September, which suggested the Tory leader's claim to have been an insurance broker was exaggerated at best (Clark and Radwanski 2019). The *Globe* could find no evidence Scheer held the licence "required by law to work as an insurance agent or broker in Saskatchewan" (ibid.).

Ottawa bureau chief Robert Fife, the Conservatives' favourite reporter up until that point, struck an aggressive tone during an appearance on the CTV public affairs program *Question Period* on Sunday, 29 September 2019. Fife flat out said Scheer was not an insurance broker. "He was a clerk, a gofer in an insurance office. He sold licence plates," the *Globe* reporter insisted (CTV 2019b).

The details of the *Globe* story about Scheer may seem less significant in news terms than the furor triggered by the sets of photos of the prime minister in blackface. But in the "peripheral cue" world of political communications, the gaffe was most significant. The Yale school's theories about the impact of the messenger on the message were developed in the 1950s – but the Conservative campaign brain trust clearly didn't fully appreciate the extent to which Scheer's ability to deliver a message about "trust" had been compromised by the controversy over his citizenship and his CV. It proved a grievous miscalculation.

Long-time Conservative strategist Kory Teneycke was among those who publicly questioned a political leader who decides to make trust the focus of his campaign, then lays claim to a credential he hasn't earned on his CV. Teneycke – who led the post-election charge to force Scheer to step down as party leader – identified a central flaw in the Conservative communications strategy when he observed, "Just go through all the things that prove Andrew Scheer is not as advertised, the same as Trudeau, and you get quite a list" (Thomson and Platt 2019, A7).

Canadian voters may not have been all that fussed about whether Scheer was a licensed insurance broker or not. But the perception he had been less than honest about his professional past played to the long-standing Liberal storyline that has become a congenial truth that Conservatives always have a hidden agenda. Scheer's evasiveness tapped into a growing uneasiness among certain electors about the Conservative leader's non-answers on issues such as abortion and same-sex marriage. In a campaign where values and leadership had replaced specific promises as the ballot question – as Alboim and Coletto assert – Scheer's evasiveness took on added electoral significance. Research conducted by the Digital Ecosystem Research Challenge focused on findings from the 2019 federal election concluded: "Anger and perceptions of hypocrisy in relation to revelation of Scheer's American citizenship were shared across political spectrum regardless of party or partisan differences" (Owen and Dubois 2020, 8). The fact Scheer didn't tell Canadians he held both American and Canadian citizenships was more telling than the fact he is a dual citizen. If their messaging missed the mark on the blackface scandal, the Conservative messaging also seriously underestimated the impact that news that Scheer's own backstory had holes in it would have on voter intentions.

Given the fact only the Liberals and the Conservatives had a realistic chance to emerge victorious in the 2019 federal election, the blackface and trust stories both had the potential to impact voter intentions in a determinant away. Leaders of the other federal parties certainly had their media moments as well, but none of them were ever in a position to win more seats than any other party, a factor in the media coverage. New Democratic Party Leader Jagmeet Singh is a visually compelling public figure. But the results of the federal election lead inevitably to the conclusion that the trend line for the federal NDP is going in the wrong direction and further suggest Singh is very much a work in progress. Former Green Party leader Elizabeth May – for all her personal charm – demonstrably never mastered the business of politics. The Greens need to learn how to translate support for environmental causes – which resulted in literally hundreds of thousands of Canadians, led by Greta Thunberg, the Swedish teenage activist, taking to the streets during the campaign – into votes (Kingston 2019). And Bloc Québécois, with its overarching focus on Quebec independence, is by definition of interest to English-language media primarily in that context.

Media as Agenda Setters

Media bias is inevitably a storyline in election campaigns, particularly in this "fake news" era.

A constituency in the Twitterverse seized on the fact the blackface photo appeared in an American publication as proof the Canadian media spends most of its time either covering up for Prime Minister Justin Trudeau or turning themselves collectively into pretzels to explain his many shortcomings – both as a political leader and as a person.

That major Canadian news organizations might be both frustrated and angered at being beaten by a foreign news organization on a story that literally was hiding in plain sight is likely. That the oversight is the result of a Canadian news industry-wide cover-up is highly unlikely. The explanation as to why *Time* ended up with the blackface photo may be as simple and straightforward as the fact the son of Michael Adamson, the source of the image, was a classmate of *Time* reporter Anna Purna Kambhampaty at Cornell (CTV 2019a). Occam's razor. That said, there is a conversation to be had about the evolution of political journalism, post-Watergate, and the place of political journalism in public discourse.

The media, as Alboim observed, feels both entitled and empowered to impose the news agenda on a political campaign, and in doing so, also seeks to impose a news agenda on political debate. The start of the 2019 federal election on September 11 provided a prime example.

A front-page story carried in that day's edition of the *Globe and Mail* reported the RCMP had not yet launched a criminal investigation into allegations of obstruction of justice in the SNC-Lavalin affair on the part of Trudeau or any of his political staff. Further, the *Globe* reported the RCMP probe was being "stymied by the federal government's refusal to lift cabinet confidentiality for all witnesses" (Leblanc and Fife 2019). The story did state the force is "examining this matter carefully with all available information." The RCMP added the force would "pause" the operation during the campaign (ibid.).

For Liberals, the *Globe* report and RCMP comment was a case of déjà vu; shades of the 2005 campaign all over again, when the federal police force announced it was conducting a criminal investigation into the leak of information from that fall's federal budget that had the potential to impact financial markets, a saga covered in some detail earlier in this work.

Trudeau was at Rideau Hall to ask Governor General Julie Payette to issue the writs for the 2019 federal election. In the normal course of events, the prime minister would have chatted with the Queen's representative, then walked out to meet the scribes assembled on the driveway in front of the residence to offer his view as to what the "ballot question" for the campaign was, and then take questions from the media. Instead, the Liberal leader found himself answering questions about SNC-Lavalin once again. It was, in the words of Alboim, "all so predictable" (Alboim 2019b). "Globe deliberately files a warmed over story to disrupt election call day and become the object of media 'news' focus," Alboim tweeted (ibid.). "Marketing, not journalism. Conservatives jump on it and raise the rhetorical stakes. PM will be forced to respond" (ibid.).

As Alboim stated, the *Globe* banner story did become the focus of news coverage of the campaign call. The Conservative opposition did raise the rhetorical stakes, insisting the RCMP had launched a criminal investigation when the force explicitly stated it had not. The *Globe* reporters, predictably, were given the first question at the "media avail" and, as Alboim noted, the paper "self-servingly follows up on its own 'story.' Others focus on Lavalin, too. The classic struggle for control over the 'news' agenda and narrative framing in political campaigns" (Alboim 2019d).

Alboim argued the day a campaign is launched is a day for "voters to hear what's on offer. That's a lesser priority for media. Welcome to Election 2019. And the pattern that will persist for

40 days" (Alboim 2019c). Alboim scoffed at media accounts that suggested launch day had been "'derailed' as if by an unseen hand. Lot of analysis of tactics and strategic imperatives for parties and minimal coverage of leader speeches and party thematics," Alboim concluded (Alboim 2019e).

A former Ottawa bureau chief for CBC and adviser to Prime Minister Paul Martin, Alboim noted his former network ran a story of "streeters" asking people "what issues were important to them with journalistic reportage and opinion that reflected none of that" (Alboim 2019f). And according to Alboim, the news story made it clear: "The gap between media and voter agendas couldn't be more obvious" (ibid.). Which begs the question: Is the "gap" between media and citizens a result of an ideological or philosophical bias – or does the answer lie elsewhere?

The Media as the Story

In an era where "fake news" accusations are tossed about with abandon, questions around media bias take on added significance. Some journalists who cover federal politics refuse to vote in federal elections as an assertion of their objectivity. Political journalists chafe at any suggestion of bias, and for that reason were concerned when the union that represents many of them in collective bargaining terms – Unifor – opted to be anti-Conservative activists in the 2019 federal election. To be fair to Unifor's Jerry Dias, he and his broader union membership have a policy and program agenda to advance. And Dias has a track record of success in working with governments to advance the interests of his membership. A quirk in election law that is the direct result of a judicial ruling allows third parties – including unions – to run paid advertising campaigns during the election period. These third parties are not allowed to declare support for a particular party but are allowed to take out ads telling voters what they oppose. And in the case of Unifor, that's the Conservative Party. Unifor's ads were uncomfortable for those reporters who are Unifor members and who cover federal politics. As the *Globe*'s Steven Chase posted, "As journalists first and foremost, we would like to make this point clear: On matters of partisan politics, Jerry Dias and Unifor do not speak for us. Please see this signed letter by Canadian journalists" (Chase 2019). The letter in question included the signatures of scores of journalists. The journalists who signed the petition deemed it important to assert their objectivity. The petition, in the view of this writer, is an affectation. Those unionized journalists chose to stay part of Unifor. Unifor is entitled to pursue a public policy agenda. If the pursuit of that policy agenda offends journalistic sensibilities, the journalists need only organize a decertification vote and join another union.

To be fair, the "media as the story" line predated the blackface revelations. In fact, the media as the story long has been an element of the political conversation in Canada.

In years past, former prime minister Jean Chrétien believed SRC – the French-language CBC – was a hotbed of separatists. Political reporters are adept at shrugging off such criticism. Political reporters are, in the main, skilled professionals who have developed their craft over years and collectively reflect the diversity of political opinion that is Canada.

But as a matter of fact, political journalism can speak in the voice of a smallish, shrinking constituency – political insiders – with stories aimed at that constituency told from a perspective that largely excludes another key constituency – voters.

If the allegations of partisan media bias are unfounded, questions about perceived bias in campaign coverage are legitimate and entirely warranted – not on the basis of personal or ideological bias, but on the basis of the bias of "news."

Going into the 2019 federal campaign, Canada's political reporters might have been well-advised to heed the caution "forewarned is forearmed." Because the fact is, as both democracies headed into election season, political reporters in Canada and the United States were warned their coverage of politics was in need of a serious upgrade.

In the days before the 2019 federal election began, and the primary season in the US was heating up, media commentator Heidi

Moore published a thread warning of the risk inherent in Twitter feeds shaping the mainstream media news agenda. Moore, a digital media strategist, has worked as a reporter and editor at publications such as the *Guardian* (US) and the *Wall Street Journal*. Her longish thread is reproduced in detail here because of the compelling nature of much of the advice Moore had to offer.

Moore encouraged political reporters to stop covering politics as marketing and optics and polls, dismissing that approach as "so 1990s ... In 1999 it was optics on cable TV. Now 'optics' means nothing. Optics where? Twitter? Facebook? Cable? Sunday shows? Town halls? Snapchat? There. Are. No. Unified. Optics," Moore declared (Moore 2019a).

Political sourcing, Moore stated, is a disaster "and needs a clean sweep" (Moore 2019b). "There is a whole generation of political reporters right now who never learned how to make phone calls, and do in-person reporting" (Moore 2019c).

Moore was scathingly critical of reporters who show up at the White House briefing room and think they've put in a hard day. "Sitting on your ass, hearing what everyone else can hear is not hard work. It's minimal presence" (Moore 2019d). Moore went on to make the point, "Hard work means talking to a lot of people. Not one comms dude who takes your call" (Moore 2019e). Twitter, Moore argues, has become a crutch for political reporters "to avoid the hard work of journalism just when the country needs them most" (Moore 2019f). The solution, according to Moore, is that editors should simply tell political reporters to get off Twitter.

Moore had more advice in her thread: stop covering the horse race; the horse race misses the story.

Moore was incensed at reporters who saw the coverage of special prosecutor Robert Mueller's investigation and report as "boring," arguing, "In fact, politics is NOT boring. Policy is NOT boring. Politics is the story of human striving" (Moore 2019g). Moore goes on to make the case "there is no story as important as the political story, and there is no journalism as trifling and petty and meaningless and careless as the US political journalism we have now" (Moore 2019h).

The Washington press corps, Moore concludes, "is completely fucking up the assignment" (Moore 2019i).

Moore's thread garnered a lot of attention among Canadian political reporters, many of whom vowed – on Twitter of course – to take her advice to heart.

And certainly many did. But the balance of coverage of the 2019 federal election for this news consumer reflected too much stenography, was largely about marketing, optics, polls, and the horse race coverage. On reflection, Arnold's confirmation that the focus group work gave the Liberal campaign an instant read on how voters were reacting to Trudeau's apology raises fundamental questions for mainstream media organizations. Preoccupied as it is with polling and party standings, the political press may have to get more strategic and creative in its approach to writing about public opinion, for example, than simply settling for a box score account of a national poll with a sample size that barely meets basic requirements. In a similar vein, news organizations focus on political messaging, particularly advertising, yet invest few if any resources in a bid to better understand whether or not the messages resonate with the audience targeted.

In terms of its editorial offering, the media need to drill deeper, which today is easier said than done. In a media ecosystem threatened by revenue streams that are drying up and readers, listeners, and viewers who are sourcing political news elsewhere, there are fewer staff jobs and an increasing reliance on freelance contributors. News bureaus in Ottawa do not have the resources that were available in the 1980s or 1990s, and with the demands of social media platforms, have meaningfully fewer journalists to produce more product. So where will liberal democracies find the well water civic journalism provides?

Trump, Twitter and Public Discourse

The blackface story, Scheer's CV, and a human interest campaign story involving an elderly couple and a Syrian refugee all reflect two fundamental realities about today's media landscape: the wisdom of Clay Shirky's description of a "media ecosystem" (2008) and Jack Germond's observation that most journalism is derivative (as cited in Patterson 2013).

A rally for People's Party of Canada Leader Maxime Bernier in Hamilton in the fall of 2019 provided one of the more interesting human interest stories of the election. Dorothy Marston, 81, and her husband were confronted by protesters looking to deny them entry. "They were … treating me like I'm a criminal," Marston said later (Taekema 2019). The confrontation was filmed, the clip went viral, and one of the protesters was identified as Alaa Al Soufi, whose family had come to Canada in 2015 and soon after opened a restaurant. The family's dedication to helping other Syrian refugees resettle was the subject of a profile in the *New York Times* (Sax 2018). However, when someone on social media identified Alaa, the family was subjected to a "barrage of death threats," according to the *Toronto Star* (2019). Initially, the family planned to close the restaurant, a decision they later revisited when the broader community stepped forward in support. The Soufi family apologized to the Marstons, and a difficult situation was resolved.

The story was covered by global media brands including the *Guardian* (Cecco 2019) and the *Washington Post* (Armus 2019). But the substantive point is that the original reporting was the direct result of work by beat reporters, such as *Toronto Star* immigration reporter Nicholas Keung and investigative reporter Diana Zlomislic (Keung and Zlomislic 2019).

The blackface story "broke" in the mainstream press. But social media in general – and Twitter in particular – played a significant role in the distribution of the "news."

Twitter is akin to January diets: individuals with Twitter accounts are constantly threatening to abandon the platform or at least swear off the site for unspecified periods of time. Twitter has raised trash talk to an art form. A consensus emerged in the Digital Ecosystem study "that the volume of negativity online had deleterious effects on Canadian democracy" (Owen and Dubois 2020, 7). And Twitter users – especially those with a public profile – often feel the need for a respite from the hateful and abusive. Further, there is a legitimate debate around the level of engagement on Twitter of the broader public.

For all the snark that can find expression on the platform, Twitter allows participants to "follow" leading thinkers and experts on the full range of policy and political issues. Further, in the context of the media ecosystem, the folks we follow constitute a rich vein of links to longer, more engaging stories, studies, or commentary.

A case can be made that America's former "commander-in-chief" was also its "Twitter-user-in-chief." Trump adviser Kellyanne Conway said simply, "Trump needs to tweet like we need to eat" (Shear et al. 2019). Trump, apparently, thought a tweet was sufficient notice to United States Congress that he may launch a war against Iran. A lengthy analysis by the *New York Times* concluded Trump "fully integrated Twitter into the very fabric of his administration, reshaping the nature of the presidency and presidential power" (ibid.).

Trump would send out a tweet and within seconds cable newscasts were interrupting programming with breathless announcements of "breaking news" (ibid.). Trump tweets were routinely embedded in the news stories of prestigious mainstream news organizations such as the *New York Times*.

One indication the president used Twitter to set America's news agenda is the fact that for a while his press secretaries stopped holding daily on-camera press briefings. Think about that fact – a press secretary that doesn't speak to the press – and what that says about Trump's approach to media relations.

Even as the economy was humming along, President Trump spent much of the fall of 2019 facing congressional impeachment hearings. A whistleblower – identified as a US intelligence official – claimed, "I have received information from multiple U.S. government officials that the President of the United States is using the powers of his office to solicit interference from a foreign country in the 2020 U.S election" (Jansen and Hayes 2019). Specifically, Trump stood accused of asking Ukrainian president Volodymyr Zelensky to conduct an investigation into former vice-president Joe Biden and Biden's son Hunter.

Trump, it is alleged, said he would only release military aide to the Ukraine if the government there agreed to investigate the Bidens – in a bid to cripple the electoral chances of Joe Biden, who was seeking the Democratic Party's presidential nomination for 2020. Congressional Democrats argued Trump's actions met the constitutional test of "high crimes and misdemeanours." Trump's Republican defenders, including the Senate majority, argued nothing untoward occurred because the Ukrainian investigation was never carried out and at the end of the day, the aid package was finally released.

The challenge for Trump in public opinion terms lay in the fact that anyone who has ever seen a Martin Scorsese or Francis Ford Coppola film understands what it means when a person in power asks someone dependent on their largesse to do a little favour. The 2020 presidential campaign may have hinged, in part, on a determination as to whether a majority of Americans were offended by that fact.

The White House was accused of trying to cover up the affair. Trump mounted much of his defence on Twitter. In fact, in a story that appeared in the 15 January edition of the *New York Times Magazine* entitled "The Fog of Rudy," written by Jonathan Mahler, Trump told radio host Rush Limbaugh, "Without Twitter, I think we'd be lost … We wouldn't be able to get the truth out" (Mahler 2020). Once the Republican majority in the Senate voted to acquit Trump in its impeachment trial, the president moved quickly to settle scores with witnesses and whistleblowers alike. And again, Twitter was Trump's instrument of choice.

That Trump was going to be active on Twitter was a given. The issue for the mainstream media was whether a presidential tweet was the beginning or the end of the news gathering process.

New York Times columnist Roger Cohen describes President Trump as "a mass-media magician. He got McLuhan – 'the medium is the message' – without reading McLuhan," Cohen observed, referring to the theories of Canadian communications scholar Marshall McLuhan (Cohen, R. 2019). In Cohen's estimation, Trump mastered the medium of Twitter and was highly skilled at using the social media platform to set the news agenda. There were hiccups to be sure. The president's congratulatory message to the 2020 Super Bowl champions the Kansas City Chiefs made the mistaken assumption the football team was based in the state of Kansas and not Missouri (Rogers, K. 2020). Trump was a "patient student" of how his tweets played on television, according to author Michael Wolff (2019, 148).

In an insightful piece posted by *The Atlantic* on 10 February 2020, writer McKay Coppins says leaders have learned how to harness the "democratizing power of social media" for their own purposes (Coppins 2020). "They no longer need to silence the dissident shouting in the streets; they can use a megaphone to drown him out," Coppins observed. Jamming is a technique of choice, as is sowing confusion. "Scholars have a name for this," Coppins reports: "censorship through noise."

Climate Change / Greta Thunberg

Social media platforms certainly created their own equivalents of the biblical David to take on the Goliaths like Donald Trump. These individuals have succeeded in inserting themselves and their cause into the media agenda setting discussion. What is less clear is whether that discussion gets reported in the legacy media on the activists' terms or on "news" terms.

Climate change activist Greta Thunberg is one such example. Hundreds of thousands of Canadian took to the streets on a sunny September afternoon in 2019 to answer the Swedish teenager's call for a climate strike. In fact, organizers claimed 500,000 people marched in Montreal, the largest protest rally in the city's history.

Prime Minister Justin Trudeau was there with his family. Trudeau met with Thunberg – who told him the Liberal government wasn't doing enough to meet the climate crisis. Trudeau was booed by fellow marchers for his decision to buy the TMX pipeline and had to be protected by his security detail when a man tried to toss an egg his way (D'Amore 2019b). News footage left the impression Trudeau's son Hadrien was unsettled by the altercation. The news accounts, highlighting voices of anger, dissent, and confrontation, positioned the prime minister as having had a bad day: not because the reporters covering the story were biased but because of the bias of news. The egg tosser made the news; the scores of marchers posing for "selfies" with the prime minister did not.

Conservative Party Leader Andrew Scheer – unlike the leaders of each of the other federal parties – decided to give the climate change marches a pass. Curiously, Scheer's campaign strategists selected a forgettable venue in Coquitlam, BC, to announce a commitment to widen expressways and freeways to make life easier for commuters in cars. As *National Post* columnist John Ivison observed, "It was a strange decision, to say the least, to schedule an announcement to build more bridges, roads and tunnels on the same day as mass climate-change protests across the country" (Ivison 2019c).

The climate change protests were the lead item on every television news cast, dominated front pages in the mainstream print media, was the talk of talk radio, and material for countless Facebook pages as granddaughters sent along photos of themselves and their friends on the march.

And that fact in itself is interesting. The Digital Ecosystem study (Owen and Dubois 2020, 75) concluded Canadians viewed the environment as an important factor in their voting decisions, Conservative Party supporters to a lesser extent. In fact, Andrew Scheer, compared to other party leaders, posted the least about climate change (ibid., 76).

While climate change was identified as an issue, even *the* issue, for large numbers of potential voters in the 2019 federal election, the news coverage tended to focus on the politics of climate change rather than the substance of the economic and public policy issues before the industrialized world as a consequence of global warming.

Long-time journalist Paul Adams, later an associate professor at Carleton's School of Journalism and Communication, explained why in a thoughtful piece carried in the Institute for Research on Public Policy's *Policy Options*. The climate crisis is "a hard sell for reporters and editors used to defining news a certain way," Adams states (2019a). Conflict and novelty are core news values. With no loud or open conflict between federal party leaders – all claim to have policies intended to address climate change – journalists struggle to find a daily news hook. "When something is routine, for example undrinkable water on reserves, it is harder to convince a morning news meeting that you should spend your time doing that story every day," Adams states (ibid.).

In the same way mainstream media struggled to cover the civil rights movement in America in the 1960s, media outlets today believe they need an event such as the September climate strike to present the climate crisis story.

Catastrophic events – hurricanes in the Caribbean or the southeastern US, forest fires in California or northern BC and Alberta – typically receive extensive news coverage. But the phenomenon itself is a more difficult news sell. Twenty or thirty years of undrinkable water is – by definition – not news. But the daily travails of people who live in these communities may constitute the biggest single program, public policy, or political issue in that community. Activists are well aware of the bias of news. First Nation communities determined to protect their ancestral lands use railway blockades to garner public attention. So how well connected is the "news" to the issues that matter most to people?

Postelection Analysis

Toronto Star columnist and Ottawa bureau chief Susan Delacourt dubbed the 2019 federal election the "tall poppy" election, drawing on the phrase that originated in Australia referring to a predisposition to cut down to size individuals who seem to be getting ahead of themselves. "The federal election was really about one thing: the humbling of our leaders," Delacourt wrote (Delacourt 2019b). "In 2019 especially, Canadians don't want larger-than-life leaders, they want leaders who make Canadians' lives larger." Delacourt followed her artful turn of phrase with the suggestion there was one overarching ballot question in 2019: "Do you want to teach Canada's politicians a lesson about humility?" (ibid.).

Yet there is a debate to be had as to whether the voters' attitude was a conscious decision, or a response? Scott Reid dubbed the fall election "the Seinfeld campaign" (Hall, C. 2019). "The whole campaign seemed so superficial to people," Reid told Chris Hall, host of the CBC's *The House*. In terms of dominant story lines in the campaign, one could argue the problems that plagued both Justin Trudeau and Andrew Scheer, in political communications terms, would fall under the heading of self-inflicted wounds. Trudeau decided to don blackface so many times he couldn't give a clear answer when asked how frequently. And it was Scheer who fibbed on his CV and didn't reveal his dual citizenship. The "news" in both instances wasn't lost on Canadian voters. But in deciding on which candidate to vote for in the 2019 federal election, the voters may have been looking for something less "newsworthy."

If, as Delacourt concludes, Canadians want leaders who can make their lives larger, they may also have been looking to political communicators and political journalists alike to help them make that assessment by creating a conversation that is less focused on today's misstep and more focused on tomorrow's solutions or opportunities.

Delacourt makes an important distinction when she states that while governing is an art, "getting elected, in the 21st century, is increasingly a science" (Delacourt 2019c). And part of that "science" is the science of communication for both political communicators and political journalists.

Theories of media effects that predate the internet are no less relevant in a social media era. Communications in general, and political communications in particular, have long suffered under the curse of the "gifted amateur." Everyone in politics thinks he or she excels at communication. Few have any foundation in mass communication or social psychology theory.

Conservative Leader Andrew Scheer, for example, might well have benefitted from some "resonance testing." Scheer, as stated earlier, denounced Trudeau as a racist, a descriptive that focus group participants in sessions organized by the Liberal campaign did not share. Scheer might have been better advised to attack

Trudeau as an embarrassment to the country, a flake, privileged, disconnected from real life and even reality.

A key element of Delacourt's story suggests political parties may have a clearer understanding of voters' preoccupations than the political press. And once again, science is at the root of that knowledge. The *New York Times* has reported "geofencing" was an outreach initiative of significance to the Trump re-election campaign (Edsall 2020). Former Trump campaign chief Brad Parscale knew where literally hundreds of thousands of unregistered conservative Catholics lived, and how to get messages to them directly on the issues that mattered to them in a bid to get them out to vote (ibid.). Geofencing was "news," the ongoing geofencing initiative, less so. News consumers, having been informed about the practice, need also be informed about what the practice produces in electoral terms.

Here in Canada, the *Star* reported the Liberal campaign had 90,000 volunteers in the field who collectively made twenty-one million "attempts" to connect personally with voters, fourteen million of these attempts during the writ period (Delacourt 2019c). By way of comparison, public opinion researchers, typically, talk to a few thousand respondents across the country for each survey they conduct.

The intelligence gathering value of these "attempts" cannot be underestimated. Door-to-door canvassers with the latest technology reporting on concerns expressed on doorsteps may help campaign strategists to come to a more informed view about what is or is not an issue with the potential to move voters. News organizations clearly do not have sufficient human resources to match the political parties on the doorstep. But perhaps political reporters should ask more questions of campaign strategists about what they are hearing and recording at the door and fewer questions about party standing in the polls.

Prior to the launch of most campaigns in North America, the media insist their reporters and columnists will not become preoccupied with the "horse race coverage" campaign narrative. It is a commitment more honoured in the breach than in the observance. This preoccupation with polls focused on party standing has also given rise to a new subject matter expert – the aggregator, an observer who pulls data from all published opinion research regardless of the source and reports the "mean" result and what that result might produce by way of seats if the results held up on election day. Polls from public research firms no one has ever heard of are routinely afforded front-page treatment in newspapers and, more problematically, are included in the calculations of the aggregators.

In the 2019 federal election, the pollsters themselves had a pretty good campaign in terms of tracking party support on a national basis. The findings of the reputable firms were within the margin of error – even though, in an era where random sampling no longer exists, margin of error disclaimers are meaningless. The "news" stories generated by these polls met the twin news tests of fairness and objectivity. The stories were "accurate." The stories just didn't tell the voters anything of real value.

Why did news organizations afford such coverage weights to horse race polls with national samples that were effectively useless in trying to assess what was happening in specific geographies? The race in Ontario is one example. That an effective and highly respected Conservative MP, Lisa Raitt, was defeated by Liberal newcomer and former Olympian Adam van Koeverden isn't a surprise in and of itself (Tubb 2019), but the fact the election in the Milton riding wasn't even close is.

When a campaign strategist as experienced as Jenni Byrne tells an audience for *The Herle Burly* podcast weeks before voting day that the Conservatives would win somewhere between three and five of Atlantic Canada's thirty-two seats (Herle 2019b), why didn't mainstream media organizations ask the Conservatives how the party planned to form a government if it couldn't win more than a handful of seats in Atlantic Canada (Britneff 2019)?

Trudeau's blackface embarrassment, in terms of coverage weights, was emphatically of significance and potentially decisive in terms of the campaign outcome. The Liberal campaign drilled down to find out what people really thought about the photos. Why didn't the mainstream media?

The significance of the SNC-Lavalin story to both the journalistic and political communities is self-evident. Reporters Robert Fife, Steven Chase, Sean Fine, and Daniel Leblanc received the John Wesley Dafoe Award for Politics at the 2020 National Newspaper Awards, as the citation reads, "for breaking the news that the Prime Minister's Office had pressured the justice minister to abandon prosecution of SNC-Lavalin, and a series of follow-up reports as the ensuing scandal grew" (National Post 2020a). Conservative Party Leader Andrew Scheer was obsessed with the story. Yet the impact of the story on voting intentions is less clear. How much do Canadian media outlets know about public attitudes about the affair? Despite the months-long fixation of Conservative MPs and the media, Hamish Marshall describes SNC-Lavalin as a "big distraction" and insists the story did not have a big impact on voter intentions. His reasoning? The issue had virtually no connection to people's day-to-day lives (Herle 2019a).

By early October, this writer couldn't shake the feeling much of the political communications from party leaders dutifully reported by the political reporters was fundamentally disconnected from voters. As is often the case in elections, the major campaigns were busy trying to buy their votes with the voters' own money through boutique tax cuts. And the campaign press was accurately and dutifully reporting what the party leaders said.

The rhetoric from party leaders seemed based on the mistaken assumption that the constituency a candidate needs to win over to win a party leadership was the same constituency a party leader needed to win over to prevail in a general election. This appeal to the "base" invariably involves "hunting the heuristics," to quote US political consultant Paul Begala (pers. notes). Campaign messages less doctrinaire may be more effective in attracting converts, to continue with Begala's analogy. A majority of Ontarians, for example, expect their federal government to do something to address the challenge of climate change. A majority of Ontarians also expect the federal government to build a pipeline from Alberta to a West Coast port. They don't see an inherent contradiction in those two positions.

Joseph Schumpeter's Creative Destruction and the Mainstream Media

Joseph Schumpeter's "gale of creative destruction" (1942, 84) is buffeting the nation's newsrooms. Technology is destroying the economic model that sustained the old media order. But a core assertion of the global social media titans may present the way forward for mainstream media companies.

If Trump is a digital sorcerer, social media platforms serve as sorcerer's apprentices.

The *Guardian* newspaper, in a piece posted Sunday, 3 November 2019, argued the fact Facebook and Twitter "spread Trump's lies" is one reason why lawmakers in Western liberal democracies must break up the social media giants (Reich 2019). The article declares, "Donald Trump lies like most people breathe." Michael Wolff, author of the bestseller *Siege*, puts it more judiciously when he states the President had a "casual regard for the literal truth" (Wolff 2019, 105).

Facebook CEO Mark Zuckerberg and Twitter's Jack Dorsey don't see that it is the job of their companies to call Trump on the lies. Facebook's further assertion that it will not verify the truth of political ads distributed on its site represents a further challenge for policy-makers in Western liberal democracies.

Democrat presidential aspirant Senator Elizabeth Warren decided to come at the issue head-on. Zeroing in on Facebook's leadership, Warren stated bluntly, "It's up to you whether you take money to promote lies" (Meisenzahl 2019).

The insistence of social media platforms that they have no responsibility to establish the accuracy of any "news" they carry and are not accountable for content on any level raises both challenges and opportunities for legacy media outlets operating in the same media ecosystem.

Because of the insistence they aren't media companies and therefore have no responsibilities for verification, social media platforms can impact political coverage even when the "news" doesn't actually make the "news." The substance of a story may never actually appear in the mainstream media. But the "details" are so widely known among political reporters that the allegation is a matter of discussion and debate.

The 2019 federal election afforded a prime example of how social media can serve this "rumour" public. The source for the narrative was the Buffalo Chronicle, an "offshore" social media news site with a publisher who readily admits his organization will create content for cash (Lytvynenko, Oved, and Silverman 2019; Baudoin-Laarman 2019).

As was the case in the blackface controversy, the allegation focused on Trudeau's time as a teacher at West Point Grey Academy in Vancouver. The online posts suggested the *Globe and Mail* was actively and aggressively pursuing another scandal (Buffalo Chronicle 2019). The blackface precedent added credibility to the – at that point – unsubstantiated allegation regarding the nature of Trudeau's relationship with a student. As Trudeau critic W. Brett Wilson posted: "Where there is smoke, there is often fire … especially in the world of @justintrudeau" (Brett Wilson 2019).

Globe and Mail reporter Marieke Walsh was tasked with asking the Liberal leader whether he had signed a non-disclosure agreement as proof of an out-of-court settlement of a civil case (Ling 2019). Walsh's question allowed other commentators to post comments. Former CBC commentator Robyn Urback, for example, tweeted "this is an extremely interesting exchange, wherein Trudeau says he did not sign a non-disclosure agreement when he left a teaching job mid-year" (Urback 2019). Urback is now a columnist with the *Globe*. At one point, the individual who was headmaster of West Point Grey Academy during the time Trudeau was teaching there issued a statement denying there was ever a scandal and speaking to the circumstances surrounding Trudeau's departure (Owen and Dubois 2020, 68).

In the end, no story ever appeared. As CTV correspondent Glen McGregor noted, "There is zero, zilch, nothing to support the claim that any political party or leader applied to any court during #elxn43 for an injunction against any news organization. That's it"

(McGregor, G. 2019). The allegations were deemed a hoax in a fact check by the international news service AFP (Baudoin-Laarman 2019). The 2020 Digital Ecosystem research "did not find any disinformation or media manipulation campaigns that succeeded in affecting the integrity of the 2019 election" (Owen and Dubois 2020, 8).

That said, the social media exchanges meant the "story" was certainly a preoccupation of political journalists covering the campaign. In a world of #MeToo, it would have been the height of irresponsibility for news organizations not to pursue the second West Point Grey Academy story. And in the not-so-old days, the story would likely have been afforded extensive coverage in *Frank* magazine. But the story, which in the end wasn't a story, was more widely known and discussed among political reporters than might have been the case in a pre-social media world.

The legacy media most certainly makes its share of mistakes.

Post-game analysis sessions in mainstream media newsrooms following the 2019 federal election were likely awkward affairs. There is no ready answer for why the Canadian media didn't know about the repeated instances of Justin Trudeau donning blackface. There is no ready answer for why – given the importance of Canada's relationship with the United States – Canada's political press did not write about the fact Andrew Scheer held dual Canadian-American citizenship when he was a candidate for the Conservative Party leadership. And why was the *Globe and Mail* the only news organization to actually break a story about Scheer's CV? These shortcomings, while significant, are not determinant in terms of media bias.

Harvard professor Thomas Patterson has written about the tendency of political journalists to cover politics from a "game" scheme, whereas voters engage in politics from a "governance" scheme. The journalistic conversation, as a consequence, can be at odds with the voter conversation.

Televised leaders' debates provide an example. Traditionally, political operatives have ascribed importance to televised leaders' debates in any general election, but particularly at the federal level.

In the past, broadcast consortiums were organized to ensure extensive airing of the debates held in each of Canada's two official languages. This time, they were organized by an independent leaders' debate commission, established by the federal government (Government of Canada 2018b).

Political reporters cover the events like judges at a prize fight, looking for the proverbial knockout punch that produced a clear winner. Advance news stories about televised leaders' debates invariably cite the exchange between Liberal leader John Turner and Conservative leader Brian Mulroney in the 1984 English-language debate as a prime example. For the record, I was Mulroney's press secretary at the time, and my recollection is that in the immediate post-game analysis of the Turner-Mulroney exchange, pundits confidently declared there had been no knockout punch. Mulroney, his campaign advisers, and the voting public believed otherwise.

US political consultant Brett O'Donnell worked with George W. Bush in 2004 and prepared Republican nominee Mitt Romney for the 2012 debate with then-president Barack Obama. O'Donnell was brought in to prepare Boris Johnson, when he was Britain's foreign secretary, for the Brexit campaign debates. The American campaign strategist encourages candidates to see televised leaders' debates as messaging opportunities. "My shtick is debates aren't really debates," O'Donnell explained to author and journalist Tim Shipman (2016, 322). "They're not about winning and losing. They are about message and moments" (ibid.). O'Donnell went on to say: "I had to coach those guys into understanding how to drive a message and then creating moments that will dominate the press coverage of the debate" (ibid.).

Boris Johnson came to understand and appreciate O'Donnell's advice to treat every question as a message opportunity.

Conservative Party Leader Andrew Scheer certainly understood what the English-language debate was about as currently constituted. In the opening moments of the debate, Scheer pounced on the first question to deliver a spirited denunciation of Trudeau as unfit for office. The attack lines were carefully scripted to lend themselves to the "clips" that dominate network newscasts and provide the raw material for the ledes of stories carried on the front pages of newspapers. And dominate they did. Scheer won the headline war in the English-language debate. What is less clear is whether Scheer connected as effectively with the voters watching the broadcast.

The English-language debate in 2019 was, in the words of Carleton journalism professor and long-time television news executive Elly Alboim, "an awesome fail" (Alboim 2019h). Alboim tweeted, "This had nothing to do with voters – it was about political bile, TV product and media PR" (ibid.). He continued, "This debate was far from the public service it should have been. The debate commission failed in its responsibility by turning the format over to TV producers –they traded pacing for incoherence. No one had the chance to develop a thought – all it rewarded was one liners" (Alboim 2019g).

That the commission's debates were uneven is self-evident. The English-language debate was roundly criticized. The commission, headed by former governor general David Johnston, was deemed responsible. "The commission handed the debate back to the same type of people to organize and got the same defects as previously existed," Carleton professor Paul Adams posted in a tweet (Adams 2019b).

The broadcast consortium that carried the English-language debate approached the broadcast from a journalistic perspective. The organizers of the French-language debate, in contrast, better understood the experience was about voters not reporters. The French-language commission debate was deemed vastly superior.

The English-language leaders' debate did produce the "news" that Brett O'Donnell's approach is intended to produce and that network executives look for. What the English-language debate failed to produce was the conversation voters were looking for.

The political conversation from the 2019 federal election seemed to disappoint candidates and columnists alike.

Veteran political columnist Andrew Coyne was so unimpressed with the electoral options on offer that in the days before the vote he wrote, "It has been, I think we can all agree, a disgraceful election … [an] intellectually vacuous marshmallow like Andrew Scheer … could not defeat a preening fraud like Trudeau" (Coyne 2019b). If Coyne was unimpressed with the electoral options, a case can be made that readers, listeners, and viewers were equally underwhelmed by much of the campaign coverage.

Mainstream media coverage of the 2019 federal election provided much "news," and the campaign media strategists developed plans to take full advantage of that "news" bias. Conservative Party Leader Andrew Scheer bet big on a predisposition to "said yesterday" style coverage. Scheer didn't even bother to release his party's electoral platform until after the televised leaders' debates. His campaign clearly made a calculation that there would be a minimum price to pay by waiting to roll out the platform rather than subjecting the platform to detailed scrutiny of journalists, the other parties, and other party leaders. And there is some evidence to suggest a significant proportion of the public couldn't care less. The Innovative Research Group posted a tweet stating "While the pundit class analyses the electoral implications of each jot of the campaign, at least half the respondents in our final poll said they had not read, seen or heard anything from each of the six parties" (Innovative Research Group 2019).

By the end of the campaign, Conservative operatives were confident of victory. That optimism slowly deflated as expected gains failed to materialize, especially in Atlantic Canada and the seat-rich suburban 905 area around Toronto, which stubbornly remained Liberal red. In the end, the Liberals dropped twenty seats and were reduced to minority status while the Conservatives picked up twenty-six seats. A resurgent Bloc Québécois enjoyed an electoral renaissance.

The federal Conservatives trumpeted the fact they won more votes than the Liberals as their silver lining in the 2019 result. But as Conservative strategist Dennis Matthews observed, the Tories have become a minority proposition with voters (Matthews 2019b). The Conservatives were nowhere in downtown Montreal, downtown Toronto, and downtown Vancouver. Its party platform included few specifics – other than a declared opposition to any form of carbon tax – on issues such as climate change, public transit, the digital economy, issues of significance to voters in Canada's major metropolitan areas. Echoing David Coletto's mid-campaign assertion, Matthews says values and emotions build political brands (Matthews 2019c). Boutique tax cuts for a 1950s Beaver Cleaver world simply didn't cut it in Le Plateau, Leslieville, or Yaletown.

The post-election political discourse in Canada focused on the alienation in the "Buffalo Republic" of Alberta and Saskatchewan. Premiers Jason Kenney and Scott Moe warned Canadians they had better listen to the frustrated voices from the resource sector or face threats to national unity. The angry voices did shape post-election coverage. "Wexit" became a story of significance.

Voters in the Buffalo Republic are frustrated their aspirations are, in turn, frustrated by voters in Ontario and Quebec – home to a majority of Canadians. Democracies are funny that way. As Obama adviser David Axelrod observed, in politics, you fish where the fish are.

Scheer fired his chief of staff and director of communications after the campaign, blaming the outcome on a communications failure. Like the Strother Martin character in the film *Cool Hand Luke*, Scheer attributed his defeat to a "failure to communicate." It may be more accurate to link the defeat to the Scheer campaign's failure to understand what the Conservative leader was communicating. With respect, a case can be made that Scheer actually did get his message out. Scheer's decision to give the climate change protests a pass and use the occasion to announce more highways for metropolitan Toronto is as tone-deaf and as unaware of the electoral significance of the climate change issue as is possible to an electorate increasingly concerned with environmental issues (Shah 2019b).

In the end, the "human sacrifice" of his senior political staff was not enough to save Scheer's job. And a media strategy was the weapon of choice for the regicide. Aided by an "animus" leak that party funds were being used to cover the cost of sending his kids to private evangelical Catholic schools, Scheer was forced to face the fact he was not going to survive the leadership review process.

The specifics of the payments for Scheer's children to attend private schools were of less significance than the signal the story sent to the party rank and file through the mainstream media that the beleaguered Conservative leader could no longer count on the support of former prime minister Stephen Harper's wing of the party. The signal couldn't have been clearer, the conclusions to be drawn obvious. Quebec partisans were already unhappy with Scheer. Doug Ford's supporters in Ontario were still smarting over the perceived slight of the premier by Scheer and his team during the campaign. During campaign stops in Ontario, Scheer avoided being seen with the province's then-unpopular premier and even had Alberta Premier Jason Kenney campaign for him in Ford's own stronghold of Etobicoke (von Scheel 2019). There was no prospect of Scheer's surviving a leadership review vote if the Harperites were looking for a leadership change as well.

Power, Politics, and the Press

"Any new means of moving information will alter any power structure whatever," Marshall McLuhan observed (1964, 92). Newspapers had precisely the same disruptive effect in an earlier time, and not just in the world of politics but also in the world of markets and finance. Yale economist Robert Shiller states, "The history of speculative bubbles begins roughly with the advent of newspapers" (Shiller 2005, 85). The media, Shiller continued, play a pivotal role in setting the stage for market moves, and then in triggering the moves themselves. News accounts set in motion "a sequence of public attention," Shiller concluded (ibid., 91). The pandemic triggered by COVID-19 – to be addressed in more detail in the next chapter – is a dramatic example.

Media effects theorists, whether of the "administrative" school or the "cultural" school, have examined power – either power in the context of the texts themselves or the power inherent in the distribution of texts.

The mainstream media once controlled the distribution process. The advertising that subsidized the content churned out in the newsrooms was tied directly to that control of the distribution process.

For those communications theorists for whom the real power lies in the distribution of texts, the power of social media platforms such as Facebook and Twitter is self-evident. That Facebook and Google earned the lion's share of digital ad revenue is a direct consequence of that power shift. Social media can also empower individuals. Trump's "power" in part was linked directly to a president's enhanced ability to distribute texts via social media, in the same way radio contributed to a breakthrough in political communications in the 1930s. And how many of us would ever have heard of a Swedish teenager named Greta Thunberg if social media platforms did not give effect to McLuhan's global village?

Legacy media's power of distribution is now limited. Media companies, therefore, will have to shift their value proposition to focus on the power of texts to inform and enlighten.

Media relations strategies are in the end designed to influence the texts and the channels of communication used to distribute those texts. As a result, these strategies are part art and part science. And institutional communications shops, whether political or financial, grew as an industry to feed the beast. The efforts of these practitioners are targeted and, as David Miller and Sally Macintyre (1998) observed, operate in a relatively closed circuit. Social media platforms increased the channels available to message purveyors but the business is fundamentally the same. Communications professionals and the interests they serve – whether institutional or individual – provide the grist for the public discourse mill.

Trump may reflect the post-literate world but the president's power was based in part on his ability to distribute texts and tweets directly to his MAGA voters. Conversely, social media platforms allow the targets of political messages to convey their response to political leaders more immediately, more directly. "Now that couch potatoes have social media, they have risen up and become active, opinionated participants," states Michael Schulman (Schulman 2019, 27).

Walter Lippmann (1922) warned a century ago, "For the most part we do not first see, and then define, we define first and then see."

The earned media strategies of many political campaigns today – whether the 2019 federal election in Canada or the 2020 presidential campaign in the US – are predicated on Lippmann's premise.

Class notes from a course taught at Carleton University by Mary Francoli, now director of its Arthur Kroeger College of Public Affairs, read, "communication of any kind fails if it does not align with the audience's interpretation of reality." Cable news networks such as Fox News or MSNBC are primary venues for creating a certain "interpretation of reality."

Academics have long argued that far from driving bias out of news, competition actually fosters it. Fox News and MSNBC would be but one illustration. Regular viewers of each cable news operation consider the other the home of fake news.

Paul Lazarsfeld and Robert K. Merton (1948) identified the conditions required for media to have an effect on an audience. The first – monopolization – suggests there is little or no opposition to the proposition being advance. The second – canalization – suggests these channels give voice to pre-existing attitudes. The final – supplementation – sees the communicator operating in conjunction with other face-to-face contact. Today's social media platforms make it possible to create Lazarsfeld and Merton's conditions. Further, an individual's media catchment basin is tailored, even idiosyncratic – news outlets of interest, individuals we "follow," the unexpected coming in the form of retweets from accounts we follow.

President Trump, for example, could speak to hosts at Fox News, confident the network would not be giving equal time to his opponents. The voice of Fox is consistent with the voice of its audience. And the president then took that message to large audiences at rallies all over the country so the folks who don red peaked caps emblazoned with Trump's promise to "Make America Great Again" can see their leader up front and personal. Progressives can mount the same campaign on MSNBC.

But for all the claims of campaign operatives about this ability to reach voters with tailored messages via social media platforms, a key constituency among voters is still consumers of editorial content.

Campaigns are won and lost on relatively small shifts among these voters, shifts that can be triggered by the broader media ecosystem.

Much was made of Trump's use of Twitter, but the president was equally conscious of the continuing reach of broadcast media, particularly television.

Before he died, literally on the job, legendary broadcast journalist Tim Russert said in the cable news era, serious politicians spent half their day either "reading, watching, talking to or preparing to talk to the media" (Columbia Journalism Review 2008). The longest-serving moderator of NBC's *Meet the Press*, Russert certainly qualified as a subject matter expert. In an earlier life, Russert had served as chief of staff for former US senator Daniel Moynihan.

Doris Graber concluded, "Television, despite its many serious shortcomings, makes major contributions to political action and to the public's understanding of political issues" (Graber 2001, 128).

British journalist Nik Gowing, in a study of the impact of television on foreign policy discussions written while a fellow at the Shorenstein Center on Media, Politics and Public Policy, concluded, "What appears on television is true and immediate and influences opinion and policy. What fails to appear effectively never happens" (Gowing 1994, 25).

Gowing's conclusion is worthy of consideration in the context of electoral politics. President Trump was seen to be a successful businessperson in no small measure because television told voters that was the case for years. And it is worth noting that in his paid media campaigns – particularly television spots – Democratic Party presidential aspirant Michael Bloomberg, who created the Bloomberg News media empire, took dead aim at this particular piece of political conventional wisdom. In classic political compare and contrast structure, Bloomberg's campaign spots scoffed at suggestions Trump was successful in businesses, with footage of failed enterprises such as Trump Air, while asserting the fact Bloomberg actually built a successful, multi-billion-dollar enterprise (CBS 2020).

Communications scholar Neil Postman made the point that television speaks with one voice: the voice of entertainment. President

Trump's relative incoherence is less problematic in a post-literate world. Bob Woodward, in his 2020 book *Rage*, notes *Dilbert* creator Scott Adams describes the approach as "intentional wrongness behaviour" (Woodward 2020, 58). Trump has demonstrated his ease in communicating in the voice of entertainment. Inspired by Fox host Lou Dobbs, Trump possesses "elementary school eloquence," according to former adviser Steve Bannon (Wolff 2019). Trump's political opponents, such as Hillary Clinton and Representative Adam Schiff, are mocked and rhetorically reduced to put-downs that lend themselves to catchy videos – "Crooked Hillary," "Shifty Schiff."

Lippmann observed the people at whom an earned media campaign is directed are like any other audience – they "engage" differently. The voters whom campaign managers target, the voters most open to conversion, read, watch, and listen less. Even in a social media era, individuals who are the primary targets of earned media campaigns often have lower media consumption habits.

Yet communications scholarship concedes communications processes most likely develop the attitudes and beliefs that affect political behaviour. European officials, for example, "think the tabloid press did more to push the UK out of the EU than anything else" (Wishart 2020, 10).

Today, an increasing number of communications processes are being carried out on the ubiquitous smartphone.

The ever increasing reliance on social media platforms for information is matched by a sharp increase in our collective reliance on mobile devices. In a study entitled "Mobile vs. Computers: Implications for News Audiences and Outlets," Shorenstein Center fellow Johanna Dunaway predicted by 2020, two-thirds of all online activity is expected to take place on mobile devices, and mobile devices are less conducive to the consumption of news (Dunaway 2016, 3). Further, the trend to mobile-only is more pronounced among Latino, Black, and low-income Americans (ibid., 7).

These trends pose a challenge for both journalism and democracy, and an informed citizenry. Dunaway concludes "the knowledge gap between America's most and least politically interested citizens has widened substantially in the last three decades and will widen further as a result of the move to mobile" (ibid., 3).

Political Discourse and Political Communication

In a piece entitled "Boris Johnson Is Headings for a Scorched-Earth Election," opinion writer Jenni Russell suggested, "The simplest way to decipher what's going on in British politics these days is not to believe a word that the prime minister says" (Russell, J. 2019). Johnson, it should be noted, was once fired as a political correspondent for literally making things up and reporting his fantasies as fact (Stubley 2019).

Skepticism in any political exchange is healthy; cynicism is problematic.

There are most certainly indications individuals interested in politics are searching for smart content.

A number of political podcasts informed political discourse during the 2019 federal campaign including former interim Liberal Party leader Bob Rae's *Political Stripes*, veteran journalist Tom Clark's *The Take*, former CBC anchor Peter Mansbridge's *The Bridge*, and *Party Lines*, cohosted by *BuzzFeed News* editor Elamin Abdelmahmoud and the CBC's Rosemary Barton. In fact, eleven million adult Canadians listened to a podcast last year (Canadian Podcast Listener 2019).

Friend and former business partner David Herle is familiar to many Canadians as one of the panellists on the CBC's Insider feature. Political operatives know Herle as chief strategist and campaign chair for former prime minister Paul Martin and Ontario premier Kathleen Wynne. To say Herle can be a controversial figure in the Liberal family is to understate the case. But even those who have been on opposite sides of the partisan wars acknowledge Herle is one of the smartest, most insightful people in Canadian politics.

Herle developed a podcast called *The Herle Burly*, fundamentally conversations with people he thought were interesting: everyone from iconic musician Robbie Robertson to American conservative columnist George Will.

The podcast, launched with limited marketing support and no initial commercial sponsorship, was soon generating 3,000 downloads an episode (pers. conversation with David Herle). But as the 2019 federal election loomed, Herle decided to switch it up a bit. He invited former Paul Martin communications director and celebrated public affairs commentator Scott Reid to join him. Reid is wicked funny and one of those people still in the room when the prime minister or premier thanks the assembled advisers for their advice and wise counsel and retreats to the inner sanctum with the closest confidants.

Herle also reached out to Jenni Byrne, a Conservative strategist of standing who has been on the other side of most of the political wars that Herle has been involved in for the last fifteen years. Byrne, too, knows of what she speaks and has clearly spent much of her professional life setting "the boys" straight, whether in boardrooms or campaign war rooms.

The result was the runaway hit of the campaign, in political media terms. The commentary was as profound as it was profane. In an era when everyone is looking for "authenticity," listeners to *The Herle Burly* heard insights and analysis articulated by three exceptional individuals who eschewed the usual practice of mouthing partisan talking points incessantly while clumsily avoiding the question put.

When Scott Reid talked about heading out to Starbucks in the early hours of the morning to write early drafts of a statement Kathleen Wynne would deliver in the 2018 Ontario election that would concede defeat a week before the campaign was actually over, listeners felt they were sitting on the stool next to him, looking forlornly out the same picture window, waiting for the sun to come up, knowing there were no rays of hope for a win, but maybe, just maybe, official party status could be secured.

Guests such as Dennis Matthews and David Rosenberg peeled back the layers of strategy behind campaign advertising.

Herle kept it all moving with a contagious laugh, blunt assessments, and insights informed in part by his day job as one of the country's best public opinion researchers and in part by a lot of long days driving the backroads of Saskatchewan as a young staffer to then-provincial Liberal leader Ralph Goodale.

By the time the campaign wound up, *The Herle Burly* had attracted 10,000 downloads for each podcast and had attracted commercial sponsors (ibid.). But of more significance, the individuals doing the downloading were the denizens of political Canada, people who live and breathe politics, people whose commitment to politics borders on obsessive compulsive disorder.

Journalism lays claim to a special role in a liberal democracy. The whole rationale in public policy terms for taxpayer support for civic journalism is the centrality of civic journalism to the democratic process. This claim is at the heart of requests to government for tax and regulatory policies to foster civic "journalism." How central the current definition of political news is to democracy is debatable. And if political journalism is not deemed by the public to be either of value or in their interest, what is the rationale for using tax dollars to fund civic journalism?

James Carey encouraged the media to move away from its historic role of informing the public and embrace a new challenge as "an agency for carrying on the conversation of our culture" (Carey 1989). For Carey, John Dewey, and other cultural theorists, the task for journalism is nothing short of the recovery of democracy. To be worthy of this public support – including direct support in the form of tax dollars – mainstream media companies, as Mitchell Stephens suggests, must provide more journalism and less news (Stephens 2014).

On one level, both politicians and the political reporters who cover them would seem to be locked into a conversation the public is both excluded from and has limited interest in.

Consumers will not pay premiums for "said yesterday" news coverage. And even political partisans do not need to pay for subscriptions to news organizations that tout the party line – online organizations such as Canada Proud or Ontario Proud fill that role faster, better, and cheaper. Anyone who wants to know the "news" from Alberta Premier Jason Kenney need only follow Kenney on Twitter. What people might pay for is smart editorial content that flows from Kenney's "news."

The mainstream media offerings too often fall short of the "value" test. The economic challenges facing news organizations are self-evident. Shrinking revenue streams mean shrinking editorial resources. And shrinking editorial resources mean shrinking editorial voices. To argue otherwise is Pollyannaish in the extreme. Mainstream media companies have literally had more than a quarter century to figure out a new business model for the internet era. Federal policy-makers have been known to mutter it isn't Ottawa's job to bail out a failing business model. Fair enough. But it is Ottawa's job to fix the tax and policy decisions that have played a role in creating that failing business model. And there is an element of self-interest in liberal democracies adopting the policies and programs designed to nurture civic journalism. Democracy itself is under siege. Civic journalism, in theory at least, can encourage the civic engagement that is democracy's lifeblood.

Civic journalism is the drinkable water of democracy; without it, liberal democracy simply cannot survive – which for those at the extreme ends of the political spectrum would be a desirable outcome to be sure.

The Trudeau government's fixation with the middle class – and those aspiring to join it – has a particular link to news. As the late Stuart Adam (Adam and Clark 2006) states, news is a particular form of culture, invented by a particular class at a particular point in history – specifically, the middle class as the Industrial Age was taking shape. Journalism may be part of the architecture of modern democracy, as the Thomas Jeffersons of the world asserted, but as the middle class retreats to McJobs in a gig economy, so too does news.

In their seminal work *The Globalization of News*, Oliver Boyd-Barrett and Terhi Rantanen argue the concept of "news" lies at the heart of capitalism (Boyd-Barrett and Rantanen 1998). News, they state, is fundamentally the repurposing of information as a commodity – for the purpose of political communication, trade, and pleasure (ibid., 1). But news repurposed in the interests of capitalism has been displaced as a primary vehicle for trade and commerce by social media platforms. There is no "mass" for the traditional mass media. In a world of social media "influencers," interests with paid messages to convey will always prefer social media platforms.

A report issued in early 2020 entitled "Digital Media at the Crossroads – 2020" analyzes the extent of the "disruption" of the Canadian content ecosystem of digital media (DM@X and Nordicity 2020). The picture for newspapers is grim. Total newspaper ad sales revenue for 2018 was $1.5 billion, down more than 18 per cent from 2016. Revenue from digital advertising is not nearly enough to offset declining print advertising revenues. Facebook and Google continue to dominate the digital ad space. At the *Toronto Star*, the study states, digital advertising has not grown significantly.

Select global brands – the *Guardian*, the *New York Times*, the *Washington Post* – are finding their way, the study states. Paywalls and digital subscriptions are now the norm.

The jobs picture is even more bleak. The study states the number of full-time positions in journalism rose steadily from 1987 to 2013. Today, the reverse is true. Full-time jobs from 2013 to 2018 fell by more than 20 per cent, from 13,000 to 10,200.

Newsrooms, bluntly put, do not reflect the country. Diversity is a major issue facing legacy news organizations.

Some 40 per cent of Canadians use Facebook for news, according to the Nordicity study (ibid., 18), but trust in social media news is generally low. Retired *Globe* reporter Rod Mickleburgh perhaps put it best in a tweet posted Friday, 17 January 2020: "Thanks to the internet, there has never been more facts and information available … Thanks to the internet, there has never been more people who could care less about facts and information. #DumbAndDumber" (Mickleburgh 2020).

The situation is somewhat better in the broadcast segment but the trend lines are not. TV advertising is in decline; it has not collapsed but there is a perception in the industry that it will, according to the Nordicity study.

Even investment guru Warren Buffett is getting out of newspapers. Buffett's love of newspapers goes back to his childhood when he delivered the evening paper door to door. To this day, Buffett takes pride in the accuracy of his toss of a rolled-up paper to the front door. Yet recently, his holding company Berkshire Hathaway sold its thirty-one dailies. "If one of the richest men on the planet has soured on newspapers, what chance do newspapers have?" said Tom Jones of the Poynter Institute, a journalism school and research centre (Smith and Chiglinsky 2020, 25).

Canada and Ontario Proud founder Jeff Ballingall, who once worked for the now defunct Sun News Network, has predicted the mainstream media giants will disappear (Ballingall, J. 2020). Many will. And the outlets left will not be giants. They may have to be national; with pages designated for local coverage in the same way the old *Ottawa Citizen* had "District" pages for stories from Carleton Place to Cobden.

Legacy media outlets may be reluctant to embrace what looks suspiciously like a boutique business. But as mystery novelist Rita Mae Brown once observed, the definition of insanity is "doing the same thing over and over again and expecting a different result" (Sterbenz 2013). Like the Swiss with watches, media companies will have to develop bespoke business models. News, therefore, is now the wrong business for media companies to be in.

News has always been about accuracy, not veracity. CNN media critic Brian Stelter has commented on the preoccupation of news reporters to be seen as neutral, which can lead news professionals to fall into the trap of presenting facts and lies in a reportorial structure that constitutes false equivalency – "the cult of both sides" (Allsop 2019).

News can be made in a tweet. Journalism cannot. Journalism and public engagement may have more, albeit limited, economic potential.

Economist Ronald Coase states, "There is no fundamental distinction between the market for goods and the market for ideas" (cited in Hesmondhalgh 2007). The mainstream media is demonstrably a diminishing choice as a primary site for the marketing of goods. The idea business may have more potential.

Journalism, Carey states, "must be examined as a corpus, not as a set of isolated stories" (Carey 1997, 148). Political journalism needs to focus on that segment of the population with heightened media consumption habits; the individuals who are in the lead position in Lazarsfeld's canonical two-step flow theory of communication, the individuals who decide election outcomes. Political communications will have to respond accordingly.

After Britain's Conservative Party won a crushing election victory, Prime Minister Boris Johnson's campaign guru and chief adviser Dominic Cummings called on "weirdos and misfits" to apply for jobs at 10 Downing Street to work on radical ideas (Syal 2020). Cummings, before being shown the door himself, decided it was time to transform how the UK government is run. A similar transformation in the skill set of the journalists covering this radically different government and the product they produce would seem in order.

If civic journalism is as central to liberal democracy as political theorists insist it is, then Canada cannot count on multinational giants such as Facebook or Twitter to foster a distinctly Canadian conversation of the type James Carey insists is the true calling of journalism. And those distinctly Canadian conversations will require more domestic platforms than the public broadcaster if it is to meet even a minimal test of free speech.

11

The Pandemic, the President, and the Prime Minister

In the second week of March 2020, the earth's axis tilted sharply, signalling more than a change in seasons.

A virus, a coronavirus described in the shorthand of newspaper headlines as COVID-19, was literally sweeping the globe.

The World Health Organization declared a pandemic. People everywhere, at the behest of their governments, were in lockdown; the world economy was literally in shutdown.

Computer and mobile device screens functioned as a collective central nervous system, as we tried to sort out what was happening in Wuhan, China, what exactly is a "wet market," and what in hell bats had to do with anything.

Social support programs of a scope and scale that dwarfed those of the Great Depression were pushed out government doors in days. Because we – collectively, employer and employee alike – sent distress signals that we could not make it to the end of the month without a quick infusion of cash. And by "quick" we meant hours and days, not weeks and months.

Suddenly individuals who work for low hourly wages – grocery store clerks, personal support workers – were deemed frontline workers, heralded for their service by some of the very politicians who in the months and years before had rolled back legislative increases in minimum wage rates and guaranteed paid sick leave.

The digital divide emerged as a factor of some significance, as did gender and race. Public health officials could post daily updates on official sites easily accessed – unless you were homeless or had limited access to the internet.

Communications theorists have long argued that in times of crisis, people look to the news, and the COVID-19 pandemic proved to be no exception.

As tallies of reported cases worldwide moved into the millions and deaths into the hundreds of thousands, news about the pandemic constituted a "media eclipse" defined by communications scholars Mireille Lalancette and Michel Lamy as a news story overshadowing "all other events happening on the planet" (Lalancette and Lamy 2020).

Even the most horrific mass murder spree in modern Canadian history – when a gunman impersonating a police officer went on a shooting spree in central Nova Scotia that left twenty-two victims, including an RCMP officer, dead – created only a partial eclipse of pandemic coverage.

Through the news we learned cocooning had become a way of life, that social distancing was the norm. If you wanted to meet a friend for drinks after work, you snapped a cap, uncorked a merlot, and sat down in front of your iPad or laptop and logged onto Zoom.

Most of the news was less than encouraging. Collectively, we'd forgotten the lessons learned during the SARS outbreak of the early 2000s. There were no cures for COVID-19 (at least not at the beginning), no vaccines, not enough protective equipment for frontline health care staff.

The president of the United States – holding an office that in earlier times might have been looked to for leadership – believed denial was an option, at least until Trump himself tested positive for the virus and, later, his son Donald Jr. did as well.

The news informed us the coronavirus was indiscriminate in infecting people.

Prime Minister Justin Trudeau went into self-isolation when he reported his wife, Sophie Grégoire Trudeau, had tested positive for COVID-19. Trudeau's residence at Rideau Cottage would become familiar to Canadians as he emerged daily to brief the national media.

His Royal Highness Prince Charles, heir to the British throne, was infected, as was his son William, the Duke of Cambridge.

British Prime Minister Boris Johnson required treatment in an intensive care unit. White House staffers also tested positive.

Trapped in their isolation, people wanted information, reliable, factual information, which in turn led to some reordering of "news makers." In a world struggling with a pandemic, expertise mattered, partisan positioning, less so.

Elected officials were front and centre to be sure – Prime Minister Justin Trudeau, Premier François Legault, and Premier Doug Ford for example. But public health officers – Dr Bonnie Henry in British Columbia, Dr Horacio Arruda in Quebec, Dr Deena Hinshaw in Alberta – dominated media coverage. Even when elected officials were present, media queries focused on what political leaders were doing to implement courses of action recommended by public health officials. Josh Greenberg, a professor of communication at Carleton University who focuses on public health, explained, "Ordinary people don't have time for celebrity peacocks when the world is burning" (Porter 2020). As Greenberg's colleague Christopher Dornan observed, "On the plus side, we're hearing next to nothing about the Kardashians these days" (Dornan 2020).

There was discussion and debate about the merits of certain of the recommendations from these public health professionals to be sure. And a fair degree of frustration, even exasperation, over what struck some media observers as inconsistencies in the medical advice and recommendations.

What was a little different this time in terms of public reaction is that because so many individuals were working from home and were online, they were in a position to watch the mainstream media at work. Reviews were mixed, at best, and because of social media platforms, these criticisms of journalistic performance received wider circulation than would have been the case in an earlier time.

The months and years ahead will be given over to debate and discussion about how we intend to organize ourselves politically, economically, and socially once the all-clear sounds on the current pandemic.

A consensus has already emerged that things will never go "back to normal," that at a minimum we will collectively be dealing with a "new normal" at best. Will we ever again agree to be wedged like a sardine into commercial airliners? Will we ever again sit right next to another person in a theatre? Will a crowded bar retain its appeal? How inclined will we be to get on the subway at rush hour? Will there be a rush hour, or will people who work in the knowledge economy keep working from home?

With the multiplicity of bailout programs for entrepreneurs and employees alike, have we all become wards of the state in fact, if not in theory? Is big government back? What will global supply chains look like going forward? What do we think about foreign investment laws? Competition laws? Privacy laws? The FAANGs?

Debates around these foundational issues will be spirited, immediate, interconnected, and protracted. Media, both social and legacy, will be a site for these debates.

As the pandemic dragged on, the primacy of legacy and mainstream media was reasserted, long-standing media effects theories were revisited, and most significantly the role of media "gatekeepers" was restored.

Consider the case of Donald John Trump.

Presidents of the United States arguably have more ability than any other political figure on the planet to make news, and Donald Trump is no exception. As the *New York Times* reported 25 April 2020, "Trump's single best advantage as an incumbent – his access to the bully pulpit" (Martin, J. and Haberman 2020). But the reporters on the story conclude that access "has effectively become a platform for self-sabotage" (ibid). Boorstin (1962) concluded celebrities will ultimately be destroyed by what makes them – publicity. And Trump, the celebrity TV president, quickly became the current proof point of Boorstin's theory.

Trump, as the record shows, dismissed the risk posed by the coronavirus in the early going. In late February 2020, for example, Trump was laying claim to "a pretty good job we've done" based on his assertion there were only "15 people" with COVID-19 in

America and "the 15 within a couple of days is going to be down to close to zero" (Blake 2020).

In fact, by the end of April 2020, there were in excess of one million cases in America, with more than 60,000 deaths (Winsor and Shapiro 2020) and with epidemic modelling forecasting rising totals for both that would put the lie to Trump's prediction of a quick end to the pandemic (New York Times 2020a).

Trump was counting on a robust American economy to carry him to re-election in November 2020. But by 30 April 2020, more than thirty million Americans had applied for unemployment insurance in just six weeks (Cox 2020). Stock markets were off sharply. And economists were saying we had only just begun to feel the effects of the most abrupt shock to the global economy in modern history. Suddenly, Trump's standing with voters as measured in public opinion polls took a turn for the worse (Panetta 2020).

Prior to the pandemic, Trump's communications tools of choice were Twitter, Facebook, and mass rallies. When the president could no longer stage rallies, he decided to break with past practice and hold daily news conferences in the White House – news conferences he used for re-election, rather than crisis leadership purposes.

Initially, the legacy media were criticized for airing Trump's revisionist musings live and unchallenged to a worried population. Critics argued the uncritical coverage of Trump's messages constituted a free time political broadcast. Democratic nominee Joe Biden, they said, should be afforded equal time. Yet as the presidential press conferences continued, opinion as to the president's effectiveness began to shift.

An analysis by three *New York Times* reporters merits detailed consideration. The report states, "The transcripts show striking patterns and repetitions in the messages he has conveyed, revealing a display of presidential hubris and self-pity unlike anything historians say they have seen before. By far the most recurring utterances from Mr. Trump in the briefings are self-congratulations, roughly 600 of them, which are often predicated on exaggerations and falsehoods" (Peters, Plott, and Haberman 2020).

In time, presidential malapropisms proved determinant.

Trump's musings about the potential benefit of a little sunshine as a virus-fighting tool or chugalugging Lysol as a possible cure will likely emerge as the most oft-cited (Broad and Levin 2020), his subsequent insistence he was only kidding notwithstanding.

New York Times columnist Thomas Friedman wrote, "The Trump daily briefing has itself become a public health hazard" (Friedman 2020). Added toxicologists at Harvard in a tweet, "Please don't inject bleach or drink disinfectant. Bleach injections cause hemolysis (where your red blood cells that carry OXYGEN break apart) and cause liver damage, and many disinfectants can cause dangerous burns or bleeding in your stomach. This tweet IS medical advice" (Harvard University 2020).

Stung by the criticism, Trump, predictably, moved to an attack footing couched in his "fake news" frame. But again, Trump tripped on his own tweets when he wondered when will "all of the 'reporters' who have received Noble Prizes for their work on Russia, Russia, Russia, only to have been proven to be totally wrong (and in fact, it was the other side who had committed the crimes) be turning back their cherished 'Nobles'" (Breuninger 2020). As CTV correspondent Glen McGregor responded, "A tweet storm complaining about a prize with a name he can't spell correctly and isn't a journalism award" (McGregor, G. 2020). Trump subsequently deleted the "Noble" tweets.

The president also resurrected his attack line of the media as the enemy of the people. Trump tweeted, "There has never been, in the history of our Country, a more vicious or hostile Lamestream Media than there is right now, even in the midst of a National Emergency, the Invisible Enemy!" (Trump 2020b).

A political truism holds that governments in trouble need to identify an external enemy as well. For Trump, on multiple policy fronts that external enemy was China. The president positioned his decision to shut down most travel to the United States from China as illustrative of the effectiveness of his administration's handling of the pandemic. The "box score" of cases and deaths carried on the nation's front pages and network nightly newscasts told another story.

Unfortunately for the president, his aides and advisers began to believe his daily news conferences were hurting the president's chances of re-election more than the appearances were helping. The president himself took to Twitter to describe the news conferences with the "Lamestream Media" as not worth the time and effort (Trump 2020a).

Trump, not surprisingly, was sticking to the message track that was fundamental to his electoral success: I/we've built the most successful economy of the world – with this pandemic we are the victims of a foreign regime – and the lamestream media with their fake news is the enemy of the people. Unfortunately for Trump, in a time of pandemic the people of America were increasingly looking to their president for something else: think Winston Churchill after Dunkirk in the Second World War or the community leaders of Gander, Newfoundland, after 9/11.

Oklahoma Republican Representative Tom Cole may have put his finger on a more fundamental problem for President Trump in political communication terms. In a crisis, like the pandemic, "you've got to have some hope to sell people," Cole said (Martin, J. and Haberman 2020). "But Trump usually sells anger, division and 'we're the victim'" (ibid.). In Canada, the opposition Conservatives having settled on a "grievance" narrative as well faced the same challenge.

New York Times columnist David Brooks describes the discourse divide this way: "Even in a pandemic there are weavers and rippers" (Brooks 2020). Weavers, states Brooks, "try to spiritually hold each other so we can get through this together. The rippers, from Donald Trump on down, see everything through the prism of politics," and attach a premium to division. "Fortunately, the rippers are not winning. America is pretty united right now," Brooks concludes.

As were Canadians in the early weeks of the lockdown, although the "rippers" were still generating significant news coverage. Opposition MPs found themselves in a peculiar position. The "weavers" expected them to be supportive of emergency measures intended to provide immediate relief. The "rippers" expected opposition MPs to be more aggressive in holding a minority government to account. Individual MPs chafed at being positioned as a human kiosk for the "Service Canada" expectations of their constituents. Yet the dearth of alternative program proposals underscored the fact political parties have become vehicles for fundraising and communications aimed at "the base" at the expense of policy development, a pertinent and valuable public service.

Certain Canadians echoed Trump's analysis that blame for the pandemic lies squarely with the People's Republic of China. The Trudeau government was roundly criticized for its failure to close Canada's borders to travellers from China early on, with Health Minister Patty Hajdu accused by a *Globe and Mail* columnist of "gaslighting" Canadians as an apologist for the Communist regime (Urback 2020).

The conflict between hope rhetoric and attack rhetoric infected political discourse in troubling ways in some instances. There are examples of similar coded language in Canadian political discourse. Michelle Rempel Garner, the Conservative Party's health critic, dismissed the federal government's vaccine strategy as "just murder" (Lem 2020) – which by any objective measure would meet Jared Kushner's test of "controversy elevates message" (Woodward 2020, 288).

In dog whistle terms, Rempel Garner's question to Health Minister Patty Hajdu whether what the minister was really saying was that "Mexicans will receive a vaccine against COVID-19 before Canadians" (Smith, V. 2020) certainly qualified, as Mexico's ambassador to Canada Juan José Gómez Camacho noted when he called Rempel Garner out on Twitter, stating, "Mexico has worked hard to ensure equitable access to vaccines for all. We believe a pandemic is a time to promote solidarity, rather than showing selfishness, which could endanger us all" (Gómez Camacho 2020).

The attacks took on a particular personal dimension, especially those aimed at Dr Theresa Tam, Canada's chief public health officer. The dog whistle messaging targeted Tam's ethnicity.

Alberta Premier Jason Kenney launched an early, personal attack when questioned about Canada's failure to close borders. "This is the same Dr Tam who is telling us that we shouldn't close our borders to countries with high levels of infection and who in January was repeating talking points out of the [People's Republic of China] about the no evidence of human-to-human transmission" (Wherry 2020a).

Kenney's comment is classic dog whistle, his words carefully selected, the "studied ambiguity" referred to earlier in this work that allows for a subsequent proclamation of innocence (Haney López 2014, 130). Not that Kenney's attack went unchallenged. *Maclean's* columnist Scott Gilmore tweeted, "Most Canadian politicians would consider accusing a Chinese-Canadian civil servant of taking guidance from Beijing to be a pathetic slur and too low to stoop. For Jason Kenney, it's just another talking point" (Gilmore 2020).

Federal Conservative leadership aspirant Derek Sloan raised the rhetorical stakes further. Sloan asked of Dr Tam, "Does she work for Canada or for China?" (Boutilier 2020a). Sloan also said Dr Tam "has failed Canadians … Dr. Tam must go! Canada must remain sovereign over decisions. The UN, the WHO and Chinese Communist Propaganda must never again have a say over Canada's public health!" (Sloan 2020a). When challenged, Sloan decided to double down: "We got Dr. Tam who dutifully repeats the propaganda of a CCP government obsessed with political control and saving face. She does this because she is involved with an organization, the WHO, which is effectively controlled by that government … Dr. Tam must now either resign or be fired … Canada's Chief Public Health Officer needs to work for Canada. Not for the WHO or any other foreign entity." (Sloan 2020b). Perhaps the most significant consideration from his attack on Dr Tam was the deafening silence from the party leadership, including other leadership candidates.

David Brooks's societal descriptive of weavers and rippers (Brooks, 2020) also has implications for media coverage of the pandemic. Analysis of Canadian public opinion in the early weeks of the pandemic suggests people, in the main, were satisfied with the way governments, public health authorities, and political leaders were responding (Bricker 2020). In fact, certain political leaders –

Prime Minister Justin Trudeau, Ontario Premier Doug Ford, and Saskatchewan's Scott Moe – saw significant improvements in their personal ratings (Benzie 2020).

There were sharp and deep concerns to be sure, the high death toll of senior citizens in long-term care facilities being one obvious example. Post-pandemic commissions of inquiry and investigation are a given. But the public, in the early stage, was more focused on solutions than shortcomings. Finger pointing can wait, posing a challenge for media who are in the finger pointing business.

The bias of news is as significant a factor in the coverage of pandemics as it is in political coverage generally. The public considered the pandemic in the context of Ulrich Beck's "risk society" (Beck 1986), a forest story. People were looking to their governments for specifics as to how these governments were systematically meeting the pandemic challenge. The media's daily coverage adopted a crisis news frame, highlighting the trees: how many cases, how many deaths and where? The public wanted to know if we were making any progress in "flattening the curve," the media wanted to know why a decision taken on a Tuesday hadn't been taken a week earlier. In the fall of 2020, as people the world over faced the medical and mental challenges of the "second wave," the availability of vaccines emerged as the dominant story line. The media coverage of the Trudeau government in the main was confrontational, even accusatory, and occasionally irresponsible.

There were other, distinct challenges for media in terms of news coverage.

To state the obvious, it is difficult to cover the most significant human interest story during a time when contact with humans is so severely limited. Reporters, like everyone else, were restricted in their movements. The relative isolation breeds a reliance on traditional sources, the proverbial "knowns." Outliers and contrarians were identified, their challenges of existing protocols and procedures duly reported. Dr Samir Sinha, director of geriatrics at Toronto's Mount Sinai Hospital, for example, warned families of the risk loved ones were facing in seniors' residences (Picard,

A. 2020) before the full extent of that tragedy in Ontario and Quebec became known. Dr Sinha's provocative comments were, by his own description, intended to send the kind of signal to others in the type of elite discourse network identified by Aeron Davis.

In a piece carried in the 15 April edition of the *National Post*, McGill's Andrew Potter made the point it is not a crime to disagree with health officials, and that Canada "needs more contrarian thinking on coronavirus pandemic measures" (Potter 2020). Yet readers, viewers, and listeners chaffed at the tone and tenor of some of the media coverage that reflected the kind of contrarianism Potter argues Canada needs. "People are fed up with the media for many reasons," posted Bill Brady (Brady 2020). "They are snarky, focused on gotcha movements, pretend they speak on behalf of Canadians, have inherent bias ..."

Thomas Patterson's "negative bias" of news is a factor (Patterson 2016). News stories by definition seize on what is wrong, what isn't working, who didn't get a cheque, what employer isn't eligible for a pandemic bailout. By the middle of May 2020, nearly eight million Canadians had applied for just one federal assistance program, the Canada Emergency Response Benefit – out of a total population of thirty-eight million. People who applied on a Tuesday reported the money was in their bank accounts on Thursday, a remarkably efficient distribution of funds. By way of comparison, an individual would be hard pressed to get their own money out of an investment account in less than four working days. At the same time, 1.7 million employees were having their wages subsidized by Ottawa (Government of Canada 2020). News accounts didn't report the successes. Yet over time, newscasts, news stories, and interviews on public affairs television and radio featured those for whom the process had proved to be less than seamless. Understandable from a news perspective. Irritating for governments seeking to reassure.

The media preoccupation with "tick-tock" stories – who did what, when – take on a particular significance during a pandemic. Media queries focus on what did you know, when did you know it, and what did you do about it? The ensuing narrative reflects a story arc of public health authorities playing catch-up ball, with a subtext certainly worth pursuing around whether the Chinese government had been as forthcoming with the world as was necessary. The *Daily Mail* reported on 2 May 2020 that an alleged intelligence briefing for the "Five Eyes" – the United States, the United Kingdom, Australia, Canada, and New Zealand – concluded China "lied about the human-to-human transmission of coronavirus, made whistleblowers disappear, and refused to help nations develop a vaccine" (Sharp, Elsom, and Tapsfield 2020). The report was leaked initially to Murdoch media in Australia, then recycled though the Murdoch-controlled Fox News network in the United States. It was also, according to the *Daily Beast*, completely bogus (Banco, Rawnsley, and Cartwright 2020). *Guardian* columnist Kevin Rudd insists the report, widely dismissed as "fake news," was all in aid of getting Trump re-elected (Rudd 2020).

Social media commentary differentiated between health reporters and the political press. The *Globe and Mail* is a net beneficiary from the insights and expertise of health reporter André Picard, an eight-time nominee for the National Newspaper Awards and past recipient of a Michener Award for public service journalism. Picard, it should be noted, has been a staff reporter at the *Globe* since 1987. Reviews of the political press were less flattering. The criticism notwithstanding, a consensus emerged Canadians need the media in this time of turmoil.

Like Trump, Prime Minister Justin Trudeau met the media daily, but took a decidedly different approach from a political communications perspective. Trudeau's strategy flowed from an acknowledgement of the importance of the symbolic arena in challenging times.

When his wife Sophie Grégoire Trudeau tested positive for COVID-19, Trudeau self-isolated with his family at his Ottawa residence at Rideau Cottage. Media availability sessions were scheduled for mid-morning, and in addition to the message of the day, Trudeau communicated a broader message about the need for social distancing and self-isolation. Once Grégoire Trudeau was cleared and she and the family headed to the second official residence at Harrington Lake, Trudeau remained at Rideau Cottage, by way of reinforcing the message that everyone with the ability to work from home should do precisely that.

Trudeau's daily appearances irritated critics, who wondered why he wasn't going in to work as was the case for other ministers, notably Deputy Prime Minister Chrystia Freeland. Trudeau, they argued, was using his daily media session to avoid tough questions from opposition parliamentarians. But in a world where eye trumps ear, what Canadians saw every day of the crisis was a prime minister patiently answering reporters' questions, including the questions that would have benefitted from some more thought in advance. And the strategy worked for a while. However, a year later, the Rideau Cottage media availability sessions were communicating something else entirely – that after a calendar year, the Canadian government had not made sufficient progress in dealing with the pandemic to allow the prime minister to go to his office – not exactly the message a political leader wants to convey.

The prime ministerial media availability sessions were followed each day by a news conference, led by Freeland, along with Dr Tam and a rotating coterie of cabinet ministers responsible for the policy areas or program specifics being rolled out. Trudeau was predisposed to leaving media queries on specifics to his ministers. But every once in a while, Trudeau would cut to the chase with a simple, straightforward declaration intended for us all. "Enough is enough. Go home and stay home" being but one example (Chase and Dickson, 2020). We should not have "soldiers taking care of seniors" another (Berthiaume 2020).

National Post columnist John Ivison learned firsthand lessons about the perils of being judged a "ripper" by "weavers" (Brooks 2020). The veteran political journalist penned a column that appeared under a headline that read, "John Ivison: Trudeau's Lavish Handouts Risk Turning Workers into Welfare Slackers" (Ivison 2020). The words "lavish" and "slackers" never actually appear in Ivison's piece, a point lost on the editor who crafted the headline and attributed the descriptive to the *Post* columnist. Ivison's musings did not occur in isolation. Former Tory cabinet minister and journalist Peter Kent articulated the challenge as "finding the precarious balance between emergency support … and human nature" (Kent 2020). Conservative Party finance critic Pierre Poilievre dismissed the various aid packages as "a gigantic experiment in *Freakonomics*" (Breen 2020). A working group at the C.D. Howe Institute that suggested Trudeau's programs create conditions for moral hazard was a source for Ivison's musings, none of which saved Ivison from the social media equivalent of a medieval stoning. Ivison was trending within minutes of his story being posted, he was attacked personally, and held accountable for all the corporate sins – real and imagined – of his employer, Postmedia. And in the following days, when the Canadian Press reported Postmedia would be seeking at least $20.3 million in coronavirus-related wage subsidies, howls of outrage at the company's perceived hypocrisy were posted on Twitter.

Canadians, in the main, were prepared to let governments at all levels get on with the job of dealing with the pandemic. Support for virtually every government – both federal and provincial, as measured in published public opinion polls – grew through the early weeks of the COVID-19 crisis. The federal Liberals, for example, had the support of 40 per cent of respondents to a poll conducted by Abacus published 23 June 2020 – an 11-point lead over the Opposition Conservatives (Anderson and Coletto 2020b). Abacus notes that just prior to the pandemic, the Liberals and the Conservatives were within a point of each other in published polls (ibid.). The Liberals led every age group, and among both women and men, in the Abacus poll of 2,979 respondents conducted between 12 June 2020 and 21 June 2020 (ibid.).

And then along came the WE Charity controversy. The "rippers" had their issue.

The specifics were featured in lead items on national newscasts and splashed across the front pages. The government had set up a $900 million-plus program to help students who weren't likely to find summer jobs given government decisions to put the economy fundamentally into an induced coma. The Trudeau government subsequently announced officials had reached out to the WE charity to administer the program through a contribution agreement, and not through a competitive process (CBC 2020c). The charity was asked to connect tens of thousands of students with volunteer opportunities. Each student would be paid for blocks of hours worked – roughly $10 an hour (McGregor, J. 2020). Some 35,000 individuals applied for the program in the week following the announcement (CBC 2020c). WE Charity was to receive $43.53 million to administer the effort, with $8.75 million of that amount eligible for sharing with partnering charities (ibid.).

Given the scope, scale, and time constraints, the federal government insisted WE Charity was the only entity with the organizational heft to take on the assignment (Tasker 2020a). Other charities (CBC 2020c) and the union representing federal government works begged to differ (Public Service Alliance Canada 2020).

The "rippers" pounced. Seizing on the close ties between the Trudeau family and the charity, Opposition MPs accused the federal government of playing favourites. The charity, they insisted, was in dire financial straits and had been bailed out by their Liberal friends with a billion-dollar untendered contract. And in the case of former finance minister Bill Morneau, the opposition attacks were more focused and personal. Morneau, they said, was in a direct conflict – the charity had paid $41,000 to cover the costs of a trip Morneau and his family had made to Kenya in the summer of 2017 and a trip to Ecuador later in the year (CBC 2020c).

Daily headlines trumpeted the "wiggle" disclosures needed to give the story legs. The prime minister's mother, Margaret Trudeau, had been paid some $250,000 in fees for speaking at WE events (ibid.). His brother Alexandre received a further $32,000 for speaking at eight events (ibid.). The prime minister's wife, Sophie Grégoire Trudeau was identified as a host of a podcast for the group entitled WE Well-Being (ibid.). The charity also paid out $200,000 to cover expenses incurred by the prime minister's mother, his brother, and his wife (ibid.).

Morneau's daughter, it was reported, worked for the charity in the travel department (ibid.). A second daughter had appeared at WE Day events (ibid.). And when both Trudeau and Morneau acknowledged they had not recused themselves from the cabinet discussion to hand the program over to WE Charities to run, the Conservative and NDP MPs decided they had everything they needed to ask Ethics Commissioner Mario Dion to launch an investigation into allegations of a conflict of interest (ibid.).

Commons committees demanded the prime minister and Morneau appear for questioning (CBC 2020b). Certain of Trudeau's cabinet ministers were less than sure-footed before the Commons committee. Certain of the public servants summoned to appear were underwhelmed (Emmanuel 2020).

The Opposition's media strategy was effective much of the time, although on occasion, certain of the charges reflected the old adage "never let the facts get in the way of a good story." Certain pundits mocked Morneau and Trudeau with a disdain the scribes wore well. There was talk of the government falling. The Trudeau government's decision to prorogue Parliament didn't remove the saga from the front pages.

Both Trudeau and Morneau apologized for not recusing themselves from the cabinet discussion. Morneau immediately reimbursed the charity the full $41,000 of expenses incurred by himself and his family (CBC 2020c).

The political price exacted from the Liberals was both immediate and significant. The spring party's boomlet of support with the voting public evaporated. Once again working Canadians were left to wonder how any person could lose track of who paid for what for trips to Kenya and Ecuador – countries few Canadians will ever see in their lifetimes. And they weren't sure how the prime minister could be unaware of the fees members of his family were receiving for appearances.

By the end of August, Morneau's career in elected politics was over. He resigned his seat as MP for Toronto Centre and tendered his resignation as the country's minister of finance scant hours after an August meeting with the prime minister (Zimonjic and Cochrane 2020). Morneau said he would pursue the secretary general's position with the Organisation of Economic Co-operation and Development (ibid.), a campaign Morneau later abandoned.

The controversy spelled the end of WE activity in Canada. Co-founders Marc and Craig Kielburger decided to wind down activities at home, and that the fallout from the controversy made fundraising difficult (Tasker 2020b).

In November 2020, Ethics Commissioner Dion dropped his investigation into Morneau's trips. "I am of the view that you did not accept a gift from WE Charity," Dion's ruling states (Tasker 2020c). "I accept that you genuinely believed you had paid for the entire cost of both trips, including the portion of the trip that involved the use of non-commercial chartered aircraft" (ibid.). Dion did say he would continue his investigation as to whether Morneau breached the Conflict of Interest Act by failing to recuse himself from cabinet deliberations (ibid.).

Matthew Torigian, a former police officer and former deputy solicitor general of Ontario, was retained by a board member of WE's American charity to conduct a review of over 5,000 pages of documents related to the case. In an opinion piece carried in the *Toronto Star*, Torigian concludes, "The case is clear: WE Charity was not looking for a lifeline. It didn't get special treatment. It was properly approached by the bureaucracy. And neither the charity nor its co-founders stood to profit from the CSSG [Canada Student Service Grant] ... But a story like that doesn't sell papers or threaten to bring down a government" (Torigian 2020). A former chief of police in Waterloo, Ontario, Torigian cited his extensive experience overseeing hundreds of complex investigations. He concluded Morneau's demise "was one of many casualties of the rush to judgment made by politicians, the media, and ordinary Canadians about the awarding of the Canada Student Service Grant (CSSG) to WE Charity" (ibid.). "The biggest casualty, of course, was WE Charity itself."

Media critics, including *Canadaland*, who played a major role if not the leading media role in the WE Charity saga, criticized the

Star for not making it clear Torigian's work had been commissioned by a party with a vested interest in WE. *Canadland*'s Jesse Brown tweeted, "This is a humiliating degradation of the Toronto Star, @IreneGentle. The 'exonerating' reports were commissioned by the Stillman Foundation. You do not disclose that David Stillman was a member of WE Charity's board and a major WE donor" (Brown, J. 2020).

What the media didn't do is challenge Torigian's work.

By the fall of 2020, the Trudeau government appeared to have weathered the WE Charity storm, at least politically. An Abacus poll in November 2020 suggested the Liberals had established a comfortable eight-point lead over the Opposition Conservatives among decided respondents – 38 per cent to 30 per cent – support that in a general election would put the Liberals in majority government territory (Anderson and Coletto 2020a). The WE Charity controversy was less determinant in terms of voters than the media coverage weights would suggest.

News consumers were familiar with the "woulda, coulda, shoulda" specifics of the Morneau saga in particular. A narrative built on the assertion Morneau had used his position to personal advantage in the end was rejected by many. The coverage from Ottawa-based reporters adopted a "game" schema, the narrative evolving around questions of the political impact of the controversy, an impact that had relatively little to do with the daily lives of people, unless you were a student looking for a summer job or had some connection to the WE Charity.

The controversy that emerged in the fall of 2020 over the timing and availability of COVID-19 vaccines was altogether different. Canadians, like the rest of the world, had been locked down for months. Early successes in containing the spread of the virus and a consequential relaxing of contact rules led to a second wave that was far more serious and deadly. Opposition Leader Erin O'Toole made it clear as far as the Conservative Party was concerned, the distribution plan for the vaccines was everything. In his response to the Trudeau government's economic update 30 November 2020,

O'Toole said, "Without a plan for vaccines, there can be no long-term plan for our economy" (CBC 2020d).

The media adopted a "game" schema for the vaccine story, a narrative focused on how many vaccines were available in Canada, how many vaccines had been administered, and how did those totals compare to the situation in other countries including Israel, Australia, the United Kingdom, and particularly the United States. It was also a story that had a direct impact on the entire population, and if the first test of media effects is relevance, it is hard to imagine a more relevant story. The prime minister admitted that a lack of manufacturing capability might result in Canada and Canadians being at the back of the line in terms of access to the vaccine (Boyd 2020). The governing Liberals tried to blame previous Conservative governments for policy and funding decisions that took the federal government out of the vaccine manufacturing business (Lum 2020). The strategy was as ineffective as it was ill-considered. First, the public has no tolerance for incumbents who look to the past to ascribe blame. Voters believe they have already held elected officials accountable for past failings by voting the previous government out of office. For voters, the instruction is simple: you asked for the job, we gave you the job, so do the job. And the defence rings particularly hollow when the current government has been on the job for five years.

As long-time Liberal strategist and *The Herle Burly* podcast host David Herle warned, "Every day that a vaccine is being distributed in the U.S. but not in Canada will be the worst day of the Trudeau government's life" (Herle 2020d).

Through 2020, the pandemic surfaced certain clear patterns. The public valued expertise – in public health officers, in political leaders, and in journalists providing the media coverage deemed essential.

Ironically, the very pandemic that heightened citizen desire for an informed media threatened the very existence of that media. In the spring of 2020, former Torstar board chair John Honderich reported readers were coming to the *Star*'s website in record numbers; the number of unique site visits was at near record highs, as were subscriptions. "You are proving all the research that says that in times of crisis readers usually turn to 'legacy media'" (Honderich 2020a). The *Star*, as a public service, placed much of the paper's COVD-19 coverage outside paywalls, even as advertising revenues evaporated. Postmedia reported "huge declines" in ad revenues (Sagan 2020).

In the UK, a poll concluded the *Guardian*'s coverage of the pandemic was substantially better than coverage in any other British newspaper (Waterson 2020a). But in a story carried in the 19 April 2020 edition of the paper, *Guardian* columnist Jane Martinson warned "we must act before the coronavirus sinks the press as we know it" (Martinson 2020). Added former *Globe* journalist Mathew Ingram, "for some this could become an extinction event" (Ingram 2020). In the first two months of the coronavirus crisis, more than 30,000 media employees in the United States had been subjected to layoffs, pay cuts or furloughs, Gannett reported (Boehmer 2020). One of those was Joe Sonka of Louisville's *Courier Journal* who won a Pulitzer in early May for revealing the scandals hidden in an outgoing Kentucky governor's pardons and was scheduled to begin his second stint of unpaid furlough the following week (Lexington Herald Leader 2020).

On Saturday, 2 May 2020, the publishers of Canada's major newspapers sent an urgent message to the Trudeau government. A joint editorial, signed by Torstar CEO John Boynton, stated, "Around the world, governments are moving to correct an historical inequality that dates back to the birth of digital platforms" (Toronto Star 2020).

Citing precedents in France and Australia, where governments were moving to stop Facebook and Google from exploiting tax loopholes and making billions of dollars off the backs of original content producers, Boynton called on Canada's federal government to follow suit. "The situation is urgent, with media companies suffering huge advertising revenue declines because of the coronavirus pandemic" (ibid.). Both France and Australia had declared their determination to have appropriate measures in place by July. "That means paying for copyrighted content and sharing the advertising dollars and data that flow from it." Boynton's editorial concluded, "The model exists. The need is clear. Let's apply those principles of fairness in Canada, and do it now" (ibid.).

Newspaper operators the world over believe they are bearing the cost of good journalism. The "Cairncross Review" in the UK, for example, suggests a tax be levied against digital platforms like Facebook to fund payments to the news organizations that supply them with local public interest news content (Cairncross Review 2019). In the UK, facing a government crackdown triggered by its dominant position in online advertising, Facebook announced an agreement with mainstream news outlets that will pay them millions a year to license articles (Waterson 2020b). Facebook curators will select what they consider the main stories of the day. Facebook will determine what stories to select based on how deeply sourced the work is, how timely, whether it offers an interesting angle. In other words, Facebook would seem to be signalling its intent to pay for original reporting. Articles selected will appear in a dedicated section on Facebook.

Globe columnist Andrew Coyne, a model of consistency on the issue, argues Google and Facebook aren't the cause of the newspaper industry's ills and taxing them won't solve the problem. "What will? Making better newspapers, and convincing people to pay for them. I wish it were more complicated, but it isn't," Coyne concludes (Coyne 2020).

At the *Toronto Star*, Coyne's challenge will be taken up by new owners. As markets closed Tuesday, 26 May 2020, Torstar chair and former publisher John Honderich announced the company had been sold to the private equity firm NordStar Capital for just under $52 million (Rubin 2020). "While it is far from easy, the time has come to pass the torch," Honderich said in a column carried on the *Star*'s front page (Honderich 2020b). "The torch, in this case, is control of the *Toronto Star, Hamilton Spectator, Waterloo Region Record, St. Catharines Standard*, three other dailies, some 70 weeklies and a host of digital and special investments" (ibid.). Former Trudeau adviser Gerald Butts tweeted, "The end of the last progressive

Canadian daily newspaper. It had become inevitable I suppose, but still sad to see it happen. #RIP" (Butts 2020). Butts's tweet triggered a few arched eyebrows among *Star* supporters. Butts, a former principal secretary in the Prime Minister's Office, was on the receiving end of numerous representations from print media leaders, including leaders from the *Star*. Butts, it was said, offered the industry everything short of real help.

The *Toronto Star* has long been one of Canada's largest-circulation newspapers. As a former *Star* correspondent, the fact the sale price is but a fraction of what the company was worth a decade earlier stings. The paper's financial circumstances have been deteriorating steadily. COVID-19 began to impact results late in the first quarter. "The problems intensified as March turned to April," the company said (Jones, J. 2020). The new owners Jordan Bitove and Paul Rivett believe a private entity structure is better suited to meet the challenges ahead. "The harsh realities of the news media business are ill-suited to the quarter-bound short-term focus of shareholders. A private structure is needed and we have the patience and willingness to invest in Torstar's long-term transformation," the new owners said in a joint statement (Rubin 2020). Added Bitove, "We believe in news. With this transaction we can ensure a future for world-class journalists and world-class journalism befitting the paper's storied history" (ibid.).

In presentations prepared for corporate clients all over the world, economic forecasters at global consulting firms are agreed the pandemic has already produced a recession, with the rate of economic decline expected to be three times what it was after the 2007–09 Great Recession. A report from the McKinsey & Company, for example, addressed the prospect of "permanent and possibly irreversible damage" to our lives and our livelihoods (Smit, et al. 2020).

As headlines tallied the spread of the coronavirus in places such as Zimbabwe and Yemen, Western liberal democracies announced plans for a first reopening. Concerns as to whether the health care system could manage the tsunami of patients and whether there was enough protective equipment for frontline health care workers gave way to growing anxiety about the economic consequences of the pandemic.

Economies, as former federal deputy finance minister Scott Clark observed, were basically induced into coma as the most effective response to the emergency (Herle 2020a). Bringing economies out of that coma will be a longer, trickier process.

Collectively, we decided big government was needed to fight the pandemic. Government, effectively, became the country's dominant employer. Canada all but introduced a guaranteed basic income.

Our businesses, after a decade of growing profits, soaring share prices, handsome bonuses for corporate leaders, share buybacks for shareholders, cheap loans, and cheaper labour, told government they would be shedding workers within days and would be back for bailouts.

The Economist described the shift as "the most dramatic extension of state power since the second world war" (Economist 2020a). The size of government may not shrink so quickly afterwards.

There will be hard and intensely personal questions put. Parliamentarians, who didn't hesitate to tell Canadians they had to start working from home, will have to come up with a better explanation as to why they must be physically present in Ottawa to deliver on their mandate to hold the government accountable.

How will cottagers who pay full property taxes to local municipal governments react to being told they should stay in the city during the pandemic? Do provinces – including provinces that rely on federal transfer payments such as equalization – have the right to erect blockades at provincial borders to keep other Canadians out? And how will seniors – having paid taxes all their working lives – react to being told that in a triage world, they may be denied medical treatments available to others? These examples are intended to be illustrative and are by no means exhaustive.

Canada and other Western liberal democracies need a new economy for this new normal, a new economy that recognizes and accepts the need for new societal norms. But to do that Western liberal democracies will need a new public discourse led by a new media ecosystem. The shift must begin with the political parties themselves.

An incident in the fall of 2020 proved most revealing. Prime Minister Justin Trudeau had scheduled a late Friday afternoon call with Opposition Leader Erin O'Toole 27 November. The press office in the PMO released a "readout" to the media claiming Trudeau had scolded O'Toole for COVID-19 misinformation being promulgated by Conservative critics – before the call occurred. "This is awkward," O'Toole spokesperson Melanie Paradis said of the readout that was issued at 4.34 p.m. "The call isn't until 5.15 p.m. today" (National Post 2020b). The PMO immediately admitted they'd screwed up (ibid.). But the real issue is more fundamental. Liberals like to see themselves as "weavers" and not "rippers," yet here they were touting the fact their leader was ripping O'Toole, which sounded a lot like the kind of politics Trudeau was allegedly calling out.

The "readout" was the worst kind of command-and-control, one-to-many, top-down talking point communications that is supposedly passé. And a written attack at that. The approach smacks of control at the centre, limits engagement, and affords no opportunity for any meaningful exchange with the journalists who will be covering the story. Neil Macdonald, a long-time CBC correspondent and columnist, said the Friday foul-up is typical of media relations in Trudeau's Ottawa. "Does anyone thing [*sic*] anything this government says is unrehearsed or transparent? When I was a columnist, I would get precisely identical non-answers from multiple departments. Eventually, I stopped bothering to call. And then I stopped listening" (Macdonald 2020).

How is a political figure or their media relations person supposed to create the kind of engagement liberal democracies need if the media has stopped calling and stopped listening? If, as referenced earlier in this work, truth is cumulative, how do you build truth with a single printed missive of trash talk? Wouldn't public affairs programming be of more value to citizens if the panellists and pundits had actually had extended, meaningful exchanges with principals?

Liberal democracies are wrestling with one fundamental question – what does a post-pandemic world look like?

Policy deliberations in Canada will focus on technology, on supply chains and what that implies for foreign relations, on our traditional reliance on the extraction of natural resources, on infrastructure including communications technology, on the efficient and effective delivery of government services, on social programs designed for an earlier age that proved ill-suited for a gig economy, on the long-term care of our seniors, on child care as economic policy.

Conservative Party Leader Erin O'Toole sees the debate differently, "because this is what it's come down to. A clash of vision between the 'somewheres' and the 'anywheres,'" said O'Toole in his response to the November 2020 Economic Update (Wherry 2020b). Echoing former prime minister Stephen Harper, and Robert Merton more than seventy years before, O'Toole spoke of "those who love their trade, their pursuit, and are loyal to local businesses, versus those who the government wants to flock to a trendy job that is in no way connected to the community or the betterment of the country. And while the Prime Minister seems to think that every Canadian can simply work on their laptop from the local café, that's not reality, nor is it what Canadians want," O'Toole concluded (ibid.).

In terms of issues discussed in this work, that debate will be enhanced with a robust and free press with the skills required to meet the challenge of the Enlightenment. And if securing a new financial footing for domestic media outlets on a universal basis involves improving the bargaining power of Canadian media outlets by allowing them to negotiate collectively rather than individually with social media giants, Canadian parliamentarians shouldn't hesitate to act. Social media giants have long profited from our collective online activity. A tax related to the successful commercialization of that activity by companies such as Facebook and Google is worthy of consideration. And if a government elected by the people of Canada decides to earmark proceeds from that windfall tax to newspapers, that's the business of government –

the allocation of resources. Canada's government has decided it is in our collective interest to have a domestic airlines industry. A healthy Canadian media ecosystem warrants similar consideration.

The pandemic story – both economically and politically – unfolded somewhat differently in the US than in Canada in part because of an urgency imposed by the 2020 presidential election campaign.

President Trump, by the first week of May 2020, had abandoned any leadership role regarding the management of the pandemic to focus on his re-election in general and the reopening of the economy in particular. In early May, Trump's former campaign director Brad Parscale was encouraging people to download the Trump 2020 app "For nearly three years we have been building a juggernaut campaign (Death Star). It is firing on all cylinders. Data, Digital, TV, Political, Surrogates, Coalitions, etc.," Parscale tweeted. "In a few days we start pressing FIRE for the first time," Parscale tweeted (Parscale 2020a). "I didn't give our campaign the name Death Star, the media did," Pascale continued. "However, I am happy to use the analogy … Laugh all you want, we will take the win!" (Parscale 2020b). The Death Star, as aficionados of the *Star Wars* franchise can attest, is a planet-killing super-weapon. However, Parscale's embrace of the descriptive is curious to say the least. As Chris D. Jackson, a Joe Biden supporter, noted in a tweet, "I'm taking it you don't know what happened to the Death Star?" (Jackson, C.D. 2020).

Parscale's delivery system may represent a "new form of propaganda that wasn't really possible until the digital age," as described by *Vox* writer Sean Illing (Illing 2020). But the strategy behind the political messages to be delivered will be easily recognized by anyone who has watched professional or college football over the last thirty or forty years. Former White House adviser Steve Bannon is on record as saying, "The Democrats don't matter … The real opposition is the media. And the way to deal with them is to flood the zone with shit" (ibid.). "Flood the zone" is a football term for an offensive strategy that seeks to dominate a defence by placing more players in one section of the field than the defence can cover. Think multiple wide receivers converging on a single cornerback.

Bannon said Team Trump sought to saturate the media ecosystem with disinformation, false news, and multiple announcements, and by doing so they would "overwhelm the media's ability to mediate" (ibid.). The premise is simple enough: you give the media so much to cover, the media lacks the resources to cover it all in any detail. The answer to "flooding the zone" in football is for the defence to switch to man-on-man coverage, which in terms of holding President Trump to account means more, not fewer, journalistic resources.

The Republican strategists worked to introduce an "October surprise" into the campaign narrative, settling on the business dealings of Biden's son Hunter as the instrument of choice. A former business partner of Hunter Biden was willing to go on the record with his claim that Joe Biden was not only aware of but had profited from his son's business activities (Lipton, Vogel, and Haberman 2020). Trump went so far as to suggest the *Wall Street Journal* was about to break the story in some detail (Smith, B. 2020b). The president, it turned out, was a little too far forward on his skis.

One of the more interesting aspects of campaign 2020 was the re-emergence of media gatekeepers. Editors and reporters at major news organizations like the *Wall Street Journal* did journalism – questioning the provenance of documents, insisting on the right to examine evidence – and in so doing reintroduced the ability of news professionals to influence the media and political agenda.

In 1897, Mark Twain was contacted by a reporter from the *New York Journal* asking if reports the American humourist was dying in poverty in London had any basis in fact. Twain responded: "Just say the reports of my death have been greatly exaggerated." So it is with mainstream media. While advocates of social media platforms are inclined to use anachronistic descriptives of legacy media, the 2020 presidential campaign reinforced Shirky's view of media as an ecosystem and by extension gave journalism and journalism's gatekeepers an opportunity to reassert their value.

In a final bit of irony, President Trump went to war with Twitter over a dispute about "truth." Trump, who, as *New York Times* reporters Peter Baker and Daisuke Wakabayashi state, "built his political career on the power of a flame-throwing Twitter account," signed an executive order 28 May 2020 that set out to strip social media companies such as Google, Facebook, and Twitter of the liability protection afforded them in federal law (Baker and Wakabayashi 2020). The president was incensed Twitter had begun to append "get the facts" warnings to certain of Trump's posts alleging voter fraud (ibid.). The president argued Twitter's actions reflected an anti-conservative bias in social media. The president's critics basically laughed out loud, suggesting Trump's executive order to force Twitter and others to be more aggressive about policing tweets for accuracy would harm one person above all else – President Trump himself (ibid.).

The Biden campaign, in contrast, was reportedly less preoccupied with social media outlets such as Twitter. "It's very simple. We turned off Twitter. We stayed away from it," said one campaign aide (Socolow 2020). Ironically, according to the analytics company Conviva, Biden's Twitter feed generated more engagement than Trump's did in September 2020 (Wagner, K. 2020).

As the presidential campaign heated up in the US through the summer of 2020, the pandemic emerged as the dominant issue, both for those preoccupied from a public health perspective and for those preoccupied by the price being exacted from the US economy by the shutdown.

Democratic Party nominee Joe Biden decided to use the symbolic arena of the campaign to position himself as a role model, wearing a mask whenever he appeared in public, keeping large public gatherings to a minimum, respecting the advice regarding social distancing.

Trump took a decidedly different approach. The president certainly understood the pandemic was the issue for the American electorate. Thanks to extraordinary access to the president and his closest advisers, *Washington Post* associate editor Bob Woodward was able to provide readers of his bestseller *Rage* with verbatim exchanges that provided invaluable insights into Trump's thinking.

People such as South Carolina Senator Lindsey Graham impressed upon the president that his opponent in the campaign was the pandemic and not Biden. Trump, in turn, told Woodward, "I was unlucky with the virus," not fully appreciating Graham's point that the job is "unfair to everybody ... it's part of being president ... things happened" (Woodward 2020, 350).

Graham believed Trump had to show the American public that he could provide the leadership required to deal with the pandemic. Instead, Trump decided the best way to "Make America Great Again" was to ignore the scientists and the public health experts and basically ignore the risk – which he did even when struck by the virus himself.

Trump opted for mass rallies, where he appeared maskless and played to the crowds' baser instincts with not so subtle hints he would fire leading immunologist Dr Anthony Fauci at an appropriate time. Trump's defence of his defiance was linked to the economy; the president argued if he listened to the scientists the country would find itself in a massive depression. At a campaign appearance in Nevada, Trump told the good people of Carson City that the state capital would become "a ghost town" if Biden was elected president (Rindels and Messerly 2020).

New York Times columnist Maureen Dowd thought it "unfathomable that the president of the United States would turn himself into a public health menace. But he has" (Dowd 2020). The prestigious *New England Journal of Medicine* said that Trump had "recklessly squandered lives" (New England Journal of Medicine 2020).

Trump's rallies became "super-spreader" events. News accounts of high-ranking administration officials infected by the virus after attending a Trump rally or White House event became a daily occurrence. Not even the death of Herman Cain (Ortiz and Seelye 2020), a presidential candidate in 2012 and ardent Trump supporter, two weeks after attending a Trump rally in Tulsa, Oklahoma, resulted in any change in the president's behaviour.

As columnists such as Nicholas Kristof insisted, "this pandemic may be the greatest failure of governance in the United States since the Vietnam War" (Kristof 2020).

Trump was insisting the crisis was manufactured by the mainstream press and predicted "when it gets a little warmer, it miraculously goes away" (Woodward 2020, 244). The president likened the virus to "a flu" and used his Twitter account to tell voters, "WE CANNOT LET THE CURE BE WORSE THAN THE PROBLEM ITSELF" (ibid., 289). Researchers at Cornell University analyzed thirty-eight million articles about the pandemic in the English-language media and concluded Trump personally generated nearly 38 per cent of the overall "misinformation conversation" (Stolberg and Weiland 2020).

Trump's personal invective directed against his opponents was central to his messaging, dismissing Biden as "totally unqualified ... mentally" (Global News 2020) and vice-presidential nominee Kamala Harris as a "monster" and a "communist" (Thompson, E. 2020).

And the president made certain he was providing a steady stream of material for the rumour public, retweeting a post, for example, advancing the theory that Obama had SEAL Team 6 killed and that the SEALs had actually killed one of Osama bin Laden's body doubles (Subramaniam and Lybrand 2020). Trump defended the original tweet as an "opinion," insisting people are entitled to make up their own minds on the specifics. "I'll put it out there. People can decide," Trump said at a town hall in Miami (Caralle and Mulraney, 2020). In David Brooks's world of "weavers" and "rippers" (Brooks 2020), President Trump decided he would be the Ripper-in-Chief.

Woodward, after multiple and extensive conversations with Trump, wrote, "I can only reach one conclusion: Trump is the wrong man for the job" (Woodward 2020, 392). Yet tens of millions of Americans disagreed.

Pulitzer Prize-winning columnist Peggy Noonan, writing in the *Wall Street Journal*, offered an inferential perspective on Trump's appeal. "He's crazy," Noonan said. "And it's kind of working" (ibid., 257). But as the former speech writer for Ronald Reagan added, "Crazy doesn't last. Crazy doesn't go the distance. Crazy is an unstable element that, when let loose in an unstable environment, explodes" (ibid.). And in the minutes and hours after the polls closed 3 November 2020, Trump moved immediately to create an unstable environment, looking for an explosion.

The results of the election, to the outside world, appeared conclusive. Democrat Joe Biden won 306 electoral votes compared to 232 for the incumbent president (Politico 2020) and prevailed in the popular vote with nearly eighty million votes (Riccardi 2020).

Yet Trump used social media outlets such as Twitter to attack the legitimacy of the election itself, claiming repeatedly, sometimes in all caps tweets, that he won the election (Trump 2020e), that the results were rigged (Trump 2020d), and that electoral fraud was commonplace in cities he did not hesitate to name, cities with significant African American populations (Badger 2020). Trump unleashed lawyers led by former New York mayor Rudy Giuliani in courtrooms in key states won by Biden that had been carried by Trump in 2016.

Trump's constant refrain of "fix" was designed to undermine the confidence of Americans – and the world – in the integrity of the electoral process. His denunciation of "fake news" was designed to undermine the credibility of any media criticism with the general public, leaving what *Washington Post* columnist Eugene Robinson described as "a dystopian landscape of weaponized disinformation" (Harvard Kennedy School 2020). His use of Twitter to fire administration officials who failed to follow his instructions to the letter – like former defense secretary Mark Esper – was intended to destabilize public servants (McEvoy 2020b).

Described by Project Lincoln activist Stuart Stevens as a "racist who doesn't understand America" (Stevens 2020), Trump eschewed the usual coded language of dog whistle politics to directly attack the competence and integrity of public officials in communities with significant minority populations. And he continued to mock the media's preoccupation with the COVID-19 pandemic, even as the number of cases in the United States surpassed twelve million and the number of deaths topped 250,000 (New York Times 2020d). Trump, for example, took to Twitter to suggest the nation's doctors were inflating the number of coronavirus cases to make more money (Lee, B.Y. 2020).

Trump and his acolytes fought to establish "rigged" as the dominant news frame around any election outcome story. Trump's message to reporters, reduced to bumper sticker rhetoric, was relatively straightforward – COVID is fake, the mainstream media is fake, Trump won the election until it was stolen from him.

The first televised debate of the presidential campaign, for example, provided a startling, even unsettling example of Trump's determination to use confusion and chaos as weapons. CNN political correspondent Dana Bash described the exchange on air as a "shitshow" (Benton 2020). At one point, an exasperated Biden told Trump to "shut up, man" (Groppe and Fritze 2020) – and Biden was supposedly the voice of calm reason. It is worth noting, however, that 73.1 million Americans tuned into the first debate compared to eighty-four million viewers from the first Trump/Clinton debate in 2016, according to AC Nielsen (Abbruzzese and Byers 2020).

"It will surprise no one that has watched him closely for the past few years that the president would end his campaign with reality-denying on such an epic scale," wrote Susan B. Glasser (Glasser 2020). Media fact checkers had a field day challenging Trump's tweets and campaign declarations that people should believe only what he – Trump – told them. But the fact is the news accounts continued to report Trump's assertions basically verbatim, imbedding tweet texts into the very news stories that took issue with the accuracy of the things the president said. As Glasser noted, "there is no news cycle without Trump."

CBC Washington correspondent Paul Hunter, in conversation with host Anna Maria Tremonti and Joy Malbon, CTV's Washington bureau chief, at a post-election event organized by the Canadian Journalism Foundation, summarized the challenge for reporters succinctly. Journalists, said Hunter, have to think through a number of questions about their craft in including "how to deal with the shiny things ... the tweets" (Canadian Journalism Foundation

2020). Journalists, Hunter said, jump on Trump's missives. "How do you not? He is the President" (ibid.). And Trump, said Hunter, "is very good at what he does."

The president, through the campaign and the immediate post-campaign period, imposed his will on the Republican Party, a party Stevens says "has fully embraced white grievance politics" (Stevens 2020). "It's the Trump party now," said Malbon (Canadian Journalism Foundation 2020).

Somehow, ballots that were acceptable to re-elect or elect Republican senators such as Senate Majority Leader Mitch McConnell were not deemed acceptable for presidential election purposes.

Despite the fact that more than 65 per cent of eligible voters cast a ballot – the highest percentage total for voter turnout since 1908 (Schaul, Rabinowitz, and Mellnik 2020) – and that Republicans actually increased the number of seats in the House of Representatives (Kilgore 2020), Trump and his chorus of supporters insisted the election was stolen.

Trump's lawyer Rudy Giuliani seemed to melt down – literally and figuratively – at a news conference 19 November 2020. And Sidney Powell, briefly a legal adviser to Trump, insisted, "What we are really dealing with here, and uncovering more by the day, is the massive influence of communist money through Venezuela, Cuba, and likely China in the interference with our elections here in the United States" (Gilbert 2020). Powell, it should be noted, was relieved of her legal duties shortly thereafter (Sonmez and Dawsey, 2020). And in a deposition in a libel case brought against her, Powell offered a novel defence – arguing in essence that no rational person would believe anything she said.

Biden, for his part, stuck to a positive message, insisting he'd work as hard for those who didn't vote for him as he would for those who did (Maclean's 2020a). Biden told voters it was time "to put the harsh rhetoric of the campaign behind us," that it was time "to unite, to heal" (ibid.).

Trump took a diametrically opposite approach. As presidential historian Douglas Brinkley observed, "Donald Trump is a bull who carries his own china shop with him" (Waters 2020).

The president racked up more votes than he did in his successful 2016 campaign, more votes in fact than any losing candidate had ever received (Riccardi 2020). He was, the pundits said, the middle finger candidate, a symbol of resistance to the woke culture, to those who historically have dominated American public life. Trump's strategy, according to *Merchants of Doubt* author Naomi Oreskes, may eventually trigger his fall. "The risk is that he takes the country with him" (Waters 2020).

And therein lies the problem.

In an editorial that appeared in the 18 October 2020 edition of the *New York Times*, the board asserted, "Donald Trump's re-election campaign poses the greatest threat to American democracy since World War II" (New York Times 2020b). The editorial went on to state, "He is a man unworthy of the office he holds" (ibid.). What the editorial did not address was the issue of the threat Trump posed to American democracy even in defeat.

Trump repeatedly, and consistently, used the mainstream media to undermine the confidence of the American people in the integrity of their electoral system. In tweets, at news conferences, in meetings with state officials summoned – arguably illegally – to meetings in the White House, Trump brayed he had won the election, that the election was rigged, and that the victory he secured on election day was stolen from him by "crooked" inner-city machine politicians. Trump made the same claims in 2016 – even when he won – by way of explaining his loss to Hillary Clinton in the popular vote. At a rally the night before the election, the president declared the result "a fraud on the American public" (Macleans 2020b) and promised his supporters "as soon as the election is over, we're going in with our lawyers" (Smith, A. 2020).

Every presidential utterance, in whatever form, was intended to communicate a message that the process and the people who run it were crooked and corrupt and were denying Trump a victory legitimate voters had bestowed on him. Trump's messaging suggested even those people he was counting on were corrupt, starting with the Supreme Court of the United States, having dropped a not so subtle hint during the campaign itself that the nation's highest court, bolstered by Trump appointees, would come to his rescue (Economist 2020c).

The president was executing against a strategy his son-in-law Jared Kushner summarized for Bob Woodward: "Controversy elevates message" (Woodward 2020, 288). Mainstream news organizations dutifully reported Trump had no proof to back up his assertions, that his lawyers could offer no proof when they appeared in courtrooms across America to mount their legal challenges, that the lawyers representing the president in Arizona went out of their way to insist they weren't claiming anyone had stolen the election, the president's declarations to the opposite effect notwithstanding (Berenson 2020).

The news accounts reported how challenge after challenge by Trump advocates was tossed, how a few Republicans were prepared to call out Trump for his behaviour, how the administration intimidates government officials into refusing to participate in the transition process, and the corporal's guard of Trump administration officials who were prepared to acknowledge the president's defeat. Even former Bush adviser Karl Rove said the corruption story being spun by Trump forces would involve a conspiracy "on the scale of a James Bond movie" (Perkins and Beaumont 2020).

But the philosophy behind the Big Lie technique holds that if you repeat the lie loud enough and long enough, people will believe you. And people did believe Trump's big lie, both in America and in Canada. As Biden's deputy communications director Bill Russo stated, "If you thought disinformation on Facebook was a problem during our election, just wait until you see how it is shredding the fabric of our democracy in the days after" (Hamilton 2020).

A Reuters/Ipsos survey concluded about half of all Republican voters believe Donald Trump rightfully won the US election but that it was stolen from him by widespread voter fraud (Kahn 2020). And an Angus Reid Institute survey in Canada reported nearly one in five Canadians agree with Trump's assertion that the US election was unfair (Leavitt 2020). Perhaps more revealing, 41 per cent of Conservative Party voters

said the election wasn't fair and should be contested (ibid.). Support
for Trump's position was significantly stronger in Alberta, Saskatchewan, and Manitoba (ibid.). Shachi Kurl, of the institute, told the *Star*,
"There's always been a significant segment of people in this country
who have, if not perhaps been enamoured with Donald Trump's personality, have certainly supported his policy stances," she said. "We
continue to see that" (ibid.).

Biden, in sharp contrast to Trump, couched every post-election
comment in the language of reason, of inevitability, regretting the
president's conduct but largely dismissing it as of no consequence.

NYU professor Jay Rosen takes a decidedly different view of
Trump and Trumpism. "To me, this is the top story in politics every
day. A counter-majoritarian party has to be counterfactual, or it
cannot live. To satisfy its core supporters it wrecks institutions. The
fuel source is destruction. Biden is not ready. His party is not ready.
The press is not ready" (Rosen 2020c).

So how does the press get ready?

Delivering the Theodore H. White Lecture on Press and Politics
at the Shorenstein Center on Media, Politics, and Public Policy,
Washington Post columnist Eugene Robinson said "our job is to be
heard and to be believed." In a world that includes "voices that
are not even remotely tethered to facts," Robinson says the media
needs "to be loud. I think we need to be loud, bordering on obnox-
iously loud ... We need to be repetitious about it ... And finally, I
think that we need to work together in defence of truth ... We need
to challenge lies every single time." Robinson, to circle back to a
comment by *Post* editor-in-chief Marty Baron referenced earlier,
believes the "work" of journalism is "war." Robinson's final word:
"We are at war, and we need to act like it."

Adds *Axios* co-founder and chief executive officer Jim VandeHei,
"I legitimately fear now that we're going to have a decoupling ...
not just like 'two Americas'... We are literally going to have two
Americas where half the country gives up on a lot of the work we
do" in the news. "If we lose this war on truth ... we're screwed"
(Stelter 2020).

As the clock ran down on the Trump administration, journalists took the time to reflect on the way the mainstream media in particular had covered the president. In an opinion piece carried in the *New York Times*, Jorge Ramos stated flatly, "We journalists should have been tougher on Mr. Trump, questioning his every lie and insult. We should not have let him get away with his racism and xenophobia. We should never again allow someone to create an alternative reality in order to seize the presidency" (Ramos 2020).

Trump's truth – self-centred, self-interested, arguably self-destructive – in the end did not hold up under the intense scrutiny of the mainstream media in a campaign context.

In Canada, Trudeau's truth seemed largely aspirational, more signalling of intent than delivering results.

The social media's truth underscored the significance of constant and ongoing adjustments to algorithms on our perception of reality.

The legacy media's truth is that the descriptive "mass" no longer applies.

And for the public, their truth signals an ongoing debate between Robert Merton's metropolitans and locals, too often articulated in angry, confrontational language.

12

Trump – A Final Tweet

In the end, according to *New York Times* columnist Michelle Goldberg, "the world agrees that Trump is exactly the man his fiercest critics said he was" (Goldberg 2021). Presidential historian Douglas Brinkley was even more dismissive, insisting, "He is the bottom of the barrel of American presidents" (Recount 2021).

As he took his leave of the White House 20 January, public opinion research reported Trump's approval rating was the lowest of his presidency (Elliott, J.K. 2021). And the riotous siege of Capitol Hill two weeks earlier – a siege Trump effectively called for – was a factor in the sharp drop in approval for a president who had spent his four years in office rewriting many of the rules of what is both expected and acceptable in word and deed from a head of state.

Liz Cheney, the congresswoman from Wyoming whose father Richard had served in the same house and subsequently served as vice president, was certainly direct in her denunciation of America's forty-fifth president. Cheney stated there had "never been a greater betrayal by a President of the United States of his office and his oath to the Constitution" than Mr Trump's incitement of the mob that attacked the Capitol (Politico 2021). "The President of the United States summoned this mob, assembled the mob, and lit the flame of this attack," Cheney continued as she made her case for impeachment, a case that ultimately carried the day in the US House of Representatives (ibid.). "Everything that followed was his doing" (ibid.).

Five people dead. Elected officials threatened by hundreds of rioters. The Speaker's office occupied, looting, the braying of slogans for the benefit of television cameras, images of a breakdown in social order beamed round the world on mainstream and social media alike.

A chain of events his opponents insist was triggered by Trump himself.

In a story entitled "The Inciter-in-Chief," *New Yorker* editor David Remnick quoted Trump's speech to a "Save America Rally" on the Ellipse urging his supporters to march on the Capitol. "If you don't fight like hell, you're not going to have a country anymore," the president declared. "I'll be there with you" (Remnick 2021). And of course he wasn't. When the storming of the Capitol occurred, Trump was watching it all on TV.

The protesters themselves apparently took Trump's message to heart. Texas realtor Jenna Ryan, now facing charges for her participation in the riot, said, "I thought I was following my president. I thought I was following what we were called to do. He asked us to fly there. So I was doing was [*sic*] he asked us to do" (Begnaud 2021). As communications scholar Christopher Dornan noted in a tweet, "Sure enough, this is shaping up to be the line of defence" (Dornan 2021).

The situation at the Capitol, on one level, was symbolic of Trump's administration in general, as well as his relationship with his supporters. He promised to stand with them and then didn't: whether you were a coal miner from West Virginia or an activist ready to storm the Capitol.

The images provided the descriptives, thousands of angry protesters assembled on the Mall, before storming the Capitol and the halls of Congress with the stated purpose of frustrating the counting of Electoral College votes, thereby delaying the confirmation of Joseph R. Biden Jr. as America's forty-sixth president.

As investigators from the Federal Bureau of Investigation began the process of laying literally hundreds of charges against the would-be insurrectionists (Wise and Lucas 2021), the evidence included videos they posted themselves on social media sites such as Facebook and Parler. Futurist and internet strategist Jesse Hirsh in his *Metaviews* newsletter stated, "I'm blown away by just how incredible the coverage of the social media coup in DC and its fallout has been on TikTok" (Hirsh 2021).

The physical assault on the Capitol Hill police became the symbol of a broader assault on American democracy. The irony of members of Congress, having taken their oath of office as a result of the same ballots being contested at the presidential level, was apparently lost on scores of Republican lawmakers.

Certain lawmakers were determined to hold Trump accountable. The evidence, lawmakers said, could be found in Trump's own words, recorded on video. The wording of the impeachment charge brought by the House of Representatives is an effective piece of political communication – succinct, yet severe in its judgment: a sole charge of "incitement of insurrection."

Having called for the removal of "the weak congresspeople," Trump went on to declare, "Because you'll never take back our country with weakness. You have to show strength and you have to be strong" (Goldberg 2021).

Trump stands as the first president in US history to be impeached twice (Blackall 2021). Yet his hold on the Republican Party was such that the outcome of the subsequent Senate vote was preordained.

Ronald J. Deibert, director of the Citizen Lab at the Munk School of Global Affairs and Public Policy, in his seminal work *Reset: Reclaiming the Internet for Civil Society*, notes, "Social media are increasingly perceived as contributing to a kind of social sickness" (Deibert 2020, 5). These same social media also provide the visual "record" of the expression of these social ills.

The White House correspondents who hit the campaign trail with Trump will undoubtedly pen insightful books that will chronicle the complete story of the 2020 presidential campaign. But for the purposes of this conversation, Trump's leave-taking and the uprising he triggered warrant further consideration on three key points: the impact of his attack rhetoric on public discourse in Western liberal democracies, on public institutions including the media, and on the public policies that impact the platforms where the debate takes place.

Once the results of the 2020 presidential election were tallied, President Trump's personal "to do" list had but a single assignment:

undermine the confidence of the American people in a cornerstone of any democracy – the electoral process.

The president, for all intents and purposes, stopped functioning as the nation's chief executive officer. The White House announcement of the president's daily schedule was reduced to farce. Issued daily, the statement read, "President Trump will work from early in the morning until late in the evening. He will make many calls and have many meetings" (Bump 2021). Lorne Michaels's writers at *Saturday Night Live* were hard pressed to come up with anything more absurd for their skits.

What the president did work at was his Twitter feed, sowing distrust and dissention, with his oft-repeated refrain that the election had been stolen from him and his supporters.

A comprehensive story filed by a team of *New York Times* reporters carried in the 31 January 2021 edition set out in detail Trump's seventy-seven-day campaign to subvert the election, a campaign the reporting team that included Maggie Haberman described as, "A lie that Mr. Trump had been grooming for years" that "finally overwhelmed the Republican Party," a lie promulgated by the "surround-sound right wing media" (Rutenberg et al. 2021). The story states, "With each passing day the lie grew, finally managing to do what the political process and the courts would not: upend the peaceful transfer of power that for 224 years had been the bedrock of American democracy" (ibid.). The post-campaign campaign, the piece asserts, was "one final norm-defying act of a reality-denying presidency."

In an article carried on CNN for example, Trump declared, "If you count the legal votes I easily win. If you count the illegal votes, they can try to steal the election from us" (Wagner, M. et al. 2020). Days later, *Business Insider* quoted Trump as saying, "We believe these people are thieves. The big city machines are corrupt" (Dzhanova 2020). Acolytes such as former House Speaker Newt Gingrich picked up the same song sheet but added a conspiracy theory line or two to the chorus. Appearing on Fox News, Gingrich said the result was "a corrupt, stolen election" that was "financed

by people like George Soros" referring to the international finan-
cier (Aivalis 2020). "We think we have evidence of a lot of it,"
Gingrich said (ibid.). If the Trump camp did have evidence, the former president's lawyers couldn't produce it in courthouses from
Arizona, to Pennsylvania, Michigan to Georgia (Wagner, M. et al.
2020). The Department of Homeland Security's Cybersecurity and
Infrastructure Security Agency issued a statement that "There is
no evidence that any voting system deleted or lost votes, changed
votes, or was in any way compromised" (Sanger, Stevens, and
Perlroth 2020). Trump's attack on the integrity of the electoral
system had been road-tested in 2016. Trump first raised the issue
during the 2016 campaign itself before the outcome was known
and then after he was declared elected by way of explaining why
he lost the popular vote to Hillary Clinton (Graham 2016).

In the course of his re-election bid, Trump had promised in
advance of voting day that as soon as the election is over, "We're
going in with our lawyers" (Smith, A. 2020). And during the campaign itself, Trump had told supporters at a rally in Reading,
Pennsylvania, "if we win on Tuesday or, thank you very much
Supreme Court, shortly thereafter" (Fearnow 2020).

The message couldn't have been clearer – either Trump wins or he
will call on his supporters to contest any result he doesn't like by any
means possible, and all those folks he appointed to the judicial branch
of government will uphold his worldview. The scope and scale of the
systemic corruption inherent in these few phases would once have
been shocking in the agora that is the American public sphere.

The courts, to the intense relief of many, proved to be more
principled than Trump had either anticipated or promised his
supporters. But if Trump's lawyers lost in the decisive court cases
brought forward, the president enjoyed a significant measure of
success in the court of American public opinion.

To establish some context, Trump received in excess of seventy-
four million votes in the 2020 presidential election (Guardian (US)
2020) – a significantly higher total than he received in victory in
2016 (Hall and Gal). Further, the former president held his vote –

nine of ten individuals who voted for Trump in his first run for the nation's highest elected office voted for him in 2020 as well (Medina and Russonello 2020). And an unsettling 86 per cent of Trump voters told pollsters they do not trust the integrity of the vote (Bump 2020). In fact, a Monmouth University poll reported 77 per cent of respondents who voted for Trump believe Joe Biden won the election because of fraud (Reich 2020). Literally tens of millions of Americans bought into the lie.

Trump loyalists were fed a steady diet of conspiracy-theory assertion from the former president and his legal advisers, "voices not even remotely tethered to facts," as Eugene Robinson put it (Harvard Kennedy School 2020). Trump's one-time lawyer Sidney Powell, who had earlier represented Michael Flynn, said in an appearance on C-SPAN, "What we are really dealing with here and uncovering more by the day is the massive influence of communist money through Venezuela, Cuba and likely China and the interference with our elections here in the United States" (Kessler 2020).

These challenges to the results are incredibly damaging.

Literally scores of Republican members of Congress voted to contest the legitimacy of the outcome, once the smoke of the occupation of Capitol Hill 6 January had cleared (Zhou 2021). Trump's legal challenges to the election outcome enjoyed widespread support among his supporters such as former Senate majority leader Mitch McConnell. The senator from Kentucky said the former president was "100 percent within his rights to look into allegations of irregularities and weigh his legal options" (Fandos and Cochrane 2020). The manner in which Trump sought to force the issue was perceived as something else again. The former president pressed his advisers to see whether Republican legislatures, for example, could pick pro-Trump electors for the Electoral college in key states, as Maggie Haberman put it, to "deliver him the electoral votes he needs to change the math and give him a second term" (Haberman 2020).

On another occasion, Trump dragged Elections Canada into the equation, retweeting a statement from the entity that runs federal elections in Canada that stated, "We use paper ballots counted by hand in front of scrutineers and have never used voting machines or electronic tabulators to count votes in our 100-year history" (Press 2021).

Subsequently, prosecutors told reporters from the *New York Times* that it was increasingly likely a criminal investigation would be launched into Trump's attempts to overturn election results in Georgia (Fausset and Hakim 2021). In a conversation that was taped, Trump pressured Secretary of State Brad Raffensperger to "find" the 11,780 votes needed to declare him the victor (Shear and Saul 2021).

The democratic cost of their irresponsibility warrants further consideration. In their compelling work *How Democracies Die*, Steven Levitsky and Daniel Ziblatt state, "the abdication of political responsibility by existing leaders often marks a nation's first step toward authoritarianism" (Levitsky and Ziblatt 2019, 5). The authors say citizens should start to worry when political leaders – either in words or in actions – reject the rules of the game, challenge the legitimacy of opponents, tolerate or encourage violence, and express a willingness to curtail civil liberties of any person or institution that does not share the leaders' worldview. Levitsky and Ziblatt state people should worry when a political leader embraces even one of these four strategies. Trump gives voice to all four. And the Trump supporters who stormed the Capitol echo the president's worldview.

Political parties, historically, have been democracy's gatekeepers. In America at least, the Republican Party has all but abdicated this role. "The Republican Party is no longer salvageable," tweeted Larry Sabato (Sabato 2021). A number of Bush-era Republicans would appear to share that view, as dozens of individuals who served in the Bush administration confirmed to Reuters they were leaving the GOP, calling it "the cult of Trump" (Reid, T. 2021). And a vote to strip first-term congresswoman Marjorie Taylor Greene of her House committee assignments – for her reported endorsation of anti-Semitic conspiracy theories and suggestions school shootings that plague America were staged and that 9/11 didn't happen – constituted a moment of truth for congressional Republicans (Wu and King 2021).

An "us versus them" subtext is easily detected in the attack rhetoric of today's politics. Louisiana Senator John Kennedy provided a textbook example during an appearance with Sean Hannity on Fox News in February 2021. Kennedy was chastising Senator John Kerry – Biden's climate czar – for using a private jet on his travels. But Kennedy quickly pivoted to a broader attack. "I try to see grace everywhere I can," Kennedy said in his folksy manner (Kennedy, J.N. 2021). But the American people, Kennedy quickly added, are "so tired of being lectured by the managerial elite … who think they're special" (ibid.). Lest anyone be confused about who exactly Kennedy was referring to, he provided this description, "The tuna tartare crowd who live in the expensive condos with high ceilings and important art on the wall." Kennedy, for the record, attended Vanderbilt, the University of Virginia School of Law, and Magdalen College at Oxford – elite universities all!

An analysis of the election day results reflects the societal divide referred to in the previous chapter first identified by sociologists Lazarsfeld and Merton (1948) between "metropolitans" and "locals."

In Merton's world, Conservative critics say Justin Trudeau is decidedly a metropolitan. Donald Trump, on the other hand, is a local. Trump's businesses are, essentially, a variation on a theme focused on local markets. To the extent Trump travels, it invariably includes time at a golf course. Turnberry may be in Scotland, and the golf course has some truly spectacular holes, but its look and feel is not a radical departure from Trump golf courses in Florida or New Jersey.

After a strong finish in the closing days Trump won election day, according to a poll conducted by Public Opinion Strategies, but to his electoral misfortune, most voters had made up their minds well in advance (2020). Exit polls suggest that in the end, the 2020 presidential campaign came down to the pandemic, regardless of whether the story was framed as a public health story or an economic story (Medina and Russonello 2020).

Opinions on which framing was more important and therefore determinant in electoral terms tended to fall along partisan lines, according to research conducted on behalf of a consortium of news organizations by Edison Research (ibid). More than 40 per cent of voters said it was the most important issue in helping them to decide how to vote, far more than any other issue, according to the survey results.

Trump certainly thought the pandemic was determinant. "Before the plague came, I had it made," Trump said at an election rally 20 October (Lach 2020). "I wasn't coming to Erie," Trump said to a partisan crowd assembled in the Pennsylvania city. "I have to be honest. There was no way I was coming. I didn't have to" (ibid.). Full marks to the former president for candour. "Because that's the thing about Donald Trump," Susan Glasser concluded (Glasser 2020). "If you listen long enough, he tells you everything you need to know."

Trump was overwhelmingly the candidate of choice for men, his numbers among non-college educated white men were crushing (Public Opinion Strategies 2020). The former president was also the electoral choice of rural men, rural women (Morin 2016), and predictably, the rich. With the exception of the rich, these groups believe Trump appreciates and shares their sense of grievance, whether that grievance is economic or societal in nature.

As *New York Times* columnist Paul Krugman observed, "the divide in US politics now is more about education and metropolitan growth than traditional regional orientation. Thx to Atlanta, GA now more educated than most of the 'blue wall'" (Krugman 2020).

Trump was the candidate of choice for that element of white America concerned with "woke" culture. Rich Lowry, editor of the *National Review,* wrote 26 October 2020, "Trump is, for better or worse, the foremost symbol of resistance to the overwhelming woke cultural tide that has swept along the media, academia, corporate America, Hollywood, professional sports, the big foundations, and almost everything in between" (Lowry 2020). "To put it in blunt terms, for many people, he's the only middle finger available – to brandish against the people who've assumed they have the whip hand in American culture."

Arguably, the single most lasting and problematic consequence of the Trump era in terms of political discourse, both in the United States and in Canada, is the accelerated conversion of small "c" conservative movements into counter-majoritarian movements.

As NYU professor Jay Rosen observes, counter-majoritarian political rhetoric tends to be counter-factual (Rosen 2020c). And presumably because these movements are counter-majoritarian, the leadership tends to be preoccupied with the base. Rosen's concern is heightened by his belief that progressives, such as President Biden and the Democratic Party leadership, are not ready for this kind of a fight; a fight that features aggressive speech to advance repressive initiatives intended to disenfranchise the "different" – however the speaker defines different. Nor is the press, Rosen says (ibid.).

Trump's decrying of "fake news" constituted a constant refrain in his campaign pitch. And if literally tens of millions of Americans believe the presidential election was hijacked, those beliefs were shaped in no small measure by messages from the president on social media, dutifully repeated by the mainstream press.

Mexican American journalist and author Jorge Ramos has written about the media's coverage of Trump, "which over time normalized his rude, abusive and xenophobic behavior." This new normal, Ramos says, "was great for ratings, but not for civility or democracy" (Ramos 2020).

CNN's Daniel Dale's journalism afforded the former *Toronto Star* writer near cult status during the presidential campaign as he subjected Trump's every tweet and public statement to a fact check.

Yet Trump and his supporters are demonstrably untroubled by inconsistencies in their story or direct contradictions in their actions. The fact a ballot is deemed valid when affirming an election to Congress yet the same ballot is suspect at the presidential level is but one example. An assertion of the democratic rights of the people as justification for lawbreaking is another.

This counter-majoritarianism has surfaced in Canadian political discourse as well, in part because certain of the same conditions, and therefore certain of the grievances, exist on both sides of the border. "Downtown elites" are a preferred target for email solicitations from Conservative fundraisers in Canada at both the federal and provincial level.

Speaking with political strategist David Herle, host of *The Herle Burly* podcast, economist and author Jeff Rubin said, "If you look at the conditions that led to the rise of populism in either the UK or the US, those same conditions exist in Canada." What's different is there has yet to be a populist political expression of that discontented, screwed middle class. "This vacuum will be filled" (Herle 2020c).

The issue is whether new Conservative Party Leader Erin O'Toole is inclined to fill the vacuum.

Since taking over as party leader in 2020, O'Toole has declared his intention to work to broaden the Conservative Party's appeal. The decision of his parliamentary caucus to expel MP Derek Sloan is considered a proof point that O'Toole will be less tolerant of extremist expressions. The specific trigger in Sloan's case was a donation to his leadership campaign from an individual linked to neo-Nazi groups. O'Toole however insisted the caucus decision to show Sloan the door was the result of a pattern of similar behaviour by the Conservative MP over a period of time (Levitz 2021).

But O'Toole's descriptive of "somewheres" and "anywheres" referenced in an earlier chapter is completely aligned with the US conversation between red states or blue states; the coasts versus fly-over states. O'Toole's argument resonates with some voters. A report in *The Economist*, for example, estimated 60 per cent of the jobs that pay $100,000 a year or more can be done from home, but only 10 per cent of the jobs that pay less than $40,000 a year can be done remotely (Economist 2020d).

But O'Toole's standard political tactic of compare and contrast can get trickier than the Conservative leader may fully appreciate, especially in a country like Canada with successive and significant waves of immigrants.

Consider the case of Deputy Prime Minister Chrystia Freeland, who is also Canada's minister of finance. Freeland was born and raised in Alberta, "somewhere" in O'Toole's world. Gifted academically, Freeland graduated from Harvard and was a Rhodes Scholar at Oxford – "anywhere" places. Freeland began her career in journalism as a stringer, a somewhere post, but also worked for the *Financial*

Times, the *Globe and Mail* and Reuters – anywhere publications. An author – somewhere work – but of an international bestseller, which is the world of anywhere. In television interviews, Freeland peppers her answers with references to her Alberta roots and her lawyer father's farm – to the intense irritation of O'Toole's somewhere constituency, a constituency that for reasons that would require deeper analysis see Alberta Premier Jason Kenney, who grew up in a leafy, affluent town on the shores of Lake Ontario, as more of a somewhere guy. Or at least they did until the pandemic came along.

Solving the puzzle may be the key to O'Toole's declared intent to make the Conservative Party "a moderate, pragmatic, mainstream party ... that sits squarely in the centre of Canadian politics" (MacDougall 2021).

Attack language is troublingly often an element of counter-majoritarian speech. In an interview with *Toronto Star* national columnist Susan Delacourt, Prime Minister Trudeau used stark language to articulate his voice of that brand of populist politics: "simple answers ... the government is good for nothing, our institutions don't work well, burn them all down and start from scratch" (Delacourt 2021).

On social media platforms, the attack language can be both intensely personal and beyond the bounds of acceptable.

And a reader's ability to relate is limited to some extent by their own personal experience. Men, for example, can express their solidarity with women attacked on social media. Yet for most men, the attacks they've had to weather are relatively limited – being dismissed as an asshole, at the worst, a fuckin' asshole. Women are subjected to a whole other level of hate. Supriya Dwivedi, who appears regularly on cable news public affairs panels, signed off as host of the 640 morning show in Toronto after tolerating years of abuse and personal threats. Dwivedi summarized her situation when she posted this statement: "But I'm sure you can all appreciate just how f-ed up it is when you start getting rape threats that target your 15 month old" (Dwivedi 2020). That political debate could degenerate to this level is so offensive that words to respond fail.

A story line from the 2020 presidential campaign that will continue to preoccupy the public policy community flows from the decision by Facebook and Twitter to shut Donald Trump down (Cohen, L. 2021).

Trump, some argue, made Twitter. "Over the course of his presidency, Trump did for Twitter what James Dean did for the open-top sports car," writes Dan Brooks in a column carried in the *Guardian* (Brooks 2021). Trump, the piece posits, was a genius at Twitter, and while his behaviour was "unbelievably irresponsible," no political figure "was better at posting."

Kurt Wagner, writing in *Bloomberg Businessweek*, states, "His constant use of the social network has made it more politically relevant than ever before, and many Americans learned to turn to Twitter to keep track of what Trump is thinking" (Wagner, K. 2020). Trump fired his secretary of defence – Mark Esper – on Twitter (McEvoy 2020b).

And he launched the final swing of his 2020 presidential campaign with a tweet. "The Fake News media is riding COVID, COVID, COVID all the way to the Election," Trump tapped out. "Losers!" (Glasser 2020).

Susan B. Glasser, covering the final swing for the *New Yorker*, concluded, "A pretty good distillation of his closing message: COVID is fake; the media is fake. Don't believe anything except what I tell you" (ibid.). Prudence would suggest caution is an appropriate approach to the president's feed. Trump's Twitter account, according to *The Logic*'s Martin Patriquin, was "arguably the internet's most read compendium of lies, spite, and knuckle-dragging fury" (Patriquin 2020).

In the end, the post-election social media postings from Trump in the run-up to the 6 January storming of the Capitol forced Facebook and Twitter to take action.

Section 230 of the Communications Decency Act allows internet companies to police their own sites while relieving these same companies of any liability for the user-created content their platforms host (New York Times 2020c). In practical terms, the companies could not be held liable for anything Trump posted, while holding the right to shut him down at their discretion.

And they did.

"In the end, two billionaires from California did what legions of politicians, prosecutors and power brokers had tried and failed to do for years," wrote Kevin Roose in the *New York Times* (Roose 2021). "They pulled the plug on President Trump." Facebook barred Trump through to the end of his term in office. "We believe the risks of allowing the president to continue to use our service during this period are simply too great," said CEO Mark Zuckerberg (Isaac and Conger 2021). Twitter's ban was permanent. And therefore the company's explanation more detailed. "After close review of recent Tweets from the @realDonaldTrump account and the context around them – specifically how they are being received and interpreted on and off Twitter – we have permanently suspended the account due to the risk of further incitement of violence" (Twitter 2021). Twitter's statement went on to make the point that, "In the context of horrific events this week, we made it clear on Wednesday that additional violations of the Twitter Rules would potentially result in this very course of action."

Trump's tweet stating he would not be attending the 20 January inauguration, for Twitter, was the proverbial bridge too far. The presidential post read, "To all those who have asked, I will not be going to the Inauguration on January 20th." Twitter interpreted the messaging as a signal to Trump supporters contemplating further disruptive action that Trump would not be personally present at the ceremony. In other words, feel free to storm the barricades. "Our public interest framework exists to enable the public to hear from elected officials and world leaders directly. It is built on a principle that the people have a right to hold power to account in the open" (ibid.). "However, we made it clear going back years that these accounts are not above our rules entirely and cannot use Twitter to incite violence."

The decision by the two social media behemoths was immediately denounced – by right-wing Republicans and civil libertarians alike. Former UN ambassador Nikki Haley, believed to harbour presidential aspirations, said, "Silencing people, not to mention the President of the US, is what happens in China not our country. #unbelievable (Haley 2021). Parler, a social media network similar to Twitter and funded by the Mercer family of Breitbart News and Cambridge Analytica fame (Ecarma 2020), saw a surge in users (Dawson, T. 2021).

Media observers pointed out the obvious: there were no shortage of media platforms available to Trump even if Twitter wasn't one of them. The "silencing" argument seemed a stretch. Presidents were able to connect with electors before social media platforms were invented.

But Kate Ruane, the lawyer for the American Civil Liberties Union, offered an interesting perspective. "We understand the desire to permanently suspend him now, but it should concern everyone when companies like Facebook and Twitter wield the unchecked power to remove people from platforms that have become indispensable for the speech of billions – especially when political realities make those decisions easier" (Colarossi 2021). Zuckerberg and Twitter president Jack Dorsey hold no public office, yet have "a kind of authority that no elected official on earth can claim," Ruane concluded (Roose 2021). CNN's John King subsequently noted that without a Twitter account, Trump is "eerily silent now" (Stelter 2021). There is no overstating the threat posed to liberal democracies when two commercial entities – albeit behemoths – can decide who does and does not get access to today's public square.

Guardian columnist Dan Brooks states, "The argument for Trump as the greatest Twitter user of all time is that he made the platform relevant" (Brooks 2021). However, Brooks adds, "The lesson, probably, is that Twitter should never be so relevant again."

In Canada, the federal government has decided the decisions as to what should or should not be taken down from social media sites should not be left exclusively to the companies. Canada's Charter includes a provision to improve "reasonable limits" on individual rights, which allows governments to ban hate speech.

Heritage Minister Steven Guilbeault, in late January 2021, announced take-down rules are coming (Curry 2021a). The new rules will require social media companies to remove illegal or hateful content from their sites. The federal government is acting on joint recommendations from the Public Policy Forum and the Canadian Race Relations Foundation. In a report commissioned by the government, the PPF concluded, "internet giants like Google and Facebook are not doing enough to review and remove dangerous content on their platforms" (ibid.).

The PPF study recommends the federal legislation, to be introduced in the spring of 2021, include a call for a powerful federal regulator to oversee social media and an "e-tribunal" where concerns over individual posts can be aired (ibid.).

The debate over federal regulations will be spirited, both in Canada and the United States, and will not be restricted to lawmakers. Project Lincoln activists in the US for example – a group that includes many disgruntled Republicans who worked actively to defeat Trump – have stated publicly they consider Facebook an anti-democratic institution and that the social media platform will be the group's "next fight" (Herle 2020b). The new federal rules, Guilbeault said in a statement, will require the companies to do exactly that, by requiring the companies to remove the offensive content "before they cause more harm and damage" (Curry 2021a).

Canadians, said the minister, are asking the government to hold social media companies accountable. A poll conducted for the foundation by Abacus Data reported 80 per cent of the 2,000 survey respondents expressed support for the removal of hateful or racist content (ibid.). How governments in countries with relatively small populations plan to force mega-multinationals to do anything remains to be seen.

Trump's use of Twitter for political purposes most emphatically extended his communication reach. As Wagner states, "His constant use of the social network has made it more politically relevant than ever before, and many Americans learned to turn to Twitter to keep track of what Trump is thinking" (Wagner, K. 2020).

With eighty-eight million-plus followers (Andrews 2021), Trump was able to connect directly. In a social media expression of Lazarsfeld's iconic two-step flow of communication, those followers could extend the former president's reach further with retweets.

Media, notably Fox News, extended Trump's message reach further still. Former White House staffer and author David Frum raised an interesting point when he tweeted, "I've often wondered whether a reason Canadian politics has been more moderate in the 21st c than UK, US, or Australian politics is that there are no Murdoch-owned media properties in Canada" (Frum 2021b).

Trump's social media reach, in turn, led to swollen follower totals for anyone in the former president's orbit. *New York Times* correspondent Maggie Haberman, the Trump whisperer of the White House press corps, had more than 1.5 million followers at the conclusion of the 2020 presidential campaign.

The debate as to whether Trump's use of Twitter was to a strategy or more a matter of a knee-jerk reaction to a momentary interest is ongoing. The answer may lie in an observation from Haberman, who knew her subject well enough to predict Trump would do better on election night than some were predicting and who penned an intriguing portrait of Trump as a "man who is both smarter and less competent than his enemies believe" (Smith, B. 2020c).

Haberman dismissed any suggestion Trump's post-vote conduct was to a master plan. "There is no grand strategy. President Trump is simply trying to survive from one news cycle to the next," the subtitle of Haberman's article read (Haberman 2020). Yet for the seventy-seven days of transition, Trump's use of Twitter allowed the former president to continue to set much of the news agenda.

President Biden has signalled his intent to use Twitter more sparingly than his predecessor. During the campaign, Biden told reporters, "If I'm elected, you won't have to worry about my tweets" (Glasser 2020).

President Biden's determination "to unite, to heal" America will require few or any words, he says (Wilkie 2020). "To make progress, we must stop treating our opponents as our enemy," the president said (Strauss 2020). To give effect to his efforts at reconciliation, Biden told American voters, "I'll work as hard for those who didn't vote for me as those who did" (Phillips, A. 2020).

The challenge of Biden's "ask" is that special media platforms operate based on algorithms that reward attack rhetoric – a commercial consideration former president Trump figured out. As Ronald J. Deibert states, "The engine at the heart of the business model – which prejudices sensational, extreme, and emotional content – amplifies our baser instincts, creates irresistible opportunities for malfeasance, and helps pollute the public sphere" (Deibert 2020, 172). This "pollution" of the "public sphere" is a factor in today's political discourse. The attacks can be personal or institutional or both. The former governor general of Canada offered her resignation after an independent audit cited allegations of a toxic work environment created – in part – by abusive language, public humiliation, and yelling (Platt and Nardi 2021).

The shift in the business model outlined by Deibert based on "the collection and monetization of the personal data of users" led directly to the emergence of social media platforms as primary sites of public discourse (Deibert 2020, 14). Instead of newspapers, or television channels, Facebook, Google, Twitter, and other sites had the eyeballs to sell. Algorithms rewarded interest. Political messaging was geared to algorithms.

During his time in office, Trump's tweets met Twitter's test of sensational and extreme. The "present mindedness" Innis (1991) was so concerned with produced a social media platform that stripped context, was emphatically of the moment, and spared people like Trump the burden of truth prior to "publication" and "dissemination."

Twitter, on occasion, censored Trump, blocked Trump, slapped warnings on Trump tweets, but only after the message was "out."

Facebook similarly impacted political messaging.

If emotional content works on social media, why would anyone be surprised that Prime Minister Trudeau spends much of his media time signalling intent. The prime minister's constant virtue signalling irritates his political opponents, for a host of reasons, not the least of which is that in social media terms, it works.

Social media has exposed other "truths" as well. The mainstream media is no longer mass. Its traditional revenue stream – advertising –

has dried up like an Arizona *arroyo*. Newspapers running blank front pages asking readers what we'd do if the newspaper wasn't there may discover the answer isn't as simple as government bailouts or a "tax" in all but name on social media platforms. Journalism will have to become a new business and like many other segments of society, produce a product people are prepared to pay for. Reporters will have to acquire new skills and new expertise – Jay Rosen suggests journalists become "experts in verification."

The public's truth has also been shaped by social media. Twitter in particular can be an angry, confrontational place. Things that in years past were considered best left unsaid now get said, potentially to wider audiences.

An arbitrator in early 2021 ruled the CBC had violated a temporary employee's privacy rights over remarks made in personal social media accounts found on a company computer. Without getting into the details of Ahmar Khan's case, one factoid of interest was the arbitrator's support of the notion you can't fire an employee for "privately criticizing their bosses – even if in crude terms" (Gollom 2021). If we fired everyone who called their boss an asshole, "this country would be facing a severe labour shortage," arbitrator Lorne Slotnick ruled (ibid.). Employees have undoubtedly been making such remarks on the shop floor forever. But in a social media era, the definition of what constitutes "in private" can get interesting.

Our political conversations are just as aggressive.

The sense of grievance over globalization's impact on countries or communities is expressed in aggressive language that questions the validity of contracts, the intentions of long-time trading partners, the integrity of multinational corporations, the rule of law. David Ricardo's law of comparative advantage is set aside, the Canadian debate over COVID-19 vaccines in early 2021 being one example. When the European Union issued a formal statement to the effect Canada will get the vaccines the federal government has contracted for, the statement is dismissed by Opposition members of Parliament as meaningless (Raycraft and Cochrane 2021). And in fairness, for Donald Trump, terms and conditions of trade agreements were in fact meaningless, so the skepticism is understandable, if regrettable for those who believe in liberalized trade.

Both examples speak to what Levitsky and Ziblatt describe as a loss of "mutual toleration" and "institutional forbearance" (Levitsky and Ziblatt 2019). Extreme partisan polarization leads to a questioning of the legitimacy of a political opponent. The right-wing media in the United States, for example, viciously attacks any Republican legislator that does not toe the party line. Said former Senate majority leader Trent Lott, "if you sway the slightest from the far right, you get hit by the conservative media" (ibid., 172). A loss of institutional forbearance means ignoring convention in favour of a limited, yet expansive, use of power – a Senate majority in the United States refusing to endorse a president's nominee to the Supreme Court in the last year of the president's mandate, then insisting on the right to approve the nominee of a president that shares the majority's political affiliation in the last week of that president's mandate.

Both trends constitute a threat to democracy, according to Levitsky and Ziblatt, and both are accelerated by the "explosion of alternative media, particularly cable news and social media" (ibid., 56).

The Canadian communications scholar Harold Innis (1991) believed powerful, advertising-driven media constituted a threat to Western civilization. The result, said Innis, was a media obsessed with "present-mindedness." Trump, and his use of Twitter, raised "present-mindedness" to new heights. With his tweets, Trump forced the mainstream media to play his game. The media invariably reported what Trump tweeted in an unfiltered manner, even if they later insisted the former president's offerings were lies.

Trump may, as former prime minister Brian Mulroney suggested in a conversation with Peter Mansbridge and Bruce Anderson on their podcast, need Twitter "to get to his cult-like supporters" (Mansbridge 2020), but the broader public caught up to the news Trump was making through the coverage of mainstream media outlets.

By way of illustration, Trump accused doctors in the United States of inflating the numbers of deaths attributed to COVID-19 to make more money. "Our doctors get more money if somebody dies from COVID," he claimed. "You know that, right?" Trump said (Glasser 2020). "When in doubt, choose COVID. … You get, like, two thousand dollars more. It's true." The crowd in attendance responded with a chant: "Fire Fauci" (ibid.) – a reference to Dr Anthony Fauci, director of the National Institute of Allergy and Infectious Diseases, who, according to the bio posted on the institute's website, has advised seven presidents on domestic and global health issues, and in recent months, has become one of the more recognizable authorities on the pandemic in America. Trump's response: "Don't tell anybody. But let me wait till a little bit after the election" (ibid.).

The exchange was recorded in detail in a *New Yorker* article. Writer Susan B. Glasser's piece did state, "This is what we will remember, and that he has chosen to campaign for a second term by pretending that a deadly pandemic is not happening on his watch" (ibid.).

Trump's attacks on the Biden family are another illustration, generating media interest about the business activities of Biden's son Hunter. The hashtag #BidenCrimeFamiily [*sic*] is "effective because it's simple," writes Emily Dreyfuss (2020). Trump, basic-ally, reduces everything – even complex issues – to the social media equivalent of a bumper sticker. And constant repetition of the mes-sage makes it all sound true – the 2020 equivalent of "Crooked Hillary." Dreyfuss says the hashtag includes a deliberate typo in a bid to circumvent Twitter's internal search results.

In the end, Trump's time in office, in many ways, was summar-ized in the manner of his leaving. As media scholar Larry Sabato put it, "A predictably disgraceful ending to the worst presidency in U.S. history" (Sabato 2020).

In a televised speech to the nation 7 November 2020, Joe Biden declared, "I sought this office to restore the soul of America" (Feiner 2020). He condemned Trump as one of the "most irrespon-sible presidents in American history" (Greve 2020), both in the immediate terms in the context of Trump's handling of the pan-demic and in the longer term, in the context of the damage the president's language has inflicted on the American body politic and its institutions.

At seventy-eight, Biden became the oldest person to take the oath of office for president in US history. His electoral pitch was fundamentally a pitch for unity. Where Trump dismissed the pandemic as a media exaggeration, Biden pledged a "full-scale, wartime effort" (Stolberg 2021) to combat an infection that has claimed more American lives than the Second World War (Haltiwanger 2021).

Where Trump declares, "the Media is just as corrupt as the Election itself" (Trump 2020f), Biden's press secretary tells reporters, "President-elect Biden believes that the media is a critical piece of our democracy; that transparency is incredibly important" (Rosen 2020b). The former president, in frustration, told his followers "Nevada is turning out to be a cesspool of Fake Votes" (Trump 2020c). Biden called on his fellow citizens to "put the harsh rhetoric of this campaign behind us" (Biden 2020). "We must end this uncivil war" (Keenan, E. 2021).

As congresswoman Liz Cheney noted, when an unruly mob literally stormed the barricades on Capitol Hill 6 January, "The president [Trump] could have immediately and forcefully intervened to stop the violence. He did not" (Washington Post 2021).

Biden will most certain face his own challenges in the Oval Office.

His assertion in the wake of the 6 January riots that "this is not who we are" (Telegraph 2021) seems Pollyannish at best. As David Remnick stated in the *New Yorker*, "Surely, these events are *part* of who we are, *part* of the American picture. To ignore those parts, those features of our national landscape, is to fail to confront them" (Remnick 2021).

On the final day, Trump opted not to attend the Biden inauguration, becoming the first president to do so since Andrew Johnson refused to attend the swearing in of Ulysses S. Grant in 1869. CNN's John King said of the former president, "He is angry, he is sullen, he is sulking." Senator Mitt Romney, a former presidential nominee for the Republican Party, said, "I would prefer to see a more graceful departure but that's not in the nature of the man" (McEvoy 2020a).

In the last hours as the nation's leader, Trump pardoned scores of people, including former adviser Steve Bannon. Again, Bannon's pardon was most symbolic. As California Democrat Adam Schiff observed, "Steve Bannon is getting a pardon from Trump after defrauding Trump's own supporters into paying for a wall that Trump promised Mexico would pay for. And if that sounds crazy, that's because it is" (Egan and Madani 2021).

Trump's leave-taking created a media opportunity for his many critics. Author David Frum tweeted, "There's a legend building among the non-deadend Trumpers, that Trump had a decent record before some arbitrary date: before the election, before the pandemic. It needs to be stressed that Trump was a crook, charlatan, bigot, thug, and incompetent from the start to the end" (Frum 2021a).

Self-centred and seized of his self-interest, Trump doesn't share the stage. On what John King said was "a page-turning day in America," Trump and his family emerged from the White House, boarded Marine One for the short flight to Joint Base Andrews, spoke briefly to a smallish crowd, then boarded Air Force One for the flight to his Florida residence at Mar-a-Lago. Before climbing the stairs to the plane, Trump took a few minutes to tell the world how hard his family had worked, how much his administration had accomplished in four years, insisted he had laid the foundation for any success the Biden administration might enjoy, and reminded the world one last time that the pandemic of COVID-19 was the "China virus ... We all know where it came from" (Chayes 2021).

Then the forty-fifth president of the United States took his leave, to a soundtrack he personally selected that included Frank Sinatra's cover of "My Way" and, more curiously, the 70s hit "YMCA" by the Village People (Watts 2021). Minutes before he walked up the stairs to board Air Force One for the last time, Trump told the assembled crowd, "this has been an incredible four years" (BBC 2021). And then the forty-fifth president of the United States told the world, "we will be back in some form" (Haberman 2021). As French-speaking reporters would say, *à suivre* – to be continued.

An Election Endnote

In August of 2021, Prime Minister Justin Trudeau called a federal election only he and his political advisers wanted.

Buoyed by public opinion polls suggesting he had built a double-digit lead in public support over his parliamentary opposition, Trudeau decided a snap summer election might just produce a Liberal majority government.

An election about nothing in particular in its early days became an election about him. The Liberal lead in public opinion polls disappeared like a snowbank in spring. Former *Toronto Star* editor Borden Spears's assertion that truth is cumulative became Trudeau's new truth. The charismatic new leader of 2015 who led a smallish rump of Liberal MPs to power largely on the basis of his personal appeal was forced to confront a deep-seated antipathy toward him personally. And that antipathy ran deepest among many who had once stood with him. Former justice minister Jody Wilson-Raybould, thanks mainly to the *Globe and Mail*, had the highest public profile of the disaffected. But coffee shop and corridor conversations with long-time Liberals suggested Wilson-Raybould was hardly alone.

The election, dismissed by columnist and political scientist David Moscrop as a waste of money and time, produced a new Parliament that looked a lot like the old Parliament (Moscrop 2021). The Liberals elected candidates in 158 ridings – up three from the seats held when the election was called, but short of the sought-after majority. The Conservative Party of Canada won top prize for running on the spot – 119 seats in the previous Parliament, 119 seats in the new. The Conservatives did well in the towns, not so well in the cities. The Bloc Québécois solidified its claim as the defenders of all things

Quebec. With thirty-four MPs, the BQ exceeded expectations from the campaign's early days and were a factor in denying Trudeau his majority. With twenty-five seats, the NDP remains the fourth-place party, and a distant fourth at that. The New Democrats were shut out in Atlantic Canada and held the party's single seat in Quebec, a national party in name only. The Greens won two seats with dramatically fewer voters. The People's Party of Canada got some votes but no seats. Voter turnout was middling though well below the 2019 and 2015 federal elections.

There will be much for political scientists and the pundits who populate television's political panels to analyze in their campaign post-mortems. How did urban millennials – a key constituency in Trudeau's rise to power – become so disappointed, even disillusioned? Was the Trudeau government all signal and no substance? Did the Liberals lose sight of what British political adviser Marc Stears describes as "the politics of everyday life ... the politics of the ordinary" (Economist 2021). How deep is Canada's urban-rural divide? And is that divide the emerging threat to national unity?

For purposes of this work, there is clearly a need for post-election conversations about both political journalism and political discourse. The first and most obvious question is whether the political journalism provided by the mainstream media meets the test of the public interest and more fundamentally, is even of interest to the public? Does the mainstream media's definition of what constitutes the news of the day align with the public's perception of what voters need to make an informed electoral choice? Journalism's "game" schema has always been in conflict with the public's "governance" schema, to use Thomas Patterson's language. The media's fixation with polls is a prime example. Every poll published anywhere by any company is parsed and picked through in a bid by media to tell the public who is "winning." Columns proclaiming emerging trends appear routinely, the shift attributed to ridiculously small sample sizes from regions. Political operatives, and the voting public, have long understood national polls are of limited value.

The media's role in agenda setting is well-established and candidates for public office ignore that reality at their peril. When he emerged from his meeting with Governor General Mary May Simon to confirm the election call, Trudeau had to know the assembled scribes would have one overarching question: Why now? Inexplicably, the prime minister didn't have an answer that stood up to any public scrutiny at all. Trudeau failed to frame the ballot question, and in doing so created an initial impression that he had put his partisan interest ahead of the public interest with the early election call.

In the days that followed, news stories identified multiple areas of "public interest," from forest fires in British Columbia to the disastrous collapse of the government in Afghanistan and subsequent takeover by the Taliban and the Delta-variant fourth wave of the COVID-19 pandemic that had left Canadians' concern for their health somewhat short-tempered.

The negative tone of news accounts convinced Liberal supporters on Twitter that the parliamentary press gallery had picked sides. In fact, the very structure of news stories was the source of the prime minister's discomfort. As set out in an earlier chapter, news stories identify a problem and the individual with the power to either solve the problem or make it worse. In mid-August, there was no shortage of problems. Trudeau was positioned as someone with the power to do something about the problems. Fed by opposition commentary, an overarching story line took hold that Trudeau wasn't tending to the problems because he was busy campaigning in an election the vast majority of Canadians believed the country didn't need just then. For those who question whether media coverage affects public opinion, the fact support for the governing Grits tanked in the campaign's early weeks warrants consideration.

As is often the case when a party's earned media strategy is flawed, certain Liberal strategists compounded the prime minister's problems by leaking stories that buttressed opposition charges the early election call was as cynical as it was opportunistic. The most spectacular example was the case of the Liberal operative who leaked a story that the campaign was canvassing Liberal candidates looking for "big ideas" that might be included in the party platform.

Conservative Party Leader Erin O'Toole and New Democratic Party Leader Jagmeet Singh could generate generally positive press for themselves by providing daily clips supportive of the "we don't need this election" story line. The fact the Conservatives had introduced numerous motions of non-confidence in the government during the minority Parliament – in essence asserting an election was in fact necessary immediately – didn't fit the media narrative and therefore was conveniently largely overlooked.

The very nature of news further contributed to the prime minister's perception problems. News, by definition, highlights the exception, what didn't work. The fact government may have successfully distributed literally millions of support payment cheques during the pandemic isn't news. The fact Joe Smith or Jane Jones didn't get his or her cheque is news. And as readers of any of Harvard professor Thomas Patterson's work can attest, this journalistic structure is by definition, anti-government. The risk for any incumbent government is that these failures or breakdowns become a metaphor for overall government competence, drinking water in First Nations communities being a prime example. (In the interests of full disclosure, my daughter Christiane Fox is the deputy minister of Indigenous Services Canada and since her appointment in the fall of 2020 has been responsible with her colleagues for getting the water advisories on reserves lifted.)

For reporters pursuing these story lines, the issue is simply holding people in power accountable, and the journalists in question rightly bristle at any suggestion of a partisan bias. But what is less clear is whether the bias of news creates a public discourse that is largely disconnected from the preoccupations of the public the media purports to serve.

The story of the Afghan interpreters and support workers caught in place when the Taliban swept into power is illustrative. Canadian journalists who had spent time covering the story when Canadian troops served there were dismayed that the Afghanis who had risked their lives to support Canada and Canadians were "abandoned" by the Trudeau government. The story dominated front pages and led newscasts for days. Journalists such as former CTV correspondent Kevin Newman and the *Globe and Mail*'s Mark MacKinnon provided firsthand accounts of their efforts to get threatened Afghanis to safety. Canada stood accused of leaving friends to face the wrath of the Taliban, our diplomats were called cowards, our evacuation efforts dismissed as an unmitigated disaster. And all blame was laid squarely at the feet of the prime minister. Retired military officers who had led Canadian troops in Afghanistan were sharply critical. The *Globe and Mail* referenced a poll that concluded almost half of Canadians disapproved of the Trudeau government's handling of the Afghanistan evacuation (Fife 2021). Ipsos Public Affairs CEO Darrell Bricker was quite correct when he wrote, "As long as Afghanistan leads the news the Liberals will struggle with getting their message out" (Bricker 2021). Struggle the Liberals did, for the several days Afghanistan led the news. Nightly tracking opinion polls reported the Conservative campaign had momentum, and that the public's perception of party leader Erin O'Toole was more positive.

Yet there is at least a question as to whether voters shared the media interest in the story. Indeed, there is a question as to whether media owners and executives shared the interest of their journalists in the Afghanistan question. Not one major Canadian news organization – including Canada's public broadcaster, the CBC – assigned a reporter to cover the story on the ground. The story was a story told by DMs and Zoom calls, without the benefit of any eyewitness journalistic accounts.

In the Abacus (Coletto 2021) polls measuring the top issues impacting voting intentions, reducing the cost of living led the list, followed by improving Canada's health care system and then dealing with climate change. Representing Canada internationally? Bottom of the list. And pollster and long-time Liberal strategist David Herle – creator of the popular podcast *The Herle Burly* and its spinoff *Curse of Politics* – reported that in a focus group discussion with undecided voters, the Afghanistan issue simply did not come up.

This fundamental conflict between political journalism and public discourse surfaced in the televised leaders' debates as well. The only English-language debate was roundly denounced as an unmitigated disaster, described by one seasoned Ottawa hand as a "drive-by smear" (Bryden 2021). The moderators chosen by the broadcast consortium saw the debates as an exercise in journalistic accountability. They were asking the leaders questions about promises made and not kept, policy failings past and present, and platform proposals of debatable merit. The voting public, in turn, wondered why the leaders weren't allowed to debate each other, why the format prohibited leaders from responding to a direct attack from a rival, why leaders with absolutely no prospect of ever forming a government were afforded equal time – one more example of television's structural false equivalency.

For Trudeau, the debate fiasco could fall under the heading of a self-inflicted wound. It was the prime minister who set up a debate commission under former governor general David Johnston with instructions to come up with a better format for the leaders' debates – a key feature of Canadian federal elections for the past forty years. It was the prime minister who named Craig Kielburger of WE fame as a member of the commission's advisory board before replacing him. And it was the commission that decided to turn the debates over to a consortium of broadcasters. Broadcasters – surprise surprise – developed a format for television, which, as former CBC journalist and journalism professor Paul Adams notes, emphasizes novelty, conflict and journalistic-style accountability (Adams 2021).

The public, in sharp contrast, were looking to get the measure of the men and woman who would lead the nation; their values, their ideas, their specific proposals on the big issues of our time. The journalist moderators certainly hammered the prime minister for his failure to deliver on promised electoral reform, the WE scandal, and the calamity of the evacuation of Canadian citizens and their dependants from Afghanistan. But Ontario Liberal MPP Mitzie Hunter wondered why, an hour into the ninety-minute debate, the issue of child care had yet to be raised, and the debate was seventy-seven minutes in before CTV's Evan Solomon raised a question about the economy.

Carleton professor and long-time CBC journalist Adrian Harewood spoke to the "journalistic accountability" side of the ensuing debate when he tweeted, "Those five opening questions for the party leaders by @ShachiKurl were among the most pointed and critical that I have ever heard in a federal party leaders debate. She challenged them all, made them uncomfortable and created some real tension. It was a masterclass" (Harewood 2019).

Others begged to differ. "Does Shachi Kurl realize she is the moderator for a National Leader's Debate for Prime Minister & not a reporter at a hostile presser?" asked Conservative strategist Jenni Byrne (2021). Former New Brunswick Liberal leader Kevin Vickers took it a step further: "Will there not be any accountability for this?" Vickers asked in a tweet. "The rude manner in which all the leaders were treated. The moderators debating with the leaders, I tuned in to hear leaders' views not theirs. I salute all the leaders for their professionalism and patience" (Vickers 2021). Airing as it did in the same time slot as Canadian tennis sensation Leylah Fernandez's electrifying run at the US Open, the televised leaders' debate may have attracted less viewer interest than in elections past. But the public backlash against both the format and the moderators would suggest more discussion is needed on whether the needs of journalism and the needs of the public are reconcilable in the current format.

The English-language televised leaders' debate also unveiled some of the challenges Canadian journalists and voters alike face in any discussion of societal divisions, whether based on values or race, and more specifically systemic racism. And again the role of the moderator was at the centre of the controversy.

Moderator Shachi Kurl prefaced a question to Bloc Québécois Leader Yves-François Blanchet with the statement: "You deny that Quebec has problems with racism," referring to provincial laws 96 and 21, which directly and particularly impact religious minorities, anglophones and allophones. Kurl then went on to state: "For those outside the province, please help them understand why your party also supports these discriminatory laws" (Caruso-Moro 2021).

The question had an immediate and transformational impact on the political debate in Quebec. Linking racism and discrimination to Quebecers rather than the laws themselves was key. Bloc Québécois Leader Yves-François Blanchet, who personifies egotism, responded with righteous indignation. O'Toole, Trudeau, and Singh, determined not to be caught on the wrong side of Quebec public opinion, moved quickly to distance themselves from the implications of Kurl's question – and in doing so, alienated some voters in English Canada who saw their positioning as a craven attempt at appeasement. The exchange was analyzed in detail by political journalists, some of whom do not read, write, or speak French and don't have an opinion on Quebec issues until they have had a chance to catch up with columnist Chantal Hébert's appearance on the CBC's At Issue panel.

Kurl's defenders argued the question was both legitimate and well put. Others criticized Kurl for being tone-deaf in the way she put the question, ironic given the fact BIPOC (Black, Indigenous, and people of colour) journalists in Canada have long criticized other media voices for their insensitivity to the realities of the BIPOC and LGBTQ+ communities.

The People's Party of Canada and leader Max Bernier brought a different dimension to the campaign story, with PPC supporters providing a daily "news" event to keep the story alive.

Pollsters at about the halfway point of the thirty-six-day campaign began to detect a groundswell of support for the far-right party. Easily dismissed in its formative years as a fringe movement, the PPC asserted itself into nightly news cycles with actions that fed media requirements for action, conflict, confrontation. Protests, noisy mostly; often punctuated with abusive profanity-laced attacks against the prime minister and his wife, Sophie Grégoire Trudeau. Incredibly, at one point the debate focused on whether a protester threw rocks or gravel at the Liberal leader. When the protests began to target hospitals and frontline hospital workers, the reports moved up the newscast. Anti-vaxxer language added to the appeal from a media perspective, given the fact COVID was the story.

The coverage, however, was the kind of coverage afforded any group outside the mainstream; the coverage once reserved for suburban teenagers, for example. The coverage also pushed the Afghan story down network news lineups, giving Trudeau an opportunity to flip the construct of news stories to his advantage. The Liberal leader was finally in a position to talk about the pandemic, vaccines, and his plan for Canada's post-pandemic future. Suddenly, Trudeau was in a position to advance himself as the person with the power to do something that had a direct impact on people's lives. The Liberal leader was able to advance his "pro-vaccine" argument and, in classic political "compare and contrast" language, let voters decide whether O'Toole's reluctance to insist all his candidates be vaccinated was an issue. Liberal organizers cancelled a scheduled event in Bolton, Ontario, because of the security risk – underscoring the significance and therefore the news value – of the protests. Trudeau, in subsequent appearances, was seen standing up to the protesters. Liberal strategists would later identify the sequence of events as the campaign's turning point.

The story began to shift somewhat when the pollsters began to suggest support for the PPC was reaching double digits and threatening to divide the right-of-centre vote.

The journalistic community began to debate what constituted appropriate "next steps" in terms of how and if the PPC should be covered. Columnists such as *Globe* veterans Andrew Coyne and John Ibbitson set out to make the case the PPC was entitled to be heard. Coyne, for example, wondered why the Green Party's Annamie Paul was invited to participate in the leaders' debate when her party was in free fall, while Bernier was excluded. Ibbitson argued media coverage needed to get past the protest and start covering the grievance that for some is the root cause of the anger. Others, such as *Star* columnist Shree Paradkar, wrote: "Disheartening to see established journalists irresponsibly arguing for legitimacy of a far-right party that seeks to overturn the essence of who we believe we are. None of this is about freedom of speech" (Paradkar 2021). The divide reflects an ongoing debate in newsrooms across North America, with emerging journalistic voices arguing in favour of "activist" journalism and rejecting the traditional adherence to journalistic objectivity as an affectation.

Political journalism, and political discourse during the 2021 federal campaign, included reported references to the "Americanization" of political discourse in Canada, invariably linked to comfortable assertions that comments of this type do not reflect who we are as a people. But former radio talk show host and political commentator Supriya Dwivedi challenges the premise. "Anyone who is surprised at these protests has not been paying attention to the political discourse in this country for quite some time," Dwivedi posted. "Canadian journalists would rather tell themselves that Americans are to blame than objectively analyze the right-wing misinformation network that is thriving in this country" (Dwivedi 2021). And that was before the PPC party leader denounced certain journalists by name as "idiots," dismissed their work as "disgusting smear jobs," and encouraged supporters to "play dirty" when dealing with journalists (Reynolds 2021).

Pollster Frank Graves retweeted a column by the *Globe*'s John Doyle entitled "Enough Already with the Demonization of CBC's Rosemary Barton" during the election campaign. Barton, wrote Doyle, generated more mail for his in-basket "than any person or show on TV ... The mail that comes in about her is mostly hate mail. Heaven only knows what Barton herself receives" (Doyle 2021). Frank Graves now has a sense of the depth of the depravity of some of the commentary. In response to his retweet of the Doyle column, Graves tweeted, "I have received a plethora of horrid responses that are completely outside of boundaries of civility" (Graves 2021b). "It may be my imagination but th elevel [*sic*] of toxic sludge that permeates Twitter today is making it increasingly useless as a tool of debate and information" (Graves 2021a).

Thomas C. Leonard's observation that the media is a primary site of political discourse in Western liberal democracies and that journalism provides much of the shorthand of political discourse is now a debatable proposition. Where are the "safe spaces" for reasoned political debate? What language is acceptable for that debate? Are Canadians in denial about who and what they are?

Vote efficiency is the name of the game, and as former Trudeau adviser Gerald Butts tweeted, "Vote efficiency isn't accidental" (Butts 2021). Campaign operatives demonstrably no longer see mainstream media as the central nervous system for connecting with voters. Singh's experiment with TikTok is illustrative; Facebook, YouTube, WhatsApp, Instagram and Twitter are all integral to the message mix.

In fact, on the last day of the 2021 federal campaign, with the polls showing his party in a dead heat with the Liberals, Conservative Party Leader Erin O'Toole scheduled only two public events, and slipped out the back door from the first event to avoid the media travelling with him, his handlers insisting there would be no media availability session that day, and no opportunity to put any questions to the Conservative leader. On a lot of days, Conservative Leader Erin O'Toole spent more time campaigning from his Ottawa television studio – dubbed the "O'Toole Box" by CTV's Glen McGregor – than he did on tour (McGregor 2021). More efficient, according to his strategists.

Veteran political journalism John Ivison noted, "This team has run a strong, positive campaign. Why invite this kind of coverage at the 11th hour?" (Ivison 2021).

The answer would make for a good and badly needed conversation.

References

Abbruzzese, J., and D. Byers. 2020. "About 73.1 Million People Tuned in to First Debate – and Most Stayed the Entire Time." *NBC News*, 30 September. Retrieved 23 November 2020. https://www.nbcnews.com/news/all/about-73-1-million-people-tuned-first-debate-most-stayed-n1241587.

Adam, G.S. 2009. "Jim Carey and the Problem of Journalism Education." *Cultural Studies* 23, 2: 157–66.

Adam, G.S., and R.P. Clark. 2006. *Journalism: The Democratic Craft.* New York, Oxford: Oxford University Press.

Adams, P. 2019a. "Why Election Coverage Neglects Climate Change." Public Policy Forum, 25 September. Retrieved 30 September 2019. https://policyoptions.irpp.org/magazines/september-2019/why-election-coverage-neglects-climate-change/.

– (@padams29). 2019b. "The Commission handed the debate back to the same type of people to organize and got the same defects as preciously existed. 4/." Twitter, 8 October. Retrieved 29 November 2019. https://twitter.com/padams29/status/1181551108113731584?s=20.

Adatto, K. 1990. "Sound Bite Democracy: Network Evening News Presidential Campaign Coverage, 1968 and 1998," Research Paper R-2. Shorenstein Center on Media, Politics and Public Policy, June. Retrieved 1 June 2018. https://shorensteincenter.org/wp-content/uploads/2012/03/r02_adatto.pdf?x78124.

Aivalis, C. 2020. "Newt Gingrich on Fox News BLAMES George Soros for Stealing Election from Donald Trump." YouTube, 8 November. Retrieved 27 January 2021. https://www.youtube.com/watch?v=Qgeta4awWdU.

Akin, D. 2017. "Finance Minister Bill Morneau Has Been Getting at Least $65K a Month from Firm He Regulates." *Global News*, 19 October. Retrieved 4 September 2019. https://globalnews.ca/news/3813503/finance-minister-bill-morneau-millions-dividends/.

Alba, D., and J. Nicas. 2020. "As Local News Dies, a Pay-for-Play Network Rises in Its Place." *New York Times*, 20 October. Retrieved 12 November 2020. https://www.nytimes.com/2020/10/18/technology/timpone-local-news-metric-media.html.

Alboim, E. 2019a. "Framing the Campaign: Trust and Values." Earnscliffe Strategy Group, 23 September. Retrieved 29 September 2019. https://earnscliffe.ca/en/news-and-insight/framing-the-campaign-trust-and-values/.

– (@ealboim). 2019b. "Globe deliberately files a warmed over story to disrupt election call day and become the object of media 'news' focus. Marketing not journalism. Conservatives jump on it and raise the rhetorical stakes. PM will be forced to respond. It is all so predictable … (1)." Twitter, 11 September. Retrieved 29 October 2019. https://twitter.com/ealboim/status/1171791314414985216?s=20.

– (@ealboim). 2019c. "(2) Today should be a day for voters to hear what's on offer. That's a lesser priority for media. Welcome to Election 2019. And the pattern that will persist for 40 days." Twitter, 11 September. Retrieved 29 October 2019. https://twitter.com/ealboim/status/ 11717918905025658995?s=20.

– (@ealboim). 2019d. "And the Globe gets the first question and self-servingly follows up on its own 'story.' Others focus on Lavalin too. The classic struggle for control over the 'news' agenda and narrative framing in political campaigns." Twitter, 11 September. Retrieved 29 October 2019. https://twitter.com/ealboim/status/1171799369789640704?s=20.

– (@ealboim). 2019e. "Day One: Media drive SNC and Bill 21 into Launch Day and then say Launch Day was 'derailed' as if by an unseen hand. Lots of analysis of tactics and strategic imperatives for parties and minimal coverage of leader speeches and party thematics (1)." Twitter, 11 September. Retrieved 29 October 2019. https://twitter.com/ealboim/status/1171967585610608640?s=20.

– (@ealboim). 2019f. "(2) On CBC TV The National, a wonderful irony. 'Streeters' asking people what issues are important to them with journalistic reportage and opinion that reflected none of that. The gap between media and voter agendas couldn't be more obvious." Twitter, 11 September. Retrieved 29 October 2019. https://twitter.com/ealboim/status/1171968561067298817?s=20.

– (@ealboim). 2019g. "This debate was far from the public service it should have been. The debate commission failed in its responsibility by turning the format over to TV producers – they traded pacing for incoherence. No one had the chance to develop a thought – all it rewarded was one liners (1)." Twitter, 7 October. Retrieved 20 January 2020. https://twitter.com/ealboim/status/ 1181387950229266433?s=20.

– (@ealboim). 2019h. "(3) Most of all, viewers and voters had little chance to hear what they wanted to hear most – who would be best to lead the country, what their vision for the country was. This had nothing to do with voters – it was about political bile, TV product and media PR. An awesome fail." Twitter, 7 October. Retrieved 20 January 2020. https://twitter.com/ealboim/status/1181389082175430657?s=20.

Alexander, C. (@calxandr). 2018. "When Trudeau kills pipeline projects & drives business away from Canada's oil patch, he costs us jobs, lowers our standard of living & empowers dictators like Putin." Twitter, 21 December. Retrieved 4 February 2019. https://twitter.com/calxandr/status/1076168933378539521.

Alexander, D. 2018. "New Details About Wilbur Ross' Business Point to Pattern of Grifting." *Forbes Magazine*, 7 August. Retrieved 27 August 2018. https://www.forbes.com/sites/danalexander/2018/08/06/new-details-about-wilbur-rosss-businesses-point-to-pattern-of-grifting/.

Allen, D., and J. Light, eds. 2015. *From Voice to Influence.* Chicago: University of Chicago Press.

Allen, J., and A. Parnes. 2017. *Shattered: Inside Hillary Clinton's Doomed Campaign.* New York: Crown.

Allport, G.W., and L. Postman. 1947. *The Psychology of Rumor.* New York: Henry Holt.

Allsop, J. 2019. "Both Sides." *Columbia Journalism Review*, 16 December. Retrieved 27 April 2020. https://www.cjr.org/the_media_today/both-sides-impeachment-trump.php.

Amanpour, C. (@camanpour). 2017. "We must always be truthful, not neutral. I learned from the Bosnia war never to draw false moral equivalence." Twitter, 18 August. Retrieved 4 August 2019. https://twitter.com/camanpour/status/898551020242046976?s=20.

Anderson, B., and D. Coletto. 2017a. "Newspapers in Peril? ... Canadians Unworried." Abacus Data, 16 June. Retrieved 18 November 2019. https://abacusdata.ca/newspapers-in-peril-canadians-unworried/.

– 2017b. "Trump Attracts Most Canadians' Attention; Jobs, Climate Change & Khadr Hot Button Issues." Abacus Data, 21 July. Retrieved 18 November 2019. http://abacusdata.ca/trump-attracts-most-canadians-attention-jobs-climate-change-khadr-hot-button-issues/.

– 2019. "Election Poll: A Sensational Week, Yet a Tight Race Remains." Abacus Data, 23 September. https://abacusdata.ca/a-sensational-week-yet-a-tight-race-remains/.

– 2020a. "Liberals Lead by Eight as Canadians Say Their Vote Is Tied to COVID-19 Response Plan." Abacus Data, 16 November. Retrieved 27 November 2020. https://abacusdata.ca/liberal-conservative-vote-november-polling-abacus-data//

– 2020b. "Liberals Up by 11 as Conservatives Stuck Below 30%." Abacus Data, 23 June. Retrieved 16 November 2020. https://abacusdata.ca/canadian-politics-poll-vote-june-2020-abacus-data/.

Anderson, C., E. Bell, and C. Shirky. 2012. "Post-Industrial Journalism: Adapting to the Present." Tow Center for Digital Journalism, 27 November. Retrieved 19 August 2018. https://towcenter.org/research/post-industrial-journalism-adapting-to-the-present-2/2018.

Andrews, T.M. 2021. "Trump Was a Center of Gravity on Twitter. What's It Like without Him?" *Washington Post*, 11 January. Retrieved 30 January 2021. https://www.washingtonpost.com/technology/2021/01/11/trump-twitter-ban-reaction/.

Arendt, H. 1968. *The Origins of Totalitarianism.* New York: A Harvest Book.

Armus, T. 2019. "After Their Son Was Doxed, Death Threats Forced a Syrian Family to Shutter Their Restaurant. Police Are Investigating." *Washington Post*, 10 October. Retrieved 21 February 2020. https://www.washingtonpost.com/nation/2019/10/10/syrian-family-closes-restaurant-after-son-doxed-death-threats/.

Associated Press. (n.d). "Anonymous Sources." *Associated Press.* Retrieved 18 November 2019. https://www.ap.org/about/news-values-and-principles/telling-the-story/anonymous-sources

Auletta, K. 1992. *Three Blind Mice: How the TV Networks Lost Their Way.* New York: Vintage Books.

– 2013. "Freedom of Information." *New Yorker*, 30 September. Retrieved 18 November 2019. https://www.newyorker.com/magazine/2013/10/07/freedom-of-information.

– 2014. "Outside the Box: Netflix and the Future of Television." *New Yorker*, 3 February. Retrieved 27 July 2018. https://www.newyorker.com/magazine/2014/02/03/outside-the-box-2.

Austen, I. 2019. "What Justin Trudeau Doesn't Regret in the SNC-Lavalin Affair." *New York Times*, 17 May. Retrieved 27 May 2019. https://www.nytimes.com/2019/05/17/world/canada/snc-lavalin-justin-trudeau-federal-election.html.

Axelrod, D. 2015. *Believer: My Forty Years in Politics.* New York: Penguin Books.

Axworthy, T. 2017. "Sovereignty in 2017: Its Meaning for Canada and the World." Conference, Massey College, Toronto, 31 March.

Badger, E. 2020. "The Cities Central to Fraud Conspiracy Theories Didn't Cost Trump the Election." *New York Times*, 16 November. Retrieved 21 November 2020. https://www.nytimes.com/2020/11/16/upshot/election-fraud-trump-cities.html.

Bagdikian, B.H. 1992. *The Media Monopoly.* Boston: Beacon Press.

Bain, G. 1994. *Gotcha! How the Media Distort the News.* Toronto: Key Porter Books.

Baker, P., and D. Wakabayashi. 2020. "Trump's Order on Social Media Could Harm One Person in Particular: Donald Trump." *New York Times*, 29 May. Retrieved 29 May 2020. https://www.nytimes.com/2020/05/28/us/politics/trump-jack-dorsey.html.

Balkissoon, D. 2020. "I Tried to Talk to My Bosses about Racism at Work." *Chatelaine*, 17 June. Retrieved 19 July 2020. https://www.chatelaine.com/opinion/racism-at-work/.

Ballingall, A. 2017. "John Honderich, Andrew Coyne Debate If Government Should Step In to 'Save Journalism.'" *Toronto Star*, 7 June. Retrieved 7 September 2019. https://www.thestar.com/news/canada/2017/06/06/john-honderich-andrew-coyne-debate-if-government-should-step-in-to-save-journalism.html.

Ballingall, J. (@JeffBallingall). 2020. "Business is getting tribal. Tell authentic stories and build out your audiences and communities. As the media giants fall, brands that can speak directly to their stakeholders and consumers will rise the fastest." Twitter, 14 January. Retrieved 31 January 2020. https://twitter.com/JeffBallingall/status/1217090415918243840?s=20.

Ball-Rokeach, S., and M. DeFleur. 1976. "A Dependency Model of Mass-Media Effects." *Communication Research* 3, 1: 3–21.

Banco, E., A. Rawnsley, and L. Cartwright. 2020. "Busted: Pentagon Contractors' Report on 'Wuhan Lab' Origins of Virus Is Bogus." *The Daily Beast*, 17 May. Retrieved 21 May 2020. https://www.thedailybeast.com/pentagon-contractors-report-on-wuhan-lab-origins-of-coronavirus-is-bogus.

Barry, W., and J. Madison. 1822. "James Madison to W.T. Barry." 4 August. Manuscript/mixed material. Retrieved 29 September 2019. https://www.loc.gov/item/mjm018999/

Barstow, D., S. Craig, and R. Buettner. 2018. "Trump Engaged in Suspect Tax Schemes as He Reaped Riches from His Father." *New York Times*, 2 October. Retrieved 6 September 2019. https://www.nytimes.com/interactive/2018/10/02/us/politics/donald-trump-tax-schemes-fred-trump.html.

Barstow, D., S. Craig, R. Buettner, and M. Twohey. 2016. "Donald Trump Tax Records Show He Could Have Avoided Taxes for Nearly Two Decades, the Times Found." *New York Times*, 1 October. Retrieved 19 November 2019. https://www.nytimes.com/2016/10/02/us/politics/donald-trump-taxes.html.

Barton, R. (@rosiebarton). 2018. "Um. I don't understand how this happened …" Twitter, 21 June. Retrieved 25 June 2018. https://twitter.com/RosieBarton/status/1009877712524185600.

Baudoin-Laarman, L. 2019. "Canada's National Newspaper Was Not Barred from Publishing a Scandal Involving PM Trudeau." *AFP Fact Check*, 9 October. Retrieved 24 March 2020. https://factcheck.afp.com/canadas-national-newspaper-was-not-barred-publishing-scandal-involving-pm-trudeau.

Bauerlein, M. 2008. *The Dumbest Generation: How the Digital Age Stupefies Young Americans and Jeopardizes Our Future.* Toronto: Penguin Books Canada.

Bayly, L. 2019. "Stock Market Sell-Off Was Due to a 'Glitch,' Says Trump." *NBC News*, 2 January. Retrieved 4 September 2019. https://www.nbcnews.com/business/markets/stock-market-sell-was-due-glitch-says-trump-n953881.

Bayne, D. 2017. "Mike Duffy: Trial by Media in a Post-Truth World." In *More Tough Crimes: True Cases by Canadian Judges and Criminal Lawyers.* book 3 in the *True Cases*, edited by W. Trudell, and L. Shyba. Calgary: Durvile Publications.

BBC. (@BBCBreaking). 2021. "'This has been an incredible four years, we've accomplished so much together' Donald Trump speaks, for the final time as US President, saying 'it's been something very special, we've accomplished a lot' bbc.in/2KvcH7d." Twitter, 20 January. Retrieved 31 January 2021. https://twitter.com/BBCBreaking/status/1351887427737149442?s=20.

Beaujon, A. 2013. "Scott Pelley: 'We're Getting the Big Stories Wrong, Over and Over Again.'" *Poynter*, 13 May. Retrieved 25 June 2018. https://www.poynter.org/news/scott-pelley-were-getting-big-stories-wrong-over-and-over-again.

Beck, U. 1986. *Risk Society: Towards a New Modernity.* London and Newbury Park, CA: Sage Publications.

Beckett, C. 2016. "What Does the Trump Triumph Mean for Journalism, Politics and Social Media?" *Polis: Journalism and Society at the LSE*, 13 November. http://blogs.lse.ac.uk/polis/2016/11/13/what-does-the-trump-triumph-mean-for-journalism-politics-and-social-media/.

Begnaud, D. (@DavidBegnaud). 2021. "BREAKING: 'I thought I was following my president. I thought I was following what we were called to do. He asked us to fly there. So I was doing was he asked us to do.' That's TX realtor Jenna Ryan who was arrested today by FBI after being at the D.C. riot." Twitter, 15 January. Retrieved 26 January 2021. https://twitter.com/DavidBegnaud/status/1350254179218911232?s=20.

Bell Canada Enterprises. 2007a. "*BCE* News Release." *BCE*, 29
    March. http://www.bce.ca/news-and-media/releases/show/
    bce?page=1&perpage=10&year=2007&month=3&keyword=.

– 2007b. "*BCE* Reviewing Strategic Alternatives: Includes Privatization Talks with
    Canadian-Led Consortium." News release. *BCE*, 17 April. http://www.bce.ca/
    news-and-media/releases/show/bce-reviewing-strategic-alternatives-includes-
    privatization-talks-with-canadian-led-consortium.

– 2007c. "Another Consortium Enters Privatization Talks with *BCE* – Strategic Review
    Process Continues." News release. *BCE*, 23 May. http://www.bce.ca/news-and-media/
    releases/show/another-consortium-enters-privatization-talks-with-bce-strategic-
    review-process-continues?page=1&perpage=10&year=2007&month=5&keyword=.

– 2007d. "*BCE* Strategic Review Process: Another Consortium Enters Privatization
    Talks." News release. *BCE*, 5 June. Retrieved from http://www.bce.ca/news-and-
    media/releases/show/bce-strategic-review-process-another-consortium-enters-
    privatization-talks?page=1&perpage=50&year=2007&month=6&keyword=.

– 2007e. "Strategic Review Process: *BCE* Signs Non-Disclosure and Standstill
    Agreement with TELUS Corporation to Explore Possibility of a Business
    Combination." News release. *BCE*, 20 June. http://www.bce.ca/news-and-media/
    releases/show/strategic-review-process-bce-signs-non-disclosure-and-standstill-
    agreement-with-telus-corporation-to-explore-possibility-of-a-business-combinatio-
    n?page=1&perpage=50&year=2007&month=6&keyword=.

– 2007f. "BCE Reaches Definitive Agreement to Be Acquired by Investor Group Led by
    Teachers, Providence and Madison – BCE Board Recommends Shareholders Accept
    C$42.75 (US$40.13) Per Share Offer." News release. *BCE*, 30 June. http://www.
    bce.ca/news-and-media/releases/show/bce-reaches-definitive-agreement-to-be-
    acquired-by-investor-group-led-by-teachers-providence-and-madison-bce-board-
    recommends-shareholders-accept-c4275-us4013-per-share-offer.

Bell, E. 2016. "Facebook Is Eating the World." *Columbia Journalism Review*, 7 March.
    https://www.cjr.org/analysis/facebook_and_media.php.

– 2017. "Technology Company? Publisher? The Lines Can No Longer Be Blurred."
    Guardian, 2 April. https://www.theguardian.com/media/2017/apr/02/facebook-
    google-youtube-inappropriate-advertising-fake-news.

– 2018. "Why Facebook's News Feed Changes Are Bad News for Democracy."
    Guardian, 21 January. https://www.theguardian.com/media/media-blog/2018/
    jan/21/why-facebook-news-feed-changes-bad-news-democracy.

– 2019. "Facebook and Twitter Are Growing into the Mainstream." *Guardian*, 2 June. Retrieved 20 September 2019. https://www.theguardian.com/media/commentisfree/2019/jun/02/social-platforms-facebook-debate-regulation.

Bell, E., O. Taylor, P. Brown, C. Hauka, and N. Rashidian. 2017. "The Platform Press: How Silicon Valley Reengineered Journalism." Tow Center for Digital Journalism, March. Retrieved 7 September 2019. https://academiccommons.columbia.edu/doi/10.7916/D8M90G7N/download.

Benkler, Y. 2006. *The Wealth of Networks: How Social Production Transforms Markets and Freedom*. New Haven, CT, and London: Yale University Press.

Benton, J. 2020. "Don't Give Up on Presidential Debates." *The Atlantic*, 1 October. Retrieved 23 November 2020. https://www.theatlantic.com/ideas/archive/2020/10/debates-still-matter/616559/.

Benzie, R. 2020. "Political Leaders Have Seen Approval Ratings Surge during the COVID-19 Pandemic, Poll Finds." *Toronto Star*, 6 May. Retrieved 7 May 2020. https://www.thestar.com/politics/provincial/2020/05/06/political-leaders-have-seen-approval-ratings-surge-during-the-covid-19-pandemic-poll-finds.html.

Berenson, T. 2020. "Donald Trump and His Lawyers Are Making Sweeping Allegations of Voter Fraud in Public. In Court, They Say No Such Thing." *Time*, 20 November. Retrieved 21 November 2020. https://time.com/5914377/donald-trump-no-evidence-fraud/.

Bergen, M. 2017a. "Google Follows Facebook in Unfurling Subscription Tool for News Publishers." *Globe and Mail*, 18 August. https://beta.theglobeandmail.com/report-on-business/international-business/google-follows-facebook-in-unfurling-subscription-tool-for-news-publishers/article36029520/.

– 2017b. "Google Extends Helping Hand to Publishers." *Globe and Mail*, 19 August.

Berger, P.L., and T. Luckmann. 1966. *The Social Construction of Reality. A Treatise in the Sociology of Knowledge*. New York: Anchor Books.

Berthiaume, L. 2019. "Lawyer for 2nd Charged in Shipbuilding Leak Case Says Client Will Plead Not Guilty." *Global News*, 5 March. Retrieved 5 September 2019. https://globalnews.ca/news/5023761/shipbuilding-leak-case-matthew-matchett/.

– 2020. "What You Need to Know about the Military's Assistance to Long-Term Care Homes." *National Post*, 23 April. Retrieved 2 May 2020. https://nationalpost.com/pmn/news-pmn/canada-news-pmn/trudeau-says-military-short-term-solution-to-caring-for-seniors.

Biden, J. (@JoeBiden). 2020. "It's time to put away the harsh rhetoric, lower the temperature, and listen to each other again. To make progress, we must stop treating our opponents as our enemy. We are not enemies. We are Americans." Twitter, 29 November. Retrieved 31 January 2021. https://twitter.com/JoeBiden/status/1333198053499490304?s=20.

Bilton, R. 2016. "How One Washington Post Reporter Uses Pen and Paper to Make His Tracking of Trump Get Noticed." NiemanLab, 9 September. Retrieved 4 September 2019. https://www.niemanlaborg/2016/09/how-one-washington-post-reporter-uses-pen-and-paper-to-make-his-tracking-of-trump-get-noticed/.

Blackall, M. 2021. "First Thing: Trump Becomes First President to Be Impeached Twice." *Guardian*, 14 January. Retrieved 27 January 2021. https://www.theguardian.com/us-news/2021/jan/14/first-thing-trump-becomes-first-president-to-be-impeached-twice.

Blackwell, K., and H. Ruja. 1994. *A Bibliography of Bertrand Russell.* London: Routledge.

Blackwell, T. 2018. "Ford Win Was a Sure Thing, Thanks to the 'Literally Thousands' of Targeted Online Ads, Says Campaign Official." *National Post*, 8 June. Retrieved 11 June 2018. http://nationalpost.com/news/politics/ford-win-was-a-sure-thing-thanks-to-the-literally-thousands-of-targeted-online-ads-says-campaign-official.

Blake, A. 2020. "Timeline: Trump's Efforts to Downplay the Coronavirus Threat." *Washington Post*, 31 March. Retrieved 1 May 2020. https://www.washingtonpost.com/politics/2020/03/12/trump-coronavirus-timeline/.

Block, J., J. Alter, and S. McCarthy. 2018. *Breslin and Hamill: Deadline Artists.* Edited by G. Bartz, and A. Gandini. Aired 15 November on HBO.

Boehmer, G. (@GabeBoehmerWF). 2020. "'Since March, more than 30,000 #media company employees in the United States have been subjected to layoffs, pay cuts or furloughs. @Gannett said that most of its 24,000 employees would take one-week furloughs in April, May and June.'" Twitter, 5 May. Retrieved 21 May 2020. https://twitter.com/GabeBoehmerWF/status/1257798108169134085?s=20.

Boessenkool, K. (@kenboessenkool). 2019. "Two things: 1. The rise in Conservative fortunes in the 06 election predated RCMP letter and continued on the same trajectory after. The idea that this is why Harper won is hogwash. 2. Someone in Goodale's Department was charged and found guilty." Twitter, 17 August. Retrieved 13 October 2019. https://twitter.com/KenBoessenkool/status/1162809587747020800?s=20.

Boorstin, D. 1962. *The Image: A Guide to Pseudo-Events in America.* 1987, 25th anniversary edition. New York: Atheneum.

Booth, W.C. 2009. *The Rhetoric of* RHETORIC: *The Quest for Effective Communication.* Malden, MA: Blackwell Publishing.

Boston Globe. 2018. "Journalists Are Not the Enemy." *Boston Globe*, 15 August. Retrieved 20 August 2018. https://www.bostonglobe.com/opinion/editorials/2018/08/15/editorial/Kt0NFFonrxqBI6N qqennvL/story.html.

Boudette, N.E. 2017. "Ford Will Build Electric Cars in Mexico, Shifting Its Plan." *New York Times*, 7 December. Retrieved 5 August 2019. https://www.nytimes.com/2017/12/07/business/ford-plant-electric.html.

Boutilier, A. 2019. "Trudeau Takes Aim at Big Tech, Announces 'Digital Charter.'" *Toronto Star*, 16 May. Retrieved 25 November 2019. https://www.thestar.com/news/canada/2019/05/16/trudeau-takes-aim-at-big-tech-announces-digital-charter.html.

–2020a. "'Does She Work for Canada or for China?' Conservative MP's Attack on Dr. Theresa Tam Draws Fire." *Toronto Star*, 23 April. Retrieved May 20, 2020. https://www.thestar.com/politics/federal/2020/04/23/does-she-work-for-canada-or-for-china-conservative-mps-attack-on-dr-theresa-tam-draws-no-comment-from-andrew-scheer.html.

– 2020b. "As Ottawa Mulled Regulations for Tech Giants, Facebook Tried to Recruit Public Servants." *Toronto Star*, 29 October. Retrieved 15 November 2020. https://www.thestar.com/politics/federal/2020/10/28/this-is-a-very-unhealthy-relationship-as-ottawa-mulled-regulations-for-tech-giants-facebook-tried-to-recruit-public-servants.html.

Boyd, A. 2020. "Why Canada Can't Make Its Own COVID-19 Vaccine – and How to 'Fix' the Problem Before the Nex Pandemic." *Toronto Star*, 25 November. Retrieved 27 November 2020. https://www.thestar.com/news/canada/2020/11/25/why-canada-cant-make-its-own-covid-19-vaccine-and-how-to-fix-the-problem-before-the-next-pandemic.html.

Boyd-Barrett, O., and T. Rantanen, eds. 1998. *The Globalization of News*. London: SAGE Publications Ltd.

Bradshaw, J., and C. Dobby. 2015. "Bell Media President Kevin Crull Ousted over Journalistic Meddling." *Globe and Mail*, 9 April. Retrieved 7 September 2019. https://www.theglobeandmail.com/report-on-business/bell-announces-departure-of-media-head-kevin-crull-over-journalistic-meddling/article23864190/.

Brady, B. (@sharemyopinion). 2020. "Not typical posturing. People are fed up with the media for many reasons. They are snarky, focused on gotcha movements, pretend they speak on behalf of Canadians, have inherent bias, focused on the next article, click bait. Can't forget the self important ones, who know everything." Twitter, 5 April. Retrieved 1 May 2020. https://twitter.com/sharemyopinion/status/1246748949677031424?s=20.

Breen, K. 2020. "Conservative Finance Critic Says Coronavirus Programs Amount to 'Freakonomics.'" *Global News*, 26 April. Retrieved 2 May 2020. https://globalnews.ca/news/6870332/coronavirus-freakonomics-conservative/.

Brett Wilson, W. (@WBrettWilson). 2019. "Where there is smoke there is often fire … especially in the world of @JustinTrudeau #KingOfHypocrisy." Twitter, 5 October. Retrieved 28 November 2019. https://twitter.com/WBrettWilson/status/1180587122371096578?s=20.

Breuninger, K. 2020. "Trump Deletes 'Noble Prizes' Tweets as He Struggles with Coronavirus Message." *CNBC*, 27 April. Retrieved 1 May 2020. https://www.cnbc.com/2020/04/27/coronavirus-trump-deletes-noble-prizes-tweets-as-he-struggles-with-message.html.

Breuninger, K., and D. Mangan. 2019. "WikiLeaks' Julian Assange Charged with 17 New Criminal Counts, Including Violating Espionage Act." *CNBC* 23 May. Retrieved 7 September 2019. https://www.cnbc.com/2019/05/23/wikileaks-co-founder-julian-assange-charged-with-17-new-criminal-counts.html.

Brewster, M. 2019. "Norman Was Told by Harper Cabinet to Talk to Quebec Shipyard about Leasing Deal." *CBC News*, 13 May. Retrieved 4 September 2019. https://www.cbc.ca/news/politics/mark-norman-supply-ship-davie-harper-mackay-1.5134548.

Brewster, M., and K. Harris. 2019. "'I Acted with Integrity': Mark Norman Claims Exoneration after Crown Stays Breach-of-Trust Charge." *CBC News*, 8 May. Retrieved 25 November 2019. https://www.cbc.ca/news/politics/mark-norman-breach-trust-charge-dropped-1.5127463.

Bricker, D. (@darrellbricker). 2018. "Given amount I've been reading about the relationship between social media and voter opinion in #onpoli, it's important to separate the fake from the real. Our social media analysis shows that nearly 20% of all social media activity in this campaign generated by bots." Twitter, 26 May. Retrieved 31 May 2019. https://twitter.com/darrellbricker/status/1000452192686424064.

– 2019a. "Liberals (31%, -3) Shed Support as Tories (40%, +4) Capitalize in Wake of Jody Wilson-Raybould Testimony." *Ipsos*, 5 March. Retrieved 4 October 2019. https://www.ipsos.com/en-ca/news-polls/Liberals-Shed-Support-Tories-Capitalize-in-Wake-of-Jody-Wilson-Raybould-Testimony.

– (@darrellbricker). 2019b. "I'm looking at the numbers and see what I see. There's no votes to gain going right. As for Twitter, about 1% of Canadians Tweet on a regular basis. Tells you how representative it is." Twitter, 18 July. Retrieved 13 October 2019. https://twitter.com/darrellbricker/status/1151954083118505984?s=20.

– (@darrellbricker). 2019c. "It's tedious how these lazy stories become accepted history. The Goodale issue did not decide the election. Gun crime moved the 905. Law and order carried the day." Twitter, 17 August. Retrieved 10 September 2019. https://twitter.com/darrellbricker/status/1162893964296499203?s=20.

– (@darrellbricker). 2019d. "What LPC has on its side is time. This isn't the last week of the campaign. Events could intervene. Problem is, they don't control events. No ad, no war room trick, nothing campaign controls will change this. Now relying on other parties to screw things up. 6/n." Twitter, 21 September. Retrieved 5 December 2019. https://twitter.com/darrellbricker/status/1175424076053123072?s=20.

– (@darrellbricker). 2019e. "Ah, no. A smart move with marginal impact. CPC vote actually grew a little through the weekend not the other way around. John Ivison: Barack Obama – the man who won the Canadian federal election | National Post." Twitter, 13 November. Retrieved 27 November 2019. https://twitter.com/darrellbricker/status/1194671316051415045?s=20.

– 2020. "Canadians Supportive of Wide-Ranging Measures to Battle COVID-19, Including Some Surveillance." *Ipsos*, 9 April. Retrieved 20 May 2020. https://www.ipsos.com/en-ca/news-and-polls/Canadians-Supportive-Of-Wide-Ranging-Measures-To-Battle-COVID19-Including-Some-Surveillance.

Brinkley, D. 2012. *Cronkite.* New York: Harper.

Britneff, B. 2019. "Ridings to Watch." *Global News*, 6 October. Retrieved 27 April 2020. https://globalnews.ca/news/5943737/ridings-to-watch-atlantic-canada/.

Broad, W.J., and D. Levin. 2020. "Trump Muses about Light as Remedy, but Also Disinfectant, Which Is Dangerous." *New York Times,* 24 April. Retrieved 1 May 2020. https://www.nytimes.com/2020/04/24/health/sunlight-coronavirus-trump.html.

Brodie, I. (@irbrodie). 2018a. "I hope the new federal subsidy program will let Canadian reporters get right on top of this story. wsj.com/articles/a-war …" Twitter, 26 November. Retrieved 4 February 2019. https://twitter.com/irbrodie/status/1067217523601358848.

– (@irbrodie). 2018b. "High quality journalism will want to show how climate change is expanding ag production in Alberta." Twitter, 26 November. Retrieved 7 September 2019. https://twitter.com/irbrodie/status/1067217658444046337?s=20.

– (@irbrodie). 2019a. "There may be a need to regulate the post-judicial career of
   Supreme Court and other judges." Twitter, 17 August. Retrieved 10 September
   2019. https://twitter.com/irbrodie/status/1162589280587272192?s=20.

– (@irbrodie). 2019b. "But the scandal here is that three retired Supreme Court judges,
   including one retired chief Justice, thought it was ok to squeeze the federal Attorney
   General about a criminal prosecution!" Twitter, 17 August. Retrieved 10 September 2019.
   https://twitter.com/irbrodie/status/1162589587488702464?s=20.

– (@irbrodie). 2019c. "After writing all those dicta about the rule of law!" Twitter,
   17 August. Retrieved 10 September 2019. https://.twitter.com/irbrodie/
   status/1162589859845791744?s=20.

– (@irbrodie). 2019d. "At the rate this story is disappearing, I doubt we'll see a
   question about it at the debate. Back to climate change, abortion and white
   supremacy, all with a straight face." Twitter, 20 September. Retrieved 29 September
   2019. https://twitter.com/irbrodie/status/1175084850786816001?s=20.

Brooks, D. 2020. "Why the Trump Ploy Stopped Working." *New York Times*, 30
   April. Retrieved 1 May 2020. https://www.nytimes.com/2020/04/30/opinion/
   coronavirus-unity.html.

– 2021. "Now That He's Been Banned We Can Say It: Donald Trump Was a Genius at
   Twitter." *Guardian*, 12 January. Retrieved 29 January 2021. https://www.theguardian.
   com/commentisfree/2021/jan/12/banned-donald-trump-genius-twitter.

Brown, I. 2009. "Give Me Twitter or Give Me Death." *Globe and Mail*, 28 March, F1.

Brown, J. (@JesseBrown). 2020. "This is a humiliating degradation of the Toronto
   Star, @IreneGentle. The 'exonerating' reports were commissioned by the Stillman
   Foundation. You do not disclose that David Stillman was a member of WE Charity's
   board and a major WE donor." Twitter, 4 November. Retrieved 19 November 2020.
   https://twitter.com/JesseBrown/status/1324126827846246405?s=20.

Bryden, J. 2020. "Trudeau Revisits Blackface Embarrassment during Black History Month."
   CBC News, 25 February. Retrieved 4 March 2020. https://www.cbc.ca/news/politics/
   justin-trudeau-blackface-1.5475399.

Buffalo Chronicle. 2019. "Trudeau Is Rumored to Be in Talks with an Accuser to Suppress
   an Explosive Sex Scandal." *Buffalo Chronicle*, 7 October. Retrieved 28 November 2019.
   https://buffalochronicle.com/2019/10/07/trudeau-is-rumored-to-be-in-talks-with-an-
   accusor-to-suppress-an-explosive-sex-scandal-that-may-force-him-from-office/.

Bump, P. 2020. "More Than 8 in 10 Trump Voters Think Biden's Win Is Not
   Legitimate." *Washington Post*, 11 November. Retrieved 2 February 2021.

https://www.washingtonpost.com/politics/2020/11/11/more-than-8-in-10-trump-voters-think-bidens-win-is-not-legitimate/

– 2021. "How Trump's 'Many Meetings' Final-Days Schedule Compares with Past Presidents." *Washington Post*, 14 January. Retrieved 27 January 2021. https://www.washingtonpost.com/politics/2021/01/14/how-trumps-lots-meetings-final-days-schedule-compares-with-past-presidents/.

Burke, J.L. 2018. *Robicheaux*. New York: Simon and Schuster.

Butts, G. (@gmbutts). 2020. "The end of the last progressive Canadian daily newspaper. It had become inevitable I suppose, but still sad to see it happen. #RIP." Twitter, 8 August. Retrieved 16 November 2020. https://twitter.com/gmbutts/status/1292136870772715521?s=20.

Byers, D. (@DylanByers). 2017. "FACEBOOK timeline: – didn't happen – happened, but was small – ok, semi-big – ok, it reached 126 million, but no evidence it influenced them." Twitter, 30 October. Retrieved 29 September 2019. https://twitter.com/DylanByers/status/925125114152214528.

Caddell, P. 1976. "Initial Working Paper on Political Strategy." 10 December.

Cadwalladr, C. 2018. "'Plucky Little Panel' That Found the Truth about Fake News, Facebook and Brexit." *Guardian*, 28 July. Retrieved 10 September 2019. https://www.theguardian.com/politics/2018/jul/28/dcms-committee-report-finds-truth-fake-news-facebook-brexit.

– 2019a. "Facebook's Role in Brexit – and the Threat to Democracy." *TED Talk*, April. Retrieved 2 May 2019. https://www.ted.com/talks/carole_cadwalladr_facebook_s_role_in_brexit_and_the_threat_to_democracy/transcript?language=en.

– 2019b. "My TED Talk: How I Took On the Tech Titans in Their Lair." *Guardian*, 21 April. Retrieved 2 May 2019. https://www.theguardian.com/uk-news/2019/apr/21/carole-cadwalladr-ted-tech-google-facebook-zuckerberg-silicon-valley.

Cadwalladr, C., E. Graham-Harrison, and M. Townsend. 2018. "Revealed: Brexit Insider Claims Vote Leave Team May Have Breached Spending Limits." *Guardian*, 24 March. Retrieved 23 May 2020. https://www.theguardian.com/politics/2018/mar/24/brexit-whistleblower-cambridge-analytica-beleave-vote-leave-shahmir-sanni.

Cahalane, C. 2012. "Martyn Lewis: 'Media Should Report Solutions.'" *Positive News*, 11 September. https://www.positive.news/2012/society/media/8386/martyn-lewis-media-report-solutions/.

Cairncross Review. 2019. "A Sustainable Future for Journalism." *Cairncross Review*, 12 February. Retrieved 21 May 2020. https://assets.publishing.service.gov.uk/

government/uploads/system/uploads/attachment_data/file/779882/021919_
DCMS_Cairncross_Review_.pdf.

Campbell, A., P. Converse, W. Miller, and D. Stokes. 1960. *The American Voter*. New
York: Wiley.

Campbell, K. (@AKimCampbell). 2019a. "And no, I don't wish anyone, anywhere,
the horror of being hit by a Category 4 Hurricane. But not everyone can have the
protection of a fortress like Mar a Lago, built to be hurricane-proof! Trump will
not bear the cost of his immoral abdication of the climate challenge!" Twitter,
29 August. Retrieved 3 September 2019. https://twitter.com/AKimCampbell/
status/1167215649241722880?s=20.

– 2019b. "I have deleted my tweet about the hurricane & Mar a Lago and sincerely
apologize to all it offended. It was intended as sarcasm-not a serious wish of
harm. Throwaway lines get a life of their own on Twitter. I shd know better. Mea
culpa." Twitter, 30 August. Retrieved 3 September 2019. https://twitter.com/
AKimCampbell/status/1167457272814948353?s=20.

Canadian Heritage. 2019. "The Government of Canada Supports Canadian Journalism
to Ensure the Vitality of Democracy." *Cision Newswire*, 22 May. Retrieved 10 May
2020. https://www.newswire.ca/news-releases/the-government-of-canada-
supports-canadian-journalism-to-ensure-the-vitality-of-democracy-822434599.html.

Canadian Journalism Foundation. 2015. "Nick Davies in Conversation with Gillian
Findlay." *CJF J-Talks*, 24 September. Toronto.

– 2016. "Building Bloomberg News." *CJF J-Talks*, 25 October. Toronto.

– 2018a. "When the Media Becomes the News: Covering Media, Power and Politics."
CJF J-Talks, 24 April. Toronto.

– 2018b. "Building Trust in Media." *CJF J-Talks*, 2 May. Toronto. http://cjf-fjc.ca/j-
talks/building-trust-media.

– 2018c. "How Trump Got Rich: The Real Story. Susanne Craig Talks with Julian Sher."
CJF J-Talks, 8 November. Toronto.

– 2019a. "Trust, Truth and Trump: A Conversation with Margaret Sullivan." *CJF J-Talks*,
28 May. Toronto.

– 2019b. "An Evening Celebrating Excellence in Journalism." *CJF-Talks*, 13 June.
Toronto.

– 2020. "After the U.S. Election: What's Next?" *CJF J-Talks*, 12 November. Toronto.
Retrieved 21 November 2020. https://cjf-fjc.ca/j-talks/after-us-election-
what%E2%80%99s-next.

Canadian Podcast Listener. 2019. Retrieved 24 March 2020. https://www. canadianpodcastlistener.ca/home#report.

Canadian Press. 2019. "A Leak, a Probe, a Case Closed: A Timeline of the Mark Norman Saga." *City News*, 8 May. Retrieved 12 October 2019. https://toronto.citynews. ca/2019/05/08/a-leak-a-probe-a-case-closed-a-timeline-of-the-mark-norman-saga/.

Caralle, K., and F. Mulraney. 2020. "Donald Trump Says 'People Can Decide for Themselves' If Osama Bin Laden's Body Double Was Killed and Says QAnon 'Are Strongly Against Pedophilia' as He Is Challenged on Conspiracy Theory Tweets." *Daily Mail*, 16 October. Retrieved 23 November, 2020. https://www.dailymail.co.uk/news/article-8845971/Trump-says-people-decide-challenged-conspiracy- theory-tweets.html.

Carey, J. 1989. *Communication as Culture: Essays on Media and Society*. London, New York: Routledge.

– 1997. *A Critical Reader*. Edited by E.S. Munson, and C.A. Warren. Minneapolis, MN: University of Minnesota Press.

– 2000. "Journalism and Democracy Are Names for the Same Thing." *Nieman Reports*, Summer Edition. Retrieved 8 November 2019. http://niemanreports.org/articles/journalism-and-democracy-are-names-for-the-same-thing/.

– 2008. *Communication as Culture: Essays on Media and Society*. Revised edition. New York & London: Routledge.

Carmody, D. 1994. "Time Responds to Criticism over Simpson Cover." *New York Times*, 25 June. Retrieved 25 November 2019. https://www.nytimes.com/1994/06/25/us/time-responds-to-criticism-over-simpson-cover.html.

Carper, A. 1995. "Paint-by-Numbers Journalism: How Reader Surveys and Focus Groups Subvert a Democratic Press." Discussion paper D-19. Shorenstein Center on Media, Politics and Public Policy, April. https://shoren steincenter.org/wp-content/uploads/2012/03/d19_carper-LR.pdf.

Carr, D. 2010. "WikiLeaks Taps Power of the Press." *New York Times*, 12 December. Retrieved 7 September 2019. https://www.nytimes.com/2010/12/13/business/media/13carr.html.

Castells, M. 2009. *The Rise of the Network Society: The Information Age: Economy, Society, and Culture*, volume 1, 2nd edition. Hoboken, NJ: John Wiley and Sons.

Cater, D. 1959. *The Fourth Branch of Government*. Boston: Houghton, Mifflin.

CBC. 2005. "Gomery Inquiry: A Summary of the Testimony. *CBC News Online*, 3 June. Retrieved 30 October 2019. https://www.cbc.ca/news2/background/groupaction/publicinquiry.html.

– 2006. "Mulroney Settles Suit against Peter C. Newman." CBC *News*, 12 June. Retrieved 8 September 2019. https://www.cbc.ca/news/can ada/mulroney-settles-suit-against-peter-c-newman-1.587281.

– 2017a. "Quebec Government Outlines $36M Plan to Help Struggling News Industry." CBC *News*, 5 December. Retrieved 9 September 2019. https://www.cbc.ca/news/canada/montreal/quebec-newspapers-1.4433347.

– (@CBCTheNational). 2017b. "Rosemary Barton presses Prime Minister Justin Trudeau about his decision to vacation on the private island owned by the Aga Khan." Twitter, 20 December. Retrieved 29 September 2019. https://twitter.com/CBCTheNational/status/943584705575755776.

– 2018. "Ontario Votes 2018: Poll Tracker: Latest Polls and Projections." CBC *News*, 6 June. https://newsinteractives.cbc.ca/onvotes/poll-tracker/.

– 2019a. "Paul Godfrey Steps Down as Postmedia CEO as Company Announces $1.4M Loss." CBC *News*, 10 January. Retrieved 9 September 2019. https://www.cbc.ca/news/canada/toronto/paul-godfrey-steps-down-as-postmedia-ceo-as-company-announces-1-4m-loss-1.4974050.

– 2019b. "PM Denies Bombshell G&M Report," part 1, Power Panel. *Power & Politics*, 7 February. Retrieved 11 April 2019. https://www.cbc.ca/news/politics/powerandpolitics/pm-denies-bombshell-g-m-report-part-1-power-panel-1.5010766.

– 2019c. "'Mark Norman Should Be the Next Chief of the Defence Staff,' Peter MacKay." *Power & Politics*, 10 May. https://www.cbc.ca/player/play/1520656963768.

– 2019d. "The Power Panel Breaks Down Former Prime Minister Kim Campbell's Now-Deleted Tweet about Hurricane Dorian and Trump's Mar-A-Lago Resort." *Power & Politics*, 30 August. Retrieved 3 September 2019. https://www.cbc.ca/player/play/1595956803792.

– 2019e. "What We Know about Justin Trudeau's Blackface Photos – and What Happens Next." CBC *News*, 20 September. Retrieved 23 September 2019. https://www.cbc.ca/news/politics/canada-votes-2019-trudeau-blackface-brownface-cbc-explains-1.5290664.

– 2020a. "Objectivity Is 'the View From Nowhere' and Potentially Harmful: Expert." *The Sunday Edition*, 10 July. Retrieved 18 July 2020. https://www.cbc.ca/radio/thesundayedition/objectivity-is-the-view-from-nowhere-and-potentially-harmful-expert-1.5639304.

– 2020b. "Trudeau Agrees to 1 Request to Testify on WE Controversy – as 2nd Committee Asks for Him Too." CBC *News*, 22 July. Retrieved 16 November 2020. https://www.cbc.ca/news/politics/justin-trudeau-we-charity-contract-1.5659172.

– 2020c. "The WE Charity Controversy Explained." *CBC News*, 28 July. Retrieved 16 November 2020. https://www.cbc.ca/news/canada/we-charity-student-grant-justin-trudeau-testimony-1.5666676.

– 2020d. "There Can Be No Plan for the Economy without a Vaccine Distribution Plan: O'Toole." *CBC News*, 30 November. Retrieved 1 December 2020. https://www.cbc.ca/news/politics/vaccine-distribution-economy-otoole-1.5822886.

CBS. (@*CBS*News). 2020. "CBS News asked @MikeBloomberg – who is campaigning in California during the Iowa Caucuses – about his feud with President Trump, and whether people want to see two billionaires fighting on Twitter. Bloomberg: 'Two billionaires? Who's the second one?'" Twitter, 3 February. Retrieved 27 February 2020. https://twitter.com/*CBC*News/status/1224546051941683202?s=20.

Cecco, L. 2019. "Toronto Syrian Restaurant Owners Defy Death Threats to Stay Open." *Guardian*, 10 October. Retrieved 21 February 2020. https://www.theguardian.com/world/2019/oct/10/syrian-restaurant-soufis-toronto-canada.

Chafkin, M., and S. Frier. 2017. "Mark Zuckerberg's Fake News Problem Isn't Going Away." *Bloomberg Businessweek*, 25 September, 51.

Chan, K. 2018. "Mark Zuckerberg a No-Show at Rare International Lawmakers Meeting on Facebook." *Global News*, 27 November. Retrieved 4 August 2019. https://globalnews.ca/news/4703327/mark-zuckerberg-international-lawmakers-facebook/.

Chase, S. 2007. "Foreign-Led Telecom Bids Must Obey Existing Cap, Flaherty Says." *Globe and Mail*, 11 April, B7.

– (@stevenchase). 2019. "As journalists first and foremost, we would like to make this point clear: On matters of partisan politics, Jerry Dias and Unifor do not speak for us. Please see this signed letter by Canadian journalists." Twitter, 20 September. Retrieved 5 December 2019. https://twitter.com/stevenchase/status/1175120311248928769?s=20.

Chase, S., and J. Dickson. 2020. "'Go Home and Stay Home,' Trudeau Tells Canadians." *Globe and Mail*, 23 March. Retrieved 1 May 2020. https://www.theglobeandmail.com/politics/article-go-home-and-stay-home-trudeau-tells-canadians/.

Chayes, M. 2021. "Trump Leaves White House for Last Time as President." *Newsday*, 20 January. Retrieved 26 January 2021. https://www.newsday.com/news/nation/trump-biden-inauguration-1.50125301.

Chiacu, D., and S.N. Lynch. 2018. "White House Adviser Says Canada's Trudeau 'Stabbed Us in the Back.'" 10 June. https://www.reuters.com/article/us-g7-summit-kudlow/white-house-adviser-says-canadas-trudeau-stabbed-us-in-the-back-idUSKBN1J60MU.

Chiu, J. 2020a. "Canadian Media Outlets Challenge the Government to Save the Industry with New Measures to Rein In Big Tech." *Toronto Star*, 22 October. Retrieved 15 November 2020. https://www.thestar.com/politics/federal/2020/10/22/canadian-media-outlets-challenge-the-government-to-save-the-industry-with-new-measures-to-rein-in-big-tech.html.

– 2020b. "Why Canada's Media Industry Is in More Danger Than You Think – and What We Can Do to Save It." *Toronto Star*, 9 November. Retrieved 15 November 2020. https://www.thestar.com/business/2020/11/09/why-canadas-media-industry-is-in-more-danger-than-you-think-and-what-we-can-do-to-save-it.html.

Chowdhury, R. 2020. "The Forever Battle of a Journalist of Colour: Dalton Camp Award Winning Essay." *Toronto Star*, 11 July. Retrieved 18 July 2020. https://www.thestar.com/opinion/contributors/2020/07/11/the-forever-battle-of-a-journalist-of-colour-dalton-camp-award-winning-essay.html.

Chozick, A. 2019. "With 'Talking to Strangers,' Malcolm Gladwell Goes Dark." *The New York Times*, 30 August. Retrieved 14 September 2019. https://www.nytimes.com/2019/08/30/business/malcolm-gladwell-talking-to-strangers.html.

Cillizza, C. 2018. "Donald Trump Just Said Something Truly Terrifying." CNN, 25 July. Retrieved 6 September 2019. https://www.cnn.com/2018/07/25/politics/donald-trump-vfw-unreality/index.html.

Cision. 2017. "The World in 2018 from The Economist Highlights Key Global Themes to Watch for Next Year." CISION *Newswire*, 20 November. Retrieved 29 May 2020. https://www.prnewswire.com/news-releases/the-world-in-2018-from-the-economist-highlights-key-global-themes-to-watch-for-next-year-300558659.html.

Clark, A. 2010. "The Man Who Blew the Whistle on Bernard Madoff." *Guardian*, 24 March. Retrieved 15 October 2019. https://www.theguardian.com/business/2010/mar/24/bernard-madoff-whistleblower-harry-markopolos.

Clark, C. 2017. "Trudeau Treated the Conflict-of-Interest Rules with Unbearable Lightness." *Globe and Mail*, 20 December. Retrieved 6 November 2021. https://www.theglobeandmail.com/opinion/trudeau-treated-the-conflict-of-interest-rules-with-unbearable-lightness/article37400080/.

Clark, C., and A. Radwanski. 2019. "Andrew Scheer, a Work in Progress: Where the Conservative Leader Comes From and How He Really Thinks." *Globe and Mail*, 28 September. Retrieved 31 October 2019. https://www.theglobeandmail.com/politics/article-andrew-scheer-a-work-in-progress-where-the-conservative-leader-comes/.

Clark, R.P. 2006. "James Carey: A Model for Journalists and Scholars Alike." *Poynter*, 23 May. Retrieved 20 October 2019. https://www.poynter.org/archive/2006/james-careya-model-for-journalists-and-scholars-alike/.

Clinton, H. 2017. *What Happened.* New York: Simon & Schuster.

CNN. 2019. "CNN Fact-Checks Trump's National Address." *CNN Cuomo Prime Time*, 9 January. Retrieved 9 May 2020. https://www.cnn.com/videos/politics/2019/01/09/fact-check-trump-address-border-security-john-king-daniel-dale-cpt-vpx.cnn.

Coben, H. (@HarlanCoben). 2016. "On Aleppo he sounds like a fifth grader giving a book report on a book he never read. #debatenight." Twitter, 19 October. Retrieved 29 September 2019. https://twitter.com/HarlanCoben/status/788927907733307393.

Cohen, B.C. 1963. *The Press and Foreign Policy.* Princeton, NJ: Princeton University Press.

Cohen, C.J., and J. Kahne. 2012. "Participatory Politics: New Media and Youth Political Action." Youth and Participatory Politics Research Network, June. Retrieved 18 April 2019. https://ypp.dmlcentral.net/sites/all/files/publications/YPP_Survey_Report_FULL.pdf.

Cohen, L. 2021. "Twitter and Facebook Lock Trump's Accounts, Take Down Video of His Message to Supporters." *CBS News*, 7 January. Retrieved 29 January 2021. https://www.cbsnews.com/news/trump-twitter-facebook-accounts-locked/.

Cohen, R. 2019. "Trump and His Henchmen in the Flames." *New York Times*, 4 October. Retrieved 18 November 2019. https://www.nytimes.com/2019/10/04/opinion/trump-impeach.html.

Colarossi, N. 2021. "ACLU Counsel Warns of 'Unchecked Power' of Twitter, Facebook after Trump Suspension." *Newsweek*, 9 January. Retrieved 29 January 2021. https://www.newsweek.com/aclu-counsel-warns-unchecked-power-twitter-facebook-after-trump-suspension-1560248.

Cole, D. 2019. "An Indictment in All but Name." *New York Review of Books*, 23 May.

Coletto, D. (@colettod). 2019a. "I think the Conservatives were winning the campaign in the first week. Set agenda on affordability and were focused on that. Blackface photos blew that up. Turned what was becoming a 'transactional' election into one about values and character. #elxn43." Twitter, 26 September. Retrieved 29 September 2019. https://twitter.com/Colettod/status/1177264535486550016?s=20.

– (@colettod). 2019b. "We will have new data out likely tomorrow. Finished a survey of 2,000 people this morning. But I'm increasingly convinced that the blackface controversy may end up helping the Liberals and Trudeau. How so? By shifting the agenda of the election. THREAD #elxn43." Twitter, 26 September. Retrieved 29 September 2019. https://twitter.com/Colettod/status/1177264534182080518?s=20.

– (@colettod). 2019c. "AN OBAMA EFFECT? 63% of Canadians have a favourable impression of @BarackObama. Most say his endorsement of @JustinTrudeau won't impact their vote. 1/4 say they are more likely to vote Liberal as a result. #elxn43." Twitter, 19 October. Retrieved 27 November 2019. https://twitter.com/Colettod/status/ 1185597662898208768?s=20.

Collins, E. 2016. "Les Moonves: Trump's Run Is 'Damn Good for CBS.'" *Politico*, 29 February. https://www.politico.com/blogs/on-media/2016/02/les-moonves-trump-cbs-220001.

Columbia Journalism Review. 2008. "Tim Russert." *Columbia Journalism Review*, 13 June. Retrieved 17 February 2020. https://archives.cjr.org/behind_the_news/tim_russert.php.

Commission on Freedom of the Press. 1947. *A Free and Responsible Press. A General Report on Mass Communication: Newspapers, Radio, Motion Pictures, Magazines and Books*. Chicago: Chicago University Press.

Common, D., and C. Gomez. 2018. "RCMP 'Sloppy' and 'Negligent' in Investigating Colten Boushie's Death, Say Independent Experts." *CBC News*, 6 March. Retrieved 12 October 2019. https://www.cbc.ca/news/canada/saskatchewan/rcmp-sloppy-and-negligent-in-invest igating-colten-boushie-s-death-say-independent-experts-1.4564050.

Competition Bureau. 2015. "Competition Bureau Statement Regarding the Proposed Acquisition by Postmedia Network Inc. of the English Language Newspapers of Quebecor Media Inc." Position Statement, 25 March. Retrieved 10 May 2020. https://www.ic.gc.ca/eic/site/cb-bc.nsf/eng/03899.html.

Connelly, M. 2009. *The Scarecrow*. New York: Little, Brown and Company.

Conservative Party of Canada. (@CPC_HQ). 2019. "This has been Trudeau's objective all along: to eliminate the industry with no regard for the hundreds of thousands of Canadians who rely on it. #cdnpoli." Twitter, 26 June. Retrieved 29 September 2019. https://twitter.com/CPC_HQ/status/1143836804505690112.

Coppins, M. 2020. "The Billion-Dollar Disinformation Campaign to Reelect the President." *The Atlantic*, 10 February. Retrieved 4 March 2020. https://www.theatlantic.com/magazine/archive/2020/03/the-2020-disinformation-war/605530/.

Couldry, N., and A. Hepp. 2011. "Conceptualizing Mediatization: Call for Papers for a Special Issue of 'Communication Theory.'" *International Communication Association Journal* 39, 9. Retrieved 8 March 2020. https://cdn.ymaws.com/www.icahdq.org/resource/resmgr/Newsletters_Archive/2011/NOV11.pdf.

Cox, J. 2020. "US Weekly Jobless Claims Hit 3.84 Million, Topping 30 Million over the Last 6 Weeks." *CNBC*, 30 April. Retrieved 1 May 2020. https://www.cnbc.com/2020/04/30/us-weekly-jobless-claims.html.

Coy, P. 2016. "The Sunny Side of Trump." *Bloomberg News*, 17 November.

Coy, P., and K. Dmitrieva. 2019. "Alexandria Ocasio-Cortez Is the Darling of the Left, Nightmare of the Right." *Bloomberg Businessweek*, 17 January. Retrieved 2 April 2019. https://www.bloomberg.com/news/features/2019-01-17/alexandria-ocasio-cortez-s-big-ideas-for-taxes-and-medicare.

Coyne, A. 2017. "Why the Media Should Say No to a Government Bailout." *National Post*, 16 June. Retrieved 6 December 2019. http://nationalpost.com/opinion/andrew-coyne-why-the-media-should-say-no-to-a-government-bailout/wcm/0c6f682f-ebcb-46a9-9034-423e01f14db3.

– 2019a. "It's When You Read Details of Media Bailout That the Chill Sets In." *National Post*, 20 March. Retrieved 2 April 2019. https://nationalpost.com/opinion/andrew-coyne-its-when-you-read-details-of-media-bailout-that-the-chill-sets-in.

– 2019b. "Can't the Liberals and Conservatives Both Lose?" *National Post*, 18 October. Retrieved 29 November 2019. https://nationalpost.com/news/politics/election-2019/andrew-coyne-cant-the-liberals-and-conservatives-both-lose.

– 2020. "Google and Facebook Didn't Cause the Newspaper Industry's Ills, and Making Them Pay Won't Fix Them." *Globe and Mail*, 5 May. Retrieved 8 May 2020. https://www.theglobeandmail.com/opinion/article-google-and-facebook-didnt-cause-the-newspaper-industrys-ills-and/.

CPAC. 2019. "Mark Norman and Marie Henein Full Press Conference." CPAC video file, 8 May. Retrieved 12 October 2019. https://www.youtube.com/watch?v=FJ6Q337NUWg.

Craig, S. 2016. "'We Have No Other Tools': CBC Asks Ottawa for More Than $300 Million in New Funding to Go Ad Free." *National Post*, 28 November. Retrieved 6 December 2019. http://business.financialpost.com/news/we-have-no-other-tools-cbc-asks-ottawa-for-more-than-300-million-in-new-funding-to-go-ad-free.

– 2019. "You Must Be This Conservative to Ride." *Canadaland*, 12 August. Retrieved 9 September 2019. https://www.canadalandshow.com/the-conservative-transformation-of-postmedia/.

Crawley, M. 2018. "Corporations Fuelled Ontario Proud's Pro-PC Election Spending." *CBC News*, 11 December. Retrieved 6 September 2019. https://www.cbc.ca/news/canada/toronto/ontario-proud-election-advertising-spending-1.4941210.

CTV. 2019a. "Source of Trudeau 'Brownface' Photo Says Only Motive Was Public's Right to Know." *CTV News*, 27 September. Retrieved 29 September 2019. https://toronto.ctvnews.ca/source-of-trudeau-brownface-photo-says-only-motive-was-public-s-right-to-know-1.4613782.

– (@ctvqp). 2019b. "The Globe and Mail's @RobertFife has more on the story revealing Andrew Scheer never really was a licensed insurance broker, despite claiming to be one. #ctvqp #cdnpoli #elxn43." Twitter, 29 September. Retrieved 30 October 2019. https://twitter.com/ctvqp/status/1178338729573912576.

– 2020. "Omar Khadr's Sister Suing Federal Government after She Was Barred from Flying Back to Canada." *CTV News*, 2 November. Retrieved 22 November 2020. https://headtopics.com/ca/omar-khadr-s-sister-suing-federal-government-after-she-was-barred-from-flying-back-to-canada-16626911.

Cudmore, J. 2015. "Davie Interim Supply Ship $700M Deal Delayed by Liberals." *CBC News*, 20 November. Retrieved 7 May 2020. https://www.cbc.ca/news/politics/davie-supply-ship-liberals-halt-1.3327039.

Culkin, J. 1967. "A Schoolman's Guide to Marshall McLuhan." *Saturday Review*, March: 51–3, 70–2.

Cupp, S.E. (@secupp). 2018. "The press is not the enemy of the people. The press is the enemy of the powerful, unaccountable and corrupt. The unjust, unethical, and dishonest. The bully, the blowhard. The cover up, run around and false pretense. Let's be clear: that's made the press the enemy of one person." Twitter, 16 August. Retrieved 10 September 2019. https://twitter.com/secupp/status/1030113973851570176?s=20.

Curran, J., and J. Seaton. 2003. *Power without Responsibility: The Press, Broadcasting, and New Media in Britain.* 6th ed. London and New York: Routledge.

Curran, R. (@reicurran). 2020. "Some personal news: I am very excited to be joining the Facebook Canada public policy team, effective today." Twitter, 18 May. Retrieved 15 November 2020. https://twitter.com/reicurran/status/1262368658589958149?s=20.

Currie, R.J. 2009. "Remarks by Richard Currie, 2009 Ivey Business Leader of the Year." Presentation and Gala Dinner, Royal York Hotel, Toronto, 14 October.

Curry, B. 2021a. "Heritage Minister Says Takedown Rules Coming, Welcomes Calls for New Social-Media Regulator." *Globe and Mail*, 27 January. Retrieved 29 January

2021. https://www.theglobeandmail.com/politics/article-heritage-minister-says-takedown-rules-coming-welcomes-calls-for-new/.

– 2021b. "Report Calls for Powerful New Federal Body to Regulate Social Media." *Globe and Mail,* 27 January. Retrieved 31 January 2021. https://www.theglobeandmail.com/politics/article-report-calls-for-powerful-new-federal-body-to-regulate-social-media/.

Curry, B., and T. McMahon. 2019. "Privacy Commissioner Takes Facebook to Court over Data Breaches." *Globe and Mail,* 25 April. Retrieved 7 September 2019. https://www.theglobeandmail.com/canada/article-their-privacy-framework-was-empty-facebook-blasted-by-canadian/.

Dahlberg, T. 2019. "Indianapolis Colts Quarterback Andrew Luck Makes the Only Decision He Can, Retiring at 29." *Toronto Star*, 25 August. Retrieved 10 September 2019. https://www.thestar.com/sports/football/2019/08/25/oft-injured-colts-quarterback-andrew-luck-announces-retirement-at-29.html.

Dale, D. (@ddale8). 2019. "Trump won the Pennsylvania county where he's speaking now by 18 points. He tells the crowd that he thinks it was '28 points.'" Twitter, 13 August. Retrieved 6 September 2019. https://twitter.com/ddale8/status/1161339166690631681?s=20.

– 2020. "Fact Check: In Bid to Win Michigan, Trump Makes False Claims about the State's Auto Industry." *CNN*, 2 November. Retrieved 22 November 2020. https://www.cnn.com/2020/11/02/politics/fact-check-michigan-auto-jobs-trump-obama/index.html.

D'Amore, R. 2019a. "Trudeau Says Video of Him in Blackface Shot during 'Costume Day' for River Guides." *Global News*, 20 September. Retrieved 17 February 2020. https://globalnews.ca/news/5929780/trudeau-blackface-video-quebec-2/.

– 2019b. "Arrest at Montreal Climate Strike after Protester Reportedly Throws Egg at Trudeau." *Global News*, 27 September. Retrieved 30 September 2019. https://globalnews.ca/news/5960896/trudeau-climate-march-montreal/.

Davey, K. 1986. *The Rainmaker: A Passion for Politics.* Toronto: Stoddart.

Davidson, W. 1983. "The Third-Person Effect in Communication." *Public Opinion Quarterly* 47, 1: 1–15. http://doi.org/10.1086/268763.

Davies, C. 2016. "All the Presidents' Den: Trump Follows the Gilded Trail to the 21 Club." *Guardian*, 18 November. Retrieved 30 April 2020. https://www.theguardian.com/us-news/2016/nov/18/21-club-new-york-trump-manhattan.

Davis, A. 2000. "Public Relations, Business News and the Reproduction of Corporate Elite Power." *Journalism* 1, 3: 282–304. http://doi.org/10.1177/146488490000100301.

– 2002. *Public Relations Democracy: Politics, Public Relations and the Mass Media in Britain.* Manchester and New York: Manchester University Press.

– 2003. "Whither Mass Media and Power? Evidence for a Critical Elite Theory Alternative." *Media, Culture & Society* 25, 5: 669–90.

– 2006a. "Media Effects and the Question of the Rational Audience: Lessons from the Financial Markets." *Media, Culture & Society* 28,4: 603–25.

– 2006b. "The Role of the Mass Media in Investor Relations." *Journal of Communication Management* 10, 1: 7–17. http://doi.org/10.1108/13632540610646337.

– 2007a. "The Economic Inefficiencies of Market Liberalization: The Case of Financial Information in the London Stock Exchange." *Global Media and Communication* 3, 2: 157–78.

– 2007b. *The Mediation of Power: A Critical Introduction.* New York: Routledge.

Davis, A., and E. Seymour. 2010. "Generating Forms of Media Capital Inside and Outside a Field: The Strange Case of David Cameron in the UK Political Field." *Media, Culture & Society* 32, 5 (September): 739–59.

Dawson, M. 2017. "The Trudeau Report." Office of the Conflict of Interest and Ethics Commissioner, 20 December. Retrieved 27 September 2019. https://ciec-ccie.parl.gc.ca/en/publications/Documents/InvestigationReports/The%20Trudeau%20Report.pdf.

Dawson, T. 2021. "Trumpism Moves to Parler: The Alternative Social Media Platform Sees a Surge in Popularity." *National Post*, 8 January. Retrieved 4 February 2021. https://nationalpost.com/news/trumpism-moves-to-parler-the-alternative-social-media-platform-sees-a-surge-in-popularity.

Dawson, T., and V. Subramaniam. 2019. "'I'm Really Sorry': Justin Trudeau Admits Wearing Brownface at 2001 Costume Party." *National Post*, 18 September. Retrieved 29 September 2019. https://nationalpost.com/news/politics/election-2019/yearbook-photo-surfaces-of-trudeau-wearing-brownface-costume-in-2001.

Debates of the Senate. 1995. "Debates of the Senate. Official Report." *Hansard*, volume 135, issues 40–89, 1486, 30 March. Retrieved 4 October 2019. http://parl.canadiana.ca/browse/eng/s/debates/35-1.

DeCloet, D. 2007. "Shut Out, Could Telus Turn Hostile?" *Globe and Mail*, 27 June, B1.

DeCloet, D., and S. Stewart. 2007. "The Man Who Won the Auction for the Biggest Prize in Canada." *Globe and Mail*, 2 July, B1.

Deibert, R. 2017. "From Russia, with Tainted Love." *Citizen Lab*, 25 May. Retrieved 13 June 2018. https://deibert.citizenlab.ca/2017/05/from-russia-with-tainted-love/.

– 2020. *Reset: Reclaiming the Internet for Civil Society.* Toronto: House of Anansi Press Inc.

Delacourt, S. 2013. *Shopping for Votes. How Politicians Choose Us and We Choose Them.* Madeira Park, BC: Douglas & McIntyre.

– 2018. "As Politicians and Social Media Take a Beating, Trudeau Praises Traditional Journalism." *Toronto Star*, 12 November. Retrieved 16 November 2018. https://www.thestar.com/politics/political-opinion/2018/11/12/as-politicians-and-social-media-take-a-beating-trudeau-praises-traditional-journalism.html.

– 2019a. "Jody Wilson-Raybould Rewrote the Book on How to Lose Your Job." *Toronto Star*, 2 April. Retrieved 11 April 2019. https://www.thestar.com/politics/political-opinion/2019/04/02/jody-wilson-raybould-rewrote-the-book-on-how-to-lose-your-job.html.

– 2019b. "The Federal Election Was Really about One Thing: The Humbling of Our Leaders." *Toronto Star*, 7 November. Retrieved 18 November 2019. https://www.thestar.com/politics/political-opinion/2019/11/07/the-federal-election-was-really-about-one-thing-the-humbling-of-our-leaders.html.

– 2019c. "How the Liberals Won – an Inside Look at the Targeting and Tactics That Got Trudeau Re-Elected." *Toronto Star*, 23 November. Retrieved 25 November 2019. https://www.thestar.com/politics/2019/11/23/how-the-liberals-won-an-inside-look-at-the-targeting-and-tactics-that-got-trudeau-re-elected.html.

– 2021. "'I'm an Introvert' and Doug Ford 'Wears His Heart on His Sleeve': What Justin Trudeau Has Learned during the Pandemic." *Toronto Star*, 30 January. Retrieved 30 January 2021. https://www.thestar.com/politics/federal/2021/01/30/im-an-introvert-and-doug-ford-wears-his-heart-on-his-sleeve-what-justin-trudeau-has-learned-during-the-pandemic.html.

Democracy Now. 2005. "Bill Moyers Responds to CPB's Tomlinson Charges of Liberal Bias." *Democracy Now*, 16 May. Retrieved 9 September 2019. https://www.democracynow.org/2005/5/16/bill_moyers_responds_to_cpbs_tomlinson.

Department of Finance Canada. 2018. "Fall Economic Statement 2018: Investing in Middle Class Jobs." Retrieved 10 May 2020. https://budget.gc.ca/fes-eea/2018/docs/statement-enonce/fes-eea-2018-eng.pdf.

Desbarats, P. 1996. *Guide to Canadian News Media*, 2nd ed. Toronto: Harcourt Brace Jovanovich Canada.

Desilver, D. 2019. "Clinton's Impeachment Barely Dented His Public Support, and It
    Turned Off Many Americans." *Pew Research Center*, 3 October. Retrieved 17 February
    2020. https://www.pewresearch.org/fact-tank/2019/10/03/clintons-impeachment-
    barely-dented-his-public-support-and-it-turned-off-many-americans/.

de Vreese, C.H. 2017. "Political Journalism in a Populist Age." *Shorenstein Center
    on Media, Politics and Public Policy*, 11 December. https://shorensteincenter.org/
    political-journalism-populist-age/.

De Vynck, G. 2020. "Former Google CEO Calls Social Networks 'Amplifiers for Idiots.'"
    Bloomberg, 21 October. Retrieved 15 November 2020. https://www.bloomberg.
    com/news/articles/2020-10-21/former-google-ceo-calls-social-networks-
    amplifiers-for-idiots.

Dickson, J. 2018. "As 2019 Federal Election Looms, Pierre Poilievre Rejoices in
    Agitating the Liberals." *Global News*, 27 December. Retrieved 4 September 2019.
    https://globalnews.ca/news/4797615/pierre-poilievre-2019-election-liberals/.

Digital, Culture, Media and Sport Committee. 2018. "Disinformation and 'Fake News':
    Interim Report." Fifth Report of Session 2017–19. UK House of Commons, 29 July.
    Retrieved 27 August 2018. https://publi cations.parliament.uk/pa/cm201719/
    cmselect/cmcumeds/363/363.pdf.

DM@X and Nordicity. 2020. *Digital Media at the Crossroads*. http://www.nordicity.com/
    de/cache/work/139/DM_X2020%20-%20No rdicity%20-%20The%20Digital%20
    Media%20Universe%20in%20Canada%20-%20Final%20Report.pdf.

D'Mello, C. 2019. "Poll Suggests Support for PCs Has 'Collapsed,' Ford Now Less
    Popular Than Wynne." *CTV News Toronto*, 24 May. Retrieved 18 December 2019.
    https://toronto.ctvnews.ca/poll-sug gests-support-for-pcs-has-collapsed-ford-
    now-less-popular-than-wynne-1.4435061.

Dornan, C. 2017a. "*Dezinformatsiya: The Past, Present and Future of 'Fake News.'*" Series
    of reflection papers, Canadian Commission for UNESCO, 30 March. https://
    en.ccunesco.ca/search#q=Dezinformatsiya.

– 2017b. "Post<Riposte" Episode 4. *Creative Comms*, 23 October. Podcast. https://
    carleton.ca/sjc/2017/episode-4-creative-comms/.

– (@CTDornan). 2018a. "Nope. This gives them too much credit. Let's recall the
    words of Deep Throat: 'Forget the myths the media's created about the White
    House. The truth is, these are not very bright guys, and things got out of hand.'"
    Twitter, 21 June. Retrieved 25 June 2018. https://twitter.com/CTDornan/
    status/1009954919565045760.

– (@CTDornan). 2018b. "A sample of how and why Trump uses Twitter. This is Trump sitting on the sofa watching the game with his cronies, commenting on the play, complaining about strategy, bragging that he would do better. Except we're his cronies, right there on the sofa in his Fireside Chatroom. twitter.com/realDonaldTrum …" Twitter, 3 November. Retrieved 5 November 2018. https://twitter.com/CTDornan/status/1058912230593441792.

– 2020a. "Science Disinformation in a Time of Pandemic." *Public Policy Forum*, June. Retrieved 19 July 2020. https://ppforum.ca/wp-content/uploads/2020/06/ScienceDisinformation-PPF-June2020-EN.pdf.

– (@CTDornan). 2020b. "On the plus side, we're hearing next to nothing about the Kardashians these days." Twitter, 18 March. Retrieved 30 April 2020. https://twitter.com/CTDornan/status/1240425870239707140?s=20.

– (@CTDornan). 2021. "Sure enough, this is shaping up to be the line of defence." Twitter, 16 January. Retrieved 26 January 2021. https://twitter.com/CTDornan/status/1350629467484512256?s=20.

Dowd, M. 2020. "King Kong Trump, Losing His Grip." *New York Times*, 24 October. https://www.nytimes.com/2020/10/24/opinion/sunday/trump-losing-his-grip.html

Dreyfuss, E. 2020. "Trump's Tweeting Isn't Crazy. It's Strategic, Typos and All." *New York Times*, 5 November. Retrieved 31 January 2021. https://www.nytimes.com/2020/11/05/opinion/sunday/trump-twitter-biden-misinformation.html.

Driedger, S. 2008. "Creating Shared Realities through Communication: Exploring the Agenda-Building Role of the Media and Its Sources in the E. coli Contamination of a Canadian Public Drinking Water Supply." *Journal of Risk Research* 11, 1–2: 23–40.

Dubois, E., J. McGuire, and T. Owen. 2019. "Policy Options Pre-Election Breakfast Series: Electoral Integrity and Disinformation." *Institute of Research on Public Policy*, 7 May. Retrieved 10 June 2019. https://policyoptions.irpp.org/magazines/may-2019/electoral-integrity-disinformation/.

Dunaway, J. 2016. "Mobile vs. Computer: Implications for News Audiences and Outlets." Discussion paper series #D-103. *Shorenstein Center on Media, Politics and Public Policy*, August. Retrieved 8 December 2019. https://shorensteincenter.org/wp-content/uploads/2016/08/Mobile-vs-Computer-News-Johanna-Dunaway-2016.pdf.

Dwivedi, S. (@supriyadwivedi). 2020. "3/ Being able to talk into a mic for a living is an incredible privilege, and I'm so grateful for everyday I had. But I'm sure you can all appreciate just how f-ed up it is when you start getting rape threats that target your 15 month old." Twitter, 27 November. Retrieved 30 January 2021. https://twitter.com/supriyadwivedi/status/1332326254545088514?s=20.

Dyroff, C. 2018. "Here's How Much Cellphones Have Actually Changed over the Years." *Insider*, 25 July. Retrieved 13 October 2019. https://www.insider.com/the-history-of-the-cellphone-2018-7.

Dyson, E. 1997. *Release 2.0: A Design for Living in the Digital Age*. New York: Broadway Books.

Dzhanova, Y. 2020. "Trump Cites the 'Best Pollster in Britain' in Baseless Claims That Biden Stole the Election, but That Pollster Is Accused of Lying about Having a PhD." *Business Insider*, 8 November. Retrieved 2 February 2021. https://www.businessinsider.com/trump-cites-questionable-pollster-to-back-up-clai-illegitimate-election-results-2020-11.

Ecarma, C. 2020. "Parler Is Becoming the Right's Safe Space for Election Denial." *Vanity Fair*, 16 November. Retrieved 4 February 2021. https://www.vanityfair.com/news/2020/11/parler-safe-space-for-trump-election-denial.

Economist. 2001. "Broadband Blues." *The Economist*, 21 June. Retrieved 18 December 2019. https://www.economist.com/business/2001/06/21/broadband-blues.

– 2016a. "The Party Declines." *The Economist*, 5 March. Retrieved 12 May 2020. https://www.economist.com/united-states/2016/03/05/the-party-declines.

– 2016b. "How It Happened." *The Economist*, 12 November. Retrieved 18 December 2019. http://www.economist.com/news/united-states/21710028-donald-trump-won-fewer-votes-mitt-romneyin-2012-hillary-clinton-did-much-worse.

– 2016c. "The Trump Era." *The Economist*, 12 November. Retrieved 18 December 2019. https://www.economist.com/leaders/2016/11/12/the-trump-era.

– 2016d. "Donald Trump's Conflicts of Interest." *The Economist*, 26 November. Retrieved 18 December 2019. https://www.economist.com/news/business/21710828-weakness-trump-inc-may-pose-more-problem-its-sprawl-donald-trumps-conflicts.

–2017a. "The Trump Presidency Is in a Hole." *The Economist*, 1 April. https://www.economist.com/news/leaders/21719794-and-bad-americaand-world-trump-presidency-hole.

– 2017b. "The Future of Bannonism." *The Economist*, 25 August. Retrieved 15 August 2019. https://www.economist.com/united-states/2017/08/25/the-future-of-bannonism.

– 2017c. "Capitol Punishment." *The Economist*, 28 October.

– 2017d. "Briefing: Social Media and Politics." *The Economist*, 4 November.

– 2017e. "Do Social Media Threaten Democracy?" *The Economist*, 4 November. https://
www.economist.com/news/leaders/21730871-facebook-google-and-twitter-were-
supposed-save-politics-good-information-drove-out.

– 2017f. "Once Considered a Boon to Democracy, Social Media Have Started to
Look Like Its Nemesis." *The Economist*, 4 November. Retrieved 9 August 2018.
https://www.economist.com/briefing/2017/11/04/once-considered-a-boon-to-
democracy-social-media-have-started-to-look-like-its-nemesis.

– 2018. "Even If America Wins Concessions, Worry." *The Economist*, 31 March.
Retrieved 8 August 2018. http://media.economist.com/news/leaders/21739654-
donald-trumps-trade-policy-economically-muddled-and-politically-toxic-even-if-
america-wins.

– 2019a. "Bagehot: The Followership Problem." *The Economist*, 2 May, 49.

– 2019b. "Click Here to Buy Libra." *The Economist*, 22 June, 9.

– 2019c. "Trump's Tweet Divides Americans." *The Economist*, 17 July. Retrieved 3 April
2020. https://www.economist.com/graphic-de tail/2019/07/17/trumps-tweet-
divides-americans.

– 2019d. "Briefing Hungary, the Entanglement of Powers." *The Economist*, 29 August, 10.

– 2019e. "Facebook Turns 15." *The Economist*, 2 February. https://www.economist.
com/united-states/2019/02/02/facebook-turns-15.

– 2019f. "Imperial Purple." *The Economist*, 23 February, 4.

– 2020a. "The State in the Time of COVID-19." *The Economist*, 26 March. Retrieved 4 May
2020. https://www.economist.com/leaders/2020/03/26/the-state-in-the-time-of-
covid-19.

– 2020b. "How Objectivity in Journalism Became a Matter of Opinion." *The Economist*,
16 July. Retrieved 18 July 2020. https://www.economist.com/books-and-
arts/2020/07/16/how-objectivity-in-journalism-became-a-matter-of-opinion.

– 2020c. "Would the Supreme Court Hand Donald Trump a Second Term?" *The
Economist*, 3 October. Retrieved 30 November 2020. https://www.economist.com/
united-states/2020/10/03/would-the-supreme-court-hand-donald-trump-a-
second-term.

– 2020d. "The Year When Everything Changed." *The Economist*, 16 December.
Retrieved 3 February 2021. https://www.economist.com/leaders/2020/12/19/
the-year-when-everything-changed.

Edge, M. 2019. "A New Book Tries to Make the Case for Government Help for
Canada's Media Giants – and Fails." *The Tyee*, 5 September. Retrieved 9 September

2019. https://thetyee.ca/Mediacheck/2019/09/05/New-Book-Canadian-Media-Giants/.

Edsall, T.B. 2020. "Trump's Digital Advantage Is Freaking Out Democratic Strategists." *New York Times*, 29 January. Retrieved 4 February 2020. https://www.nytimes.com/2020/01/29/opinion/trump-digital-campaign-2020.html.

Egan, L., and D. Madani. 2021. "Trump Pardons Steve Bannon Along with Dozens of Others in Final Hours in Office." *NBC News*, 20 January. Retrieved 26 January 2021. https://www.nbcnews.com/politics/donald-trump/trump-pardons-steve-bannon-along-dozens-others-final-hours-office-n1254754.

Eggers, W.D., and P. Macmillan. 2013. *The Solution Revolution: How Business, Government, and Social Enterprises Are Teaming Up to Solve Society's Toughest Problems.* Watertown, MA: Harvard Business Review Press.

Elliott, J. 2019. "Congress Scraps Provision to Restrict IRS from Competing with TurboTax." *ProPublica*, 5 June. Retrieved 15 October 2019. https://www.propublica.org/article/congress-scraps-provision-to-restrict-irs-from-competing-with-turbotax.

Elliott, J.K. 2021. "Donald Trump Leaves Office with Worst Job Approval Rating in History." *Global News*, 20 January. Retrieved 26 January 2021. https://globalnews.ca/news/7587657/donald-trump-final-approval-rating/.

Eltzroth, C. (@clay1016). 2018. "This has to be the best headline I've seen on the US/EU tarriff 'Hit the Chevy with a levy and tax your whisky and rye' #Tarriffs #bourbon #steel #Aluminum #TicTocNews @tictoc." Twitter, 6 March. Retrieved 14 October 2019. https://twitter.com/Clay1016/status/970964976616792065?s=20.

Emmanuel, R. 2020. "WE Charity Deal 'In Process' of Being Cancelled: Qualtrough." *iPolitics*, 12 August. Retrieved 16 November 2020. https://ipolitics.ca/2020/08/12/we-charity-deal-in-process-of-being-cancelled-qualtrough/.

English, K. 2010. "Is Twitter a Threat to Journalistic Credibility?" *Toronto Star*, 19 June. Retrieved 26 August 2018. https://www.thestar.com/opinion/public_editor/2010/06/19/english_is_twitter_a_threat_to_journalistic_credibility.html.

– 2016. "I Should Have Listened to My Dad about Donald Trump." *Toronto Star*, 11 November. Retrieved 26 August 2018. https://www.thestar.com/opinion/public_editor/2016/11/11/i-should-have-listened-to-my-dad-about-donald-trump-public-editor.html.

– 2017. "Criteria for Anonymous Sources: How the Star Handles Unnamed Interviewees in Its Political Coverage." *Toronto Star*, 10 June. Retrieved 19 December 2019 from ProQuest.

Entman, R.M. 1989. "How the Media Affect What People Think: An Information Processing Approach." *The Journal of Politics* 51, 2 (May): 347–70.

– 1993. "Framing: Toward Clarification of a Fractured Paradigm." *Journal of Communication* 43, 4 (December): 51–8.

Environmental Protection Agency. 1973. *Working Papers in Alternative Futures and Environmental Quality.* Office of Research and Development. Washington Environmental Research Centre. Environmental Development Studies.

Epstein, E.J. 1974. *News from Nowhere: Television and the News.* New York: Vintage Books.

– 1975. *Between Fact and Fiction: The Problem with Journalism.* New York: Vintage Books.

Erman, B. 2007a. "Under Fire, Sabia Triggers Battle for BCE." *Globe and Mail*, 18 April, B1.

– 2007b. "BCE Bondholders Eye Lawsuit Over Deal." *Globe and Mail*, 12 July, B1.

Erman, B., S. Stewart, and J. McNish. 2007. "Teachers, U.S. Fund Providence Made Moves on BCE Buyout." *Globe and Mail*, 10 April, B1.

Ettema, J.S., and T.L. Glasser. 1984. "On the Epistemology of Investigative Journalism." Presented at the Annual Meeting of the Association for Education in Journalism and Mass Communication (67th, Gainesville, FL, 5–8 August 1984). https://eric.ed.gov/?id=ED247585.

Etter, L. 2017. "What Happens When the Government Uses Facebook as a Weapon?" *Bloomberg Businessweek*, 12 December. Retrieved 19 December 2019. https://www.bloomberg.com/news/features/2017-12-07/how-rodrigo-duterte-turned-facebook-into-a-weapon-with-a-little-help-from-facebook.

Everett-Green, R. 2017. "Quebec Offers Plan to Help Newspapers While Ottawa Does Nothing." *Globe and Mail*, 15 December. Retrieved 9 September 2019. https://www.theglobeandmail.com/opinion/quebec-offers-plan-to-help-newspapers-while-ottawa-does-nothing/article37354647/.

Fallows, J. 1996a. *Breaking the News: How the Media Undermine American Democracy.* New York: Pantheon Books.

– 1996b. "Why Americans Hate the Media." *The Atlantic*, February. Retrieved 29 September 2019. https://www.theatlantic.com/magazine/archive/1996/02/why-americans-hate-the-media/305060/.

Fandos, N., and E. Cochrane. 2020. "Republicans Back Trump's Refusal to Concede, Declining to Recognize Biden." *New York Times*, 13 November. Retrieved 31 January 2021. https://www.nytimes.com/2020/11/09/us/politics/republicans-trump-concede-2020-election.html.

Farnsworth, C.H. 1993. "Governing Tories in Canada Routed by Liberal Party." *New York Times*, 26 October. Retrieved 5 August 2019. https://www.nytimes. com/1993/10/26/world/governing-tories-in-canada-routed-by-liberal-party.html.

Fausset, R., and D. Hakim. 2021. "Atlanta Prosecutor Appears to Move Closer to Trump Inquiry." *New York Times*, 18 January. Retrieved 31 January 2021. https://www. nytimes.com/2021/01/15/us/politics/atlanta-prosecutor-trump-election.html.

Fawcett, M. 2019. "Political Polls Are Flawed. Can AI Fix Them?" *The Walrus*, 17 October. Retrieved 17 February 2020. https://thewalrus.ca/political-polls-are-flawed-can-ai-fix-them/.

Fearnow, B. 2020. "Trump Says Election Will Be Decided after November 3, 'Thank You Very Much Supreme Court.'" *Newsweek*, 31 October. Retrieved 27 January 2021. https:// www.newsweek.com/trump-says-election-will-decided-after-november-3-thank-you-supreme-court-1543809.

Feiner, L. 2020. "Read Joe Biden's First Speech as President-Elect." *CNBC*, 7 November. Retrieved 31 January 2021. https://www.cnbc.com/2020/11/07/read-joe-biden-acceptance-speech-full-text.html.

Feran, T. 2019. "Plain Dealer Lays Off a Third of Unionized Newsroom Staff." *Cleveland.com*, 1 April. Retrieved 5 April 2019. https://www.cleveland.com/news/2019/04/plain-dealer-lays-off-a-third-of-unionized-newsroom-staff.html.

Feuer, A. 2018. "6 Takeaways from Michael Cohen's Guilty Plea." *New York Times*, 21 August. Retrieved 8 September 2019. https://www.nytimes.com/2018/08/21/nyregion/michael-cohen-guilty-plea-trump-takeaways.html.

Fife, R. 2017. "Ottawa Pays Out $10.5-Million to Khadr amid Potential Legal Battle." *Globe and Mail*, 6 July. Retrieved 19 December 2019. https://www.theglobeandmail. com/news/politics/omar-khadr-settlement-federal-government-guantanamo-bay/arti cle35581403/.

Fife, R., and J. Dickson. 2019. "Conservative Leader Andrew Scheer Holds Dual Canadian-U.S. Citizenship, Had Attacked Michaëlle Jean on Same Issue." *Globe and Mail*, 3 October. Retrieved 24 March 2020. https://www.theglobeandmail.com/politics/article-conservative-leader-andrew-scheer-holds-dual-canadian-us-citizenship/.

Fife, R., S. Chase, and S. Fine. 2019. "PMO Pressed Wilson-Raybould to Abandon Prosecution of SNC-Lavalin." *Globe and Mail*, 7 February. Retrieved 11 April 2019. https://www.theglobeandmail.com/politics/article-pmo-pressed-justice-minister-to-abandon-prosecution-of-snc-lavalin/.

Fini Zanuck, L., dir. 2017. *Eric Clapton: Life in 12 Bars*.

Fitzpatrick, K., and C. Bronstein, eds. 2006. *Ethics in Public Relations: Responsible Advocacy*. Sage: Thousand Oaks, CA, London, New Delhi.

Fitzwater, M. 1995. *Call the Briefing! Reagan and Bush, Sam and Helen: A Decade With Presidents and the Press*. New York: Times Books.

Flint, P.B. 1995. "Robertson Davies, 82, Dies, Chronicler of Moral Battles; Considered for Nobel." *New York Times*, 4 December. Retrieved 26 August 2018. https://archive. nytimes.com/www.nytimes.com/books/97/08/24/reviews/davies-obit.html.

Forcese, C. 2008. "Repatriation of Omar Khadr to Be Tried under Canadian Law; An Overview of the Case against Omar Khadr and the Prospect of Canadian Criminal Jurisdiction." Retrieved from University of Ottawa, Faculty of Law, January. http://aix1.uottawa.ca/~cforcese/other/khadrrepatriation.pdf.

Ford, P. 2018. "Where's Our Digital EPA?" *Bloomberg Businessweek*, 18 March. Retrieved from Bloomberg Businessweek.

Fox, B. 1999. *Spinwars: Politics and New Media*. Toronto: Key Porter Books Limited.

– 2018. "Cabinet Reset an Opportunity for a Policy Reset in Support of 'Civic Journalism.'" *Toronto Star*, 22 July. Retrieved 20 December 2019. https://www. thestar.com/opinion/contributors/2018/07/22/cabinet-reset-an-opportunity-for-a-policy-reset-in-support-of-civic-journalism.html.

Fox, E.J. 2016. "Let Fran Lebowitz Soothe All Your Election-Related Worries." *Vanity Fair*, 20 October. Retrieved 2 May 2019. https://www.vanityfair.com/news/2016/10/fran-lebowitz-trump-clinton-election.

Fox, W. 1997. "Junk News." Discussion Paper D-26. Shorenstein Center on Media, Politics and Public Policy, August. https://shorensteincen ter.org/wp-content/uploads/2012/03/d26_fox.pdf?x78124.

Frank, T. 2016. *Listen, Liberal: What Ever Happened to the Party of the People?* New York: Metropolitan Books.

Frankel, M. 1995. "Journalism 101." *New York Times*, 22 January. Retrieved 5 September 2019. https://www.nytimes.com/1995/01/22/magazine/word-image-journalism-101.html.

Fraser, G. 1989. *Playing for Keeps: The Making of the Prime Minister, 1988*. Toronto: McClelland & Stewart.

Freeze, C. 2017. "B.C., Britain Investigate Role of Canadian Tech Firm AggregateIQ in Brexit Vote." *Globe and Mail*, 14 December. Retrieved 20 December 2019. https://www.theglobeandmail.com/news/national/bc-britain-investigate-role-of-canadian-tech-firm-aggregateiq-in-brexit-vote/article37340241/.

Friedman, T.L. 2017. "Where Did 'We the People' Go?" *New York Times*, 22 June. Retrieved 15 August 2019. https://www.nytimes.com/2017/06/21/opinion/where-did-we-the-people-go.html.

– 2020. "We Need Herd Immunity from Trump and the Coronavirus." *New York Times*, 25 April. Retrieved 1 May 2020. https://www.nytimes.com/2020/04/25/opinion/coronavirus-immunity-trump.html.

Friends of Public Broadcasting. 2019. "Unfriend Facebook." *Globe and Mail*, 2 May, A6.

Frier, S., and G. Smith. 2017. "Media Companies Are Getting Sick of Facebook." *Bloomberg Businessweek*, 19 June, 21.

Friscolanti, M. 2015. "'You Are Free to Go,' Judge Tells Omar Khadr." *Maclean's*, 17 May. Retrieved 4 August 2019. https://www.macleans.ca/news/canada/you-are-free-to-go-judge-tells-omar-khadr/.

Frum, D. 2011. "When Did the GOP Lose Touch with Reality?" *New York*, 28 November. Retrieved 21 December 2019. http://nymag.com/news/politics/conservatives-david-frum-2011-11/index3.html.

– 2018. *Trumpocracy: The Corruption of the American Republic*. New York: Harper.

– (@davidfrum). 2021a. "There's a legend building among the non-deadend Trumpers, that Trump had a decent record before some arbitrary date: before the election, before the pandemic. It needs to be stressed that Trump was a crook, charlatan, bigot, thug, and incompetent from the start to the end." Twitter, 16 January. Retrieved 4 February 2021. https://twitter.com/davidfrum/status/1350578796265676804?s=20.

– (@davidfrum). 2021b. "I've often wondered whether a reason Canadian politics has been more moderate in the 21st c than UK, US, or Australian politics is that there are no Murdoch-owned media properties in Canada." Twitter, 27 January. Retrieved 30 January 2021. https://twitter.com/davidfrum/status/1354422456170246146?s=20.

Fulton, K. 2000. "News Isn't Always Journalism." *Columbia Journalism Review* 39, 2: 30. https://go.gale.com/ps/anonymous?id=GALE%7CA63563075.

Gallant, J. 2020. "Media Organizations Still Waiting for Rollout of Key Federal Government Support Program." *Toronto Star*, 16 October. Retrieved 15 November 2020. https://www.thestar.com/news/canada/2020/10/16/media-organizations-still-waiting-for-rollout-of-key-federal-government-support-program.html.

Galloway, G. 2017. "Ottawa Passes Legislation to Protect Journalists' Anonymous Sources from Police." *Globe and Mail*, 4 October. Retrieved 21 December 2019.

https://beta.theglobeandmail.com/news/politics/ottawa-passes-legislation-to-protect-journalists-an onymous-sources-from-police/article36497819/.

Gans, H. 1980. *Deciding What's News: A Study of CBS Evening News, NBC Nightly News, Newsweek and Time.* New York: Vintage Books.

Geddes, J. 2015. "How the Liberals Took Down the Tories." *Maclean's,* 20 October. Retrieved 15 August 2019. https://www.macleans.ca/politics/ottawa/trudeaumania-how-the-liberals-took-down-the-tories/.

Gerbner, G., L. Gross, M. Morgan, and N. Signorielli. 1980. "The 'Mainstreaming' of America: Violence Profile No. 11." *Journal of Communication* 30, 3: (September): 10-29.

Gergen, D. 2000. *Eyewitness to Power: The Essence of Leadership Nixon to Clinton.* New York: Simon and Schuster.

Ghobari, M. 2015. "Gunmen Hold Yemeni Official to Try to Derail New Constitution." *Reuters,* 17 January. Retrieved 8 September 2019. https://www.reuters.com/article/us-yemen-security/gunmen-hold-yemeni-official-to-try-to-derail-new-constitution-idUSKB N0KQ0AI20150117.

Gilbert, D. 2020. "Trump's Lawyer Sidney Powell Is Hardcore QAnon." *Vice,* 11 November. Retrieved 21 November 2020. https://www.vice.com/en/article/wx8n8w/trumps-lawyer-sidney-powell-is-hardcore-qanon.

Gilder, G. 1994. *Life after Television.* New York: Norton.

Gilliam, F., and S. Bales. 2001. "Strategic Frame Analysis: Reframing America's Youth." *UCLA: Center for Communications and Community.* https://escholarship.org/uc/item/5sk7r6gk#main.

Gillmor, D. (@dangillmor). 2018. "Dear Journalists, you don't have to let liars use you as loudspeakers. Here's how you can deal with a challenge that, so far, you've failed to address in any useful way." Twitter, 15 June. Retrieved 17 June 2018. https://twitter.com/dangillmor/status/1007703044794957824.

Gilmore, S. (@Scott_Gilmore). 2020. "Most Canadian politicians would consider accusing a Chinese-Canadian civil servant of taking guidance from Beijing to be a pathetic slur and too low to stoop. For Jason Kenney, it's just another talking point." Twitter, 14 April. Retrieved 14 May 2020. https://twitter.com/Scott_Gilmore/status/1250042417333653504?s=20.

Gingras, R. 2016. "Digital Journalism Will Find Its Models with the Right Tools." *Globe and Mail,* 18 November. Retrieved 28 December 2019. https://beta.theglobeandmail.com/report-on-business/rob-commen tary/digital-journalism-will-find-its-models-with-the-right-tools/article32895532/.

Gitlin, T. 1980. *The Whole World Is Watching: Mass Media in the Making & Unmaking of the New Left.* Berkeley, CA, and Los Angeles: University of California Press.

– 1998. "Public Sphere or Public Sphericules?" In *Media, Ritual and Identity*, edited by T. Liebes and J. Curran, 168–75. London: Routledge.

Glaberson, W. 1994. "The Nation: Raking Mud; The New Press Criticism: News as the Enemy of Hope." *New York Times*, 9 October. Retrieved 28 September 2019. https://www.nytimes.com/1994/10/09/weekinreview/the-nation-raking-mud-the-new-press-criticism-news-as-the-enemy-of-hope.html.

Glasser, S.B. 2020. "Donald Trump's 2020 Superspreader Campaign: A Diary." *The New Yorker*, 3 November. Retrieved 21 November 2020. https://www.newyorker.com/news/letter-from-trumps-washington/donald-trumps-2020-superspreader-campaign-a-diary.

Glavin, T. (@TerryGlavin). 2019. "And by the way, there will be foreign interference in the October federal election. The Liberal government is quite right about that. But it won't be Russia making the most mischief. It will be China, it will be in spades, and the target will be Andrew Scheer's Conservatives." Twitter, 8 May. Retrieved 19 October 2019. https://twitter.com/TerryGlavin/status/1126211034723667973.

Global News. 2019. "Singh on Trudeau in Blackface, Brownface: It's a 'Pattern of Behaviour.'" *Global News*, 19 September. Retrieved 29 September 2019. https://globalnews.ca/video/5927015/singh-on-trudeau-in-blackface-brownface-its-a-pattern-of-behaviour/.

– 2020. "Donald Trump Calls Biden 'Mentally Unqualified' to Serve as President." *Global News*, 17 October. Retrieved 23 November 2020. https://globalnews.ca/video/7403826/donald-trump-calls-biden-mentally-unqualified-to-serve-as-president.

Globe and Mail. 2005. "Editorial Opinion: The Income Trust Mess." *Globe and Mail*, 30 December, A14.

– 2019. "Donald Trump Isn't a Secret Russian Agent. He's Just a (Very) Bad President." *The Globe and Mail*, 24 April. Retrieved 18 December 2019. https://www.theglobeandmail.com/opinion/editorials/article-no-donald-trump-is-not-a-secret-russian-agent-hes-just-a-visibly/.

Goldberg, M. 2021. "The Inevitable." *New York Times*, 15 January. Retrieved 26 January 2021. https://www.nytimes.com/2021/01/15/opinion/trump-second-impeachment.html.

Goldstein, L. 2019. "Trudeau Was Teflon, Now He's Velcro." *Toronto Sun*, 9 May. https://torontosun.com/opinion/columnists/goldstein-trudeau-was-teflon-now-hes-velcro.

Gollom, M. 2021. "CBC Wrong to Fire Reporter Who Told News Site He Was Forced to Delete Tweet Critical of Don Cherry: Arbitrator." *CBC News*, 14 January. Retrieved 5 February 2021. https://www.cbc.ca/news/canada/khan-cbc-canadaland-tweet-cherry-fired-arbitor-1.5873539.

Gómez Camacho, J.J. (@JJGomezCamacho). 2020. "Mexico has worked hard to ensure equitable access to vaccines for all. We believe a pandemic is a time to promote solidarity, rather than showing selfishness, which could endanger us all. @erinotoole @MichelleRempel." Twitter, 24 November. Retrieved 26 November 2020. https://twitter.com/JJGomezCamacho/status/1331367745552781313?s=20.

Gooch, T. 2017. "We Must All Create a Culture of Respect in the Twittersphere." *Toronto Star*, 25 June. Retrieved 28 December 2019. https://www.thestar.com/opinion/commentary/2017/06/25/we-must-all-create-a-culture-of-respect-in-the-twittersphere-gooch.html.

Gordon-Reed, A. 2018. "Female Trouble." *New York Review of Books*, 8 February. Retrieved 9 August 2019. https://www.nybooks.com/articles/2018/02/08/hillary-clinton-female-trouble/.

Gormley, J. 2018. "The Hour of the Big Stories." *CJME/CKOM*, 12 March. https://soundcloud.com/980cjme_650ckom/gormley-the-hour-of-the-big-stories-march-12.

Government of Canada. 2006. "Report of the Events Relating to Maher Arar: Analysis and Recommendations." *Commission of Inquiry into the Actions of Canadian Officials in Relation to Maher Arar.* http://publica tions.gc.ca/collections/Collection/CP32-88-1-2006E-AR.pdf.

– 2018a. "Budget Plan 2018: Supporting Local Journalism." https://www.budget.gc.ca/2018/docs/plan/chap-04-en.html.

– 2018b. "Democratic Institutions." *The Leaders' Debates Commission.* https://www.canada.ca/en/democratic-institutions/news/2018/10/the-leaders-debates-commission.html.

– 2020. "Canada Emergency Wage Subsidy (CEWS)." Canada Revenue Agency, 14 May. Retrieved 21 May 2020. https://web.archive.org/web/20200518034821/html. https://www.canada.ca/en/revenue-agency/services/subsidy/emergency-wage-subsidy/cews-statistics.html.

Gowing, N. 1994. "Real Time Television Coverage of Armed Conflicts and Diplomatic Crises: Does It Pressure or Distort Foreign Policy Decisions." Working paper series #1994-1. Shorenstein Center on Media, Politics and Public Policy, Spring. Retrieved 13 December 2019. https://shorensteincenter.org/wp-content/uploads/2012/03/1994_01_gowing.pdf.

Graber, D. 1988. *Processing the News: How People Tame the Information Tide*, 2nd revised edition. New York: Longman Group.

– 2001. *Processing Politics: Learning from Television in the Internet Age.* Chicago and London: University of Chicago Press.

Graff, G.M. 2017. "Trump Force One Is Ready for Takeoff." *Bloomberg Businessweek*, 14 March. Retrieved 2 January 2020. https://www.bloomberg.com/news/features/2017-03-14/trump-force-one-is-ready-for-takeoff.

Graham, D.A. 2016. "The Lasting Damage From Trump's False 'Voter Fraud' Allegations." *The Atlantic*, 28 November. Retrieved 4 February 2021. https://www.theatlantic.com/politics/archive/2016/11/trump-vote-fraud/508868/.

Green, J. 2019. "Elizabeth Warren Is Done Playing It Safe." *Bloomberg Businessweek*, 29 July, 38.

Greenberg, J. (@josh_greenberg). 2019a. "I would also note the important broker role played by a key intermediary – the PR strategist – both within and outside parties, advising on media relations, timing of announcements, key messaging, etc. Leon Mayhew's work super valuable in this context." Twitter, 5 April. Retrieved 11 April 2019, from https://twitter.com/josh_greenberg/status/1114161381182451719.

– 2019b. "Finally, there's no doubt in my mind that JWR and JP received effective tactical advice about how to hit back at PMO with maximum impact: Fife leak, drip release strategy, Wells interview, published caucus letter &c. All calculated and carefully executed with sharp precision." Twitter, 5 April. Retrieved 8 April 2021. https://twitter.com/josh_greenberg/status/1114174916918558722?s=20.

Greenspon, E., and T. Owen. 2018. "Democracy Divided: Countering Disinformation and Hate in the Digital Public Sphere." The Shattered Mirror Series. *Public Policy Forum*, August. Retrieved 26 August 2018. https://www.ppforum.ca/wp-content/uploads/2018/08/DemocracyDivided-PPF-AUG2018-EN.pdf.

Greenwood, J. 2007. "BCE-Telus Deal Best." *National Post*, 18 April, FP5.

Gregg, A. 2017. "What Canadians Think of the News Media." *Policy Options*, 10 February. Retrieved 24 May 2020. https://policyoptions.irpp.org/magazines/february-2017/what-canadians-think-of-the-news-media/.

Greve, J.E. 2020. "Biden Condemns Trump as One of the 'Most Irresponsible Presidents in American History.'" *The Guardian*, 19 November. Retrieved 28 January 2021. https://www.theguardian.com/us-news/2020/nov/19/joe-biden-donald-trump-irresponsible-president-history.

Grieco, E. 2019. "U.S. Newsroom Employment Has Dropped by a Quarter since 2008, with Greatest Decline at Newspapers." *Pew Research Center*, 9 July. Retrieved 6 August 2019. https://www.pewresearch.org/fact-tank/2019/07/09/u-s-newsroom-employment-has-dropped- by-a-quarter-since-2008/.

Groppe, M., and J. Fritze. 2020. "As Trump Continues to Interrupt during the Debate, Biden Says, 'Will You Shut Up, Man?'" *USA Today*, 29 September. Retrieved 23 November 2020. https://www.usatoday.com/story/news/politics/elections/2020/09/29/biden-asks-trump-shut-up-president-keeps-interrupting-debate/3582754001/.

Grynbaum, M.M. 2017. "Trump Strategist Stephen Bannon Says Media Should 'Keep Its Mouth Shut.'" *New York Times*, 27 January. Retrieved 2 January 2020. https://www.nytimes.com/2017/01/26/business/media/stephen-bannon-trump-news-media.html.

Guardian (US). 2020. "US Election Results 2020: Joe Biden's Defeat of Donald Trump." *The Guardian* (US edition), 8 December. Retrieved 3 February 2021. https://www.theguardian.com/us-news/ng-interactive/2020/dec/08/us-election-results-2020-joe-biden-defeats-donald-trump-to-win-presidency.

Gul, M. 2019. "'Absolute Garbage': Vancouver Sun Op-Ed Draws Backlash, Criticized as Racist." *City News*, 7 September. Retrieved 9 September 2019. https://www.citynews1130.com/2019/09/07/absolute-garbage-vancouver-sun-op-ed-draws-backlash-criticized-as-racist/.

Haberman, M. 2020. "Trump Floats Improbable Survival Scenarios as He Ponders His Future." *New York Times*, 12 November. Retrieved 30 January 2021. https://www.nytimes.com/2020/11/12/us/politics/trump-future.html.

– 2021. "Trump Departs Vowing, 'We Will Be Back in Some Form.'" *The New York Times*, 22 January. Retrieved 31 January 2021. https://www.nytimes.com/2021/01/20/us/politics/trump-presidency.html.

Haberman, M., G. Thrush, and P. Baker. 2017. "Inside Trump's Hour-by-Hour Battle for Self-Preservation." *New York Times*, 9 December. https://www.nytimes.com/2017/12/09/us/politics/donald-trump-president.html.

Haberman, M., and K. Rogers. 2018. "'Drama, Action, Emotional Power': As Exhausted Aides Eye the Exits, Trump Is Re-Energized." *The New York Times*, 10 June. Retrieved 11 June 2018. https://www.nytimes.com/2018/06/10/us/politics/trump-turnover.html.

Habermas, J. 1989. *The Structural Transformation of the Public Sphere: An Inquiry into a Category of Bourgeois Society.* Translated by T. Burger. Cambridge: MIT Press.

Hachten, W., and J. Scotton. 2011. *The World News Prism: Digital, Social and Interactive*, 8th edition. Oxford: Wiley-Blackwell.

Haley, N. (@NikkiHaley). 2021. "Silencing people, not to mention the President of the US, is what happens in China not our country. #Unbelievable." Twitter, 8 January. Retrieved 29 January 2021. https://twitter.com/NikkiHaley/status/1347693768825180160?s=20.

Hall, C. 2019. "China Turns Up the Heat and Canada Pushes Back." *CBC*, The House, 20 December. Retrieved 20 January 2020. http://13533.mc.tritondigital.com/CBC_THE_HOUSE_FROM_CBC_RADIO_P/media-session/1ce05213-a915-40ea-a83e-03b88b8b4771/thehouse-087JRqC4-20191220.mp3.

Hall, M., and S. Gal. (n.d.). "How the 2020 Election Results Compare to 2016, in 9 Maps and Charts." *Business Insider*. Retrieved 28 January 2021. https://www.businessinsider.com/2016-2020-electoral-maps-exit-polls-compared-2020-11.

Hall Jamieson, K. 1989. "Context and the Creation of Meaning in the Advertising of the 1988 Presidential Campaign." *American Behavioral Scientist* 32, 4: 415–24. doi:https://doi.org/10.1177/0002764289032004007

– 2000. *Everything You Think You Know about Politics – and Why You're Wrong*. New York: Basic Books.

Haltiwanger, J. 2021. "More Americans Have Now Died from COVID-19 than the Number of US Troops Killed during World War II." *Business Insider*, 20 January. Retrieved 31 January 2021. https://www.businessinsider.com/more-americans-dead-covid-19-us-battle-deaths-wwii-2020-12.

Hamby, P. 2013. "Did Twitter Kill the Boys on the Bus? Searching for a Better Way to Cover a Campaign," #D-80. Shorenstein Center on Media, Politics and Public Policy, September. https://shorensteincen ter.org/wp-content/uploads/2013/08/d80_hamby.pdf.

Hamer, D. (@DavidHamer_1951). 2019. "Fine to say, but you don't know who is leaking what. My point is that Mr. Fife might want to ask why they're leaking and what axes his sources are grinding before he publishes. The Arar affair should have taught him and others a lesson." Twitter, 24 February. Retrieved 12 April 2019. https://twitter.com/DavidHamer_1951/status/1099626521705279488.

Hamilton, I.A. 2020. "A Top Biden Staffer Accused Facebook of 'Shredding the Fabric of Our Democracy' – Yet Another Sign the Social-Media Giant Should Fear the New Administration." *Business Insider*, 10 November. Retrieved 21 November 2020.

https://www.businessinsider.com/biden-bill-russo-facebook-misinformation-social-media-attack-2020-11.

Haney López, I. 2014. *Dog Whistle Politics: How Coded Racial Appeals Have Reinvented Racism and Wrecked the Middle Class.* New York: Oxford University Press.

Harper's Magazine. 2020. "A Letter on Justice and Open Debate." *Harper's Magazine,* 7 July. Retrieved 20 July 2020. https://harpers.org/a-letter-on-justice-and-open-debate/.

Harris, G., and M. Eddy. 2016. "Obama, with Angela Merkel in Berlin, Assails Spread of Fake News." *New York Times,* 17 November. Retrieved 2 January 2020. https://www.nytimes.com/2016/11/18/world/europe/obama-angela-merkel-donald-trump.html.

Harris, K. 2019. "Wilson-Raybould Tables New Documents on SNC-Lavalin File, Release Expected Friday." *CBC News,* 27 March. Retrieved 4 September 2019. https://www.cbc.ca/news/politics/wilson-raybould-justice-committee-documents-1.5073415.

Harris, R. 2017. *Munich.* Toronto: Random House Canada.

Harvard Kennedy School. 2011. "A Conversation with David Carr and Danah Boyd." *Harvard Kenney School,* 14 December. Retrieved 28 January 2020. https://www.youtube.com/watch?v=yNFBVp3gyHg.

– 2020. "The Challenges Facing the Media on November 3rd and Beyond, with Eugene Robinson." Theodore H. White Lecture on Press and Politics. Harvard Kennedy School, 28 October. Retrieved 21 November 2020. https://iop.harvard.edu/forum/challenges-facing-media-november-3rd-and-beyond.

Harvard University. (@Harvard_Tox). 2020. "Please don't inject bleach or drink disinfectant. Bleach injections cause hemolysis (where your red blood cells that carry OXYGEN break apart) and cause liver damage, and many disinfectants can cause dangerous burns or bleeding in your stomach. This tweet IS medical advice." Twitter, 24 April. Retrieved 1 May 2020. https://twitter.com/Harvard_Tox/status/1253626240537448450?s=20.

Hedges, C. 2010. *Death of the Liberal Class.* Toronto: Knopf Canada.

Hemmadi, M. 2018. "Facebook Can Claim Its Very Busy Man in Ottawa Is Not a Lobbyist. Here's How." *Maclean's,* 5 April. Retrieved 2 January 2020. http://www.macleans.ca/politics/ottawa/what-facebook-is-not-doing-in-ottawa/.

Hennessey, K. 2016. "Breaking Tradition, Trump Doesn't Permit Journalists to Cover His First Meeting with Obama." *PBS News Hour,* 10 November. Retrieved 30 April

2020. https://www.pbs.org/newshour/politics/breaking-tradition-trump-doesnt-permit-journalists-cover-first-meeting-obama.

Herle, D. 2018. "Kory Teneycke, Campaign Manager to Doug Ford." *The Herle Burly*, 21 June. Retrieved 25 June 2018. https://www.theherleburly.com/episodes/2018/6/21/kory-teneycke-campaign-manager-to-doug-ford.

– 2019a. "Hamish Marshall." *The Herle Burly*, 24 December. Retrieved 7 January 2020. https://www.theherleburly.com/episodes/2019/12/24/hamish-marshall.

– 2019b. "Raw Politics with Jenni Byrne and Scott Reid." *The Herle Burly*, 23 September. https://www.stitcher.com/podcast/air-quotes-media/the-herle-burly/e/64106351.

– 2020a. "Canada's COVID-19 Economic Response with Scott Clark + the Political Panel." *The Herle Burly*, 31 March. Retrieved 6 May 2020. https://www.theherleburly.com/episodes/scottclark-panel.

– 2020b. "Stuart Stevens of the Lincoln Project and Author of 'It Was All a Lie.'" *The Herle Burly*, 28 October. Retrieved 2 February 2021. https://www.theherleburly.com/episodes/stuart-stevens.

– 2020c. "Jeff Rubin + the Political Panel with Jenni and Scott." *The Herle Burly*, 17 November. Retrieved 29 January 2021. https://www.theherleburly.com/episodes/jeffrubin-polipanel.

– 2020d. "Adrienne Spafford + the Political Panel #MailbagEdition." *The Herle Burly*, 24 November. shorturl.at/pvyCH.

– (@TheHerleBurly). 2020e. "They were effective until they weren't. Trudeau made them counterproductive with a flawless campaign performance. A good lesson – 'Don't base your campaign on a proposition your opponent can disprove.'" Twitter, 28 January. Retrieved 31 January 2020. https://twitter.com/TheHerleBurly/status/1222371888950861824?s=20.

– (@TheHerleBurly). 2020f. "'If you look at the conditions that have led to the rise of populism in either UK or US, those same conditions exist in CAN. What's different is there has yet been a populist political expression of that discontented, screwed, middle-class. This vacuum will be filled.' @JeffRubin." Twitter, 19 November. Retrieved 21 November 2020. https://twitter.com/TheHerleBurly/status/1329607319043379207?s=20.

Herman, Edward S., and N. Chomsky. 1988. *Manufacturing Consent: The Political Economy of the Mass Media.* New York: Pantheon Books.

Hesmondhalgh, D. 2007. *The Cultural Industries,* 2nd edition. Los Angeles, London, New Delhi, Singapore: Sage Publications.

Hess, S. 1984. *The Government/Press Connection: Press Officers and Their Offices.* Washington: Brookings Institution.

–1996. *Presidents & the Presidency: Essays.* Washington, DC: Brookings Institution.

Hindman, M., and V. Barash. 2018. "Disinformation, 'Fake News' and Influence Campaigns on Twitter." The Knight Foundation, October. Retrieved 11 October 2018. https://kf-site-production.s3.amazonaws.com/media_elements/files/000/000/238/original/KF-DisinformationReport-final2.pdf.

Hirsh, J. 2018. "The Policy Deficit Behind Canadian Artificial Intelligence." *Centre for International Governance Innovation*, 13 February. Retrieved 27 March 2018. https://www.cigionline.org/articles/policy-deficit-behind-canadian-artificial-intelligence.

– 2019. "Could Banking Regulation Rein in Social Media Giants?" *Centre for International Governance Innovation*, 22 February. https://www.cigionline.org/articles/could-banking-regulation-rein-social-media- giants.

– 2021. "Is This China's Technology Moment?" *Metaviews*, 14 January. Retrieved 3 February 2021. https://metaviews.substack.com/p/is-this-chinas-technology-moment.

Honderich, J. 2020a. "COVID-19 Made Us Reinvent Our Newsroom on the Fly. The Mission Is Simple: We Must Tell the Story." *Toronto Star*, 23 March. Retrieved 1 May 2020. https://www.thestar.com/opinion/2020/03/23/covid-19-made-us-reinvent-our-newsroom-on-the-fly-the-mission-is-simple-we-must-tell-the-story.html.

– 2020b. "'So We Pass the Torch.'" *Toronto Star*, 26 May. Retrieved 27 May 2020. https://www.thestar.com/business/opinion/2020/05/26/so-we-pass-the-torch.html.

Hood, S., and T. Tabary-Peterssen. 1997. *On Television.* London: Pluto Press.

Horgan, C. 2017. "Why Canadians Are Closer to Losing Their News Than They Think." *Maclean's*, 21 June. https://www.macleans.ca/culture/canadians-losing-news-facebook/.

Horton, D., and R. Wohl. 1956. "Mass Communication and Para-Social Interaction: Observation on Intimacy at a Distance." *Psychiatry* 19, 3: 215–229.

Houpt, S. 2017. "Guelph's Post-Mercury Blues: How an Ontario City Is Coping without Its Local Newspaper." *The Globe and Mail*, 21 July. Retrieved 2 January 2020. https://www.theglobeandmail.com/news/national/guelph-mercury-ontario/article35731429/.

– 2019. "Trudeau Has Lost Control of the Image He Built for Himself." *The Globe and Mail*, 19 September. Retrieved 22 December 2019. https://www.theglobeandmail.com/arts/article-trudeau-built-an-image-for-himself-now-he-faces-the-daunting-task-of/.

Hovland, C., I. Janis, and H. Kelley. 1953. *Communication and Persuasion: Psychological Studies of Opinion Change*. New York: Yale University Press.

Howse, A. 2019. "The Federal Conservatives Photoshopped Justin Trudeau into a Campaign Ad and Some Canadians Say It's Racist." *Narcity*, 28 June. Retrieved 24 May 2020. https://www.narcity.com/news/ca/conservatives-photoshopped-justin-trudeau-into-a-campaign-ad-and-canadians-are-calling-it-racist.

Huckabee, M. (@GovMikeHuckabee). 2019. "Sick & twisted-fmr Canadian PM wishes hurricane to hit Mar-A-Lago. @realDonaldTrump won't be there to get hurt, but many ppl, including service workers, families, etc would be hurt and property destroyed. Are liberals this hateful?" Twitter, 30 August. Retrieved 3 September 2019. https://twitter.com/GovMikeHuckabee/status/1167433741964328960?s=20.

Ignatius, D. 2017. "How to Protect Against Fake 'Facts.'" *Washington Post*, 23 November. Retrieved 28 November 2020. https://www.washingtonpost.com/opinions/getting-back-to-facts/2017/11/23/ebd6a12e-cfb9-11e7-81bc-c55a220c8cbe_story.html.

Illing, S. 2020. "'Flood the Zone with Shit': How Misinformation Overwhelmed Our Democracy." *Vox*, 6 February. Retrieved 21 May 2020. https://www.vox.com/policy-and-politics/2020/1/16/20991816/impeachment-trial-trump-bannon-misinformation.

Ingram, M. (@mathewi). 2020. "It's hard to imagine an industry more poorly prepared for a global pandemic than the media. Even before the coronavirus, the industry was reeling from a series of body blows, and for some this could become an extinction event. For a few, it already has." Twitter, 20 April. Retrieved 1 May 2020. https://twitter.com/mathewi/status/1252206639584817159?s=20.

Innis, H.A. 1950. *Empire and Communications*. Oxford: Oxford University Press.

– 1991. *The Bias of Communication*. Toronto: University of Toronto Press.

Innovation, Science and Economic Development Canada. 2018. "Terms of Reference: Broadcasting and Telecommunications Legislative Review." Retrieved 6 June 2018. https://www.ic.gc.ca/eic/site/110.nsf/vwapj/terms_of_reference_EN.pdf/$FILE/terms_of_reference_EN.pdf.

Innovative Research Group. (@InnovativeRG). 2019. "#cdnpoli #elxn43 While the pundit class analyses the electoral implication of each jot of the campaign, at least half the respondents in our final poll said they had not read, seen or heard anything for each of the 6 parties. Click for our final report: hubs.ly/H0llY1y0." Twitter, 20 October. Retrieved 29 November 2019. https://twitter.com/InnovativeRG/status/1186087200485715971?s=20.

Ireland, N. 2016. "CBC/Radio Canada Asks for $400M in Increased Government Funding to Go Ad-Free." *CBC News*, 28 November. Retrieved 2 January 2020. https://www.cbc.ca/news/canada/cbc-radio-canada-ad-free-proposal-1.3871077.

Isaac, M. 2016. "Facebook, in Cross Hairs after Election, Is Said to Question Its Influence." *The New York Times*, 12 November. Retrieved 2 January 2020. https://www.nytimes.com/2016/11/14/technology/facebook-is-said-to-question-its-influence-in-election.html.

Isaac, M., and K. Conger. 2021. "Facebook Bars Trump through End of His Term." *The New York Times*, 7 January. Retrieved 29 January 2021. https://www.nytimes.com/2021/01/07/technology/facebook-trump-ban.html.

Isenstadt, A. 2020. "GOP Memo Urges Anti-China Assault over Coronavirus." *Politico*, 24 April. Retrieved 1 May 2020. https://www.politico.com/news/2020/04/24/gop-memo-anti-china-coronavirus-207244.

Ivison, J. 2013. "Duffy and His Co-Accused Fail to Go Along Quietly, Much to the Chagrin of the PMO." *National Post*, 22 October. Retrieved 2 January 2020. http://nationalpost.com/opinion/john-ivison-duffy-and-his-co-accused-fail-to-go-along-quietly-much-to-the-chagrin-of-the-pmo.

– 2019a. *Trudeau: The Education of a Prime Minister.* Toronto: Signal/McClelland & Stewart.

– (@ivisonj). 2019b. "A future Liberal government would provide $2,000 travel bursaries to send Canadians camping. I think that might be the stupidest thing I've heard so far in this election." Twitter, 26 September. Retrieved 29 September 2019. https://twitter.com/IvisonJ/status/1177255274779915397?s=20.

– 2019c. "Climate Change Plan Myopic: Do Voters Care?" *National Post*, 28 September, A6.

– 2019d. "Barack Obama – the Man Who Won the Canadian Federal Election." *National Post*, 13 November. Retrieved 27 November 2019. https://nationalpost.com/opinion/john-ivison-barack-obama-the-man-who-won-the-canadian-federal-election.

– 2020. "Trudeau's Lavish Handouts Risk Turning Workers into Welfare Slackers." *National Post*, 28 April. Retrieved 2 May 2020. https://nationalpost.com/news/canada/john-ivison-trudeaus-lavish-handouts-risk-turning-workers-into-welfare-slackers.

Iyengar, S., and D. Kinder. 1987. *News That Matters: Television and American Opinion.* Chicago: University of Chicago Press.

Jackson, C.D. (@ChrisDJackson). 2020. "I'm taking it you don't know what happened to the Death Star?" Twitter, 7 May. Retrieved 8 May 2020. https://twitter.com/ChrisDJackson/status/1258399920161259522?s=20.

Jackson, E. 2018. "Rogers Media Axes 75 Jobs, Slashing One-Third of Its Digital Content and Publishing Team." *National Post*, 14 June. Retrieved 9 September 2019. https://business.financialpost.com/telecom/media/rogers-cutting-one-third-of-digital-content-and-publishing-team-about-75-jobs.

Jackson, H. 2019a. "Scheer Says He Will Stand by Candidates Who Have Made Mistakes If They Apologize." *Global News*, 15 September. Retrieved 17 February 2020. https://globalnews.ca/news/5905237/scheer-candidates-mistakes-apologies/.

– 2019b. "Trump 'Surprised' by Photos, Video of Trudeau in Brownface, Blackface." *Global News*, 20 September. Retrieved 23 September 2019. https://globalnews.ca/news/5929146/trump-trudeau-blackface/.

Jamieson, N. (@nljco). 2016. "I appreciate the irony of tweeting this but its worth a read RT How the Internet Is Loosening Our Grip on the Truth." nyti.ms/2e1ipMJ." Twitter, 2 November. Retrieved 15 October 2019. https://twitter.com/nljco/status/793773982025646080.

Jansen, B., and C. Hayes. 2019. "House Democrats' Report on the Impeachment Inquiry Finds Trump Has Solicited Foreign Interference in the 2020 Election." *USA Today*, 3 December. Retrieved 5 December2019. https://www.usatoday.com/story/news/politics/2019/12/03/house-democrats-conclude-trump-solicited-foreign-interference/2591967001/.

Jarvis, J. 2018. "The Spiegel Scandal and the Seduction of Storytelling." *Medium.com*, 24 December. Retrieved 5 April 2019. https://medium.com/whither-news/the-spiegel-scandal-and-the-seduction-of-storytelling-bfed804d7b21.

Jennings, J. 2002. "Deaths of the Intellectual: A Comparative Autopsy." In *The Public Intellectual*, edited by H. Small, 110–29. Oxford: Blackwell Publishing Company.

Johnston, M. 2017. "Q&A: Paul Godfrey, the CEO Who's Presiding over the Postmedia Newspaper Chain's Rapid Decline." *Toronto Life*, 7 February. Retrieved 2 January 2020. https://torontolife.com/city/business/qa-paul-godfrey-ceo-whos-presiding-postmedia-newspaper-chains-rapid-decline/.

Jones, A. 2009. *Losing the News: The Future of the News that Feeds Democracy*. New York: Oxford University Press.

Jones, J. 2020. "Toronto Star Owner Torstar to Be Sold, Taken Private in Deal Worth $51-Million." *Globe and Mail*, 26 May. Retrieved 27 May 2020. https://www.theglobeandmail.com/business/article-family-trust-agrees-to-sell-the-toronto-star-and-other-news papers-to/.

K, Astrid. (@littlered_ace). 2018. "I'm not married, have no kids, have a job that pays well, and have investments. There isn't a major party who offers me anything, I'm basically nothing more than an ATM to them." Twitter, 17 November. Retrieved 4 February 2019. https://twitter.com/littlered_ace/status/1063880999350734849.

Kahn, C. 2020. "Half of Republicans Say Biden Won Because of a 'Rigged' Election: Reuters/Ipsos poll." *Reuters*, 18 November. Retrieved 21 November 2020. https://www.reuters.com/article/us-usa-election-poll/half-of-republicans-say-biden-won-because-of-a-rigged-election-reuters-ipsos-poll-idUSKBN27Y1AJ.

Kahneman, D. 2011. *Thinking, Fast and Slow.* Toronto: Doubleday Canada.

Kambhampaty, A.P., M. Carlisle, and M. Chan. 2019. "Justin Trudeau Wore Brownface at 2001 'Arabian Nights' Party While He Taught at a Private School." *Time*, 18 September. Retrieved 23 September 2019. https://time.com/5680759/justin-trudeau-brownface-photo/.

Kang, C., N. Fandos, and M. Isaac. 2017. "Russia-Financed Ad Linked Clinton and Satan." *New York Times*, 1 November. Retrieved 2 January 2020. https://www.nytimes.com/2017/11/01/us/politics/facebook-google-twitter-russian-interference-hearings.html.

Katz, E., and P. Lazarsfeld. 1955. *Personal Influence: The Part Played by People in the Flow of Mass Communications.* New York: Free Press.

Kearns Goodwin, D. 2013. *The Bully Pulpit: Theodore Roosevelt, William Howard Taft, and the Golden Age of Journalism.* New York: Simon & Schuster.

Keenan, D. 2012. "My Thwarted Attempt to Tell of LIBOR Shenanigans." *Financial Times*, 26 July. Retrieved 15 October 2019. https://www.ft.com/content/dc5f49c2-d67b-11e1-ba60-00144feabdc0.

Keenan, E. 2021. "'We Must End This Uncivil War': Joe Biden May Be Ready, but Is America?" *Toronto Star*, 20 January. Retrieved 31 January 2021. https://www.thestar.com/news/world/2021/01/20/its-time-to-end-this-uncivil-war-joe-biden-may-be-ready-but-is-america.html.

Kellner, D. 2018. *Television and the Crisis of Democracy.* London: Routledge.

Kennedy, D. 2017. "No More 'Paper of Record.'" *Media Nation*, 4 January. Retrieved 26 August 2018. https://dankennedy.net/2017/01/04/no-more-paper-of-record-mcgrory-offers-more-details-on-the-globes-reinvention/.

Kennedy, H. 2017. Data Power 2017 Conference. *Researching Data Power: Looking Forwards.* Carleton University, Ottawa.

Kennedy, J. 2019. "Trudeau's Not a Fake Feminist, Despite How His Foes Paint Him." *Ottawa Citizen*, 5 April. Retrieved 11 April 2019. https://ottawacitizen.com/opinion/columnists/kennedy-trudeaus-not-a-fake-feminist-despite-how-his-foes-paint-him.

Kennedy, J.N. 2021. "Kennedy Talks Climate Hypocrisy with Fox News's Sean Hannity." *Fox News*, 3 February. Retrieved 5 February 2021. https://www.youtube.com/watch?v=dBbJe5eIs1w.

Kenney, J. (@jkenney). 2019. "Congrats to Vice-Admiral Mark Norman on his exoneration. The charges brought against him were an outrage. I was proud to work with him on successful interim supply ship procurement. Govt effort to block and politicize the project should be investigated." Twitter, 8 May. Retrieved 15 October 2019. https://twitter.com/jkenney/status/1126191158843981824.

Kent, P. (@KentThornhillMP). 2020. "Finding the precarious balance between emergency support … and human nature." Twitter, 28 April. Retrieved 2 May 2020. https://twitter.com/KentThornhillMP/status/1255101543302520832?s=20.

Kentish, B. 2016. "Donald Trump Has Lost Popular Vote by Greater Margin Than Any US President." *The Independent*, 12 December. Retrieved 28 November 2020. https://www.independent.co.uk/news/world/americas/us-politics/donald-trump-lost-popular-vote-hillary-clinton-us-election-president-history-a7470116.html

Kessler, G. 2020. "Fact-Checking the Craziest News Conference of the Trump Presidency." *Washington Post*, 19 November. Retrieved 28 January 2021. https://www.washingtonpost.com/politics/2020/11/19/fact-checking-craziest-news-conference-trump-presidency/.

Keung, N., and D. Zlomislic. 2019. "Syrian Family Closes Restaurant, Confirms Son Was Target of Death Threats after Political Protest." *Toronto Star*, 8 October. Retrieved 21 February 2020. https://www.thestar.com/news/gta/2019/10/08/restaurant-founded-by-syrian- refugee-family-closes-amid-allegations-of-death-threats.html.

Key Jr, V.O., and M. Cummings. 1966. *The Responsible Electorate*. Cambridge: Belknap Press.

Kilgore, E. 2020. "Republicans Make Shocking Gains in the House." *New York Magazine*, 4 November. Retrieved 21 November 2020. https://nymag.com/intelligencer/2020/11/republicans-pull-off-shocking-gains-in-the-u-s-house.html.

Kim, R. (@RichardKimNYC). 2020. "Okay, I did not sign THE LETTER when I was asked 9 days ago because I could see in 90 seconds that it was fatuous, self-important drivel that would only troll the people it allegedly was trying to reach – and I said as much." Twitter, 7 July. Retrieved 20 July 2020. https://twitter.com/RichardKimNYC/status/ 1280592642645114880?s=20.

Kingston, A. 2019. "If Only Hugs Were Votes." *Maclean's*, 22 October. Retrieved 24 March 2020. https://www.macleans.ca/politics/green-party-elizabeth-may-election-2019/.

Kochkodin, B. 2017. "Trump Is Shattering His Own Tweet Records." *Bloomberg News*, 13 November. Retrieved 4 January 2020. https://www.bloomberg.com/news/articles/2017-11-13/trump-is-shattering-his-own-tweet-records-with-non-stop-barrage.

Kolhatkar, S. 2019. "Elizabeth Warren Made Her Name Criticizing Wall Street. Can Her Economic Proposals Set Her Apart From Her Primary Rivals?" *New Yorker*, 24 June, 38.

Kovach, B., and T. Rosenstiel. 2007. *The Elements of Journalism: What Newspeople Should Know and the Public Should Expect*, 2nd Edition. New York: Three Rivers Press.

Koza, H. 2007. "Private Equity LBOs Are Putting the Squeeze on Bondholders." *Globe and Mail*, 6 April, B11.

Krashinsky Robertson, S. 2018. "Rogers Seeks Buyer for Magazine Assets." *Globe and Mail*, 15 August. Retrieved 8 September 2019. https://www.theglobeandmail.com/business/article-rogers-looking-to-sell-eight-of-its-digital-and-print-magazine-assets./.

Kristof, N. 2020. "America and the Virus: 'A Colossal Failure of Leadership.'" *New York Times*, 22 October. Retrieved 20 November 2020. https://www.nytimes.com/2020/10/22/opinion/sunday/coronavirus-united-states.html.

Krugman, P. (@paulkrugman). 2020. "What we're seeing is that the divide in US politics now is more about education and metropolitan growth than traditional regional orientation. Thx to Atlanta, GA now more educated than most of the 'blue wall' 2/." Twitter, 8 November. Retrieved 28 January 2021. https://twitter.com/paulkrugman/status/1325466251062341632?s=20.

Kruse, M. 2017. "Johnstown Never Believed Trump Would Help. They Still Love Him Anyway." *Politico*, 8 November. Retrieved 2 January 2020. https://www.politico.com/magazine/story/2017/11/08/donald-trump-johnstown-pennsylvania-supporters-215800.

Kurtz, H. 1998. *Spin Cycle: Inside the Clinton Propaganda Machine.* New York, London, Toronto, Sydney, Singapore: The Free Press.

– 2001. *The Fortune Tellers. Inside Wall Street's Game of Money, Media, and Manipulation.* New York: Touchstone.

Lach, E. 2020. "'Before the Plague Came, I Had It Made': Trump Strikes a Doubtful Note in Pennsylvania." *New Yorker*, 21 October. Retrieved 31 January 2021. https://

www.newyorker.com/news/campaign-chronicles/before-the-plague-came-i-had-it-made-trump-strikes-a-doubtful-note-in-pennsylvania.

Lakoff, G.P., and G. Duran. 2018. "Trump Has Turned Words into Weapons. And He's Winning the Linguistic War." *The Guardian*, 13 June. Retrieved 2 January 2020. https://www.theguardian.com/commentisfree/2018/jun/13/how-to-report-trump-media-manipulation-language.

Lalancette, M., and M. Lamy. 2020. "COVID-19 and the Total Eclipse of the News." *Policy Options*, 3 April. Retrieved 6 May 2020. https://policyoptions.irpp.org/magazines/april-2020/covid-19-and-the-total-eclipse-of-the-news/.

Lammer, A., M. Linsky, and E. Ratliff. 2020. "#398: Dean Baquet." *Longform*, 26 June. Retrieved 18 July 2020. https://longform.org/posts/longform-podcast-398-dean-baquet.

Lanchester, J. 2016. "How Economic Gobbledygook Divides Us." *The New York Times Magazine*, 1 November. Retrieved 30 September 2019. https://www.nytimes.com/2016/11/06/magazine/how-economic-gobbledygook-divides-us.html.

Lanham, R. 2007a. *The Economics of Attention: Style and Substance in the Age of Information*. Chicago and London: University of Chicago Press.

– 2007b. *Style: An Anti-Textbook*. Philadelphia: Paul Dry Books.

Lasswell, H. 1935. *World Politics and Personal Insecurity*. New York: McGraw-Hill.

– 1948. "The Structure and Function of Communication in Society." In *The Communication of Ideas*, edited by L. Bryson, 37–51. New York: Institute for Religious and Social Studies.

Laughland, O. 2018. "Trudeau 'Stabbed Us in Back' on Trade, Says Trump Chief Economic Adviser." *The Guardian*, 11 June. Retrieved 4 September 2019. https://www.theguardian.com/us-news/2018/jun/10/justin-trudeau-donald-trump-tariffs-g7-north-korea-summit.

Lazarsfeld, P., B. Berelson, and H. Gaudet. 1944. *The People's Choice: How the Voter Makes Up His Mind in a Presidential Campaign*. New York: Columbia University Press.

Lazarsfeld, P., and R. Merton. 1948. "Mass Communication, Popular Taste, and Organized Social Action." In *The Communication of Ideas*, edited by L. Bryson, 95–118. New York: Harper.

Lazer, D., M. Baum, N. Grinberg, L. Friedland, K. Joseph, W. Hobbs, and C. Mattsson. 2017. "Combating Fake News: An Agenda for Research and Action." Shorenstein Center on Media, Politics and Public Policy, 2 May. https://shorensteincenter.org/wp-content/uploads/2017/05/Combating-Fake-News-Agenda-for-Research-1.pdf.

Leavitt, K. 2020. "Nearly One in Five Canadians Agree with Trump's Assertion the U.S. Election Was Unfair." *Toronto Star*, 18 November. Retrieved 21 November 2020. https://www.thestar.com/politics/federal/2020/11/18/nearly-one-in-five-canadians-agree-with-trumps-assertion-the-us-election-was-unfair.html.

Leblanc, D. 2016. "Liberal MPs Urge Facebook to Curb Fake News in Bid to Preserve Politics." *Globe and Mail*, 17 November. Retrieved 2 January 2020. https://beta.theglobeandmail.com/news/politics/liberal-mps-urge-facebook-to-curb-fake-news-in-bid-to-preserve-politics/article32911547/.

– 2018. "Facebook Canada Contracts Independent Fact Checkers to Combat 'Fake News.'" *Globe and Mail*, 26 June. Retrieved 7 September 2019. https://www.theglobeandmail.com/politics/article-facebook-canada-contracts-independent-fact-checkers-to-combat-fake/

Leblanc, D., and R. Fife. 2019. "Ottawa Blocks RCMP on SNC-Lavalin Inquiry." *Globe and Mail*, 10 September. Retrieved 29 October 2019. https://www.theglobeandmail.com/politics/article-ottawa-blocks-rcmp-on-snc-lavalin-inquiry/.

Le Conte, M., and J. Waterson. 2016. "Why Did Vote Leave Donate £625,000 to a 23-Year-Old Fashion Student during the Referendum?" *BuzzFeed News*, 2 August. Retrieved 23 May 2020. https://www.buzzfeed.com/marieleconte/vote-leave-donations.

Lee, B.Y. 2020. "Trump Claims Doctors Are Overcounting Covid-19 Deaths to Make More Money; Physician Groups Say Otherwise." *Forbes*, 27 October. Retrieved 21 November 2020. https://www.forbes.com/sites/brucelee/2020/10/27/trump-claims-doctors-overcounting-covid-19-coronavirus-deaths-to-make-more-money/.

Lee, E. 2020. "Bari Weiss Resigns from New York Times Opinion Post." *New York Times*, 14 July. Retrieved 19 July 2020. https://www.nytimes.com/2020/07/14/business/media/bari-weiss-resignation-new-york-times.html.

Lem, G.T. (@gtlem). 2020. "Conservative Health Critic Michelle Rempel Garner accuses the Liberal Government of MURDER #cdnpoli #COVID19." Twitter, 18 November. Retrieved 29 November 2020. https://twitter.com/gtlem/status/1329224784119533569?s=20.

Leonard, T.C. 1986. *The Power of the Press: The Birth of American Political Reporting*. New York and Oxford: Oxford University Press.

– 1995. *News for All: America's Coming-of-Age with the Press*. New York: Oxford University Press.

Levine, A. 1993. *Scrum Wars: The Prime Ministers and the Media*. Toronto: Dundurn Press.

Levitsky, S., and D. Ziblatt. 2019. *How Democracies Die*. New York: Broadway Books.

Levitz, S. 2021. "O'Toole Defends Decision to Oust Controversial MP Derek Sloan." *CTV News*, 23 January. Retrieved 29 January 2021. https://www.ctvnews.ca/politics/o-toole-defends-decision-to-oust-controversial-mp-derek-sloan-1.5279618.

Lewis, M. 2010. *The Big Short: Inside the Doomsday Machine*. New York: W.W. Norton & Company.

– 2014. *Flash Boys: A Wall Street Revolt*. New York: W.W. Norton & Company.

Lewis, R. 2018a. *Power, Prime Ministers, and the Press: The Battle for Truth on Parliament Hill*. Toronto: Dundurn.

– (@Robert_L_Lewis). 2018b. "Total magazine revenue for @rogers publishing less than half of what Maclean's alone generated in 1980s. #macleans globe2go. newspaperdirect.com/epaper/showlin ..." Twitter, 16 August. Retrieved 19 August 2018. https://twitter.com/Robert_L_Lewis/status/1030081046539202562.

Lexington Herald Leader. 2020. "The Best of Times, the Worst of Times. Kentucky Journalism Needs Your Support." *Lexington Herald Leader*, 7 May. Retrieved 21 May 2020. https://www.kentucky.com/opinion/editorials/article242563286.html.

Lichterman, J. 2016. "Nearly Half of U.S. Adults Get News on Facebook, Pew Says." *Pew Research Center*, 26 May. https://www.niemanlab.org/2016/05/pew-report-44-percent-of-u-s-adults-get-news-on-facebook/.

Lietaer, J. (@jasonlietaer). 2019. "If the CEO of Tim Hortons were found to have been in blackface, the same people defending Mr Trudeau would mount a ferocious online campaign and boycott its coffee and donuts. The CEO would be gone in less than 24 hours. Any CEO would be fired by the Board. That is a fact." Twitter, 20 September. Retrieved 29 September 2019. https://twitter.com/jasonlietaer/status/1175130094697951233?s=20.

Lilleker, D.G. 2006. *Key Concepts in Political Communication*. London, Thousand Oaks CA, New Delhi: Sage Publications Ltd.

Lincoln, A. 1894. *Political Debates between Abraham Lincoln and Stephen A. Douglas in the Celebrated Campaign of 1858 in Illinois*. Cleveland, OH: Burrows Bros. Company.

Ling, J. 2019. "Rumours of a Suppressed Globe Story about Justin Trudeau Are Bullshit." *Canadaland*, 8 October. Retrieved 28 November 2019. https://www.canadalandshow.com/rumours-of-suppressed-trudeau-affair-story-are-bullshit/.

Lippmann, W. 1920. *Liberty and the News*. New York: Harcourt, Brace and Howe.

– 1922. *Public Opinion*. New York: Harcourt, Brace and Co.

Lipton, E., K.P. Vogel, and M. Haberman. 2020. "Questions and Answers about the Bidens and a Deal in China." *The New York Times*, 25 October. Retrieved 23 November 2020. https://www.nytimes.com/2020/10/25/us/politics/bidens-china.html.

Lizza, R. 2016. "Kellyanne Conway's Political Machinations." *The New Yorker*, 17 October. Retrieved 2 January 2020. https://www.newyorker.com/magazine/2016/10/17/kellyanne-conways-political-machinations.

Lowery, W. 2020. "A Reckoning over Objectivity, Led by Black Journalists." *The New York Times*, 23 June. Retrieved 18 July 2020. https://www.nytimes.com/2020/06/23/opinion/objectivity-black-journalists-coronavirus.html.

Lowry, R. 2020. "The Only Middle Finger Available." *National Review*, 26 October. Retrieved 28 January 2021. https://www.nationalreview.com/2020/10/the-only-middle-finger-available/.

Lum, Z.-A. 2020. "Trudeau Blames Conservatives For Canada's Vaccine Manufacturing Decline." *Huffington Post*, 25 November. Retrieved 28 November 2020. https://www.huffingtonpost.ca/entry/canada-vaccines-trudeau-conservatives_ca_5fbedb65c5b66bb88c63f66d.

Lundy, M., and T. Cardoso. 2019. "Federal Budget 2019 Highlights: 10 Things You Need to Know." *Globe and Mail*, 19 March. Retrieved 2 April 2019. https://www.theglobeandmail.com/politics/article-federal-budget-2019-highlights-10-things-you-need-to-know/.

Lytvynenko, J., M.C. Oved, and C. Silverman. 2019. "The Canadian Election's Surprise Influencer Is a Buffalo Man Targeting Canadians with Viral Disinformation." *BuzzFeed News*, 18 October. Retrieved 24 March 2020. https://www.buzzfeednews.com/article/janelytvynenko/matthew-ricchiazzi-buffalo-chronicle-trudeau-claims.

MacDougall, A. 2020. "Derek Sloan's Rhetoric Is Only a Symptom of a Bigger Conservative Party Problem." *Globe and Mail*, 27 April. Retrieved 1 May 2020. https://www.theglobeandmail.com/opinion/article-derek-sloans-rhetoric-is-only-a-symptom-of-a-bigger-conservative/.

Macdonald, N. (@TypesAndSpells). 2020. "Does anyone thing [sic] anything this government says is unrehearsed or transparent? When I was a columnist, I would get precisely identical non-answers from multiple departments. Eventually, I stopped bothering to call. And then I stopped listening." Twitter, 28 November. Retrieved 1 December 2020. https://twitter.com/TypesAndSpells/status/1332711686265053184?s=20.

Maclean's. 2020a. "Joe Biden's Latest Election 2020 speech: 'I'm Confident We'll Emerge Victorious.'" *Maclean's*, 4 November. Retrieved 21 November 2020. https://www.macleans.ca/politics/joe-bidens-latest- election-2020-speech-im-confident-well-emerge-victorious/.

– 2020b. "U.S. Election 2020, Trump's Speech: 'This Is a Fraud on the American Public.'" *Maclean's*, 4 November. Retrieved 21 November 2020. https://www.macleans.ca/politics/u-s-election-2020-trump-transcript-this-is-a-fraud-on-the-american-public-this-is-an-embarrassment-to-our-country/.

Madison. 2019. "Conservative Senator Rips Trudeau over 'Secret' Mark Norman Settlement." *The Post Millennial*, 2 July. Retrieved 23 May 2020. https://thepostmillennial.com/conservative-senator-rips-trudeau-over-secret-mark-norman-settlement.

Madrigal, A.C. 2017. "What Facebook Did to American Democracy." *The Atlantic*, 12 October. Retrieved 24 May 2020. https://www.theatlantic.com/technology/archive/2017/10/what-facebook-did/542502/.

Mahler, J. 2020. "The Fog of Rudy." *New York Times*, 15 January. Retrieved 25 January 2020. https://www.nytimes.com/interactive/2020/01/15/magazine/rudy-giuliani.html.

Maier, M. 2007. "Journalism without Journalists: Vision or Caricature?" Discussion Paper Series #D-40. Shorenstein Center on Media, Politics and Public Policy, November. https://shorensteincenter.org/wp-content/uploads/2012/03/d40_maier.pdf?x78124.

Manjoo, F. 2016. "How the Internet Is Loosening Our Grip on the Truth." *New York Times*, 2 November. Retrieved 7 January 2020. https://www.nytimes.com/2016/11/03/technology/how-the-internet-is-loosening-our-grip-on-the-truth.html.

Mansbridge, P. 2020. "The Right Honourable Podcast – Brian Mulroney Joins The Race Next Door (#16) with Bruce Anderson and Me." *The Bridge with Peter Mansbridge*, 30 October. Retrieved 31 January 2020. https://www.thepetermansbridge.com/episodes/the-right-honour able-podcast-brian-mulroney-joins-the-race-next-door-16-with-bruce-anderson-and-me.

Martelle, S. 2005. "And That's the Way Cronkite Still Is." *Los Angeles Times*, 30 September. Retrieved 30 April 2020. https://www.latimes.com/archives/la-xpm-2005-sep-30-et-cronkite30-story.html.

Martin, D. 2018. "Time for Trudeau to Take Aim at Trump's Base." *CTV News*, 14 June. Retrieved 12 October 2019. https://www.ctvnews.ca/politics/don-martin-s-blog/don-martin-time-for-trudeau-to-take-aim-at-trump-s-base-1.3974051.

Martin, J., and M. Haberman. 2020. "Nervous Republicans See Trump Sinking, and Taking Senate with Him." *New York Times*, 25 April. Retrieved 1 May 2020. https://www.nytimes.com/2020/04/25/us/politics/trump-election-briefings.html.

Martinson, J. 2020. "We Must Act before Coronavirus Sinks the Press as We Know It." *The Guardian*, 19 April. Retrieved 1 May 2020. https://www.theguardian.com/media/commentisfree/2020/apr/19/journalism-coronavirus-press-google-news.

Massolin, P. 1996. "Context and Content: Harold Innis, Marshall McLuhan and George Grant and the Role of Technology in Modern Society." *Past Imperfect* 5: 81–118. https://doi.org/10.21971/P7D302.

Masthead. 2016. "The End of an Era. Rogers Media Sells Off Some of Their Iconic B2B Media Brands in November." *Masthead*, 25 November. Retrieved 9 September 2019. http://www.mastheadonline.com/news/the_end_of_an_era._rogers_media_sells_off_some_of_their_iconic_b2b_media_brands_in_november/.

Mattelart, A. 1994. *Mapping World Communication: War, Progress, Culture*. Minneapolis, MN, London: University of Minnesota Press.

Matthews, D. (@DennisJMatthews). 2019a. "He's not a normal political candidate, he's a brand. A celebrity who has built, and continues to build, something that can withstand even the most damaging circumstances. #cdnpoli #elxn43." Twitter, 26 September. Retrieved 29 September 2019. https://twitter.com/DennisJMatthews/status/ 1177219090135638016?s=20.

– (@DennisJMatthews). 2019b. "1. In pursuit of 40% popular vote, have Conservatives accidentally become a minority proposition with voters? What ever happened to the Silent Majority. Make a broader appeal and fall short instead of trying to tack on extra voters to the 1/3 …" Twitter, 25 October. Retrieved 30 January 2020. https://twitter.com/DennisJMatthews/status/11877443418187777600?s=20.

– (@DennisJMatthews). 2019c. "2. Values and emotions build political brands. Conservatives mostly stuck on taxes and finances (cognitive arguments). Why do we think values and emotions are the exclusive territory of Liberals or Trudeau?" Twitter, 25 October. Retrieved 30 January 2020. https://twitter.com/DennisJMatthews/status/11877444454725242887?s=20.

Mayer, J. 2016. *Dark Money: The Hidden History of the Billionaires Behind the Rise of the Radical Right*. Toronto: Doubleday.

McChesney, R.W. 2013. *Digital Disconnect: How Capitalism Is Turning the Internet against Democracy*. New York: The New Press.

McCombs, M., and D. Shaw. 1972. "The Agenda-Setting Function of Mass Media."
    Public Opinion Quarterly 36, 2 (January): 176–87. https://www.jstor.org/
    stable/2747787.

McCullough, D. 1991. *Brave Companions: Portraits in History.* New York: Simon and
    Schuster.

McDaniel, C.-G. 1987. "Book Review: Reading the News." *Newspaper Research Journal*
    8, 4: 85–6. https://doi.org/10.1177/073953298700800408.

McDougall, A. 2021. "MacDougall: O'Toole Should Place Morality at the Heart
    of His Plan." *Ottawa Citizen*, 28 January. Retrieved 30 January 2021. https://
    ottawacitizen.com/opinion/macdougall-otoole-should-place-morality-at-the-
    heart-of-his-plan.

McEnteer, J. 1991. "Changing Lanes on the Inside Track: The Career Shuttle between
    Journalism, Politics and Government." Discussion Paper D-8. Shorenstein Center on
    Media, Politics and Public Policy, May. https://shorensteincenter.org/wp-content/
    uploads/2012/03/d08_mcenteer.pdf.

McEvoy, J. 2020a. "Mitt Romney Says Trump Won't Disappear: 'He's the 900-Pound
    Gorilla When It Comes to the Republican Party.'" *Forbes*, 8 November. Retrieved 31
    January 2021. https://www.forbes.com/sites/jemimamcevoy/2020/11/08/mitt-
    romney-says-trump-wont-disappear-hes-the-900-pound-gorilla-when-it-comes-to-
    the-republican-party/?sh=3edf12ac6399.

– 2020b. "Trump Fires Defense Secretary Mark Esper over Twitter." *Forbes*, 9
    November. Retrieved 21 November 2020. https://www.forbes.com/sites/
    jemimamcevoy/2020/11/09/trump-fires-defense-secretary-mark-esper-over-twitter/.

McGinniss, J. 1969. *The Selling of the President 1968.* New York: Trident Press.

McGregor, G. 2015. "Trudeau among Wealthy Canadians He Says Benefit from Small-
    Business Tax Deductions." *Ottawa Citizen*, 9 September. Retrieved 4 September
    2019. https://ottawacitizen.com/news/politics/trudeau-among-wealthy-
    canadians-he-says-benefit-from-small-business-tax-deductions.

– (@glen_mcgregor). 2019. "There is zero, zilch, nothing to support claim that any
    party or leader applied to any court during #elxn43 for an injunction against any
    news organization. That's it." Twitter, 6 October. Retrieved 28 November 2019.
    https://twitter.com/glen_mcgregor/status/1180886280932134912?s=20.

– (@glen_mcgregor). 2020. "A tweet storm complaining about a prize with a name he
    can't spell correctly and isn't a journalism award." Twitter, 26 April. Retrieved 1
    May 2020. https://twitter.com/glen_mcgregor/status/1254501789572960257?s=20.

McGregor, J. 2020. "Paying Volunteer Students Less Than Minimum Wage Was Federal Government's Idea, Says WE Charity." *CBC*, 21 July. Retrieved 16 November 2020. https://www.cbc.ca/news/politics/student-aid-volunteer-we-charity-trudeau-pandemic-coronavirus-covid-1.5656622.

McKeen, A. 2020. "'THIS SAYS IT ALL': Trump Retweets Elections Canada in Apparent Attempt to Call American Voting System into Question." *Toronto Star*, 17 November. Retrieved 23 November 2020. https://www.thestar.com/news/canada/2020/11/17/this-says-it-all-trump-retweets-elections-canada-in-apparent-attempt-to-call-american-voting-system-into-question.html.

McKenna, B. 2017. "CBC's Digital Shift Is Helping to Kill Local News Outlets." *Globe and Mail*, 1 December, B1–2.

McLean, C. 2007a. "Suitors Bank on Changes to Foreign Ownership." *Globe and Mail*, 18 April, B8.

– 2007b. "Sabia Says Options Still Open for BCE." *Globe and Mail*, 7 June, B1.

McLean, C., S. Stewart, J. McNish, and S. Chase. 2007. "Telus-BCE Union Would Be 'An All-Canadian Solution': Entwistle." *Globe and Mail*, 21 June. Retrieved 6 September 2019. https://www.theglobeandmail.com/report-on-business/telus-bce-union-would-be-an-all-canadian-solution-entwistle/article22624942/.

McLean, C., S. Stewart, E. Reguly, and J. McNish. 2007. "Losers Refuse to Back Down after Teachers Wins BCE War." *Globe and Mail*, 2 July, A1.

McLean, C., A. Willis, B. Erman, and L. McLeod. 2007. "Teachers Enters Race for BCE Buyout." *Globe and Mail*, 6 June, B1.

McLuhan, M. 1964. *Understanding Media: The Extensions of Man.* New York: McGraw-Hill.

McManus, J.H. 1994. *Market-Driven Journalism: Let the Citizen Beware?* Thousand Oaks, CA, London, Delphi: Sage Publications.

McNish, J., C. McLean, and S. Stewart. 2007. "Telus Puts Brakes on BCE Bid – For Now." *Globe and Mail*, 27 June, A1.

McQuigge, M., and N. Thompson. 2017. "'I'm Going to Be Lost': Residents across Ontario Upset over Community Newspaper Closures." *Global News*, 28 November. Retrieved 9 September 2019. https://globalnews.ca/news/3885139/ontario-community-newspapers-closures/.

Meachem, J. 2015. *Destiny and Power: The American Odyssey of George Herbert Walker Bush.* New York: Random House.

Medina, J., and G. Russonello. 2020. "Exit Polls Showed the Vote Came Down to the Pandemic Versus the Economy." *New York Times*, 3 November. Retrieved 31

January 2021. https://www.nytimes.com/2020/11/03/us/politics/exit-polls.html.

Meisenzahl, M. 2019. "Facebook Made the Unusual Decision to Push Back Directly on Elizabeth Warren and Her Criticism of the Company, but Its Attempt to Defend Itself Backfired Spectacularly." *Business Insider*, 14 October. Retrieved 4 February 2020. https://www.businessinsider.com/facebooks-elizabeth-warren-tweet-about-trump-impeachment-ads-backfires-2019-10.

Menon, V. 2019. "Why Trudeau's 'Deeply Regrettable' Blackface Apology Just Doesn't Cover It." *Toronto Star*, 20 September. Retrieved 23 September 2019. https://www.thestar.com/entertainment/opinion/2019/09/20/trudeaus-blackfacebrownface-scandals-show-the-narcissist-underneath-it-all.html.

Mickleburgh, R. (@rodmickleburgh). 2020. "Thanks to the internet, there has never been more facts and information available … Thanks to the internet, there has never been more people who could care less about facts and information. #DumbAndDumber." Twitter, 17 January. Retrieved 22 February 2020. https://twitter.com/rodmickleburgh/status/1218217145634451457?s=20.

Miège, B. 1987. "The Logics at Work in the New Cultural Industries." *Media, Culture & Society* 9, 3: 273–89.

Milbank, D. 2019. "Trump Boasted about Making Air Force One Cheaper. He Didn't." *Washington Post*, 7 August. Retrieved 6 September 2019. https://www.washingtonpost.com/opinions/trump-boasted-about-making-air-force-one-cheaper-he-didnt/2019/08/07/75316ad6-b946-11e9-a091-6a96e67d9cce_story.html.

Miliband, R. 1973. *The State in Capitalist Society*. London: Quartet Books.

Miller, D., and S. Macintyre. 1999. "Risk Communication: The Relationships between the Media, Public Beliefs and Policy-Making." In *Risk Communication and Public Health*, edited by P. Bennett, and K. Calman. Oxford: Oxford University Press.

Montpetit, É., E. Lachapelle, and S. Kiss. 2017. "Does Canadian Federalism Amplify Policy Disagreements? Values, Regions and Policy Preferences." No. 65. *Institute for Research on Public Policy*, September. http://irpp.org/wp-content/uploads/2017/09/study-no65.pdf.

Moon, N. 1999. *Opinion Polls: History, Theory and Practice*. Manchester: Manchester University Press.

Moore, H. (@moorehn). 2019a. "How on earth are you going to straight-facedly write a hot take about 'optics' in 2019? In 1999 it was optics on cable TV. Now 'optics' means nothing. Optics where? Twitter? Facebook? Cable? Sunday shows? Town halls? Snapchat? There. Are. No. Unified. Optics." Twitter, 25 July. Retrieved 8 December 2019. https://twitter.com/moorehn/status/1154562047725789185?s=20.

– (@moorehn). 2019b. "Political sourcing is a disaster right now and needs a clean sweep, both of sources and of methods. EICs and political editors should work with reporters to comb source lists and find the weak spots. Why so many centrists? Why does every story sound like Rahm Emanuel wrote it?" Twitter 25 July. Retrieved 8 December 2019. https://twitter.com/moorehn/status/ 1154563200035065857?s=20.

– (@moorehn). 2019c. "Sourcing methods. There's a whole generation of political reporters right now who never learned how to make phone calls and do in-person reporting. They show up at events and they email (!!!!) and DM people they want to talk to, who are mostly oleaginous comms people." Twitter, 25 July. Retrieved 8 December 2019. https://twitter.com/moorehn/status/1154564487925686274?s=20.

– (@moorehn). 2019d. "They are also lazy AF. They consider showing up in a room with other reporters – the WH press room, the WH pool, the Mueller hearing – to be hard work. Sitting on your ass hearing what everyone else can hear is not hard work. It's minimal presence. Hard work is context." Twitter, 25 July. Retrieved 8 December 2019. https://twitter.com/moorehn/status/1154565414921412610?s=20.

– (@moorehn). 2019e. "Hard work means talking to a LOT of people. Not the one comms dude who takes your call. 10–15 people for a decent news story. 40 or more for a feature. Right now we're seeing two-source stories consistently – the journalism MINIMUM. It's insufficient in complex times." Twitter, 25 July. Retrieved 8 December 2019. https://twitter.com/moorehn/status/1154565958884896768?s=20.

– (@moorehn). 2019f. "But seriously: Get your reporters off Twitter. They are disgracing themselves, political journalism, and journalism in general. Twitter has become a crutch for them to avoid the hard work of journalism just when the country needs them most. Set a limit on Twitter hours." Twitter, 25 July. Retrieved 8 December 2019. https://twitter.com/moorehn/status/1154569572835635203?s=20.

– (@moorehn). 2019g. "In fact, politics is NOT boring. Policy is NOT boring. Politics is the story of human striving. It's the story of how we build our societies and what humans in 2019 think society should look like. It's rich in wins, losses, big things at stake, lives on line." Twitter, 25 July. Retrieved 8 December 2019. https://twitter.com/moorehn/status/1154572035206656005?s=20.

– (@moorehn). 2019h. "This. Is. Our. Future. As. Humans. There is no story as important as the political story, and there is no journalism as trifling and petty and meaningless and careless as the US political journalism we have now. It is bloodless, meaningless, cold, useless." Twitter, 25 July. Retrieved 8 December 2019. https://twitter.com/moorehn/status/1154573398087000064?s=20.

– (@moorehn). 2019i. "Politics right now is the biggest story in American history since the Civil War. It's corruption, treason, cyberwar, racial hatreds, women and POC finding a voice and real power for the first time in decades. And the DC press corps is completely fucking up the assignment." Twitter, 25 July. Retrieved 8 December 2019. https://twitter.com/moorehn/status/1154574680726081536?s=20.

Morin, R. 2016. "Behind Trump's Win in Rural White America: Women Joined Men in Backing Him." *Pew Research Center*, 17 November. Retrieved 3 February 2021. https://www.pewresearch.org/fact-tank/2016/11/17/behind-trumps-win-in-rural-white-america-women-joined-men-in-backing-him/.

Morris, D.Z. 2016. "Trump's Digital Team Orchestrating 'Three Major Voter Suppression Operations.'" *Fortune*, 30 October. Retrieved 6 September 2019. https://fortune.com/2016/10/30/trump-voter-supression-operations/.

Morrow, A. 2018. "Trump Signs Executive Order Ending Family Separation Policy at Mexican Border." *Globe and Mail*, 20 June. Retrieved 26 January 2020. https://www.theglobeandmail.com/world/us-politics/article-trump-signs-executive-order-ending-family-separation-policy-at-mexican/.

Moscrop, D. 2019. *Too Dumb for Democracy? Why We Make Bad Political Decisions and How We Can Make Better Ones*. Fredericton: Goose Lane Editions.

Mozur, P., and M. Scott. 2016. "Fake News on Facebook? In Foreign Elections That's Not New." *New York Times*, 17 November. Retrieved 26 January 2020. https://www.nytimes.com/2016/11/18/technology/fake-news-on-facebook-in-foreign-elections-thats-not-new.html.

Mullainathan, S., and A. Shleifer. 2005. "The Market for News." *American Economic Review* 95, 4: 1031–53.

Mullen, J., and S. Saifi. 2016. "Whatever Happened to Guy Who Tweeted about Raid That Killed Osama bin Laden?" *CNN*, 20 January. Retrieved 7 September 2019. https://www.cnn.com/2016/01/20/asia/osama-bin-laden-raid-tweeter-sohaib-athar-rewind/index.html.

Mundt, E. (@edwinmundt). 2019. "So @CPC_HQ memed a doctored photo by combining a picture of Justin Trudeau with a Getty Images stock photo and ran a Photoshop Plug-in to darken his skin tones. I suspect we'll see more of this. (h/t @

BinAnimals) #cdnpoli." Twitter, 26 June. Retrieved 29 September 2019. https://twitter.com/edwinmundt/status/1144034988377223170.

Murphy, C., and Z. Haylock. 2020. "New York Times Publisher Calls Tom Cotton Op-Ed 'Contemptuous.'" *New York Magazine*, 5 June. Retrieved 19 July 2020. https://www.vulture.com/2020/06/new-york-times-writers-speak-out-against-tom-cotton-op-ed.html.

Murphy, R. 2006. "A Tory Gift from Left Field." *Globe and Mail*, 14 January, A23.

Muse Abernathy, P. 2014. *Saving Community Journalist: The Path to Profitability*. Chapel Hill, NC: The University of North Carolina Press.

National Post. 2020a. "The Globe and Mail Wins Leading Eight National Newspaper Awards at Virtual Ceremony." *National Post*, 1 May. Retrieved 1 May 2020. https://nationalpost.com/pmn/news-pmn/canada-news-pmn/the-globe-and-mail-wins-leading-eight-national-newspaper-awards-at-virtual-ceremony.

– 2020b. "PMO Sends Readout of Trudeau Scolding O'Toole Over 'COVID Misinformation' in Phone Call. Before the Call." *National Post*, 28 November. Retrieved 1 December 2020. https://nationalpost.com/news/politics/pmo-sends-readout-of-trudeau-scolding-otoole-over-covid-misinformation-in-phone-call-but-the-call-hadnt-happened.

Naughton, J. 2016. "A Moment of Truth amid the Fake News for Mark Zuckerberg." *The Guardian*, 20 November. Retrieved 26 January 2020. https://www.theguardian.com/commentisfree/2016/nov/20/fake-news-facebook-mark-zuckerberg-donald-trump.

– 2017. "Move Fast, Zuckerberg, or Hate Will Kill Facebook." *The Guardian*, 28 May. Retrieved 26 January 2020. https://www.theguardian.com/commentisfree/2017/may/28/hate-speech-facebook-zuckerberg-content-moderators.

Naylor, B., and T. Keith. 2017. "Trump Defends Charlottesville Comments at Phoenix Rally." *NPR*, 22 August. Retrieved 7 September 2019. https://www.npr.org/2017/08/22/545226284/trump-heads-to-arizona-to-push-border-wall-funding-rally-supporters.

Neuharth, A.H. 1989. *Confessions of an S.O.B.* New York: Doubleday Books.

Neuman, W., M. Just, and A. Crigler. 1992. *Common Sense: News and the Construction of Political Meaning*. London and Chicago: University of Chicago Press.

Neuman, W., and L. Guggenheim. 2011. "The Evolution of Media Effects Theory: A Six-Stage Model of Cumulative Research." *Communication Theory* 21, 2 (May): 169–96. http://doi.org/10.1111/j.1468-2885.2011.01381.x

Neustadt, R.E. 1960. *Presidential Power: The Politics of Leadership*. New York: Wiley.

New England Journal of Medicine. 2020. "Dying in a Leadership Vacuum." *The New England Journal of Medicine*, 8 October. Retrieved 19 November 2020. https://www.nejm.org/doi/full/10.1056/NEJMe2029812.

New York Times. 2020a. "Models Project Sharp Rise in Deaths as States Reopen." *New York Times*, 4 May. Retrieved May 11, 2020. https://www.nytimes.com/2020/05/04/us/coronavirus-live-up dates.html

– 2020b. "End Our National Crisis." *New York Times*, 18 October. Retrieved 21 November 2020. https://www.nytimes.com/interactive/2020/10/16/opinion/donald-trump-worst-president.html.

– 2020c. "How to Take On the Tech Barons." *New York Times*, 30 October. Retrieved 15 November 2020. https://www.nytimes.com/2020/10/30/opinion/tech-companies-data.html.

– 2020d. "Covid-19 Live Updates: U.S. Passes 12 Million Total Cases." *New York Times*, 20 November. Retrieved 21 November 2020. https://www.nytimes.com/live/2020/11/20/world/covid-19-coronavirus#us-records-12-millionth-case-as-virus-surge-gathers-speed.

Newman, N., R. Fletcher, A. Kalogeropoulos, and R.K. Nielsen. 2019. "Digital News Report 2019." *Reuters Institute for the Study of Journalism*. https://reutersinstitute.politics.ox.ac.uk/sites/default/files/2019-06/DNR_2019_FINAL_1.pdf.

Newton, K. 1999. "Mass Media Effects: Mobilization or Media Malaise?" *British Journal of Political Science* 29, 4: 577–99.

Nickle, R. 2017. "Visual Deceptions: National Geographic and the Pyramids of Giza." *Medium*, 28 February. Retrieved 15 August 2019. https://medium.com/engl462/visual-deceptions-national-geographic-and-the-pyramids-of-giza-3fee6d448d0d.

Noelle-Neumann, E. 1973. "Return to the Concept of Powerful Mass Media." *Studies in Broadcasting* 9: 67–112.

– 1974. "The Spiral of Silence: A Theory of Public Opinion." *Journal of Communication* 24, 2: 43–51. http://doi.org/10.1111/j.1460-2466.1974.tb00367.x.

Nowak, P. 2007. "Hasten Bid Review: Telus; Play for Bell Could Lose to Private Equity Firms." *National Post*, 26 June.

Obama, B. (@BarackObama). 2019. "I was proud to work with Justin Trudeau as President. He's a hard-working, effective leader who takes on big issues like climate change. The world needs his progressive leadership now, and I hope our neighbors to the north support him for another term." Twitter, 16

October. Retrieved 27 November 2019. https://twitter.com/BarackObama/ status/1184528998669389824?ref_src=twsrc%5Etfw.

Oliver, C. 2016. *Unleashing Demons: The Inside Story of Brexit.* London: Hodder and Stoughton.

Oliver, T.R. 2006. "The Politics of Public Health Policy." *Annual Review of Public Health* 27: 195–233.

Ortiz, A., and K.Q. Seelye. 2020. "Herman Cain, Former C.E.O. and Presidential Candidate, Dies at 74." *New York Times,* 3 August. Retrieved 20 November 2020. https://www.nytimes.com/2020/07/30/us/politics/herman-cain-dead.html.

Orwell, G. 1945. "You and the Atom Bomb." *Tribune Magazine,* 19 October.

Orwin, C. 2016. "Trump Didn't Win Only Because Clinton Lost." *Globe and Mail,* 11 November. Retrieved 19 November 2020. https://www.theglobeandmail.com/ opinion/trump-didnt-win-only-because-clinton-lost/article32804705/.

O'Sullivan, D. 2019. "Twitter Co-Founder Calls President Trump 'Master of the Platform.'" *CNN Business,* 22 May. Retrieved 28 May 2019. https://www.cnn. com/2019/05/22/tech/president-trump-twitter-ev-williams/index.html.

Owen, T. (@taylor_owen). 2016. "If you think #fakenews is a problem now, wait until @facebook builds a metaverse. my essay on journalism in VR @cjr cjr.org/the_ feature/vi …" Twitter, 9 December. Retrieved 5 September 2019. https://twitter. com/taylor_owen/status/807347858227634176.

– 2017a. "Is Facebook a Threat to Democracy?" *Globe and Mail,* 19 October. https:// beta.theglobeandmail.com/opinion/is-facebook-a-threat-to-democracy/ article36661905/.

– 2017b. "How Internet Monopolies Threaten Democracy." The 2017 Dalton Camp lLcture on Journalism. *CBC Ideas,* 15 December. Retrieved 7 December 2020. https:// podcastaddict.com/episode/44459288.

Owen, T., and E. Dubois, eds. 2020. "Understanding the Digital Ecosystem: Findings from the 2019 Federal Election." Digital Ecosystem Research Challenge. Retrieved 7 March 2020. https://b1c9862c-6924- 4cfd-9cbe-6c6f0144a777.filesusr.com/ ugd/38105f_c2beb2fbbe5f46199f bc2f636ace59ee.pdf.

Packer, G. 2016. "Will Our Democratic Institutions Contain Trump?" *The New Yorker,* 21 November. Retrieved 1 February 2020. http://www.newyorker.com/ magazine/2016/11/21/will-our-democratic-institutions-contain-trump.

Panetta, A. 2020. "Trump's Bump Goes Bust: Polls Point to Rising Disapproval as Voters Sour on U.S. President's Pandemic Response." *CBC News,* 25 April.

Retrieved 22 May 2020. https://www.cbc.ca/news/world/trump-bump-gone-1.5543277.

Papenfuss, M. 2018. "Canada 'Will Not Be Pushed Around': Justin Trudeau to Trump." *Huffpost Canada*, 10 June. Retrieved 28 May 2019. https://www.huffingtonpost.ca/2018/06/10/justin-trudeau-canada-not-pushed-around-trump-g7_a_23455128/.

Parliament of Canada, House of Commons. 2016–17. Standing Committee on Canadian Heritage, 42 Parliament, 1st Session, Meetings 4–68, February–June. https://www.ourcommons.ca/Committees/en/CHPC/StudyActivity?studyActivityId=8800976.

– 2016a. Standing Committee on Canadian Heritage, Number 015, 42nd Parliament, 1st Session, 12 May. Retrieved 10 May 2020. https://www.ourcommons.ca/DocumentViewer/en/42-1/CHPC/meeting-15/evidence.

– 2016b. Standing Committee on Canadian Heritage, Number 027, 42 Parliament, 1st Session, Meeting 27, 29 September. http://www.ourcommons.ca/DocumentViewer/en/42-1/CHPC/meeting-27/evidence.

Parscale, B. (@Parscale). 2020a. "For nearly three years we have been building a juggernaut campaign (Death Star). It is firing on all cylinders. Data, Digital, TV, Political, Surrogates, Coalitions, etc. In a few days we start pressing FIRE for the first time." Twitter, 7 May. Retrieved 8 May 2020. https://twitter.com/parscale/status/1258388669544759296?s=20.

– 2020b. "I didn't give our campaign the name, Death Star, the media did. However, I am happy to use the analogy. The fact is, we haven't used it yet. Laugh all you want, we will take the win!" Twitter, 7 May. Retrieved 8 May 2020. https://twitter.com/parscale/status/1258402017590104067?s=20.

Pasquale, F. 2015. *The Black Box Society: The Secret Algorithms That Control Money and Information*. Cambridge, London: Harvard University Press.

Patriquin, M. 2020. "Quebec Ink: What's a Nice Guy Like Patrick Pichette Doing at a Place Like Twitter?" *The Logic*, 5 October. Retrieved 29 January 2021. https://thelogic.co/news/quebec-ink/quebec-ink-whats-a-nice-guy-like-patrick-pichette-doing-at-a-place-like-twitter/.

Patterson, T. 1994. *Out of Order*. New York: Vintage Books.

– 2013. *Informing the News: The Need for Knowledge-Based Journalism*. Toronto: Vintage.

– 2016. "News Coverage of the 2016 General Election: How the Press Failed the Voters." *Shorenstein Center on Media, Politics and Public Policy*, December. https://

shorensteincenter.org/wp-content/uploads/2016/12/2016-General-Election-News-Coverage-1.pdf.

– 2017. "News Coverage of Donald Trump's First 100 Days." *Shorenstein Center on Media, Politics and Public Policy*, 18 May. https://shoren steincenter.org/wp-content/uploads/2017/05/News-Coverage-of-Trump-100-Days-5-2017.pdf.

Perkins, T., and P. Beaumont. 2020. "Donald Trump's Baseless Vote Fraud Claim Opens Cracks in Republican Ranks." *The Guardian*, 7 November. Retrieved 21 November 2020. https://www.theguardian.com/us-news/2020/nov/06/republicans-break-ranks-with-donald-trump-over-baseless-vote-claim.

Peters, J.W., E. Plott, and M. Haberman. 2020. "260,000 Words, Full of Self-Praise, from Trump on the Virus." *New York Times*, 26 April. Retrieved 1 May 2020. https://www.nytimes.com/interactive/2020/04/26/us/politics/trump-coronavirus-briefings-analyzed.html.

Petty, R., and J. Cacioppo. 1986. "The Elaboration Likelihood Model of Persuasion." *Advances in Experimental Social Psychology*, 19: 123–205. http://doi.org/10.1016/S0065-2601(08)60214-2.

Pew Research Center. 2017. "Large Majorities See Checks and Balances, Rights to Protest as Essential for Democracy." *Pew Research Center*, March 2. Retrieved 20 June 2018. http://assets.pewresearch.org/wp-content/uploads/sites/5/2017/03/02134825/03-02-2017-Democratic-values-release2.pdf.

Phillips, A. 2020. "Joe Biden's Victory Speech, Annotated." *Washington Post*, 7 November. Retrieved 31 January 2021. https://www.washingtonpost.com/politics/2020/11/07/annotated-biden-victory-speech/.

Phillips, G. 2017. "Keynote Address." Data Power Conference, Carleton University. Ottawa

Picard, A. 2020. "If You Can Get Your Relatives Out of Seniors' Homes, Try to Do So as Fast as You Can." *Globe and Mail*, 2 April. Retrieved 1 May 2020. https://www.theglobeandmail.com/canada/article-if-you-can-get-your-relatives-out-of-seniors-homes-try-to-do-so-as/.

Picard, R.G. 2006. "Journalism, Value Creation and the Future of News Organizations." Research paper R-27. Shorenstein Center on Media, Politics and Public Policy, spring. Retrieved 29 July 2018. https://shorensteincenter.org/wp-content/uploads/2012/03/r27_picard.pdf?x78124.

Plank, L. (@feministabulous). 2018. "This is 100% bait. This is an effective strategy to get the media to criticize her wardrobe so that they can criticize the media for criticizing her wardrobe and delegitimize us as fake news." Twitter, 21 June. Retrieved 25 June 2018. https://twitter.com/feministabulous/status/1009894668082012166.

Platt, B., and C. Nardi. 2021. "Rideau Hall a 'Toxic Workplace' with 'Screaming, Aggressive Conduct,' Workers Tell Payette Workplace Review." *National Post*, 28 January. Retrieved 4 February 2021. https://nationalpost.com/news/politics/rideau-hall-was-toxic-work place-with-screaming-aggressive-conduct-workers-told-payette-workplace-review.

Politico. 2020. "Joe Biden Has Been Declared the Winner, Toppling Donald Trump after Four Years of Upheaval in the White House." *Politico*, 20 November. Retrieved 20 November 2020. https://www.politico.com/2020-election/results/president/.

– 2021. "Read Liz Cheney's Full Statement in Support of Trump's Impeachment." *Politico*, 12 January. Retrieved 2 February 2021. https://www.politico.com/news/2021/01/12/liz-cheney-trump-im peachment-statement-458394.

Pope, K. 2016. "Here's to the Return of the Journalist as Malcontent." *Columbia Journalism Review*, 9 November. https://www.cjr.org/criticism/journalist_election_trump_failure.php.

Porter, C. 2020. "From Behind the Scenes to the Forefront: Canada's Public Health Officers." *The New York Times*, 10 April. Retrieved 30 April 2020. https://www.nytimes.com/2020/04/10/world/canada/coronavirus-bonnie-henry.html.

Postman, N. 1985. *Amusing Ourselves to Death: Public Discourse in the Age of Show Business.* New York: Penguin Books.

– 1992. *Technopoly: The Surrender of Culture to Technology.* New York: Knopf.

Potter, A. 2020. "It's Not a Crime to Disagree with Health Officials." *National Post*, 15 April. Retrieved 1 May 2020. https://nationalpost.com/opinion/andrew-potter-canada-needs-more-contrarian-thinking-on-covid-19-measures.

Press, J. 2018. "Trudeau Says Politicians Must Use Social Media for Good, Despite Others' Polarizing Twitter Tactics." *Globe and Mail*, 12 November. Retrieved 16 November 2018. https://www.theglobeandmail.com/canada/article-trudeau-says-politicians-must-use-social-media-for-good-despite/.

– 2021. "Inside Elections Canada after Trump's Tweet on Voting Machines." *The Globe and Mail*, 3 January. Retrieved 31 January 2021. https://www.theglobeandmail.com/politics/article-inside-elections- canada-after-trumps-tweet-on-voting-machines/.

Proudfoot, S. 2019. "Jody Wilson-Raybould's Trail of Political Breadcrumbs." *Maclean's*, 8 February. Retrieved 11 April 2019. https://www.macleans.ca/politics/ottawa/jody-wilson-rayboulds-trail-of-political-breadcrumbs/.

Public Opinion Strategies. 2020. "Post Election Analysis." *Public Opinion Strategies*, 4 November. Retrieved 28 January 2021. https://pos.org/post-election-national-survey-2/.

Public Policy Forum. 2017. "News, Democracy and Trust in the Digital Age." The Shattered Mirror Series, *Public Policy Forum*, January. https://shatteredmirror.ca/wp-content/uploads/theShatteredMirror.pdf.

– 2018. "Mind the Gaps: Quantifying the Decline of News Coverage in Canada." The Shattered Mirror Series, *Public Policy Forum*, 25 September. Retrieved 11 October 2018. https://www.ppforum.ca/wp-content/uploads/2018/09/MindTheGaps-QuantifyingTheDeclineOfNewsCoverageInCanada-PPF-SEPT2018.pdf.

Public Service Alliance Canada. 2020. "PSAC Pushes Back against WE Charity Contracting Out at Finance Committee." PSAC, 30 July. Retrieved 16 November 2020. http://psacunion.ca/psac-pushes-back-against-we-charity-contracting.

Pugliese, D. 2018. "Supply Ship Mark Norman Fought for Now on Its Way to Support RCN during Major Exercise." *Ottawa Citizen*, 13 April. Retrieved 8 September 2019. https://ottawacitizen.com/news/national/defence-watch/supply-ship-vice-admiral-mark-norman-fought-for-now-on-its-way-to-support-rcn-during-major-exercise.

– 2019. "Vance and the Senior Leadership Have a Change of Heart about Mark Norman." *Ottawa Citizen*, 10 May. Retrieved 2 February 2020. https://ottawacitizen.com/news/national/defence-watch/vance-and-the-senior-leadership-have-a-change-of-heart-about-mark-norman.

Pullen, J.P. 2017. "Al Franken to Facebook: How Could You Not Connect the Dots on Russian Election Interference?" *Fortune*, 31 October. Retrieved 2 February 2020. http://fortune.com/2017/10/31/franken-facebook-russia-investigation/.

Pynchon, T. 1973. *Gravity's Rainbow*. New York: Viking Press.

Quinn, G. 2017. "Trudeau's Vacation Broke Ethics Rules, Canadian Commissioner Says." *Bloomberg*, 20 December. Retrieved 9 August 2018. https://www.bloomberg.com/news/articles/2017-12-20/trudeau-vacation-broke-ethics-rules-canadian-commissioner-says.

Ramos, J. 2020. "What I Learned from My Brush with Trump." *New York Times*, 4 December. Retrieved 6 December 2020. https://www.nytimes.com/2020/12/04/opinion/international-world/trump-ramos-authoritarianism-media.html.

Raycraft, R., and D. Cochrane. 2021. "EU Says It Has Authorized Vaccine Delivery to Canada." *CBC News*, 2 February. Retrieved 5 February 2021. https://www.cbc.ca/news/politics/eu-vaccine-export-controls-covid-variants-1.5897991.

Read, M. 2016. "Donald Trump Won Because of Facebook." *New York Magazine*, 9 November. Retrieved 25 August 2019. https://nymag.com/intelligencer/2016/11/donald-trump-won-because-of-facebook.html.

Recode. 2017. "Washington Post Executive Editor Marty Baron at Code Media." *Code Media*, 16 March. https://www.recode.net/2017/3/16/14950658/video-watch-washington-post-executive-editor-marty-baron-code-media.

Recount. (@therecount). 2021. "Is Trump the worst ever? Historian @TimNaftali: 'I argue that [Trump] has surpassed in awfulness …' Historian Douglas Brinkley: 'Yeah, I do agree with that. I think he is the bottom of the barrel of American presidents.'" Twitter, 20 January. Retrieved 26 January 2021. https://twitter.com/therecount/status/1351872501664673792?s=20.

Regan, M.P. 2019. "Powell Speaks, Trump Tweets, China Reacts, Markets Freak. Repeat." *Bloomberg Businessweek*, 8 August, 24.

Reguly, E. 2007. "A Peek into the Pages Of KKR's Playbook." *Globe and Mail*, 27 April, B8.

Reguly, E., and A. Willis. 2007. "U.S. Equity Firm Stalks BCE, Plots Takeover." *The Globe and Mail*, 29 March, A1.

Reich, R. 1987. *Tales of a New America*. New York: Random House.

– (@RBReich). 2018. "We have become so overwhelmed by the corruption and attacks on democracy emanating from the White House that the EPA can roll back clean air laws, potentially killing thousands of Americans, and it goes barely noticed. The damage being done to the country is truly unfathomable." Twitter, 24 August. Retrieved 27 August 2018. https://twitter.com/RBReich/status/1033069989924749313.

– 2019. "Facebook and Twitter Spread Trump's Lies, So We Must Break Them Up." *The Guardian*, 3 November. Retrieved 3 December 2019. https://www.theguardian.com/commentisfree/2019/nov/02/facebook-twitter-donald-trump-lies.

– 2020. "America Is Being Subjected to a Stress Test – and Republicans Are Failing." *The Guardian*, 22 November. Retrieved 4 February 2021. https://www.theguardian.com/commentisfree/2020/nov/22/trump-republicans-discredit-election-stress-test.

Reid, S. 2019. "Some People (See: Justin Trudeau) Are Judged by a Different Set of Rules." *Globe and Mail*, 26 September. Retrieved 29 September 2019. https://www.

theglobeandmail.com/opinion/article-some-people-see-justin-trudeau-are-judged-by-a-different-set-of/.

Reid, T. 2021. "Dozens of Bush-Era Republican Officials Leaving GOP, Calling It 'Cult of Trump.'" *Globe and Mail*, 1 February. Retrieved 2 February 2021. https://www.theglobeandmail.com/world/us-politics/article-dozens-of-bush-era-republican-officials-leaving-gop-calling-it-cult-of/.

Reliable Sources. (@ReliableSources). 2017. "'Mistakes are precisely the reason that people should trust the media … it's the process of bringing truth to light,' says Atlantic Senior Editor @davidfrum snpy.tv/2iNTSe8." Twitter, 10 December. Retrieved 15 October 2019. https://twitter.com/ReliableSources/status/939894319699447814.

Remnick, D. 2016. "Obama Reckons with a Trump Presidency." *New Yorker*, 18 November. Retrieved 4 September 2019. https://www.newyorker.com/magazine/2016/11/28/obama-reckons-with-a-trump-presidency.

– 2021. "The Inciter-in-Chief." *New Yorker*, 9 January. Retrieved 26 January 2021. https://www.newyorker.com/magazine/2021/01/18/the-inciter-in-chief.

Rempel Garner, M. (@MichelleRempel). 2018. "This is a sentiment that is pervasive among a set of the leftist elite political class in Canada. 'Cars are soooo outdated, why should we make them?' 'Oh Alberta, you and your dirty little jobs, it's about time the industry collapsed.' The 'let them eat cake' idiocy of the left. t.co/EqCJs6NaMn." Twitter, 26 November. Retrieved 4 February 2019. https://twitter.com/MichelleRempel/status/1067078261375520768.

Riccardi, N. 2020. "Biden Approaches 80 Million Votes in Historic Victory." *Associated Press*, 19 November. Retrieved 20 November 2020. https://apnews.com/article/election-2020-joe-biden-donald-trump-politics-elections-372af3b89bc1f5f0f6d7f8c80025a9b0.

Rindels, M., and M. Messerly. 2020. "At Carson City Airport Rally, Trump Promises Hard-Hit Nevada an Economic Revival." *Nevada Independent*, 18 October. Retrieved 19 November 2020. https://then evadaindependent.com/article/at-carson-city-airport-rally-trump-promises-hard-hit-nevada-an-economic-revival.

Rogers, E. 1962. *Diffusion of Innovations*. New York: The Free Press.

Rogers, K. 2020. "Trump Mistakenly Congratulates Kansas City, Kan., on Its Super Bowl Win." *New York Times*, 2 February. Retrieved 6 February 2020. https://www.nytimes.com/2020/02/02/us/politics/trump-kansas-city-chiefs-tweet.html.

Roose, K. 2021. "In Pulling Trump's Megaphone, Twitter Shows Where Power Now Lies." *New York Times*, 9 January. Retrieved 29 January 2021. https://www.nytimes.com/2021/01/09/technology/trump-twitter-ban.html.

Rose, J. (@JonathanRose). 2017. "Govt's need to use the language of citizens not bureaucracies. Few will want to 'offer input on a revised draft of a framework.'" Twitter, 11 June. Retrieved 15 October 2019. https://twitter.com/JonathanRose/status/873930175322435584.

Rosen, J. 2009. *The Laura Flanders Show*. GRITtv: *Jay Rosen: The Church of the Savvy*, 1 December. https://www.youtube.com/watch?v=m s548AkFP5s.

– 2010. "The Afghanistan War Logs Released by Wikileaks, the World's First Stateless News Organization." *PressThink*, 26 July. Retrieved 29 July 2018. http://pressthink.org/2010/07/the-afghanistan-war-logs-released-by-wikileaks-the-worlds-first-stateless-news-organization/.

– 2011. "Why Political Coverage is Broken." *ABC News*, 30 August. Retrieved 28 September 2019. https://www.abc.net.au/news/2011-08-30/rosen---why-political-coverage-is-broken/2862328.

– 2017. "Getting Granular with the Claim That Trump Is Some Media Wizard." *PressThink*, 28 May. Retrieved 2 February 2020. http://pressthink.org/2017/05/getting-granular-claim-trump-media-wizard/.

– (@jayrosen_nyu). 2018. "Or, on the same point – how did journalists come to see themselves a society's storytellers and what are the costs of this misfit self-conception? – read @jeffjarvis on the Der Spiegel scandal, which is all about this. The seduction of storytelling." Twitter, 25 December. Retrieved 5 April 2019. https://twitter.com/jayrosen_nyu/status/1077608242484862977.

– (@jayrosen_nyu). 2020a. "Baquet: 'Black and Latino journalists have told us that we only accomplished half of what we set out to do, and they're right.' (44:04) We set out to diversify the newsroom, he said, but we thought these diversely talented people wanted to be just like us – and they do not! 9." Twitter, 4 July. Retrieved 9 July, 2020. https://twitter.com/jayrosen_nyu/status/1279485371550662656?s=20.

– (@jayrosen_nyu). 2020b. "By the way, the Biden campaign's press secretary said yesterday, 'President-elect Biden believes that the media is a critical piece of our democracy; that transparency is incredibly important.' Thought you might want to know that." Twitter, 9 November. Retrieved 31 January 2021. https://twitter.com/jayrosen_nyu/status/13258117177734019073?s=20.

– (@jayrosen_nyu). 2020c. "To me, this is the top story in politics every day. A counter-majoritarian party has to be counterfactual, or it cannot live. To satisfy its core supporters it wrecks institutions. The fuel source is destruction. Biden is not ready. His party is not ready. The press is not ready." Twitter, 17 November.

Retrieved 21 November 2020. https://twitter.com/jayrosen_nyu/status/ 1328741577070612480?s=20.

Rosenthal, J. 2009. "The Mogul at Play." *New York Times*, 9 January. Retrieved 4 August 2019. https://www.nytimes.com/2009/01/11/books/review/Rosenthal-t.html.

Rubin, J. 2020. "Torstar to Be Sold, Taken Private in $52-Million Deal." *Toronto Star*, 26 May. Retrieved 27 May 2020. https://www.thestar.com/business/2020/05/26/ torstar-to-be-sold-taken-private-in-52-million-deal.html.

Rudd, K. 2020. "The Murdoch Media's China Coronavirus Conspiracy Has One Aim: Get Trump Re-Elected." *The Guardian*, 7 May. Retrieved 8 May 2020. https://www.theguardian.com/media/2020/may/08/murdoch-media-china- coronavirus-conspiracy-trump-kevin-rudd.

Russell, A. 2016. "'Mind-Boggling and Shocking': Judge Slams Harper PMO in Mike Duffy Verdict." *Global News*, 22 April. Retrieved 7 September 2019. https:// globalnews.ca/news/2655906/mind-boggling-and-shocking-judge-slams-harper- pmo-in-mike-duffy-verdict/.

Russell, J. 2019. "Boris Johnson Is Heading for a Scorched-Earth Election." *The New York Times*, 26 October. Retrieved 31 October 2019. https://www.nytimes. com/2019/10/26/opinion/boris-brexit-conservatives.html.

Rutenberg, J., J. Becker, E. Lipton, M. Haberman, J. Martin, M. Rosenberg, and M.S. Schmidt. 2021. "77 Days: Trump's Campaign to Subvert the Election." *The New York Times*, 31 January. Retrieved 2 February 2021. https://www.nytimes. com/2021/01/31/us/trump-election-lie.html.

Sabato, L. 1991. *Feeding Frenzy: How Attack Journalism Has Transformed American Politics*. New York: Free Press.

– (@LarrySabato). 2020. "Everyone expected Trump to be a poor loser. He is, inventing nonexistent fraud & making flimsy excuses. But GOP 'leaders' are coddling him, indulging his stubborn delusions. A predictably disgraceful ending to the worst presidency in U.S. history. #Shame." Twitter, 8 November. Retrieved 31 January 2021. https://twitter.com/LarrySabato/status/1325463560043057152?s=20.

– (@LarrySabato). 2021. "The Republican Party is no longer salvageable – at least a sane center-right version the country needs as an alternative. I resisted accepting this for a long time. But Trump, Jan 6, Greene et al made me face it. Not sure what's next & best, or how to get there." Twitter, 29 January. Retrieved 2 February 2021. https://twitter.com/LarrySabato/ status/1355272574800953348?s=20.

Safia Khan, F. (@farrahsafiakhan). 2019. "What high school student today uses Facebook?" Twitter, 29 August. Retrieved 10 September 2019. https://twitter.com/farrahsafiakhan/status/1167181563123130373?s=20.

Sagan, A. 2020. "Postmedia to Lay Off 80 Employees, Permanently Close 15 Newspapers as COVID-19 Hits Revenue." *Globe and Mail*, 28 April. Retrieved 1 May 2020. https://www.theglobeandmail.com/business/article-postmedia-to-lay-off-80-employees-permanently-close-15-newspapers-as/.

Sallot, J. 2006. "U.S. Authorities Quietly Examining Income-Trust Case." *Globe and Mail*, 7 January, A8.

Sandman, P.M. 1993. *Responding to Community Outrage; Strategies for Effective Risk Communication*. American Industrial Hygiene Association.

Sanger, D.E., M. Stevens, and N. Perlroth. 2020. "Election Officials Directly Contradict Trump on Voting System Fraud." *New York Times*, 12 November. Retrieved 4 February 2021. https://www.nytimes.com/2020/11/12/us/politics/election-officials-contradict-trump.html.

Sax, D. 2018. "Toronto Suddenly Has a New Craving: Syrian Food." *The New York Times*, 12 January. Retrieved 21 February 2020. https://www.nytimes.com/2018/01/12/dining/toronto-syrian-food.html.

Schaul, K., K. Rabinowitz, and T. Mellnik. 2020. "2020 Turnout Is the Highest in Over a Century." *Washington Post*, 5 November. Retrieved 21 November 2020. https://www.washingtonpost.com/graphics/2020/elections/voter-turnout/.

Schefter, A. (@AdamSchefter). 2019. "Filed to ESPN: Andrew Luck has informed the Colts he is retiring from the NFL, per source. There will be a press conference Sunday to make it official, but Luck is mentally worn down, and now checking out." Twitter, 24 August. Retrieved 10 September 2019. https://twitter.com/AdamSchefter/status/1165435636893016064?s=20.

Scherer, S. 2019. "Canadian Lawmakers Fume after Facebook's Zuckerberg Snubs Invitation." *Reuters*, 28 May. https://ca.reuters.com/article/domesticNews/idCAKCN1SY208-OCADN.

Schiffrin, A. 2011. *Bad News: How America's Business Press Missed the Story of the Century*. New York: The New Press.

Schramm, W. 1947. "Measuring Another Dimension of Newspaper Readership." *Journalism Quarterly* 24, 4: 293–306. doi:https://doi.org/10.1177/107769904702400401.

– 1949. "The Nature of News." *Journalism Quarterly* 26, 3: 259–69. https://doi.org/10.1177/107769904902600301.

Schudson, M. 1995. *The Power of News.* Cambridge, MA: Harvard University Press.

Schulman, M. 2019. "Superfans: A Love Story." *New Yorker*, 16 September.

Schumpeter, J.A. 1942. *Capitalism, Socialism, and Democracy.* New York, London: Harper & Brothers.

Scotsman Leader Comment. 2018. "Leader Comment: A Denunciation of Donald Trump." *The Scotsman*, 12 July. Retrieved 15 August 2019. https://www.scotsman.com/news/opinion/leader-comment-a-denunciation-of-donald-trump-1-4767577.

Senate of Canada. 2013. "Senators Statements: Orders of the Day." 2nd Session, 41st Parliament, volume 149, issue 11, 4 November. Retrieved 18 March 2020. https://sencanada.ca/en/content/sen/chamber/412/debates/011db_2013-11-04-e.

Serebrin, J. 2018. "La Presse to Become Non-Profit." *National Post*, 9 May, F1.

Shah, M. 2019a. "Green Party Leader Speaks Out about One of Her Own Candidates Wearing Blackface in the Past." *Global News*, 21 September. Retrieved 4 November 2019. https://globalnews.ca/news/5934682/green-party-candidate-blackface/.

– 2019b. "Climate Change Emerges as One of the Top Ballot-Box Issues among Voters: Ipsos Poll." *Global News*, 9 October. Retrieved 17 February 2020. https://globalnews.ca/news/6006868/climate-change-federal-election-issue-poll/.

Sharp, R., J. Elsom, and J. Tapsfield. 2020. "Bombshell 'Five Eyes' Western Intelligence Dossier Claims China Lied about Human-to-Human Transmission, 'Disappeared' Whistle-Blowers and Refused to Help Other Countries Prepare a Vaccine for Coronavirus." *Daily Mail*, 2 May. Retrieved 2 May 2020. https://www.dailymail.co.uk/news/article-8279859/Bombshell-intelligence-lays-bare-China-lied-coronavirus-outbreak.html.

Shaygan, T. 2018. "Former National Post Reporter Takes Helm as U of C's Journalist-in-Residence." *The Gauntlet*, 27 February. Retrieved 18 June 2018. http://www.thegauntlet.ca/former-national-post-reporter-takes-helm-as-u-of-cs-journalist-in-residence/.

Shear, M.D., M. Haberman, N. Confessore, K. Yourish, L. Buchanan, and K. Collins. 2019. "How Trump Reshaped the Presidency in Over 11,000 Tweets." *New York Times*, 2 November. Retrieved 3 December 2019. https://www.nytimes.com/interactive/2019/11/02/us/politics/trump-twitter-presidency.html.

Shear, M.D., and S. Saul. 2021. "Trump, in Taped Call, Pressured Georgia Official to 'Find' Votes to Overturn Election." *The New York Times*, 5 January. Retrieved 31 January 2021. https://www.nytimes.com/2021/01/03/us/politics/trump-raffensperger-call-georgia.html.

Shenk, D. 1997. *Data Smog: Surviving the Information Glut*. New York: HarperCollins.

Shiller, R. 2005. *Irrational Exuberance*, 2nd ed. New York: Broadway Books.

Shipman, T. 2016. *All Out War: The Full Story of Brexit*. London: William Collins.

Shirky, C. 2008. *Here Comes Everybody: The Power of Organizing without Organizations*. New York: Penguin Group.

– 2011. "The Political Power of Social Media." *Foreign Affairs* 90, 1 (January / February): 28–42.

Shorenstein Center on Media, Politics and Public Policy. 2015. "Riptide: What Really Happened to the News Business." Interview with Kara Swisher. https://www.digitalriptide.org/person/kara-swisher/.

Shribman, D. 2017. "With a GOP-Led Congress, a New Washington Takes Shape." *Globe and Mail*, 2 January. Retrieved 18 July 2019. https://www.theglobeandmail.com/news/politics/globe-politics-insider/as-trump-prepares-to-take-office-a-new-washington-takes shape/article33469929/.

Shufelt, T. 2018. "Rogers Lays Off One-Third of Its Digital and Publishing Employees." *Globe and Mail*, 14 June. Retrieved 15 June 2018. https://www.theglobeandmail.com/business/article-rogers-lays-off-one-third-of-its-digital-and-publishing-employees/.

Sides, J., and L. Vavreck. 2013. *The Gamble: Choice and Chance in the 2012 Presidential Election*. Princeton and Oxford: Princeton University Press.

Siebert, F.S., T. Peterson, and W. Schramm. 1956. *Four Theories of the Press: The Authoritarian, Libertarian, Social Responsibility and Soviet Communist Concepts of What the Press Should Be and Do*. Urbana: University of Illinois Press.

Siegel, J. (@Joelmsiegel). 2018. "Stumbled across this 1998 Giuliani speech. Wow: 'Too many immigrants work and pay taxes but are still being deprived of the basic benefits they deserve … It's simply unfair to target hardworking people simply because they have not yet become citizens.' nyc.gov/html/records/r …" Twitter, 15 June. Retrieved 26 August 2018. https://twitter.com/joelmsiegel/status/1007707317884915713.

Silcoff, S. 2007a."Why Private Equity?" *National Post*, 30 March, FP1.

– 2007b. "Teachers Says Group Set for Possible Bid for BCE; Canadian-Led." *National Post*, 14 April, FP1.

– 2007c. "BCE Might Widen Field of Bidders; Pension Funds Would Pool Money for Any Purchaser." *National Post*, 28 April, FP1.

– 2007d. "Entwistle Too Shrewd to Call." *National Post*, 3 May, FP1.

– 2007e. "Speculators Look to Ring Up Tidy Profits by Shorting BCE Shares." *National Post*, 10 May, FP10.

– 2007f. "Teachers, Cerberus Eyeing BCE; Canwest as Partner?" *National Post*, 19 May, FP7.

– 2007g. "Captain Canuck to Bell's Rescue?; Telus CEO Paints Bid as Corporate Nationalism." *National Post*, 22 June, A1.

– 2007h. "Teachers VP Says Trust Decision Set Up Bell Deal; PROMPTED ACTION; Board's Openness to Change Stirred Dealmakers." *National Post*, 3 July, FP8.

Silver, N. 2012. *The Signal and the Noise: Why So Many Predictions Fail – but Some Don't.* New York: The Penguin Press.

– (@NateSilver538). 2016a. "I'll put it like this: Clinton would almost certainly be President-elect if the election had been held on Oct. 27 (day before Comey letter)." Twitter, 11 December. Retrieved 19 October 2019. https://twitter.com/NateSilver538/status/807987340941684736.

– (@NateSilver538). 2016b. "Comey had a large, measurable impact on the race. Harder to say with Russia/Wikileaks because it was drip-drip-drip. 53eig. ht/2fvuQNl." Twitter, 11 December. Retrieved 26 August 2018. https://twitter.com/NateSilver538/status/807984392480161793.

– 2017. "The Comey Letter Probably Cost Clinton the Election." The Real Story of 2016, Part 10. Part 10. *FiveThirtyEight*, 3 May. https://fivethirtyeight.com/features/the-comey-letter-probably-cost-clinton-the-election/.

Silverman, C. 2016a. "How Teens in the Balkans Are Duping Trump Supporters with Fake News." *BuzzFeed News*, 3 November. Retrieved 8 September 2019. https://www.buzzfeednews.com/article/craigsilverman/how-macedonia-became-a-global-hub-for-pro-trump-misinfo.

– 2016b. "This Analysis Shows How Fake Election News Stories Outperformed Real News on Facebook." *BuzzFeed News*, 16 November. Retrieved 6 February 2020. https://www.buzzfeed.com/craigsilver man/viral-fake-election-news-outperformed-real-news-on-facebook.

Simpson, J. 2006. "The Mounties Shouldn't Horse Around in This Election." *The Globe and Mail*, 6 January, A15.

Singer, P.W., and E.T. Brooking. 2018. *Like War: The Weaponization of Social Media.* Boston, New York: Houghton, Mifflin, Harcourt.

Skoler, M. 2009. "Why the News Media Became Irrelevant – And How Social Media Can Help." *Nieman Reports*, 16 September. Retrieved 26 July 2018. http://niemanreports.org/articles/why-the-news-media-became-irrelevant-and-how-social-media-can-help/.

Slaby, M. 2013. "Mapping the New World: Lessons from the Obama Campaigns," #D-82. Shorenstein Center on Media, Politics and Public Policy, September. Retrieved 6 November 2021. https://shorensteincenter.org/wp-content/uploads/2013/09/d82_slaby.pdf.

Sloan, D. (@DerekSloanCPC). 2020a. "Dr. Theresa Tam, Canada's Chief Public Health Officer, has failed Canadians. Dr. Tam must go! Canada must remain sovereign over decisions. The UN, the WHO, and Chinese Communist propaganda must never again have a say over Canada's public health! #cdnpoli." Twitter, 21 April. Retrieved 1 May 2020. https://twitter.com/DerekSloanCPC/status/1252738270632558599?s=20.

– 2020b. "Dr. Theresa Tam must be fired. Here's my email from Tuesday in case you missed it. #cdnpoli." Twitter, 23 April. https://twitter.com/DerekSloanCPC/status/1253452758075744257?s=20.

Smit, S., M. Hirt, K. Buehler, S. Lund, E. Greenberg, and A. Govindarajan. 2020. "Safeguarding Our Lives and Our Livelihoods: The Imperative of Our Time." McKinsey & Company, March 23. https://www.mckinsey.com/business-functions/strategy-and-corporate-finance/our-insights/safeguarding-our-lives-and-our-livelihoods-the-imperative-of-our-time.

Smith, A. 2020. "Trump Says He's Sending in His Lawyers as Soon as the Election Ends to Review Swing State Votes." *NBC News*, 2 November. Retrieved 21 November 2020. https://www.nbcnews.com/politics/2020-election/trump-begins-rally-blitz-playing-hits-lamenting-cold-n1245691.

Smith, B. 2020a. "Marty Baron Made The Post Great Again. Now, the News Is Changing." *New York Times*, 28 June. Retrieved 18 July 2020. https://www.nytimes.com/2020/06/28/business/media/martin-baron-washington-post.html.

– 2020b. "Trump Had One Last Story to Sell. The Wall Street Journal Wouldn't Buy It." *New York Times*, 25 October. Retrieved 1 December 2020. https://www.nytimes.com/2020/10/25/business/media/hunter-biden-wall-street-journal-trump.html.

– 2020c. "The Trump Presidency Is Ending. So Is Maggie Haberman's Wild Ride." *New York Times*, 8 November. Retrieved 30 January 2021. https://www.nytimes.com/2020/11/08/business/media/trump-maggie-haberman.html.

Smith, G., and C. Chiglinsky. 2020. "What Use Does Wall Street Have for Newspapers." *Bloomberg Businessweek*, 10 February.

Smith, M., J. Levin, and M. Bergen. 2017. "Why It Took Google So Long to End Shady Rehab Center Ads." *Bloomberg Businessweek*, 26 September. Retrieved 6

February 2020. Bloomberg Businessweek: https://www.bloomberg.com/news/features/2017-09-26/why-it-took-google-so-long-to-end-shady-rehab-center-ads.

Smith, V. 2020. "Vaccine Race: Mexican Ambassador to Canada Angered by Conservatives." *Canada Live,* 25 November. Retrieved 26 November 2020. https://canadalive.news/2020/11/25/vaccine-race-mexican-ambassador-to-canada-angered-by-conservatives/.

Snyder, T. 2019. *On Tyranny: Twenty Lessons from the Twentieth Century.* New York: Tim Duggan Books.

Social Blade. 2019. "Twitter Statistics on Social Blade/Twitter Stats." Retrieved 25 August 2019. https://socialblade.com/twitter/user/realdonaldtrump.

Socolow, M. (@MichaelSocolow). 2020. "'It's very simple. We turned off Twitter. We stayed away from it. We knew that the country was in a different headspace than social media would suggest.' I would love to hear more about this." Twitter, 7 November. Retrieved 23 November 2020. https://twitter.com/MichaelSocolow/status/1325264133311311872?s=20.

Solon, O. 2016. "Facebook's Failure: Did Fake News and Polarized Politics Get Trump Elected?" *The Guardian,* 10 November. Retrieved 8 February 2020. https://www.theguardian.com/technology/2016/nov/10/facebook-fake-news-election-conspiracy-theories.

Sonmez, F., and J. Dawsey. 2020. "Giuliani Releases Statement Distancing Trump Campaign from Lawyer Sidney Powell." *Washington Post,* 22 November. Retrieved 27 November 2020. https://www.washingtonpost.com/politics/2020/11/22/giuliani-releases-statement-distancing-trump-campaign-lawyer-sidney-powell/.

Soufan, A. (@Ali_H_Soufan) .2018. "Unfortunately, the Russian strategy paid off: In PA, Stein received 49,678 votes. Trump won by 46,765 votes. In WI, Stein received 31,006 votes. Trump won by 22,177 votes. In MI, Stein received 51,463 votes. Trump won by 10,704 votes. nbcnews.com/politics/natio ... via @NBCNews." Twitter, 22 December. Retrieved 5 February 2019. https://twitter.com/Ali_H_Soufan/status/1076500928809836545.

Southey, T. 2016. "The Problem with Fake News Is Not Supply. It's Demand." *Globe and Mail,* 18 November. Retrieved 8 February 2020. https://www.theglobeandmail.com/opinion/the-problem-with-fake-news-is-not-supply-its-demand/article32924694/.

Springsteen, B. 2016. *Born to Run.* New York: Simon and Schuster.

Squires, J.D. 1993. *Read All About It! The Corporate Takeover of America's Newspapers.* New York: Time Books.

St. Catharines Standard. 2019. "All the Chair's Men Wins National Award for Investigative Journalism." *St. Catharines Standard*, 4 May. https://www.stcatharinesstandard.ca/news-story/9337226-all-the-chair-s-men-wins-national-award-for-investigative-journalism/.

Stahl, L. 1999. *Reporting Live*. New York: Touchstone.

Stead, S. 2019. "In Defence of Confidential Sources." *Globe and Mail*, 22 February. Retrieved 11 April 2019. https://www.theglobeandmail.com/public-editor/article-in-defence-of-confidential-sources/.

Stelter, B. 2020. "Axios CEO: I Fear a 'Decoupling' of America." *CNN*, 11 November. Retrieved 28 November 2020. https://www.cnn.com/videos/business/2020/11/22/axios-ceo-i-fear-a-decoupling-of-america.cnn.

– (@brianstelter). 2021. "Without a Twitter account, Trump 'is eerily silent now,' @johnkingCNN says. 'In some ways that's calming. In other ways, to those who are worried about his erratic behavior, it is unnerving …'" Twitter, 10 January. Retrieved 29 January 2021. https://twitter.com/brianstelter/status/1348271773243080704?s=20.

Stephanopoulos, G. 1996. "Every Political Reporter." *American Journalism Review* 18, 1–5.

Stephens, M. 2009. "Beyond News: The Case for Wisdom Journalism." #D-53. Shorenstein Center on Media, Politics and Public Policy, June. https://shorensteincenter.org/wp-content/uploads/2012/03/d53_stephens.pdf?x78124.

– 2014. *Beyond News: The Future of Journalism*. New York: Columbia University Press.

Stephenson, M. (@MercedesGlobal). 2019. "Question for the #cdnpoli [vote jpg] twitterverse: is there any previous occasion/precedent where MPs have called for an officer of Parliament to testify and it has been blocked? #SNCLavalin." Twitter, 21 August. Retrieved 7 September 2019. https://twitter.com/MercedesGlobal/status/1164301054286209024?s=20.

Stephenson, M., and J. Armstrong. 2019. "Video Shows Trudeau in Blackface in 3rd Instance of Racist Makeup." *Global News*, 19 September. Retrieved 17 February 2020. https://globalnews.ca/news/5922861/justin-trudeau-brownface-video/.

Sterbenz, C. 2013. "12 Famous Quotes That Always Get Misattributed." *Business Insider*, 7 October. Retrieved 24 March 2020. https://www.businessinsider.com/misattributed-quotes-2013-10.

Stevens, S. (@stuartpstevens). 2020. "Trump is a racist who doesn't understand America. To support him you have to be comfortable with a racist president.

The Republican Party has fully embraced white grievance politics. I helped elect many of these. I never thought it possible. But I was wrong." Twitter, 22 September. Retrieved 27 November 2020. https://twitter.com/stuartpstevens/status/1308575998678454273?s=20.

Stewart, S. 2007. "Three Funds Look to Join CPP, Bypassing Teachers in BCE Hunt." *The Globe and Mail*, 23 April, B1.

Stewart, S., and D. DeCloet. 2007. "It Was Mountains of Cash (and Some Last-Minute Calls from an Alberta Glacier) That Finally Helped Put Teachers Over the Top." *Globe and Mail*, 2 July, B1.

Stewart, S., and A. Willis. 2007. "BCE Advisers Push for Hasty Coronation." *Globe and Mail*, 23 June, B7.

Stewart, S., A. Willis, and J. McNish. 2007. "CPP Partners Walk Away from BCE Bid." *Globe and Mail*, 26 June, B1.

Stolberg, S.G. 2021. "Biden Rolls Out 'Full-Scale, Wartime' Coronavirus Strategy, Including Requiring Masks on Some Planes, Trains and Buses." *New York Times*, 21 January. Retrieved 31 January 2021. https://www.nytimes.com/2021/01/21/us/politics/biden-rolls-out-full-scale-wartime-coronavirus-strategy-including-requiring-masks-on-some-planes-trains-and-buses.html.

Stolberg, S.G., and N. Weiland. 2020. "Study Finds 'Single Largest Driver' of Coronavirus Misinformation: Trump." *New York Times*, 30 September. Retrieved 23 November 2020. https://www.nytimes.com/2020/09/30/us/politics/trump-coronavirus-misinformation.html.

Strauss, D. 2020. "'This Is the Time to Heal': Joe Biden Addresses Americans in Election Victory Speech." *The Guardian*, 8 November. Retrieved 31 January 2021. https://www.theguardian.com/us-news/2020/nov/07/joe-biden-speech-us-election-win-kamala-harris.

Stubley, P. 2019. "Boris Johnson: The Most Infamous Lies and Untruths by the Conservative Leadership Candidate." *The Independent*, 24 May. Retrieved 16 February 2020. https://www.independent.co.uk/news/uk/politics/boris-johnson-lies-conservative-leader-candidate-list-times-banana-brexit-bus-a8929076.html.

Stursberg, R. 2012. *The Tower of Babble: Sins, Secrets and Successes Inside the CBC*. Vancouver, Toronto, Berkeley: Douglas and McIntyre.

– 2016. "Cultural Policy for the Digital Age." Paper presented at Cultural Policy for the Digital Age: A Discussion. Ottawa: University of

Ottawa. https://techlaw.uottawa.ca/sites/techlaw.uottawa.ca/files/culturalpolicyforthedigitalage.pdf.

– 2017. "Same Media Market, Same Rules." *National Post*, 12 January, FP7. Retrieved 14 May 2020 from ProQuest.

Subramaniam, T., and H. Lybrand. 2020. "Fact-checking the Dangerous bin Laden Conspiracy Theory That Trump Touted." CNN, 15 October. Retrieved 23 November 2020. https://www.cnn.com/2020/10/15/politics/donald-trump-osama-bin-laden-conspiracy-theory-fact-check/index.html.

Sullivan, A. 2020a. "Is There Still Room for Debate?" *New York Magazine*, 12 June. Retrieved 18 July 2020. https://nymag.com/intelligencer/2020/06/andrew-sullivan-is-there-still-room-for-debate.html.

– 2020b. "See You Next Friday: A Farewell Letter." *New York Magazine*, 17 July. Retrieved 19 July 2020. https://nymag.com/intelligencer/2020/07/andrew-sullivan-see-you-next-friday.html.

Sullivan, M. 2016. "What TV Journalists Did Wrong – and the New York Times Did Right – in Meeting with Trump." *Washington Post*, 22 November. Retrieved 13 May 2020. https://www.washingtonpost.com/lifestyle/style/what-tv-journalists-did-wrong--and-the-new-york-times-did-right--in-meeting-with-trump/2016/11/22/54fe17ba-b0d3 11e6-8616-52b15787add0_story.html.

Sulzberger, A.G. 2019. "A Campaign Targeting Our Staff." *New York Times*, 25 August. Retrieved 10 September 2019. https://www.nytco.com/press/a-campaign-targeting-our-staff/.

Sunstein, C.R. 2013. *Simpler: The Future of Government*. New York: Simon and Schuster.

Sun Tzu. 1964. *The Art of War*. Translated by S.B. Griffith. Oxford: Clarendon Press.

Surowiecki, J. 2012. "Private Inequity." *New Yorker*, 30 January. Retrieved 10 February 2020. http://www.newyorker.com/magazine/2012/01/30/private-inequity.

Swaim, B. 2015. *The Speechwriter: A Brief Education in Politics*. New York: Simon and Schuster.

Swisher, K. 2019. "Trump and Twitter, Together Forever." *New York Times*, 10 July. Retrieved 10 September 2019. https://www.nytimes.com/2019/07/10/opinion/trump-twitter-census.html.

Syal, R. 2020. "Dominic Cummings Calls for 'Weirdos and Misfits' for No 10 Jobs." *The Guardian*, 2 January. Retrieved 2 January 2020. https://www.theguardian.com/politics/2020/jan/02/dominic-cummings-calls-for-weirdos-and-misfits-for-no-10-jobs.

Taekema, D. 2019. "Woman with Walker, Called 'Nazi Scum' by Protesters at Bernier Event, Speaks Out." *CBC News*, 2 October. Retrieved 21 February 2020. https://www.cbc.ca/news/canada/hamilton/dorothy-marston-bernier-protest-mohawk-1.5305661.

Tait, C. 2007a. "No Deal without All Wireless, Says Telus Chief." *National Post*, 26 June, FP1.

– 2007b. "Is Telus Merely Stalling?; 'Doesn't Make Sense'; Telco Blames 'Inadequacies' of Bid Process." *National Post*, 27 June, FP4.

Tait, C., and S. Deveau. 2007. "New Bid for BCE Likely; Telecom Giant Denies Discussions with U.S. Firm." *National Post*, 30 March, A1.

Tasker, J.P. 2017. "Government Formally Apologizes to Omar Khadr, as Andrew Scheer Condemns 'Disgusting' Payout." *CBC News*, 7 July. Retrieved 23 May 2020. https://www.cbc.ca/news/politics/cabinet-explain-omar-khadr-settlement-1.4194467.

– 2020a. "Trudeau Says Only WE Charity Can Administer $900 Million Student Grant Program." *CBC*, 29 June. Retrieved 16 November 2020. https://www.cbc.ca/news/politics/trudeau-we-charity-1.5631278.

– 2020b. "WE Charity Winding Down Operations in Canada after Student Grants Scandal." *CBC*, 9 September. Retrieved 16 November 2020. https://www.cbc.ca/news/politics/we-charity-winding-down-operations-1.5717899.

– 2020c. "Commissioner Drops Ethics Investigation into Morneau's WE Charity Trips." *CBC*, 29 October. Retrieved 16 November 2020. https://www.cbc.ca/news/politics/ethics-commissioner-morneau-we-charity-trips-1.5781995.

Taylor, J. 2017. "Americans Say Civility Has Worsened under Trump; Trust in Institutions Down." *NPR*, 3 July. Retrieved 7 September 2019. https://www.npr.org/2017/07/03/535044005/americans-say-civility-has-worsened-under-trump-trust-in-institutions-down.

Tedesco, T. 2007a. "'Shot across the Bow' of BCE; Largest Shareholder 'Exploring' Its Options." *National Post*, 10 April, A1.

– 2007b. "BCE Would Not Be Pushed." *National Post*, 18 April, A1.

– 2007c. "Dealmaker's Parting Shot; Corporate Statesman Richard Currie Dismisses Critics of Bell Canada's Sale as 'Amateurs.'" *National Post*, 5 July, FP3.

Tedesco, T., and L. McLeod. 2007. "Teachers Has US$25B for BCE Bid; Source Says Citigroup Providing Financing for Pension Giant's Move." *National Post*, 11 April, FP1.

Tedesco, T., and S. Silcoff. 2007a. "Telus Plans Bid for Bell; Purchase Would Face Regulatory Hurdles." *National Post*, 21 June, A1.

– 2007b. "Bell Gets Two $41 Offers; CPP, Teachers Groups; All-Cash Bidders Front-Runners, Sources Say." *National Post*, 29 June, FP1.

Telegraph. 2021. "'This Is Insurrection': Joe Biden's Speech in Full as US Capitol Is Stormed." *The Telegraph*, 8 January. Retrieved 1 February 2021. https://www.telegraph.co.uk/news/2021/01/06/insurrection-joe-bidens-speech-full-us-capitol-stormed/.

Tharoor, I. 2016. "'Fake News' Threatens Germany's Election, Too, Says Merkel." *Washington Post*, 23 November. Retrieved 10 February 2020. https://www.washingtonpost.com/pb/news/worldviews/wp/2016/11/23/fake-news-threatens-germanys-election-too-says-merkel/.

The Drew Berquist Show. 2013. "IED Construction Video with Omar Khadr (Trial Video)." *The Drew Berquist Show*, 4 November. https://www.youtube.com/watch?v=-EQjYowsBgc

Thompson, E. 2018. "More Needed to Prevent Foreign Interference in Canadian Elections, Watchdog Says." *CBC News*, 27 August. Retrieved 10 October 2018. https://www.cbc.ca/news/politics/canada-elections-facebook-twitter-1.4799688.

– 2020. "Trump Insults Harris as 'a Monster' Morning after Vice Presidential Debate." *ABC News*, 8 October. Retrieved 23 November 2020. https://abcnews.go.com/Politics/trump-insults-harris-monster-mor ning-vice-presidential-debate/story?id=73498918.

Thompson, P.A. 2009. "Market Manipulation? Applying the Propaganda Model to Financial Media Reporting." *Westminster Papers in Communication and Culture* 6, 2: 73–96.

Thomson, S., and B. Platt. 2019. "Not Ready For Primetime." *National Post*, 26 October, A7.

Timberg, C. 2017. "Spreading Fake News Becomes Standard Practice for Governments across the World." *Washington Post*, 17 July. https://www.washingtonpost.com/news/the-switch/wp/2017/07/17/spreading-fake-news-becomes-standard-practice-for-governments-across-the-world/.

Tomasky, M. 2017. "Trump: The Scramble." *New York Review of Books*, 6 April.

– 2018. "The Worst of the Worst." *New York Review of Books*, 22 February. Retrieved 5 September 2019. https://www.nybooks.com/articles/2018/02/22/trump-wolff-worst-of-the-worst/.

Toobin, J. 2016. "Clinton Investigation Mania, Part 2." *New Yorker*, 14 November. https://www.newyorker.com/magazine/2016/11/14/clinton-investigation-mania-part-two.

Topp, B. 2010. *How We Almost Gave the Tories the Boot: The Inside Story behind the Coalition*. Toronto: James Lorimer & Company.

Torigian, M. 2020. "Forensic Analysis Exonerates WE Charity and the Canadian Government." *Toronto Star*, 3 November. Retrieved 16 November 2020. https://www.thestar.com/opinion/contributors/2020/11/03/forensic-analysis-exonerates-we-charity-and-the-canadian-government.html.

Toronto Star. 2019. "Hate Will Never Win." *Toronto Star*, 11 October. Retrieved 21 February 2020 from ProQuest.

– 2020. "An Urgent Message to the Government of Canada from the Publishers of Canada's Major Newspapers." *Toronto Star*, 2 May. Retrieved 2 May 2020. https://www.thestar.com/opinion/2020/05/02/an-urgent-message-to-the-government-of-canada-from-the-publishers-of-canadas-major-newspapers.html.

Toughill, K. 2016. "Does Democracy Need Newspapers? Maybe Not So Much." *Toronto Star*, 22 January. Retrieved 10 February 2020. https://www.thestar.com/opinion/commentary/2016/01/22/does-democracy-need-newspapers-maybe-not-so-much.html.

Tower, T. 2018. "Concordia Announces a New Institute for Investigative Journalism." *Concordia News*, 14 June. Retrieved 15 June 2018. http://www.concordia.ca/cunews/main/stories/2018/06/14/concordia-announces-a-new-institute-for-investigative-journalism.html.

Tremonti, A.M. 2018. "The Current for May 31, 2018." Radio broadcast. *CBC*, 31 May. Retrieved 30 October 2019. https://www.cbc.ca/radio/thecurrent/the-current-for-may-31-2018-1.4684322.

Trump, D. (@RealDonaldTrump). 2016. "Boeing is building a brand new 747 Air Force One for future presidents, but costs are out of control, more than $4 billion. Cancel order!" Twitter, 6 December. Retrieved 4 September 2019. https://twitter.com/realDonaldTrump/status/806134244384899072?s=20.

– (@RealDonaldTrump). 2018a. "Based on Justin's false statements at his news conference, and the fact that Canada is charging massive Tariffs to our U.S. farmers, workers and companies, I have instructed our U.S. Reps not to endorse the Communique as we look at Tariffs …" Twitter, 9 June. Retrieved 8 September 2019. https://twitter.com/realDonaldTrump/status/1005586152076689408?s=20.

– (@RealDonaldTrump). 2018b. "PM Justin Trudeau of Canada acted so meek and mild during our @G7 meetings only to give a news conference after I left saying that, 'US Tariffs were kind of insulting' and he 'will not be pushed around.' Very dishonest & weak. Our Tariffs are …" Twitter, 9 June. Retrieved 8 September 2019. https://twitter.com/realDonaldTrump/status/1005586562959093760?s=20.

– (@RealDonaldTrump). 2018c. "'I REALLY DON'T CARE, DO U?' written on the back of Melania's jacket, refers to the Fake News Media. Melania has learned how dishonest they are, and she truly no longer cares!" Twitter, 21 June. Retrieved 25 June 2018. https://twitter.com/realDonaldTrump/status/1009916650622251009 and https://twitter.com/realDonaldTrump/status/1005586152076689408?s=20.

– (@RealDonaldTrump). 2018d. "Mike Pompeo is doing a great job, I am very proud of him. His predecessor, Rex Tillerson, didn't have the mental capacity needed. He was dumb as a rock and I couldn't get rid of him fast enough. He was lazy as hell. Now it is a whole…" Twitter, 7 December. Retrieved 4 February 2019. https://twitter.com/realDonaldTrump/status/1071132880368132096.

– (@RealDonaldTrump). 2018e. "The only problem our economy has is the Fed. They don't have a feel for the Market, they don't understand necessary Trade Wars or Strong Dollars or even Democrat Shutdowns over Borders. The Fed is like a powerful golfer who can't score because …" Twitter, 24 December. Retrieved 5 February 2019. https://twitter.com/realDonaldTrump/status/1077231267559755776

– (@RealDonaldTrump). 2019a. "So horrible to watch the massive fire at Notre Dame Cathedral in Paris. Perhaps flying water tankers could be used to put it out. Must act quickly!" Twitter, 15 April. Retrieved 18 April 2019. https://twitter.com/realDonaldTrump/status/1117844987293487104.

– (@RealDonaldTrump). 2019b. "Chairman Kim has a great and beautiful vision for his country, and only the United States, with me as President, can make that vision come true. He will do the right thing because he is far too smart not to, and he does not want to …" Twitter, 2 August. Retrieved 15 October 2019. https://twitter.com/realDonaldTrump/status/1157306452228366336?s=20.

– (@RealDonaldTrump). 2020a. "What is the purpose of having White House News Conferences when the Lamestream Media asks nothing but hostile questions, & then refuses to report the truth or facts accurately. They get record ratings, & the American people get nothing but Fake …" Twitter, 25 April. Retrieved 1 May 2020. https://twitter.com/realDonaldTrump/status/1254168730898173953?s=20.

– (@RealDonaldTrump). 2020b. "There has never been, in the history of our Country, a more vicious or hostile Lamestream Media than there is right now, even in the midst of a National Emergency, the Invisible Enemy!" Twitter, 27 April. Retrieved 1 May 2020. https://twitter.com/realDonaldTrump/status/1254767509460234243?s=20.

– (@RealDonaldTrump). 2020c. "Nevada is turning out to be a cesspool of Fake Votes. @mschlapp & @AdamLaxalt are finding things that, when released, will be absolutely shocking!" Twitter, 9 November. Retrieved 31 January 2021. https://www.thetrumparchive.com/?results=1&searchbox=%22%5C%22Nevada+is+turning+out+to+be+a+cesspool+of+Fake+Votes%5C%22%22.

– (@RealDonaldTrump). 2020d. "Heartwarming to see all of the tremendous support out there, especially the organic Rallies that are springing up all over the Country, including a big one on Saturday in D.C. I may even try to stop by and say hello. This Election was Rigged …" Twitter, 13 November. Retrieved 21 November 2020. https://twitter.com/realDonaldTrump/status/1327319294057848832?s=20.

– (@RealDonaldTrump). 2020e. "I WON THE ELECTION!" Twitter, 15 November. Retrieved 20 November 2020. https://twitter.com/realDonaldTrump/status/1328200072987893762?s=20.

– (@RealDonaldTrump). 2020f. "The Media is just as corrupt as the Election itself!" Twitter, 21 November. Retrieved 31 January 2021. https://www.thetrumparchive.com/?search box=%22the+media+is+just+as+corrupt+as+the+election+itself%22.

Tubb, E. 2019. "Does Your Local Candidate Make a Difference? How Some GTA Races Could Be Decided by Star Power." *Toronto Star*, 12 September. Retrieved 8 December 2019. https://www.thestar.com/politics/federal/2019/09/12/does-your-candidate-make-a-difference-how-some-but-not-many-gta-races-may-be-decided-locally.html.

Tucher, A. 1994. *Froth and Scum: Truth, Beauty, Goodness, and the Ax Murder in America's First Mass Medium.* Chapel Hill, NC: The University of North Carolina Press.

Tuchman, G. 1978. *Making News: A Study in the Construction of Reality.* New York: Free Press.

Tuck, S., and S. McCarthy. 2007. "Takeover Talk Catches Ottawa Off Guard." *The Globe and Mail*, 30 March, B4.

Tufekci, Z. 2017. "We're Building a Dystopia Just to Make People Click on Ads." TEDGlobal, 27 October. https://www.ted.com/talks/zeynep_tufekci_we_re_building_a_dystopia_just_to_make_people_click_on_ads/.

Tunney, C. 2016. "Kellie Leitch Defends 'Anti-Canadian Values' Survey Question." *CBC News*, 2 September. Retrieved 4 September 2019. https://www.cbc.ca/news/politics/leitch-responds-survey-question-1.3746470.

Tur, K. 2017. *Unbelievable: My Front-Row Seat to the Craziest Campaign in American History.* New York: Dey Street Books.

Tversky, A., and D. Kahneman. 1974. "Judgment under Uncertainty: Heuristics and Biases." *Science* 185, 4157: 1124–31.

Twitter. 2021. "Permanent suspension of @realDonaldTrump." Twitter, 8 January. Retrieved 29 January 2021. https://blog.twitter.com/en_us/topics/company/2020/suspension.html.

United States Government. 1971. *Congressional Record: Proceedings and Debates of the United States Congress*, vol. 117, part 35. US Government Printing Office.

Urback, R. (@RobynUrback). 2019. "This is an extremely interesting exchange, wherein Trudeau says he did not sign a non-disclosure agreement when he left a teaching job mid-year." Twitter, 4 October. Retrieved 28 November 2019. https://twitter.com/RobynUrback/status/1180173286484987904?s=20.

– 2020. "Canadians Have Been Gaslit on China." *Globe and Mail*, 30 April. Retrieved 1 May 2020. https://www.theglobeandmail.com/opinion/article-canadians-have-been-gaslit-on-china/.

Vieira, P. 2007. "Flaherty's Tax Conundrum; BCE Privatization Could Cost Him $800-Million." *National Post*, 18 April, FP3.

Vlessing, E. 2013. "'Amazing Race Canada' Outpaces Rival U.S. Reality Series with Debut Season." *The Hollywood Reporter*, 18 September. Retrieved 10 December 2019. https://www.hollywoodreporter.com/news/amazing-race-canada-outpaces-rival-631664.

Vogel, K.P., and J.W. Peters. 2019. "Trump Allies Target Journalists over Coverage Deemed Hostile to White House." *The New York Times*, 25 August. Retrieved 1 April 2020. https://www.nytimes.com/2019/08/25/us/politics/trump-allies-news-media.html.

von Scheel, E. 2019. "Why Scheer Campaigns with Kenney but Not Ford." *CBC News*, 28 September. Retrieved 17 February 2020. https://www.cbc.ca/news/politics/scheer-campaigns-kenney-1.5301549.

Vosoughi, S., D. Roy, and S. Aral. 2018. "The Spread of True and False News Online." MIT Initiative on the Digital Economy Research Brief,"8 March. http://ide.mit.edu/sites/default/files/publica tions/2017%20IDE%20Research%20Brief%20False%20News.pdf.

Waddell, C. 2019. "Government Funding for Journalism: To What End?" *The Conversation*, 21 March. Retrieved 2 April 2019. https://theconversation.com/government-funding-for-journalism-to-what-end-113978.

Wagner, D., R.W. Miller, N. Penzenstadler, K. McCoy, and D. Slack. 2020. "For These Trump Supporters Primed to Disbelieve Defeat, Challenging the Election Was a Civic Duty." *USA Today*, 3 December. Retrieved 27 January 2021. https://www.

usatoday.com/in-depth/news/2020/12/03/trump-lawsuits-challenging-election-michigan-arizona-pennsylvania-georgia/6425725002/.

Wagner, K. 2020. "Trump and Twitter Enter a New Phase in a Tortured Relationship." *Bloomberg Businessweek*, 13 November. Retrieved 23 November 2020. https://www.bloomberg.com/news/articles/2020-11-13/twitter-twtr-s-trump-treatment-will-change-when-he-leaves-the-white-house.

Wagner, M., M. Mahtani, M. Macaya, F. Alfonso III, V. Rocha, and A. Wills. 2020. "Election 2020 Presidential Results." *CNN*, 6 November. Retrieved 27 January 2021. https://www.cnn.com/politics/live-news/trump-biden-election-results-11-05-20/h_86803fe1e19a5825dbc47bf5aa677a7a.

Waldman, S., and C. Sennott. 2019. "A Future without the Front Page." *The New York Times*, 1 August. Retrieved 7 September 2019. https://www.nytimes.com/2019/08/01/us/news-deserts-future.html.

Wallace, C. 2017. "Facing Digital Turmoil, Journalism Goes Back to School." *Toronto Star*, 6 May, IN1.

Wall Street Journal. 2020. "America's Jacobin Moment." *Wall Street Journal*, 22 June. Retrieved 19 July 2020. https://www.wsj.com/articles/americas-jacobin-moment-11592867349.

Walsh, D., M. Raju, and S. Collinson. 2017. "House Republicans Pull Plan to Gut Independent Ethics Committee after Trump Tweets." *CNN*, 3 January. Retrieved 7 September 2019. https://www.cnn.com/2017/01/02/politics/office-of-congressional-ethics-oversight-of-ethics-committee-amendment/index.html.

Walsh, M. 2018. "With Wynne Out, Ontario Proud Sets Its Sights on Trudeau." *iPolitics*, 15 June. Retrieved 17 June 2018. https://ipolitics.ca/article/with-wynne-out-ontario-proud-sets-its-sights-on-trudeau/.

Walsh, R. (@toccataprima). 2018. "OUTRAGEOUS: I can't access a @CBC podcast without joining Facebook. I thought I had opened a new account as ALTERNATIVE to access via Facebook. Now getting repeatedly pinged with messages to confirm the Facebook account that I have created. And @cbc is a taxpayer's media outlet!" Twitter, 11 December. Retrieved 5 February 2019. https://twitter.com/toccataprima/status/1072471260708421635.

Wang, S. 2017. "Twitter Isn't Taking Fake News Seriously." *Bloomberg Businessweek*, 23 October, 22.

– 2018. "Canada's The Logic Is a New Subscription News Outlet Focused on the Innovation Economy, à la The Information." Nieman Lab, 12 June. Retrieved

30 August 2018. http://www.niemanlab.org/2018/06/canadas-the-logic-is-a-new-subscription-news-outlet-focused-on-the-innovation-economy-a-la-the-information/.

Wardle, C., and H. Derakhshan. 2017. "Information Disorder: Toward an Interdisciplinary Framework:" Report DGI(2017)09. Council of Europe, 27 September. Retrieved 10 October 2018. https://rm.coe.int/information-disorder-toward-an-interdisciplinary-framework-for-researc/168076277c.

Warnica, R. 2019. "In an Inspired Performance, Norman Lawyer Marie Henein Did Incalculable Damage to the Trudeau Brand." *National Post*, 9 May. Retrieved 24 February 2020. https://nationalpost.com/news/canada/in-an-inspired-performance-henein-did-incalculable-damage-to-the-trudeau-brand.

Warzel, C., and A. Ngu. 2019. "Google's 4,000-Word Privacy Policy Is a Secret History of the Internet." *New York Times*, 10 July. Retrieved 10 September 2019. https://www.nytimes.com/interactive/2019/07/10/opinion/google-privacy-policy.html.

Washington Post. 2021. "Opinion: President Trump Deserved Impeachment. The Senate Must Convict Him Quickly." *Washington Post*, 13 January. Retrieved 1 February 2021. https://www.washingtonpost.com/opinions/president-trump-deserved-impeachment-the-senate-must-convict-him-quickly/2021/01/13/746e3b2c-55cd-11eb-a931-5b162d0d033d_story.html.

Waters, J. 2020. "Biden Nears Record 80m Votes as Trump Persists in Trying to Overturn Result." *The Guardian*, 19 November. Retrieved 21 November 2020. https://www.theguardian.com/us-news/2020/nov/19/biden-latest-votes-record-amid-trump-legal-challenges.

Waterson, J. 2016. "Vote Leave, the Canadian IT Company, and the £725,000 Donations." *BuzzFeed News*, 30 November. Retrieved 23 May 2020. https://www.buzzfeed.com/jimwaterson/vote-leave-the-canadian-it-company-and-the-ps725000-donation.

– 2020a. "Guardian Tops Poll of National Papers for Coronavirus Coverage." *The Guardian*, 28 April. Retrieved 1 May 2020. https://www.theguardian.com/media/2020/apr/28/guardian-tops-poll-of-national-papers-for-coronavirus-coverage.

– 2020b. "Facebook to Pay UK Media Millions to License News Stories." *The Guardian*, 1 December. Retrieved 1 December 2020. https://www.theguardian.com/technology/2020/dec/01/facebook-to-pay-uk-media-millions-to-licence-news-stories.

Watkins, E. 2018. "Peter Navarro Says 'There's a Special Place in Hell' for Justin Trudeau." *CNN*, 10 June. Retrieved 4 September 2019. https://www.cnn.

com/2018/06/10/politics/peter-navarro-justin-trudeau/index.html.

Watts, M. 2021. "Frank Sinatra's 'My Way' Serves as Musical Bookends for Trump's Presidency." *Newsweek*, 20 January. Retrieved 4 February 2021. https://www.newsweek.com/frank-sinatras-my-way-serves-musical-bookends-trumps-presidency-1563088.

Watzman, N. 2017. "Is It Time to Revisit Liability Immunity for Facebook, Twitter and Their Online Platform Cousins?" *Trust, Media & Democracy*, 22 November. Retrieved 10 May 2020. https://medium.com/trust-media-and-democracy/revisiting-liability-immunity-for-facebook-twitter-and-their-online-platform-cousins-c45a3ab15696.

Waxman, O.B. 2021. "As Trump Plans to Skip Biden's Swearing In, Here Are 3 Other U.S. Presidents Who Dodged Their Successors' Inauguration." *Time*, 19 January. Retrieved 26 January 2021. https://time.com/5928537/trump-biden-not-attend-inauguration-history/.

Webster, J., and T. Law. 2019. "Former Canadian Prime Minister Apologizes after Tweeting She Hoped Hurricane Dorian Would Strike Mar-a-Lago." *Time*, 31 August. Retrieved 30 March 2020. https://time.com/5665303/canada-prime-minister-rooting-hurricane-dorian-trump-apologizes/.

Wehner, P. 2018. "The Full-Spectrum Corruption of Donald Trump." *New York Times*, 25 August. Retrieved 27 August 2018. https://www.nytimes.com/2018/08/25/opinion/sunday/corruption-donald-trump.html.

Weiss, B. (@bariweiss). 2020. "The civil war inside The New York Times between the (mostly young) wokes the (mostly 40+) liberals is the same one raging inside other publications and companies across the country. The dynamic is always the same. (Thread.)" Twitter, 4 June. Retrieved 18 July 2020. https://twitter.com/bariweiss/status/1268628680797978625.

Weiser, B., and A. Watkins. 2019. "Cesar Sayoc, Who Mailed Pipe Bombs to Trump Critics, Is Sentenced to 20 Years." *New York Times*, 5 August. Retrieved 6 September 2019. https://www.nytimes.com/2019/08/05/nyregion/cesar-sayoc-sentencing-pipe-bombing.html.

Wells, P. 2019. "Justin Trudeau, Imposter." *Maclean's*, 4 March. Retrieved 5 September 2019. https://www.macleans.ca/politics/ottawa/justin-trudeau-imposter/.

Westerståhl, J. 1983. "Objective News Reporting." *Communication Research* 10, 3: 403–24.

Wherry, A. 2018. "Jagmeet Singh's Question-Popping Photo Op and the Vague Limits of Touchy-Feely Transparency." *CBC News*, 18 January. Retrieved

8 September 2019. https://www.cbc.ca/news/politics/jagmeet-singh-
engagement-photo-analysis-wherry-1.4491147.

– 2019. *Promise and Peril: Justin Trudeau in Power.* New York: HarperCollins.

– 2020a. "Governments Will Make Mistakes during the Pandemic – and They
Won't Be Able to Pin Them on 'Experts.'" CBC *News*, 15 April. Retrieved 1 May
2020. https://www.cbc.ca/news/politics/kenney-tam-pandemic-coronavirus-
covid-1.5532290.

– (@AaronWherry). 2020b. "Here's the passage from O'Toole's speech in the
House, responding to the fall economic statement." Twitter, 30 November.
Retrieved 1 December 2020. https://twitter.com/AaronWherry/
status/1333562538789924866?s=20.

Whipple, C. 2017. *The Gatekeepers: How the White House Chiefs of Staff Define Every
Presidency.* New York: Crown.

Wilkie, C. 2020. "Biden Calls for Unity and Healing After Electoral College Certifies
His Victory." CNBC, 14 December. Retrieved 31 January 2021. https://www.cnbc.
com/2020/12/14/biden-calls-for-unity-and-healing-after-electoral-college-
cements-his-victory.html.

Williams, J. 2020. "Here's the Choice: Fall into Line or Shut Up." *The Times*, 16 July.
Retrieved 19 July 2020. https://www.thetimes.co.uk/article/heres-the-choice-fall-
into-line-or-shut-up-wcmg3bds8.

Willis, A. 2007a. "Battle Begins for Lucrative BCE Fees." *Globe and Mail*, 19 April, B16.

– 2007b. "Will BCE Be Holding a One-Bidder Auction?" *Globe and Mail*, 24 April, B25.

Willis, A., and E. Reguly. 2007. "Telus's BCE Play May Drive Off Rival Bids." *Globe and
Mail*, 22 June, B1.

Willis, A., and S. Stewart. 2007a. "Teachers Garners Support for BCE Bid." *Globe and
Mail*, 16 April, B1.

– 2007b. "Trailing in Auction, Cerberus Touts Bid." *Globe and Mail*, 29 June, B1.

Willis, A., L. McLeod, and B. Erman. 2007. "For Would-Be Buyers of BCE, a Fresh
Hunt for Partners." *Globe and Mail*, 1 May, B1.

Willis, A., J. McNish, and C. McLean. 2007. "BCE Mulls Radical Changes with
Industry under Pressure." *Globe and Mail*, 30 March, B1.

Willis, A., S. Stewart, and B. Erman. 2007. "BCE Faces Push for Open Bidding." *Globe
and Mail*, 25 April, B1.

Windrem, R. 2018. "Russians Launched Pro-Jill Stein Social Media Blitz to Help Trump
Win Election, Reports Say." NBC *News*, 22 December. Retrieved 8 September 2019.

https://www.nbcnews.com/politics/national-security/russians-launched-pro-jill-stein-social-media-blitz-help-trump-n951166.

Winsor, M., and E. Shapiro. 2020. "US Coronavirus Death Toll Surpasses 60,000 and 100 Bodies Found in Trucks Outside NYC Funeral Home." *ABC News*, 30 April. Retrieved 1 May 2020. https://abcnews.go.com/Health/coronavirus-updates-us-federal-inmate-dies-covid-19/story?id=70399771.

Winter, C. 2017. "How Scott Adams Got Hypnotized by Trump." *Bloomberg Businessweek*, 22 March. Retrieved 24 February 2020. https://www.bloomberg.com/news/features/2017-03-22/how-dilbert-s-scott-adams-got-hypnotized-by-trump.

Wise, A., and R. Lucas. 2021. "Hundreds Identified, More Than 100 Arrested in Connection with Capitol Insurrection." *NPR*, 26 January. Retrieved 27 January 2021. https://www.npr.org/sections/insurrection-at-the-capitol/2021/01/26/960861088/hundreds-identified-more-than-100-arrested-in-connection-with-capitol-insurrecti.

Wishart, I. 2020. "The One Who Got Away." *Bloomberg Businessweek*, 27 January.

Wolff, M. 2018. *Fire and Fury: Inside the Trump White House*. New York: Henry Holt and Company.

– 2019. *Siege: Trump under Fire*. New York: Henry Holt and Company.

Woodward, B. 2018. *Fear: Trump in the White House*. New York: Simon & Schuster.

– *Rage*. 2020. New York: Simon & Schuster.

Wright, Mason. (@thismason). 2020. "A statement from the elected union executive representing Globe and Mail workers." Twitter, 11 June. Retrieved 19 July 2020. https://twitter.com/thismason/status/1271138049037041664?s=20.

Wu, N., and L. King. 2021. "House Will Vote Thursday to Remove Rep. Marjorie Taylor Greene from Her Committees." *USA Today*, 3 February. Retrieved 4 February 2021. https://www.usatoday.com/story/news/politics/2021/02/03/marjorie-taylor-greene-house-vote-removing-her-committees/4373488001/.

Wu, T. 2016. *The Attention Merchants: The Epic Scramble to Get Inside Our Heads*. New York: Knopf.

– 2017. "How Twitter Killed the First Amendment." *New York Times*, 27 October. Retrieved 24 February 2020. https://www.nytimes.com/2017/10/27/opinion/twitter-first-amendment.html.

– (@superwuster). 2019. "Purposefully or not, Trump has successfully changed the national political conversation from gun control to Greenland." Twitter, 21 August. Retrieved 7 September 2019. https://twitter.com/superwuster/status/1164372348537069569?s=20.

Yahoo Finance. 2007. "BCE Inc. Shares Historical Data Mar. 28, 2007 – Mar. 30, 2007."
   Table. Retrieved 14 May 2020. https://ca.finance.yahoo.com/quote/BCE.TO/
   history?period1=1175040000&period2=1175299200.

Yakabuski, K. 2007a. "What a Bell Deal Means to Quebec." *Globe and Mail*, 18 April, B9.

– 2007b. "Teachers Chief Questions Role of Brass in Deal." *Globe and Mail*, 5 July, B3.

Yglesias, M. 2018. "4 Political Science Lessons from Kanye West's Embrace
   of Donald Trump." *Vox*, 3 May. https://www.vox.com/policy-and-
   politics/2018/5/3/17311906/kanye-west-donald-trump-political-science.

Zhou, L. 2021. "147 Republican Lawmakers Still Objected to the Election Results after
   the Capitol Attack." *Vox*, 7 January. Retrieved 28 January 2021. https://www.vox.
   com/2021/1/6/22218058/republicans-objections-election-results.

Zilio, M. 2019. "Obama Warns about Effects of Fake News on Democracies during
   Address in Ottawa." *Globe and Mail*, 31 May. Retrieved 24 February 2020. https://
   www.theglobeandmail.com/politics/article-obama-warns-about-effects-of-fake-
   news-on-democracies-during-address/.

Zimonjic, P., and D. Cochrane. 2020. "Bill Morneau Resigns as Finance Minister and MP,
   Will Seek to Lead OECD." *CBC*, 17 August. Retrieved 16 November 2020. https://www.
   cbc.ca/news/politics/bill-morneau-justin-trudeau-decision-1.5689890.

Zito, S. 2016. "Taking Trump Seriously, Not Literally." *The Atlantic*, 23 September.
   Retrieved 24 February 2020. https://www.theatlantic.com/politics/
   archive/2016/09/trump-makes-his-case-in-pittsburgh/501335/.

Zittrain, J. 2014. "Facebook Could Decide an Election without Anyone Ever Finding Out."
   The New Republic, 1 June. Retrieved 24 February 2020. https://newrepublic.com/
   article/117878/information-fiduciary-solution-facebook-digital-gerrymandering.

An Election Endnote References

Adams, P. (@padams29). 2021. "Those voter needs are to a degree at odds with many
   conventional media (television) values, such as an emphasis on novelty (many
   viewers haven't heard even the stump pitches at this point), conflict, face-pace, and
   journalistic-style accountability." Twitter, 10 September. Accessed 21 September
   2021. https://twitter.com/padams29/status/1436299239852814346?s=20.

Bricker, D. 2021. "Darrell's Campaign Week – Afghanistan, a 2-Tier Scare Tactic and the
   Tories' Ontario Surge." *Global News*. 27 August. Accessed 23 September 2021. https://
   globalnews.ca/news/8147374/darrell-bricker-campaign-digest-afghanistan-905/.

Bryden, J.. 2021. "Leaders' Debates Commission Under Fire After Controversial English Debate." *Toronto Star.* 10 September. Accessed 22 September 2021. https://www.thestar.com/politics/federal-election/2021/09/10/leaders-debates-commission-under-fire-after-controversial-english-debate.html?rf.

Butts, G. (@gmbutts). 2021. "Vote efficiency isn't accidental. All three Trudeau Liberal campaigns were among the most efficient in [Canadian flag image] history. The unsung team of super geniuses put together and led by @tompitfield at Data Sciences deserves a lot more credit than they've ever received. #Elxn44 [VOTE image] (43 and 42)." Twitter, 21 September. Accessed 22 September 2021. https://twitter.com/gmbutts/status/1440347519284760580?s=20.

Byrne, J. (@Jenni_Byrne). 2021. "Does Shachi Kurl realize she is the moderator for a National Leader's debate for Prime Minister & not a reporter at a hostile presser? #awkward #cringe." Twitter, 9 September. Accessed 21 September 2021. https://twitter.com/Jenni_Byrne/status/1436135238439165955?s=20.

Caruso-Moro, L. 2021. "'None of Your Business': Legault Calls out 'Ridiculous' Question on Quebec Secularism, Language Laws During Federal Debate." *CTV News.* 10 September. Accessed 21 September 2021. https://montreal.ctvnews.ca/none-of-your-business-legault-calls-out-ridiculous-question-on-quebec-secularism-language-laws-during-federal-debate-1.5580572.

Coletto, D. 2021. "Canadian Election Update." Abacus Data, 9 September. Accessed 20 September 2021. https://mailchi.mp/abacusdata/worth-a-look-childrens-health-in-covid-509485?e=e335936325.

Doyle, J. 2021. "Enough Already with the Demonization of CBC's Rosemary Barton." *Globe and Mail.* 21 September. Accessed 23 September 2021. https://www.theglobeandmail.com/arts/television/article-enough-already-with-the-demonization-of-cbcs-rosemary-barton/.

Dwivedi, S. 2021. "Don't Blame Canada's Vitriolic Election on U.S. Politics. It's as Canadian as It Gets." *Washington Post,* 14 September. Accessed 23 September 2021. https://www.washingtonpost.com/opinions/2021/09/14/canada-election-vitriol-trudeau-conservative-party/?utm_source=twitter&utm_medium=social&utm_campaign=wp_opinions.

Economist. 2021. "Bagehot: Orwell, Priestley and the Politics of the Ordinary." *The Economist,* 21 January. Accessed 21 September 2021. https://www.economist.com/britain/2021/01/23/orwell-priestley-and-the-politics-of-the-ordinary?utm_campaign=editorial-social&utm_medium=social-organic&utm_source=twitter.

Fife, R. 2021. "Almost Half of Canadians Disapprove of Trudeau Government's Handling of Afghanistan Evacuations." *Globe and Mail*. 3 September. Accessed 23 September 2021. https://www.theglobeandmail.com/politics/article-almost-half-of-canadians-disapprove-of-trudeau-governments-handling-of/.

Graves, F. (@VoiceOfFranky). 2021a. "It may be my imagination but th elevel of toxic sludge that permeates Twitter today is making it increasingly useless as a tool of debate and information . A shame actually . Once again the toxic minority are disrupting things." Twitter, 22 September. Accessed 24 September 2021. https://twitter.com/VoiceOfFranky/status/1440734896406683657?s=20.

— (@VoiceOfFranky). 2021b. "Welcome to the new Twitter (or maybe it is not new). I retweeted a column by John Doyle re. Rosie Barton . I thought it was an interesting read. I am taking the retweet down as I have received a plethora of horrid responses that are completely outside of boundaries of civility." Twitter, 22 September. Accessed 23 September 2021. https://twitter.com/VoiceOfFranky/status/1440734373830008850?s=20.

Harewood, A. (@CBCAdrianH). 2019. "Those five opening questions for the party leaders by @ShachiKurl were among the most pointed and critical that I have ever heard in a federal party leaders debate. She challenged them all, made them uncomfortable and created some real tension. It was a masterclass. #elexn44" Twitter, 9 September. Accessed 21 September 2021. https://twitter.com/CBCAdrianH/status/1436151393195335683.

Ivison, J. (@IvisonJ). 2021. "This team has run a strong, positive campaign. Why invite this kind of coverage at the 11th hour?" Twitter, 19 September. Accessed 21 September 2021. https://twitter.com/IvisonJ/status/1439727549290979329?s=20.

McGregor, G. (@glen_mcgregor). 2021. "'Coffee (which I don't have yet) is for closers.'" Conservative campaign is on the road today (kind of), headed to Glengarry - Prescott - Russell, a Liberal-held riding near Ottawa that CPC won under PMSH. Then it's back to the O'Toole Box for the rest of day." Twitter, 14 September. Accessed 23 September 2021. https://twitter.com/glen_mcgregor/status/1437784519264935943?s=20.

Moscrop, D. (@David_Moscrop). 2021. "It's unfair to say the election was a waste of money. It was also a waste of time." Twitter, 21 September. Accessed September 22, 2021. https://twitter.com/David_Moscrop/status/1440360656314650624?s=20.

Paradkar, Shree. 2021. "Federal Election Campaign in a Sad State as the Powerful Attack Female Journalists of Colour and Defend the People's Party." *Toronto Star*. 18 September. Accessed 21 September 2021. https://www.thestar.com/politics/

political-opinion/2021/09/18/federal-election-campaign-in-a-sad-state-as-the-powerful-attack-female-journalists-of-colour-and-defend-the-peoples-party.html.

Reynolds, C. 2021. "Twitter Requires Maxime Bernier to Delete Tweet Sharing Reporters' Emails." *CTV News*. 23 September. Accessed 24 September 2021. https://www.ctvnews.ca/politics/twitter-requires-maxime-bernier-to-delete-tweet-sharing-reporters-emails-1.5597839.

Vickers, K. (@KVickers). 2021. "Will there not be any accountability for this? The rude manner in which all the leaders were treated. The moderators debating with the leaders, I tuned in to hear leaders views not theirs. I salute all the leaders for their professionalism and patience." Twitter, 10 September. Accessed 21 September 2021. https://twitter.com/KVickers/status/1436317181814452227?s=20.

Index